Rhodon

*Rhodri*

# A Political Life
# in Wales and Westminster

## Rhodri Morgan

UNIVERSITY OF WALES PRESS

2017

*www.uwp.co.uk*

*British Library CIP Data*
A catalogue record for this book is available from the British Library

ISBN     978-1-78683-147-7
eISBN    978-1-78683-148-4

The University of Wales Press acknowledges the financial support of the Welsh Books Council.

Typesetting and layout by Chris Bell, CB Design
Printed by CPI Antony Rowe, Melksham

# Contents

**Foreword**  Kevin Brennan and Mark Drakeford                    vii

List of illustrations                                            xvii

1   **The Cradle of Belief**  1939–1963                             1

2   **The Next Twenty-Four Years**  1963–1987                      41

3   **MP Morgan: Mainstream or Maverick**  1987–1997              77

4   **Leadership Contests**  1997–1998                            119

5   **They Got Us Surrounded**  1998–1999                         137

6   **Getting the Show on the Road**  1999–2000                   157

7   **Earning Respect**  2000–2003                                185

8   **The Heyday That Wasn't**  2003–2007                         259

9   **Working with Plaid**  2007–2009                             287

10  **No Back-Seat Driving**  2010–2017                           329

    Index                                                         341

# Foreword

OUR FRIEND AND MENTOR Rhodri Morgan left this book very largely, but not finally, finished when he died so unexpectedly on 17 May 2017. He had been working on the final details right up to the day of his death. A preface had been planned, to explain the approach taken in the book, and to thank those many individuals who had contributed to it. Now, some of that at least falls to us. Our main qualification for doing so is that we knew and worked with Rhodri throughout his career as a public politician, and continued to do so right up to his death.

For the present task, this is only a very partial set of credentials. The book is far more than an account of elected office. It is quite certainly not – and was never intended to be – a book of historical record. Rather, it is an account of a life from the unique perspective of the person who actually lived it: personal, compelling, individual in tone as well as content. In the early weeks after his death, reading these pages proved at times a painful experience in a way never intended, because the author's voice can be so unmistakably be heard. Readers and students many years from now can be confident that the text reads as its author spoke. In life, Rhodri enjoyed gossip and story-telling, and used figurative language to illustrate his point. Many historians have written of how the great Texan president Lyndon Baines Johnson would secure the attention of interlocutors by grabbing their lapels and holding them close. In later years, as Chancellor of Swansea University, Rhodri formed his own links with the University of Texas, including with members of the Johnson family and, though never physical in his approach, Rhodri's conversational technique was actually not so different to the Texan's. He grabbed your attention, drew you in close, and held you there with the strength of his words rather than the force of his hands, until the encounter was over.

How, then, was this book produced? The essential answer is by recollection, amplified by conversation. Much has been written, both during Rhodri's career and since his death, about his phenomenal memory, and all that you have read is true. He had an astonishing ability to absorb, retain and recall information of all sorts, from complex technical research to apparently casual conversation. Moreover – and even more remarkably – he had an ability to summon up and synthesise material across time and across apparently disparate subjects. During the period of the gestation and preparation this autobiography, we have lost count of the number of people who have told us of conversations in which Rhodri drew out and discussed events that he wanted to pin down for inclusion in the book. Nevertheless, a core group of people have been involved throughout its production, and because Rhodri is now unable to thank them himself, we want to make sure that we do so on his behalf.

As readers will discover, a significant portion of this book is given over to exploring the family experiences that shaped Rhodri's life. No one was more important to him in his early years than his brother, Prys – Professor Prys Morgan – and their relationship remained central to many aspects of Rhodri's life as First Minister. If ever an issue relating to the Welsh language cropped up, Prys would be consulted. In the highly unlikely event that a gap emerged in Rhodri's knowledge of Welsh geography – a village not yet visited, a hamlet unheard of, a minor road not travelled – Prys would fill the gap. Faced with a speech to make where visitors from outside Wales were to be present, Prys would be relied upon to find some family connection or intertwining of national histories, around which twenty minutes of information and entertainment could be crafted. All of these contributions can be found in the weft and weave of this book, not on the surface necessarily, but in the patterns of thought and depth of understanding that lie beneath it.

For the political chapters of this book, Rhodri relied on a close group of individuals who had been present throughout or during a large part of his career. The book would not have reached its state of near-readiness without the consistent help of Jane Runeckles, a Special Adviser during Rhodri's tenure as First Minister, and a regular reminder to him of the need to commit those memoirs to paper; Lawrence Conway, a civil servant like no other, whose presence at Rhodri's side at almost every moment made him an indispensable sounding board for the evolving text; and, latterly, Jo Kiernan, political journalist, media adviser and, in the context of this book, a driving force to get it over the line. Their assistance covered all facets of the book, from helping to generate its content to shaping its final form. Those who knew Rhodri, even by reputation, will not to be shocked to learn that the second of these tasks was at least as challenging as the first. In one version of the book, a particular chapter had been allocated between eight and ten thousand words, but a first (still incomplete) draft of that chapter weighed in at 56,000 words! Every author needs an editor and, in this regard, the input of the whole team at the University of Wales Press is of note – specifically Sarah Lewis as Head of Commissioning, Siân Chapman as Production Manager, and Dafydd Jones as Editor of the Press, each of whom has played an important part.

We would not have the book at all without the patient determination of Professor Mike Sullivan of Swansea University. Very soon after his retirement from the National Assembly, Rhodri wrote a version of the material that appears in the early chapters. Then he lost interest – or at least was overtaken by other events, including becoming Chancellor of Swansea University. Mike and Rhodri were already acquainted. Mike had chaired the very first exercise to identify and select Labour candidates for the inaugural Assembly election, and had worked as both a specialist and special adviser inside the Welsh Government, being particularly influential in and around the formation of the One Wales administration and in shaping the children's rights agenda of which Rhodri was so proud. During his Chancellorship at Swansea, it was Mike who brought Rhodri back to the idea of an autobiography, by pitching it to him as part of a double act in which the Morgan book would be accompanied by a Sullivan text, telling the same story of devolution from a more analytical and academic perspective.

In part, at least, this notion of companion volumes helps explain some of the barer passages that might otherwise strike the reader in Rhodri's own text. There are significant events and long-term developments which are conspicuous mainly by their absence or brief treatment. Some of this material, understandably, Rhodri regarded as better developed in the less personal account that Mike had contracted to produce. Then there was the volume of material on the cutting room floor. Quite simply, not everything could be included, and neither was everything meant to be included. The publisher had initial thoughts of newspaper serialisation, and certainly Rhodri was already planning and immensely looking forward to a book tour; both of these would require material held back to bring readers and purchasers through the door. And who was to say, in any case, that this one book would be the last?

Because it is the only book to be produced by Rhodri himself, of course, we wanted to use the opportunity of this foreword to outline some of the themes which in many ways he was too modest to claim himself. A great deal of what made Rhodri such a remarkable politician did not seem all that remarkable to him – to a degree that escapes all but a very few other practitioners of the political arts, he naturally possessed those qualities, and this book is remarkable for the understated claims it makes for some very emphatic achievements. And, because the man himself loved lists – lists of everything, ten things to do today, eight people to appoint to the Cabinet, fifteen best left-footed full-backs never to have played for Wales – we have compiled a brief list of what appear to us to be key dimensions of Rhodri's contribution as First Minister that a casual reading of the book might not otherwise reveal.

## Putting devolution back on track

Rhodri really wanted Welsh devolution to work. He was a true believer in what devolution could achieve for Welsh prosperity and Wales's standing in the world. When the first months of the new Assembly descended into rancorous contention and bitter partisan arguments, a real danger was posed to the future of the very devolution that had been won on the narrowest of mandates. In our experience, the Assembly of February 2000 sat on a knife-edge. It was by no means certain that it would survive, let alone thrive, as an institution. Rhodri saw it as his central mission to put devolution back on track and to reach a stage where, rather than wanting to get rid of the Assembly, the Welsh people would be incensed if a future Tory Government tried to take it away. The fact that the second devolution referendum gave such emphatic support to extending the powers of the Welsh Assembly is a key part of Rhodri's legacy in embedding the roots of devolution more deeply in the democratic soil of Wales. For him, it was a delicate and fragile flower to be nurtured, grown organically, and never to be taken for granted.

Few organisations owe their history to one individual, but the fact that there was a future for devolution owed more to Rhodri than to anyone else.

## Being a bridge between Wales and Westminster

Striking the right balance between emphasising the autonomy of the new devolved Assembly and Government in Wales, and working effectively with the UK Government in Westminster, was an absolutely key quality that Rhodri possessed. In a way, Tony Blair did him a huge favour by being so vehemently opposed to Rhodri becoming Welsh Labour leader in the first place, because no one could subsequently accuse him of being in the pocket of the Prime Minister. But Rhodri loved Westminster and the House of Commons, and enjoyed interacting with politicians at a UK level. This unique combination of qualities allowed him to be the kind of effective bridge between Wales and Westminster that was essential to the success of Welsh devolution. In a way quite hard to imagine now, nearly twenty years on, the earliest period of devolution relied on personal as much as institutional relationships. It was of enormous value, at a time when the rulebook was still being written, to know that any Westminster minister would return a Rhodri Morgan phone call. To be so fully at home in two such different places was a rare quality, and it was to the huge advantage of devolution that, just at the point when it mattered the most, the project was in the hands of someone who was decidedly at home in both.

## Working across the aisles: coalitions with progressive parties

Before Rhodri, the Labour Party in Wales was too often beset by the kind of blinkered tribalism that was becoming increasingly arcane in a world where the old certainties of class and employment were breaking down. A long-standing supporter of electoral reform, Rhodri knew that the narrow victory in the 1997 referendum could never have been achieved without the promise of pluralism practically expressed in a proportional electoral system. As a result, he knew that Labour would have to reach out to other parties with a progressive agenda, and be prepared to share power and influence when it did not command a majority in the Assembly. Before Rhodri's tenure as First Minister, the early months of the first Assembly constituted the original coalition of chaos. A daily deal had to be cobbled together to stop the opposition parties from being able to direct the Labour administration to carry out policies in which the latter did not believe. This was the madness of the Assembly's first set of Standing Orders, combined with the weakness of an administration led by a leader who had not commanded popular support. The discussions with the Liberal Democrats about forming a stable coalition after Rhodri became First Minister were the best-kept secret in Welsh politics (perhaps the only secret ever kept in the history of Welsh politics); it is ironic that Rhodri, a great advocate of Freedom of Information when he was Chair of the House of Commons Public Administration Select Committee, should have been responsible for this particular political subterfuge. It was a necessary venal sin, however, because any indication of what was going on would have allowed the old tribalists to block any talk of coalition. Instead, Rhodri committed an enormous amount of personal political capital to put in place a government that brought stability and a clear, progressive programme to the Assembly.

This progressive pluralism triumphed again when Rhodri successfully formed a coalition with Plaid Cymru in 2007 to form the One Wales Government. No small part of these arrangements was Rhodri's ability to reach across aisle and be trusted not to betray an agreement. Most people in the Labour Party define themselves in opposition to the Conservatives: they know they are Labour because they know they could never be Tory. For some, however, the opposing touchstone of socialism is nationalism, and the notion that Labour could be in government with Plaid Cymru was not only difficult to imagine, it was anathema. The story of how the One Wales Government came about has been told elsewhere, and Rhodri's account is provided in this book. He is, as ever, more modest about his own part than an objective history would provide. Without his personal authority, unstintingly deployed in keeping Labour in government, combined with an instinctive understanding that power could be shared in order to be retained, the future of the Labour Party as well as of devolution would have been very different, and a good deal more troubled.

### Politics rooted in economics: a 'socialist of the Welsh stripe'
In the era of New Labour, Rhodri remained confidently and determinedly himself – 'classic Labour', as he often described his own position. One way in which he was very much in the Labour mainstream lay in his consistent belief in the

shaping impact of economic opportunities on the lives of people. In his famous Clear Red Water speech, he amended the text as drafted to refer to himself as a 'socialist of the Welsh stripe', a reference to the industrial as well as cultural heritage he brought to his politics. Nobody would have survived for long in Rhodri's office as First Minister without knowing that unemployment figures were published at 9:30 am on the third Wednesday of the month – they were anticipated almost as eagerly as news of the latest Welsh rugby squad. The basic belief that economic relationships shaped social relationships ran as a thread from his early days working in the South Glamorgan Economic Development Department right through to his year as the first Economic Development Secretary in the first Welsh Government. It was, he told us, his ideal job. When the time came, however, Rhodri wanted to be First Minister because he believed he was the best person qualified to make a success of it – though being First Minister also brought a weight of responsibility that he may have worn lightly, but which never went away. Economic Development, by contrast, was a job that he relished because it spoke to the practical socialist in him, creating the conditions in which people could make a success of their lives.

## Policies rooted in everyday life

Rhodri's natural ability to communicate with people of every background meant that he was acutely attuned to what really mattered to people. With his academic background he could easily have been a policy wonk, but his policies were genuinely rooted in everyday life. Campaigning with Julie on Merthyr Road in Whitchurch, Rhodri could talk to a pensioner sat at the bus stop and point out that the journey they were about to take on the bus was free thanks to the bus pass provided by the Welsh Labour Government. Similarly, the constituent emerging from the chemist with a newly-filled prescription could be reminded easily of the practical benefits of Rhodri's brand of pragmatic socialism.

Less than a decade after he voluntarily stepped down from being First Minister, today's changed circumstances of security make Rhodri's own way of life seem more remarkable, doing his own shopping, paying at the gate to watch Cardiff Blues play rugby, making his own sandwiches, ironing his own shirts. For ten years, Wales had a First Minister whose address and telephone number remained in the directory (which was still in those days delivered to every house) and their availability, he said, was barely ever abused.

Monday mornings in Rhodri's office had a routine. Sometime after about ten o'clock, the phone would ring. The person on the other end would say, 'I met Rhodri at the frozen fish counter in Tesco's on Saturday' – or the Riverside market on Sunday, or while out walking the dog on Friday – 'and he said to be sure to phone in this morning and remind him about what I told him'. And he had, and he did, and he wanted to know the result, because this was never an act: Rhodri was genuinely and unfailingly interested in what people from any walk of life had to tell him, believing that everyone in their own way was an expert, and that everyone had their own story to tell.

## Picking the right people

Rhodri had a knack for picking the right person for the job. He gave early notice of this aptitude with his first Cabinet appointment. Christine Gwyther had been Alun Michael's Agriculture Minister, but had got off to a rocky start, not least when Welsh livestock farmers discovered she was a vegetarian, after which she was unfairly targeted by the opposition parties in a way that undoubtedly carried elements of misogyny. Rhodri knew she was not the right person for the job, but also knew he could not allow the other parties to hound her out of office. A spirited defence was organised, which exposed the misogyny particularly of the Welsh Tories in their attacks, and which saved his Minister from a vote of no confidence. But Rhodri was unsentimental about the fact that he needed to make a change and shortly afterwards, at a time of his choosing, replaced Christine with Carwyn Jones. It was an astute choice and a timely one as Carwyn deftly handled the foot-and-mouth crisis of 2001. Rhodri's first Cabinet appointment, of course, went on to be his successor.

During the first Assembly term, the agreement with the Liberal Democrats required that a review be undertaken of this earliest period of devolution, to report early in the second term. Finding the right person to chair the review was a challenge. Accusations that Labour took its orders from London meant that it could not be someone tainted by New Labour, and it also had to be someone whose report would resonate both within and beyond Wales. In choosing Ivor Richard, Rhodri found someone who had been at the very top of the UK Government, serving in the first Blair Cabinet, but whose distance from the then-Prime Minister was well known. He was also someone who had been a heavyweight figure on a world and European stage, yet whose Welsh roots were incontrovertible. The Richard Commission Report became another early turning point in devolution, which proposed a strengthening of the National Assembly and of the Welsh Government, not because of the deficits of the first term but because of its successes.

The decision to ask Gerry Holtham to review the funding issues of devolution was similarly astute. The review was a condition of Plaid Cymru's participation in the One Wales government, but Plaid had no strong candidate in mind to carry it out. Gerry was a relatively rare figure – Labour aligned, formidably cerebral, but with a personal career in the world of finance, and Welsh to boot. The Holtham Report was that even rarer thing – a document that even the UK Treasury treated with respect and which has lasted a decade as the basis for any serious discussion of the way in which Wales is funded. There is some justice in the belief that choosing the right people is a political skill, which leaves among the most lasting legacies. It was a talent that Rhodri possessed to a high degree, and that helped shape some of the most fundamental decisions of devolution.

### Promoting women

In the book, Rhodri says that his criterion for appointing people to his Cabinet was always whether or not he felt they were of the calibre to be a senior minister at a UK level. It was a matter of course for him that, in practice, this involved appointing women to all the most senior posts in his administrations. When he carried out his first major Cabinet reshuffle, in creating the partnership administration with the Liberal Democrats, he brought three new women into Ministerial office: Jenny Randerson from the Lib Dems, and Sue Essex and Jane Davidson from Labour. By the time he retired, women had been responsible for every Cabinet portfolio, other than economic development – and that was put right when Edwina Hart took on the job throughout the fourth Assembly.

Outside Ministerial appointments, his record was similarly strong. The fight for gender equality inside the Labour Party was very familiar to him, and from close quarters. That the result would be a Labour Group in the second Assembly made up of 19 women and 11 men exceeded every expectation. When it came to appointing a new Permanent Secretary to the Welsh Government, he opted for the first woman to hold that post in the devolution era; when it came to appointing a Presiding Officer, he was a strong supporter of Rosemary Butler, his only regret being that he had failed to secure her nomination as Deputy Presiding Officer as early as October 2000.

### Creating Welsh Labour

In 1997, when the chance for devolution came about, Rhodri very quickly decided that he would stand for the Assembly and the Welsh Labour leadership. He understood more than anyone that devolution would change everything – and that devolution under Labour would fail if Labour in Wales was perceived as a branch office of Labour HQ in London. In a real sense, that was the moment at which Welsh Labour was born. Rhodri knew that for Wales to embrace devolution, the leader would not just have to be *from* Wales but would need to be seen to have been *made in* Wales; and for Labour to succeed in the devolution era, the party would have to be unambiguously Welsh in its identity. It is, of course, easy to be wise after the event, but at the time none of this was uncontested. Scottish Labour colleagues, in the early years of devolution, could not always disguise a rather baffled condescension at the Welsh Labour determination to create an identity which was distinctive and different from the successful Blairite brand. Rhodri understood, rather better, the political need to prevent any space opening up between being Labour and being Welsh. Scottish nationalism has thrived on its ability to persuade many voters that being Scottish can only find its political expression by voting SNP. While facile accusations of crypto-nationalism were to be heard in Westminster, the triumph of the Welsh Labour mission was perhaps best seen most recently in the way in which candidates ran on an overtly Welsh Labour ticket at the 2017 General Election, emphasising Labour's devolution achievements and prominently featuring the Welsh Labour leader. Both the nature and the outcome of that campaign, at the start of which Rhodri continued play such an active part, were a direct legacy of his vision of Labour's relationship to devolution.

Rhodri Morgan accomplished that rarest of political feats, confounding the dictum that all political careers end in failure. Certainly, in the thirty years that followed his first election in 1987, the only leader of any political party at Westminster to buck the trend was the late John Smith, who died suddenly without having faced the challenge of being in government. Rhodri retired at a time of his own choosing, and with levels of popularity exceeding even those that marked his arrival as First Minister. The outpouring of affection and appreciation that came in response to his sudden death demonstrated just how much, almost a decade after his retirement as First Minister, he retained a grip on the public imagination as a symbol of Wales in the twenty-first century. As we said at the start of this foreword, reading the final lines in this book, still so close to the shock of his death, remains a difficult experience. Rhodri himself remained, to the end, optimistic and forward-looking, always more interested in what could be achieved tomorrow than in dwelling on what has happened in the past.

It would be unthinkable to conclude this foreword without noting Julie Morgan's huge contribution to Rhodri's life and political career. As Rhodri points out in the book, it was she who shaped his earliest active involvement in Labour politics, and it was her political activism that triggered his own pursuit of democratic office. For thirty-five years, one or other or both was involved at the highest levels of politics while retaining the strongest sense of personal and family life. Theirs was one of the most remarkable of political partnerships, and it would take another book fully to do justice to the huge contribution that Julie Morgan has made to the politics of Wales and to the story told in this book. In the hugely difficult weeks following Rhodri's death, Julie demonstrated the most enormous strength, sustaining family members and sharing both her grief and her memories with the huge circle of Labour activists and Welsh citizens who want, always, to share with her their affection for Rhodri. Hard as it must be, we hope that she too will read this book and recognise in it the relish for life, for Labour and for Wales, which springs from every page.

*Kevin Brennan and Mark Drakeford*
*July 2017*

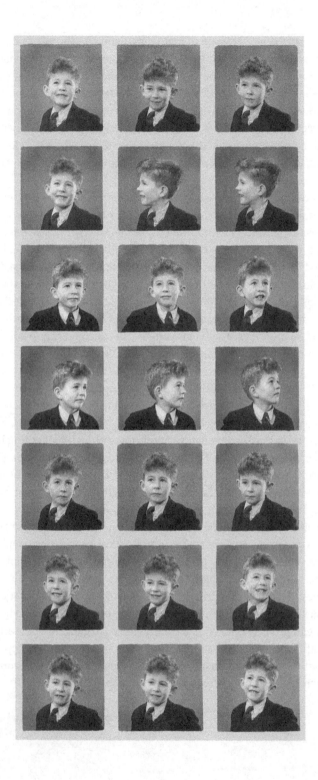

# List of illustrations

2009 (cover) photograph by Terry Morris.

**Summer in the early 2000s,** on Mwnt beach (inside jacket), photograph © Wales Online.

1946, aged six (p. xvi).

2009, on the summit of Snowdon (p. 338), photograph © Stephen Ford/Alamy.

**Colour photographs**

1940, aged twelve months.

1943, aged three, with brother Prys aged six.

**Spring 1948,** Radyr School.

1955, the back yard in Radyr. Rhodri's parents, T. J. and Huana Morgan.

**July 1955,** the back yard in Radyr. Standing, Prys and Rhodri; sitting, Rhodri's grandfather John Rees, Rhodri's mother Huana Morgan, and the family's guest Boris Collbring from Sweden.

1961, going to Harvard.

1964, St David's Day dinner at Eastgate Hotel, Oxford. The guest speaker was Rhodri's father T. J. Morgan, seated centre with Huana Morgan; Rhodri is standing, fifth from the left, and Prys fourth from the right.

1964, campaigning with Jim Callaghan.

**Autumn 1985,** shortly after moving to Michaelston-le-Pit. Rhodri, T.J., Huana and Prys.

1987, campaigning with Denis Healey.

June 1987, with Julie at the Cardiff West count, elected MP for the first time.

1988, abseiling from the Holiday Inn, Cardiff, to raise funds for youngsters in Ely to visit Africa. © Wales Online.

1988, training with Alun Michael for the London Marathon. © Wales Online.

1989, with Neil Kinnock, leader of the Labour Party.

1997, with Julie, celebrating thirty years of marriage, mid-election campaign.

July 2000, with Prys and Huana Morgan at Swansea Brangwyn Hall, to receive the Swansea University Honorary Fellowship for Huana at the age of 95. © Wales Online.

October 2000, the Partnership Agreement coalition Cabinet with the Liberal Democrats.

2001, with Tony Blair during the General Election campaign. © Wales Online.

March 2002, Ground Zero, New York.

2003, launching the European Year of Disabled People.

2003, the Service of Reconciliation at St Augustine's Mission, Rorke's Drift, South Africa.

2005, celebrating the first Wales Grand Slam since 1978. © Wales Online.

2007, with the Prime Minister of New Zealand, Helen Clark.

July 2007, the One Wales coalition Cabinet with Plaid Cymru.

2008, with star pupils at Fitzalan High School.

September 2008, at the closing ceremony of the Ryder Cup, Valhalla Golf Club, Louisville.

Summer in the early 2000s, on Foel y Mwnt. © Wales Online.

June 2009, conquering Snowdon with Lawrence Conway.

May 2016, with Julie at her Cardiff North count. © Wales Online.

June 2016, the EU referendum campaign in Pontypridd, with Paul Murphy, Carwyn Jones and Peter Hain. © Wales Online.

June 2016, campaigning during the EU referendum with grandson Jaydon. © Wales Online.

# one

# The Cradle of Belief
## 1939–1963

I N SOME WAYS I had a very Welsh childhood. I was brought up in a Welsh-speaking family, albeit in the English-speaking village of Radyr in the Taff Valley, five miles north of Cardiff. Cardiff was not the capital city of Wales until I was fifteen, and it was also overwhelmingly English-speaking. Mine was also a very British childhood too. I was a war baby, born in September 1939. My early life was utterly dominated by the war, with John Snagge intoning the news in that plummy voice on the BBC Home Service giving updates on how we were doing in El Alamein, D-Day, Burma, and how the Red Army was marching westward after Stalingrad and so on. September 1939 must have been a hell of a time to bring a new child into the world. On the whole, though, I'm glad I was born.

There were bits and bobs of a European childhood too, with our Czech refugee neighbours, the Sussemilchs, in and out of our house all the time. You could say it was a British Empire-influenced childhood as well. By the time I was in secondary school, I found myself growing up while the sun was setting on the British Empire. The coincidence of the Suez crisis of 1956 coming along while I was in the Lower Sixth Form in Whitchurch Grammar School, which served the northern fringes of Cardiff, just at the time when you were encouraged to start to think for yourself cannot be underestimated.

My parents, Thomas John Morgan and Huana Rees, met when they were studying their honours degrees in Welsh at the newly opened university in Swansea in the 1920s. They came from the almost adjoining villages of Glais and Ynystawe in the Lower Swansea Valley. They had never met each other before university, because my mother lived in Port Talbot from the age of ten until she was twenty-four. No one can be objective about their parents, but I have the impression that they were a bit of a golden couple around the campus.

Although my father won a state scholarship, it was a minor miracle that he reached the giddy heights of higher education. He was born in 1907. His father, William, was a coal miner but had long periods without any work, especially after 1920. When my father passed with some ease his School Certificate (today's GCSE equivalent) in 1922, he told the headmaster at Pontardawe County School that he was leaving school to get a job in a bank. He wanted to contribute to the family's meagre income. Most of his friends were leaving anyway, so peer group pressure must have come into it.

In those days, to get a job in a bank your parents had to post a bond of £100 in case you stole the petty cash. Some chance of getting a £100 bond from an unemployed miner's household. But my father's pride told him that work and not the Sixth Form was his destiny. At fifteen years of age, you know it all!

Wasting his life was what my father proceeded to do over the next few months. None of his friends had jobs or apprenticeships. The sympathetic care-taker of the Institute in Clydach let my father play billiards all day – until his old headmaster nabbed him on the way home for tea. The head had dreamt up a ruse. He asked my father if he still had his rugby boots. My father said yes, and the head then explained that the First XV were a few players short for Saturday. Would my father like to play? 'Yes', he said. 'Well, there you are. You're in the team. Just one little detail – you'll have to come back to school. Don't worry about that job in the bank. Any time you get a job, you can leave straight away.' 'No problem, okay, I'll see you Saturday' (and Monday and Tuesday etc., of course!). I think my father must have been getting bored with non-stop billiards by then, and he will-ingly fell for the headmaster's little trick.

He flew through his Highers, as A levels were known back then, despite the missing months. That's how he earned his state scholarship and entrance into Swansea to study his honours degree in Welsh and play rugby for the college team. Had it not been for that amazing pastoral care by the grammar school headmaster, my father would never have met my mother.

Her route to the same university campus at Singleton Park was different but equally tortuous. By the time she was sitting her A level equivalent exams, the Rees family were living in Port Talbot. They came from Ynystawe in the Swansea Valley, but had moved after my grandfather's grocery business had collapsed. He then became the company secretary of a small coal-mining company in the Afan Valley.

When my mother was revising for her examinations, alone in the house one evening, there was a thunderous knock on the door. My mother opened the door to four men in heavy overcoats and black-brimmed hats, with just a touch of the Four Horsemen of the Apocalypse about them. One asked, 'Is John Rees at home?' 'No', my mother answered quite truthfully, 'he's at a prayer meeting'. 'And well he might be', was the riposte, as the four turned on their heels. They were bailiffs of some kind, come to serve a notice on my grandfather.

He must have managed to get out of this financial crisis somehow. He returned to Ynystawe, where he was a long-standing deacon of Moreia Baptist Chapel. He got hold of a coal lorry, and established the coal delivery business that served the family well until he retired at seventy-two. He was known as 'Rees y Glo' to the Welsh speakers in the area – 'Rees the Coal' to the English speakers. The effect of the coal-mining company's problems on my mother, given the timing, could have been quite severe. She was so sick with worry that she seriously underperformed in the examinations, but got into university on her teacher's recommendation.

If my grandfather had been made bankrupt, I don't suppose she would have been able to go to Swansea, but she did. So my parents were studying Welsh within a year of each other, and met. My father asked my mother to go with him to listen to the violin competition in the Patti Pavilion at the Inter-College Eisteddfod. It was a piece by César Franck. There were six competitors, and my future parents sat through it all.

My mother must have been a bit impressed by this rugby-obsessed miner's son from the other side of the Swansea Valley. He must have been very culturally clued up too to listen to hour after hour of César Franck.

When my mother finally took him home to meet her parents in Ynystawe, the four of them sat through a rather nervous tea. After my father left, my mother asked her parents what they thought of him. 'Siarad gormod', was my grandfather's terse reply – 'Talks too much'. My grandfather was a man of religion. He left the speaking to the preacher in any communal gathering. As the senior deacon in the chapel, he was the only one allowed to fill the gaps in the sermon with 'Amen' or 'Hallelujah'. I used to be terribly impressed by this obvious sign of status.

My parents didn't get married until 1935. They must have been courting for ten years. They both had masters degrees in Welsh by then. My mother's was on poetry appreciation. My father was more into linguistics and the parallels between Middle Welsh and Middle Irish. This had involved him spending a year at University College Dublin in 1928. He told me he almost had a nervous breakdown doing his MA – it was a combination of overwork and a huge row with his professor and supervisor, Henry Lewis, who thought my father's theories were plain wrong. There might have been some added stress from his immersion in the Irish language, seen as essential to his academic work – he lived in Dublin in a 'No English Spoken Here' lodging house, run by a redoubtable Republican landlady called Miss Coyle, who had apparently been a gun-runner for the IRA in the civil war a few years previously.

I think giving up rugby far too early was a big loss to him. If you're studying hard, you need some physical recreation to balance body and mind, and my father had always played rugby. He was carrying an annoying shoulder injury, but his lifestyle in Dublin did not abide by the dictum of 'Healthy Mind in a Healthy Body'. It was all work and no play.

These days, a row or two with your supervisor over a key part of your PhD thesis is par for the course, but in the much narrower field of Welsh linguistics back in the late 1920s it would have felt far more threatening. My father must have been close to panic that all his hard work in earning his state scholarship and First Class Honours in Welsh was not going to lead to a job in academia after all.

My father did get his MA (PhDs were little known back then), despite his professor's criticisms, and was appointed to the staff of the Welsh Department of the University College of South Wales and Monmouthshire, Cardiff, in 1930.

In 1929, my mother had got her first job teaching Welsh in Rhymney at the county secondary school known as 'The Lawns'. That makes it sound quite plush, but in 1929 it was anything but. The Rhymney Coal & Iron Company had closed the iron works in 1928, and the unemployment rate had soared to 75 per cent in the town. Rhymney sits at the top of the valley of the same name, and was known as the last Welsh-speaking town in Monmouthshire. Rhymney was the western part of the Ebbw Vale constituency, and 1929 was also the year in which the area first elected its firebrand new MP Aneurin Bevan. He was from Tredegar, just three miles (and one mountain) east of Rhymney. Tredegar had changed from Welsh- to English-speaking around the turn of the century, but Rhymney had not.

Tom Price, the headmaster at 'The Lawns', met my mother at the station. They walked together up the main street to the school. Most of the shops were boarded up. Out of the corner of his eye, he could see my mother becoming grad-ually dispirited at the dismal appearance of the place. He may have worried that she was going to turn round and get on the next train home. 'It may look pretty depressed now, Miss Rees, but don't forget – Tom Jones the Cabinet comes from here!' Tom Jones wasn't a Cabinet Minister. He was much more important than that. He was the Deputy Cabinet Secretary and the great fixer behind every gov-ernment decision throughout the interwar years.

At her first staffroom tea break on her first Monday, my mother was totally disconcerted by a question from one of her new colleagues. 'Which councillor did you have to buy the three-piece suite for?' *Out of left field* doesn't come close. It turned out that every one of the other teachers, all appointed in happier but more crooked times, had had to buy a three-piece suite from the Roath Furnishing Company in Cardiff for one of the councillors, all in order to secure their jobs.

They must have omitted to make that arrangement in my mother's case, either because Rhymney County School was the only school in Monmouthshire where Welsh was taught, or because they anticipated a real recruitment problem in depression-hit Rhymney. Whatever the reason, my mother never had to pay anyone to get her first (or second and last) teaching appointment. That was the only good thing about the job. In every other way it was a searing experience.

The kids were starving. They had no change of clothing. They couldn't concentrate – except on Fridays.

Eastbourne had apparently adopted Rhymney. A van containing food parcels would arrive from the south coast and distribute the contents around the town. Each family would have enough for a square meal on Thursday nights and a breakfast on Friday morning and, as a result of full bellies, they'd be all bright-eyed and bushy-tailed on Friday. That was Teaching Day. Mondays through to Thursdays were survival days.

My mother did two years in Rhymney and then, courtesy of a wonderful reference from Tom Price, no doubt grateful that my mother had lasted two years, got a job at Glan-y-Môr Secondary School in Swansea. That meant she could live at home. She never forgot the dreadful experience of being interviewed by the full Swansea council –'Sixty old men', as she recalled it throughout her life. It wasn't an interview for a headship or even a departmental head. Just a normal teaching job. 'What did any of those old men know about the teaching of Welsh?' she would rail when the family took her for birthday meals in the old Swansea Guildhall, which was by then the Dylan Thomas Centre. It was where the dreadful interview had taken place, and the experience would come flooding back to her.

My mother never spoke as much about the four years she taught in Glan-y-Môr as about the two years in Rhymney. It wasn't as dramatic. She'd mastered the art of teaching.'Never smile before Easter'was one of her guiding principles. Living in Ynystawe and working five miles away in Swansea made courtship just a bit more practical. My parents eventually got married in 1935 in Moreia Chapel, Ynystawe, where my grandfather was a deacon. Just six people present, and they didn't include my father's brother and sister or his parents. That caused a bit of upset in Glais, but my parents always did things their own way. Whether it was to save money or a certain diffidence towards any form of display, I'm not sure. I used to ask my mother and father about this when a small boy. I always asked them separately and I never got a satisfactory answer.

All I do know from family legend is that my Uncle Aylwin, the best man, was only asked to be best man on the night before. When asked, he first said he couldn't possibly do it because he didn't have a clean collar. Whatever the reason for going economy class for the wedding, Julie and I followed suit when we got married more than thirty years later (on my father's birthday) in April 1967, as also did my daughter and son-in-law when they were married in 1998.

My mother's teaching career ended in 1935. Married women were not allowed to teach in state schools, not since an edict of the National Government in 1931, I believe, to help spread the jobs around. It was a terrible waste of my mother's teaching talents, but she never complained about it. She thought the rule was tough but fair in the Hungry Thirties. Why should some families have two bread-winners when other families didn't have one?

My father had a permanent safe job in Wales in the 1930s. Not many people could say that. Almost all of my father's graduating class and his pals in the Swansea university college rugby team had had to leave Wales to get teaching jobs. Claude Davey, my father's centre partner went to teach in the Manchester area, played for Sale rugby club and went on to captain Wales to victory over the All Blacks in 1935. Idwal Rees, later head of Cowbridge Grammar School, had to start off teaching in Fettes in Edinburgh, Tony Blair's alma mater; he also played in that victorious 1935 team, at which time he was a player for Edinburgh Wanderers. Watcyn Thomas was another Swansea teammate, and briefly a rival for my mother's attentions until shooed off firmly by my father; he became a star player for Moseley, and Wales while teaching at King Edward VII School in Birmingham, and then captained Wales to its first ever victory at Twickenham in 1933. All of them had to leave Wales. My father did not.

Now they were married, my father could move out of digs and my mother could leave home. The newly-wed Morgan family rented a house in Radyr, a suburban village in the Lower Taff Valley on the railway line from Cardiff to Merthyr and the Rhondda Valleys. The house was bang in the centre of the village next door to the Wesleyan Methodist English language chapel. 'Bang' is the operative word as well, because all road accidents in Radyr took place on the crossroads outside our house, and the wounded were always brought into our front room to wait for the ambulance, dripping blood on our carpet.

I'm still puzzled as to how my parents chose the house in Radyr. Many young academics, especially those with radical leanings, chose the Rhiwbina Garden Village. That was the Hampstead of Cardiff. But I think it was the same reason as the six person wedding – a fear of public display and a loss of privacy, and the compulsion to join in things. My father wanted the freedom to get on with his studies with minimum distractions.

With a ten minute railway commute to the university and the no. 33 bus to central Cardiff stopping outside the house, the location was undoubtedly convenient. It was no. 32 Heol Isaf. Radyr might have appealed to them as the ideal place to raise children because it was surrounded by fields and forests. My brother Prys arrived on 7 August 1937, and I followed on 29 September 1939, twenty-six days after Britain declared war on Germany.

Being on the banks of the Taff, Radyr is built on quite a steep slope; the bottom part of the village was totally dominated by the railway marshalling yards. We were all brought up with our mother's milk in the belief that Radyr Sidings were the largest in the UK after Clapham Junction. The sidings needed to be that big because the railway wagons coming down from the Valleys, full of coal to be exported to all the bunkering stations to refuel Royal Navy and Merchant Navy vessels all around the world, had to have a holding pond somewhere until a ship was available in Cardiff Docks. By the time my brother and I came along, the glory days of Cardiff Docks had gone. In the 1880s Cardiff competed with New York as the largest port in the world on tonnage; by the 1940s, New York had edged slightly ahead of Cardiff!

Right at the top of the slope was the golf club, and it was the area where the captains of industry lived in substantial merchant's houses. Radyr was always said not to need a village inn. That was because 'the folks on the hill' near the golf club could use its bar as their local. Thirsty railwaymen living near the river could hitch a lift on a passing loco to Llandaff North, where there were four pubs next to the station, only five minutes away. Not that my parents wanted a pub next door, a chapel was fine, but they were always conscious that all the residents of Heol Isaf were somehow caught in the middle of a quite socially divided village. That middle part was quite popular with BBC Wales and university staff. It was not so much the home of the intelligentsia as of the in-telly-Welshia!

If my parents chose Radyr as an idyllic place to raise their children, they were proved right. It was idyllic. Loads of fields and forests to explore. Climbing trees or playing football or cricket, it had everything you could want. My speciality was climbing trees. My brother's was damming streams.

Even as young boys, we were conscious of a class divide because it emerged as an educational divide. Probably a third of the children in Radyr went to a private junior school called Mrs Stanford's Academy. They would then pass on to the Llandaff Cathedral School at the age of nine to prepare to go to Clifton or other public schools when they were thirteen. My late uncle Dewi was six when the General Strike of 1926 happened. He remembered being stoned by the children in Mrs Stanford's as he walked past it up to the council school on the nine days of the strike.

A majority of the kids in the council school came from the adjoining village of Morganstown. No one from Morganstown was privately educated. It was only a mile from the one village to the other over Fisher's Hill. Fisher's Hill got that name from the Fisher family who owned Tŷ Mynydd, the big house on the hill. Tŷ Mynydd became famous retrospectively as the home of the Dahl family when young Roald was growing up. But the Fisher family would prove just as significant, at least for me, later on in life. The Fishers were the biggest shareholders in the Taff Vale Railway Company. In 1901, the company won a test case to be allowed to sue the RMT's predecessor railway workers' union – the Amalgamated Society of Railway Servants – for its assets, following a very damaging strike and lockout. It was this judgement and its severe implications for the finances of trade unions that caused the newly-formed Labour Party to become a parliamentary party: to get that judgement reversed. No Colonel Fisher, no Labour Party in Parliament.

In September 1939, the war started and my mother went into 'confinement' as it was called then, at Mrs Gill's Nursing Home in Connaught Road in Roath, Cardiff. It was a big Edwardian wealthy merchant's villa, converted for maternity purposes.

In the fortnight before I arrived, my mother had nothing to do except read with increasing alarm of the German Blitzkrieg sweeping its way through Poland.

My mother discussed with Mrs Gill the local implications of all this for her. 'I'm in the attic. Wouldn't I be safer in the basement? The Germans might start bombing here.' My mother had strong nesting instincts, you see. Anyway, Mrs Gill's reply was classic Cardiff – the confident Cardiff that had once been the largest port in the world – 'Don't you worry, my dear. These old Cardiff houses are built very solidly.' I don't actually know whether my mother prevailed and if I was born in the basement, or up in the attic with my mother having bought into Mrs Gill's vision of the Luftwaffe's biggest bombs bouncing harmlessly off the slate roof of the nursing home.

When my father went down to register me, he was rebuffed. He told the registrar that the baby boy was to be named HYWEL RHODRI MORGAN. The pesky petty bureaucrat of a registrar put his foot down. Hywel was apparently okay, but he refused to register the Rhodri bit. 'That's not a proper name', he announced. 'Well, it is now', said my father, 'write it down!' The registrar duly did. My father was six feet tall, which is quite tall by Welsh standards and I think he had quite a lot of natural authority.

Whether it was a reaction to the registrar's opposition to the name Rhodri that prompted my parents to use it in preference to Hywel, my actual first name, I don't know. It's not uncommon for boys in Wales to be known by their middle name. Anyway, both Hywel and Rhodri were kings of medieval Wales, Hywel Dda (Hywel the Good), Wales's great law-giver, and Rhodri Fawr (Rhodri the Great), a warrior king. Hywel the Good and Rhodri the Great. No pressure there then. But it was Rhodri that I went by.

I say 'went by', but that's not quite accurate. In the chapel and at home and among relatives, I did indeed go by 'Rhodri'. But no one else could pronounce it. It wasn't that difficult to say really, but the two big guttural Rs in one word seemed to grate on anglicised tongues. I had Rory, Roderick, Roger or even Rogery thrown at me – anything and everything but Rhodri. Nowadays, Wales's nursery and junior schools are crawling with little Rhodris, but back in the 1940s the name was unknown. My parents were twenty years ahead of their time.

The only time my moniker caused me a problem was when I became an MP in 1987. I had a phone call from the *Western Mail* asking if I felt any differently now about my involvement in the destruction of the television transmitter near Aberystwyth in my student days. I'd been waiting for the question for about twenty years, after spotting an interesting factoid in the reporting of the court case involving half a dozen militant Welsh language student activists from Aberystwyth in the late 1960s, who had deliberately vandalised the transmitter and phoned the police to tell them what they'd done. One of those Aber students was called Rhodri Morgan.

I remember thinking back then, oh-oh! I wonder when that'll bounce back on me? Everybody thinks there's only one Rhodri Morgan in the whole of Wales. So I was ready when the court case was disinterred from a dirt-digging database and given to the *Western Mail*. I simply said, 'I was never a student at Aberystwyth. I'm fifteen years older than this other Rhodri. I don't know where you'd find him – probably a respectable job in the BBC by now, but in any case "it wisna me!" as the Scots would say.'

Morgan wasn't a problem. It is said to be the only Welsh family name that English vicars or registrars of births, deaths and marriages have never changed or misspelt. Morgan always stays beautifully unmangled. Rhys may be changed to Rees, Llwyd to Lloyd, ap Dafydd to Davies etc., but Morgan always stays Morgan.

The overall effect of my name is that I don't have to say where I'm from. I might have to say where in Wales I'm from, but never whether I'm from Wales or another country. That is settled by my name.

I wasn't a healthy child. The Dr Spock of the 1930s was another American called Dr Truby King, and my mother swore by his every word. His books on child-rearing were based on the premise that no parent wanted to have a 'winnicky child'. Quite right too. To toughen baby up, therefore he advised bathing the baby in a little tub filled with hot soapy water as normal, but then to finish off by pouring a jug of cold water over the baby's head!

That's exactly what my mother did with my brother in 1937, but she must have felt it was a bit cruel because she didn't do it to me when I came along in 1939. Maybe she thought the war was enough for baby Rhodri to cope with. The upshot was that my brother never caught colds sniffs and sneezes. Indeed, he's a year-round swimmer in the sea at Caswell Bay even today. I always caught everything going round. Perhaps Dr Truby King was right – so if only my mother had poured a jug of cold water over me every night, I would have grown up healthy instead of winnicky. I would obviously have gone on to play rugby for Wales if my mother hadn't lost her nerve. But rather than blame my mother for my not making it into the starting XV for Wales, I think I'll blame Hitler for invading Poland in September 1939.

I was worse than winnicky on one occasion. I nearly passed away. This was at Christmas-time in 1942. We were staying at my grandparents' house in Ynystawe. I was just past my third birthday and developed pneumonia. Antibiotics had been invented, but they were reserved for the troops. Not enough tests had been done on side-effects to release them for use among the civilian population.

It must have been a desperate time for the four grown-ups gathered around my bedside with my grandparents' family doctor. Pre-antibiotics, there was no actual treatment apart from keeping a big fire going in the bedroom. With my grandfather being a coal merchant, that part at least was not a problem. My temperature kept going up and up and I was delirious.

Instead of my fever going up another notch to where it would have been game over for me, my temperature came down the other side to massive relief all round. I survived, but there are always after-effects to pneumonia, scarring on the windpipe and so on. So as I wended my way through school, I was missing about six weeks every year. I was very quick at making up the work. That was no problem, but it was annoying that the promised corporeal maturing, at which point I would finally grow out of it, whatever *it* was, took a long time to come. I had an X-ray to see if I had a shadow on the lung when I was eleven. I presume the dreaded shadow, if there had been one there, would have meant TB. Anyway, the good news was no shadow.

By the time I was fifteen I knew far more about health issues than I should. Not just about my personal health problems, but others' way outside the family too. Near our home and again even nearer to my grandparents' home, two American Nissen hut-style hospitals suddenly appeared as D-Day approached. Rhydlafar (known as 'Redlaver') hospital was thrown up to deal with all the anticipated wounds and injuries from the Normandy landings, and then the advance through France. That was a mile west of our house in Radyr. What is now Morriston Hospital north of Swansea had exactly the same purpose. That was just a short walk from Ynystawe, where my grandparents lived.

My brother and I used to sneak over to the hospital and see the wounded in their wheelchairs, or pottering around with Zimmer frames and covered with bandages. The other kids gathered there used to shout, 'Got some gum, chum?' through the fence. My brother had spotted an entirely different transatlantic scrounging opportunity. All the wounded soldiers had been issued with ocarinas – they were like a cross between a mouth organ and a recorder, ideal for learning to play 'Home Sweet Home' and 'Home on the Range'. So my brother's plea through the fence was 'Got a spare ocarina, chum?'

My own contact with the real world of hospitals from the inside came from ear, nose and throat problems, and lungs. When I became First Minister, I used to tease the Tories by boasting that I'd been treated in a private hospital, hoping they would be scandalised and issue angry press statements on the hypocritical nature of my support for the NHS. They never fell for it.

But I was the only active politician old enough to be able to compare treatment in NHS and private hospital care. I'd had my adenoids out before the NHS was founded, and then had my tonsils out under the NHS. My verdict was that NHS care was far superior. That was because when I needed a pee in the private hospital in 1947, they gave me an empty milk bottle, but in the NHS hospital in 1949 they gave me a proper receptacle to pee into.

Then came my grandmother's massive health crisis, cancer of the womb. My grandparents moved in with us after selling up in Ynystawe so that my grandmother could be admitted to what is now known as Velindre Hospital – at that time part of Whitchurch Hospital – the first cancer hospital in Wales. This was early version radiotherapy, which wasn't available in the Swansea area.

My father and mother had only just dipped their toes into the property market, finally buying the house at no. 32 Heol Isaf after fourteen years of renting it. Now, a year later they had to sell it so that we could have an extra bedroom for the grandparents. It wasn't that traumatic a house move – just eight doors up the road to no. 16. This was in the summer when I was leaving the junior school to join my brother in Whitchurch Grammar School, just south of Velindre and Whitchurch hospitals and the minaret-like tower that we could see from our front bedroom window on the opposite side of the River Taff.

My mother had accompanied grandmother to see the oncologist, and she was in a bit of a state when she got home. She needed to talk to my father but he wasn't there. So she unburdened herself on my brother and me. The consultant had warned my grandmother that the side-effects of the radiotherapy were going to be very severe and very painful. 'How painful?' asked my grandmother. 'Well', he replied, 'do you remember childbirth?' 'Yes, of course', my grandmother said. 'Well, the pain of this treatment is going to be a thousand times worse than childbirth. But your heart is as strong as a horse's, so you should be able to cope with it!' was his clincher. I don't know. Perhaps he'd missed the bedside manner module at medical school.

She did have the treatment and it was painful, but at least it was successful for a while. Then, the cancer returned. Back then there was no way you could have a second dose of radiotherapy. There was no escaping the long job of simply nursing my grandmother as she got weaker and weaker on ever-increasing doses of morphine. Indeed, it was my job to get the morphine from the chemists. I would run down to the shops, sign the poisons register, nip into the next-door newsagents and get the *Dandy* and the *Beano* as my reward for running the errand. Then I'd walk home, head buried in the comics, blissfully unaware of the powerful opiate in the little paper bag in my pocket. Signing the poisons register was just normal for me at twelve years old.

My grandmother, Jane Rees, finally passed away in January 1952. The morphine despite ever-increasing dosages was no longer able to counter the pain, and her heart finally gave out. As with many children, the death of a grandparent is the first experience you have of mortality. It didn't hit me as anything sudden or unexpected. She'd been dying for a long time. Courtesy of my supplying the morphine, I suppose she had become a drug addict. That was the only way to cope with the pain 'a thousand times worse than childbirth'.

What it was like for my grandfather, I cannot imagine. He would sit next to her in the bedroom, dutiful as a deacon to the end. She would moan in pain. He could do absolutely nothing about it and developed this coping mechanism of moaning with her. He couldn't think of anything else to do. The noise used to fill the whole house. He must have felt just as powerless when his son David died of diphtheria at five years old.

About six months before she died, something happened which definitely had a formative influence on me. My grandmother had a day's remission. It was on a Sunday. When I told my strictly Sabbatarian Auntie Mary Ann later that day that my grandmother had done some washing in the morning, my aunt disapproved. I was as angry as only teenagers can be about the 'No washing on the Sabbath' issue, and I never felt the same about Welsh chapel values after that.

I was probably far too confused by then. I'd already had a taste of three different kinds of Nonconformist chapel religion. Until 1946, when petrol became available again and our pre-war Morris 8 was back in action, we'd had no option but to attend Sunday School next-door at the English Wesleyan Methodists. We sang 'All Things Bright and Beautiful' every week.

With petrol coupons available, the language of religion turned to Welsh – Congregationalist in Gwaelod-y-Garth for the morning service, and then the Baptist Sunday School in the Hayes Tabernacle in the centre of Cardiff in the afternoon. Even today, 'All Things Bright and Beautiful' doesn't sound right to me in Welsh, and the Lord's Prayer doesn't sound right in English.

My father by this time had liberated my thinking quite a bit by referring to himself as a 'rationalist'. This may have come from his being baptised by a Communist Congregationalist, the famous Reverend T. E. Nicholas – Niclas y Glais, to give him his popular name in Welsh. Niclas was a great poet, a noted pacifist, a famous Congregationalist minister and, by all accounts, a terrible dentist.

With my father's background, I've never been able to work out why he never went in for politics himself. All the influences were there on him, but somehow he managed to pass them all on to me while totally eschewing them himself. I recall his fascinating account of an open-air meeting in Swansea that he'd attended around 1930 to listen to Tom Mann, leader of the 1889 London Dock Strike, attacking the Mond-Turner accords (an early attempt at capital and labour getting together in the common interest).

My father once explained why we always had *The Sunday Times* as our Sunday paper, and never *The Observer*. It might have seemed odd for a left-leaning person to insist on buying a Kemsley-owned Tory-supporting newspaper like *The Sunday Times* – I'd assumed that it was because the rugby coverage was so much better – but it was nothing to do with that. It was all about the Spanish Civil War. *The Observer* had supported Franco, and the paper had not yet been forgiven by my father.

Anti- or pro-Franco – that was a bigger social divide in South Wales than anywhere else in Britain. Left-wing miners volunteered for the International Brigade. Buccaneering sea captains from Cardiff, like Ham & Egg Jones and Potato

Jones, were proud to run the gauntlet of Franco's naval blockade. No Spanish navy was going to stop them delivering their food cargo up to Bilbao. Basque orphans were taken in with welcoming arms.

The added political edge in Wales was that the founding father of Plaid Cymru, Saunders Lewis, was pro-Franco. A Methodist minister's son born in the bosom of the Liverpool Welsh community, Lewis had converted to Catholicism. Given Franco's promise to crush nationalist ambitions in Catalonia and the Basque country to defend their respective languages, you might have thought that Lewis would empathise with those small nations' rights to their own identity and at least some element of self-government. But for Lewis, the Catholicism came before the solidarity of small nations. He was well out of step with what most people in Wales thought.

Saunders Lewis was a lecturer in the Welsh Department at the university in Swansea when my mother and father were students there. He'd taught them poetry appreciation. My mother had been heavily influenced by his lectures. Lewis had then come to public notice in 1936 (or notoriety) when he and two others, D. J. Williams, a schoolteacher from Fishguard, and the Reverend Lewis Valentine had carried out a semi-symbolic attempt at arson at a new bombing school being built in preparation for the impending war at Penyberth on the Llŷn Peninsula in north-west Wales.

My father was an admirer of Saunders's plays and poems, but not of his politics. It all came to a crunch at the National Eisteddfod in Denbigh in August 1939, the last eisteddfod festival held before the Second World War and seven weeks before I was born. My father travelled on his own to the eisteddfod as an adjudicator in the short story and other prose competitions. He was billeted for the week at Garthewin, a local manor house belonging to R. O. F. Wynne, like Saunders Lewis a Catholic convert. The other 'lodger' for the week was Saunders Lewis himself, who was adjudicating some of the poetry competitions.

Each morning over breakfast, Lewis and Wynne would rejoice at Franco's victory in the Spanish Civil War that April. The phrase 'A fine upstanding Christian Gentleman' would be trotted out regarding Franco. My father could barely keep down his boiled egg and toast.

An even bigger divide opened up in 1943. Hard though it is now to imagine, university graduates had two votes at general elections – one where they lived, and one for their university seat, regardless of where they lived. This arrangement was abolished in 1948. But, in 1943, the University of Wales MP died, and there was a by-election.

There was hue and cry among the Welsh intelligentsia for Saunders Lewis to be given a 'free run' for the seat. Saunders would be adopted as a Plaid Cymru candidate and Labour, Liberals and the Conservatives would desist from fielding candidates.

The theory was that Plaid Cymru would never ever win a seat at a general election, and the only way in which Plaid Cymru would ever have its voice heard in the House of Commons was via the University of Wales seat – and only then if the other parties did not field candidates.

Despite the pressure to give Saunders a free run, people like my father and his old boss W. J. Gruffydd, the Professor of Welsh at Cardiff, an ex-Plaid member himself, thought the 'free run for Saunders' idea was barking. Gruffydd ran as a Liberal with my father as his agent, and he won. They repeated the same feat at the 1945 General Election, before the whole university seat nonsense was done away with.

My father once said to me that Saunders had upset him enormously, not only on account of his views on Franco. Lewis had pronounced that the Welsh working class should not emerge from their poverty until they had learnt to appreciate the Welsh language and culture. To say that to my father in the Hungry Thirties – a miner's son from the Valleys just when the Valleys were being devastated by unemployment, poverty and massive emigration – was insensitivity of the highest order.

Basically, if you thought like Saunders, you would wish that the Industrial Revolution had never happened. If Saunders could have taken Wales back to a pre-Industrial and pre-Reformation Catholic Wales, as a country of small farms and small businesses, he'd have been over the moon.

That, in a way, is still the fundamental divide over what is the No. 1 problem for Wales. Is it replacing the jobs lost in coal and steel and tinplate in the Valleys and the slate quarrying areas of north-west Wales, or is it how to save the Welsh language from being drowned by immigration to the Welsh-speaking heartlands (Y Fro Gymraeg).

My father's job during the war was in the Ministry of Labour. He'd been called up but was considered too old for the fighting part, and had become the secretary of the Tribunal on Conscientious Objectors and Reserved Occupations. He was, in a way, a civil servant and a serviceman and a seconded university lecturer all at the same time. When I became a regular drinker in the Old Arcade pub in Church Street in the middle of Cardiff in the 1960s, I had no idea it was where my father used to meet his old boss W. J. Gruffydd once a week during the war for a pub lunch, so that my father could stay in touch with what was happening back in the Welsh Department in Cardiff.

My father must have found it a massive change to be out of academia for six years, but everyone else was on the move as well, doing things they'd never done before. He enjoyed being secretary of the Tribunal. I can't have been more than five years old when my father came back from a Tribunal visit to North Wales once. He told the family over tea about this little incident where an eighteen-year-old would-be conscientious objector had appeared before them.

He was very religious. He'd claimed that he couldn't fight because of his pacifist principles. All very standard stuff for the three Tribunal members – Professor d'Albuquerque, the trade union representative Herbert Hiles of the Bakers Union, and an employer rep, whose name never came up. None of the three spoke any Welsh. The chairman asked the young man to give the Tribunal some idea of the frequency of his chapel attendance. 'As seldom as I can, sir!' came his surprising reply. There was consternation all round until my father asked the young man in Welsh if he could answer that question in Welsh. It was 'often' not 'seldom', obviously.

My mother wasn't keen on my father's undoubted skills as an administrator. 'I thought I'd married a poet', she used to wail only half-jokingly. Back in the 1930s, she was complaining that the poet she thought she'd married was only writing prose or was only interested in linguistics. Then during the war and even more strongly later on when my father became Registrar of the University of Wales in 1951, the wail of complaint went, 'I thought I'd married a poet and found out too late that I'd married an administrator!'

Welsh poetry meant a lot to my mother, having studied it under Saunders Lewis at Swansea for her BA and MA courses. How much influence that had on her political views, I can't say. Quite a bit had soaked in. She was hugely enthusiastic about Gwynfor Evans's victory in the Carmarthen by-election in the Summer of 1966, in that 'A new dawn has broken over Wales' kind of way that tends to greet any Plaid Cymru electoral success. If I had a pound for every time I've heard that expression, I could have abolished income tax in Wales when I was First Minister.

I know you should never judge a man by his handshake, but I had been very struck by the limpness of Gwynfor's on the only occasion I met him, when I was an undergraduate and he had been the guest of honour of the Dafydd ap Gwilym, the Welsh society at the University of Oxford. I should probably blame my fellow students. Many of them supported Plaid, and they may have pumped Gwynfor's hand so hard that it was no surprise it was so limp by the time he got to me!

The family influence on me came from this carefully constructed peace agreement between my mother – more Plaidish – and my father – more socialist. It basically meant that they didn't argue about politics, certainly not party politics in front of the children.

One thing they definitely could agree on was that kids should not be going to school hungry. My mother had experienced the impossibility of teaching kids poetry appreciation or anything else if they went to school hungry in her first teaching job in Rhymney from 1929–31. My father had experienced going to school hungry himself. The kindness of his teachers had kept him going, teachers who brought leftover crusts or toast in paper bags to school and discreetly placed them on the desks of the hungry kids. If there was no paper bag with a crust in it, my father's head would slowly drop onto the desk for a little sleep.

It wasn't all happy days or fun and games for my father, even when his own father was in work. Health and safety was appalling by today's standards. My father would come home from school some days to find my grandfather fast asleep in the passageway. It was oxygen deprivation in the levels – the shallow entrance mines around Glais – that caused the problem. The miners were breathing in methane and all sorts while working flat out physically to get the coal.

My grandfather had originated from Landore (Glandŵr in Welsh) in the Lower Swansea Valley, which had been the world capital of the copper industry. There was one very specific reason why my grandfather was so proud of coming from Landore – there was Welsh royal blood there. Dickie Owen, who had captained Wales to victory in 1905 over the otherwise invincible All Blacks, was from Landore. 'Never forget', he would boast to my father and his older brother Gwyn, 'Dickie Owen's full name is Richard MORGAN Owen. He's your uncle. Our family!'

These reminiscences and views that my father had did certainly steer me towards politics, though they steered him away from it. Why was that? For me, politics became the top priority. For him, I think it was number three or four. His priority was to get and keep your safe job, and there weren't many around in Wales in the 1930s. Second was his love of the intricacies of the Welsh language, with all its infernal soft mutations which make it so hard to master well. Third, maybe, was rugby, which he'd given up at twenty-two. He certainly got a huge amount of enjoyment from watching it.

I absorbed an awful lot of my politics by osmosis from him and his instinctive bias to the left, so much so that it became the big thing for me in a way that it never had been for him.

My mother was not a miner's daughter. Her parents on both sides were small-business people, what Stalin would have contemptuously referred to as *kulaks*. My grandfather on that side of the family came from a small-holding above the Swansea Valley. My grandmother's family had farmed, but by the time of her upbringing they had a pony and trap business in the industrial suburb of Llansamlet in the Lower Swansea Valley, opposite Landore.

There was much more politics from the gene pool coming down to me from my mother's family. Far more of it than in my father's exceedingly humble origins. My mother's father, John Rees the grocer, then coal merchant, and Baptist chapel deacon, had been chairman of Llangyfelach Parish Council around the turn of the century. Not that I knew that when I became an MP! He sat as an Independent, but he would instinctively have supported the Lloyd George Liberals especially on issues such as the Disestablishment of the Church in Wales. That was a massively popular cause at the time, in part because it abolished the tithe, the tax on all to pay for church schools for the few.

My great-grandfather Thomas Rees had been a leading light in the tenants' rights movement against oppression from the landlords. He had given evidence, much praised for its cogency, to the Commission on Land Reform in the 1890s. He had married into the family of the really famous Morgans of Wales – not my father's family, not Henry Morgan the pirate's, not Cliff Morgan the outside half's family, but the Morgans of Cwmcile Farm.

Unbiased? Of course I am! At the height of the Rebecca Riots against the toll-gates in south-west Wales, on 23 July 1843, there was a fracas at Cwmcile Farm, where my great-great-great-grandfather Morgan Morgan lived – not far north of the M4, north-west of Swansea, close to where Morriston Hospital now stands. Colonel Napier, the very first Chief Constable of Glamorgan, arrived at six on the Sunday morning to make some arrests. I don't know when the British police started to go about their business unarmed, but Colonel Napier was definitely 'tooled up'.

David Williams, the doyen of modern Welsh historians, describes what happened in his 1955 classic *The Rebecca Riots*:

> The family objected vigorously to being disturbed on the Sabbath … the whole family set about the two police officers. The father belaboured them with his stick and the mother with a bar of iron which she snatched from the fire, while the sister threw a saucepan of boiling water at them. Out of doors they got Napier (yes, this is the armed Chief Constable we are talking about!) and in the struggle the sister cut his head with a reaping hook. They tried to seize his pistol, but he succeeded in freeing his arm and shot a younger brother in the stomach. This increased their fury. Yet another brother Rees attacked with a hammer and Henry, who had come downstairs, with a hatchet. Napier who was now on his feet floored the farmer with his fist and then fired his pistol again, so that Henry ran away. The shots brought one of the other policemen on the scene. With his help, the two officers secured the wounded boy and took him and the elder brother Mathew to Swansea. In the afternoon a company of the 73rd Foot reached Cwmcile and arrested both mother and daughter and the brother Rees. The father was recognised in Swansea the following day, enquiring about his wounded son and he, also was arrested.

That was a nice quiet Welsh Sunday in the countryside, wasn't it?

Maybe they didn't understand the concept of the police as the new law enforcers. There could have been a bit of Welsh–English language confusion. They might have been utterly scandalised by the attempt to make the arrest on the Sabbath. You might imagine that a yeoman farmer family with quite a lot to lose might have done a quick calculation of the risks – that would normally have told an elderly couple, confronted by an armed Chief Constable and a police inspector, not to go in for outright frontal attack.

The consequences of what they did were incalculable and could at the very least have ended in transportation to Botany Bay, if not worse. I used to speculate at Welsh Labour fund-raising dinners that if my great-great-great-grandparents had been shipped to Botany Bay, I'd be addressing them not as Rhodri Morgan, First Minister of Wales, but as visiting guest speaker Bruce Morgan, Premier of New South Wales!

They never were transported. Their status as ultra-respectable although notoriously stubborn yeoman farmers stood them in good stead a few months later at the trial. I still find my mind in a boggle trying to picture the scene on the Sunday afternoon, when forty soldiers of the 73rd Regiment of Foot arrived at the farm to arrest my great-great-great-grandmother.

I had some unexpected support from *The Times* when I was running against Alun Michael for the Labour leadership in early 1999. William Rees Mogg, by then retired from the editor's chair but still an occasional columnist (and father of the self-caricaturing young fogey Tory MP Jacob Rees Mogg) supported my candidacy. He expressed bafflement that Tony Blair opposed me standing for the job, saying that I'd been superbly well educated at Oxford and Harvard. I spoke Welsh fluently. My father had been a professor. Why, it was almost as if I'd been genetically engineered to lead the Welsh Assembly.

Well, I somehow doubt that it was the genes I inherited from my great-great-great-grandmother Esther, who wrestled in the Cwmcile Farm yard with Colonel Napier the Chief Constable, that William Rees Mogg was commending me for having in my genetic CV – what he meant was that I'd been to Oxford.

Some of the Cwmcile stubbornness genes may have passed on to my grandfather John Rees. An individual of very few words, the worst criticism he would make of any man in the chapel or village was that he went with the flow –'mynd gyda'r afon' in Welsh. That meant being less bound by a guiding set of principles and prepared to rely too much on the opinion of the majority. Indeed, he was so inclined to stick to his own views that his own mother warned her prospective daughter-in-law not to marry him. He was far too stubborn to be married to any woman!

What I may have absorbed as an attitude is a sense that authority is not a matter of hierarchy handing down doctrine, and expecting automatic acceptance of it by the flock.

John Rees, my mother's father, was one of that first generation of Welsh children to attend state schooling after the Forster Education Act provided for universal and compulsory primary education until the age of eleven. That was a consequence of the Gladstone Liberal landslide of 1868. It was a traumatic experience for that first generation of kids to go to school, because they only spoke Welsh and the education was provided only through the medium of English.

This was the era of the Welsh Not, the dunce's cap device used to discourage Welsh being spoken in the playground. My grandfather claimed that this was never a problem for him and his two younger brothers, Tommy and Willy. At the approach of the playground supervisor wielding the Welsh Not, the three brothers would sprint for the wall, climb over it 'Colditz' style and play in the woods and fields all day. The girls with their hooped skirts couldn't do that. Despite this inherited rebellious streak, he did well enough in school to be employed in his final school year until he left aged twelve as a 'pupil teacher' – which meant helping the slower learners with their sums for a few pennies a week.

When my grandfather was three, the family was evicted from Ty'n y Waun, the small farm they had occupied under a 'nine lives' tenancy since the 1550s. They moved to nearby Blaen 'r Olchfa. It was from there that my grandfather went to Pen Clun school, before becoming an apprentice grocer in Ynystawe. He moved his chapel membership from Salem Llangyfelach to Moreia Ynystawe, where he became a deacon at nineteen, and remained one for sixty years.

My final memory of my grandfather was an emotional moment at his funeral in 1954. As we were leaving the chapel in the hearse for the cemetery, I was sat in the passenger front seat. An elderly lady was tapping my window, and I wound down the window to see her face with tears streaming down. She grasped my wrist like a claw – I can still feel that vice-like grip pinching through my flesh down to the bone – and she said in Welsh, 'If it wasn't for your grandfather John Rees, a lot of people in this village would have starved. We'll never forget what he did for us.' My grandfather had kept on extending credit to striking miners. He was initially backed up by his suppliers, like Weavers Mill down on Swansea Docks, but eventually the suppliers withdrew their credit and my grandfather got into severe financial difficulties. But he had done what he thought was right to help stop miners' children from starving.

When I delivered my maiden speech in the House of Commons in 1987, I was thinking of Margaret Thatcher having been hugely influenced by her grocer father in Grantham – I'm not sure whether Margaret Thatcher ever had that experience at her father Alf's funeral, of a lady digging her fingers into her wrist and saying, 'If it wasn't for Alf Roberts, a lot of children in Grantham would have starved.'

When the shop went downhill, and then later the small coal mine in Cwmavon north of Port Talbot turned out not to have much coal in it, the family income depended for a while on my grandmother's earning power as a piano teacher and a seamstress. She was unusual in being determined to be an independent earner in the family – that's why my mother's values were coloured by that small-business upbringing, and especially about the risks of businesses going wrong. Getting into university and a safe job in academia or the professions was far safer.

Politics was far too chancy. If my father had thought of making a mid-career switch to politics, he certainly had the contacts. After our family had settled in Radyr, from 1935 onwards, one of our neighbours and a university colleague of my father's on the daily commute to Cathays Park was Hilary Marquand. He was the Professor of Industrial Relations, but better known as the author of the Grand Plan for the revitalization of the South Wales Valleys, first published in 1931, and then an improved version in 1936. He was elected MP for Cardiff East in 1945, and became a junior Minister immediately. He finally got into the Cabinet in 1951 when Aneurin Bevan, along with Harold Wilson and John Freeman, resigned over the imposition of prescription charges. Marquand was Bevan's replacement as Minister of Health and Housing for just six months or so before Labour lost power in the 1951 General Election. His son David carried the political tradition on by becoming the MP for Sutton in Nottinghamshire in the 1960s.

Another contact was Arthur Jenkins, the Parliamentary Private Secretary to Clem Attlee, Labour leader and Churchill's Deputy Prime Minister during the Second World War. Jenkins was the MP for Pontypool, and used to park his car in our drive when he visited Hilary Marquand. The Marquands didn't have a drive. The Jenkins vehicle was a rather ostentatious Armstrong Siddeley, and he would cross the road in his even more ostentatious astrakhan coat! Arthur's son Roy also became an MP in 1945, and became a Labour Chancellor of the Exchequer and Home Secretary – before becoming the founder of the SDP after returning from a stint as President of the European Commission. The Jenkins–Marquand connection established by the two fathers continued with the two sons. When Roy Jenkins got the top job in Europe as President of the European Commission in 1976, he took David Marquand to Brussels to be his *Chef de Cabinet*. That relationship was forged in our drive at no. 32 Heol Isaf.

Of course, my father had left academia for the Ministry of Labour after being called up during the war. That had been very fulfilling. The other part of his war service was in the Ely Home Guard, keeping the Luftwaffe at bay with the ack-ack batteries. His great friend in the Home Guard was the artist Ceri Richards. Like my father, he was Welsh-speaking from the Swansea area, and a lecturer in Cardiff School of Art. I suppose you could describe them as the provisional wing of the Ely Home Guard.

On one occasion, the pair of them went to their sergeant to ask whether the unit should have more training – they hadn't hit any German aircraft, just a greenhouse on the other side of Cardiff. The sergeant listened to their plea patiently, then let loose. 'Morgan, Richards – you don't understand, do you? The purpose of this ack-ack battery is not to hit German aircraft. It is to make a hell of a lot of noise so that the good burghers of Cardiff can sleep soundly in their beds knowing that their city is being properly defended!' That put them in their place.

While my father was doing his overnights in Ely, my mother, brother and I had to endure the occasional air-raid near Radyr. If the air-raid siren went off, we certainly knew about it. The siren was located on the police station roof next door, about five yards from our bedroom. When it went off, my mother would pick up my brother and me, take us downstairs, pull out the rough hessian canvas camp bed (I can still smell that hessian) and we would all sleep together there in the cupboard under the stairs until morning.

Sleeping in a cupboard now and again was hardly a major deprivation during wartime. Our friends, the Sussemilchs, who lived opposite our house knew what war was really like. The father had fought in the International Brigade in the Spanish Civil War. Then he returned to Czechoslovakia when the Germans invaded the Sudetenland after the Munich betrayal. As a Communist, he then headed east, leaving the mother Klara, daughter Hertha and son Bruno aged eight, to fend for themselves.

My survival skills were never tested like Bruno's. All I had to contend with was going to Radyr School in 1944 when it was swollen to twice its normal size by the evacuees. For that first year of school, you just did not know who you would find yourself walking with, to or from the school. It was more like a United Nations school than a village school. There were Cockney kids. There were Brummie kids, Coventry kids, Maidstone kids, Glasgow kids, Motherwell kids. Some evacuees had their parents with them, and most were billeted with Radyr families. Others were not strictly evacuees but arrived under the 'Directed Labour' scheme, the head of the house having been directed to jobs in the Cardiff area. There was no choice about it. The government would find you a requisitioned house, but you had no choice about the job.

I started school in the official sense in 1944. But I'd already been attending a kind of school on Saturday morning. This was the Welsh-speaking school in Tŷ'r Cymry in an unprepossessing bay-window terraced house, just around the corner from the Lord Mayor's official residence in Gordon Road, Cardiff. It had been donated in the late 1930s to the tiny minority of Welsh-speaking families in Cardiff to serve as a focal point for Welsh language and culture activities. The donor was Lewis Evans, a residential landlord.

For those unfamiliar with Cardiff's history, it was first a Roman garrison, then a Norman fort, then a little fishing port, before the explosive arrival of the coal industry just to the north. One thing Cardiff had never been was Welsh-speaking. My parents had been involved in doing up the Tŷ'r Cymry house so that it was habitable for children's activities on Saturday mornings. My brother Prys and I were founder pupils of that school. You can think of the Tŷ'r Cymry Saturday school as the forerunner of all the Welsh-medium schools in Cardiff, where there are now sufficient primary schools to feed three sizeable secondary schools.

By the time I flew through the eleven-plus in 1950 to attend Whitchurch Grammar School, I had already attended three schools. First, the Welsh-medium Saturday school from 1942. Then the United Nations evacuee-swollen school for the year 1944–5. Then from 1945 until 1950, a nice quiet Anglo-Welsh village school complete with a spare classroom. If I had to guess which one had most influence on my leanings towards politics, I'd have to nominate that first year in the all-UK UN-type school. It was such an eye-opener.

I'd also tasted three different varieties of Christianity, albeit all Nonconformist. I had attended an English Wesleyan Methodist Sunday School until 1945. Then morning service at Bethlehem Congregationalist Chapel in Gwaelod-y-Garth, only three miles north of Radyr but far more Welsh – and then we attended the Hayes Tabernacle Welsh Baptist Sunday School in the afternoons. Was I confused about religion? You bet I was.

Gwaelod-y-Garth was very different socially to Radyr. It's a hill village on which the film *The Englishman who went up a Hill but came down a Mountain* was based. It gave me an experience of life in a Welsh village rather than a Cardiff suburb.

The most significant learning experience I had in the grammar school came in February 1952. This was one month after my grandmother had passed away. We were all called into the school hall mid-morning to be told that the King had died. When my brother had gone to the grammar school in 1948, the head was Arthur Richard, the uncle of Ivor Richard, a member of Tony Blair's first Cabinet in 1997 as Labour leader in the Lords. Arthur had retired by the time I started there in 1950. The head making the out-of-the-blue announcement about the sudden passing of King George VI was Wyndham Jones.

He told this special assembly that school was suspended for the day. The side gate on Church Road that we Radyr boys used to get into the school would be closed, so that all pupils would leave via the main gate. That way, we would see the flag at half-mast on the British Legion building opposite. We were all to file out in a dignified manner with no running or jostling. Once past the flag, we could then proceed home in good order. He didn't say we should bow our heads or salute the flag, but he came pretty close.

The half-dozen of us from Radyr got on the first train available. We'd just settled into our seats when the carriage was filled by a late rush of workers from the Melin Griffith tinplate works, the only big factory anywhere near the school. They'd obviously been given a half-day as well. We all bunked up close together in our school uniforms to make room for the late arrivals in their uniforms – greasy overalls, that is. Most of them would be travelling on, way past Radyr, to their homes in the Valleys.

One of the workmen had managed to buy a copy of the special early edition of the local evening paper, the *South Wales Echo*. It had a half-inch-wide black edge all the way round the front page, and a massive banner headline 'THE KING IS DEAD'. Underneath that was a huge picture of the newly-widowed Queen Elizabeth the Queen Mother wearing a veil, but visible underneath her a brave-looking quizzical Mona Lisa-like half-smile.

One of the overalled workmen must have muttered some words of commendation for her apparent dignity in grief – but another workman did not share that view, and uttered two words in a strong Valleys accent which I can still hear to this day. 'Brazen bitch', he said very firmly, as some kind of judgement from the depths. There was a stunned silence. We uniformed grammar school boys had been in some kind of cocoon of middle-class respectability since being called to the school hall an hour before. Those two words, uttered with such certitude, had burst the bubble we'd been in. As for me, I had no idea what the words meant. All I knew was that they weren't meant as a compliment.

I raced home from the station. My mother was there as mothers always were in those days. I was full of both bewilderment and excitement about the incident. 'What does "brazen bitch" mean?' That's all I wanted to know. It would solve the mystery of the universe. My mother cautiously asked why I needed to know, and I explained what had happened in the overcrowded railway carriage. She then said I must never use those words – but, for the purpose of background information, what lay behind it was that not everyone in the Valleys thought the Royal Family was so wonderful.

Until the bursting bubble on that day, I don't think I had ever considered how someone could challenge the symbolic icons of the British establishment. Of course, millions had voted Labour in 1945 to get rid of Churchill, but he was back in now. You could be against Churchill, but surely not against the Royal Family? I was a genuine war-baby and a ration-book baby anyway – half the map in our school geography books was coloured red. That's how our world was, surely. Now, there was a crack in it.

The drip-feed effect of the war on me came about mainly because I'd never known anything else. I'd been issued with my ration book even before I had a name – my ration book said simply 'Baby Morgan'. Once you'd entered the system as 'Baby Morgan', you were always 'Baby Morgan'. Even when my mother and I went to buy my first pair of long trousers, the clothing coupons still said 'Baby Morgan'.

I had seen a gang of Italian prisoners-of-war digging out the huge snow drifts in December 1944 on the A4119, the Llantrisant Road, which cut Radyr off from Cardiff. I'd seen Field Marshal von Rundstedt walking along the Bridgend bypass, interned in the Island Farm prisoner-of-war camp while awaiting trial at Nuremberg. I have vague memories of D-Day and VE Day, and of the Labour landslide. I have very strong memories of the evacuees going home, of the VJ Day giant bonfire celebrations down at the village cricket field, and hearing dance music on some kind of rigged sound system and seeing husbands and wives dancing together. Not my parents, though, because while my father had allegedly been an excellent mover on the dancefloor, my mother either couldn't or wouldn't.

Two other things denoted the end of the war within our family. One involved my father going down to Cardiff Market and buying examples of all the fruit that we hadn't tasted during the war. My brother might possibly have had some taste-bud memories of exotic fruit, but not me. Bananas were wonderful. Pomegranates were unbelievably disappointing. Coconuts were somewhere in between.

The other thing he did was to buy a rugby ball. This coincided with my brother starting violin lessons next to Whitchurch Library and park, also next to Velindre Hospital, where my grandmother was to receive her cancer treatment a few years hence. While my brother went through the torture of his hour's violin lesson with Miss Dorothy Morgan, quite a martinet of a teacher, my father and I repaired to the park. Up and down and up and down we ran, passing the ball to each other. Occasionally my father would throw a dummy to me. I always bought it. That had been my father's great gift as a centre three-quarter back in the 1920s, and it certainly fooled me every time.

What really struck me about my father on those occasions was the expression of childlike delight and relaxation on his face that I'd never seen before. If you think of that great cliché of post-war British prisoner-of-war films, where the fiendish German capturer says to the captured plucky Brit, 'For you, Tommy, the war [pronounced "ze vor"] is over', well, that's how it was for my father. That smile of happiness meant that for him the war was definitely over. That's when I realised rugby touched a part of my father's psyche that nothing else could. He might have been in his late thirties and a heavy smoker, but he was enjoying himself as much as in his Glais boyhood. Now he was teaching his son how to play rugby and tried (but ultimately failed) to teach him how to pick which pass was the dummy.

My father had a level of physical coordination that I could never match. I never saw him dancing the Charleston, but I do remember him killing a mouse with a volume of the *Encyclopaedia Britannica*! In my mind's eye, I can still see him sat in a kitchen chair casually reading the *Encyclopaedia*. A cube of cheese had cunningly been placed six inches away from the skirting board where the mouse-hole had appeared. Out came the mouse, delighted at the ending of cheese rationing. In one movement, my father closed the *Encyclopaedia* and aimed it at the nibbling mouse, flattening it.

I fear that if my father ever dreamt I might one day play rugby for Wales, by giving me a good start with that rugby ball, I must have been a severe disappointment. I was far too skinny, far too slow off the mark, far too easily tackled in possession. I was simply a good rugby-watcher.

My father bought three season tickets for us – my brother and me and him – to watch Cardiff RFC play every other Saturday at the Cardiff Arms Park, where Wales played for the first season when rugby resumed after the war. That was after a break of seven seasons. I lapped it up, but my brother did not. He would bring a sketch-pad along, and would spend the match sketching the crowd or details of the stanchions holding up the roof of the stand.

Because of the rugby starvation during the blank years of war, the crowds for the club games were huge. Cardiff had great pulling power for players from the Valleys, from Glamorgan and Gwent or further west. The centre pairing that Cardiff had in Bleddyn Williams and Jack Matthews was arguably the best centre pairing ever to have played the game in Wales or anywhere else. Haydn Tanner, the scrum-half, was again arguably the best in the world, and only Gareth Edwards can touch his achievements, despite Tanner like the others of that era having missed out on the best seven years of their careers. There was plenty of spending power around as the late 1940s was an era of post-war reconstruction, where demand for coal and steel seemed limitless. There was no return to the 1930s and the Great Slump.

During the summer of 1948, my father and I occasionally went to the Glamorgan cricket ground backing onto the rugby stadium, and that was the miracle year in which Glamorgan finally won the County Championship, despite being known in some quarters as 'Middlesex Seconds', so many Lord's rejects did they have in the team!

What all these experiences were doing for me was building up a Welsh wall of inner self-confidence. I love R. S. Thomas's poetry but I've never been able to recognise the picture of *Gwalia Deserta*, a nation in permanent decline, which inspires his poetry. Beautifully depressing wonderful verse. I grew up in a parallel universe to R.S. My Wales was doing okay and I was convinced that I was in the right place, the right city and the right country.

Of course, there was a strong sense of Britishness as well. But if Britishness meant British Empire-ness, the Britain where half the world map was coloured red, then that was going down the pan pretty quickly during my progress through grammar school. But I didn't lament the Empire's passing.

Not everyone would have agreed with my view. We had a steady trickle at the grammar school of returnee children from the Empire, whose parents had had good jobs in India, Malaya and so on. When I was at the school dinner table in the Fifth Form, I heard a conversation between two of these returnee children, three years younger than me, which left me so gobsmacked that I didn't even respond to it. One lad (ex-India) said to a girl (ex-Dutch East Indies), 'We taught them all they know!' Inwardly, I recoiled. I had read about white people in the colonies thinking these thoughts and uttering them in white-only company, but now I'd actually heard with my own ears two people spouting such drivel right in front of me! It wasn't in a play or a Rudyard Kipling poem, but at our school dinner table.

The Suez adventure in October 1956 went nowhere, and did nothing except confirm that Britain was no longer a world power. That happened when I was in the Lower Sixth. The collapse of the Suez adventure was quite a heady cocktail for me in my formative years. The Soviet Union was in the international doghouse over the brutal repression of the Hungarian Uprising, and now Anthony Eden had managed to upset the Americans and the Soviets at the same time by invading Egypt to try to take back the Suez Canal.

It was almost like a real-life version of a script from *The Goon Show*. That programme's weekly utterly anarchic exploration of British establishment pomposity had a big effect on me and my generation. The Goons' Trans-Africa Aeroplane Canal could easily have been Suez. My father found *The Goon Show* too anarchic. I loved it. He preferred *Take It From Here*.

I did once need my father to explain me the hidden meaning of one little passage in *The Goons Show* which had slipped past the BBC censors, something about an obscure eastern European country ruled by a hapless Royal Family dynasty called the Eidelbergers. Following the death of the old King, his courtiers discussed what to do about the succession, and one of them pronounced, 'We don't want another Eidelberger on the throne!'

The studio audience went into paroxysms. It was probably the first time anyone in Britain had ever had the chance to poke fun at *a*, if not *the* Royal Family. You've never heard laughter like it. I couldn't get the joke, to my eternal shame, sophisticated teenager though I thought I was. It went clean over my head. I had to go into the study where my father was reading. I asked him what was so funny? He gently explained that 'Eidelberger' could be read as 'Idle bugger'. We don't want another idle bugger on the throne, of course, of course. I went back into the living room thumping my forehead with the flat of my hand. The audience was still laughing. How did they get that past the censors? It was a moment of liberation, although I didn't get it at first. Even Auntie Beeb could be liberated.

When and how did that liberation fit in with my grasp of politics? The Conservatives were back in charge. They'd won enough marginal seats to get back in in 1951. One of those marginals was Barry – that was our parliamentary seat – and I knew that there were a lot of Tories in Radyr. Indeed the parents of my two best friends were Tories. One of them would rail against the iniquities of the red tape restrictions on private business of the post-war Labour Government. I knew that my parents didn't seem to share those frustrations of the government's attempts to rebuild the economy post-war, while introducing the National Health Service and so on.

The General Election of October 1951 was the first one at which I attended a political meeting. The Korean War was in full swing. Barry was such a marginal seat that the Labour victor in the 1945 landslide, Lynn Ungoed-Thomas, had decided to switch to a safer Labour seat in Leicester. To everyone's surprise, Labour had held on in 1950, courtesy of Alderwoman (but always known as Alderman) Dorothy Rees. She was one of a very rare breed. She was a Welsh woman MP.

After eighteen months as our MP, she was coming to Radyr Church Rooms, our village hall, in her campaign to save the seat. She probably shouldn't have bothered. But she was coming. So at just twelve years of age I insisted to my mother that we go. My brother came too. Wild horses would not have dragged my father there, but my mother knew it was part of my education. When we arrived, I understood why my father didn't want to be there. Bearpits didn't come close.

The Conservatives had thrown the kitchen sink at the seat, going to the extent of persuading the Liberals not to field a candidate. The Conservative Raymond Gower ran as a Conservative and Liberal! The late Alun Emlyn-Jones, who had done pretty well in 1950, had to stand down. He was later to be my landlord in 1964, when Neil Kinnock and I rented the old Emlyn-Jones family home at 40 Cyncoed Road, where Lloyd George always stayed on his many visits to Cardiff.

I never realised that Radyr had quite so many Hooray Henries until that meeting. They were sure they were going to win. The warm-up speaker, Lord MacDonald of Gwaun Ysgor, an ultra-moderate North Wales miners' leader ennobled by the Attlee Government, lapped up all the heckling and all the shouts of 'What about the Ground Nut Scheme? What about rising prices?', and threw it back.

It was very different when Dorothy Rees arrived and started her speech. The crowd hadn't got their piece of meat with Lord MacDonald. They heckled Dorothy Rees mercilessly with all the 'What about rising prices?' stuff twice as loud. She had a thin and reedy voice, and she just couldn't make herself heard. After ten minutes, she left the stage in tears, the same stage where the dinner ladies had doled out the school dinners when I was in the village school two years before. She had never experienced crowd hostility like this. I looked across our row. I saw very respectable business types I knew who walked down past our old house every day wearing bowler hats and suits and carrying briefcases and brollies, on their way to Radyr station, the very picture of Radyr respectability. Now they were screaming abuse and barracking through cupped hands. They were just short of baying for blood!

Labour lost the seat. If the Liberals had stood, Labour might have saved it. Who knows? Dorothy Rees went back to local government as an Alderman of Glamorgan County Council. Raymond Gower went on to become a semi-permanent fixture in the Commons as the MP for Barry, subsequently renamed the Vale of Glamorgan, right through to my election as Labour MP for the adjoining seat of Cardiff West in 1987. Sir Raymond died of a massive heart attack in February 1989 while canvassing in the Pontypridd by-election. The consequential

Vale of Glamorgan by-election in May 1989 allowed Labour to win the seat back after thirty-eight years! John Smith, a close friend of mine, beat Rod Richards, later to be the first Tory leader in the Welsh Assembly. That victory in 1989 was the first Labour win from the Conservatives in a by-election since Fulham in 1935.

Sir Raymond deserved better than to be sent out by the Tories on a freezing cold February day in Tonyrefail, canvassing up a steep hill for a totally lost cause. He was a thoroughly nice guy. Indeed it was probably his unfailing courtesy that killed him. A more aggressive Tory MP would have told the by-election agent where to get off when asked to climb the steep hills of Tonyrefail, where there were no Tory votes anyway, just to save the party's deposit. When I arrived in the House in 1987, Sir Raymond knew that I lived in his constituency. He took me around the House, like a favourite uncle. He showed me the best arm chairs in the Commons Library for a snooze during late night sittings. Being a very gentle soul, he would have been horrified by what was meted out on Dorothy Rees in Radyr that day. But politics is a rough old trade.

That political meeting in Radyr Church Rooms was very formative for me. It certainly was dramatic seeing the Labour candidate leave the stage in tears. Perhaps the account my Uncle Dewi gave in the Radyr School centenary leaflet about his being stoned on the way to the council school by boys from Mrs Stanford's (private) Academy during the 1926 General Strike was not so far-fetched after all! The hecklers could easily have been the same persons, twenty-five years on!

But 1951 obviously didn't put me off politics. Indeed, in 1955, when Labour was the challenger, I doubled up. Not only did I attend the Labour meeting, I went to the Conservative one as well! Dan Jones was the Labour candidate, later MP for Burnley, and father of Dari Taylor, the MP for Stockton after 1992. I also asked my first question at the Raymond Gower meeting, about freedom for Cyprus. I was living through this transformation in Britain's status as a truly Great Power in 1945, having defeated Hitler but now sliding into the subsequent loss of Empire. What future did the country called Britain have? We read the *News Chronicle* at home. It was very good in covering the decolonisation of Africa and the French, Belgian, Portuguese and British colonies struggling and heaving their way towards independence. We also read the *Western Mail*, which was good for the rugby, the births, deaths and marriages, but did not follow a progressive agenda.

Around this time my grandfather passed away. I had spent a lot of time with him. He paid for my comics then read them himself. We spent time together in the garage sawing wood together and making toys. It was his younger brother Tommy who was the joiner/carpenter in the family. My grandfather was an untrained but natural carpenter. I still make little Pinocchio-type figurines out of six-inch lengths of broom handles for my grandchildren just as he did for me, but mine are nowhere near as good.

About a year before he died, he stopped reading my comics and took up reading the Bible again. He knew in his bones that his time was coming. He started with Genesis and went all the way through to the end of the Book of Revelations, reading a chapter a night. Then, a fortnight later, he was gone. His kidneys had failed. He went into the Royal Infirmary. He was diagnosed with uraemia and that was it (it was then that I had the experience in the hearse with the lady with the vice-like grip).

The way that my grandfather knew his time was coming was that he couldn't dig the garden any more. If a man couldn't even dig the garden over to ready the tilth for the spring vegetable planting season, that man was no use to anyone. Worse still was the fear of becoming a burden on the family and on society. If there was one person who could not abide the thought of being a burden on the family, it was my grandfather, John Rees. He embodied the Protestant ethic in its purest if extreme Welsh Nonconformist form. Of course, we were all relieved that he had reached the end of the Book of Revelations before his kidneys failed, but they weren't going to fail until the job was done, were they? He knew he had enough strength left to read the Bible, one chapter every night, and only then would his kidneys stop working.

Shortly after that, my mother went through a huge argument with herself over whether to return to teaching. The Conservatives had abolished the rule barring married women from teaching. She'd been twenty years out of the class-room, but had kept up with the curriculum by marking 'A' level scripts for the Central Welsh Board, predecessor of the WJEC. I don't know how much she discussed the question with my father or how much use he was to her on it. But I do know that I once had the following bizarre conversation with her.

She cornered me playing table football in the front room. She said she was going to work her fingers to the bone. She was determined to go back to teaching and throw herself into it as never before. And the money she earned was to pay for me to go to Winchester – to send me away to a very posh albeit highly intel-lectual public school, not a hearty rugger and cold showers one. My mother had actually gone to the trouble of getting the Winchester prospectus. It was the first I'd heard of me going away to school.

Although I was always top of the class in Whitchurch, my parents, or at least my mother, may have thought I wasn't being stretched enough. I was still reading comics rather than books (proper books). I certainly didn't read any book that wasn't written by Enid Blyton. I used to do my homework in twenty minutes and then I was out playing. She had a point, but I just ignored her really and carried on playing table football. I heard no more about it.

I think my mother noticed how unimpressed I'd been by her offer to work her fingers to the bone to help me have a public-school education, with all that might mean for my accent. It was a maternal guilt trip that went horribly wrong.

The likeliest reason for her getting the Winchester College prospectus was that she was casting around for reasons for going back to teaching. Paying the fees to transform me from rough diamond to Oxbridge material was one way of persuading herself to take the plunge back into the classroom.

The only person who would definitely have been impressed would have been Tony Blair, who would probably have made me Foreign Secretary in 1997 – except that I would probably never have been selected as a Labour MP in the first place.

So I never went to Winchester, and she never went back to teaching. Instead, she threw herself into starting a branch of the Women's Institute in Radyr. Radyr's womenfolk, mostly in those days non-working women, did need something like that. It was a huge success. There weren't enough Welsh speakers in the village to form a pioneering branch of what would be the Welsh-language equivalent – Merched y Wawr, formed later in 1967 – so the WI it would have to be.

Soon after, I did get into reading proper books having accidentally discovered Ernest Hemingway via *The Old Man and the Sea*. I read it under the blankets in one go, and was soon devouring everything by him and by John Steinbeck.

A year after my grandfather's death in 1956, my brother won an Open Scholarship to study History at Oxford (or *read* History, to use the correct Oxford form). In those days, Oxbridge colleges required National Service first, so my brother joined the RAF. After the statutory six weeks square-bashing, he then spent most of his two-year stint studying, not *reading* this time, Russian at the School of Oriental and African Studies in London University under the auspices of the Joint Services School for Languages.

While my brother was away, my father suffered a massive heart attack at the age of fifty. At about four in the morning our GP, Dr Fraser finally agreed to come round to the house, after the third desperate phone call from my mother. Each of the previous calls had received the 'Oh, it's probably just acute indigestion!' responses, with the promise of a housecall in the morning. Fair point, as my father did suffer from occasional bouts of indigestion. But my mother knew this was different, she made that life-saving third phone call, and the doctor finally came to the house.

What my mother knew but Dr Fraser did not was that my father hadn't slept for a week, agonising over whether to accept the offer of the University Chair in Welsh at Swansea or to continue as Registrar of the University of Wales. He was completely torn.

When I had the same heart attack scenario fifty years later, I went through the same palaver of 'indigestion or heart attack'. In my case, it was the stressful build up to the 'recall' Welsh Labour Conference on whether to accept the Labour–Plaid Cymru coalition agreement in July 2007. My father's heart attack was in October 1957. When the doctor did eventually get to us, he took one look at my father and phoned for an ambulance. 'Heart attack', he said. That was when my mother woke me from my slumber in the next bedroom. I went into my parents' bedroom, and there was my father crumpled up in pain, sat in a chair looking more like seventy than fifty.

I had an immediate vision of life without my father, and burst into tears. My father must have been thinking the same, and seemed to find some indefinable comfort in my tears. 'And well you might cry', he croaked in Welsh. We sat together waiting for the ambulance, contemplating a future in which he might very well not be around. My mother was downstairs saying goodbye to the doctor and making tea.

When the ambulance arrived, the driver blanched when he saw my father's condition. He apologised for coming single-handed. He'd been told it was a walking wounded job, not a stretcher one, and told my mother and this tall stick-like youth of eighteen standing before him (me) that somehow we would have to carry my father downstairs and out to the ambulance in a chair, with the driver holding the chair legs and me holding the chair back. That twenty minutes from going into my parents' bedroom, seeing my father's pain-twisted grey face and bursting into tears, and now the reality of carrying him downstairs was when I grew up. I had to. A year before, I doubt very much that I could have done it.

Fortuitously and fortunately the year before, I had got a bit self-conscious as thin boys of seventeen do about how skinny my arms were. I had started to do a bit of DIY body-building in the bedroom with my big portable radio. Years later, as I explained this episode to my children about the body-building with a radio set, they would go off into peals of laughter. They were thinking of the modern tranny. Even a sparrow couldn't do chest expanding with a tranny, they said. They couldn't conceive of 1950s portable radios powered by car batteries with chunky leather straps.

Rather like my grandfather's kidneys lasting just long enough to finish his marathon Bible-reading stint, my arms were just about capable of hanging to that chair-back for dear life, down the stairs and out to the ambulance. My father was off work for nine months, with the first four spent in hospital. That included Christmas – the best Christmas he'd ever had, my father always used to say. I'm not sure if that was a comment on us not giving the Yuletide festival much of a go in our house, or whether it was his best Christmas simply because he was still alive.

So, in the space of two years, I'd gone from being No. 4 Male in the Morgan household to being No. 1, which was all a bit sudden. Years later, I saw a television programme in which my father described his feelings at being carried downstairs in that chair by me and the ambulanceman. It was so strange, he said, to think of me being his baby boy and dependent on him, to now suddenly and effectively him being the child and dependent on me.

Because my father was the University Registrar, he was provided with a private room on the NHS. It had his name, Dr T. J. Morgan on the door. This next event could only happen in Wales. An old man burst into my father's room and cried, 'Teddy! Teddy! I saw you score that try that beat the All Blacks in 1905! I was there! And now it's so wonderful to meet you! What a day that was, eh?' My father wasn't even born in 1905 and, in any case, if your affectionate name is Teddy your initials are going to be E. not T. But that wasn't going to stop an over-enthusiastic Welsh rugby fan retiring happily to his grave believing he had met the rugby immortal who had scored the try that beat the All Blacks in 1905!

I'm not certain that my father did much to correct the old man's error. Fair's fair after all, Dickie MORGAN Owen, the Welsh captain on that day of days in 1905, was a distant uncle. So genetically, my father had been there.

My father lived for another twenty-nine years after that major heart attack. That was a pretty good recovery by the standards of the day and for a previous heavy smoker, who'd given up his thirty- or forty-a-day habit at the age of forty-four. He had one really bad relapse with another heart-attack, this time combined with a stroke, when he was seventy-two. The whole family was convinced he wouldn't be able to come back from that. But somehow he did, and had another seven years of pretty good quality of life, still researching aspects of Welsh family names with my brother. When my father died with the book on Welsh family names not quite finished, my brother was able to complete it.

The key thing for me is whether my father – had he been given the choice – would have preferred me to be a really outstanding centre three-quarter playing for Wales, or the first First Minister of Wales. He'd have thought about it for a bit. He really disapproved of politics as a dirty game, but not perhaps to be avoided at all costs. He was very disappointed by the miserable failure of the 1979 referendum, and died eleven years before the just successful 1997 referendum. So many rugby-mad fathers in Wales stand on muddy touchlines watching junior rugby wondering if their son is ever going to get a cap – but in the end, that's a short-term thing. Careers in rugby are over by the time you're thirty-five. So chalking up devolution for Wales and climbing to the top of that devolution tree, I think he would have said that was more important than an international cap! But maybe only just.

Somehow, I progressed through the Sixth Form studying Latin, French, and my favourite subject German. As my brother had done, I stayed on into the mythical Third Year Sixth after my 'A' levels to sit the Oxford Common Entrance, and got in with an Open Exhibition, a minor version of the Open Scholarship. That was not bad considering I had the worst possible interview imaginable to get into St John's College – you could have filmed it as a 'How Not To Get Into Oxford' instructional video for state school pupils. The don interviewing me was Will Moore, allegedly not a crusty old ivy-covered typical old school Oxford academic, but you could have fooled me that day.

The student wannabes all had to sit in Moore's room in the college buildings – the same room he used for his tutorials, which had six armchairs. So, in effect, you heard the interviews of the applicants who went in before yours started. Every one of the other boys seemed to be head boy and vice-captain of the First XV or deputy head boy and captain of the First XV! I was none of those things. I was a prefect, I suppose, but useless at rugby.

The really well-coached sixth-formers would get up from their chairs and cross over to Will Moore's well-stocked bookshelves, pretend to be terribly interested in a title on the spine, then thoughtfully take it off the bookshelf and open it at page 322 or whatever and pretend to see something very significant therein. It was so blatant, it made me want to puke. I shrank deeper and deeper into my armchair fearing the worst, for when my turn would come.

Will Moore's first question in this barking confident voice, 'Now then, Morgan, which is your favourite Shakespeare play?' 'I'm not doing Eng. Lit.!' went through my mind. All I could come up with was, 'I haven't got one, sir.' 'Oh, but you must have! Shakespeare is your national poet!' I so wanted to respond, 'Oh no, he's not sir, Dafydd ap Gwilym is my national poet!' – or even if I'd really let go, 'Doesn't it occur to you, sir, that with a name like Rhodri Morgan I might not actually be English?'

But no, caution overrode. I couldn't do the bit about Dafydd ap Gwilym, because it would inevitably lead to questions about what I knew about him – close to bugger all, really. The second super-stroppy approach would have worked in the late 1960s but not the late 1950s. I was, after all, trying to get into this university. I mumbled my way incoherently through the rest of the interview as it went from bad to worse. It was truly dreadful on an epic scale.

But somehow, they didn't just admit me, they gave me a minor scholarship as well. I must have done okay on the written examinations, sufficient to over-top the zero I probably got for the interview. Or they must have seen the contrast between a respectable showing in the written and the mumbling answers to all the interview questions as the signs of a chronically shy yet budding genius with a personality problem! And I never caught sight of any of the well-coached supremely confident guys who had been in that interview hell-hole the following October. Presumably, they never made it.

A day or so after my nineteenth birthday, I became a student instead of a schoolboy. Looking back on my school career, journalists have often asked me who, among all my teachers, had really inspired me to do great things many years later. The nearest to an inspirational teacher I ever had was Mervyn Powell Davies, my maths teacher in my first two years at Whitchurch Grammar School. He was also the school deputy head. Sadly, he left to become General Secretary of the Association of University Teachers, and we never saw him at the school again.

What inspired me about his conduct in the classroom was that, halfway through the maths lesson, he would switch from writing right-handed on the board to left-handed. The reason for doing so was not to show off his ambidextrousness – it was because the girls all sat next to the window and couldn't see what he was writing when right-handed, because their view would be blocked by his head and shoulder.

Before getting to university, I had done two jobs out in the real world. I'd sold books in Beti Rhys's bookshop in the Castle Arcade in the middle of Cardiff. That was just for the week, and I was paid £4 and 10 shillings. I enjoyed every minute working in the bookshop because it was in the run-up to Christmas and last-minute present-buying was the order of the day. Thrill of the week was selling *A History of the Rhondda* to the late Gareth Griffiths who had played in the Cardiff and Wales XV, both sides that had beaten the All Blacks in 1953.

Then, in my last pre-university summer, I worked for six weeks labouring on the Whitchurch bypass with the Glamorgan County Council direct labour force. Six grammar schoolboys amid fifty or more genuine navvies and bull-dozer drivers – mainly from the Bridgend area and all over the Valleys – plus one outlier, a guy from Tiger Bay, who used to taunt me mercilessly about my pigeon chest and non-existent biceps. From his face, you could see an amazing mixture of ethnic origins – Chinese and Arab and West Indian, all mixed together. One day, at the lunch-break in our shed, he'd seen my face fall half a mile when I opened my lunch pack. I'd forgotten to put in any tea! He pushed his billy can over and said, 'You are, kid, 'ave arf mine.'

The great thing that Oxford did for me was enable me to switch to PPE – Politics, Philosophy and Economics – after two terms of the first year. Starting off studying Modern Languages, but rapidly growing disillusioned with them as a long-term prospect, I really didn't know what to do about it. The famous Will Moore, who had admitted me despite the ghastly interview, was on a visiting professorship in the USA at the time. We St John's College German students were shipped across to Queen's College, which was said to have the best German student group. They were very good, too, out of my league really. Many of them seemed to have lived for a time in Germany or to have a German mother.

For French, we had a Scottish post-doctoral researcher, Dr Alan Falconer. He seemed to be a normal human being. Many of the dons were not. Eccentricity was highly prized. I started attending lectures by Dr Enid Starkie on the French Romantic poets – she wore piles and piles of layers of clothing, wound around and around her, including on top of her head. She was the 'Gomorrah' half of the infamous 'Wadham and Gomorrah' partnership – the other half being Maurice Bowra, the Master of Wadham College, just behind St John's. Starkie might have been the world's greatest expert on Rimbaud, but I just couldn't take her seriously. I stopped going to her lectures (and, indeed, many other lectures too).

At the end of the second term, we all sat Prelims. They were Oxford's equivalent of end-of-year exam, but Oxford had to be different. I did reasonably well, but Dr Falconer asked me to see him. He told me that I ought to switch to PPE. The same thought had been forming in my brain, but I had no idea that students could switch courses. It was just a dream for me and not a plan. I took his recommendation up with enthusiasm and went to see Dr Mabbutt, the moral philosophy don and deputy head of St John's – and a member of the human race, quite unlike his superior Dr Costin, the college president.

At first, he was quite encouraging, but a week later came the bad news. PPE was full. I would have to continue studying languages. What I did next was totally out of character. I immediately responded back with, 'Well, if I finish my degree in Modern Languages, can I then come back and do PPE?' Where did that decisiveness come from? I have no idea. Anyway, it was what Dr Mabbutt wanted to hear. The following day he told me I was okay to switch to PPE.

Catching up with what I'd missed in those first two terms was tricky – teaching yourself symbolic logic from a textbook was not easy. I'd always been strong at maths, and symbolic logic was akin to algebra. Samuelson's *Foundations of Economic Analysis* was the basic textbook by the MIT economics guru. I lapped that up. St John's was strong in Philosophy and in Economics, but hopeless at Politics. Only two Oxford colleges had specialist Politics tutors in those days, and St John's wasn't one of them. Our tutor, the late Michael Hurst, preferred teaching Modern History, the history that by Oxford's definition stopped at 1914. What was worse, when we studied American politics, it became apparent that Hurst hated America. He would give us a reading list of textbooks written by people with very un-English names – he'd wave his arm dismissively and say, 'You can read about all this in Ogg and Zink.' You could see from the contempt in his voice – 'Why can't American professors have proper English names?' – Hurst had certainly never read Ogg and Zink himself!

The American Rhodes scholars doing their graduate BLitt degrees did their best to help me and make up for the deficiencies of the official tutoring. I made lifelong friendships with almost all of them – that's why, in 1961, I went to Harvard from where many of them had graduated in the first place. They were my saviours time and time again, because they could give me reading lists on American politics that our tutor Mr Hurst hadn't heard of.

My three years at Oxford coincided with the ending of the 'Do your National Service first' rule. If I'd been three months older, I would have been caught in the net just as my brother had been in 1956. As a result, for the second time in my educational life, I caught up with my brother. The first time was back in 1948, when I was put into the scholarship class two years early because of ability in maths. Of course, I couldn't actually sit the eleven-plus until I was ten, but I was in the class readying myself for it for three years in a row. Now here, in 1958, it happened again because of the abolition of National Service. Those three years, 1958–61, were the crossover years. Everything in the university was very crowded. But the difference those two years away from home made to the relative maturity of the two groups of students was astonishing.

We young ones straight from home moaned constantly about the food. The ex-National Servicemen thought college food was wonderful because they'd survived on army and NAAFI food and tea for two years. I couldn't sleep because the college beds lacked any springs, but the ex-servicemen found the bedsprings excellent. We youngsters found getting up in the morning hard – it was no incentive to have to face the baleful glare of the Cyclops-like fried egg staring up at us from the plate. Those only two years older than us were all up and about at half past seven, having shaved already, which was probably an hour later than they'd have got up in the Army, so they were happy as Larry.

In one way, it was a bit odd to have an older brother in the same year at the same college, but at other times quite handy. In my first week, I went into Hall for the evening meal. I was a smidgen late, and sat down at the only empty place available. I didn't know a soul on the table – they were Oxford aesthetes, I suppose, busy discussing composers and the relative merits of various symphonies. One of them thought it would be polite to try to bring me in on this. 'Who's your favourite composer?' he essayed. It was the dreaded 'What's your favourite Shakespeare play?' question all over again. Why didn't anyone in Oxford give you an easy starter-for-five question like 'Which football team do you support?'

Anyway, following my nightmare interview with Will Moore, I was wised up. I said that my brother was the music expert in the family, and he was over there, somewhere else in Hall –'A walking encyclopaedia', I said, 'back in Form One in the grammar school, the music teacher had asked the class if they could name the two famous composers born in 1685. No one put up their hand. The teacher looked straight at my brother and said, "Morgan, I thought you knew something about music. Now name the two!" My brother responded by pointing out that there were in fact three, and not two, famous composers born in 1685 – Bach, Handel and Scarlatti!'

That would shut up these Oxford aesthetes, I thought. Some of us from Wales know a bit about music. But no, one of them had the perfect comeback: 'How very interesting. And which of the Scarlattis was that? Alessandro or Domenico?' I was in the big league now, I had to accept, I was in Oxford, not the grammar school.

Harry, the elderly porter, was one of my influences in Oxford. Far more influential than W. C. Costin the College President ('Principal' to you or me). Costin was like something straight out of Evelyn Waugh. You had breakfast with the President in the First Year, lunch with him in Year Two, and dinner in Year Three. At the breakfast he was in miserable mood because he'd not been able to go on the expected holiday to Kenya with his great friend Rear-Admiral Frobisher, all because of 'this dreadful Jumbo Kenyatta business'. He meant the Mau Mau, and what the Mau Mau would have made of Costin if he had gone to Kenya I can't imagine. What did I have in common with this person? Less than nothing, I thought.

Harry, though, was a different kettle of fish. He encapsulated the whole of twentieth-century British social history in one lifetime. As a young man in rural Oxfordshire, he'd walked to South Wales at the turn of the century to get a job in the mines. He was underground at the next-door pit in Abertridwr when the almighty explosion at the Universal Colliery in Senghennydd happened in 1913, killing 440 men and boys, Britain's worst ever mining explosion. He'd been brought up to the surface to hurry up the road to the Universal Colliery and help out with the rescue. He had a voice like a rusty concrete mixer. By the 1930s, of course, came the reverse migration from the Welsh Valleys to Oxford to get jobs in the car factories.

With a lot of help from my Rhodes Scholar circle of friends, I was offered a place to study Politics and Economics at Harvard, at the Graduate School for Arts and Sciences. I earned a Second Class Honours in PPE – Oxford, doing everything differently to other British universities, did not at that time split its Second Class Honours into 2.1s and 2.2s. That way, all those with an Oxford Second Class Honours could claim – rightly or wrongly – that it was the equivalent of a red-brick 2.1. All I cared was that I'd got into Harvard, and my father had dug out of the University Registry files a scholarship programme for which I was the only applicant that year, the Thomas and Elizabeth Williams Scholarship for anyone from Glamorgan going to Graduate School in the USA. And I was better off than most American graduate students, because the Williams Scholarship paid towards maintenance, which was almost unheard of in the USA.

I had this odd feeling at Harvard of being completely at home. How could that be? How could I feel more at home in Harvard, some 3,000 geographic miles from my home in Wales, than in Oxford just a hundred miles from Radyr? When I was First Minister, Sir Michael Scholar, who was by then the President of St John's (maybe ten presidents after Costin), asked me to come to dinner at High Table. They had, after all, made me a Fellow (much as Tony Blair had nominated me to the Privy Council). So I was the Rt. Hon. Rhodri Morgan. I tried my best to explain to Sir Michael that if I had more respect for a semi-retired porter like Harry than for the college president, I would feel a bit of a fraud going back for a meal at High Table. I think he sort of understood.

In 1961, maybe even today, to most Americans Harvard is terribly *olde worlde*. Degree certificates were still issued in Latin. It was the only American university still doing that. Whatever the BA or MA degree you might be heading for, well, Harvard just had to be different – the Harvard degrees were AB and AM. Harvard did not call Political Science by that name – it was Government, just to be different. For me, that turned to be brilliantly predictive! I got the degree of AM in Government from Harvard in 1963, and by 1999 I was an AM in Government. Very clever institution, Harvard!

It wasn't just Ivy League, it was ivy-covered. But to me, after Oxford, it seemed terribly modern. I lived in a graduate block of rooms designed by Walter Gropius, he of the Bauhaus school. The Politics and Economics professors were all markedly non-eccentric, they were even fully paid-up members of the human race. In addition, all the professors in those two departments were pretty hyped-up by the sense of involvement with the new Kennedy Administration in Washington. A lot of Harvard academics had already gone to Washington to join the Kennedy team, and many others were waiting by the phone for the call that could change their lives. You could almost feel that I was being taught by the team that was now running America.

The high point of my two years there was a lunch in the Harvard Staff Club, in which the invited guest was Dick Goodwin, one of Jack Kennedy's favourite speech-writers. There were a dozen people in that room, and I was one of them. That would never have happened at Oxford. How did I get on the guest list to hear all the latest gossip from an administration insider like Dick Goodwin? I wasn't even American. I did feel privileged. I asked Goodwin during a lull what were they going to do about the United Fruit Company, a megabucks American fruit plantation company operating in Central America that had become a hate symbol for Latin Americans? It did give me even more of a taste for politics than going to the Radyr Church Rooms ten years previously to see Dorothy Rees booed off the stage in tears. I wanted more of this politics business.

There was a low point, though, and it was pretty awful. That was Cuba weekend in October 1962. I went as normal to my lecture on Latin American Politics. This was just after the President's broadcast to the nation about the Soviet missiles shortly to be emplaced in bunkers in Cuba. The professor, John Plank, himself soon to be off to Washington, said that he wouldn't be giving the normal lecture that morning because 'None of us might be here by the end of the week!' *The Times* (in London, not New York) defence correspondent, Alun Gwynne Jones, later a Defence Minister in Harold Wilson's Government in 1964, ennobled as Lord Chalfont, had run a story in the paper saying he wasn't convinced that the alleged missile silos were anything of the kind. From his examination of the aerial photographs, they could, he claimed, be 'bicycle sheds'.

I essayed this alternative view to the fifty or so students and Professor Plank. Harvard students never hiss or boo, but they did that morning. It was dreadful. Anyway, I've always thought that Alun Gwynne Jones *should have gone to Specsavers*, whether he was the star defence expert at *The Times* or not! If he had, it would certainly have saved me a lot of embarrassment. The USA is not used to the threat of invasion – Pearl Harbour apart. Cuba weekend was like a premonition of 9/11.

Harvard students would have seen themselves as very far removed from crude half-baked nationalist 'USA! USA! USA!' sentiments. Unthinkable in normal times, but they were under threat and pretty nationalistic that day. I got hissed and deservedly so for parroting that ridiculous bicycle sheds theory.

One of the side-effects of the Cuban Missile Crisis was that Teddy Kennedy romped home in the by-election for the Massachusetts Senate seat, which had been vacated by his older brother Jack becoming President. The control exercised by the Kennedy family over the Democratic Party in the state was so complete that the seat had been left open for two years to wait for Teddy to reach his thirtieth birthday, the minimum age at the time then to be eligible to stand. Teddy had a bad reputation around the Harvard campus because of the incident where he'd got a friend to sit a Spanish examination. He was being challenged pretty strongly from the left by a Bernie Sanders-type Independent, a Harvard History professor called H. Stuart Hughes. The Hughes insurgency came crashing down on Cuba weekend, but was already imploding after a radio interview Hughes had given. This was when he was away from his minders just for once. The Boston radio reporter asked him if he could sum up what his candidacy was all about. 'Yes, sure', said the overly honest professor, 'I'm an atheist, a socialist and a pacifist!' 'There goes the ball-game!' yelped the reporter, thrilled with his scoop! The mastery of the one-liner in American politics is something I grew to love and admire.

We all survived, and World War Three never happened, and I got my AM. The key moment of my time at Harvard was the advice I was given by Sam Beer, the professor of British Politics. He said I should consider trying to get a job with the Labour Party. It was a bit like Dr Falconer, four years earlier advising me to switch from Modern Languages to PPE. There was a double message there in both instances. Dr Falconer was telling me that I wasn't that great at languages, not by Oxford standards anyway, but also that he'd spotted something in my general contributions to seminars indicating a talent for PPE. Now it was Sam Beer, and I did get on really well with him, but he was telling me 'You're never going to make it as an academic. You'd be better off going for a career in politics, not studying it, but doing it.' Academia was not what I was cut out for.

I'd packed a lot into my two years. I'd been down to New Orleans and to lots of jazz concerts. Jim Crow still ruled in the South. It was an oddly quaint name for the colour bar. The colour bar itself wasn't at all quaint. As traditional jazz fanatics, my fellow student Graham Cooper and I had gone to a jazz concert in the French Quarter where George Lewis and his band were playing. The audience in a converted chapel, the St Peter's Preservation Hall, was a hundred per cent white, mostly college students from the all-white state universities of Arkansas and Alabama, whose American football teams had qualified to play in the city's Sugar Bowl.

Graham and I waited for the crowd to leave and then, rather daringly, we approached George Lewis himself. He had been in on the start of jazz as a young man in 1920s New Orleans. He came outside into the night air to join us. He and the band had just come back from a tour of British university campuses, where trad jazz was all the rage. I then summoned up the courage to ask him, really stupidly, whether we could all go for a drink somewhere. Now wouldn't that be a great idea? Well, yes, it would, but not in a segregated city like 1961 New Orleans. If you've ever wanted to know what the expression 'He looked straight through me' really meant, well that was it. The old man looked straight through me. I kicked myself as soon as I realised that the look meant 'Don't you understand what Jim Crow actually means? Do you want to get me into trouble?' It was all there in that look.

I did two summer camps with a Quaker foundation called the Encampment for Citizenship, the first in Berkeley, California, and the second just before travelling home on the top of El Yunque mountain in Puerto Rico. Just after finishing the six weeks in Puerto Rico, I had to head up to Montreal to catch the Empress of England liner to Liverpool, by way of Greenock, along with two gap year students, Kathy Williams from Caernarfon, and her Scottish flatmate Morag. They'd persuaded another flatmate, Frank Follick, to drive us to Montreal crossing the US–Canada via a narrow road through a forest with no customs or border post on it. That way, I wouldn't have any trouble with the IRS, the US tax authorities and my precious $200 that I'd earned in Puerto Rico.

I had visited forty of the fifty states, plus Puerto Rico and the Virgin Islands, and I enjoyed so many different mind-broadening experiences that would stay with me for ever. I felt really sorry for all the St John's graduates who had gone straight into the Treasury, the Foreign Office, ICI or Shell, without that layer of fun and occasionally frightening experiences that I'd had all over the vast expanses of the USA.

I caught the train from Liverpool to South Wales. My mother and father had arranged to meet me at Pontypool Road station, ten miles north of Newport. How on earth we made that arrangement and made it stick without the aid of a telephone message, let alone emails or texts, I do not know. But work it did. I didn't feel my best due to an abscess, and my parents didn't feel too clever either after a bit of a disastrous experiment in taking a cruise holiday. Still, I was home. I was a very different person to the one who went away – I'd filled out a lot physically, and mentally as well, but I had no wish to live anywhere else apart from Wales. The thing was to find a job, and a route into political engagement.

I was coming up to twenty-four, and it was to be twenty-four more years before I became an MP. So I thought that my formative years were over at twenty-four, but actually in politically formative terms they were only half over.

# two

# The Next Twenty-Four Years 1963–1987

I HAD ARRIVED BACK in Wales just before my twenty-fourth birthday. My mother, father and brother were by now well ensconced in Swansea. My father was the Professor of Welsh, my brother was still doing his Oxford history DPhil, and my parents together had bought this beautiful house for £5,000 in Bishopston near Caswell Bay, on the Gower Peninsula but very much at the Swansea end of it. It was an easy commute into the university's Singleton Park campus, where my parents had first met in 1924.

I had to find a job and I got one in October 1963 as a tutor-organiser with the Worker's Educational Association (WEA). So many of my successors as WEA tutor-organisers in the South Wales region went on to become Labour MPs, it became the candidates' training academy. I was the first of them into the WEA, but it took me twenty years to get nominated for a seat. Neil Kinnock, who succeeded me in my tutor job, Llew Smith MEP and then MP, Allan Rogers MEP then MP, Ron Davies MP, and Wayne David MP, they all progressed straight from the WEA to full-time political careers. I did not. I left the WEA in 1965 and wasn't selected until 1985. But parliamentary selection for a safe Labour seat in the Valleys or a marginal seat on the coastal belt are really matters of being in the right place at the right time. I could possibly have been selected to fight Cardiff North in 1966. The Labour candidate all signed, sealed and selected, Meurig Williams, had a last-minute change of heart about standing and just pulled out. The local party was stunned. What warm bodies were available that could fill in at the last minute? If I was still at the WEA, I might have got it.

I was approached but it turned out that I was ineligible because I wasn't a union member. I'd been a union member when working for the WEA, but I went in for town planning and I was a Graduate Trainee in the Cardiff Planning Department. I'd reacted allergically very badly to the dust in the old building where the department was, and missed the first fortnight after my first day at work, and that was the fortnight during which the NALGO team recruitment process took place for signing up new employees of the Council into the union. They never came round to asking me again, and I never thought to rectify the omission. It was my fault. The upshot was that Ted Rowlands won the nomination and got elected in the Labour landslide. I never gave it a second thought after that. It was just one of those what-ifs. Ted couldn't hold what was basically a Conservative seat in 1970 – nobody expected him to – he then won a by-election in Merthyr, and had a long career in Westminster. I had no regrets.

If you are a political animal in your mid-twenties, you have to try to build a three-legged stool. You need an outlet for your political interests, you need a paid job or even an actual career (which may in turn not be compatible with a political career), and then you may wish to get married and have a family. That last leg of the stool was much the most important to me. I suspect that if I had become an MP in 1966 at far too young an age, the marriage and children and grandchildren part of my life would have taken a very different course. It might never have happened at all.

Looking at the careers of Tony Blair, Gordon Brown, Neil Kinnock and Harold Wilson, you see a pattern – if you want to reach the top in the Labour Party, you need to be in the House of Commons before you're thirty. I'm glad I wasn't.

I had joined the Labour Party in December 1963. I climbed up the stairs of no. 36 Churchill Way in the centre of Cardiff, an address with a brass plate on the outside saying 'Cardiff South & Penarth Labour Party'. I had noticed that brass plate when visiting the WEA Regional office in Charles Street, which ran parallel to Churchill Way. The ground floor and first floor were solicitor's offices overspilling from no. 34 and belonging to Leo Abse and Cohen – Abse was the Labour MP for Pontypool.

I knocked the door and walked in. The two persons inside were Paddy Kitson, the full-time agent for Jim Callaghan, and Jack (later Lord) Brooks. I said I didn't live in the constituency, but that I wanted to help Jim get re-elected whenever the general election was called. Jim was the Shadow Chancellor of the Exchequer, but at the 1959 election his majority had been cut to less than a thousand by Michael Roberts, a local headteacher and later MP for Cardiff North from 1970 to 1982. Paddy gently explained that to join a particular Labour Party, like Cardiff South & Penarth, you actually had to live in that same constituency. I lived in Pontypridd from Monday to Friday, then in the family home in Bishopston outside Swansea at weekends, so I had a problem.

I must have stayed there an hour. Jack Brooks mentioned that he and Paddy had been discussing C. L. R. James, the West Indian cricket writer and historian of anti-slavery rebellion in the Caribbean. Luckily, I'd heard of C. L. R. James.

This was the opposite of my interview with Will Moore to get admission to Oxford University five years earlier. This time, we were all on the same wavelength. We agreed that I would be given a membership card, but I would need to move into the Cardiff South & Penarth area to live as soon as possible. Paddy also mentioned that he too was looking for a better flat. If I found a sizeable one, he would be interested in a joint move, along with his current flatmate, a Cardiff University student called Neil Kinnock. I could meet Neil if I wanted to that evening in the Alexandra Hotel, a pub just across the road from Queen Street station, just a few hundred yards or so from the students' union, where Neil apparently spent most of his time. After that, there was to be a Labour fund-raiser at the Ocean Club in Tremorfa.

I went back up to Pontypridd in my mini-van to where I was living in digs. My address was the Welshest address of all time – it was Rhodri Morgan c/o Mr and Mrs Ivor Jones, Maes-y-Dderwen, 1 Pant-y-Graigwen Road, Graigwen, Pontypridd, Glamorgan, Wales (that last bit was totally unnecessary really). My American friends who received my letters with that address all thought I'd made it up just to impress them – no such place could possibly exist! I explained to Mrs Jones that I would probably be moving out in the New Year, and she was fine with that. I think she'd noticed that I was spending far more of my social time in Cardiff than in Pontypridd.

So back down to Cardiff in my mini-van, which was easy to park anywhere, and I went into the Alex. I saw Paddy Kitson in one corner with a flame-haired student. And a very nice-looking girl in a green dress. Paddy introduced me to Julie Edwards and Neil Kinnock. Julie, he explained, was a postal vote canvasser – that was her holiday job, but in term-time she was studying English at King's College London.

Postal vote canvassers were paid £5 a week. She'd done it through the summer holidays and was now getting a few extra weeks' worth of princely £5 wages during the Christmas holidays. Postal votes were hard to come by in those days. Not only did you have to have some kind of mobility or illness problem to qualify, but a nurse or GP had to counter-sign the application. Still, maximising the number of postal votes you could get signed up in safe Labour areas like the huge council estate in Llanrumney had already been spotted as being well worth the effort in seats such as Cardiff South & Penarth, which were classed as marginal. Although I was chronically shy about asking girls if I could take them home, I did manage to summon up the courage to ask Julie. I think my fear was rejection really, but Julie didn't reject me. I owe a lot to having my mini-van in the Ocean Club car park – you couldn't go wrong with a mini-van. The upshot of all this was that Julie and I hit it off, I couldn't believe my good fortune really.

The following day, I went flat-hunting. In the Chris John estate agent's window on the Hayes, there was an advert for a furnished flat in Cyncoed Road suitable for a share and £5 a week! I dashed back over to the Labour office to see if 40 Cyncoed Road was in Cardiff South. Miraculously, it was albeit the last house in the constituency – everything north of it was in Cardiff North. We (me, Paddy and Neil, plus a fourth person, Wil Roberts from Chwilog in North Wales, by now sadly the late Wil Roberts of Blaenau Ffestiniog) signed all the forms, and leased the flat from January for one year.

The flat was pure gold. It was the ground floor of the old family home of the late Alun Emlyn-Jones, the Liberal candidate in the Barry constituency in 1950, who had then been prevailed upon to pull out in 1951 so that the Tory Raymond Gower could have a straight shot at Dorothy Rees, the sitting Labour MP. Lloyd George had also stayed at 40 Cyncoed Road on innumerable occasions on visits to Cardiff.

One minor problem, at least for Neil, was the six-monthly health and safety inspection by his formidable mother. As I would always say of my own mother, 'Once a schoolteacher, always a schoolteacher!' You could safely say of Neil's mother, 'Once a district nurse, always a district nurse!' I can still hear that commanding voice ringing out from the bathroom, 'Neil, these towels are filthy! Get them washed!' Thank goodness my mother never came to visit.

Everything had moved so quickly. I definitely felt I'd landed on my feet. I'd been a member of the Oxford University Labour Club, but I cannot recall anyone mentioning that actually joining the Labour Party itself involved signing up to join in the place where you lived. That separate step entitled you to go to ward meetings. It was just never mentioned. Now, I could go to Roath Ward meetings. Bizarrely, I reckon I was the only Labour MP who had been to a Democratic Party branch meeting in America (in Lewiston, Idaho) before I'd been to a Labour Party branch meeting in Britain! Roath Ward was untypical, it has to be said – we had two members of the branch whose main occupation was composing opera libretti. If there had been a competition to see which branch of the Labour Party was the brainiest, it would have been a close run between Roath and some esoteric corner of Hampstead every year.

The librettists were busy composing operas, so I was elected to represent the ward on the monthly meeting of the constituency General Management Committee. I was also made Constituency Youth Officer (because I was younger than anyone else), which put me on the Executive Committee, the inner sanctum. So I saw Jim Callaghan in action every month. He would get the train down from London on a Friday afternoon, and then attend the monthly constituency meeting in the evening. On Saturday mornings, he would hold a surgery, accompanied by his super-efficient secretary, Ruth Sharp (she had been in the secret service SIS throughout the war, and it was stamped all over her). Once you got past the SIS briskness, she was the embodiment of charm, but in a very SIS way. Jim would then catch the train back to London on Saturday afternoon, as did most MPs in those days who visited their constituencies rather than lived in them. By now, of course, most Labour MPs live in the area they represent, and visit the House of Commons from Monday to Thursday.

We enjoyed our politics as much as possible. We took the meaning of 'party' politics literally – every Saturday night, we would either have a proper party or at least take a 'carry out' bag of flagons from the Alex in central Cardiff back to the flat, with the Old Arcade taking over as our home pub after the Alex closed down. On one Friday night, we knew that Jim would unusually be staying down until the Sunday, and we boldly asked Jim, the Shadow Chancellor, if he'd like to come to a Saturday night party. To our surprise, he said he would, and when it became known that Jim was coming to our party, Ken Morgan came down from Swansea because he wanted to lobby Jim on the importance to Wales of the federal status of the University of Wales. Despite the excellent dance music I'd bought back from America, Jim's presence did inhibit everyone else, to the extent that he complained himself , 'When's this party going to liven up then?' 'As soon as you bugger off, Jim!' were the words of the unminced reply he got from Jack Brooks. That was what you would call a Splott putdown!

It was lucky that no thunderbolts descended on the flat after the Splott putdown, when you think that in that room were a future Prime Minister (Jim Callaghan), a future Labour Party leader (Neil Kinnock), a future First Minister of Wales (yours truly) and three future Labour peers and, respectively, Leader of South Glamorgan County Council, Vice-Chancellor of Aberystwyth, and an international Development Minister (Jack Brooks, Ken Morgan and Glenys Kinnock). After Jim left, the party did eventually liven up, but that putdown was a never-to-be-forgotten moment.

In the spring of 1964, the first ever demonstration in Wales was organised against an all-white South African sports team. It was that country's bowls team, and they were playing against Wales at Sophia Gardens. We were granted police permission to march along Queen Street with banners and then to picket the match itself. Not only was Queen Street an incredibly busy shopping thoroughfare – especially the stretch from Littlewoods past M&S, Woolworths to Boots, with C&A and BHS on the other side – it was also the main east–west road traffic route through South Wales.

All these demonstrations started from the Alex, just to give Neil Kinnock and Glenys Parry (later Kinnock) maximum time to get students not quite as committed as themselves to down one last pint before coming out onto the street.

As the South African bowls team came past in their coach, they were shaking their heads in a mixture of disbelief and contempt that their right to represent the whole of South Africa was being questioned. The other lesson from that day was to never trust the anarchists. We had done all the work to get the police permission to march and sing, a peaceful demo only was what we had promised. As soon as we got close to Sophia Gardens, the half-dozen anarchists marching with us broke off, ran along the embankment above the bowling green, and threw their placards onto the greens, hoping to do enough damage to ruin the playing surface. They'd taken a free ride on our backs.

We didn't know when that year's election would be called. It couldn't go beyond October 1964, because the five year maximum term would be up, but it could be called at any time before then. In the end, to give the 'Maudling boom' of 1963–4 as much time as possible to work its magic, the election was held right at the end of the five-year period. Harold Wilson won a majority of just four votes in the House. Reggie Maudling, the outgoing Chancellor, left the incoming Chancellor Jim Callaghan the customary note, saying 'Sorry, old cock, that the finances are in such a mess' (a remarkable forerunner of the Liam Byrne 'There's no money left' note addressed to George Osborne in 2010).

The press interest in Cardiff South & Penarth seat was huge. Not only was Jim Callaghan the second most important figure in the Labour hierarchy, but his opponent was Ted Dexter, the former England Test match captain. I was told that the Cardiff South & Penarth Tories had decided that they'd got agonisingly close to winning with Michael Roberts in 1959, and now, with one more heave, they could do it in 1964. They thought, quite wrongly, that the dashing Ted would go down a treat with the ladies, and go down a bomb with cricket-loving West Indians in Tiger Bay, and so forth. But they were wrong on all counts.

The problem with Ted Dexter was his total political inexperience, and so he didn't do any public meetings until the Monday of election week itself. Then he was down to speak in Splott – Neil Kinnock and I went down to hear him and maybe heckle him, just to see how he would stand up to a bit of Welsh fast bowling. A lot would depend on the audience too – although it was Labour heartland territory, there were Conservatives in Splott living mainly in the terraced houses with bow windows and front gardens. Chairing the meeting was G. V. Wynne-Jones, the BBC Wales rugby commentator with the full-on RAF officer drawl. He could out-English the English any day. Dexter spoke from notes and then took questions. He'd asserted that Labour governments always end in financial chaos, and when it came to questions I was first on my feet to ask if he knew of any evidence that the 1924 Labour Government had ended in financial crisis – and, furthermore, that the reason the 1929–31 Labour Government faced financial chaos when it came in was the 1929 Wall Street Crash, not to mention that the problems in 1951 were a consequence of the inflation caused by the Korean war. Amazingly, Ted Dexter said in reply that I obviously knew far more about the subject than he did! 'So you agree with me then?' I asked him. 'Yes', he said glumly, 'perhaps you should come up here and speak.' Total batting collapse. This was the Dorothy Rees meeting in Radyr Church Rooms thirteen years previously, but in reverse. And, of course, members of the British officer class do not blub. Anyway, at Dexter's invitation to go up and speak, I climbed onto the school desk I was sat at, at which G. V. Wynne-Jones drew the meeting to a premature close.

I don't think Jim Callaghan was very pleased when we reported back to the campaign HQ. He thought the *South Wales Echo* might receive an official Conservative complaint that Labour vandals had wrecked their public meeting, but they didn't dare complain – they just hid Ted Dexter away again. If ever a man was out of his depth, that was him. I did feel sorry for him. In all my long political life, I am not sure there was ever a higher point than that night in Splott. To say it whetted my appetite for politics is a total understatement. We did all feel in that campaign that it was a crucible of left and right, right and wrong, Tory establishment versus Labour righteous anger. I felt anger at BBC reporting of *our* election. *Newsnight* hadn't been invented. Before that it was *Gallery*, hosted by Ian Trethowan, the Jeremy Paxman of his day, albeit far more wooden. He'd deigned to come down and do a colour piece of reportage on this fascinating battle between Jim Callaghan and Ted Dexter. Shadow Chancellor versus England cricket captain.

Trethowan had found an elderly black Labour supporter to interview in the guy's home – I can still see him sat in his armchair, being stitched up by the interviewer. After the elderly gentleman had given half a dozen reasons for supporting Labour at the general election, Trethowan finished the interview by asking if he knew the name of his local candidate. The guy struggled for a bit, then said he thought it was Clark. 'Cut!', they must have whooped, the black voters in South Cardiff don't even know Jim Callaghan's name! That was the end of the piece. The conclusion you were invited to draw was that of voter ignorance; truly appalling. Actually what the guy had done was to remember the name of Bill Clark, the local candidate in the council elections a few months before. That's what he'd been asked and the ignorance was entirely Ian Trethowan's. How the screen of our television set survived that night I know not.

Just before election day, teams of us had to go out and collect and mail the postal votes duly completed, with all the necessary signatures and medical counter-signatures by Julie and her two fellow canvassers – Peter Stead, later Professor of Cultural History at the university in Swansea, and Jenny Morris, later the first wife of Jim's son Michael, who was studying economics at university in Cardiff. If you wanted an example of the perfect dilemma for those in party politics, I had such a one on the Llanrumney council estate – you could use it really as a case-study on the rights and wrongs in training election returning officers or applicants for jobs at the Electoral Commission.

I arrived at a council house to pick up a vote and post it. The elderly lady qualified for a postal vote because she had advanced Parkinson's. Her middle-aged daughter was her live-in carer, and the lady hadn't voted yet – the three of us sat around the kitchen table so that she could vote. She told me that she liked

Mr Callaghan a lot, she was strong Labour, and that she was really proud to be voting for Jim. But, as I looked on in horror, her hand with the pen jerked uncontrollably as she went to put the cross on the voting slip and it went from the Callaghan column to the Dexter column just below. Having done what she had to do, a beatific smile came over the lady's face. 'There', she said, 'I've done it!' I didn't know what to say. The voter intent was clear, but the cross was in the Dexter column. Although I got a ferocious telling off back at campaign HQ, I went with the beatific smile and the sense of pride in marking that cross, and posted it off. 'But that was one of OUR votes!' I was told, 'The intent was clear, you should have ripped it up at least!'

Jim won easily, but his problems were just beginning. There was a run on sterling as Labour announced that it was proceeding with its manifesto promise to raise the old age pension to £5 a week for a single person, and £8 for a married couple. When a month later we had our first meeting of the General Management Committee, with our MP being no longer Shadow Chancellor but the *actual* Chancellor, Jim seemed to have aged about ten years in four weeks. His hair seemed to have whitened. It was obvious that the Gnomes of Zurich were keeping him and Harold Wilson awake at night. You don't hear much now about the Gnomes of Zurich – they were the bankers and financial speculators who were betting against the British pound now that Labour was in charge.

Jim had to spend a lot of time with Lord Cromer, the Governor of the Bank of England, who was spending much of his time in turn talking to his American opposite number in the Federal Reserve and the IMF. Harold Wilson was on the phone to President Johnson, getting help to defend the pound. Three years later, the struggle to defend the pound was abandoned, and the pound sterling rate went down from $2.80 to $2.40. Jim resigned as a point of honour on the devaluation. Harold Wilson made his ill-judged broadcast to the nation, using the 'pound in your pocket has not been devalued' folksy message of reassurance, for which he was mercilessly pilloried.

What Harold Wilson did not do was provide troops for the Vietnam war – why Tony Blair didn't do the same thing in 2003, I still don't know. Wilson came under huge pressure to chip in with some combat troops to fight alongside the ever-increasing numbers of GIs. Lyndon Johnson's Texan mindset was that he'd done Wilson a few favours in getting him his loan facility from the IMF to help defend the pound – so now Wilson owed Johnson, who wanted some British troops in Vietnam. Wilson refused. Did Tony Blair in 2003 simply not know what Harold Wilson had done between 1964 and 1970, despite the enormous pressure he had been under? Or did Blair really want to be in the regime change battle with George W. Bush against Saddam Hussein? It's a minor political miracle that we didn't get dragged into the Vietnam war, and we should be thankful for small mercies.

Julie was much more oriented to direct action-style politics than I was. She was a fully paid-up member of CND. She went on Aldermaston marches and, later, to Greenham Common. By and large, I preferred organising our own demos against all-white sporting teams coming from South Africa. I liked dreaming up good slogans to paint onto placards. YCHAFI APARTHEID was my best one, although I've never been sure of the correct spelling of *Ychafi*. For those unfamiliar with it, it's what a Welsh mother shouts at a toddler in a park who is about to pick up some dog mess. *Ychafi*! It is the most expressive Welsh word ever. Maybe alongside *pili-pala*, the wonderful Welsh for butterfly.

Of course, I had to render YCHAFI on the reverse side of my placard as UGHAVEE to help the monoglot English in Wales to latch on to its pronunciation. *Ychafi* isn't really meant to be written down. It is one of those words of command that we Welsh have inherited as a matter of Darwinian evolutionary necessity since we came down from the trees. I don't know what the equivalent terms of absolute prohibition are in other languages. I don't think you get the same force from an American mother crying out GROSS! to her precious toddler about to pick up dog mess in the park.

Julie and I did take part in the anti-Vietnam march in 1968 that finished up at the American Embassy in Grosvenor Square. I hated every minute of it. An old school friend, Robin Okey, by then a rising star in the History Faculty at the University of Warwick, tried to engage us in the new technique of alternating phase of walking and running on the march. I can't remember what the ostensible purpose of that bit was, but I'd rarely felt so stupid.

The other bit of direct action I did do was to paint NYE FOR PRYE on Splott Bridge. Who painted it there originally is lost in the midst of time. Perhaps it was an act of teenage rebellion by the young John Humphrys, who grew up just around the corner, long before he progressed to the BBC's *Today* programme. But when British Rail finally got round to repainting Splott Road bridge under their twenty-year planned maintenance schedule, NYE FOR PRYE got painted over. This was sacrilege – it was the Checkpoint Charlie, the main point of entry into the Independent Socialist Republic of Splott. The NYE FOR PRYE sign was where you had to show your passport. Of course, Splott Road bridge is now the main access point to the Independent Yuppified Up-and-Coming Suburb of Splott. Times do change. Anyway, it was at about three in the morning, and Julie and I plus Paddy Kitson set off from Julie's grandmother's house a mile away. We had a paint pot and a brush, and with shaking hands we got the job done. No cop car came speeding by to pull us all in. I'm not Banksy. In fact I felt more like Guy Fawkes. It wasn't pretty, but it got the job done and it lasted another twenty-five years until the dreaded painters returned.

What Jim Callaghan did not have to worry about in this period was support from his constituency party. We had waited thirteen years for a Labour Government, which was now delivering the old age pension increase and on abolition of the widows' earning rule – that meant a huge amount to Julie, because her mother Grace was a widow and earning. It had meant a great deal personally to Jim as well, as he had been brought up by a mother widowed when he was a year old.

I used to quite regularly attend Fabian Society weekend schools at Beatrice Webb House in Dorking, on the top of Box Hill. The atmosphere was a bit too 'Hampstead house party' for my taste, but Bill Rodgers, later of the SDP Gang of Four, did informally offer me the job of being the Assistant General Secretary. Shirley Williams was the General Secretary and Bill was the Chairman in that period of the Harold Wilson Labour Government elected in 1974. That was the nearest I ever got to following the advice of my old Harvard Politics Professor Sam Beer, that I should try to get a job working for the Labour Party. I explained to Bill Rodgers that I liked coming to London on visits or for a weekend, but I didn't want to live in London. I wanted to be based in Wales. Cardiff was my scene.

I left the WEA in the summer of 1965 to become a trainee town planner. It was all a ghastly mistake and I wasted eighteen months there, a very unhappy bunny indeed. Labour had finally won control of the City Council, and really only had two manifesto commitments – the first being the move towards comprehensive education, and the other being the establishment of a City Planning Department. I got caught in the middle of the age-old dispute in town planning between those who love drawing lines on maps of land use, and those like me who saw it in terms of economic planning.

The newly-established department was also caught up in one of the planning corruption court cases involving several prominent city councillors. At one point, for weeks on end, we had police officers from the Cardiff Fraud Squad tramping up and down our corridors removing enormous piles of files. The councillors were put on trial in the early 1970s, but all of them were found not guilty on the judge's instructions when it was ruled that the evidence did not meet the test of a conspiracy. This was a forerunner of the much bigger trials of councillors and officers and top civil servants and architects – the set of trials involving T. Dan Smith (Leader of Newcastle), Gerald Murphy (Leader of Swansea), Sydney Sporle (of Wandsworth Council), J. G. Poulson (one of the UK's biggest architects), and many others – all being found guilty of corruption in local government planning and housing.

Late in 1966, I joined the Welsh Office. That was a fascinating experience, because if the Welsh Office had not been set up in 1964 by the incoming Wilson Government, there would have been no foundation stone there for the Assembly in 1999 to have an administration capable of supporting a government and legislature directly elected by the people of Wales. I was there for six of those crucial thirty-five years, when Wales was gradually building up its capacity for running its own affairs.

Jim Griffiths, MP for Llanelli, was the first Secretary of State for Wales. He had been deputy leader of the Labour Party in the mid-1950s, which gave weight to ensuring the commitment for a separate Cabinet Minister with a Department of State was included in the 1964 election manifesto. But what the new shiny Welsh Office took over was a branch office of the Department of Housing & Local Government, combined with a branch office of the Department of Transport, but only in respect of highways. On top of that little lot, a Department of Economic Planning was set up, which didn't do any actual economic planning – it did lobbying of Whitehall departments with actual executive powers whenever anything relating to Wales came up, whether it be an NCB coalmine closure programme or a series of defence cuts, the Welsh Office could lobby against it in Cabinet.

What I found fascinating was the difference in mentality between those civil servants who operated as if they were still in a branch office of the Department of Housing & Local Government, and those who could see the potential working of a separate Department of State with its own Cabinet Minister to bang the Cabinet table if needs be. That was the line of thinking of the group led by John Clement, who had been secretary of the old Advisory Council for Wales and Monmouthshire in the 1950s. In Whitehall, John was suspected of having gone native, which was the worst thing Whitehall top brass could imply of any official working in the colonies or, in this case, the Celtic Fringe. John had been shifted to Whitehall to straighten his native bias, but now he was back.

This all came to a head over the relocation of the Royal Mint from Tower Hill in London. Scotland was determined to have it relocated up there to help deal with job losses in the shipyards, and the north-east of England wanted it for similar reasons. The Scottish Office had already been around for a century, and how could the infant Welsh Office hope to compete with the Scottish Office's massive inbuilt extra experience of lobbying government?

What made the battle for the Mint far more complicated was that the new Driver and Vehicle Licensing Agency was up for grabs at the same time. This had been provisionally earmarked for the expanded London overspill town of Peterborough. Additionally, there was a relatively minor 300-job prospect for accommodating an office to administer the new Regional Development Grants. The old guard with the branch office mentality counselled the Welsh Office not to go for all three – Whitehall would think the Welsh Office was being greedy and Wales might end up with nothing. John Clement was having none of that, and was strongly supported by my new boss, D. T. M. Davies. The upshot of all this was that Wales did bid for *and win* all three projects! The Royal Mint still employs a thousand people in Llantrisant, and the DVLA still employs over four thousand civil servants in Swansea.

The Welsh Office seemed to have bitten off more than it could chew with its promise of an economic plan for Wales. It had a title. *Wales: The Way Ahead.* It was being re-drafted for the sixteenth time when I arrived there. People were going nuts over it. Most of the sections to be contained within it were being contributed by the non-devolved branch offices of Whitehall ministries in Wales. The Welsh Office had to pull it all together and make it look semi-coherent. But the Welsh Office officials did not have any final over-ride of the bits coming in from other departments – everything from Education, Agriculture, Trade and Industry, and even the Post Office!

The Secretary of State by then was Cledwyn Hughes. He had succeeded Jim Griffiths after the 1966 Labour landslide, and had been the most passionate of all Welsh Labour MPs about the importance of putting a Welsh stamp on things and increasing the power of the Welsh Office. But he had come to the Welsh Office from the Foreign and Commonwealth Office, where he had earned his spurs as a Minister of State. I don't know if he had arrived in Cardiff with an impression already formed that the calibre of the officials did not compare with the smooth-talking diplomats he had been working with at the FCO, or if he formed that impression after his arrival.

Whichever way around it was, he got the FCO to supply him with a retired diplomat of world-wide experience, Sir Anthony Rumbold, with an armful of letters of distinction after his name to do the killer seventeenth and final redraft of *Wales: The Way Ahead.* He took away the drafts of all the sections and chapters, and promised to return in three weeks with it all done with true FCO spit and polish applied. The sow's ear of the provincial oiks would be transformed into a Foreign Office silk purse. It was a shattering blow to the morale of the officials in Wales, but it was the Secretary of State's choice.

On the big day of his return with the final draft, the conference room was all ready. Twenty-five rather cowed Welsh Office officials were assembled around the table to have the finished article work presented to them on the basis that Sir Anthony would show them how to do things properly. 'Comme il faut', and so forth. The great man took off his mackintosh, hung it up, patted the leather briefcase that he had carried all around the world with him, telling one and all that the precious document was all in there. A little hiccup as he sat down – he couldn't find the keys to the briefcase. 'Not to worry', he reassured everybody, 'must be in my coat.' Over he walked to the coat-stand – no, sadly, it was not in his mac pocket – tried his jacket and trousers again – definitely no key.

'Terribly sorry, gentlemen. I've left the key to my briefcase in London. I don't suppose there is anyone in this room who knows how to get into a locked diplomatic briefcase?' I wasn't in the room, but my boss D. T. M. Davies was. 'Yes', he said, 'I'm sure I can get it open in two minutes.' 'I'd be most grateful if you could', said the by now slightly flustered Sir Anthony. When my boss came into the room, I shared with him down the corridor, he handed me the briefcase and went into his desk drawer to fetch an Ever Ready razor blade. He said to me,

'Stretch the top of the briefcase apart as tight as you can.' He then ripped it open, along the full length of the briefcase, with the Ever Ready, and took it back to the conference room. Sir Anthony was in love with that briefcase. It had history – diplomatic history – and now it had been ruined. 'You'll have to pay for a new one', he glared – a classic emperor's new clothes moment, and the score was Welsh Office 1–Foreign Office 0. Sir Anthony Rumbold wasn't superman, but a fallible old buffer after all.

The incident with the Ever Ready was the talk of the entire Welsh Office. Sir Anthony's redraft was considered nothing very special. The clerk in the supplies and expenses office, Tony Hopkins, who wouldn't normally say boo to a goose, was emboldened resolutely to refuse to pay for the new briefcase on the grounds that it was all Sir Anthony's fault anyway. A little corner of the UK, still afflicted by a kind of colonial psychology, had won a battle for freedom.

That issue of the calibre of officials in the old Welsh Office, and now the Welsh Government, has not entirely gone away. Even now, I hear comparisons usually adverse to the Welsh civil service compared to the Scottish civil service, 'lack of ambition' frequently at the heart of them. There was certainly a sharp difference in attitude to Whitehall. In the old Scottish Office and in the Scottish Government since 1999, you earned your promotions up the ladder by giving your Whitehall opposite numbers a bloody nose. In Wales, at least until recently, you ONLY got promotion if you hadn't upset your elders and betters in Whitehall!

From mid-1968 to the end of 1969, I had an eighteen-month secondment to Bristol to work on the Severnside Physical Planning Unit. It was one of three mega-planning projects intended to create three new city-regions with a population of a million each. The other two were in Humberside and Tayside. The aim was to accommodate the huge increase in population expected from the baby-boomers coming to their maximum fertility phase in the 1960s and 1970s. The UK's population was expected to grow from 50 million to 70 million before the 2001 Census, and no one had told the demographers about the pill. The increase never happened, and I wasted another eighteen months of my life just as I had in the Cardiff City Planning Department. It was good experience though, working in Bristol in a cross-border Welsh–English way.

Whenever I hear the Migration Watch pressure group or, indeed, UKIP claim that concern about migration is about space not race, I always feel inclined to remind people that the alleged horrors of the UK population reaching 70 million by 2035 constitutes a far far slower rate of growth than we thought we were dealing in those far off pre-pill days in the late 1960s!

In the meantime, Julie and I had got married and three children had arrived by the end of 1969. Marriage and children also meant moving to Dinas Powys in the Vale of Glamorgan – it was only a two-bed council flat, but it never felt overcrowded. That was in part because my mother-in-law Grace also owned a caravan in St Mary's Well Bay, just west of Lavernock Point. We spent four or five months of each summer and autumn living there.

Commuting into Cardiff from Lavernock Point wasn't that much further than from Dinas Powys. Julie and I would get up at around six in the morning, take the children down for a paddle on the beach, with each adult getting in for a quick swim, and then back to the caravan for breakfast. It was idyllic.

Switching my Labour Party membership to the Vale of Glamorgan Labour Party was a bit of a culture shock. In Cardiff South, we were proud to have the Chancellor of the Exchequer as our local MP. Then, in my year in Cardiff North in 1966–7, we had the young Ted Rowlands who became a junior Minister in no time at all. Labour had failed to dislodge Sir Raymond Gower in the Vale of Glamorgan even in the 1966 landslide, and there did not seem to be the same connection with the world outside Barry. The Dinas Powys branch put me on the Vale of Glamorgan General Management Committee. There was correspondence from Labour Party headquarters inviting parties to choose a delegate to attend the Annual National Conference in Brighton. An alpha-male type character said, 'Well, no, we won't be doing anything like that. Total waste of time for us. We're only interested in what happens on the Barry Town Council!'

Then I burst in with 'If every constituency party thought like that, there wouldn't be a Labour Party!' Then there was a big argument over whether the party could afford to send a delegate. Rail fares and hotel bills in Brighton and subsistence – it could all mount up. I remembered that a friend of a friend was doing a Masters at Sussex University and had a flat in Brighton. I said I'd go as the delegate if they paid my rail fare only – I'd sleep on the floor and eat freebie food at the fringe meetings – so they agreed for me to go. That was my first Labour Annual Conference.

The fringe meetings were fantastic, and not just for the freebie food. The conference itself I didn't find so interesting – that was in part because most young delegates like me stayed up until four every morning drinking in the Grand Hotel, making new friendships and swapping ideas on energy policy or the future of industrial policy. In the mornings, I think we were not fully engaged and were only really coming to by the time the lunchtime fringe meetings were starting. I've probably missed ten of the fifty Annual Conferences since 1967. People don't stay up until four in the morning any more. They don't have the stamina like we had, and they're a whole lot more sensible as well.

I was very happy with my work at the Welsh Office as a research officer, but there were a couple of problems. The first was that I was a civil servant, and that was not really compatible with an open political interest. As a researcher, I wasn't in a politically restricted post, but when Labour lost power in 1970, neither I nor any of the other Welsh Office staff had experience in working for Tory Ministers.

Ironically, when that did happen, I found it more stimulating than working for Labour Ministers. I can only explain away this oddity because it just simply put you on your mettle. The same applied when I worked for Chris Chataway at the Department for Trade and Industry in 1972–4.

The other problem was that I didn't really agree with one of the fundamental tenets of the regional shape of industrial South Wales that my boss D. T. M. Davies was putting forward. He didn't want Cardiff to have any new industry because it was the capital of Wales. We should, therefore, be trying to build it up as the office centre, with as little industry as possible. Cardiff, as a result, did not have Assisted Area status, which would have enabled the government to award grants for incoming industry. What made it even tougher for Cardiff was that any industry in the city had every incentive to leave and move to an Assisted Area in Llantrisant or Caerphilly, less than ten miles away. The need for new industry to move into the Valleys was desperate with coal closures coming thick and fast, as coal could not compete with oil at 25¢ cents a barrel – not $25 dollars but 25¢! Still, the Valleys would not benefit much if the main new industries were coming from Cardiff not London.

The other lesson was that many officials in the Welsh Office didn't have the experiences that I had had in the southern strip of Cardiff, below the main line railway to Paddington, across the NYE FOR PRYE bridge. They just assumed that Cardiff was a smaller version of the three historic capitals in the British Isles – London, Edinburgh and Dublin – which was patently not true. Cardiff had been a steel-making centre since 1898. There were 12,000 steelworkers in Cardiff in 1970. If anything happened to those steel jobs, the workers weren't all going to be able to switch to office work. I think I was pretty much on my own in my views on what Cardiff, as a capital city for Wales, was for.

You could have invented the expression 'across the tracks' to describe Cardiff in that era. Civil servants didn't live below the railway line. That other Cardiff was an unknown city to most of them, but I'd cut my political teeth down there. The shops in the city centre did not employ any black or mixed-race counter staff. There was, effectively, a colour bar. Around 1970, Littlewoods became the first big store to breach the colour bar. I did a lot of my food shopping in Littlewoods in Queen Street – my bulk protein purchases, for our growing brood and my sandwiches. I needed cheese and tins of tuna fish, Littlewoods had a strong line in both. I was often served by the same mixed-race seventeen-year-old. I doubt very much if she was aware that she was the first person of colour on the counter actually serving customers in Cardiff, a city that was quite proud of its multi-ethnic tolerance.

Thirty years later, I was at the annual gala thousand-pounds-a-ticket dinner during the Labour Annual Conference. Labour front-benchers were asked to attend. Of course, we didn't pay anything – it was our business leaders and friends who paid the thousand pounds each to have access to us ministers of HMG or the 'devolveds'. I struck up a conversation with Peter Moores, a leading member of one of the warring factions that split the Littlewoods stores dynasty apart, and I mentioned how important shopping at Littlewoods in Queen Street had been to my family's growing food needs back in the early 1970s. I threw in the line about my suspicion that Littlewoods was the first store to employ black counter staff, and the outbreak of delight on his part was amazing to behold. He was hopping up and down with unbridled joy. 'Yes! Yes!' he said between hops. 'That was me. I introduced that policy first in Cardiff and Liverpool, of course, then all around the country. You wouldn't believe the struggle I had, first inside the family. Then the stick we got from the other stores. You wouldn't credit it!' I had obviously made his day.

My experiences gave me a kind of advantage over those officials on the admin and research side who had never been across the tracks in Cardiff. But they were political experiences. I couldn't really use them if I wasn't involved directly in politics. And this was a period of my life when my political involvement was minimal. Politics was taking a definite back-seat compared to fatherhood and husbandhood. Making a living had to come first.

It's odd how interwoven Julie's career moves and mine have been. It's always been Julie doing something first, then that spurring me on to have a go at something. Nothing ever planned. At the end of 1971 came one example. Julie got a job at Sully Hospital, an amazing place doing path-breaking work on heart valve replacement. The vacancy was for a hospital almoner (as hospital social workers were called before 1974), and Sully was just two buses from Dinas Powys. And wonder of wonders, it had a crèche! With three children below school age, that was a huge advantage.

So what did I do? I applied for, and got, the job as an economic adviser at the Department of Trade and Industry in London. Pretty much the same pattern emerged in 1985, when Julie put her name forward to be a county councillor. She was chosen for Plasnewydd Ward, very near where she was brought up in Roath, and she won the seat by just fourteen votes. The excitement of that wafer-thin winning margin must have been too much for me. I immediately started seriously to look for a parliamentary seat and, luckily for me, I was selected later that year. If Julie hadn't become a councillor, would I have let events drift by and missed out altogether on a political career? Maybe.

So the two of us start our new jobs together. Julie couldn't drive, so I used to drive our newly-acquired motorhome into the old school-yard of Chapter, the new municipal arts centre in Cardiff, by now arguably the best in Britain. Julie and I had been involved in getting Chapter started. I knew no one would steal our motorhome because the rest of the vehicles parked there were all police cars belonging to Canton Police Station next-door.

I'd get there at around seven on a Monday morning and then walk across to Cowbridge Road, western Cardiff's main east–west thoroughfare, with buses into the city centre and the railway station every five minutes. The morning buses were so packed at that time of day, with scores of cleaning ladies from the Ely council estate further out west, that I'd sometimes be practically hanging out of the back of the bus, feet barely lodged on the edge of the platform, real Calcutta-style. But this was full-employment Britain! And I had to catch that 7:25 Pullman train to Paddington to be at my Whitehall desk by 9:30.

By the time of my election campaign to win Cardiff West fifteen years later, Britain was no longer in full employment. I suggested to my agent, Andy Pithouse, that we capitalise on the packed buses leaving Ely for the city centre at around seven in the morning. I was a keen runner, and if we found two or three others willing to join me, we could run alongside the buses with our VOTE MORGAN signs and slogans on our vests and track-suit tops. It was good exercise, but the early morning buses were half-empty.

That Pullman early morning InterCity special train was so important because after Newport it ran direct to Paddington. What is more, it was given priority over any freight trains in its path. It was as reliable as British Rail could be. We left Cardiff Central at 7:25 am and got into Paddington at 9:10 am. It was then a mad rush down into the waiting arms of the Bakerloo, out into the fresh air at Charing Cross, a sprint across Trafalgar Square and onto the one-a-minute no. 3 or 159 bus going down Whitehall to Horseferry Road, and into my office.

That was a chaotic time to be working in central London. The IRA campaign on mainland Britain was in full swing. The wounded were always brought to Westminster Hospital, right opposite my office. Likewise, the Westminster Fire Station was just up from my office.

Working conditions couldn't have been worse, but the upshot was that the timing of my arrival couldn't have been better. The Heath Government had just done its famous U-turn, at the end of 1971 which has spooked the modern Tory Party ever since. Under pressure from the Upper Clyde Shipbuilders sit-in and the collapse of Rolls-Royce, Heath had agreed to intervene over the threatened shipyards on the Clyde – he'd nationalised Rolls-Royce and introduced a new regional policy, which is what I was working on. U-turns were what Margaret Thatcher was determined never to do. U-turns were what George Osborne pretended never to do; it all went back to the mythology of what happened in that U-turn at the end of 1971.

The new regional policy came into being in March 1972, and continues to form the basis of regional policy today. The definition of Assisted Areas was laid down, the grants levels and the cost-per-job maximum limits were set up. The UK as a whole, and then each region or nation, had an Industrial Development Advisory Board, which comprised (in principle, at least) teams of hard-nosed business people who could prevent over-enthusiastic ministers and naive officials from being conned into subsidising non-viable projects.

I was working for the late Chris Chataway, one of my great sporting heroes – he ran the third lap to pace Roger Bannister to the first ever four-minute mile on the Iffley Road track in Oxford back in May 1954 (it would probably have been the other way round if Chataway could have kicked his chain-smoking habit!). As it was, Chataway broke several world records and won an Olympic medal in Melbourne 1956. What he would have achieved without the nicotine in his lungs beggars the imagination. He was also a very genial One Nation Tory, who really did believe in industrial intervention. He had been brought in to replace Nicholas Ridley, who most certainly did not believe in industrial intervention. Ridley, another chain-smoker, had risen to the dizzy heights of being one of the Thatcher inner-Cabinet of true believers by the time I became an MP in 1987.

Another bonus of being in London was going to the House of Commons once a month and meeting up with Neil Kinnock. I loved the atmosphere in the Strangers Bar, but I didn't like to go there too often because Neil had to buy all the rounds. Strangers were welcome, but weren't allowed to buy a round. I had a lot of disagreements with Neil – he was very hostile to devolution, and he was hostile to the Llantrisant New Town project which never actually went ahead, a huge mistake in my opinion. I was as passionately for devolution back then as I am now, but Neil and I went back so far that you could have a good up-and-downer over your differences without it affecting your friendship.

When the recruitment drive came on for the first wave of UK civil servants to join the Eurocracy in Brussels, I applied for an interview, thinking my ability in French and German would be useful. It certainly was vital when I became a Eurocrat in 1980, but not so much in 1973. I didn't get a sniff, which was probably for the best. Commuting home would then have become a monthly not weekly jaunt. The DTI was full of good people, usually grammar school ex-pupils from the provinces, most of them with degrees in Economics – that was quite unlike the Treasury, which was full of public schoolboys who had done Classics or History. Five years ago, I mentioned this social divide to an expert on the British civil service, who just smiled and said, 'And what makes you think things have changed?'

The steel industry was state-owned in that period. The last big project I worked on was the ten-year-programme to modernise the industry submitted to the Government by the British Steel Corporation. It was hugely overblown, based on a big programme of closures in Ebbw Vale, Shotton, East Moors Cardiff, and all of their equivalents in England and Scotland. There were going to be huge investments in Redcar, Port Talbot and Hunterston. The Secretary of State for Industry was the late Peter Walker, destined to become the Secretary of State for Wales in 1987 – being sent off to Wales was the equivalent in the Thatcher Government to the Siberian power station in the Stalin era, ideal for dissidents you couldn't completely dispose of. But in 1973, Peter Walker was a key ally of Ted Heath. Most of us officials thought the whole ten-year-programme was utterly unrealistic. At one point, a very senior official, trying to persuade Peter Walker to kick it into touch, asked, 'Secretary of State, would you put your own money into it?' Walker replied, 'No, but I think it's in the national interest!'

Finally, in February 1974, I got my dream job back in Cardiff. The new two-tier structure of local government had come into force in a shadow sense with the elections of May 1973, which Labour had won handsomely, but the old all-purpose Cardiff City Council did not go out of existence until May 1974. The new South Glamorgan County Council was making all its appointments and getting itself sorted during that year, and I was appointed from a shortlist of five to be the new Industrial Development Officer. I started work in February, two months before the new authority took over, without a department, staff or office. I didn't mind. I was back where I belonged. I just hoped I'd have more luck trying to forge a reasonable career in local government than my dreadful foray into town planning ten years earlier.

Until the new County Hall on Newport Road was ready, all of us new staff had to share a huge room in the back of the City Hall. I enjoyed doing that job so much, I would have carried on for ever if the European Commission job had not come around in 1980. We were facing the massive threat of 4,500 job losses at the East Moors steelworks, and with no local source of steel the even bigger headcount in the Guest Keen steel works next-door (Europe's largest re-rolling complex) might be threatened. But it was the kind of job I'd always wanted. Politics could wait, and thoughts of a political career dropped off the radar completely.

But some experiences from that job were like gold later on. When the new County Council got up to speed, we announced the setting up of the Wentloog Industrial Park – a 300-acre industrial estate east of the city, on low-lying land between the main railway line and the sea wall. There was nothing significant about that, except for the objection from Blaenau Gwent Council, which meant there had to be a public inquiry. I was in the witness box for two days. The Blaenau Gwent Council's barrister, Aubrey Myerson, tried to rough me up, but I gave as good as I got.

We were a terribly pro-active council. We subsequently promoted a Parliamentary Bill to give ourselves powers to introduce all sorts of by-laws and to have powers to promote industry. That, in turn, meant me doing a marathon session of evidence before a House of Lords Scrutiny Committee. Clustered around the Houses of Parliament are the offices of that most arcane of professions, the parliamentary agents, whose job it is to promote (or oppose) private bills. The agents have to be licenced by Parliament. There are only half a dozen of them. They are like the Aztec high priesthood. Ours were Sharpe Pritchard, whose premises just around the corner from Parliament were a bit gloomy, fusty and musty. They didn't do 'modern'. The senior partner was a bit like that too. He was straight out of a Pall Mall gentlemen's club.

During some small talk over the coffee before our meeting started, the senior partner mentioned that this long hot dry summer of 1976 meant very little decent fishing. 'How are the salmon doing in Wales?' he asked me. 'Well, with a couple of friends, we caught five last weekend.' He was very jealous. 'How did you manage that?' 'With a beach net on Harlech beach in North Wales', I said, adding, 'Have you ever used a beach net?' He looked horrified, so I explained: 'I was in about three feet of water holding one end of the net. My friend Dai walked around in a semi-circle up to his shoulders in the water, dragging the other end, and we hit this little school of salmon. We landed them, bopped them on the head with a flagon full of cider from the Spar, put them in the fridge overnight and barbecued them on the Sunday at Llyn Cwm Bychan – a wonderful local beauty spot. Fantastic flavour.'

I hadn't made up a single word of it. The senior partner from Sharpe Pritchard didn't quite die of shock, but his face was tinged with a mixture of jealousy and fascination about a world of angling totally removed from his gentlemen's very proper fly-fishing hobby. The Welsh clearly lived on a different planet. He then ran through the five Lords who would be asking the questions – they were four life peers and one Scottish hereditary. He analysed their reputations and what they were likely to ask. One Lord was a 'lightweight', as he called him, Lord Energlyn, the statutory Welshman they'd put on the committee. He was a professor of Geography at Nottingham University – Geography didn't count, and Nottingham didn't count either, a lightweight academic from a red-brick university who had never served on a Royal Commission. Dismissed. You'd never invite him for a weekend's fly-fishing on the Test. I don't know what the man would have made of Theresa May, an Oxford Geography graduate becoming Prime Minister!

Anyway, the committee was highly skilled at probing. It was a pretty good advertisement for the Upper House, although it didn't change my views on the principle of the non-elected chamber. It's a hangover from feudal times. The Scottish hereditary Earl Cathcart was the most persistent, but at the end of my session of two days of evidence, he winked at me as I was wrapping up my notes and whispered, 'Well done, m'boy!' Now, did that experience of the Houses of Parliament give me a taste of life in the Mother of Parliaments? Did it implant a seed? Maybe it did. I remember Tony Blair telling me that his tastebuds were awakened for a possible future life in the Houses of Parliament by his experience as a junior barrister in the chambers attending a session of the Law Lords. In effect, that was Britain's Supreme Court, and it was handing down a judgement. The only thing the junior barrister attending had to do was literally attend, listen and pick up the copy of the judgement, and then head back to the chambers. But, just occasionally, one of the Law Lords might ask a question on a technicality, so you had to read up on everything the night before. On this occasion, one of their Lordships did ask a question, and the young Blair, a totally unknown junior barrister, made a good fist of at least pretending to know the answer. I don't know if he too got a wink and a 'Well done, m'boy!' as I did, but Tony told me that this was the moment when he first thought, 'This building is where I want to be and where I belong.' It was never that definitive with me, but a seed was certainly planted.

I wouldn't have wanted to move from my job as Industrial Development Officer except for one thing. It happened in 1979. The Conservatives had won control of the County Council in 1977, and I was switched, without being asked, to the Planning Department. I was mightily cheesed off. I couldn't walk out of the Planning Department, telling *them, all of them*, to stuff their job as I'd done in 1966. By now I was married with three small children and, what is more, an actual mortgage. Julie and I had bought no. 3 Millbrook Road, Dinas Powys, in 1974. We'd sweated blood to buy it, then modernise and extend it, creating two extra bedrooms in the roof-space. It had a wonderful shed out the back for all my tools, and the kids loved the back garden with its treehouse and basketball hoop. But escape from local government was at hand.

Some jobs are just meant to be for you. This one was. In the spring of 1980, I'd seen an advertisement for the Head of the European Commission Office for Wales. I knew that Gwyn Morgan, who had previously held the post, had moved on to head up the Commission's office in Canada. I'd been to the offices at 4 Cathedral Road once or twice, and noticed that the advert had reappeared in the summer. They were obviously struggling to fill it. I was puzzled, because I'd assumed that a steelworkers union official, Brian Connolly, who had been seconded from his union to work for Gwyn at the Commission Office, was certain to succeed him. I knew Brian from the campaign to save the East Moors steelworks in Cardiff and, just by chance, I bumped into him near Cardiff Castle. 'What's going on with that job then?' I asked, 'I thought you would be a snip for it.' 'Oh no', he explained, 'I don't have a university degree and I don't speak French or German or Welsh. Why don't you go for it, Rhodri?' 'No', I said, 'I don't want to be involved in all that party-giving and receptions and all that! It's just not me.' But from that moment, I couldn't get the idea out of my head. I was a bit like my father in 1957. I just couldn't make up my mind. I was like a donkey caught between two equidistant piles of straw.

Finally, I did get the application form but did nothing about it. I remembered the closing date was a Monday morning. Eventually, I got quite worked up about the idea. 'I want that job', I was finally thinking. I really did want it. On the Sunday afternoon I completed the form, and did quite a good job. Then, to my absolute horror, I noticed that the closing date, that is the Monday morning just eighteen hours away, was for the application form to be received in Brussels, not in the office in Cathedral Road in Cardiff. I'd thrown away my chance! Then I remembered that Win Griffiths, the MEP for South Wales elected the previous year lived in our village – perhaps he would be flying out to Brussels the following morning. Sadly, his wife Ceri told me that Win had travelled out early to Brussels, which was no use to me but at least she was able to give me the home numbers of the other two Welsh Labour MEPs – Ann Clwyd and Allan Rogers. I rang Ann Clwyd's number. She was in London and wasn't going to Brussels that week. Right, last chance. Allan Rogers. Yes, he was home, and yes, he was flying to Brussels on Monday morning, and yes, he would drop the application form off to the personnel department on his way to his office at the Parliament building. So all I had to do was to drive to Hengoed in the Rhymney Valley to drop the envelope off and he, Allan Rogers, duly delivered it to the correct address. That was a close shave!

I was interviewed at the London head office of the Commission in the plushest address in London – Kensington Palace Gardens. George Scott, the Head of the London office, led the interview. I only knew him as an ex-*Panorama* reporter and as a serially unsuccessful Liberal candidate, but the people who had come over from Brussels to interview me were probably more important. Aneurin Rhys Hughes, who had succeeded Gwyn Morgan as student president at both Aberystwyth and the whole of the UK, was there to test me on my Welsh and sensitivity to Welsh issues. He also tested me on my French. There was a German national there from personnel who could test my German. It was smiles all round. I ticked all the boxes! Just for once in my life, my chaotic university career which had started off in Modern Languages before switching to PPE after one year worked in my favour big time.

A week after the interview, I received a phone call to go to Brussels urgently. The personnel official was utterly mysterious about it – he said that I must be ready to meet a 'certain person' while I was there. That would be after my medical and a whole load of form-filling. Joining MI5 was probably less creepy!

The mystery summons to meet this 'certain person' never transpired. I worked out that the 'certain person' who was thought to want to meet me was the President of the Commission, Roy Jenkins. Pity really. I could have said to him, 'Ah, Roy, your father used to park his Armstrong Siddeley in our drive!' Jenkins was a God-like figure in Brussels. I never met him at all during my time in the job – he was up on Mount Olympus and, in any case, was going back to the UK in 1981. Was he really going to take an interest in who was Head of the Wales Office? I don't think so.

The Europe job was the last non-political job I did. Although that isn't entirely accurate, because the European Commission Head Office for Wales job was actually highly political. There were no restrictions on political activity for any holder of the post – it was quite unlike the British civil service. The absence of a bar on politics for Eurocrats was based on the rules of the German civil service. The irony was that it was the British who wrote the rules for the German civil service in 1948! As part of the de-Nazification strategy after 1945, the highest priority was to persuade civil servants, teachers and anyone else of a democratic stripe to stand for public office at all levels after the traumas of those twelve Nazi years, 1933–45, in rebuilding the democratic map of Europe. It was quite a relief not to have to worry about political activity. My predecessor Gwyn Morgan (no relation) had hoped to be selected as the Labour MEP candidate for the South East Wales constituency in the inaugural European Parliament elections of 1979. He was beaten to the nomination by Allan Rogers (who had hand-delivered my application for the job to the Brussels personnel department). If I had been looking for a job that was part politics and part policy, I found it, albeit inadvertently.

I started work at 4 Cathedral Road on 1 October 1980. Two big euro-developments came into effect on the same day which had a massive impact on Wales. One was the Sheepmeat Regime, the other was the Davignon Plan for the steel industry (a crisis measure to deal with the collapse in demand for steel and the need to eliminate as much as possible of surplus capacity). The Sheepmeat Regime was a bit too easy for one or two to exploit, as it was a subsidy per head of sheep – a headage payment. There was too much incentive just to increase the size of the national sheep flock. Indeed the number of sheep in Wales did shoot up from eight million to over ten million. The Davignon Plan was an entirely different kettle of fish. It was potentially totally disastrous for Wales. It wasn't a question now of the closure of the old-fashioned steelworks based on open-hearth technology, like Ebbw Vale, East Moors in Cardiff and Shotton. What we were now facing was a big question mark over the two remaining major works at Port Talbot and Llanwern, which were based on modern Basic Oxygen steel-making technology. But if nobody was buying steel, could they survive?

Governments were banned from subsidising steelworks, except for severance and redundancy and retraining payments for those who had lost their jobs. So, a lot of my work arose from being right in the thick of the steel crisis.

Gwyn Morgan had used the office to promote the whole idea of UK European membership. That was not surprising, given that the referendum had only taken place in 1975. I could hardly follow that promotional modus operandi. I had voted against in the referendum, and that was well known in the Cardiff area. I'd participated in debates as an 'anti'. That was despite being a committed European, fluent in German and French and so on. For me it was simply the case that Edward Heath had cheated – he'd promised that he would not take the UK into the Common Market without the full-hearted consent of the British people. The damage caused by him reneging on that implicit promise of a referendum (what else could 'full-hearted consent' possibly mean?) has bugged the whole issue of the UK's membership ever since – with the recent disastrous consequences.

My modus operandi was much more soft focus, more to do with helping to re-train steelworkers, and helping arrange loans for any companies moving into steel-making regions that were haemorrhaging jobs. It was about promoting the use of the European Regional Development Fund to local authorities, to help build new highways like the Ely Link Road and the Grangetown Link Road in Cardiff. It was all about trying to help everyone in Wales to understand that the EEC had some good programmes of assistance. They might appear to be unfamiliar, but I was there to overcome such unfamiliarity.

Although my political sympathies were well known, I used to throw popular receptions at all four Welsh party conferences. Our receptions were well attended – maybe people expected a better standard of canapés at anything marked 'European'. We were exotic. I even attended the famous Liberal Party 1982 Annual Conference in Llandudno. I was actually in the visitors gallery when David Steel made his imprecation to delegates to return to their constituencies and prepare for government!

The Conservatives were pretty well impregnable with Raymond Gower in the Vale of Glamorgan. He had not even lost his grip on the seat in the Labour landslide in 1966. We had had a good go at it in 1979 with Julie's former postal-vote canvassing colleague Peter Stead, a native of Barry, although by 1979 he was a Swansea History professor. Peter did provide us all with a moment of hilarity, when he turned up for canvassing one Sunday morning in Dinas Powys – he was still convinced at that stage that the reception he was getting on the doorstep meant he was on a winner. This is what's known as the 'candidate's delusion'.

We had a golden rule never to canvass in Dinas Powys on a Sunday morning – but the candidate had turned up, with John Smith (who eventually won the seat at the 1989 by-election). What were we to do with them? We sent them up to the posh houses by the golf courses, where we knew there were no Labour voters that might get angry over a knock on the door on a Sunday morning. At the first house, Peter and John ascended the ten steps to the door and knocked. After a while they could see, dimly through the frosted glass, a kind of fluttering of a woman in a shimmering nightdress getting to the landing and starting down the stairs. The two of them shuffled backwards away from the door out of politeness. Then an almighty crash as the four milk bottles left on the top step crashed all the way down, it's glass and milk everywhere. 'Quick', said Peter to John, 'turn your lapels over to cover the Labour rosettes!' As the lady of the house opened the door to the scene of lactic carnage outside, Peter introduced himself in a hearty voice, 'Good morning, madam, we're calling on behalf of Sir Raymond Gower, the Conservative candidate for the Vale of Glamorgan!' The lesson is never to canvass on a Sunday morning.

After the disastrous 1983 General Election, Michael Foot resigned and Neil Kinnock came down to Barry as part of his leadership campaign. He was driving himself everywhere and came to address the Vale of Glamorgan Labour Party members at the Seaview Labour Club. After closing time, he and I went over the road from the club to wind down, attracted by the amazing views over Barry Docks and the Bristol Channel beyond. It was a beautiful night and we must have chatted away until close to midnight. I told Neil that it was far too late to drive home, so why not stay the night with us in Dinas Powys, and set off back to Ealing in the morning. He wouldn't have it. He'd promised Glenys that he'd be home that night however late the hour, and that was it. If he'd promised Glenys, he could not go back on it.

He had a brand new Ford Sierra bought via the Labour Party as part of a bulk order with various trade unions for their regional organisers. He'd be home in no time along the M4, with no traffic at that time of night. With no mobile phones around to text a message or a voicemail, I just couldn't persuade him to stop the night. Anyway, the upshot was that I nearly became famous as the last person to speak to Neil Kinnock alive. The brand new German-designed Sierra flipped over on a very exposed section of the M4 at Theale, near Reading. That first batch of Sierras apparently kept flipping over when caught in crosswinds, and after all the bad publicity about Neil's near miss, the model was provided with greater adhesion via wider tyres.

In October that year, I had just arrived in Brighton for the Labour Party Annual Conference, only to miss out on the official announcement that Neil had quite handily won the leadership. I had booked in and was walking along the sea-front towards the Grand Hotel, which was the conference hotel. I bumped into Joe England, my old WEA colleague from twenty years before, who had been the South West Wales organiser while I looked after South East Wales. 'Are you going to Neil's victory party?' he asked me. I told him I had no idea there was one – which was pretty naive of me. Of course, there was bound to be one. Anyway, Joe was totally determined. 'Come on, we're going. You and I are WEA. Neil is WEA! We're going.' He had the room number. Robin Cook (also ex-WEA) had been Neil's campaign manager and was full of the joys of life. I'd never met him before, but I was very impressed. Being there gave me a good feeling. It was another brick in the wall, pointing me in the same direction. I'd been to the new leader's victory party. I'd felt an outsider with my nose stuck against the shop window until I bumped into Joe England. Now, I was a bit less of an outsider.

My bosses in Brussels knew that my job did involve being as close as possible to the Labour movement – that was my value to them. So the London office of the European Commission would always put on a big do at the Labour Conference. I had better contacts in the Labour movement than anyone in the London office, so I had to be there. They certainly wouldn't expect me to attend the UK Tory or Liberal conferences, except for that one which was actually in Wales (the Liberals in Llandudno, 1982). I used to organise lunches in the office at 4 Cathedral Road for the research officers of all four parties in Wales – I'd do the same for the journalists, print, radio and TV. Nobody else was doing this. Cardiff was a capital city, but it didn't have a quasi-diplomatic community like Edinburgh. It had long since lost the American and French full-time consulates I could remember from my youth (indeed, I got my visa to go to Harvard from the US Consulate at Windsor Place in Cardiff).

Roy Jenkins retired from the presidency of the European Commission at the end of his term in 1981. The UK had two Commission members, one Labour and one Conservative. The new pairing on the stratospheric level of the Commission were Ivor Richard (Labour) and Christopher Tugendhat (Conservative). They did their four-year terms from 1981 until 1985. They were the ones that I had most to do with. When they were in Wales, I was expected to look after them, driving them around in my official Rover 2000. Because Ivor was Welsh, he made many more visits to Wales than Christopher Tugendhat – Ivor was much more of a Welsh Commissioner than Roy Jenkins had been. Roy Jenkins's Welshness was only skin deep.

Ivor had a family background in mining as well, but on the engineering side. His was a Cardiff family. His uncle Arthur Richard was my brother's headteacher at Whitchurch Grammar School. That's a good Welsh coincidence, but not half as good as the coincidence of UKIP's Welsh Assembly leader Neil Hamilton's father. He succeeded Ivor Richard's father as chief engineer of the West Wales region of the National Coal Board at its Ammanford headquarters. We had a farewell do for Ivor in Cardiff Castle in 1985. He wasn't offered a second four-year term.

So, two things happened pretty well simultaneously. The first was that Ivor was now going to be at a loose end. What I didn't realise at the time was that he was going to be looking for a seat. His original seat at Baron's Court in London had disappeared in boundary changes in 1979. He had been a Minister of State for the Armed Forces under Jim Callaghan and, for Ivor, Jim had been a great Prime Minister. The feeling was mutual. The other thing that happened was that at his farewell do, Ivor had spoken well – but somehow, I had spoken well too. The thought struck me – 'I'm just as good as Ivor at holding an audience!' I suppose part of it was that the audience laughed at my jokes, and that's always a good sign. Anyway, the thought stuck. I could communicate. I was as good as Ivor.

The other bricks fell into place over the next few months. Julie went on the panel of candidates for the County Council. She was selected for the Mackintosh Ward at the start of 1985. It was one of those inner-city wards that could go in any direction – Tory, Liberal or Labour. The retiring councillor was a working class Tory called Stan James. The Liberals were terribly confident of taking it. But Julie won it by fourteen votes. When the result was announced, it gave the pair of us a fantastic feeling of elation – that was because of one extra canvassing session the two of us had done together on a Sunday afternoon, when all the rest of the team had been given the day off. We'd gone back over the completed sheets looking for uncontactable voters, some of whom seemed to live in flats that didn't exist. We found some of these missing properties almost hanging off the fire escapes at the back of the regular houses. Such a relief to discover these apparently non-existent flats and canvass them. We both felt that that was where those fourteen winning votes had come from.

I had been in loads of election campaigns but never one in the family that was won by such a small margin. The blue touchpaper was lit for me when Jim Callaghan announced his retirement in mid-1985. I wanted in. In early August I went down to the Star Centre on Splott Road, where my old fellow campaigner, the late Lord Jack Brooks, held court. I told him I wanted to throw my hat in the ring for the Cardiff South & Penarth vacancy, and I wanted his support. I got the bum's rush. 'Stay clear of Cardiff South', he said. Despite my persistence and my plea for him to take into account all those good times back in the mid-1960s, he wasn't having any of it. You couldn't win the nomination for that constituency without his support, but his support wasn't forthcoming. I was a bit shocked and peeved but, of course, I had had no contact with that constituency for decades. He'd promised his backing to someone else. But, to be fair to Jack, he did give me a brilliant piece of advice – just to get me off his back probably. 'Why don't you have a look at Cardiff West?' They'll be going through their selection conference very soon.' Both seats were going be picking their candidates in parallel, it seemed, but I told Jack that I couldn't compete against my family solicitor and friend, David Seligman, the unsuccessful candidate in 1983. Jack said, 'I doubt he wants to go for it again after what happened last time.' One door slammed shut, but another door might be ajar.

One positive thing was that David Seligman had definitely had a gutsful in 1983. It had been hard for voters to contemplate voting Labour for anyone not called Thomas after doing just that for every election since 1945. What made it worse for David Seligman was that the SDP candidate did have Thomas as a surname – Jeffrey Thomas, the ex-MP for Abertillery. He won 10,000 votes running for the SDP, with David Seligman for Labour second on 12,000, and the winner being Stefan Terlezki for the Tories with 14,000 votes. The seat had been uncontested in 1979 because George Thomas was the Speaker, and boundary changes in 1985 had made Cardiff West less of a Labour stronghold.

The positive aspect of the boundary changes was that my home village of Radyr had come into the constituency. It meant that I could say that I'd lived the first twenty-one years of my life in the constituency. Gaining Radyr, but losing the big Labour area of Grangetown, was not a net gain in trying to regain the seat for Labour, but it might help me. I'd also shared a flat with Neil Kinnock in 1966 in Riverside, also in Cardiff West. These things may seem small, but they do count when introducing yourself to a sceptical audience.

The really bad news was that two of the wards had already met in August, and both had chosen the chair of the constituency, Gareth Williams, as candidate. It was probably worse news for Ivor Richard, because he would be looking for support from the same centrist wing of the party as Gareth himself – I considered myself a bit more Kinnockite or Tribunite. Ivor was using the recently retired Welsh Labour Secretary Hubert Morgan to do his legwork in Cardiff West, while he was winding up his affairs in Brussels and restarting his barrister's practice in London.

For the previous year there had been a lot of pressure on me to move from my job in the Europe Office to Brussels to do some impossibly boring job processing application forms for support from the European Social Fund. Luckily, my teenage children were reaching the age where GCSEs and 'A' levels were upon us a family, and I resisted the pressure to move. I still wonder if that pressure was put on me so that I'd get out of the way and give Ivor a clear run. My appointment in Cardiff was only for three years, but custom and practice said you could get another three years out of it, if there were compassionate or family grounds for an extension – which there were.

The August–October period was absolutely frantic in the search for nominations. The selection conference was at the end of October. By that time, I really had to have one ward as a minimum, and one union branch. And that was all I eventually got. The Ely branch nominated me, and so did the construction workers section of the Transport & General. It wasn't much, but under the circumstances of coming into the race after it had all started, it wasn't disastrous. I couldn't use the Radyr born-and-bred card much, because the Radyr Branch had already nominated Gareth Williams before I'd committed myself to the race.

From what I could see of the constituency, there was here and there some hard-left militant influence, which had in turn generated an anti-militant backlash of the fairly standard (they're not taking our party away from us!) kind. The two inner-city branches of Riverside and Canton were more feminist and progressive, and did not see the Militant Group as a threat. They did not like the idea of having any enemies on the left. The party had not actually done any shortlisting – there had been only seven valid candidate nominations, so all seven had been invited to the selection conference.

But there came a bombshell at the beginning of October as Labour's Annual Conference in Bournemouth was getting underway. The candidate leading in the nomination stakes, the party chair, Gareth Williams, pulled out. He and I sat on the floor of the conference hotel in Bournemouth with our backs against the wall at about three in the morning, pint in hand, the standard yogic posture in the Labour Party for revelations and confidences to be disclosed between fellow-delegates and friends. It doesn't happen now, because it's all done on social media, but text messages will never replace the late night and early hours' conversations sat on the floor in the big hotel, pint in hand. Gareth told me that his two daughters, both under ten, had pleaded with him not to go away to London. It was fortunate that my children were all ten years older than his, and were actually tickled pink at the idea that I might be spending quite a bit of time away in London.

Gareth was blocking Ivor Richard's run for the seat to quite a degree – not only had he picked up the most moderate wards, but he'd got the GMB's support. The GMB was Ivor's union, and Jim Callaghan's too. As soon as Gareth pulled out, the GMB switched to Ivor. Gareth was asked to use his good offices to try to get all the branches supporting him to switch to Ivor as well. It eventually proved critical to me that he did not agree to that further step. The key thing was that Cardiff West's Labour nomination wasn't stitched up for anyone by the morning of the selection conference – it was genuinely open, and I was therefore in with a shout if I performed really well.

With such a long shortlist, the luck of the draw was critical. I was desperate to be first or last to speak. I was drawn fourth out of seven – that was hopeless. Then, a stroke of luck. One of the candidates from away in England, Mary Honeyball, phoned in just before proceedings started to say she'd won Norwich North the previous night, and wouldn't be coming to Cardiff. Now, if I had been party secretary, I'd have simply removed Mary Honeyball's name from the batting order and proceeded as before, but secretary Carol Cobert decided otherwise. 'We must redraw', she said, and this time I was drawn last. That was just what I wanted.

The only problem now was that it would be a long wait before I got to speak. Carol had prepared a huge plate of ham sandwiches, there was unlimited coffee, and to make sure I didn't get too jumpy from the coffee I kept eating the ham sandwiches. I don't think I've eaten so many in my life.

The candidates were all friendly, but it was a tense time cooped up together in the ante-room. My future was at stake here. I was forty-six, younger than Ivor, but still I'd be too old next time round. And when finally I did get my turn to speak, my speech was no better than average, but I think the key to my winning people over was the answer I gave to one question in particular. The unofficial leader of the progressive women's caucus tried to catch me out – which is exactly what the ten minutes Q&A is supposed to do. She picked up on a point I'd made that we had to derive special strategies to meet the different needs of the incredible diversity of Cardiff West – could I please provide examples?

Well, I went on about the sprawling council estates like Ely and Fairwater to the west, with their huge potential Labour vote. Then there was the multi-ethnic communities in the inner-city like Riverside, and as an afterthought I added that we had to serve the intelligentsia in leafy Conway Road. The whole room burst out laughing. The first joke they'd heard all morning! And it was unintentional. I didn't know that the very progressive feminist university lecturer who had asked the question did indeed live in leafy Conway Road. There was no looking back after that. I'd got credibility, they'd laughed out loud at one of my jokes. The best jokes are probably the unintended ones. It wasn't a putdown to her – everyone in the constituency would have loved to live in leafy Conway Road.

The second practically free gift I received was that Ivor had effectively blown it during his Q&A session. He'd been asked to guarantee that if elected as the MP he would take up his position full-time and give up his barrister's practice. His response was to say that it was an impertinent question – and that was a big mistake.

The upshot was that on the fourth ballot, a lot of those who had arrived committed to Ivor realised that he was never going to win and switched to me. Unwittingly, I had come through the middle in the classic manner, and won! I could barely believe it. All I had to do now was find an agent and campaign like hell to win the seat. The congratulatory phone calls from Brussels seemed to indicate that I'd achieved the impossible – maybe in Germany or France it wouldn't be possible for an ordinary bureaucrat-Eurocrat like me to defeat a Member of the European Commission – you have to remember that Ivor was seven ranks of Eurocratic pay-grades above me. But I'd won.

I was a marked man now in my office on Cathedral Road. There was no rule against political activity, but that wouldn't stop a journalist trying to sniff out a story that I was in some way misusing the office for political purposes. Brian Hoey, a distinguished ex-BBC journalist of the older generation, told me later that he tried to stand up a story along those exact lines, but it wasn't a runner. I was glad in retrospect that I'd invested so much time on inviting representatives of all the four parties to receptions at my office or out to dinner.

What really got the Thatcherites' goat was my part in exposing the fact that Margaret and Denis Thatcher had, throughout the miners' strike of 1984–5, held shares in the world's largest coal exporter. It wasn't my story at all. It was *The Mail on Sunday* wot dun it. On the first Sunday, *The Mail* broke the story that both Thatchers, Margaret and Denis, held shares in BHP, the leading Australian steel and iron mining company. Their names were there in the shareholders register in Sydney as bold as brass, unshielded by any kind of blind trust. *The Mail on Sunday* reporter with the scoop was bitterly disappointed at the low key reaction to his story, and rang me to get my reaction as a Labour candidate to see if I could give him anything fresh that would justify a second bite at the cherry. I told him that BHP, the Aussie steel company, was also the owner of Utah Mining in the USA, which in turn owned the Peabody Coal Company, the largest coal exporter in the world. I said something about an obvious conflict of interest during the miners' strike. *The Mail on Sunday* took the line on that second Sunday about how incredibly foolhardy the Prime Minister had been to own these shares in her's and Denis's name throughout the strike – if that revelation had come out in the middle of the strike the year before, it would have provoked a constitutional crisis. But the story died a death again, which shows you that timing in politics is everything. Everyone in Britain, including the NUM and the Labour Party, were so traumatised by the strike that they didn't want to open it up again in any way. Still, it made me a marked man and I had to be careful.

After five years in the office, it had got into a bit of a routine. Then something totally out of the blue would come and shake everything up. Chernobyl was one such event. It wasn't so much the explosion at the power station itself that shook everyone up in Wales, but the radioactive cloud. The radioactivity released 4,000 miles south-east of Wales in the border region of Belarus and Ukraine went up into the sky, motored north-west and finished by depositing radioactive rain over Snowdonia. My specialist colleagues in Brussels all wanted to get the local picture from Wales – it was going to have an effect on the public health risks of eating lamb from the mountain slopes in north-west Wales. I had to bone up on quite arcane subjects, such as how many becquerels of radioactivity were permissible in meat designated for public consumption and for export throughout the European Commission area. Everyone accepted that the following year's lambs would have to be destroyed, but for how long would that continue? In the end, the culling lasted almost thirty years.

Also out of left field came the near-bankruptcy of University College Cardiff in 1986. This was the institution which had given my father his first job back in 1930, and without which my mother and father would never have been able to afford to get married and give birth to my brother and me! In the mid-1980s, official UK Government policy was to shrink the higher education sector. It was too full of bolshies, especially those doing sociology and the like. So the recurrent grant was being cut so that there was less money to pay staff and cover all the overheads involved in teaching students. Two universities took a stand against this – Cardiff and Warwick. Warwick was a relatively new 1960s creation, and it had a growth strategy called 'Make half and save half'. What that meant was that the university would parlay its central position next to so many motorway connections and its shiny modern white-tile buildings to pull in a huge slug of conference income in the summer months. The 'save half' part of it was for even the vice-chancellor to travel second class on the train, which was pretty revolutionary. They jumped from thirtieth place in the league table of British universities to fifth, and never looked back. It was the making of Warwick.

Cardiff, under the ebullient Bill Bevan, did not have a strategy except to insult everyone who got in the way, especially the key man in the funding of all universities, Sir Peter Swinnerton-Dyer, chairman of the University Grants Committee. Bevan called him 'Peter Spin-Drier', not a bad joke, except that this was the guy who controlled the purse-strings. Cardiff was haemorrhaging money and the local branch of the academic trade union, the Association of University Teachers, passed a vote of no confidence in Bevan. They also asked the four local Labour candidates to meet the union's executive. Jim Callaghan was the only Labour MP left in Cardiff after the 1983 debacle, and he was about to retire. The four of us candidates turned up to meet the AUT – Alun Michael (Cardiff South & Penarth), me (Cardiff West), Jon Owen Jones (Cardiff Central) and Steve Tarbet (Cardiff North). We all agreed that Bevan was becoming a danger to the several thousand jobs at the university. Just as we were concluding that he was a liability, putting thousands of jobs in mortal danger, Bill Bevan adopted a strategy which was the polar opposite of ours – it was to join the Labour Party so that he could enlist Labour support, and what's more, he lived in Cardiff West. This was by now a cause célèbre in all the London papers. I went public and told *The Independent*, then in its pomp, that I disapproved of Bevan joining the Labour Party – that was the only time I ever did that, and Bevan took the hint.

To be fair to Principal Bevan, now and again he did have periods of sober clear-headedness in which a glimmer of a strategy would appear. One such glimmer was to wait until the property boom boomed sufficiently for him to sell off the land and buildings of the Department of Domestic Science in Llandaff (Cooks' College to everyone else) opposite the BBC Wales television centre for top dollar, that would clear the debts. And Margaret Thatcher with Nigel Lawson damn near bailed him out. The Lawson boom was driving up house prices and land prices to ridiculous levels as the months rolled by into 1987, just as had happened with the Reggie Maudling Boom of 1964 and the Tony Barber boom of 1973–4. That's how the Tories sought to win elections, with the house price boom feelgood factor. The Cooks' College site was worth £1 million in 1986, but £3 million by 1987. But Bevan needed the money in 1986. The university simply ran out of money, and Bevan ran out of time. The staff didn't get paid for four months. I opined gloomily that if Labour invented the Open University, then the Tories were inventing the Closed University. That was gallows humour.

Those of a conspiratorial cast of mind smelled a plot. The solution to University College Cardiff running out of money was to merge it with the financially stronger University of Wales Institute of Science and Technology over on the other side of Cathays Park. That was the old Cardiff Technical College, it was far less prestigious than University College Cardiff. Its Principal was the late Sir Aubrey Trotman-Dickinson, who had allegedly been a friend of Margaret Thatcher when they were fellow Chemistry students for four years at Oxford. So, she wanted Sir Aubrey to be given the job of merging the two institutions. In the end, that was what happened, but with a massive dowry by the standards of the time of £30 million to rebuild the Newport Road Engineering Faculty campus of University College Cardiff.

What these experiences about the near death of University College Cardiff gave me was a foretaste of what being an MP would be like. That was if I could get the votes in. Another more directly personal one-on-one experience with a voter came when an elderly gentleman from Riverside wrote to me on his wife's behalf. It was the curse of the elderly, severe arthritis of the hip, the hip equivalent of housemaid's knee. His wife was in agony half the time, and they'd been to the consultant who had told them there was a three-year waiting list. However (and you can sense what's coming here), if they were willing to pay £2,500, she could have her replacement hip in three weeks. What did I advise? Use up all the savings on a new hip or keep on waiting. I rang up my cousin's husband (she and he were both NHS consultants, although not in orthopaedics) and asked for advice. He said to tell them not to go private. I should write to the GP on their behalf, and emphasise how much pain she was in and that she should be moved up the priority as an emergency. She should be reclassified as urgent. I couldn't write on MP House of Commons notepaper as I was just a candidate –'Prospective Parliamentary Candidate' is not nearly as impressive on the letterhead, but the upshot was that the lady got her operation pretty quick, and I got a massive ego boost from that little exercise. This is what being an MP is going to be like, I thought, writing letters on constituents' behalf to get them operations or council houses, whatever it might be. Bring it on!

I had met George Thomas in the meantime and, although there was something a bit oleaginous about George, he did give me sound advice. It's all about Ely. Winning Cardiff West is all about Ely. If you can get them to come out to vote, they will vote Labour. Getting them to come out isn't the easiest, but if you can do it, you will be elected. So I spent the next twelve months introducing myself to the people of Ely. I had one key ally, Bryn Devonald, who said he was willing to come out with me rain or shine, freezing or warm. He and I had a map, and we worked from street to street and from house to house introducing me. 'Good evening, I'm Rhodri Morgan. I'm standing for Labour at the next election. Hope you'll be voting for me.' Nothing more scientific than that. I've no idea if what I was doing was winning me any votes, but the hostility towards the Tory MP Stefan Terlezki in Ely was palpable. Sometimes, it had a rational basis. One enraged elector told me, 'He's useless. When he took over Cardiff City they were in Division Two. Now they're in Division Four!' Once it was downright racist –'That Polish pig! I'd never vote for him!' the man shouted, as I retreated hurriedly down the garden path muttering 'Ukrainian actually …'. Bryn and I wore out loads of shoe leather.

The constituency party got into campaigning mode as the election came into view. I had been selected eighteen months before that election, because Cardiff West was a key marginal, along with Newport West and Bridgend. These seats were strung out along the M4. They were new boundaries ready for the 1983 election, and were all won by the Tories. Clwyd South had the same status in North Wales. Our constituency party, as a fighting force, was hamstrung by a left–right divide. I didn't think it was healthy that I'd walk into the room in the old Amalgamated Society of Woodworkers regional HQ above a shop on Cowbridge

Road to be faced with this 'bride and groom' divide. Progressives – self-styled and militant and the feminist left on one side of the aisle, and the trade union and moderate wing on the other side. Fortunately, that all disappeared after we won the election.

We had the benefit of weekend training schools on campaigning for all candidates in standing in winnable marginals in Wales, plus their agents and press officers. Labour's top experts would come down to the Carmarthenshire Adult Education Residential Centre at Ferryside, a stunning location on the Tywi estuary south of Carmarthen and opposite Llanstephan Castle. The scenery was as impressive as the calibre of experts sent down was not – or then again, perhaps I have a problem with experts from head office. I had the same issue with the lectures from Templeton College Oxford and Arthur Andersen that keen shadow front-benchers expecting Ministerial appointment had to listen to just before the election in 1997. Or perhaps I simply suffer from a deference deficiency.

In Ferryside, my deference bypass came to the fore when one of the experts down from London asked us all to participate in a little exercise in sensitivity training with regard to what we should wear on candidate duty, all depending on different audiences. She asked us naive country bumpkins, 'What would you wear normally?' We all said a suit and tie – I almost said 'A suit and tie, miss!' We had two female candidates. They introduced a bit of variety into the monotonous 'suit and tie' responses. Then the lecturer made it a little bit harder. 'What would you wear before a youthful audience?' We all agreed that we would wear jeans and a sweater, so as not to look too authoritarian. Then she brought in her killer question, which we all saw coming a mile off. 'Ah, but what would you wear if it was a black and ethnic minority audience?' I put my hand up and said with a straight face, 'I'd wear a grass skirt and carry a spear!' The woman nearly died. 'Is he real?' she must have thought. 'Are they all like this in Wales? They're in the Stone Age!' And so forth. I couldn't wait to go to the pub. As a bonding session, the weekend was great. That was also true for the two Templeton College Oxford weekends ten years later, the only difference being that there are no pubs in the Oxford area serving Felinfoel beer and exempt from anything remotely resembling closing time, as was the case in Ferryside!

When the three weeks of the election campaign came in May–June, it was a march to victory. Not in the UK as a whole, but across South Wales and for Clwyd South in North Wales. Neil Kinnock wrote me a lovely letter afterwards, saying 'Yours was one of the most uplifting results on an otherwise depressing night all round.' I really enjoyed campaigning. I found that I wasn't shy about talking to total strangers. I'd just walk along the crowded shopping streets of Cardiff West, especially the main suburban district centre of Cowbridge Road in Canton, and button-hole everybody I could catch the eye of. I wasn't exactly kissing babies, but I was pressing the flesh. One little surprise was that not a day went by without somebody coming up to me and talking Welsh. It had never occurred to me how important speaking Welsh was going to be in a seat like Cardiff West.

I would often start campaigning by running in with a group of four joggers all the way from Ely to Transport House where we had our campaign HQ. Then out amid the shoppers. Then maybe a mid-morning press conference with a visiting VIP. Then canvassing and loudspeaker work. Then more more door-knocking in the evening. Then a visit to a pub to end the day, and home for a few hours' sleep. All candidates live on adrenaline. One memory I treasure is the day of the envelope stuffing for the free postal delivery of the manifesto, organised like a military operation. I arrived to give encouragement to the troops on the Sunday morning. It was politically the most beautiful sight and sound possible, a hundred or more diligent activists in total concentration stuffing envelopes, and in the corner was John Abraham playing the *Moonlight Sonata* with full right pedal down on the Transport & General's piano.

There were a few unforgettable blips in those final stages of the campaign. My official nomination meeting was to mark the kick-off for the campaign itself. We hadn't booked a VIP guest to do the speech nominating me – all you need is something akin to a best man's speech at a wedding, but preferably without any *double entendres.* At the last minute, the campaign committee picked up a rumour that Clive Jenkins was staying at the Angel Hotel, which was then Cardiff's number one hotel, and only two hundred yards from our HQ in Transport House Wales. Clive was the General Secretary of the ASTMS trade union, he was from Port Talbot, and his voice was very high-pitched with an accent that had never been Richard Burtonised. He was widely credited with securing massive union backing in 1983 for Neil Kinnock's successful leadership bid. He agreed to speak at the last minute in my nomination, and over the bridge he came with partner Muriel Turner in tow. They were both on the stage with me, and Gareth Williams the chair. When his turn came, Clive gave an impassioned plea with both barrels on why everyone in that hall should be out there for three weeks, night and day, to get me elected, and he listed my apparently many virtues – 'This outstanding young man with huge future leadership potential', and so on. Then Clive must have realised that he didn't actually know my name, and he tried to cover this up by leaning across to me and stage-whispered, 'What's yewer name again?' Clive's discreet stage whisper could have been heard back in the Angel Hotel, and the hall collapsed in laughter.

The other blip was in the pre-election day final Labour rally in Cardiff City Hall on the Wednesday night. Not in London but in Cardiff, because Neil Kinnock was a Welsh MP. The MC was the actor-comedienne Miriam Karlin. Neil, Glenys and their teenage children Stephen and Rachel, seventeen and fifteen respectively, all stood in the front row while Miriam Karlin called us candidates standing in the Tory-held marginal seats up onto the stage one by one. We were all going to line up behind Neil and Glenys at the back of the stage. There were at least a thousand people in the audience. Although it wasn't quite as good as having Stanley Baker addressing a pre-election rally of many thousands with Harold Wilson in Ninian Park football ground, which had happened twenty years before, the atmosphere was still pretty enthusiastic. Expectations were high of winning quite a few of those seats lost in the 1983 disaster. Behind the candidates was the backdrop featuring Labour's new long-stemmed soft-focus market-tested Red Rose. I was the last one called up, and bounded up to great cheering from the Cardiff West members in the audience, all of which stopped dead in its tracks when the Red Rose disappeared off the backdrop as I brushed past it to go to stand directly behind the Kinnocks. I had knocked the polystyrene rose with my shoulders, which are rather wide, not deliberately but a Freudian Slap maybe – Neil turned to see what the commotion was, and said to his bewildered daughter Rachel as I stood there with a bit of polystyrene fake rose stem in my hands, 'S'alright Rachel, I used to live with this guy!'

Election day was the perfect day for a Labour campaign. Unbroken sunshine all day and very long. It was still sunny at nine-thirty in the evening. In Ely, notorious for its reluctance to come out, I saw a husband and wife strolling down to the polling station at twenty-to-ten taking advantage of the gorgeous weather. You can't ask for more than that. I was on the loudspeaker all day with Colin Adams, my driver, taking me up and down every street. After hours on the loudspeaker your messaging gets a little bit samey. In Archer Road at the Bullring end of Ely, where some buses feared to go, a municipal bus-driver motioned us past. I went for variation and ordered the passengers over the loudspeaker, 'Have a whip-round for the driver!' 'I wish', said the driver as we went past. At least it proved that the loudspeaker was working. We won by over 4,000 votes. I was an MP!

*three*

# MP Morgan: Mainstream or Maverick? 1987–1997

D ESPITE THOSE training weekends we had, there is nothing that can actually prepare you for being an MP. The training was all about how to be a good candidate, not a good MP – there is no way of preparing you for life as an MP. It is so much up to the individual public servant you want to be. What do you want to specialise in? Do lots of committee work, as Alan Williams Swansea West advised? Or was committee work a complete waste of effort, as Dennis Skinner advised all new MPs. Looking back now at my parliamentary baptism in the summer of 1987, I have no idea whether I was doing well or not. *The Times* did a crit of all the maiden speeches of the 1987 intake – most of the new MPs were Labour because of the swing of the pendulum since 1983 – and they awarded joint-first to mine and Alistair Darling's speech. My mother and brother, inveterate *Times* readers, were thrilled. They could have, and probably should have, crucified me for speaking more than twice as long as the advised ten minutes. I spoke for twenty-two minutes!

So, if I was doing well and throwing myself into things, why did the Labour Whips punish me by putting me on the Dartford-Thurrock Crossing Bill? This was the gigantic new bridge over the Thames – filling in the missing link in the M25. It was a PFI scheme and, because there were objections, had to go through a Hybrid Bill Committee. Everyone on that committee had upset the Whips except for the chairman, Sydney Chapman. On the Labour side, John Reid (later the all-purpose Cabinet Minister for practically everything) knew why he had got on the wrong side of the Whips. 'Gorgeous' George Galloway was born to upset the Whips Offices at every opportunity – he was unwhippable. The other Conservatives were all doing hard-labour for rebelling on something. They all wanted to know what I had done wrong. I would protest that I had no idea what, and I still don't know. Being on the committee was a bind. It was hard work, but it was like doing an ordinary nine-to-five job with an hour off for lunch. That's what I had been doing for the previous twenty-five years, mind you. So for about two months I became one of Britain's leading experts on vortex load-shedding on cable-stayed suspension bridges. I've forgotten it all now. Kent and Essex County Councils were the objectors, because there was no wind-shielding on the bridge. They had consulting engineers to present the case for wind-shielding. Their expert was in the witness box for five days and stood up to it very well. It reminded me very much of the time I gave evidence to their Lordships on the South Glamorgan Bill. I couldn't quite repeat Earl Cathcart's wink to me when I'd finished, whispering 'Well done, m'boy!' Instead, I asked the expert witness if he'd heard the Irish joke to end all Irish jokes, in which an Irish navvy desperate for a job turns up to try to get a start on the Severn Bridge. The foreman tells him, 'No job for you, son! You know nothing about welding!' 'Ask me anything about welding', says the desperate navvy. The foreman says 'Okay then, what is the difference between a joist and a girder?' Then comes the reply, 'Now wasn't it Joyce who wrote *Ulysses* and wasn't it Goethe who wrote *Faust*?' The speed-writers who back then recorded verbatim every word of Committee proceedings in Parliament had forty fits trying to cope with the double meanings!

So was I actually doing well? Or had I upset somebody. Were they trying to take me down a peg? If so, why? Was it because I had stopped the return to Parliament of Ivor Richard?

The Labour Whips did try to take new MPs who deserved the treatment down a peg or two. The late Ray Powell, the Accommodation Whip (and father of Janice Gregory, who held a similar role in the Welsh Assembly until 2016) was a past master at this. Ray controlled the allocation of MPs' offices. Ken Livingstone got the full Ray Powell treatment. He made about six attempts to see Ray to get some kind of office in or near the House. He'd made an appointment. Ken knocked nervously on the door, and entered. Ray pretended to be busy writing. Then, after two minutes' nib-scratching in near-silence and a pleading cough from Ken, Ray, without looking up, asks 'Name?' Ken just disappeared without trace in Parliament after that, until the Mayoralty came along more than a decade later.

I did get new offices far more quickly than Ken Livingstone, so I couldn't complain. My first office for four weeks was in the Cloisters – this was said to be the room where Charles I had been left to compose himself before going to the scaffold! My next office, my first *proper* office, was shared with six other Labour MPs – three Welsh, namely the two Pauls Flynn and Murphy, and my next-door constituency MP, Alun Michael; two English MPs, Elliot Morley and Eric Illsley; and one Scot, John McFall. There was almost as much history attached to this office as to the Cloisters – it was in 1 Old Palace Yard, in a house belonging to the House of Lords but standing on the site of a much older house which Guy Fawkes and the gunpowder plotters had used to dig their tunnel under the Yard to blow up Parliament! Guy Fawkes – burnt at the stake.

In May 1989, when we had the Vale of Glamorgan by-election, I wasn't appointed as the Liaison MP whose job is to coordinate all the visits to the constituency by MPs, front-bench and back-bench, during the three weeks of campaigning. I thought I would automatically be Liaison MP, simply because I was the only Labour MP who lived in the constituency. I didn't think I would have to ask Neil Kinnock to lobby for the position. It was a fairly prestigious perk that couldn't go to anyone else, could it? But it did. It went to Alun Michael. So I was on the wrong side of the Whips Office. In May 1989, of course, I knew why the Whips Office would want to do me down – it was all about the Barrage. I had made my opposition to the Cardiff Bay Barrage clear, but the Labour Whips had somehow convinced themselves into believing that supporting the Barrage was official Labour Party policy, although it wasn't. So there was no mystery for me in 1989 (but I still don't know what I'd done wrong in 1987).

As with the Dartford-Thurrock Crossing Hybrid Bill Committee in 1987, I gained a huge learning experience from my home seat by-election in the Vale. John Smith, the eventual victor, stayed in our house at Michaelston-le-Pit for most of the campaign, as he'd moved to live in Swansea after failing to win the seat in 1987. He helped build the granny flat in our house in 1983, when he was still a carpenter, so he knew everything about the place. John and his wife Kathy were obliged to follow by-election instructions from Labour HQ to a tee. They had to go up to see Barbara Follett to be Folletised; to describe Ken and Barbara Follett's place in Cheyne Walk, Chelsea, as 'a nice house' is a bit of an injustice. Middle Eastern sheikhs would have sold off their country's oil wells to own a place like that. After a cup of tea and a bit of small talk, Barbara tried to size John up. How much of a task was it going to be to get John to look smart, really smart, for the by-election. 'Where do you buy your suits, John?' she asked. 'Oxfam', he replied, deadpan. 'Oh, very funny', said Barbara. 'I like that one, good gag!', chipped in Ken, laughing. 'No, I'm serious', said Barbara, trying to look businesslike, 'where actually do you buy your suits?' 'I'm serious too!', said John, 'Oxfam!' 'Okay', said Barbara – she'd sized it up by now – 'Ken, you're the same size as John, go and get four of your suits for him from the wardrobe. You've got hundreds!' The thing about that by-election was that it had the feel of an impending win from the start. And that was despite Labour never having won a mid-term seat from the Tories since 1935. One of the best lessons for me from the Vale by-election came from Robin Cook, then Labour's Shadow Health Minister. He had been on the stage with John Smith and Julian Tudor Hart, veteran pro-NHS campaigning medic, at the public meeting in Dinas Powys held in the junior school my children had attended. Julian Tudor Hart had made a brilliant speech, contrasting the NHS with American healthcare. He said an American doctor once suggested surgery to his patient with suspected appendicitis – 'Your appendix is worth more to me than it is to you!' A week later, I heard Robin use exactly the same words in a public meeting in Barry!

The variety of experiences you get as a new MP kept on coming in 1987. The first by-election of the new Parliament came within a month. Sir Brandon Rhys Williams, a Welsh aristocrat and Lord of Miskin Manor died just after re-election – he was the MP for Kensington, one of the nearest seats to the House of Commons, and it was very winnable for Labour. It had the biggest divide between rich and poor of any seat in the country, with palatial mansions cheek by jowl with dreadfully neglected council blocks with broken windows and foul-smelling lift shafts. We had no excuse not to go out canvassing. The Labour candidate, Ann Holmes, had an excellent level of credibility. I was door-knocking a street of mansions. I wouldn't have bothered to knock on one particularly impressive palace door, except that the family name was ffitch – not Ffitch, but ffitch. I'd never met anyone whose family name didn't start with a capital letter! Here was my chance at the house of Sir Rodney ffitch, and my social curiosity overcame my political conviction that knocking this door was a total waste of time.

There were massive curved stone steps to ascend, then a wide portico. A double staircase was visible heading up to the first floor, which made the big houses near the golf course in Dinas Powys look like hovels. I rang the doorbell. This was a palace ffit for a ffitch. On the landing, I could see a man in a smoking jacket – I'd never seen a man emerging dressed in a smoking jacket before, except on the West End stage. He started down the stairs and disappeared from view for twenty seconds. I started to laugh – what was I going to say to him? By the time he opened the door, I was laughing fit to burst. He saw my Ann Holmes Labour rosette and understood immediately why I was laughing. He waved his cigar at me, as I tried to utter the standard canvasser's patter between giggles – 'Good evening, Sir Rodney, I'm canvassing on behalf of …'.'You can stop right there', he said,'Of course, I'm not of your persuasion myself, but if you try the door to the basement flat round the side of the building, you might get better luck. There are two social workers living down there!'He was right too.

We missed winning that by-election by fewer than six hundred votes. Neil Kinnock got quite down about the near miss. What a good start to Parliament it would have been if we'd done it. But as in sport,'would have','could have' and 'should have' are the three commonest phrases in the game of politics. Neil was under huge pressure all the time, so I don't blame him for getting down over these things. *The Daily Express* had a policy to use only two headlines from day to day – one was ANOTHER MAGGIE TRIUMPH and the other one was ANOTHER KINNOCK DISASTER. *The Daily Mail, The Sun* and *The Daily Telegraph* weren't that much subtler. Margaret Thatcher seemed untouchable, but of course she was gone within three years – but from the 1987 perspective, you would have thought thirty-three years was more likely.

When Neil had a bit of a down day, his Parliamentary Private Secretary Adam Ingram would organise a 'Cheer up Neil with a curry!' evening. Adam would book the restaurant, and John Reid and I were the core guests because we could reminisce and yak away until the cows came home about rugby, football, Nye Bevan, Jim Callaghan, Harold Wilson, the Tredegar Town Band, everything under the sun without drifting into the unavailing battle against Thatcher. I remember Paul Boateng coming along once, and he got the hang of it straight away. One who didn't was Tony Blair, who came and ate but stared into space most of the time, looking for all the world as though he was desperate to be somewhere else. Anywhere else.

In October came a big test of the government's authority. The October hurricane – usually referred to these days as the Michael Fish Hurricane – was nothing to do with the government. It coincided with the stock market crash reducing the value of shares by over 25 per cent. What threatened the government was that the crash coincided with the week of the public sale of its 49 per cent stake in BP. The government response was to suspend the advertising aimed at the retail investor, the small guy, the people known as the 'Sids', while it worked out whether the share sale could proceed at all. I managed to pounce at Prime Minister's Questions. I asked Thatcher if the suspension of the advertising campaign meant that the government now thought that BP shares were a bit too risky for the small investor? Thatcher answered very slowly and deliberately working her face as though she was trying to keep her food down. It's funny how non-tribal even a tribal place like the House of Commons can be at times – Andrew Mackay, a Tory Whip, collared me outside the Chamber to say, 'Very clever question, you could see she was struggling there.' I replied, saying that I had noticed the outbreak of Prime Ministerial Tension.

The excitement when at ten o'clock at night, a few days later, the Chancellor Nigel Lawson announced the amended and highly conditional go-ahead to the share sale, was absolutely crackling, especially for new boys like me. I sat right behind John Smith, the genial Scotsman who was Shadow Chancellor, and the usual courtesy of the Minister providing a copy of his statement to the Shadow Minister, half an hour before a statement to the House had not applied. It was probably only being finalised by Lawson at the last minute. Smith was reading the two pages given to him by the Chancellor on the dot of ten o'clock, as his great friend Donald Dewar was completing a highly technical speech on Social Security. John Smith had told Dewar to keep rabbiting on until he'd had a chance to read Lawson's statement and give himself a few seconds to get his thoughts in order – I saw him tug the bottom of Donald Dewar's suit jacket as soon as he'd read it through. 'What a trouper!', he said of Dewar, turning to us keen learners on the bench behind him. Then he listened respectfully to Lawson announce that the share sale was going ahead but with the proviso that the government would buy back any shares the public wanted to return. With Smith's quickie response that 'This privatisation is the first one with a measure of re-nationalisation built in!', it was brilliant to watch past-masters at parliamentary procedure plying their craft. They'd learnt a lot doing the *Observer Mace* student debating competition, which Glasgow University had won on many occasions. With that foundation in place, the House of Commons wasn't a daunting place.

Donald Dewar could seem quite otherworldly at times. When, in the year 2000, he and I found ourselves doing the same job as First Ministers of Scotland and Wales respectively, we were at the Labour Party Conference and Ulster TV wanted to interview us together on devolution. The Northern Ireland Assembly was suspended at the time. so we were the next best thing. As we were having our microphones fitted, Dewar turned to me with that typical slightly pained and strained look on his face, and asked, 'Rhodri, is it true that your official car has the special registration number plate TAFF 1? A journalist has asked me if I shouldn't follow your example and have a JOCK 1 number plate.''No, Donald', I replied, 'it was just a quip I made in my conference speech just now.' JOCK 1 definitely was not Donald!

But in 1987, Dewar was a part of my crash course in learning how the House of Commons worked. Another future First Minister took a different view on how to get to grips with the Mother of Parliaments – Alex Salmond, who also entered the House of Commons in 1987. His crash course was to get ejected from the House, which did his reputation in Scotland no end of good. It proved he was a fighter in Scottish eyes. The thought of proving my street-fighter credibility by getting ejected by the Speaker for breaching the rules never occurred to me, I must admit. It was learn, learn, learn from the likes of John Smith and Donald Dewar as far as I was concerned.

In my first year as an MP, I served on the Standing Committee Stage for three Parliamentary Bills – the Housing Bill, the Steel Privatisation Bill, and the annual Finance Bill. Anthony Bevins of *The Independent* did an analysis of the workloads of MPs on Standing Committees, and wrote that I was being ridiculously overworked. I enjoyed doing line by line scrutiny of bills – some people enjoy it, some find it a bore. We were never going to bring the Government down by outvoting them when they had a majority of over a hundred. All you could hope to do was embarrass the Government into making changes here and there. The Housing Bill was a real whopper of a bill, with 140 clauses. It spent over four months in Committee. When it was all over, the MPs involved from both sides of the House sauntered along the corridor together heading for the lift down to the Strangers Bar where, by tradition, the two front-benchers who'd been leading on the monster bill would buy their respective teams of back-benchers a drink or two. The Conservative Whip on the Committee was Alan Howarth, MP for Stratford-upon-Avon, and he walked along the corridor towards the lift with me. He apologised for the fact that the Government side had not even made one concession to us by way of accepting a Labour amendment or two –'We should have, but we weren't allowed to. Orders from above', he added mysteriously. Whether he was referring to the inflexibility of Thatcher herself, or of Nicholas Ridley the Secretary of State for the Environment, I do not know.

Ridley had been next door to us for those four winter months taking the Poll Tax legislation through Committee, a monster of a bill in the other sense. What the coded message from Alan Howarth was telling me as a new-boy MP, in words that meant little to me at the time, was that the Thatcher government had got so over-confident that it and *she* in particular would be in power for ever. They had ceased caring about parliamentary custom and practice, which was to accept one or two amendments from the Opposition during the Standing Committee. It was that winter's arrogance and hubris that led to Thatcher's downfall in 1990, when the Government tried to implement the Poll Tax. She thought she was in for ever. Indeed, if she'd accepted the Michael Mates amendment to have five different levels of Poll Tax payment, she might have done twenty-two years as Prime Minister instead of just eleven. But she wouldn't hear of the gradation amendment. She didn't think she had to listen to anyone, not least someone who was a friend of the hated Michael Heseltine.

The other coded part of Alan Howarth's cosy little chat with me on that long corridor was that he was getting thoroughly disillusioned with the Tory Party. It certainly never occurred to me that ten years later he would be the Labour MP for Newport East. Not that many MPs cross the floor. One or two Labour ones left to join the Scottish Nationalists. Alan Howarth and Shaun Woodward went from the Tories to Labour under Tony Blair, and found safe Labour seats too. The most famous was Churchill, who 'ratted and re-ratted' as he put it, from Conservative to Liberal and then back again, without significant damage to his career prospects. That was unique. The one I remember hearing about first was Sir Hartley Shawcross, a Labour Attorney-General under Attlee in 1945–51, and who became known as Sir Shortly Floorcross! I wish I had thought of that!

To keep body and soul together, I joined the Lords and Commons Tennis Club. We played from nine until ten on the courts belonging to Westminster School. There were regular matches, but I only once played for the team itself against the Bank of England at Roehampton. Playing parliamentary tennis meant playing mostly with Tory MPs and their wives – we Labour tennis types were outnumbered. On the courts and on the walks back to the House to get changed, I did learn a lot about Tory MP psychology – they could be unbelievably indiscreet and nasty about their colleagues.

When the Housing Bill came back onto the floor of the House of Commons for its Report Stage – one last look at its wording, and one last go for the Opposition to put forward amendments – either new ones or rehashes of ones already voted down in Committee – Nicholas Ridley was there all the time as Secretary of State. And time is the Opposition's only weapon when it has a huge majority against it. The same band of ten Labour MPs controlled the Report Stage as had done on the Committee Stage, but this time we had Ridley on display and with all the journalists up in the Press Gallery watching. Only the specialist press attend committee stages. Our Whip, the late Tony Banks, outfoxed the Tory front-bench and we ran an all-night filibuster on the bill, and we eventually killed the following day's business. That was much better than Alex Salmond getting himself thrown out of the House – we were using the Commons rules against the Government. 'Big Deal', you might say, but the elation we new MPs felt was huge, and so was the publicity. The Press Gallery, especially the sketch writers, loved a bit of theatre like that.

Craig Brown, *The Times* sketch-writer, did a big page lead story on it with the headline AMID THE DETRITUS, ICH BIN EIN BINLINER! He wrote that I'd come up with the joke of the Parliament so far – the 'Ich bin ein binliner' part, based on John Kennedy's famous 'Ich bin ein Berliner' declaration in 1963 Berlin in the wake of the completion of the Wall. It was also a reference to that day's *Evening Standard* featuring a front page picture of Margaret Thatcher and Nicholas Ridley who had done a photoshoot the previous day with those hand-operated litter pickers in St James's Park promoting the virtues of 'Keep Britain Tidy'. In any filibuster, jokes come in handy – I had complimented Ridley on his Kennedyesque leadership of the Western world in litter-picking, with 'Ich bin ein binliner' being his catchphrase. 'Joke of the Parliament?' Not bad, but Parliament had only just begun.

The long drawn-out proceedings on the Cardiff Bay Barrage Bill taught me that you have to learn more about Commons procedure than any MP can possibly know. You have to rely on the Clerks to advise you. They can't take sides, of course, but they can provide an opposition MP with advice on how best to obstruct a bill. Half an hour later, they may well be advising the Government side on how best to get round the blocking manoeuvre they've just helped the opposition MP to devise. Occasionally, you can devise a precedent yourself, but only in a small way. When the Barrage Hybrid Bill Committee came to Cardiff to take evidence, it was chaired by a very fair-minded middle-of-the-road Conservative, Robert Hicks. Like many Cornishmen, he had an instinctive sympathy for the underdog. The opponents of the Barrage asked if part of the evidence could be sung rather than spoken, and he was happy that the dignity of the Mother of Parliaments would not be besmirched. He allowed, for the first time in Commons history, for evidence to be sung. Dave Burns had the honour of singing Frank Hennessy's *The Grangetown Gondolier* about life in Cardiff after the Barrage.

The Government was certainly in breach of the rules over the Hybrid Bill itself. With a Hybrid Bill, Parliament acts more like a public inquiry to establish the facts, listening to both sides, before the House makes up its mind. There is no government whip meant to be on any of the votes – but I knew there was. Austin Mitchell, Labour MP for Grimsby, was receiving all the government whipping advice, because he was receiving in his pigeon hole the government whip sheet of paper intended for Tory MP Andrew Mitchell. Austin would then, out of mischief, pass it on to me. Of course, I couldn't use the information that there was a government whip on a Hybrid Bill, because that would have got Austin Mitchell into trouble for ungentlemanly conduct.

Before we broke up for the summer, many of us new MPs were put on Select Committees. I was given a place on the Energy Select Committee, which was about to start an inquiry into the Government's White Paper on the privatisation of the electricity supply industry. Alex Salmond was put on that Committee too, although his main interest was in North Sea oil and gas. He wanted to be friends with me, but his idea of friendship with a Welsh Labour MP was to get me to agree with him that my fifty Scottish Labour MP colleagues were a useless bunch. I didn't bite.

I also became the Parliamentary Private Secretary to Roy Hattersley, the deputy leader of the Opposition. I was told that this was a very prestigious position, previously held by Tony Blair. Roy was also Shadow Home Secretary. All of this was designed to sell the job to me, because Neil Kinnock's office realised I might be a bit reluctant to do it on account of the fact I was not of the Solidarity centrist wing of the party. I didn't know Hattersley at all. The main point of interest in the job was working with, or rather observing how, Roy and his brilliant Brummie *factotum* David Hill prepared for PMQs on those occasions when Neil was away. They were so good at it, they didn't need help from me. The strategy was always the same, but it always worked. The first question to Thatcher was always an easy delivery, and the Prime Minister would always fall for it. Then would come the much faster delivery to follow up. 'Ah, but Prime Minister, let me quote what you said on this selfsame issue a year ago!' – which was the exact opposite, obviously. Either Neil Kinnock didn't have a David Hill in his office to prepare him, or his natural inclination to go in fully and frontally every time made it impossible for him to use the two-part Hattersley *modus operandi*.

I only remember one occasion when Neil flattened Mrs Thatcher at PMQs. It was just after she had appointed Professor Alan Walters, one of the 'mad monk monetarists' school of economists, as her personal economic adviser. The Chancellor, Nigel Lawson, was known to be furious, and Neil twisted the knife by referring to the number of Chancellors having doubled. She and all the serried ranks behind her seemed to be just hanging there, gaping mouths open in suspended animation, like fish out of water. Neil Kinnock's great strength was not PMQs but conference speeches. His Bournemouth speech in 1985, which saved Labour from extinction, could not have been made by anybody else but him. We over-use the phrase 'epoch-making', but Neil's Bournemouth speech definitely qualifies.

Neil had one outstanding victory over John Major five years later, when Major as Prime Minister attacked Neil for having failed to turn up to vote with the Government at ten o'clock the night before on the Cardiff Bay Barrage Bill. Neil's reply was perfectly pitched: 'If the Prime Minister had checked the Court Circular last week [as if!], he would have observed that Her Majesty the Queen and the Duke of Edinburgh did Glenys and myself the most enormous honour of inviting us to Windsor Castle for dinner and to stay the night!' Put that in your pipe and smoke it! Major looked as though he wanted the earth to open up beneath him. Still, PMQs was not Neil's strongpoint.

Back home, but this time at my mother's house in Swansea, she told me over tea of her dilemma. She had cataracts. She was eighty-two. Her ophthalmologist had told her that there was a two-year waiting list to have the operation done on the NHS, but he could fit her in privately in the Sancta Maria Hospital in about three weeks. Thousands of such conversations took place every week. My mother told him, 'Oh, I can't do that. My son's a Labour MP.' I couldn't believe she had done that. For me, my mother lived for *The Times* crossword, even more so since my father had passed away three years earlier – she absolutely had to have her eyesight. And to think she'd sort of sacrificed it for me! I just couldn't believe it, I almost felt guilty for being a Labour MP.

I explained to her that the junior Minister in the Welsh Office looking after the Health brief, Ian Grist (Cardiff Central), with whom I often shared a railway compartment home from Paddington late on Thursday night, had just brought in a new scheme to bust the waiting lists. There would be a hip factory in Rhydlafar in my constituency, a general surgery (varicose veins, hernias and piles) factory in Bridgend, and a cataract factory in Ysbyty Gwynedd in Bangor. I told my mother she must get on that scheme at once, and she found herself quite looking forward to the trip. She would be able to talk Welsh to all the nurses, and my brother or I could take her and bring her back. So, she tried to get on the scheme, and then – horror of horrors – she was turned down on the grounds that she was too old to withstand the journey. Some cataract factory! If there was one thing my mother could not abide, it was being told she was too old for something. After protests, she did eventually get the cataracts done on the NHS at Bridgend Hospital.

There were Shadow Cabinet elections in the autumn of 1988. Mo Mowlam, among my closest friends of the new intake of MPs, had asked me if I would be supporting Tony. I said yes. He was one of the best Commons performers we had. He and Gordon Brown stood out as the next generation of contenders for party leadership after the time of the Neil Kinnock and John Smith generation. When

Neil Kinnock handed out portfolios to the Shadow Cabinet, Energy went to Tony Blair, and a few weeks after that the shadow junior Minister's jobs were dished out as well. I was going to be in Tony Blair's team, and our job was to oppose the privatisation of the electricity supply industry.

What was it like working for one of the rising stars of the Labour Party? I knew there would be tensions, because it's quite hard to have a boss who's four-teen years younger than you – that just goes against the grain of human nature – but he was older than me in House of Commons years. He was part of the 1983 intake, and I was 1987. Although he was formidably bright, he turned out not to be very good at maths and science. I remember walking into his room one morning when he shoved a letter he'd received in my direction. He looked gutted. He'd written to the Secretary of State for Energy, John Wakeham, demanding that he should take action on $SO_2$ emissions from the UK's coal-fired power stations, because the sulphur dioxide was going to cause acid rain and contribute to global warming. He'd received a stinker of a reply from Wakeham, pointing out that acid rain and global warming were two very different things. 'Please tell me, Rhodri, that John Wakeham is wrong. There is a connection between acid rain and global warming. Surely, there must be!' I said 'Sorry, but acid rain can actually help stop global warming because it creates a kind of cloud cover, although you don't want acid rain either because it pollutes your upland trout streams and so forth.' He looked shattered. I wasn't very happy either because my special duties in the Shadow Energy team concerned energy and the environment. So, in fact, he really should have shown me his letter in draft before sending it. But he'd been got at by somebody.

If you put maths and science to one side, Blair could pick up the essence of a subject faster than the speed of light. Then he'd see which political angle would be best for us. The Opposition Energy team had an unofficial back-up research team just as good as the one advising the Secretary of State. The year, 1988 was one of those periods when property prices in the London area had shot up so high that mid-career civil servants had been leaving the service in droves – pay wasn't high enough to enable them to afford a house in London. We had secret missives coming from the Central Electricity Generating Board, the monolith which controlled the power stations in England and Wales. During all the negotiations going on with the Department of Energy over the future shape of the electricity industry after it had gone private, a leaked position paper from the CEGB Board would be hand-delivered anonymously to Tony Blair MP at the House of Commons.

It was this brilliant bit of back-stairs hookey briefing that enabled Blair and the team to get off to such a good start with the nuclear tax bombshell which Blair was able to launch at our first Government Energy Secretary Cecil Parkinson. For Parkinson it was rehabilitation – for Blair it was promotion. Parkinson had lost his Cabinet job in 1983 over the Sara Keays affair (in every sense of the word). After a full Parliament away from the front line, Parkinson was allowed back in. On day one, on the committee corridor upstairs, you were allowed to remove your jacket. That was strictly forbidden in the Chamber, but not upstairs. Parkinson revealed his hand-made shirt with the letters CJP monogrammed on the shirt pocket – that was a bit of one-upmanship, really. The five of us on the Labour front-bench side all looked at each and grinned. We were all tall and slim, a bit like Parkinson himself, but none of us had ever had (or dreamt of having) our initials mono-grammed onto our shirt pockets! Two of the Labour front-bench were ex-coal miners, Frank Haynes the Whip, and Kevin Barron; one was the son of a Scottish firebrand MP, John Maxton (Electricity being devolved in Scotland, though not in Wales); and Tony Blair and me. Not one monogrammed shirt between us.

Parkinson only lasted a year. The Energy Department had got into such a mess over the actual structure of the pricing system after privatisation that Thatcher had to give Parkinson, one of her all-time favourites, the heave-ho and replace him with John Wakeham, her Mr Fixer. He did manage to devise a work-able procedure to agree a pool system for wholesale and retail price-setting – it's never worked properly in the interests of the consumer ever since. Blair only stayed with Energy for two and a half years – he was judged to have had a good couple of years at Energy, but for his rise up the ladder he needed to move on and he went to Employment. I enjoyed working for him, and I once enjoyed going to a team dinner at his home in Highbury to meet Cherie (and, until they were packed off to bed, their three youngsters). I don't know whether that dinner with the Blairs was something that all Shadow Cabinet Members did, or if it was a Blair touch. Anyway, I stayed at Energy when Blair moved on. I probably should have asked Neil Kinnock for a move, but I felt that my knowledge would be useful to the incoming Energy Secretary Frank Dobson (and between us, Frank and me, we came up with what is at the time of writing the last-ever proposed measure of nationalisation to feature in a Labour manifesto – it was to re-nationalise the National Grid, which was the hinge of the electricity supply system).

Labour didn't win the 1992 Election, so the re-nationalisation of the Grid never happened. Actually, *de facto* grid nationalisation has been gradually getting closer and closer in recent times in order to ensure that the Government can achieve the de-carbonising of the economy. When the 1992 manifesto was finally approved, Frank Dobson was absolutely thrilled to be the only member of the Shadow Cabinet with a nationalisation ticket in his pocket! If Blair had stayed at Energy, my guess is that this would never have happened – Blair was one of those chameleon personalities who could make his reputation in the House of Com-mons from doing a superb job in opposing privatisation of the electricity supply, but then in government would have no qualms in dropping the whole idea.

The craft of being an MP is basically legislating and campaigning. That is why many commentators have set out the advantages to new MPs of being in

Opposition for their first five years. If you're in support of the Government, you don't learn the art and craft of legislating in quite the same way – you're just lobby-fodder really. The Minister and his team of civil servants have to do all the work of drafting the new law, and then of defending it in Committee or on the floor of the House. There are exceptions to that if you win the right in the annual Members Ballot to promote your own back-bencher's piece of legislation. I never did that, but Julie once did with great distinction getting a law onto the Statute Book on the Regulation of Sunbeds just minutes before the 2010 Parliament came to an end (after which she sadly lost her Cardiff North seat in the general election).

I was more of a guerrilla fighter. I enjoyed amending government legislation. I enjoyed using what parliamentary procedure I understood to mess up what the Government was trying to do. I regret having been forced to spend so much of my time and energy opposing the Cardiff Bay Barrage – it was certainly not how I would have chosen to spend such a big chunk of my first seven years in Parliament – but if that's the way the cookie crumbles and it's what your constituents need you to do, then you don't have a choice. Your constituents always come first. Once a battle over a Hybrid Bill like that starts, you do have to fight it all the way. If ultimately I couldn't stop the actual construction of the Barrage, at least I could secure huge improvements in protection, amendment, mitigation or compensation for my voters – which is roughly what happened. But I didn't really want to be typecast as 'The MP who Opposed the Cardiff Bay Barrage', even less as 'The MP who spoke tor two and three quarter hours in an all-night filibuster against the Cardiff Bay Barrage'. I don't regret it for a moment, but I certainly didn't want to be typecast.

The long speech was immensely enjoyable to make because it was quite a challenge not to lose my place or wander off the subject or to repeat myself. Of course, it was nowhere near the record – it's David Hunt, the former Secretary of State for Wales (1990–92 and 1994–5), who holds the record, having spoken for three and a half hours (also against a Hybrid Bill, the Mersey Docks and Harbour Bill) early in his career as a humble back-bench Merseyside MP. It didn't do his career in Parliament any harm at all.

My old friend, the late Jack Brooks, by then Lord Brooks and Deputy Chairman of the Cardiff Bay Development Corporation, told me I'd managed to trash my reputation as a new MP by proposing legalised brothels in Cardiff, the release of Rudolf Hess from Spandau Prison, and in opposing the Barrage. I didn't see it quite like that. As far as I was concerned, I was among the hardest working MPs in the new intake, having done three bills in my first year, then been Roy Hattersley's PPS, and then done the Electricity Privatisation Bill on the Labour frontbench. That was the day job. Most of the other stuff was in my spare time – I was spreading my wings, and if you can't do that as an MP then what is the point of it all when you have that huge prestige and influence by dint of those two simple letters after your name?

I did try to use my influence, such as it was, to consider a change to the nature of the Remembrance Service at the Welsh National War Memorial. I had a conversation with Cecil Rapport, ex-Tory councillor and Chairman of the Jewish ex-Servicemen's League, and that year's Chairman of the British Legion in Cardiff. What I proposed was that we invite Manfred Rommel, the son of the Desert Fox himself, to the following year's service. Rommel was Oberbürgermeister (mayor) of Stuttgart, Cardiff's twin city, a ferocious Welshophile as well as Anglophile. He could bring representatives from the retired Luftwaffe, Wehrmacht and Kriegsmarine, and we could turn it into a service of reconciliation. Rapport thought it was a brilliant idea – 'If we don't do it soon, we'll all be dead anyway!' he said. I left it with him. I didn't want to get him into trouble with the Legion, but sadly the idea went nowhere. Pity though, because we've still not had an act of reconciliation on a par with the French and Germans at Verdun.

Looking back, I would stress that I *had* 'huge prestige' with the letters MP after my name in the past tense, because I'm far from sure they would open quite so many doors today – that's partly due to the emergence of the three Celtic legislatures, and partly the effect of the expenses scandal.

MPs did have perks, mind you. Take the London Marathon, for example. Everyone involved in fund-raising and running wants to get an entry for the event. The marathon is oversubscribed tenfold but, in the case of MPs, the marathon organisers came to ask us lunchtime joggers if we would please take part. I agreed to try to get sponsorship for an African adventure for the members of two youth clubs, both run by friends of mine – John Rose, who ran the North Ely Youth Club in the heart of my constituency, and Jane Davidson, who ran the Dinas Powys Youth Club in our village. Far from a safari trip, they were going to construct a sustainable water supply project in Illuni village in Machakos province, Kenya. I wrote to my fellow MPs seeking sponsorship, and explained what the project was. Most were very good about it, others demurred quoting an unofficial bit of House of Commons custom and practice, barring MPs from asking for charitable donations for anything in another MPs constituency. With this particular project being in Kenya, the latter objection hardly counted in my eyes.

The strangest objection came from the Honourable Tom Sackville, a Bolton MP, but being a baronet of sorts he was a non-typical Boltonian. He claimed to have helped fund a project by boy scouts in his constituency that had already built a sustainable water project in Illuni village in Machakos, and it turned into one of those Humphrey Bogart as Rick Blaine in *Casablanca* moments –'Of all of the sustainable water joints in all the towns in all the world, and I do a marathon run into this one!'

The Honourable Tom was right. The selfsame sustainable water project had been started but only half finished by boy scouts from Bolton, but all was well because there was still plenty of work to be done on it. It was now going to be finished by young people from the Cardiff area. I did a fund-raising stunt for the project, which almost went horribly wrong trying to abseil down the side of the newly-built ten-storey Marriott Hotel in the centre of Cardiff. For safety purposes, abseiling involves having two harnesses strapped to the rope that lowers you when you abseil. The one under my crotch jammed – it was a horrible position to have the rope jam, and I had gone down just a tiny bit too far to drag me back up. The abseiling expert had to lean right over the parapet to untie the harness under my crotch and re-thread it. It took ages. By the time he'd finished and got it strapped correctly around me, my legs had gone totally dead. So when the command came to kick against the wall and get the abseil up and running (or down and running, to be precise), nothing happened. I was temporarily paralysed – my legs were useless – so I had to be lowered all the way without the kicking out bit, which is the whole point of abseiling. Never again! After that, actually running the marathon in 3 hours 14 minutes was a breeze!

Still, there was the compensation of having the front page of the Saturday evening *South Wales Echo* devoted entirely to a photograph of me peering over the parapet of the roof of the Marriott – trying to look calm and very definitely not looking down. 'Jim Callaghan never had a photograph as big as this!' the editor told me triumphantly. I think he meant it as a compliment – not as in 'Jim Callaghan would never have got himself involved in anything so madcap as abseiling down the side of the Marriott!' Best of all about the whole episode was the experience and the adventure that twenty or so young people, half of them from a quite deprived neighbourhood, got out of it.

That area of north Ely around the Pethybridge Road Youth Centre was the same one that exploded into a riot in 1991. The 'Ely Bread Riots' became the label that was attached to the incident, but the people of Ely, however deprived they might be classed, were certainly not short of bread. It was the very end of August, and the weather was absolutely scorching and sultry, which was half the problem. Nobody wanted to be indoors because the heat and humidity were so stifling. The flashpoint was a row between two shopkeepers in the little shopping parade serving the top end of Ely, first built in the 1920s. Their council tenancies specified what they could and couldn't sell. One shopkeeper, who was a Cardiff Maltese called Agius, didn't have the right to sell bread, but was doing so right next-door to the shop that *did* have the right to sell bread. The shopkeeper next-door was Pakistani but, unlike all the many other Pakistani shopkeepers in Ely, he was from Birmingham. All very complicated.

Riots had also broken out on the same day on the Blackbird Leys estate in Oxford, and in inner-city Newcastle, as if a switch had been thrown. I received a phone call on the Sunday morning from the Reverend Bob Morgan, vicar of the Church of the Resurrection and the key local politician in Ely, far more important than me. He was a former council leader as well. Many in Ely thought we were related, which did me no harm at all. We walked up together from the vicarage to the riot site, half a mile away, and it was like a scene from a Greek tragedy being played out in the open air. All the women-folk were sat together on a low wall outside the area housing office, opposite the shopping parade. On the central patch of grass were half a dozen police officers. Beyond them, higher up the hill, were the rioters, the local testosterone-fuelled young men spoiling for a fight with somebody, police or otherwise. They really didn't care. The press were all gathered like the Greek chorus on the south side where we – the local MP and councillors – were entering stage left. The cameras were rolling.

And what about the two shops? The Agius shop was open, but nobody was going in. The Pakistani shop was all shuttered up ... but with her back to the shutters was this bird-like figure of a woman, very much the worse for wear, kicking her heels against the shutters. 'Bang! Bang! Bang!' A member of the Agius family. And then I made a strategic mistake – I should have taken a step back and sized up the situation, and then gone over to the low wall where the womenfolk were sitting and asked what was going on. They were sticking by their menfolk and all that, and they wouldn't have minded a bit of competition between the shops over the price of a loaf, but they didn't want a riot and didn't want their neighbourhood trashed. But the wrong move that I made was to head along with the three councillors for Inspector Lewis and, as far as the young men intent on trouble were concerned, that was taking sides. There were 'sides' going on in the sense of the Cardiff Maltese versus Birmingham Pakistani shopkeepers, but along with that there were the much older 'sides' that lay in the hostility between the police and the local banditry.

No sooner had I started talking to Inspector Lewis than an egg whizzed across towards us, maybe aimed at me but it hit Inspector Lewis full in the shirt-front. Whoever it was who threw that egg from a good twenty yards away, they had a good aim. If it had hit me instead of the copper, that picture would certainly have made the front page of the *South Wales Echo*. Luckily for my street cred, it didn't. The following night, there was more trouble. By this time, young trouble-makers from all over Cardiff and Barry had congregated in the area in the hope that a right royal punch-up with the police might erupt. It didn't, and the following day the weather broke. The rains came down in bucket-loads and everyone returned to their homes and any attraction in hanging around a little parade of five shops quickly evaporated. But I knew I'd made a mistake in appearing immediately to take the side of authority when I should have tried to remain neutral – Julie would never have made that mistake.

Julie was in the meantime trying to get a parliamentary nomination. She went first for Cardiff Central, which is where her council seat, the Mackintosh Ward, was. That was the ward she'd won by just fourteen votes in 1985, but she'd been re-elected by over a thousand votes in 1989. She lost out in the nomination to Jon Owen Jones who had fought the seat and lost in 1987; he duly won it in 1992. After losing out in Cardiff Central, Julie then turned her attention to Cardiff North, the most difficult of the four Cardiff seats for Labour to win. She got the nomination, but not without coming up against the kind of problems all women candidates face and that men don't. Appearing in front of Rhiwbina Ward to make her pitch, Julie delivered her ten-minute speech and then it was ten minutes for questions. Now, Rhiwbina is the suburb of Cardiff with the lowest proportion of *Sun* readers and the highest proportion of *Guardian* readers in the entire city. Still, the first question was,'Well, it says on your leaflet that you're married.'Julie nodded. Then the killer follow-up was,'So, where's your wedding ring?' Anyway, after finally getting the nomination, Julie fought the seat against the Welsh Office Minister Gwilym Jones. She lost, but she put clear daylight between herself in second place and the Lib Dems in third, which prepared the ground for the eventual thumping win for her in Cardiff North in 1997.

We'd had four by-elections in Wales between 1987 and 1992, and all four had been won by Labour, and all with men candidates. You couldn't fault the selections in any of them, but it was proving a problem to break that pattern of men coming through who fitted the bill without any women doing likewise. Two of the by-elections were in safe Labour seats, and two were Tory-held. In the middle of the Neath by-election in 1991, Tony Blair still remained in charge of the Energy Portfolio in the Shadow Cabinet, and I was one of his juniors. He sidled over to me in a seven o'clock vote on a Thursday night to complain how ridiculous it was that he was under instructions from the by-election team to be in Neath for a press conference on Labour's Energy policy at nine o'clock the following morning – yet the Labour Whips in the Commons were not giving him the evening off to get down there, and not even letting him off the ten o'clock vote that night! It was totally ridiculous, he said, but halfway through this rant against the Whips something dawned on me – he was asking if he could stay at our house. So that's what I offered. If he could cleverly park his car under Big Ben and make sure the fuel tank was full, and if we were first through the Division Lobby by five past ten and in the car by ten past, then we would soon be on the M4. My son had then moved out, and Tony could have his room. He'd have to take the bedroom as he found it, and then it was only forty minutes maximum from our house to Neath. What could go wrong?

I was a captive audience for Tony's thoughts all the way back home. It was his very comfortable Rover, and for most of the way I just listened. Tony went on and on about London property prices. I told him he had a lovely house in Highbury, etc., but he wasn't having any of it. 'Rhodri, you should see the houses all the guys who started in our barristers chambers at the same time as Cherie and I did – they've all moved on from your Highbury type of house to really nice neighbourhoods like Holland Park and Notting Hill, houses worth a million or more. No more Islington for them.' I don't know whether I should have, but I had to try to shut him up, although he was doing the driving. 'You shouldn't be thinking like that', I said as firmly as I could, 'you've made your choice not to be a barrister, you're already in the Shadow Cabinet, and it's looking good for the next election. Then you'll be in the Cabinet, and all your old chums from your chambers will be desperately jealous of you!'

Looking back, I wonder now whether doubts had already entered Blair's mind as to whether Labour was actually going to win the 1992 General Election. What I'd said abut his old chambers chums feeling jealous would only apply if we did actually win the election. What if we didn't? Blair had an intuitive feel for how people thought in the south of England, topped up by Anji Hunter's daily reports on what people were saying on the Brighton & Lewes line commuting into London. Although she was gone, Margaret Thatcher had constructed a southern strategy to help her dominate politics for a decade. Could Labour find the way through? Blair represented Sedgefield on the edge of the Durham coalfield, but he just had a feel for southern opinion better than anyone in Labour's history. That was not just because he understood the values of Mr and Mrs Southern Voter – he actually *shared* many of those values himself, including not least the obsession with property prices as a measure of success in life.

We finally arrived at Michaelston-le-Pit at about one o'clock in the morning. I showed the future Prime Minister where the kettle, tea and coffee, milk and packets of cereals were. I had already explained to him how to get back up to the M4 and then on towards Neath for the nine o'clock press conference. I told him I wouldn't be getting up in the morning to see him off – my excuse was that I was so much older than him. I showed him the bathroom and shower switches, and the bedroom with my son's Bob Marley posters plastered all over the ceiling. I found out much later on the following day that he'd got up at around half past six, dressed and gone down to make a cup of tea, and my mother-in-law Grace was there already. She'd walked across from the granny flat, and was making herself a cup of tea. She hadn't met Tony before, and he had no idea who she was. But she broke the ice brilliantly – 'I know who you are. You're Lionel Blair, aren't you?' Well, there is a slight resemblance. Anyway, he and Grace both survived the encounter, and Tony did get to his nine o'clock press conference in Neath in time.

The other by-election later that year again fuelled hopes of an impending Labour general election victory. It was in Monmouth. I spent a lot of time on that campaign. My Labour colleagues back in London would regularly ask, 'Can we win it? Is it worth me coming down for a day or two?' Journalists asked much the same thing. I couldn't honestly answer with any confidence. The feeling on the ground was quite unlike the Vale of Glamorgan two years previously, when the campaign had the indefinable air of a Labour victory right from the start. Monmouth was very different. The Monmouth electorate was holding something back from us canvassing teams, and none of us knew what it was.

Jack Cunningham was in charge of the campaign, and Peter Mandelson was in charge of the spin-doctoring. I tried to observe Peter at work but all I could actually see him doing was staring at the television, for hours on end. He finally came up with the right look for our candidate Huw Edwards on the election leaflets. He had him photographed with jacket off but cunningly slung over his shoulder. It wasn't Huw at all. It was half casual and half formal, making him look like a cross between an itinerant tarmac-layer and 'Man at C&A'. But it did the trick. Huw was far less extrovert than our three previous by-election candidates – Kim Howells (Pontypridd), John Smith (Vale of Glamorgan) and Peter Hain (Neath). The special look devised by Mandelson overcame the impression of shyness that Huw could convey.

At last the voters of Monmouth were moving in our direction as the big day approached. Then disaster struck. At the final morning press conference, Jack Cunningham seemed to have to lost it completely. He had a right go at the Tory candidate Roger Evans. It was true that Evans was quite short and chubby – he was a barrister from Cardiff and, although a 'townie', he wore tweedy country gent clothes as if to the manor born. But for those of us sat in the audience, we had to question whether it really was right and proper for Jack to refer to Evans as 'Turd of Turd Hole', especially as we seemed to be winning. We didn't do bad language. Respectable swing voters beginning to edge towards voting Labour would be scandalised – Jack had blown it, surely. Then it transpired that it was Jack's deep-as-the-mineshaft Durham accent that had fooled everybody – it was 'Toad of Toad Hall'! And despite that momentary hiccup, Huw Edwards won the seat, and hopes of general election victory soared.

All of the opinion polls predicted a Labour win at the 1992 election, but we lost. What that must have been like for Neil Kinnock I can't imagine, because it was certainly shattering for me and Julie. Whether it was the Sheffield Rally, or the Kenneth Baker speech on immigration, or the unrelenting hostility of the *Sun*, *Mail* and *Express*, I do not know. The Sheffield Rally should have been held in Basildon if at all! All I know is that the air went out of our balloon on the Monday night before polling day. The response on the doorstep was different, palpably different, and although I wasn't panicking about Cardiff West, I certainly didn't want to go to the election eve rally in Barry. My canvassing team was desperate to go. So I let them off for the rest of the night while I carried on door-knocking. I wasn't willing to leave the streets of Ely – I could feel something slipping through our fingers like quicksilver. We'd had a good campaign until those last three days.

Edward Pearce was writing a quickie book to come out within a week of the election itself, called *Election Rides* after a similarly titled book by William Cobbett. He put a joke that I'd stolen from Ken Dodd into the book – I'd used it at a remarkably well attended public meeting in Ely, which had still been smarting from the after-effects of the Ely Bread Riots. The reputation of the area had been high, but was now at rock-bottom, and I had told the tale of a brave young man from Ely on a visit to Bristol Zoo. The lion had escaped, and the Ely boy jumped on its back as it was heading towards a group of schoolgirls. He half-nelsoned the lion until it fell limp and the keepers could tranquillise it and put it back in its cage – he was an instant hero. Then they asked where the boy was from. 'Ely', he answered, and the newspaper the following day ran the headline ELY THUG THROTTLES CHILDREN'S PET! Everyone in the audience got the point.

As soon as the Basildon result was in, horribly early on election night, we knew that we hadn't got anywhere in the south of England yet again. We hadn't won the election. All that work had been in vain. I knew we'd lost the election even before we had our count in Cardiff West. I tried to laugh off the disappointment in my victory speech from the platform and said that as a candidate mooching around in the count for hours on end, watching the bundles of votes for each candidate being heaped up, I felt a bit like a surgeon wandering around a hospital that's closing down – you can see other people's piles growing, but it's too late to do anything about it! To be honest, my heart wasn't in making up jokes for a victory speech. Winning Cardiff West in 1987 felt like a victory, but 1992 felt more like a wake. Julie and I headed off to the Lake District to try to get over the disappointment – every other Labour MP or candidate felt the same – and we booked into a hotel next to Wordsworth's birthplace. By sheer coincidence, we spotted another re-elected Labour MP, Jeff Rooker (Birmingham Perry Bar) in the same post-election gloom. We exchanged brief hellos, and that was it. I had no wish to exchange views about the election with him and I'm sure the feeling was mutual. We just wanted to retreat. That's how bad it was. The only cold comfort was the thought of how much worse it probably was for Neil and Glenys.

I doubt if any MP enjoys his or her second Parliament as much as the first. In your first Parliament, the possibilities seem endless even when you're in Opposition. In the second Parliament, you hope you will be in Government so that you can use the skills you've built up in those first four or five years. It didn't happen for those of us who came in 1987 – far worse for those like Tony Blair, Gordon Brown or Ron Davies and many others who had come in in 1983 – not forgetting poor old Jack Straw, who had entered Parliament in 1979, in continuous Opposition for thirteen years already and about to start another four or five!

First, I had a little local difficulty with Peter Mandelson to contend with. This was 1992, but it would come back to bite me in 1997. I had put down an Early Day Motion just before the election, which was still on the Commons Order

Paper after the election. It told of the day that the late David Frost had been confronted by John Birt (later to become Director-General of the BBC, but who was back then a combative *World in Action* investigative journalist) looking into Frost's business dealings. Frost had cried, and had asked Birt not to pursue the issue. I'd spoken to the interview cameraman who had been there at the Algonquin Hotel in New York to verify events, and the *Mirror* ran the story under the headline 'How Beeb Boss made Frosty Cry!' Mandelson had formerly worked for Birt while a candidate for Hartlepool between 1990 and 1992, so he had written me a note telling me I should now withdraw the whole allegation as it had been completely disproved. In the interim, I had bumped into journalist Anna Ford in Cardiff, who told me how wonderful it was that at long last an MP had taken this ghastly story of how Frost and Birt had helped each other climb the ladder of success, leaving others trailing in their wake. So, I wrote a note back to Mandelson telling him off for interfering in another MP's business. Mandelson was just a new boy at the time, and under John Smith he was not a figure of any influence at all. But by the time of the next election with Labour forming a government, a falling out with Mandelson was as bad as if not worse than falling out with Tony Blair himself.

Neil Kinnock resigned after that second election defeat. Paul Murphy and Kim Howells drove over to his house in Pontllanfraith to try to persuade him to carry on, but to no avail. I couldn't see how he could carry on, but I was really shocked that there was no proper way of saying thank you to him for the incredible service he had rendered the party. First and foremost for his storming speech at the Bournemouth Conference in 1985, and then for his nine years of leadership. He had made us electable, even though we were not eventually elected. But at the first post-election meeting of all 270-odd Labour MPs, it was as though Neil had never existed. It was brutal.

John Smith had come in as leader with huge backing from almost every corner of the party. He was an immensely affable Scot who had an edge of steel when it came to issues like devolution. He'd been Mr Devolution in the run-up to the failed project in 1979, and this was now unfinished business as far as he was concerned. He picked Ann Clwyd to be his Shadow Welsh Secretary of State, and me as one of her deputies. I hadn't been asked if I'd like anything else. I wouldn't have minded another economic portfolio – Treasury, Trade & Industry, or Employment – if I'd had the choice, but I didn't. I did the full five years of that parliament on Welsh Affairs. When John Smith's secretary rang me up to tell me that in fifteen minutes John would be wanting a word with me, I was naturally excited. I used up my ten minutes' notice to hang out the washing on the clothes line, with the cordless phone by my side. When the fateful phone call did come through, it was a little bit early and I was still hanging out the washing. After a second or two of small talk, John Smith must have sensed I was outdoors, and asked me where

I was speaking from. I told him the unadorned truth that I was hanging out the washing, which I hope he took as an example of sangfroid on my part.

Regardless of what front-bench job anyone was doing, the Maastricht Treaty was looming over everything. Parliament had to ratify the Treaty. John Major had got two big opt-outs, one on the euro and one on the Social Chapter. The latter opt-out was anathema to Labour. John Major's tactical problem was that if Labour amended the Government motion to reinstate the Social Chapter, thirty or more Eurosceptic rebels would vote with Labour to try to kill off the whole ratification process – and that's roughly what happened. It was the most exciting night of my entire parliamentary career. I voted very quickly through the Labour lobby, and shoved and elbowed my way though the crowded Chamber up to the Government end to see what was happening. The Government whips had formed a human barrier so that Tory rebels couldn't get into the Labour lobbies. I saw my local MP, the Tory new-boy Walter Sweeney, who had beaten John Smith by only nineteen votes in the Vale of Glamorgan, trying to get into the Labour lobby. He was like a slightly bewildered horse in a corral and didn't know what to do. I could hear Rod Richards (Clwyd West), part of the Tory phalanx, calling out 'Come on Walter! This way!' That tripped a switch for me, and I pretended to trip over my own shoelaces and fell forward into the phalanx, which broke the line they'd formed and Walter Sweeney walked through the gap! Complaining loudly at my tactics, the Tory Whip (whose shoulder I'd fallen heavily against) said, 'I say!' I knew I'd won when I heard that public-school exclamation.

Labour won by one vote on the night. There weren't quite enough Tory rebels really, but we got an extra vote from the Government whip who was doing the counting, the late Irvine Patnick, who hadn't noticed that the Labour Deputy Chief Whip, Don Dixon, voted twice. If you're counted through twice by sneaking back into the lobby and coming back out again, then it's the government's own fault for letting you do so. British democracy takes many different forms, and that night there were phalanxes, rugby tackles (by me anyway), and double voting. The Government lost, but returned the following day with a slightly different wording which made the Maastricht Treaty vote an issue of confidence in the Government, and losing that vote would have meant another general election (which nobody wanted). The Government got its vote through, but the Eurosceptic Tories were so enraged by the Government's tactic that they swore revenge and made John Major's life hell thereafter.

That's one of the reasons why I'm among the few who thought that *Yes Minister* and *Yes Prime Minister* were pretty tame shows. The audience imagined the programmes actually exaggerated what really happened inside government just to spice it up as entertainment – but half the time, what really happened was, and no doubt still is, twice as extreme as what they would dare put on television! *The Thick of It* got a bit closer, but nothing like the night of the Maastricht vote.

Back in my constituency office in Transport House in Cardiff, the amount of casework was pouring through the doors. If I'd been inclined towards the conspiracy theory, I would have concluded that the Tories were trying to tire out MPs by overloading us with casework. It was caused by the incompetence of the new agencies dealing with Child Support and Disability Living Allowance. MPs' offices used to be part of the redress system for those really difficult knotty problems that all bureaucracies struggle with, but now we were becoming part of the quality control process. Chuck out decisions any old how, and let the MPs' constituency case workers deal with the fallout.

If you had a fair amount of immigration casework as I did, the overload on the office got even worse. On one occasion, though, I felt I had to breach the sanctity of what constituents tell their MP in the surgery, which is akin to the confessional. This all arose over a fraudulent claim for housing benefit including the lodging allowance, after an unscrupulous local landlord came to my surgery with the case of a tenant/lodger with learning difficulties. Lodgers were supposed to get breakfast, but this lodger was barred from touching the box of cornflakes in the kitchen – it was just for show, and I finished up giving evidence against the landlord, whose admission was so brazen that I felt I had to take it up with the anti-fraud team in the Housing Benefit department of Cardiff City Council.

I was at one point part of a team of MPs visiting Moscow at the worst of the troubles during the difficult transition from state control to free market economics in the Yeltsin government era. Yeltsin didn't know what was going on, and the Russian Mafia was getting a firm grip on food distribution. Former civil servants within Ministries with state-owned industries about to be sold off would position themselves outside the door at precisely the moment when offers for these state assets were received and the envelopes containing bids were opened, and the lucky few who knew where this auction was taking place would become billionaires overnight. I wasn't being terribly superior about Russian privatisation, because I knew that it was only a more extreme version of what happened in selling off the electricity supply industry in the UK – I knew that the bosses of the South Wales Electricity Board (SWALEC), while it was the regional electricity supply nationalised industry for South Wales, did become rich overnight when the great sell-off took place. I had been appalled by that, but what was happening in Russia was far more blatant.

My introduction to the British Embassy staff at the Ambassador's official residence was bizarre in the extreme. Each MP was greeted at the door by Sir Roderick Braithwaite, the Ambassador himself. As I shook his hand, he said, 'Ah, Morgan! You must be the one from Dinas Powys!' 'That's right', I replied. 'Well my mother came from Dinas Powys!' he explained delightedly. I moved further on down the hallway to meet Sir Roderick's deputy, who introduced himself as David Manning – 'You must be Rhodri Morgan, the one from Dinas Powys!' (they'd obviously been studying the pen-pictures in advance) –'That's right', I said. Then David Manning said, 'My mother comes from Dinas Powys!' (a decade later, David Manning was the guy given credit by the Chilcott Inquiry for unsuccessfully trying to dissuade Tony Blair from writing the ludicrous 'We will be with you always' note to George W. Bush in the run-up to the invasion of Iraq – he was Sir David by then, of course). The third diplomat I met told me his name was Chris Steele. I took the initiative this time and said, 'I suppose your mother comes from Dinas Powys too?''No', he laughed, 'but my father does come from Ynysybwl!' Chris Steele is now the famous author of the controversial report on Donald Trump and what he got up to in Moscow.

Our supper the previous Sunday night in the grim hotel, only partially converted from being the ex-headquarters of the Komsomol, the old Communist Youth Organisation, had Cold War written all over it. But the same dilemma reared as over the fake and fraudulent lodging allowance in my surgery. If someone tells you something in confidence, should you then pass it on? All that was on the menu for supper was hard-boiled eggs and black bread. A young-ish Russian entrepreneur came to sit by me wanting to practise his English a bit – he was one of those who'd bought out a state-owned factory making gas masks to protect against chemical warfare, and was off to Sofia in Bulgaria the following day to try to seal a deal with Iraq and anyone else who wanted to buy this stuff. Sofia was *the* place to buy and sell defence equipment, he informed me, and he even gave me his business card. At the Embassy dinner the following night, I told the staff of my dilemma. If this guy was selling anti-chemical warfare materiel via some dodgy arms fair in Sofia, then the Foreign Office needed to know about it. But he'd been very open with me and I didn't want the guy bumped off or anything. 'Thanks for the tip-off', they said, 'it's always useful to know what's going on.' I felt queasy passing on the guy's business card … it was the same dilemma as the one in Cardiff, but in more of a John Le Carré setting.

On the subject of being bumped off, it was something that was happening in the new Russia perhaps more than in Gorbachev's USSR. One of the dinner guests sat next to me at the Ambassador's dinner was the democracy campaigner Galina Starovoitova, and we had a fascinating conversation about how to turn the discussion groups going on all over Russia into genuine Western-style political parties. Sadly, she did get bumped off, well before her dream of Russian democracy could be realised. Her killer was never identified. We Western politicians, with incredibly rare exceptions like Jo Cox or Ian Gow, don't know how lucky we are. It's the luck of the draw to be born in Wales, Poland, Germany or Russia.

Even death from natural causes can still send massive shock waves through the system. That's what happened with John Smith. He was only Labour leader for two years, dying of a heart attack at a Labour fund-raising dinner. He'd had the big warning storm-cone hoisted over him in 1988 when he had his first heart attack, at which time Gordon Brown had taken over as temporary Shadow Chancellor, and had done a brilliant job. John made a very good recovery on that occasion, losing a lot of weight by climbing a Munro every Sunday with the then Shadow Culture Secretary, Chris Smith. The heart problem seemed to be solved but, eventually, the stress of being party leader proved unrelenting. He could wipe the floor with John Major in the Commons, and didn't get the battering in the press that Neil Kinnock had endured. But the strain got to John in the end, and he stopped doing the Munro climbs on Sundays. He put back on all the weight, and the end was probably inevitable.

Ron Davies, Win Griffiths and I were doing a morning press conference for the Welsh media in the rather soul-less office block at 7 Millbank, when we got the news that John had died. We did our best to explain what he meant to us – now I think we can see clearly that John Smith was the ablest Prime Minister Britain never had. I probably felt it in my bones even on that morning. There is never time to grieve or to take stock in politics, and within twenty-four hours of John's death people were lining up to choose his successor. Events very quickly transformed into a Brown or Blair question. The two of them no longer shared an office in the Commons as they had done when I first became an MP, but they still seemed to see themselves as rising up the ladder of political promotion together.

The previous year, the pair had been encouraged by John Smith to stand for election to the Labour National Executive, for which the electorate was totally different to the Shadow Cabinet annual elections where only Labour MPs had the right to vote. Tony Blair had asked me to organise a reception in the Cardiff area for him so that he could meet as many constituencies within a ten-mile radius. Kevin Brennan, who ran my constituency office and became my eventual successor as MP for Cardiff West, alighted on Churchill's Hotel which could put on a reasonably priced wine, cheese and nibbles evening do. We sent out the invitations. We had a good response, especially strong from Radyr, the village where I'd grown up and where Tony Blair's parents, Leo and Hazel, had also lived while Tony was away at university. In fact, it was in Radyr that Hazel had spent her final days, having died there at a very untimely age. In my introductory speech, I would have to refer to Tony's Cardiff connections and especially his Radyr ones, since they were the ones he and I shared. But then a thought occurred to me – what if Tony had been traumatised by his mother's death. I rang up Anji Hunter, and explained my dilemma – would Tony be okay if I referred to his Radyr connections, despite Hazel's passing away there while in her forties? Anji felt sure it was okay.

I did my usual back-handed compliment to Tony's abilities, explaining that to get to the top in the Labour Party you had to have real brains, you had to have a very short surname, and you had to have connections with Edinburgh, the Athens of the North. Smith, Cook, Brown, Blair, Dewar, etc., all proved the point.

What's more, he could lay claim not just to superhuman brainpower, but also to Scottish (father), English (mother), and Welsh (Radyr) links. I said I wasn't sure which of the home nations he supported, so I tried to get him signed up for Wales. I joked that, with Wales having just beaten the Faroes 6–0 at football in a World Cup qualifier, a super-intelligent guy like Tony Blair here had shaken his head and said, 'Surely the Egyptian FA could put out a stronger team than that!'

After my introduction and his speech, he was immediately surrounded by the lady members from Radyr, all of whom seemed to remember his mother Hazel and were desperate to tell Tony of how fond they had been of her. He was pretty close to tears – I'd never seen him so emotional before or since. I'm not sure Anji had been right, although she knew him far better than I did. The upshot of the dual campaign to get both Tony and Gordon onto the NEC was successful, but the following year the big split between the Brownites and the Blairites burst into the open. It was inevitably going to happen at some stage. Brown and Blair were head and shoulders above any other Labour MP in their presentation skills. The ideal scenario would have been for John Smith to bring them on in Opposition, and then in senior jobs in Government, and it would then emerge which one was pre-eminent when the succession to Smith arose in due course. But we didn't have the luxury of time to settle the issue.

I pledged my support to Tony Blair. I had worked for him and I admired his kitbag of abilities. He was far less prone to the London press finding a weakness to exploit (as they'd done with Neil and the Welsh Windbag sobriquet) and Tony was 'paradigm man' in a way that Gordon Brown was not. Gordon wasn't married at that time, but Tony was Mr Normal with a wife and three kids and a house in Highbury near the Arsenal ground (even if he privately felt it should have been in Notting Hill). I hadn't really woken up to his chameleon tendencies, nor to his inclination to listen too much to Peter Mandelson's advice – I just calculated that he'd be armour-plated against *The Sun* and *The Mail*. Ergo we had a far better chance of beating John Major with Tony than with Gordon, which was all I cared about. Tony covered his own back against the posh public-schoolboy accusation by allying himself with John Prescott as his deputy party leader. You have to give him that one as a masterstroke. Yes, they were the Odd Couple of politics, but the balance worked.

I went to the victory announcement at the Agricultural Halls. There was never any doubt about the result. After idly chatting with other MPs for half an hour, I headed back towards the House of Commons, where there were nowhere near enough taxis, and then a taxi door opened and a Welsh voice beckoned. It was Delyth Evans, formerly of the BBC and now without a job having been a speech-writer for John Smith. She asked if I wanted to share the taxi, and I jumped in. Another John Smith staffer, now jobless, was in there – David Ward, who would later work for Formula 1. The taxi was stuck in a jam straight away. David Ward was looking back at the crowds milling about outside the Agricultural Halls. 'Look', he said, 'they're all back.' 'Who?' I asked. 'All the luvvies', he said, 'the celebs, the show-biz hangers-on, Mandelson has brought them all back. John would have nothing to do with any of them. Now they're back!' David was very down, because if you work for one party leader, the effect of a death is the same as a change of government. One minute you're at the centre of everything, the next minute you're out – so I should have allowed for that – but by the time they dropped me at the House of Commons, I was thoroughly depressed about the future.

I was going in through the Carriage Gates under Big Ben as Alistair Darling was coming out. 'Aren't you coming to the party?' he asked. 'What party?' 'The victory party for Tony', he said. Once again, parties were way off my radar, but it would have been no problem for me to go with Alistair. Anyway, I told him 'No, I think I'll be heading home.' I don't know why I said that, it was a bad move really, because I had voted for Tony Blair and backed him publicly. I think it was all to do with that feeling that Blair was surrounded by the wrong people, the celebs and luvvies. Not going to the victory party meant that if anyone noticed I wasn't there, they would have the right to assume that I was a disgruntled Brownite, which I certainly was not.

My reaction to the next Blair move was exactly the same. That was the move to replace Clause Four. 'Why is he doing this?' I thought. A few months after the change had gone through, I was walking on the seafront in Brighton, with Rod Richards of all people, who was doing something for the Welsh broadcaster S4C. Rod asked why Blair had replaced Clause Four, because it wouldn't advantage Labour as hardly any middle-of-the-road voters up and down the country had any idea that Clause Four ever existed. That was the only time in my life I ever agreed with Rod Richards! But it was all about the rebranding, the New Labour marketing exercise, and Clause Four was part of the rebranding. It wouldn't have happened under John Smith, who was of the one-more-heave school, the theory that when the next election came the country would be so tired and fed up with the Tories that any sensible programme for Government by Labour would see the party elected. The New Labour rebranding theory was that the image of Labour was now so negative in the south of England that the party had to change fundamentally to have any chance of winning. Back in 1988, I had heard Neil Kinnock tell a few of us new MPs that if we went moderate, we could be in power for a generation. I knew that wasn't Neil Kinnock speaking – it was Mandelson, speaking via Kinnock. John Smith, being a moderate anyway, never saw the need to change the Labour brand.

Labour MPs were forming themselves into squads that would answer any calls by a constituency Labour MP to come and explain what the new Clause Four was all about. Kim Howells came up to me in the party conference to ask if I could take his place at a meeting of Brecon and Radnor CLP. 'I'm not sure I want to be part of this exercise', I told him. I didn't want to oppose the changes now that they were underway, but neither did I want to be a part of the exercise of selling them to parties up and down the country. I was caught in the middle.

On the Welsh front, we were getting a lot of help from John Redwood in preparing for climbing Mount Devolution. In his two years as Secretary of State for Wales, he had not stayed a single night in Wales; he had made a right cobblers of miming the Welsh national anthem in public; and he'd brought forth a Welsh Local Government Reform Bill which removed one tier of local government. He made a mistake by agreeing to Ted Rowlands's plea that Merthyr had a strong historic claim to being a local authority, despite its small size, but the bill paved the way for Welsh devolution by removing the argument that devolution would give Wales too many tiers of government! Mostly, Redwood helped the case for devolution simply by being John Redwood. He had made himself into a new Tory bogeyman on a par with Margaret Thatcher. I suppose he got what he wanted from being Secretary of State for Wales, which was ultimately to get into the Cabinet. That in turn gave him the ability to resign from the Cabinet with a flourish and to lead the rebellion of the Eurosceptics against John Major – if he hadn't been in the Cabinet, he wouldn't have been able to lead what became known as 'The Charge of the Light in the Head Brigade'.

But Labour had to capitalise on the opening that Redwood's two years at the Welsh Office in Cathays Park gave us. Ron Davies and the Labour Party in Wales were not as one in deciding exactly what model of devolution we wanted. Whereas John Smith had been totally committed, Tony Blair was not. He had his doubts. So we had to work it through. In Scotland, a Convention was formed, led by Labour and with full participation of the Lib Dems, although it was boycotted by the Conservatives and the SNP. It also had civil and civic society on board, local government, the churches, and the trade unions. We had none of that in Wales. In Wales, we set up a purely Labour Commission, but we did have full permission to talk to as many of the other parties as we could, and to engage with the civic and civil sectors. I did a lot of the spadework on the Commission, and led it when it visited Caernarfon and Aberystwyth and Haverfordwest.

When the Commission met back in Cardiff, it was hard going. There was a minimalist school of thought, heavily influenced by the rejected 1979 model. Ken Hopkins was from the Rhondda Labour Party and an ex-Director of Education of Mid Glamorgan, and his favourite phrase was that the new Welsh Assembly should not have any more powers than the old Glamorgan County Council. There were one or two who wanted a big model of devolution influenced by what was emerging in the Convention in Scotland – Jim Brandon, a fiery Scot who was the steelworkers union rep on the Commission, didn't see why Wales couldn't have something similar to Scotland. The good thing about a Labour Party Commission was that when the Commission had finished its work, its report back to the Welsh party conference could be rejected but not amended. But what kind of model of devolution could we get through the Commission? There was a great deal of shouting and testosterone-fuelled argument in every session, and we finished up with something much better than in 1979.

It wasn't going to be a local government-based model. It was going to be based on transferring the powers of the Secretary of State to the new Assembly. Given the much greater powers the Secretary of State had by 1996 compared with 1979, the Assembly would be powerful. The big conflict was over legislative powers. Was it going to be simply an executive body, or would it have any power to make laws? Scotland had always had its own legal system, even though it hadn't had its own parliament since 1707, so there was a huge body of Scots law that the new Parliament there would inherit. We had very little Welsh law for the new Assembly to get its teeth into.

I was on the side of the argument in favour of legislative powers to the maximum that we could get into the report of the Commission. In the end, we out-argued minimalists like the late Ken Hopkins and the late Terry Thomas – we secured a moderate-ist report, a lot better than minimalist. It would all depend on how flexible the definition of legislative powers was eventually going to be. You might only have secondary legislative powers, but if you could use those legislative powers creatively you could achieve something. In effect, that's what happened after 1999 – we made creative use of secondary legislative powers to do significant things for Wales. The problem with the moderate model of devolution was its saleability to the Welsh public in a devolution referendum – could the package engender any enthusiasm among the voters if it was too moderate? Should Wales have had a Scottish-style Convention? Well, I'm not sure about that. Whereas the SNP, like the Tories, boycotted the Convention in Scotland, I suspect that Plaid Cymru would have agreed to take part along with the Lib Dems, which would have made the Labour representatives on it much more defensive. The likelihood of a 'No' vote when the report of the Convention was put to the Welsh Labour Party conference would have been far higher.

I think that Ron Davies, appointed Secretary of State for Wales in 1997, was happy to keep the Plaid Cymru leader Dafydd Wigley and then leader of the Welsh Lib Dems, the late Richard Livsey, on board with what was going on inside the Labour Commission. I was never invited, but Ron was having dinner regularly with the two other pro-devolution party leaders and formed a really good relationship with them. The other thing I was never invited to were the meetings with the top civil servants at the Welsh Office. I knew that my opposite numbers in the Scottish Shadow Ministers were pretty well given the run of the place in the Scottish Office, and I knew more about what Scottish civil servants were saying to the Labour Shadow Scottish Office ministerial team, all four of them, than about how the Welsh Office was responding to our plans. Either Ron had already had an intimation from Tony Blair that I wasn't going to get any kind of ministerial post in his new Government, or Ron preferred to keep an awful lot of the key cards much closer to his chest than Donald Dewar, his Scottish counterpart. Ron was a member of a group of Shadow Ministers led by Robin Cook and Clare Short which was trying to provide a forum for progressive ideas. I only found out about the group from the Pembroke MP Nick Ainger. He'd been invited, but not me. That was strange – there was an air of secrecy about the group of progressives. Ron had an exaggerated sense of privacy, which was most evident when he would announce to me and his office staff at lunchtime that he was going to walk over to Battersea Park to feed the ducks in the lake. He had a way of announcing this when he had a half of his lunchtime sandwiches left, but in a way that clearly indicated he would not welcome anyone walking over there with him.

What all the top civil servants in Scotland and Wales accepted was that the Conservatives were definitely going to lose the forthcoming election. The next government was going to be a Blair government. The New Labour opinion poll lead was over twenty points most of the time, and officials were naturally keen within professional protocols to meet the Shadow Ministers who were going to be their bosses before long. Ron established an excellent working relationship with Rachel Lomax, the Permanent Secretary at the Welsh Office. The only relationship I had with Welsh Office officialdom came out of the blue, two days before the election itself, when I had a phone call from the Health Department concerning the new cottage hospital to be built in Chepstow via the Private Finance Initiative. The official said that the bank providing the private finance was nervous about committing the money unless it was going to be backed by the incoming Labour ministerial team, and asked if I could please provide the necessary message of comfort that would persuade the bank to sign on the dotted line. I said that I could do no such thing. If I was a Minister, I would have seen the proposal, the papers and the briefings, but here I was as a Shadow Minister sat in my chair in my constituency office, having a little break before heading out canvassing again. I'd seen no documentation, so I was very sorry, but no.

Of course, it was possibly that I was better suited to guerrilla tactics than to any meetings with Rachel Lomax and her chief lieutenants. I had developed really good contacts with rebellious staff members at the Welsh Development Agency and the National Audit Office. They were supplying me with juicy tidbits of office scandal, usually involving Dr Gwyn Jones, the WDA chairman who had been appointed as a true Welsh go-getter by Peter Walker and was hugely admired by Margaret Thatcher. I worked closely with Bruce Kennedy, a journalist with HTV's *Wales This Week*. When most of the WDA's staff was scandalised by the travel itinerary proposed for the chairman's visit to Australia and the USA with a stopover on the island of Tahiti, I was given the story to 'use' as best I could. Amazingly, Bruce managed to track down the beachside hotel in Tahiti where the three from the WDA had been booked in. It only took two phone calls apparently – this was in the days before Google-type search engines. It was one of the best *Wales This Week* programmes ever, which also produced one of the best cartoons ever in the *South Wales Echo* by the legendary cartoonist Gren, showing a group of business executives of Polynesian appearance turning up at the WDA head office asking for a grant to build a grass skirt factory in the Valleys!

Another tip-off I'd received was causing huge embarrassment at the WDA where Gwyn Jones had appointed a marketing executive named Neil Smith, a man that Gwyn described as very much like himself, a go-getter. It turned out that Neil Smith had faked his reference from Peter Lloyd, the Conservative MP for Fareham. It was a bad fake, which gave Peter Lloyd's constituency as Farnham, not Fareham. Easy to check. That spelt the end of Gwyn Jones's time at the WDA, but he soon crossed Quango Avenue to take up the Chair of the BBC Broadcasting Council for Wales, carrying a seat on the UK BBC Board of Governors. When the story of the Korean LG investment was broken, it came after Gwyn Jones had barged into the newsroom after an excellently enjoyable briefing lunch with Rod Richards, still a Welsh Office minister at the time, and he told the startled newsroom that at last Wales really had hit the jackpot. It was the best thing that had ever happened – negative thoughts about the future of Wales could now be set to one side – it was going to be all positive news from now on!

Sadly, the LG investment had £247 million of Welsh Office money allocated to it, and we were still trying to sort out the financial mess left behind the project for most of the first decade of the Assembly! LG signed on the dotted line while William Hague was being blooded in Wales with his first Cabinet job as Secretary of State in 1996–7, and the European Summit meeting of the summer of 1998 had to be planned well before the election, even though it would not take place until one year later. The previous time the European Summit meeting had taken place in the UK, it was held in Scotland, and so William Hague had fought very hard for the 1998 Summit to be held in Wales. The Foreign Office had originally decided that this was out of the question because Cardiff did not have a 5-star hotel and Hague, to be fair to him, went to see an old friend. Rocco Forte, who had found himself with several hundred millions he didn't really want after the Forte family lost out in a takeover battle against the Granada Group, was asked by Hague to build Cardiff's first ever 5-star hotel in Cardiff Bay. The Cardiff Bay Development Corporation awarded a grant of several million as an incentive, and that was enough to get the stuffy old Foreign Office to withdraw their objections to Cardiff as Summit host.

The fact that the great new 5-Star St David's Hotel wasn't finished until a year after the Summit had been and gone hardly seemed to matter. It was all in the sales pitch. My involvement in the Summit came just before and just after the 1997 General Election, and preparations for the Summit went ahead under a heavy blanket of secrecy. The university in Cathays Park was going to be taken over for a week, but nobody was allowed to know why. Cardiff City Hall was to be vacated for something terribly important, but nobody knew what. Now, my philosophy at that time was that the Tory Government in London should not be allowed to believe it could do anything in Wales without me (or us, Labour), knowing about it. Wales was our country. Yes, I was being a bit possessive, but that's how I felt. 'They', the Tories in Wales, were the colonists. When Ken Hopkins blabbed at a meeting of the Labour Devolution Commission that there was something big and top secret being planned for the summer of 1998, and that it was going to be taking over most of the civic centre in Cathays Park, I worked out that the only thing that could fit the bill was the European Summit meeting.

I didn't want to break the story without checking with Robin Cook, the Shadow Foreign Secretary. I didn't mind embarrassing William Hague and John Major, but the last thing I wanted to do was embarrass Robin Cook. I thought he might have been given a confidential briefing in what the Government was proposing – logically, he should have been, as it was going to happen in 1998, well after the election. Robin would then have been sworn to secrecy (although that would have been a bit of a problem for me). Anyway, he knew nothing about the Summit meeting location. He told me to do whatever I considered best to grab the initiative on the issue, and so I broke the story in such a way as to make it sound as if Labour pressure was behind the choice of Cardiff for the Euro Summit.

After the 1997 General Election was over, my old fiend Anji Hunter came down to Cardiff to do one of her famous 'recces'. She always did these before any visit by Tony Blair to anything, both in Opposition or as Prime Minister. She asked us Labour MPs to come over for coffee to give her a break from all the Foreign Office types – although I may have done the opposite by embarrassing her, albeit with the best of intentions, when I told her in front of the mandarins about the famous air duct in City Hall. The duct was famous, because you could hear everything going on in the next room by putting your ear close to it. Anji wasn't completely confident of her position vis-à-vis the regular civil servants, and she also didn't know if I was taking the mickey. I wasn't. I had worked in City Hall back in 1974 and I knew the place. I told her and the visiting mandarins that they just had to be sure to allocate any troublesome EU country delegation to the committee room with the whispering air duct, and then the UK delegation could listen in next-door. Lots of frowns all round! Not cricket, old boy! For all her jolly hockey sticks manner, Anji Hunter was intensely loyal not just to Tony but to people like me (and herself of course) who were the original members of the Shadow Energy team back in 1988. That was when he, Blair, had first emerged as a politician of front-rank quality.

Wherever the breach with Blair came from, resulting in my not being selected as a Minister after the May 1997 landslide win, I'm sure it didn't come from Anji. I had managed to upset not just Peter Mandelson in 1992, but two other members of the Blair inner sanctum, David Miliband and Tim Allan. That was during the election campaign itself. The row with Miliband blew up over the wording of the Welsh Labour manifesto. I co-wrote the Health part of it with my Health Advisory Group. But David Miliband didn't like the wording of it – he thought its strong commitment to the NHS as the delivery vehicle, without any encouragement to private provision, would cause difficulties in England where the main Health manifesto would apply. The health unions and other campaigning bodies like the Socialist Health Association would point to the wording of the Welsh Health manifesto and demand exactly the same wording in the so-called 'main' (that is, English) manifesto. I pointed out to David that the wording we had alighted on was remarkably similar to that in the Scottish Health manifesto, but Miliband said Scotland didn't count because in England there was no read-across from Scotland as there was from Wales. I agreed with him that this read-across was there for now, but that it was surely going to change. Labour was going into the election with a commitment to devolution for Scotland and Wales, subject to a referendum – if we didn't believe in the devolution principle ourselves in writing our three Health manifestos, how were we going to persuade the public in any forthcoming referendum? I'm sure that David was working sixteen hours a day trying to coordinate everything, but he was quite short-tempered with me. He really didn't seem to expect or like anyone contesting his fearsome brainpower. We finished up with me promising to alter Labour's Welsh Health manifesto as soon as he got the Scots to change the wording in theirs! That wasn't what he wanted – I wasn't being helpful – and I suppose if Tony Blair had come on the line and explained why he was desperate to have a closer alignment between the manifestos, I would have taken the whole thing much more seriously. But David Miliband was not an MP. He was, in my mind at least, only an adviser, a paid official, who was not facing the voters in the election. He thought he was more important than me, and I thought the reverse.

The other member of Blair's inner sanctum that I managed to upset was Tim Allan, who phoned to instruct me to issue an official retraction of something I'd said about the prospects of us joining the euro in a Sunday morning programme from Cardiff City Hall. He was Tony Blair's enforcer of the message, and again, if Tony Blair himself had come on the line and asked me to do it, I might have agreed. But Tim Allan was not Tony Blair. He was one of those strange creatures who had attached themselves to the New Labour project because they were sure Blair was going to win.

I might have also upset a fourth member of the Blair praetorian guard, namely Jonathan Powell. He was the one who organised the two weekends of commando training for future Ministers in the early spring of 1997. When the Welsh Affairs Shadow team lined up in Powell's office to be given its orders to Templeton College, Oxford, I took the mickey out of Jonathan as usual. 'Are these management gurus going to be giving us marks out of ten or what?' I asked. Jonathan took the Templeton College exercise terribly seriously. Not all the front-bench teams turned up – I certainly don't remember the Scottish team attending the exercise. It was a brilliant bonding exercise but, as far as the lectures were concerned, it would have been far better if *we* had been doing the lecturing and the lecturers had been sat in the front row – half of them were from the management college, and the other half from Arthur Andersen whose sole purpose was to sell us their services.

It was my job to find us a pub for Saturday night. On the second Saturday, I hit the jackpot, finding the way across country to the Boat Inn at a lock gate on the Thames. The only problem was that we had to climb up an embankment to get to the Oxford bypass, cross it where the traffic was doing seventy miles an hour, and only then find our way to this canal barges pub right in the middle of the river.

Even more worthwhile was listening in on the next Sunday morning breakfast conversation between Doug Henderson, a Newcastle MP who was our champion marathon running colleague, telling John Cornford, one of our better lecturers, how Labour in power was going to drop all this stuff about devolution. I ate my breakfast absolutely agog, but very quietly so that Doug didn't notice I was there. Doug was a member of Jack Straw's Shadow team. He ran through the standard anti-devolution case. 'We're not going to spend most of the first two years of the first Labour Government in eighteen years mucking about on constitutional issues – we're going to need to head straight into the key issues like health, education and the economy. Definitely not devolution.' It all went into my mental notebook. That was Jack Straw speaking really, not Doug Henderson. Of course, devolution was exactly what we did spend a huge amount of parliamentary effort on during the 1997–9 period – it filled the gap while Labour carried out its manifesto promise to abide by Tory public spending.

Most of us concluded that the Templeton College personnel were going to supply marks out of ten for each of us Shadow Ministers to Jonathan Powell, or at least comments on how prepared each of us was for government. As far as I was concerned, if Powell or indeed Tony Blair himself were daft enough to believe that these management gurus from the college or the private sector had any idea what running a government department was like, then more fool them.

Where I did far better as part of Labour's central campaign machine was over health stories for the *Mirror*'s usual 'Twenty-Four Hours to Save the NHS' campaign. In the final ten days before the election, they were desperate to get stories that proved how the NHS was falling apart under the Tories. I was the only one, as I recall, to provide any stories that actually got into the *Mirror*. One

**1943,** aged three, with brother Prys aged six.

**Spring 1948**, Radyr School.

**1955,** *(left)* the back yard in Radyr. Rhodri's parents, T. J. and Huana Morgan.

**July 1955**, *(below)* the back yard in Radyr. Standing, Prys and Rhodri; sitting, Rhodri's grandfather John Rees, Rhodri's mother Huana Morgan, and the family's guest Boris Collbring from Sweden.

**1961**, *(right)* going to Harvard.

**1964**, *(below)* St David's Day dinner at Eastgate Hotel, Oxford. The guest speaker was Rhodri's father T. J. Morgan, seated centre with Huana Morgan; Rhodri is standing, fifth from the left, and Prys fourth from the right.

**1964**, campaigning with Jim Callaghan.

**Autumn 1985**, shortly after moving to Michaelston-le-Pit. Rhodri, T.J., Huana and Prys.

**1987**, *(left)* campaigning with Denis Healey.

**June 1987**, *(below)* with Julie at the Cardiff West count, elected MP for the first time.

**1988**, *(opposite left)* abseiling from the Holiday Inn, Cardiff, to raise funds for youngsters in Ely to visit Africa.

**1988**, *(opposite right)* training with Alun Michael for the London Marathon.

**1989**, with Neil Kinnock, leader of the Labour Party.

was a terribly sad but true account of an elderly and confused constituent of mine who had been taken by ambulance to Llandough Hospital. He had wandered around the hospital for the best part of a week, and then died without ever being actually admitted or seen by a nurse or a doctor. It had been in the local paper, but I made sure it got in the *Mirror.* The other story was provided for me by a top Tory quango chairman, Donald Walters. He chaired the Hospital Trust, which was hoping very much to open the new Barry Community Hospital in time for it to feature in the local Tory manifesto to try to help the hapless Walter Sweeney to defend the Vale of Glamorgan seat against John Smith. This could have resulted in another fatality but fortunately it ended up more farce than tragedy. The Trust couldn't open the hospital properly because the slates kept sliding off the roof, but the contractors McAlpine had come up with the temporary solution of putting a giant hair-net over the roof. As a result, the shiny new hospital was known by the staff as the Nora Batty Hospital (after the *Last of the Summer Wine* battleaxe). the *Mirror* absolutely lapped up that story, but mysteriously changed the sobriquet from the Nora Batty Hospital to the Ena Sharples Hospital (after the long-gone *Coronation Street* battleaxe). That probably says a lot about the age profile of *Mirror* readers.

One other useful contribution I made in the run-up to the Labour landslide was when John Major made his last Welsh Conservative party conference speech before the election. It was at the Kinsale Hall Hotel in Flintshire, and Major had concentrated his firepower on Labour's devolution plans. He didn't have much firepower left by then – his authority as Prime Minister had been badly eroded by all the sniping from the back-bench Eurosceptics and the weekly maulings by Tony Blair at PMQs. Major's line that devolution would bring about an end to 'a thousand years of history in this country' was a bit shrill and totally unhistorical. He was clearly referring to English history, not British history, which was what devolution was all about. My brother Prys pointed out to me that the King of England, a thousand years ago in AD 996, was none other than Ethelred the Unready, the nearest thing to a national joke among the many monarchs you could think of – and there were distinct parallels between him and the hapless John Major. So I fed the line about Ethelred to Blair's office, and he used it to devastating effect at the next PMQs. Blair certainly could deliver a better punchline than Gordon Brown. I'd once fed Brown a joke to use at party conference after it became known that one of the big foreign donors to John Major's campaign funds was the Greek shipping magnate John Latsis, who had previously come to public attention by funding the military takeover of the government of his homeland by the Greek Colonels. My joke was that John Latsis had gone down-market from funding Greek Colonels to funding a British Major. He used the joke, but Gordon didn't do funny lines, it wasn't in his skillset.

I am convinced now that Tony Blair had already decided I wasn't going to be in his ministerial team before the election. At the last Welsh Night party at the 1996 annual party conference, the last party conference before the General Election in May 1997, Tony Blair had come to sit at our table where Ron Davies, Win Griffiths and I were settled. I'd bought him a pint – he didn't want it, which was fair enough, he never was a pint of bitter man. When he got up to make his rallying call speech, he naturally enough praised the outstanding Shadow Welsh Affairs team, but the wording he used about me was different to what he said about Ron and Win. He referred to my 'great political future' but, reading between the lines afterwards, you could see that he meant a great political future else-where than in the Welsh Office. When, after the election dust had settled, Chris Blackhurst of *The Independent* (and later its editor) took Julie and me to lunch to help write a piece on the five Shadow Ministers who didn't become actual Ministers in the Blair Government. I mentioned my rows with Mandelson, David Miliband and Tim Allan, and Blackhurst said immediately, 'Go for the Mandelson explanation. He's the one with Blair's ear!'

Summing up that long Parliament of 1992–7 which culminated on May 1st with the first Labour victory for eighteen years, I found that I'd become far more isolated from the mainstream of Labour MPs than in the 1987–92 period. That was part political and part geographical – maybe demographics as well. The 1992 intake was more susceptible to the appeal of New Labour in all its glory. The new Clause Four may not have meant all that much in its wording, but the appeal of being a very moderate party of government-in-waiting was more of a driver for the new MPs than for previous intakes. Being in the Welsh Affairs Shadow team meant being away from the House on the Devolution Commis-sion, which meant that I met my old Labour MP colleagues in the bar or in the Chamber far less frequently.

The old divide between the centrist Solidarity Group (Roy Hattersley, John Smith, George Robertson and the like), the Tribune Group (Neil Kinnock, Gor-don Brown, and me and many others), and the Campaign Group (Jeremy Corbyn, Diane Abbott, Ken Livingstone), had all but disappeared. Everybody coming in in 1992 had joined the Tribune Group, Peter Mandelson included! It had then col-lapsed as a discussion forum and there wasn't one thereafter until the top secret Robin Cook and Clare Short group.

None of the above really adequately explains just how disastrous my two attempts to get elected to the Shadow Cabinet were. English Labour MPs, if asked, would faithfully vote for one Welsh Labour MP because they realised that if there wasn't one Welsh Labour MP elected to the Shadow Cabinet, then the party leader would have to appoint the Shadow Secretary of State from out-side the Shadow Cabinet, and that would not look good. It was a major part of my annual campaign to get Ron Davies elected to the Shadow Cabinet as top

Taff. When I put my own name forward, your average Labour MP from England couldn't understand what I was trying to do – I wasn't campaigning to undermine Ron, I just wanted to be in the Shadow Cabinet in my own right, but I couldn't get airborne at all.

So as the General Election of May 1st approached, Labour was doing great but I was far from sure that I was. I felt a bit sidelined. Then Tony Blair came up with this wizard wheeze to relaunch my political career by the snub – without a shadow of a doubt, not being picked by him to be a junior Minister in the Welsh Office was the best thing that ever happened to me.

The key point for me about Labour's great landslide win on May 1st was that Julie easily won her seat in Cardiff North by over 8,000 votes, which more than compensated for the non-arrival of the expected junior ministerial job. For Julie, it was the other way around. Her feeling of elation at winning Cardiff North was tainted by me not being given the ministerial job that I'd shadowed for five years. When they assembled the array of women Labour MPs, now numbering in excess of a hundred, to line up in front of the House of Commons for the historic Blair's Babes photoshoot, Julie refused to go. She strongly disapproved of the Blair's Babes tag anyway, but it was mostly out of solidarity with me.

The reaction in Wales to Blair snubbing me was far stronger than I would ever have anticipated. I only started to appreciate this when I was asked to deputise for George Thomas as the guest of honour at the Rhondda Labour Party annual din-ner at Tylorstown Leisure Centre. On these fairly formal occasions, the VIPs are always corralled into a side room for drinks while the hoi polloi settle in. When everybody is safely seated, we, the lineup of VIPs emerge from the sideroom. The council leader went first, then the officers of the constituency Labour Party, and then finally the local MP Allan Rogers and me. The applause around the room was thunderous. 'Hey, Allan, you're mighty popular around these parts', I whis-pered to him. 'No', he said, 'that's for you!' Only then did I start to appreciate what the people of Wales thought of the Blair snub. Years later, I was told that when the council direct labour electricians were asked to carry the chairs over to the main hall ready for the dinner, they declined to do it as beneath their craft status. 'Who's it for? George Thomas, isn't it?' asked one. 'No, it's for Rhodri Morgan', replied the foreman. 'Oh, well, that's alright then', the electricians said, 'but don't ask us to carry them back!'

There were five of us who had been Shadow Ministers who didn't get posts – three of us had shared the same room in 1 Old Palace Yard back in the 1987–92 Parliament! Eric Illsley, John McFall and me. John and I were the only ones who had shadowed the same job for five years, and then not got it when the election was won – him in Scotland and me in Wales. Maybe it was the curse of Guy Fawkes that struck us all down. The technical explanation for not being able to put all the Commons Shadow Ministers into actual ministerial posts was that because, in Government, Labour would need to appoint at least half a dozen extra Lords, so we were the sacrificial anodes to enable Labour to get government legislation through.

I presume the other four unappointed or snubbed ministers got a phone call from the new Prime Minister just as I did, to thank us for our services and to offer some sort of explanation. It wasn't a pleasurable thing for Tony to have to do, nor for me to have to listen to. He trotted out all the usual stuff about needing to be assured that all his junior Ministers were capable of developing into full Cabinet Ministers in the future – that was a laugh, I knew most of the new junior Ministers far better than he did and I could have given him a pretty accurate list of which ones were never going to make it to the Cabinet itself. And I would have been ninety per cent accurate. We both knew that the phone call was a matter of courtesy. I had no wish to get into a long discussion, and Tony must have been glad when he could put the phone down and tick me off the list. Later that day, I responded in a stinging letter where I could express myself much more freely. My guess is that he wasn't shown the letter in which I said that, for me, 'the crucifixion had come three days after the resurrection!' That's the bit that would have upset Tony, and that's the bit that would have made his staff not show him the letter.

I did feel disrespected, but I didn't feel in any way that I wasn't up to the job. Tony might not think I was up to the job, but more fool him. That was my response. The snub never gave me a moment's self-doubt. 'I coulda been a contender', to borrow the famous line from *On The Waterfront*. 'But what did you give me? A one-way ticket to Palookaville!' as Marlon Brando went on to complain. Well, my one-way ticket to Palookaville turned out to be the chairmanship of the Select Committee on Public Administration. It had never been a particularly prestigious Select Committee, but I was going to chair it and I could make of it what I wanted. It was Nick Brown, the Government Chief Whip, who offered it to me (Nick did the same job in Opposition under Jeremy Corbyn twenty years later). Nick was an ardent Brownite, but whether anyone in Gordon's team suggested I should get something, I know not. Ron may have had a hand in it, because he and Nick Brown were very good friends. It may have been Nick's own idea, because he was a natural rebel himself while loving the idea of being the Chief Whip – an unusual combination.

What the chairmanship of that Select Committee gave me was status as a friendly critic of the government. For a while, I seemed to be a fixture on the *Today* programme. They weren't interested in what critical Tories had to say about anything – the Tories were a busted flush after eighteen years in power – they were only interested in what Labour people like me thought of their own shiny new government. That friendly critic business started over the Blair Formula 1 debacle. Blair had fallen for the persuasive Bernie Ecclestone magic during a visit to Silverstone for the British Grand Prix – Ecclestone had made a donation of £1 million to the Labour Party, and then the Blair Government had joined the Kohl Government in Germany in vetoing a proposed EU-wide ban on tobacco advertising in the context of sporting events – Formula 1 included. It looked awful and it was awful. Redeeming circumstances were exceedingly hard to find. Jonathan Powell had undoubtedly failed the Templeton College School of Management test! Two out of ten at best. What he did when the story broke was to try to refer it to Lord Nolan, chair of the Special Commission on Standards in Public Life, appointed during John Major's time. Murphy's Law intervened. Lord Nolan had finished on the Friday, and the story broke on the Saturday. Lord Nolan's successor, Lord Neill, Master of All Souls College Oxford, who else, didn't take up the chair of the Special Commission until the following Monday! And in any case, the Nolan Commission was debarred from looking at individual cases.

Anyway, when I was asked to comment, I had two choices. The first was to say that Blair must have been totally naive in accepting the donation from your actual Bernie in the Ecclestone palatial de-luxe motorhome at Silverstone, but I chose the coward's exit. I said that the whole situation was the result of appalling staff work in 10 Downing Street – in other words, Jonathan Powell should shoulder the blame, though I didn't name him. 'Poor staff work' was code for Jonathan Powell. Why it took the intercession of the Master of All Souls to tell everybody that the Labour Party would have to return the £1 million donation from Ecclestone and reverse its new policy opposing the EU ban on tobacco advertising in sport beats me. A seven-year-old with a smidgen of a moral compass could work that one out. More than the poor staff work, it was the lack of any moral compass that I found alarming.

Another time when I tried to be as friendly an in-house critic as I could occurred in May 1998. It was when the Conservatives under William Hague won a numerical victory over Labour in the European Elections. William Hague was winning the jousting over Tony Blair at PMQs pretty regularly, but it didn't seem to amount to a row of beans. Hague was a clever Oxford Union-style debater, humorist and wordsmith, but never came over as an alternative Prime Minister. So he posed no danger to Blair, who had his measure. But now in 1998, the Tories had beaten Labour in a national election, albeit one that didn't matter. I was asked to do an interview on *Today*, but recorded the night before. I said that Labour had temporarily mislaid the magic recipe for blending the guacamole of New Labour with the mushy peas of Old Labour. What I then did was a little naughty. I knew that Margaret Beckett was going to be live on *Today* in the morning responding to my criticism, ultra-mild though it was. Margaret was the officially designated Minister for the *Today* programme. I rang the Downing Street switchboard and I asked to be put through to Margaret – the Downing Street switchboard can find any government minister any time, anywhere. Margaret came on the line and she twigged why I was ringing her. 'Ah, Rhodri, you're going to tell me what you're going to be saying.' 'Sharp cookie!' I thought. I don't know what the producer of the programme would have thought of that phone call but, strangely enough, Mark Damazer, the overall editor of *Today* until he went to head up Wadham College Oxford, told me a few years later that he thought I should have been Blair's Minister for the *Today* programme.

The highlight of the work of the Select Committee was the inquiry we did into spin in government. It caused severe collywobbles to my very keen New Labour colleagues on the committee. Getting Alistair Campbell in before us to give evidence caused huge excitement in the Press Gallery of the Commons – they were queuing miles down the corridor from half past seven. My rookie colleagues thought that by participating in this exercise in parliamentary accountability, they were destroying their chances of ever becoming Ministers or even getting a new bypass around their main town or a new school built. They'd be damned forever. Nothing like that happened, of course. The young Tories on the committee naturally tried to use the rapier and the sabre, the foil and the épée to damage Alistair, but never touched him. Likewise when Sir Bernard Ingham came to give evidence, and I tried to do the same. I referred to him as the 'original Professor of Rotational Medicine'. 'Was that a compliment?' I could see him thinking. But spin in government is as old as the hills.

We had Lord Irvine, by now Lord Chancellor and the original mentor of the young Tony Blair and the young Cherie Blair, both in his barristers chambers, before us. This resulted in a very undignified discussion about the cost of the wallpaper in the refurbishment of the Lord Chancellor's rooms in the House of Lords. 'You can't buy wallpaper like that in B&Q, you know', he asserted suicidally. 'Now there's a man who's never stood for election in his life', I thought. All of this innocent excitement and amusement for the journalists working the Parliament beat resulted in me getting awarded the unwanted title of the *Spectator* Parliamentarian of the Year – I was nothing of the sort – it was just that I was the one who'd got Alistair Campbell to give evidence to my Select Committee.

Meanwhile, back in Wales, we were getting ready for the referendum. Once the legislation authorising the holding of this very tricky test of public opinion in Wales had been passed, it was down to the campaign itself. Julie and I decided to start on a Saturday morning in early August on the high street in Whitchurch, the main shopping street in Cardiff North. It was horrendous. We were practically pushed out into the passing traffic by the hostility. Cardiff North had just elected a Labour MP with a sizeable majority, but the Welsh Assembly part of Labour's manifesto was a step too far. 'Get out of my way!' 'Don't bother me with all that devolution nonsense!' were some of the choicer remarks. It was going to be impossible to win if it carried on like that. We travelled down to the caravan in Mwnt that night, sunk in gloom about the referendum campaign. The following day, we'd agreed to go to Aberaeron, the county town, to campaign with the Cere-digion Labour Party. Aberaeron was the absolute reverse of Whitchurch – and that applied both to the local inhabitants and to the holidaymakers from the Val-leys. Julie and I didn't know what to make of our chances.

Labour's campaign for a 'Yes' vote in the referendum had been devised with the help of the late Philip Gould, the guru of the focus group. If we were con-fused at the beginning of August, even Gould was pretty flummoxed after the four focus groups he attended. There were two in Maesteg, a former mining town at the mid-point east–west of the Welsh Valleys, which comprised ten women and ten men. An equivalent pair of groups was arranged in Wrexham. Maesteg was still pretty depressed from the closure of the mines after the 1984–5 miners' strike. Gould was not used to the air of hopelessness, and issues like setting up a Welsh Assembly didn't seem that relevant when what a depressed population needed was group therapy, not a focus group. Wrexham came next, and ideas were begin-ning to float around in Philip Gould's head by then. They had to – there were no more focus group sessions after Wrexham.

The men's group was slightly dominated by a particularly talkative individual who lived in a probation lodging house. He'd not long come out of Walton Gaol in Liverpool after doing seventeen years for some heavy-duty crime – he was Welsh, although he spoke with a cockney accent. He was getting on the nerves of the others, all local Wrexham types, and he'd answer every question Gould would throw in as he prowled around the room before anyone could get a word in edge-ways. Gould threw in the thought, 'Do you feel pretty confused about your Welsh identity?' The cockney jailbird got in first again. 'Sort of, yeah, I do feel confused.' 'Why?' was the chorus from all around him. 'What d'you mean, you're confused?' 'Well', came his reply, 'when I was younger, I could have boxed for Wales but I couldn't have played football for Wales!' The Wrexhamites were all ears and up and running now – everyone was chipping in – 'How on earth could you have boxed for Wales but not played football for Wales?' 'Well, I was pretty good at boxing, and no fucking use at football', he said! They were all confused if not utterly floored by this point, including Gould, the great focus-groupie himself. But out of all that confusion there somehow emerged the slogan that the Assem-bly, whatever its weaknesses and virtues, would be 'A voice for Wales'. And the focus groups seemed to agree that Wales needed a voice. That's what we ran on as a slogan, and we won, but only just – a majority of one vote would have been enough, in theory at least. In the event, the majority was 6,721 and the turnout was just over fifty per cent. Nothing like as impressive as the Scottish pair of votes and the far healthier turnout north of the border.

We would never have won if we had asked the same two questions as were put to the Scots. The first was on the principle, and the second was on the right to vary income tax by three pence in the pound. We would never have won if it hadn't been for Margaret Thatcher and John Redwood – Wales needed bogey-men and women to get us out of our armchairs and down to the polling station. About twenty Labour MPs, all newly elected, were bussed down to Cwmbrân shopping centre, just north of Newport, to help in the campaign. They hadn't had much in the way of briefing, and I was their sheepdog for the afternoon. We were in the covered market hall, with me on the megaphone, which worked well under the roof. My message, 'Vote for a Welsh Assembly. It's our insurance policy against Maggie Thatcher coming back!' Sometimes, I'd vary the pitch by insert-ing John Redwood's name instead. One of the MPs with us that day, a newly-elected woman MP from London, stopped handing out leaflets, came up to me and said, 'I understand now what this is all about'. It wasn't easy really – we had just elected a Labour Government and there was huge enthusiasm for what it was going to do, so you couldn't sell the Welsh Assembly to the people of Wales on the grounds that it was going to do things differently to Tony Blair (although it eventually did!). But you could argue that Labour might not be in power for ever, and that a reborn Thatcherite government might one day get back into power at Westminster. That was a viable sales pitch.

And lastly, we would never have won without Tony Blair's half-day in Wrex-ham. John Prescott, the Deputy Prime Minister, was sent to Newport, which was not particularly effective. But Wrexham turned out in force to see Tony Blair. The half-day had all the quality of a religious visitation from on high. People were hanging out of upstairs office windows just to catch a glimpse of the great man. Now, Wrexham is a border town, just ten miles from Chester. Not natural pro-devolution territory. But the Prime Minister's visit gave us only a three-to-two adverse result. Newport, also in some ways a border town, was two-to-one against. Wrexham doing better than Newport was from our point of view down to the Blair visit and the quasi-religious fervour that came with it.

Later that same month came the Labour Party Conference in Brighton, when Donald Dewar announced that he would put his name forward for Labour leader and candidate to be the first First Minister of Scotland. From Ron Davies came there not a squeak. I bumped into the Transport & General Workers Union dele-gation from Wales – Jim Hancock, Nev Taylor, Teifion Davies and John Burgham – and told them I was going to stand. 'You're our man, Rhodri!' they said, and a die of sorts was cast. It took twelve months or so from that day to the eventual outcome of the Labour leadership ballot, with Ron finally being declared leader, only to resign a few weeks later.

# four

# Leadership Contests
# 1997–1998

O N THE AFTERNOON of Tuesday, 27 October 1998, I sat in my MP's office in the Parliament Square building opposite the House of Commons. It had the most fantastic view looking out across the garden below Big Ben and the Carriage Gates. Just as the vibrating boings of Big Ben struck four o'clock – literally on the dot at four o'clock – the phone rang. It was Peter Hain, the junior Minister at the Welsh Office, and the sensational news he had to impart was that Ron Davies, the Secretary of State for Wales and newly-elected leader of Welsh Labour in the soon to be created National Assembly for Wales, had just resigned due to an incident overnight on Clapham Common. 'Something really weird', Peter said, 'we don't know the full background. All we know is that he's gone. Alun Michael has just been promoted to the Cabinet. That will mean a vacancy to be the Labour leader in the Assembly. If you want to fill the vacancy, you've got to get in to see Blair tonight, because things will move pretty fast from now on.'

As that phone call finished, the phone rang again. It was Michael White of *The Guardian*, the doyen of parliamentary lobby journalists. He was the one I trusted and liked most, and one who was more interested in Wales than your average lobby journalist. He wanted to know whether I had any inkling that Ron had previous history indicating that he might strike up a conversation with a total stranger from the margins of society on the grass verge on the edge of Clapham Common, and then agree to go for a meal later that night with the man and his friends. I had to plead the Fifth Amendment. I didn't like doing that to Michael, but I had to have time to think and get in to see the Prime Minister. This was the ultimate hot news story, which was going to grip Westminster for months.

It wasn't quite along the lines of the John Profumo–Christine Keeler scandal of forty years previously, simply because neither the Welsh Office as a Department of State, nor indeed shortly-to-be-born Welsh Assembly, covered defence and security secrets – but it was a sensation nonetheless, the first big personal scandal to hit Tony Blair's Government.

I don't know if Michael White believed me when I stalled, claiming to be too shocked to answer him. If I had answered him completely truthfully, I would have had to have told him of a chain of events – cobbled out of rumour and fact – which did, when added together, make Ron's moment of madness and subsequent instant resignation not such a surprise for me as it was for others.

When I'd had my cup of coffee in Brighton in September 1997 with the Transport & General Workers Union Welsh delegation, the talk had naturally turned to the narrow squeak in the referendum and the big job of turning the wafer-thin victory into a successful Assembly – and above all, who was going to stand to be the Labour leader in the Assembly. Because we had all taken as given that the Labour landslide in the May of 1997 would carry through into the Welsh Assembly elections in May 1999, the Labour leader would become the very first First Secretary of Wales. While Donald Dewar, the Secretary of State for Scotland, had announced his candidature for the leadership of the Scottish Parliament, Ron had remained silent.

The whole question of who was to lead Labour in the Assembly went onto the back-burner for months. The legislation to set up the Scottish and Welsh devolution bodies still had to start its tortuous passage through Parliament. It didn't start until after the two referenda had been won, as Labour's manifesto had indicated. The Northern Ireland negotiations leading up to the Good Friday Agreement the following spring had received a lot of priority and quite rightly so. Ron's silence on whether he was interested in running for the leadership, in the meantime, remained deafening through the winter and spring of 1997–8. I don't know who the ugly duckling was in all this, but the line in Danny Kaye's song that goes 'All through the wintertime he hid himself away' seems apposite for any harbouring of swan-like ambitions. All the potential candidates had to hide themselves away in a lonely clump of weeds, waiting for the moment of the selection of candidates for the sixty seats to get going, and for the leadership issue to be sorted out later on in 1998.

The Scottish legislation to set up its first Parliament in almost three hundred years was structured quite simply. Anything *not* reserved to the UK Parliament was devolved to Scotland. The Welsh legislation was far more tortuous, because it was drafted the other way round – it tried to specify everything that *was* to be devolved to Wales. Any issue that wasn't scheduled to be devolved remained with the UK Government and Parliament, which made for a lot of trench warfare.

Through those winter and spring months of Ron Davies's radio silence on the 'will he? won't he?' question, Donald Dewar got very firmly established without any challenge as Labour's one and only conceivable candidate as Scotland's first First Minister. That couldn't happen in Wales. Ron kept his options open. Kevin Brennan, who then worked for me as my constituency caseworker and researcher, and had already agreed to be my campaign manager when the contest started, had a conversation in which Ron told him he genuinely was not sure about following Donald Dewar's lead and going for the Welsh Assembly. He knew that Labour traditionally struggled to find politicians with sufficient interest in farming and rural affairs to hold the Agriculture portfolio in the UK Cabinet, and Ron's interest and expertise in farming and the rural environment was of long standing. There would almost certainly be a reshuffle in July 1998 and, if Ron had got the Agriculture and Fisheries job in the reshuffle, that might have opened the way for me, or indeed for Wayne David, the MEP who was keen on running for the Welsh Assembly.

During those months of waiting for the passage of the legislation to be completed and the selection contest to begin, I started to hear disturbing rumours about Ron leading another life. This might be one other explanation for Ron's radio silence on the leadership vacancy. One of these rumours related to something that had happened in the Turkish Baths in Newport, an alleged gay haunt. I put it out of my mind as a bit of nastiness being spread by political opponents. I had suffered in the similar way with a story being put about by a former schoolfriend who had become a top Welsh Tory saying that I'd been cautioned by the police for picking up prostitutes in the Cardiff Docks area – this particular individual eventually issued a full apology and had to make a financial contribution to a charity, of my choice after I had approached the then Tory Party Chairman, Brian Mawhinney, for help. I knew that politics was a dirty game alright.

Then came a request for help from an investigative journalist for the *People*, Brian Radford, a former racing tipster in Wales before moving up to Fleet Street. He said he had picked up on a rumour from what he described as a very reliable source that Ron had driven himself in his private car up the A470, the main north–south road through Wales, and stopped off at a public convenience that was again known or alleged to be a gay assignation haunt. Could I confirm? 'Absolutely not!' I said. Ron was my friend, and I thought I knew him pretty well and any hint of 'another life' would not have escaped my attention. Or so I thought.

The third piece of the jigsaw came a month or so later and was much more substantial, although I only heard it third-hand. Gay Welsh Tories had very solemnly warned a prominent gay Welsh Labour figure called Neil Wooding, in no uncertain terms, that 'Ron was cottaging at the Castle Gate'. What gave this story extra political significance was that they were pretty regretful about saying this for obvious reasons, but felt they had to pass on the warning that the Tory hierarchy had the story and would detonate this unexploded bomb against Labour a few weeks before the Assembly elections if Ron became the Labour leader.

Neil Wooding then passed the warning on to the late Val Feld, later to be elected Assembly Member for Swansea East, but sadly the first AM to die in office and a huge loss to me as Labour leader in Wales. In 1998, Val was the head of the Equal Opportunities Commission in Wales, and a big wheel in the Labour movement in Swansea. She was a close friend of Julie's and passed the story about Ron on to her, who in turn told me. Three rumours in four months is bound to make you pause. In Wales, nearly everybody knows nearly everybody else .Third-hand or not, this last story meant I had to do something with it – in other words, this might be less about Ron and more about Labour's campaign for the first elections to the Assembly in May 1999 being torpedoed.

First, I had to understand exactly what this third piece in the jigsaw meant. It shows what a sheltered life I had lived up to that point that I didn't actually know what 'cottaging' was – I knew it involved the gay world and was probably illegal, but I had no idea what it actually involved. I rang Lesley Griffiths, a prominent Labour activist in Wrexham, who was a medical secretary in a clinic at Wrexham Maelor Hospital where related issues were dealt with, and asked her what exactly 'cottaging' was? After some criticism of my other-worldliness and lack of nous, she explained that it was predatory one-night-stand behaviour by gay and bisexuals, much frowned on by gays with stable same sex relationships. Apparently, 'cottagers' stood in shopping bags to disguise the fact that there was a second pair of feet inside a public toilet cubicle, in case the vice squad coppers came around with their periscope-type mirrors to look under door panels. This was all news to me.

The next question was, 'Where the hell is the Castle Gate?' I assumed it must be a pub in Caerphilly, Ron's constituency, which has its famous huge castle. I was wrong. 'The Castle Gate', it turned out, was about a hundred yards from my constituency office in Transport House. It was just across the River Taff from where my constituency of Cardiff West stopped and Cardiff Central began. All MPs pride themselves on knowing every inch of their constituencies and boundaries, but I'd missed the reference. 'The Castle Gate', a notorious pick-up point for the one-night-standers among gays and bisexuals, was the entrance to the grounds of Cardiff Castle, not Caerphilly Castle.

So, I said to Julie, 'This is going to be the most difficult phone call of my life – but I've got to do it'. Ron was a fully-fledged Cabinet Minister. He was a Secretary of State. Above all, he was my very close political and personal friend. I'd run his campaign to get on to the Shadow Cabinet, but could there be a side of him that I just didn't know anything about? It had to be sorted out, because if the three tip-offs I had received were even half true, then the reputational risks to Labour and the 1999 Assembly election campaign were enormous.

It was lucky in a way that I had been subject to the rumour that had circulated about me, so I used it as a bit of an ice-breaker. When I phoned Ron, I implied strongly that he might very well be the subject of a dirty tricks campaign to discredit him, and devolution, and Labour in Wales. Somehow, our conversation got on to discussing whether Ron was going to run for the leadership – I told him that I was definitely going to run, but that it would definitely not affect our friendship if he ran as well, assuming that might be his decision.

Ron's reaction was astonishing. He said he wasn't sure if he was going to stand. In fact, he was so fed up with life and politics in general that he might not even stand for the Assembly. In fact, he might walk away from politics altogether. He seemed to be in the depths of depression. I said, 'Ron, you're in no fit state to run for the leadership, you're having a mid-life crisis!' then he replied, 'I AM having a mid-life crisis.' I didn't twig at the time that the really astonishing part of Ron's responses to my questions was not the failure to deny any of the allegations at all, but to divert the discussion towards him being on the brink of walking away from politics altogether. I assumed at the time that his silence on the content of the rumours was a denial. After Clapham Common, I realised that his non-denial was in fact admission.

For the next few months, Ron was in denial – and I was in denial about Ron. Eventually, we did have our Labour leadership contest, which opened for nominations in late July after Tony Blair's first reshuffle was completed, with Ron neither promoted nor demoted. Much to my own surprise, I won a lot of the early leadership nominations, sometimes in constituencies that I didn't even know were holding meetings on the issue. Aberavon was the first constituency to meet in late August. I heard from the local evening paper that I had won it. I rang Malcolm Gullam, the local party Secretary to ask him if this could be true. He confirmed that I had won the nomination by twenty-one votes to eighteen. 'And I didn't even have to tell them your mother was from Port Talbot!' he said. I thought my chances were looking up. I also did okay with the two Swansea nominations a few days later.

Early signs in the T&G were also promising. The Pembrokeshire branch had met in Milford Haven, and I had won their overwhelming backing. I was T&G after all. George Wright, the T&G Welsh Area Regional Secretary, had gone up the wall when the members of the delegation to the Labour Conference the previous September told him that they'd expressed their strong support for me as a T&G member running for the leadership vacancy. George lived in Ron's Caerphilly constituency, but I suspect he would have tried his best to swing the T&G vote behind Ron regardless of that. It was more of a Labour establishment kind of feeling that drove George, not a Caerphilly constituency thing.

One way or another, after the Pembrokeshire area vote for me, T&G branches were told not to frame the debate in terms of a head-to-head between Ron and me. A subterfuge was invented by George Wright. Branches were only allowed to consider whether they supported union policy on the nomination of the candidate to be First Minister – well, of course they supported union policy. It was then left to George to determine this union policy that the branches had agreed to support. It was a Kafkaesque device.

That was the fundamental difference between the way unions balloted their members in Labour leadership contests before the Welsh leadership elections, as well as in the overall British Labour leadership elections. Today, it is absolutely clear that the members themselves vote and that their votes count. John Smith's reforms to get away from the block vote in the hands of the union general secretaries and inner sanctums had been clear. Tony Blair was elected by the unions voting on a one member one vote, OMOV, basis. So was Ed Miliband. On many occasions, Tony Blair and Margaret McDonagh, Labour's General Secretary, claimed the same methodology was used in the Welsh elections. But in the Welsh Labour leadership elections, each union was allowed discretion on how they consulted their members, and that was what George Wright exploited. If unions didn't actually want to ballot their members, they didn't have to. Some chose to while other unions didn't.

The Welsh MPs formed the third part of the electoral college. They went heavily for Ron, although I kept his majority among the approved panel of Assembly candidates down to 32–22. Of the candidates subsequently elected to the Assembly, it was 4–4. The unions went for Ron, even my own union the T&G. The party members' vote split much more evenly, but I didn't maintain the early success I'd had in Aberavon and Swansea, although I did get a majority of the constituency nominations, 14–11. The calculation that Kevin Brennan had done for me was remarkably accurate. We couldn't win because the MPs had OMOV, and so did the approved panel of candidates. The unions certainly did not, and neither did party members, with the nominations being determined by the local general committee or executive. As a general rule, the more OMOV, the better my chances.

The attack line used by the party establishment against me was relentless. It was that I couldn't be First Secretary because I hadn't already been Secretary of State. Furthermore, if the party was to back me to lead Labour into the Assembly elections, it would emasculate Ron's ability to carry out his job as Secretary of State in the period through till the Assembly elections the following May.

Kevin Brennan and I tried time and time again to persuade Ron and his campaign team to participate in hustings for party members, or to take part in television or radio debates. As far as they were concerned, Ron was far too busy as Secretary of State – or at least he and his team wanted to give everyone the impression that he was far too busy to get involved in such hustings. But the 'I'm too busy' line was undermined by his agreeing to do sequential hustings, appearing in front of party members one after the other, but never together.

Kevin and I would arrive as Ron would depart the scene, or my team and I would depart the scene just as Ron would arrive with his. We never appeared together until the very last night before polling closed, when Ron and I stood before a studio audience for the regional ITV franchise, HTV. Predictably, the question was thrown at me again from someone in the audience, 'How can you expect to be able to run the country when you have no ministerial experience?' I wasn't actually disqualified from running, but I was judged to be unqualified on the basis that the future job of first First Secretary was essentially the same as being Secretary of State in the Cabinet.

That was the only argument really, and it wasn't easy to come up with a punchy answer for it, given how nervous people in Wales were about setting off on this journey of self-determination, however limited the powers. The euphoria of the huge majority New Labour had won the previous year was still carrying over into this wish for the new job of First Secretary practically to be a semi-detached member of Tony Blair's Cabinet, which would make it all less risky.

So, in late September at the Newport Leisure Centre, the count was done and the result was announced. Ron was declared victor, and we both made our winner's and loser's gracious acceptance and concession speeches. Labour moved on with completing the selection of its candidates in all the constituencies through the twinning of seats – with one man and one woman being picked in twenty paired-off constituencies to cover the forty Westminster seats. My constituency of Cardiff West, and Cardiff North where Julie was the MP, were twinned and we were the first pair of constituencies to do our double selection together. The following day, Cardiff Central and Cardiff South & Penarth did theirs. Cardiff broke the ice, because there was less opposition to twinning and women's equality issues generally around the capital city.

The candidate selections for the regional list would come later – Labour didn't expect any great entitlement from the regional list, because the party would do too well in the individual seats.

Eight Assembly candidates had been picked for their constituencies out of the forty required, when Clapham Common happened at the end of October 1998. The following week went from the ridiculous to the surreal. My attempts to get to see Tony Blair, as Peter Hain had insisted I must do, did not succeed on Tuesday night, and was apparently not going to happen on Wednesday either despite repeated entreaties to his office. As there was no three-line whip on the Wednesday night or Thursday, Julie and I decided we had to get back home to touch base with my supporters, and to see what I could do to prepare for whatever was coming next. My hope was to persuade the party leadership that they could theoretically ask me to take over the leadership because I was the only other candidate who had run in the July–September race. It seemed a sensible solution given the total concentration by the party machinery on getting the candidates selected in the pairs of constituencies and the lack of time for another contest.

Julie and I had just got the car out through the Carriage Gates, and on to Millbank heading west along the Thames back towards Wales at about half past four on Wednesday, when the mobile phone rang. It was Bruce Grocott, Tony Blair's PPS, a very warm and friendly guy trusted by everyone, including me. He was distantly related by marriage to Alun Michael, but that would never have clouded his first-class judgement as the Prime Minister's eyes and ears. In his inimitable West Midlands drawl, he said to me, 'Rhodri, glad I've got you. Tony wants to see you. You're probably half way down the M4 b'now, I suppose …' 'Luckily', I replied, 'we're barely a hundred yards down Millbank. Not even at Lambeth Bridge yet. We'll be back in the House of Commons car park in five minutes. Is Tony in No. 10, or in the House?' 'In his office in the House.' 'Okay', I said, 'give me ten minutes.' 'Great, make it as quick as you can, he hasn't got long.' We did the proverbial taxi-driver's U-turn outside the BBC Westminster studios, and headed back to the underground car park beneath Big Ben.

The Prime Minister's office in the House of Commons is a little way down the corridor behind the Speaker's Chair – there's an outer office where all the secretaries and press officers, civil servants, MPs and anyone else waiting or wanting to see the PM mill around, no one able to do any actual work until the PM goes back over the road to Downing Street. The PM's rooms have a wonderful view over the courtyard below Big Ben.

When I arrived there practically running up the stairs, there was nobody to show me into the PM's office. After ten minutes, I was panicking. I tried to find somebody who knew what was going on, and I raised my voice above the outer office hubbub. 'Where is Bruce Grocott?' I asked. 'I'm supposed to be seeing the Prime Minister!' 'Oh', said one of the secretaries, 'I'll go in and check.' It turned out that Tony was waiting for me all the time, while I was outside waiting for him to call me in. They had expected me to just march straight in – no one in the outer office had been told to expect me. Not the most auspicious start, but Tony put me at ease straight away. He was charm and friendliness itself, just like the good old days back in 1988–9 when I worked under him in the Shadow Energy team. The years of growing distance in between just rolled away, as though all the upset over him not appointing me to the Government in May 1997 had never happened. Never has a Prime Minister's cup of afternoon tea tasted so sweet. 'I have got a chance here', I thought to myself. I thought Tony might now realise that he does need me just as he used to when he was Shadow Energy chief honcho.

I threw in a possibly unwise question that had been bugging me since Clapham Common erupted thirty-six hours earlier. 'It comes to something', I said to him, 'when Special Branch or MI5 never warned you that you were going to appoint someone to your Cabinet who was a 22-carat blackmail risk. Either they didn't know, or they didn't tell you.' Tony used his ultimate weapon for disarming the enquirer going down an inconvenient line of questioning. Start off a sentence as though you are going to give a full answer, and then let the sentence trail off before reaching any conclusion. Tony would then finish with a bit of a nod and a wink, and a few 'y'knows'. The overall effect of these unfinished sentences would be that you thought at first you'd been told something, when in fact Tony had said absolutely nothing. It was a trick Gordon Brown could not master.

What Tony Blair said was intentionally garbled, but it came out something like this: 'Well, y'know, MI5, they're not that, y'know ...'. He never actually said that MI5 were totally useless, only vaguely implied it. Neither did he say that he had no idea about Ron's double-life. What that would imply for his judgement if he *had* known is another issue. If he had had an inkling about Ron via MI5 or anyone else, it would imply a criticism of his judgement in appointing Ron at the start of the Labour Government, and then in effect re-appointing him in the July 1998 reshuffle when so many had anticipated Ron would be reshuffled out of the Cabinet.

Looking back now with clear hindsight, this was the critical exchange I had with Tony Blair over the Ron issue – did he know about the other Ron or didn't he? If he didn't know, how come? Was Ron's astonishing ability to cover his tracks so well that MI5 had no idea? The new Prime Minister's hands had been tied back in May 1997 by the Labour Party's internal rule that all members elected to the previous Shadow Cabinet by the body of Labour MPs must, without exception, be appointed to the Cabinet by the incoming Labour Prime Minister. MI5 could have warned Blair about Ron's double-life, but his hands would still have been tied by the rule. MI5 might possibly have accommodated any risk by ensuring that Ron never saw any papers that impinged on national security issues. Perhaps that was it.

What the foregoing doesn't answer is the question why Blair would then have re-appointed Ron to the Cabinet when he had a free hand to appoint in July 1998. It was only after *not* being reshuffled out of the Cabinet in July 1998 that Ron finally announced he was running for the Welsh Labour Assembly leader job, ten months later than Donald Dewar in Scotland – it would have been a huge humiliation if Ron had been reshuffled out of the Cabinet after saying he wanted to be the first First Secretary of the new Welsh Assembly.

Wayne David, MEP for South Wales Central, a previous leader of the Labour MEPs in the European Parliament and the candidate for the Rhondda, was widely rumoured to have been considering putting his name forward if Ron had lost his job in Blair's first reshuffle. Ron was not reshuffled, so Wayne stayed out of the race to be Labour leader in Wales. If Clapham Common had not supervened, Ron would in any case be out of harm's way down in the Welsh Assembly, which the security establishment may have thought to be the best solution all round. That was because the Assembly had no powers over police, the courts and law and order, let alone national security, and no blackmail risk therefore, the issue would then virtually be solved overnight. However, the political problem of the Tories or anyone else who might get wind of Ron's double-life detonating the bomb in the middle of the election campaign would very clearly not be solved by having him ensconced in the Welsh Assembly. That wouldn't have been an issue for Special Branch, but it sure as hell would have been for the Labour Party.

I had my quarter of an hour with the Prime Minister. I'd put my case, my plea for neutrality or even a hint of backing, and left it at that. I had felt some warmth, and more at ease in the company of Tony Blair than I had done for quite a few years. I felt that I was close to be being on the inside rather than on the outside. Perhaps Tony was a tiny bit grateful that I had stood against Ron. Then again, I was probably neither the first nor the last person to have a quarter of an hour's meeting with Tony Blair and feel reassured of his support, only to realise later that it was far from being the case.

The next week turned into the most surreal of the quarter century of my political life. When Julie and I got home and drove up our lane, we noticed that the curtains of our neighbours' house, the only other house on the lane, were carefully drawn and the lights very subdued – there was a special reason for that, but we didn't know it at the time. My next-door neighbours, Huw and Julia, were very much part of the political scene in Wales. Huw was Ron's chief political adviser and spin-doctor, and Julia had been my secretary since a few months after I became an MP in June 1987. The period of campaigning between Ron and me had put our relationship under some strain. Kevin Brennan, my constituency researcher, was my campaign manager, and Huw and Kevin had had a rules of engagement meeting in late July, just as the leadership race was getting under way. Huw was not allowed to be Ron's campaign manager because he was a civil servant as a special adviser, but he probably had more influence over the campaign than Ron's actual campaign manager, Angharad Davies.

There was one occasion during the campaign when the tie-up with Huw and Julia had proved very handy in keeping the peace and the good name of the Labour Party in Wales. One morning, we received a mysterious parcel through the post in my constituency office, which turned out to be a large and official, but smashed, framed photograph of Ron – that is, Ron's official portrait as Secretary of State. It had been hanging with all the other portraits of Secretaries of State going back to Jim Griffiths in the building in Cathays Park, which housed most of the Welsh Office civil servants. It's hard to credit, but someone had gone to the trouble of taking down Ron's portrait, smashing the glass, and wrapping it in brown paper to post to me. It was nice to think I had support in any quarter, but that kind of support I did not want. After a bit of tense discussion of the what-the-hell-do-we-do-with-this type, it was decided that the best way forward was for Julia to take the whole package home with her, and Huw could then take it back in to the Welsh Office and arrange for it to be repaired and rehung as discreetly as possible. We did laugh a bit about it, but it was really no laughing matter. Whoever was responsible would have lost their job if they'd ever been identified.

A week or so later, Julia had found working as my secretary too much of a strain because of how frequently Kevin and I had to discuss our campaign tactics behind my closed office door, just a few feet away from her typing desk. We'd never had to have closed doors in the office before. It was hard. It was tense, but we did all remain good friends. We just had to manage our way through this unique situation in which we found ourselves, something that could only happen in Wales.

The situation got even harder to manage two days after Ron's resignation. There was by then a real hue and cry to find Ron and doorstep him, or indeed his wife Chris. As there was no one in at Ron and Chris's home at Draethen, a little hamlet east of Caerphilly not unlike Michaelston-le-Pit, the hunt was on to find him. We quickly realised that the drawn curtains at Huw and Julia's meant Ron was actually holed up there, right next door to Julie and me. The curtains remained fully drawn day and night for about a week. A few days later, at about nine o'clock at night in the middle of a filthy rain storm, there was a knock on our door. It was a soaked through Nick Horton, the chief political reporter of the *Western Mail*. He said the paper had received a tip-off that Ron was staying with us to protect him from the press! It seemed pretty bizarre to Nick, but that's what the tip-off said.

I knew that if I invited Nick in, I would have to offer him a cup of coffee or a beer, and the likelihood of me being able to conduct a conversation with him and not reveal that Ron was in hiding next door was very low. I certainly didn't feel it was my job to tell him where Ron was, because Ron's mental state may have been too fragile to deal with a media scrum forming in the lane outside Huw and Julia's house – I would have felt responsible.

I have always felt guilty about sending Nick away into the rain. Speaking to him years later, he was able to confirm to me that he didn't even know that Huw lived next door and that the tip-off was definitely to the effect that Ron was in hiding *chez moi* not *chez Huw*. He thought it was the most unlikely tip-off he had ever received, but as he was on the night staff that Wednesday, he had to come to Michaelston to check it out.

What a sensational scoop it would have been if Ron had poked his face out from behind the curtains as Nick Horton was driving past. In the days after submitting his resignation as Secretary of State for Wales, Ron had remained the elected leader of the Labour Party in Wales. He'd become quite bolshie about that. So when Peter Hain had spoken to me on the Tuesday afternoon, he had been wrongly informed by Tony Blair and Alistair Campbell that Ron had resigned from both offices, Secretary of State and Welsh Labour leader. Ron finally bowed to the inevitable when he resigned as Labour leader on the Thursday as he was having to travel up to London to attend the ID parade to pick out Donald Fearon – the man who forced Ron to go to the cash machine, and had then kept Ron's car, because Ron couldn't remember his PIN number. It's a moot point whether Ron would have been better advised *not* to pick our Fearon in the ID parade, which would have left Fearon without a saleable story to hawk around the tabloids. Ron would then have had a far better chance of resigning quietly, citing 'personal problems'.

The sheeting rain carried on incessantly over the weekend. By Hallowe'en, which fell on the Saturday, we had a flooding problem between our houses in Michaelston-le-Pit. The Cadoxton brook running down the little valley between the two houses had burst its banks, not in the normal way but around the huge earth banks that had been dug out by the construction firm that was building a new bridge over the brook (it had been agreed as part of the planning conditions for a third house by way of a barn conversion).

These big mounds of earth were preventing the floodwater from running away into the fields. So that Julie and I could get to our house, the builders had prepared for the weekend's bad weather when they wouldn't be around by slinging sheets of 8'×4' plywood over the earth banks and, with the aid of wellies, we could just about make it to the front door of our house. On the Friday night, I just about managed to clamber my way to my home, up and over the mounds of earth which were getting more like the trenches of Flanders by the hour as the non-stop rain continued. At the point where the brook went under the old bridge, it was now running *over* the bridge instead. You just had to trust to your wellies. I parked my car up on the road, as there was no way I could drive it along the lane. Even 4×4 would have made no difference. We were pretty well blocked in and blocked out. If I was inconvenienced, Huw and Julia were becoming demented because their cesspit was next door to where the old bridge was and practically underneath the mounds of mud.

Julie and I tramped down to the brook in our wellies to go to the theatre on Saturday night, Hallowe'en. By the time we got home, the earth banks had become so impregnated and muddy, even a gung-ho ex-cross-country runner like me couldn't get across the bridge. In the pitch darkness, I had to tell Julie, 'I can't do it, it's not safe'. She was relieved. We walked back up the little hill from Huw and Julia's to the lay-by where we'd parked and we drove through our village to the far side, to park the car near the next bridge crossing the brook. The water was high there but it wasn't flooded. Then a half-mile walk along a farm track and across a field, and across a stile to the back of our house.

Our relief to get home safely was soon over when we received a frantic phone call at about 11:30 pm from our not-long married elder daughter. Her new husband was away at a scientific conference in America, and in his absence she'd gone out to a Hallowe'en party dressed as a serial killer – only to come home to the little terraced house they were renting to find the waiting police who had seen her front door wide open. It had been crow-barred open, and the television and video etc. had gone. She was on her own, and asked if she could come over and spend the night. Normally, we would have told her to come on at once, without any hesitation, but on this occasion we had to tell her, 'You can't actually get to our house except through the fields.' She didn't fancy that particular trek, and made alternative arrangements. What other surprises could the weekend possibly have in store?

On Sunday, 1 November, thirty-six hours later, No. 10 Downing Street phoned to invite me to meet the Prime Minister again on the Monday. When I discussed this with Kevin Brennan, my campaign manager, he asked me whether I was supposed to go in via the Downing Street entrance or via the Cabinet Office entrance. I checked back with Anji Hunter, gatekeeper to the Prime Minister, who checked and told me to come in via the Cabinet Office entrance at 70 Whitehall. 'That means he wants to try to persuade you not to stand', said Kevin. 'If he was okay with you running, he wouldn't have a problem with you entering via Downing Street and being seen by all the press.' 'Well, I can't not go', I said, 'I do owe him that, but I'll have to tell him straight that my leadership bid's not for sale.'

I went up overnight, and stayed at our London flat to be sure of being at 70 Whitehall well in time for nine-thirty in the morning. The German Chancellor, Gerhard Schroeder, was to meet the Prime Minister at ten, so I was met by Anji Hunter. She was somewhat more gushing than usual, but I couldn't help being very fond of her. I had to allow, though, for the possibility that this extra measure of Anji's gush might have a motive. She wasn't at the actual meeting between me and Tony. The third person present, with pencil and notepad, was Sally Morgan, the PM's political secretary (now Baroness Morgan). I got on well with her too, but I didn't know her as well as I knew Anji. Tony was sat on his sofa, and I sat in an armchair.

Tony was quite friendly to begin with. He asked if I'd had a good weekend! I told him the weird and wonderful story of the floods and us being cut off from our house – a house he knew well – my daughter's house being burgled, and her not being able to come over to stay with us. 'Apart from all that, no problem!' I said. I wasn't looking for the sympathy vote, but that would have been a good start if I was.

Then we got down to serious business. It was a tough meeting. No shouting, but there were very firm views expressed. No quarter asked or given. Absolute hammer and tongs. Chancellor Schroeder was kept waiting a quarter of an hour while the Prime Minister tried to wear me down. I would love to have seen Sally Morgan's notes. Tony Blair told me I couldn't stand for the leadership. I said I fully intended to stand. He said I didn't have any ministerial experience and I wasn't ready to take on the responsibilities of being First Secretary.

Now, this was the argument that had been thrown at me repeatedly during my fifteen-rounder with Ron Davies. Indeed, in the only actual hustings that Ron and his advisers did agree to, a local representative of the business community had aired the same argument, but I didn't think I'd dealt with it properly or really effectively then. As often happens in the cut and thrust of political debate, you think of the best answer on the way home in the car, or when you replay the events in your head in the early hours of the morning. *L'esprit de l'escalier* is what the French call it – the wit of the staircase after you've left the salon.

That answer to the 'no experience – you can't stand' canard that I couldn't come up with in the television hustings six weeks previously, I now threw in Tony Blair's face. I was ready for him. I said, 'Tony, if there was any force in that argument, Margaret Beckett would be sitting on that sofa right now and not you!' This time, it was Tony Blair, the trained barrister and legendary instant comeback expert, the man who was never lost for words, who seemed totally stunned by what I had just said. I suppose you have to conclude that the best spontaneous one-liners are in fact the ones you've thought of in advance!

Tony Blair was dumb-struck. I was looking him straight in the eye, when I delivered my salvo without actually shouting, but with every ounce of conviction I had. He couldn't form any words at all. It was almost embarrassing. Tony Blair turned his face ninety degrees and stared at the wall, trying to gather his thoughts. I felt a bit like a novice heavyweight who had got into the ring with Joe Louis and poleaxed him, and then didn't know what was supposed to happen next. I could talk the hind legs off a donkey, but Tony Blair could talk the robin off a box of starch.

I couldn't bear to look at the Prime Minister and he didn't want to look at me, so the only other place I could look was at Sally Morgan. She had adopted a sphinx-like pose with pen in the air and writing pad on the table next to the window, but with nothing to write.

I ploughed on. 'Think about it, Tony. It's not just you that never had any ministerial experience. Gordon never had any, and he's Chancellor. John Prescott never did either, and he's Deputy Prime Minister. Robin Cook never had any, and he's Foreign Secretary. And Jack Straw's Home Secretary, but he was never a Minister before. Your Government is probably the first one in British history where all five senior offices of state are held by people without any previous experience as Ministers.' Tony countered by saying that the Welsh Assembly was a brand new idea, and therefore experience was going to be essential. I slung the argument back at him, that surely he wasn't trying to claim that running Wales was going to be a more onerous job than running the whole of Great Britain, with all the defence and security decisions that he and his Ministers had to make.

Then I explained the other key reason why I felt I had to run. It was because Alun Michael, the new replacement Secretary of State, had just announced his candidacy but had a big handicap in that he wasn't on the panel of approved Labour candidates, and the list was now closed. The selection procedures had already started, and eight constituencies had already chosen their candidates (including my constituency of Cardiff West and, more importantly, Alun's own constituency of Cardiff South & Penarth). Since Alun Michael was not guaranteed to be able to find a winnable seat, it seemed pretty bizarre to ask me to stand down from a contest where I had a seat to fight, while the other wannabe didn't have one and might not be able to get a winnable seat.

Twice Tony's diary secretary came in to remind him that Chancellor Schroeder was waiting. It seemed pretty pointless to go round and round the houses on this age-old argument about how anyone can do an important job without having the experience, and how can you get experience without doing the job! We finally called it a day, and I returned to Cardiff and the mud of Michaelston-le-Pit and the muck of an internal Labour Party civil war. I do emphasise the civil, because it was a remarkably civil affair where Alun Michael and I personally were concerned.

In the same way as I felt that I absolutely had to run against Ron Davies once he'd told me that he was having a mid-life crisis and was thinking of walking away from it all and leaving politics altogether, I absolutely had to stay in the repeat version of the contest against Alun Michael because he wasn't guaranteed a winnable seat. I never had a shadow of a doubt about the correctness of my decision to stay in the race. Why couldn't the party establishment see that?

The Labour NEC now had to move quickly, if Alun was going to be able to stand. For a start, the approved candidates list had to be reopened. Alun was said to be ringing up all the Welsh Labour council leaders he knew from his time as a Labour Group Whip on Cardiff City Council to solicit support, while the NEC appointed a commission to set the rules for the election contest. It was jointly chaired by Jim Hancock (the chair of the Welsh Labour Executive and George Wright's deputy in running the Wales Region of the Transport & General – Wales is invariably known simply as 'Region 4' in the T&G), and Don Touhig (Neil Kinnock's successor as MP for Islwyn in the Gwent Valleys). Touhig was a confirmed devo-sceptic, and prided himself on being a bit of a hard man politically, but I got on pretty well with him and Jim Hancock. Indeed, Hancock was one of those who had clapped me on the back in Brighton back in September 1997 when I had told the T&G delegation that I was intending to run for the job of leading Labour in the Assembly – he was one of those who had proclaimed, 'Rhodri, you're our man.'

On Thursday, 5 November, ten days after Ron Davies's walk on the wild side of Clapham Common, this commission met to decide on the rules of the contest. The meeting was scheduled at four in the afternoon, and there was huge press interest, not just in Wales or Britain, but across Europe as well. Tony Blair and New Labour was big news, and what the press was interested in was the possible loss of New Labour's shiny patina of virtue.

Meanwhile, back at home, the floods had receded but I had an entirely different kind of domestic problem. My son was studying at the University of Glamorgan – it was a struggle, but he was just about managing to get his essays done, although they were sometimes a bit late at submission. He had written an essay to be handed in at the very latest on Friday morning – it was all there on the computer at home, but the printer had broken down and panic had set in. At teatime, I rang his older sister for help, but she said she didn't have a compatible printer at home. But she knew enough about the equipment I had in my constituency office to say that the printer there could print it off in two minutes. I felt very unsure about whether I would be able to print it off without the danger of deleting my son's essay, so I asked if she could meet me at the constituency office to do the business. 'Okay', she said, 'when?'

What complicated things was that my constituency office was on the fourth and top floor of Transport House, which was also where Labour Party Wales had its HQ, and it was also where this joint-commission of the NEC and the Welsh Labour Executive was meeting at teatime that same day. The ground rules for the contest were to be finalised and announced, and I guessed the entire building and car park would be surrounded by television crews, cars and trucks. My daughter and I agreed to meet in the car park at seven, which should give the commission plenty of time to meet, announce its decision, hold its press conference, and for the press to wander off to the nearest pub.

How wrong could I be? I left home with the computer disk at a quarter to seven, to drive into town. Shortly before seven, my mobile phone rang in its cradle – it was IRN, the radio news arm of ITN, with a simple question. 'The Labour Party Special Commission has just announced that there will be a contest for the Labour leadership in Wales to be completed by mid-February. Are you going to run?' I said, 'Yes, of course I will be running. I ran in the last race and lost, but I did get a lot of support from ordinary party members, so I will definitely be running again.'

A couple of minutes later I was at Transport House. There were so many outside broadcast trucks and those big Volvo estate cars favoured by television crews, all kinds of other cars and people swilling around, that I wondered if I'd even be able to find my daughter in the melee. We did eventually manage to meet up in the car park, and make it up to the fourth floor via the back stairs to dodge any journalists. We got to my office and printed off the essay in a few minutes. Just as we were finishing up, the phone rang. It was the Downing Street switchboard. They had tried my home number, and Julie had the unnerving experience of simultaneously talking to a journalist who had come to the house on the off-chance of getting an interview with me about whether I was running, while she spoke to the Downing Street switchboard at the same time, all without giving the game away.

Having tracked me down to my office in Transport House, where I had not been intending to stay more than five minutes, Pat McFadden's softly spoken Scottish brogue came on the line from Downing Street. He was the Prime Minister's special adviser on political issues. 'Aye, good evening, Rhodri. You've heard the announcement about the Executive's decision, I suppose?' I said that indeed I had, although I hadn't seen the details. 'You won't be making any announcement yourself tonight about whether you're running, will you? Tony will be wanting to speak to you later on tonight when he's free, before you say anything'. I said, 'Sorry, Pat, you're twenty minutes too late. I've already told IRN that I am standing.' 'Ach, well, that'll be alright then', he said, and rang off. Whether it really was alright or not, I will never know.

We had two telephone lines in the office, and I had my mobile with me. By the time the phone call from Pat McFadden was finished, all three phones were ringing. My daughter could see what was happening, and offered to act as my call handler for the next few hours. It was absolutely non-stop calls from reporters everywhere, all wanting to know if I was standing and sensing a good old-fashioned scrap. If you want to know what the phrase 'ringing off the hook' really means, well, we had it that evening. The line of media questioning was a bit short of political logic in my opinion. It wasn't, 'Can you think of any reason why you wouldn't want to stand this time, when you had a respectable level of support in the previous contest?' It was more along the lines of, 'Are you really sure that you want to take on the might of the Downing Street establishment and the Labour Party machine for the second time?' After the first round of 'Are you going to stand?' questions, the 'Is the Pope a Catholic?' response was getting dangerously close to the surface. But I knew I shouldn't use it. I could think it, but I couldn't say it.

At around half past seven, dodging the incoming flak for two minutes, I managed to contact Kevin Brennan my campaign manager in the race against Ron, and I asked if he wouldn't mind being my campaign manager again and if he could come into Transport House to relieve my daughter in her duty as telephonist. He was happy to do both. Just before he arrived, the BBC *Newsnight* programme came on the line and asked if I would come on that night to be interviewed by Jeremy Paxman. I couldn't really refuse an invitation like that. Kevin agreed to drive me up the road to the BBC Wales studios, which, like the Labour Party Wales HQ, lay in my constituency. Up we went, and on I went. It was about my thirtieth interview in a row all about the same damn simple and utterly obvious no-brainer question: 'Are you going to stand again for the Labour leadership in the Welsh Assembly?'

'Yes, of course I'm bloody standing!' was how I felt by then, but that would have been bad news – questioning the Pope's faith or the bear's toilet arrangements in the woods as alternative responses would have been infinitely worse. Actually, I was so tired by that late hour that I had almost reached a kind of philosophical plateau, and the reply that came out was another variant on the same theme – 'Does a one-legged duck swim in a circle?' Paxman seemed as dumbstruck as Tony Blair had been in his lair the previous week. I probably should have said it was a no-brainer, but I'm not actually sure that expression was so well known back in 1998.

People have asked me repeatedly since that night, 'Where on earth did you get that expression from?' I'd actually read it in *Wales on Sunday*, attributed to a Welsh rugby player out on tour in southern Africa and winning his first cap against Namibia. That was back in the amateur days and the player concerned, Phil Ford, was a carpet-fitter in Cardiff. He was asked the same kind of eejit question, 'Are you pleased to be getting your first Welsh cap on Saturday?' or some such foolery. Where he got the duck analogy from, God only knows. The pity is that although Phil Ford may have said it first, I've ended up getting all the credit. Jeremy Paxman thought it was some kind of strange druidic imprecation to ancient Celtic Gods, and could attribute to my answer absolutely no meaning known to an English gentleman. I did ask several people in Cardiff whether they had any problem understanding what I meant, and they all said they'd breathed a sigh of relief that I had not mentioned the religious denominational loyalties with regard to the Bishop of Rome, which meant I didn't lose the Catholic vote. That was the key thing. I came close to it, but I held back. It was a career-building answer for me, because not many people in politics in Wales or elsewhere have ever left the formidable Paxman lost for words. The scene was now set for the second Labour leadership contest.

# five

# They Got Us Surrounded
# 1998–1999

O N 20 FEBRUARY 1999, in the late afternoon after the result of the Labour leadership election in Alun's favour had been announced around midday down at St David's Hotel, I was returning to my campaign HQ in the Castle Arcade for a party. It was an incredibly uplifting occasion. I'd got out at the arcade entrance opposite Cardiff Castle, and it was almost like an episode of Michael Aspel's *This Is Your Life*. This was the bus-stop, where the no. 33 bus from Radyr to Cardiff used to drop me into town time after time when I was a boy. As I walked along, I passed successively the Cafe Minuet, usually known as Marcello's after the chef, purveyors of the best and cheapest pizza slices in Cardiff which had kept the campaign workers and media guests going during the campaign. Then came Beti Rhys's bookshop, where I'd had my first ever job for a week at Christmas in 1955, opposite another long disappeared shop full of memories, Bud Morgan's model shop, an absolute Mecca for all aeroplane model teenage enthusiasts in Cardiff in the 1950s.

As I walked another few yards all on my own, I could hear this lovely music coming down from the overbridge at the far end of the arcade. It was Côr Cochion, the Cardiff Red Choir, serenading me! Then the cheering started. I cannot tell you what a beautiful scene it was. The Castle Arcade is the prettiest of the many arcades in Cardiff, and that area at the ninety-degree bend including the semi-Venetian overbridge, is the prettiest part of it. I was already feeling remarkably upbeat when my walk started, but now I felt almost euphoric. How could that be possible when I'd just lost a leadership election and, indeed, lost for a second time? Now, normally for cause and effect, losing produces down-beat feelings, but not on this occasion. I just felt terrific.

To get to the root of the explanation for such a positive feeling about the outcome, you have to go back to the start of the campaign on 20 November. Kevin Brennan, my eventual successor as Labour MP but right then my campaign manager, had done a rough calculation of the likely result. We were going to lose the election by five per cent of the total electoral college. More than likely. His prediction came within one per cent of what had happened. There was no way we were going to lose the ballot of the Labour membership. Conversely, there was no way we were going to win the Trade Union section given that we had got absolutely stuffed just two months earlier, with over ninety per cent of it going to Ron Davies in the first contest. The MP and MEP, plus Assembly candidates final part of the electoral college, was harder to predict, but we were unlikely to win it. So if it was that difficult to win, what had been the point of standing at all with the rule changes that had stacked the odds against me? I told my campaign team right at the start that yes, the odds were stacked against us, but we should never forget the words of General Anthony McAuliffe, commander of the 101st Airborne at the siege of Bastogne in the middle of the Ardennes in Belgium at the height of the Battle of the Bulge in November 1944. I had had a stopover at Bastogne – with Alun Michael (strange as that might seem) in 1986. The German counter-offensive had caught the Allies napping in an appalling winter in 1944–5 that gripped the whole of Europe (I could recall four feet of snow falling on Radyr). All five roads in and out of Bastogne were controlled by the Wehrmacht, and the German commander gave the 101st Airborne two hours to surrender or be annihilated. General McAuliffe's words to his besieged troops were, 'They got us surrounded – the poor bastards!' Then he led them in a fightback until General Patton's troops relieved. That was pretty much the end of the German counter-offensive. It wasn't Hollywood. It was what actually happened. And that was what I told my merry little 101st Airborne!

Anyone who knows me would confirm that I'm not one given to Churchillian blood, sweat toil and tears rhetoric. I'm more of a wise-cracker. But Kevin did tell me years later that everyone felt a hell of a lot better after that speech. Faced with almost certain defeat, we are going to give the members a reason for believing and a reason for casting their ballots. Ah, ballots! We couldn't get quite enough of them actually to get the win – but all the ballots, we did win. When the rules for the contest were announced on 20 November, the trade unions were allowed to make up their own rules on how to consult their members – maybe ballots, maybe no ballots. When the Blair–Prescott ticket had swept the board in 1994, any unions that refused to conduct a ballot of their members couldn't take part – but now Labour was going back on that process, back to the old block vote. I went on the *Today* programme to denounce this reversal as a fix. I did go ever so slightly Churchillian this time, saying it was all very simple –'It was invented in Ancient Greece. It comes in nice folding ballot papers and it's called democracy.' I cannot tell you the number of compliments I had from my fellow MPs over that, even from those who were Ministers and who couldn't raise a finger to help me.

Even Labour Party officials were confused about that block vote issue. John Braggins, the organisation supremo at Labour's UK HQ at Millbank, came down to address the Welsh Executive. I was a member of the Executive back then, as chairman at the time of the Welsh Parliamentary Labour Party. Braggins said the taskforce had determined that the unions would have to conduct OMOV ballots but, once the union had balloted, it would be winner take all. Each union would then cast all its voting strength via a block vote determined by the majority outcome of the OMOV ballots. I don't doubt that John Braggins was telling the truth as he understood it – he genuinely believed that each union was obliged to hold a ballot, then to vote en bloc. Margaret McDonagh, the Labour General Secretary of whom I was very fond, seemed to be convinced that the Welsh Labour Party leadership election would be con-ducted along effectively the same lines as the Blair–Prescott ticket five years earlier. The first slip back into the old ways, however, was going back to the block vote, albeit one determined democratically by an OMOV among all the members. Then came the far bigger step back to the Dark Ages of the block vote when each union's executive, or even just by the regional secretary, was quietly allowed to determine which candidate to support without a ballot of the members at all. It was that second change that scuppered my chance of victory. I could have won the contest with the first slip back to the old ways, but not the second.

In the run-up to the starting gun on the leadership contest being fired on 20 November, there had been various moves to try to avoid having an election at all, which meant that in practice that I should gracefully withdraw. I wouldn't really describe it as pressure, in all honesty. Wayne David, having ceased being an MEP and previously leader of the Labour MEPs Group in Strasbourg, came to see me and Kevin. He explained the concept of a Dream Team that involved Alun being given a free run to be the Labour leader, and myself and Wayne being his twin deputies. Kevin flashed back, 'I can see the team, but what's the dream?' It was difficult to know exactly how to put it to Wayne, like me a product of the WEA, about the impracticality of my stepping down in favour of Alun. So many people who knew Alun well in the Cardiff area had told me that he was an excellent deputy, but never a leader. Psychologically speaking, Alun just wasn't that kind of personality. I told Wayne that I would be happy to lead a Dream Team with Alun and him as twin deputies, and that if Alun or Wayne wanted to lead a Dream Team then there was only one way of settling that issue. A ballot! What was there to be so afraid of?

Representations were made to Glenys Kinnock to pull out of her own race to continue as an MEP, so that she could run against me. The European elections were in June 1999, one month after the Assembly elections, and the floating of a possible Glenys Kinnock candidacy implied strongly that those who wanted to stop me – for whatever reason – were not confident that Alun was the man to do it. To be fair to Glenys, whom I had known for thirty-five years, she was definitely interested in Europe and definitely not interested in devolution. Again, I don't know how much pressure was put on her, but it didn't work.

Kevin decided that we needed a separate campaign headquarters. We had run the campaign against Ron Davies in the July–September period from the constituency office in Transport House. My office was on the fourth floor: the Labour Party Wales office was on the second floor; the Transport & General, who owned the building, were on the ground and first floor. The potential of the other camp trying to make a point of a campaign being run from a constituency office subsidised by the parliamentary office allowance was too much of a risk. Kevin knew the guy who owned the Castle Arcade from his days on the City Council, and he asked him if there was any spare office space up on the second floor. There wasn't, but Kevin was very persistent, and in the end we secured a temporary lease on the 'pad' that the guy used when he made his monthly care and repair visits from Bradford to Cardiff. All we had to do was to store his double mattress somewhere and sweep the place clean, and get some office equipment in. Faxes were the key thing for me – computers were a bit too advanced.

Then, if we were going to get an office, we would need some money to run the campaign. Kevin started to write around. My brother gave me a £2,000 loan. Next, out of the blue, there came a cheque – not a loan, but a campaign contribution for £2,000 from Mike McCarthy, the owner of Rightacres Properties (still more than active in the property market in Cardiff, indeed probably market leaders in the field). I'm still not sure why the company sent me that £2,000 cheque – I barely knew Mike McCarthy, and I can only assume that he had been speaking to his solicitor David Seligman, who was my solicitor as well. My campaign needs may have come up in conversation, and Mike's empathy for the underdog in a David vs Goliath contest could have prompted him to open his chequebook. That's all I can think of. Anyway, Kevin and I were delighted. Then, even more out of the blue, I received a cheque for £100 from novelist Jilly Cooper! Now we could get our show on the road. Paddy Kitson, who had first enrolled me into the Labour Party in 1964, and the late Chris Sheehan, who described himself to visiting journalists as an existentialist unemployed plumber, manned the phones. I left the organisation of the corresponding operation in North Wales to the Labour house owned jointly by the MP for Wrexham John Marek, and the MEP for North Wales Joe Wilson.

My cousin Nia from Beddgelert composed a *cywydd* couplet, all in strict metre with consonantal alliteration of *cynghanedd* in the proper order, which went thus:

> *Brwydrwr dros bawb yw Rhodri,*
> *Yr un iawn i'n harwain ni.*

and roughly translates as:

> *Rhodri is a fighter for everyone,*
> *The right man to lead us on.*

Songs and poems don't win you union delegate votes, of course, but they do give your campaign a lift and the feeling that God is on your side!

It's not always a disadvantage to be in that underdog position. Now a world-famous songwriter for her collaboration with Ed Sheeran on *Thinking Out Loud*, Amy Wadge was unknown back in 1998 when she wrote a song about me called *Valleys Boy* – having not long crossed the Severn Bridge from Bristol to Cardiff, she didn't fully appreciate the distinction between that part of the Taff Valley north of the Taff Gorge that counts as 'The Valleys', and those villages to the south like Radyr – Radyr sits on the banks of the Taff alright, but is never counted in Wales as part of the Valleys. Still the music and the words were very good.

Another reason why I never considered standing down in favour of the Alun Michael candidacy was that it was far from clear that he would be selected in a winnable seat. By the time in November that Alun announced that he was going to step away from his Westminster ministerial career in favour of the Assembly, the process of selecting candidates for the constituencies was well under way, with eight of the forty constituencies having already chosen. Selections in pairs under the twinning process involved two constituencies, usually adjoining, which would choose one woman and one man candidate, and then it would be jointly agreed which constituency would have the top woman candidate and which the top man. The Cardiff area had gone first, partly because twinning had caused less aggravation in Cardiff than in other areas. Cardiff West and Cardiff North had jointly chosen me and Sue Essex, the former Leader of Cardiff City Council; then we'd kind of separated out into me being allocated to Cardiff West, and Sue to Cardiff North. Easy-peasy. That was on the first Saturday, and on the Sunday Cardiff Central and Cardiff South & Penarth had jointly chosen Mark Drakeford and Lorraine Barrett, then allocated Mark to Cardiff Central and Lorraine to Cardiff South & Penarth. The latter selection had been done with the strong backing of Alun Michael, for whom Lorraine had worked as office manager since he became an MP in 1987.

Labour Party Wales officials found the ease by which the four selection processes took place in the Cardiff area a wonderful surprise, and then hoped against hope that the twinning procedure might possibly go smoothly in the rest of Wales. 'Good luck with that', we all said. The dream-like smoothness of the first four selections turned into a nightmare for Alun, because he couldn't go for his own parliamentary seat of Cardiff South & Penarth. Even if Lorraine Barrett had been willing to stand down in his favour, it would have upset the balance of one man and one woman standing in the twinned constituencies. It would have meant Mark Drakeford having to stand down as well. If that can of worms had been reopened, the Labour Party Wales team would never have been able to persuade reluctant constituencies in the Valleys to obey orders and to get on with the twinning process. So Alun had to look elsewhere.

Not only did we have the novelty of twinning to contend with, we had the panel system as well. All would-be candidates for the Assembly on the Labour side had to get on the panel. They had to be interviewed, and the panel interview team was quite formidable and highly professional. They did put you through your paces. There had been a huge row when Tyrone O'Sullivan, leader of the Tower Colliery workers' buy-out, didn't pass through the panel. I don't know what went wrong there, but he became a major loss to the Assembly. There was an appeal process, but Tyrone, despite my encouragement, didn't want to appeal. 'If they don't want me, then fair enough, I'm happy carrying on with Tower!' he said. 'I don't want to go through all that hassle again!' Other failed candidates did appeal successfully and did get selected where they were the local favourites and, in the event, usually got elected as well. The appeal process was the very opposite of the panel – the panel was super-professional and rigorous; the appeal panel was chaired by the late Terry Thomas, an old-style very Old Labour fixer, lately of the NUM and who, after the mines had mostly gone, had transferred to the GMB union. 'Are you one of us?' was all Terry was interested in. You had to have an appeal process, but to have it run by someone whose approach to candidate approval was the dead opposite of the empanelling procedure was daft. Twelve people got on the panel via the appeal process. Whichever was the right process – the panel that had rejected Tyrone O'Sullivan, or the Terry Thomas Old Labour alternative – we finished up with 160 approved candidates on the panel to cover the forty constituencies and the regional lists.

By the time the announcement came that Alun was to seek a nomination for the Assembly, the panel had been closed after hearing all of the appeals. Alun had a mountain to climb. So the panel was reopened. It could not be reopened just for Alun – that would have been too absurd. It was reopened for anyone else to apply, anyone except for those rejected candidates who had decided not to appeal (like Tyrone) or those who had appealed but been rejected by the appeal panel. And that's how Alun got on the reopened panel – as indeed did one of my future Cabinet Ministers, Jane Davidson, a successful late entrant candidate too. She was selected as 'top woman' in the twin constituencies of Pontypridd and Merthyr, and was then elected in Pontypridd. Paul Flynn, MP for Newport West and a former long-term flatmate of Alun's, got on the panel as well during this reopened window. His purpose, he said, was a touch Quixotic – namely to offer himself for selection in any constituency where Alun put himself forward. His opposition was to Alun being shoe-horned into the Assembly by the jiggery-pokery of reopening the panel, and Paul's incandescent rage could have fired a Welsh rocket to the moon if we'd had a space programme!

At the same time as constituencies were preparing to select candidates, they were also choosing whether to nominate me or Alun or the third candidate, Roger Warren Evans, who was unlikely to get into the Assembly, for the leadership. The franchise used in the contest against Ron Davies the previous autumn had been replaced. Back then, it was the constituency party management committee which chose between Ron and me. This time it was full OMOV, whereby the less active party members who didn't attend monthly party meetings would get a postal ballot form. I was more than happy with the OMOV system, although many commentators thought it would reduce my probable win in the constituency section. What I wanted and needed was the OMOV system to be used in the Trade Union section as well. Constituency parties were able to invite Alun and me to address them in an open forum, with the regular delegates present along with any other party member as well. The Blaenau Gwent Constituency Labour Party open meeting was one of those occasions when everything went right for me – it was probably the highlight of my campaign. The attendance was huge, eighty to a hundred. Blaenau Gwent had been twinned with Llanelli, sixty miles away!

I managed to defuse the issue by referring to the fact that there was a hidden part of the arrangement to twin Blaenau Gwent with Llanelli, which was that the star of the local rugby team, Byron Hayward, the outside half for Ebbw Vale, had to be transferred to Llanelli. The player's actual shock transfer had only just been announced, and was a sore point. All the men in the room laughed at that, the women weren't so amused – but when half the audience has a good laugh at one of your better jokes, it gets you nice and relaxed and everything tends to flow well from there on. I won 75 per cent of the votes that day but, of course, that was only going to have a marginal effect on the outcome of the full postal ballot.

I wasn't that worried by the three-month length of the campaign. There were conspiracy theorists among my supporters who were convinced a plot lay behind the three-month stretch of the second leadership campaign, compared to the two-month stretch for the one between Ron Davies and me. The theory was that in the extra month, Alun would have an improved chance to become better known. But taking out the Christmas and New Year break, it only gave him an extra fortnight. Every journalist who came from London to do a colour piece on the contest was struck by just two things – how much better known I was among the general public, and how we were having to manage on a penny farthing machine in this charming office upstairs in the Castle Arcade, fuelled entirely by Marcello's wonderful pizza slices. Alun Michael's campaign head-quarters in Newport Road seemed to have more computers than they knew what to do with. The public just wasn't buying this line of Tony Blair's that he hadn't judged me suitably qualified even to be a junior Minister in the Welsh Office in May 1997, which meant I clearly couldn't be good enough to lead the Welsh Assembly. Will Woodward of *The Guardian* said I had almost pop-star status among his vox pops on the streets of Cardiff. I don't know about pop-star status, but it was certainly true that when a pair of new peacocks were bought for the grounds of Cardiff Castle, and the *South Wales Echo* had invited suggestions for names for the pair, 'Rhodri and Julie' were among the read-ers' nominations. Thank goodness they eventually chose more historically apt names like Arthur and Guinevere for the pair.

It was a huge blow to the prestige of the about-to-be-born Assembly when Rachel Lomax, Permanent Secretary of the Welsh Office and soon-to-be top civil servant of the Assembly, resigned her position to become Permanent Secretary of the Department of Social Security. That was just before Christmas 1998, and it was bad news for Wales. There is no suggestion that she didn't get on with Alun, but there is every suggestion that she'd really hit it off with Ron. By established protocol, Ron had been a regular visitor to the Welsh Office for the last eighteen months of the John Major Government. Then, in the eighteen months that Ron had actually held the office of Secretary of State, the relationship of Minister and mandarin had really blossomed. I bumped into Rachel Lomax on the steps of the National Museum, just as she was coming out of one of the free lunch-time con-certs. The conversation naturally turned to how sorry I was that she was leaving Wales at such a crucial time. She said she hoped no one would think she was los-ing interest in her home country – she had just had a beautiful new house built in the heart of the Vale of Glamorgan, and certainly wasn't going to be selling it. She was going, she said, simply because the Clapham Common incident that was the downfall of Ron Davies had come as a total shock to her, and she felt she had to try to move on and reset her career. Rachel was a genuine star of the civil service, as gifted as any Permanent Secretary in any Whitehall department. Losing Rachel Lomax knocked everything sideways.

The other big development in the run-up to Christmas was that Alun's team realised the futility of the search for a constituency seat, and announced that he would be seeking the list seat as head of the four-person list for Mid & West Wales. The problem with that strategy was that it depended on Labour doing suf-ficiently badly in at least one of the two seats in the area that Labour held at West-minster falling to Plaid. Such a scenario may happen from time to time in other

PR systems of election – in Ireland, for example – but in Britain it was unheard of for a Labour leader to be campaigning and hoping his party would do badly enough for him to get in! That doesn't mean there was any sabotage of the campaigns in Dinefwr & Carmarthen East or in Llanelli, where Chris Llewellyn and Ann Garrard were the two Labour candidates. Their very disappointing failure to get elected let Alun in through the back door. Anti-Blair rage over his interference was strongest in south-west Wales. As a result, Plaid Cymru was collecting disillusioned Labour votes in swathes, which allowed Blair to have his way! If everyone had really understood how the Additional Member List system worked, they should have voted for Chris Llewellyn and Ann Garrard and got two Labour AMs in – then Alun would have been out in the cold, and Blair would have got the bloody nose they wanted to give him!

Dozens of PhDs will be written on this curious and self-contradictory phenomenon in future years. I can certainly vouch for its existence from a phone call I received late one evening, just before the actual Assembly elections in May. It was from my cousin-in-law Ray, a retired miner. He was at the Globe Inn in Glais, my father's home village in the Swansea Valley, and spoke to me in English for the first and only time in his life. He spoke in English so that everyone within earshot could hear our conversation. 'Rhodri!' he shouted above the din I could hear in the background, 'You know we're all Labour round here, well, we've decided to vote Plaid this time, one in the eye for Tony Blair, see!' Ray lived right on the edge of the Neath constituency, at its border with Swansea East. It would have made little difference there, but the same pub discussion ten miles further west or north-west down towards Llanelli or Ammanford would really have got to the heart of it. 'If we in this pub want to give Tony Blair a bloody nose, what's the best way of doing it?' Discuss. The answer was for everyone to vote Labour, true at one level, but it offended against common sense. This was really one of the problems of the PR system we had adopted. PR is a compensation mechanism – if you win a lot of constituency seats, you win fewer list seats. When people are more used to the chess games involved, they will be able to arrive at the right answer on how to achieve the desired objective before the next round of drinks! But it wasn't like that in 1999.

I was very concerned that it should be a clean fight. Alun and I had met and we'd agreed that it should be, but Millbank was throwing the kitchen sink at us in so many ways that some dirty dishwater was likely to be spilt. The messages that had come out during the contest against Ron had not been the most reassuring – it had been put about that Blair didn't consider me suitable ministerial material because he thought my house didn't look tidy (which was pretty absurd, given that Blair had only been in my house between the hours of one and seven in the morning). But it was the old isolate-before-you-denigrate technique. I rang Alistair Campbell one morning, before he set off for his Saturday afternoon rendezvous with his beloved Burnley, and told him that I'd been unimpressed by some of the mud that was thrown my way during the previous contest. I wouldn't stand for any nasty stuff about me, my house, or my family. This was all about politics. Alistair kept repeating that it wasn't 'in our interests', but I just wasn't sure whether I could trust that semi-reassurance.

So I went to see John Prescott as well. I explained my concerns that mud would be flung – there certainly wouldn't be any mud flinging from my side – but I was worried that over-enthusiastic members of the New Labour Taliban militia might think anything was fair in love, war and Labour leadership contests. 'I'll watch your back', Prescott said – this was over a whisky in his House of Commons office, and Prescott got quite convivial. 'You're more of a party man than the other feller', he said, jerking his head towards an imaginary Alun Michael over his shoulder. I'm still not sure I know what that phrase, 'more of a party man', meant in John Prescott's mind. He didn't mean social animal, an extrovert, or anything like that, and I'm pretty sure he wasn't referring to Alun's grounding in politics in the Liberal Party (I doubt if he even knew about that). Anyway, he evidently saw himself as a counterweight to the New Labour in-crowd, and promised to 'watch my back!' He did indeed do that quite literally, several years later, when at a Joint Ministerial Council meeting in Scotland Tony Blair said quite loudly in front of everyone else that my suit was terribly rumpled. Something must have flipped a switch in Prescott's brain, because he ripped into the Prime Minister. 'Don't talk so daft, Tony!' he said in everyone's hearing, 'The man's just got out of an aeroplane to get here and then a taxi, it's a boiling hot day, of course his suit is rumpled!' I was *suitably* grateful, but it was originally in the leadership campaign that I wanted him to watch my back, not two or three years later! Perhaps all the Deputy Prime Minister meant by that 'more of a party man' remark was that I was not very New Labour, and not very interested in smart turnout.

Just before Christmas, both John Humphrys and I had received awards from the Plain English Society – him for being crystal-clear at all times, and me the booby prize for my famous (or infamous) reply to Jeremy Paxman. The one-legged duck line made my career. I believe the Plain English Society receives nominations from all quarters for its best and worst prizes – I don't know which of my enemies had nominated me. They had me on the *Today* programme again to talk to Humphrys about whether there was something special about the water in Cardiff that nurtured candidates for the Plain English Awards. I had one of the loveliest letters ever from a listener to that interview on *Today*, who claimed my stories were so funny that she almost crashed the car laughing! It would have been an interesting insurance claim if she had crashed her car – 'I was laughing so hard at one of Rhodri Morgan's jokes, I drove into a tree!' The one-liner that impressed her most was one from Charles Beard, the Harvard historian, who had written in criticism of the silence of most American intellectuals during the McCarthy era, saying they were afraid to collect their thoughts lest they be accused of unlawful assembly!

The unions were now girding their loins to see if they were going to ballot members in proper John Smith-style or not. There were four big affiliated unions in Wales – the AEEU, the T&GWU, the GMB and UNISON. There were six medium sized unions – the CWU, ISTC, MSF, NUM, USDAW and ASLEF, the last of which decided to abstain. UNISON had an honourable tradition of organising workplace balloting. They were the only union to have voted for Denis Healey against Tony Benn in 1983, based on a workplace ballot. UNISON decided again that they would ballot their members in Wales – so did the NUM, the FBU and MSF. In the event, I won all those ballots. Perhaps it's possible to extrapolate that I probably would have won all the other unions if they had balloted. Another dozen PhD topics to keep political science faculties in business for years. I can't be objective, but I'd say I probably would have won the other union ballots because the spread of the types of industry and qualifications concerned among the balloting unions was pretty wide. In winning all of those, it's probably a reliable indicator of union-member opinion on the 'Alun or me' issue, but there's no way of ever being sure.

The one that hurt me the most, in the sense of felt most deeply, was the T&GWU. Alun belonged to the GMB. I belonged to the T&GWU, and the obvious assumption was that we'd have been supported by our own unions respectively – especially since that ten-minute conversation I'd had with the T&G Welsh delegation to the Labour Party Annual Conference in Brighton on that gloriously sunny day on the south coast in 1997.

But Ron got the T&G's support, even the Pembrokeshire part of the union, where they had actually balloted. When the Alun Michael vs Rhodri Morgan contest came along three months after the first one, George Wright was *unlikely* to be in the OMOV camp. George was going to pull out all the stops to use his baronial powers to get the union's block vote in the bag for Alun. The rest of the union executive, including those who had told me I was 'their man', were bludgeoned into submission. This was the same George Wright who had got the Wales Co-op Centre going with me – the same George Wright who had got me to go over the road from my European Commission Office at 4 Cathedral Road as an independent observer to certify the correctness of the ballot to continue the political levy. So why did he do it? He cannot possibly have imagined he would end up in the House of Lords – only trade union general secretaries got the ermine, not Welsh regional secretaries. Anyway, George was going to ensure that the T&G block vote went to Alun, and that was that.

I didn't expect anything from the GMB – it was Alun's union, and union solidarity counts for more in the GMB than in the T&G. UNISON was balloting its membership, and I could be confident there. The last of the four big unions was the AEEU, more of a craft union than the T&G, and the AEEU Regional Secretary didn't wield the same power. With the AEEU, it's the proudly independent delegates who hold sway. I should have had a chance there, but I made a complete hash of the opportunity.

Campaigning had restarted in earnest on 14 January with a reception thrown by Tony Blair at No. 10 for some two hundred Welsh Labour activists. The guest list didn't distinguish between pro-Alun Michael delegates, neutrals (there were fewer and fewer of these by now) and my supporters. Those closest to the Prime Minister, who had persuaded him to throw his full weight behind Alun, must still have been of the view that his clear preference carried weight with party members – which it would have done in the middle of 1997. In the September 1997 referendum campaign, I did hear of one conversation in Blaenau Gwent which would have typified Labour support at the time: 'I don't have a clue what this devolution stuff is all about, but if The Boss [Blair] says it's good for us, then I'm voting Yes!' But a lot of that lustre had worn off by January 1999, and though there wasn't that much mixing between the two lots of supporters, there was still some. When Blair addressed the reception crowd, he didn't go all partisan – the message that he was supporting Alun was designed to work subliminally.

In the mad rush to get everyone shoehorned into the taxis to catch the trains from Paddington to South Wales, I'd borrowed a tenner from a Bridgend delegate. On the train back to Wales, there were really impassioned arguments, but all in a very good humour, and I had taken part in three or four of them in different train carriages. It was a wonderful chance to talk to a semi-captive audience. As the train drew into Cardiff station, I remembered that I hadn't repaid the tenner to the Bridgend delegate, someone I might not see again for months, and the last thing you want in the final month of a leadership contest is a reputation as the guy who bums money off Labour delegates. So, in a mad rush, I dashed through the carriages to find him and eventually repaid it. The train lurched into action to leave Cardiff station – next stop Bridgend – and I made another mad dash, this time to reach the door to get off before the train carried me further west. As I did so, I caught my eyebrow heavily on the glass divider behind the seat and cut it open, in classic Henry Cooper style. I got off the train with blood pouring from the cut.

As ill-luck would have it, the AEEU delegates meeting was in Swansea the following morning. My driver, Annabelle Harle, picked me up to head west, and there was nothing to be done to disguise the cut, though at least it had stopped bleeding at the cost of a sizeable scab. I had been extra careful about brushing my hair and wearing a freshly-ironed shirt and my best suit to try and overcome any negatives among the delegates, but the suspicious among them were bound to think I'd had too much to drink at the Downing Street reception the night before. But all the extra effort at sartorial elegance did was to make me look like a pirate trying to look his best at Captain Morgan's wedding! The regional secretary tossed a coin to see who'd speak first – the coin rolled around and round (these fitters have strong wrists!) under the furniture in the Swansea Guildhall side room, and when it was finally found it came up heads for me! I should have said I'd speak second, but I opted to go first. I should have let Alun warm them up, and then when I stood up the shock of the scab over my eyebrow wouldn't have been so great. Anyway, I went first and gave one of my poorest performances of the entire campaign. I was self-conscious about the scab – I'm not saying I would have won the meeting over if I hadn't cut my eyebrow, but you know when you enter a room of largely hostile delegates that most of them are against you from the off. There was an air of coldness, nothing like what Tony Blair once experienced at the National Federation of Women's Institutes, but still cold. I would have had to be at my most persuasive to win them over, and I was anything but that. Alun, so I was told later, gave his best performance of the campaign – some way short of charismatic, but more than just competent. I was neither – all part of my throwing away an outside chance of getting the vote of the AEEU, the biggest union in Wales! And all was my own fault.

This isn't to say that Alun's campaign didn't make mistakes too, but they were less critical mistakes. If I'd won the AEEU block vote, it could have swung a lot of unions that weren't balloting over to my side. Everyone likes to be on the winning side, after all. Then Alun publicly promised a job to Ron Davies in his first Cabinet if he won the leadership election, not forgetting the Assembly election, of course. That was seen as crass and presumptuous. When it eventually came to it in May, after the Assembly elections, it was one of the few things on which I wouldn't negotiate – 'No Ron in the Cabinet, he's damaged goods!' I said very firmly. Alun was the leader by then, but he complied.

Peter Hain and a few other Labour MPs had to admit to using official House of Commons notepaper and free postage and sending out appeal letters to their party members asking them to support Alun Michael. If we'd done that, it would have brought down the Furies of hell upon us. But it was laughed off by the MPs involved as an 'administrative error' by 'new and inexperienced staff'. Ultimately, it did little damage to Alun's campaign.

What Alun's campaign was really looking for was an opportunity to throw the crypto-nationalist accusation at me and my supporters, but Kevin and I were determined not to give them the opportunity. Then I made another error in not checking the text of a letter we were sending out to all Assembly Labour candidates. It was written by the late Geoff Mungham, a sociology lecturer at Cardiff University, who had been brought in to help with drafting. He was a former colleague of Kevin's on Cardiff City Council. I can still remember gazing inertly at the draft Geoff had prepared – it just sat on my desk. I was so exhausted, I never did check it, and off it went. Nothing explosive, just some pretty anodyne comments that it was about time for Labour Party Wales to be given more autonomy. But that one word, *autonomy*, was what Peter Hain had been waiting for. Suddenly, we were deep in crypto-nat territory. I was asked to go on the *World at One* to listen to Neil Kinnock denouncing me as a crypto-nat. He'd known me a very long time – I was a very nice guy and a likeable soul, indeed a great guy to have at a party, BUT BUT BUT! He patronised me up one studio wall and down the other one. When it came to my turn I was dying to give one back on his own terms – the phrases had already formed in my mind, I was going to say what a privilege it was to be patronised by someone as eminent as Neil Kinnock, icy superior sarcasm and all that. Then I decided no, no sarcasm, and that was one of the better decisions I made – leave a story you don't want running to die a natural death.

To Geoff Mungham's credit, he was the one who came up with the brilliant line for my concession speech at the St David's Hotel: 'I don't feel like a loser today. Runner-up, Yes! Loser, No!' It buoyed me enormously, and from the cheer it got it must have buoyed my supporters as well among the three hundred people present. Geoff hit just the right note with that line. In the meantime, I have to take responsibility for not checking the letter calling for more Labour Party autonomy in Wales.

Some of the local candidates chosen in winnable seats seemed to show that my supporters were doing well, and even occasionally defeating rivals backing Alun Michael against the odds. In Clwyd West, in the centre of the North Wales coastal belt around Colwyn Bay, the local Labour MP Gareth Thomas, elected for the first time in 1997, had decided to enter his name to become an Assembly candidate. He was beaten by one of my supporters, Alun Pugh, a miner's son from the Rhondda Valley (not normally an advantage in Colwyn Bay). Alun Pugh worked in further education at Llandrillo College in Colwyn Bay, and his win came as a lovely surprise. Any selected candidate would have a big say in the final outcome of the contest. Because of the structure put forward for the third section of the electoral college, one third of the overall vote would be cast by sitting Welsh MPs, MEPs and Assembly candidates. What that meant was that each time one of my supporters won a nomination for an Assembly seat, it was the equivalent of getting 300 votes from ordinary party members, and that applied to the list members as well. The structure was wide open to abuse by the establishment because the Executive put the names in list order to the delegates for each electoral region. On four occasions, the delegates for Mid & West Wales refused the list offered – it comprised Alun Michael, Delyth Evans, Vaughan Gething and Sioned Mair Richards. Again, all the badgering and urging to do what the establishment wanted seemed only to anger party workers – it was as if the *Yes, Prime Minister* deference that the party once had to the great redeemer who had brought the Labour landslide of 1 May 1997 was, by early 1999, collapsing into *No, Prime Minister.*

It appeared extremely heavy-handed for the Labour Executive to add an extra little clause to the party's rules for selecting a leader if a vacancy arose during an Assembly term. If there did emerge such a vacancy (as in circumstances where Alun Michael didn't win a seat), the Welsh Executive would have a joint meeting with the Assembly Labour Group to elect a leader in such a meeting. In fact, the Executive would outnumber the Welsh Labour AMs – though when that eventuality did come about in February 2000, the provision proved to be a dead letter, because by then you'd be forgiven for thinking that I'd always been the natural choice of the Welsh Executive! And Tony Blair's best mate to boot!

I was surprised that the civil service allowed Alun Michael to do a meet the people tour of Wales at taxpayers' expense – it was so obvious that it was all to do with the internal Labour Party leadership contest. Officially, it was supposed to help the new Secretary of State introduce himself to the people living in the different sub-regions of Wales – the civil servants who had to sanction it as a legitimate expense should have asked themselves whether the Secretary of State would have undertaken the tour if he wasn't also fighting an internal Labour Party leadership contest. It was all sailing very close to the wind. Whether it did Alun any good in winning votes from Labour Party members is hard to say, but it fitted in with this obsession that the Prime Minister, George Wright and many others had, that being First Secretary in the Assembly was essentially the same as the job of Secretary of State for Wales.

As January drew to an end, it was all getting a bit frazzled and frantic. Labour Party members still hadn't received their ballot forms. We had been given a probable date for the postal ballot forms being dispatched, which was to be the end of the first week in February. It wasn't. The date was brought forward without anyone being notified. My campaign team only got to know because of a phone call from Liz Lewis, a North Wales area T&G organiser who was also on the Welsh Executive – 'They've brought it forward', she said breathlessly, 'the ballot forms are going out this week.' If George Wright had found out she'd given my team that key bit of information, I don't know what would have happened to Liz. When I look back on my long-term connection with the T&G, I think fondly of people like Liz Lewis and Danny Fellowes who never allowed themselves to be cowed by the boss.

My campaign chief Kevin Brennan and I could see what was going on. Three things came together. First, there was to bring forward the date of the ballots being sent out. Second was to get the *Daily Mirror's* full double-page encomium on why Alun (and not me) was the right choice – I was a maverick of no account, Alun was a worker who would deliver for the workers in Wales. I decided to bite the bullet and phoned the editor, Piers Morgan – what can only be described as an *ychafi* experience, which left me feeling oddly contaminated. Please, God, I should never be in a railway carriage on a long journey from London to Aberdeen with him – I'd encountered superciliousness before, but never on this scale. Would it do me damage? The *Mirror* was a declining force in the land, but it still outsold the *Western Mail*, the *Echo* and *Wales on Sunday* by three to one. Indeed, Wales and Merseyside were the only parts of the UK where the *Mirror* still outsold *The Sun*. But, on its own, the *Mirror* article would not be significant – it could only be effective as part of the whole strategy.

The third part of the strategy was Tony Blair's third campaign visit to Wales, on 2 February, the same day as the ballot forms arrived on people's doorsteps. Blair combined his visit to meet the members and cast his halo like a frisbee in the direction of Alun Michael with some official visits – one of which included a visit to Julie's constituency. He visited Tŷ Maeth, headquarters of the Royal College of Nursing, in the grounds of the University Hospital of Wales. The RCN had installed a new training suite and Julie, as the host MP, had to delay a visit to Denmark with the Select Committee for Welsh Affairs so that she could be present at the public unveiling of the RCN's new childcare system. So Julie found herself having to be there to host the Prime Minister as he ably skirted the leadership ballot issue during the tour of the computer-aided training set-up.

Then off the Prime Minister went, a dozen miles up the road to the University of Glamorgan at Treforest, transforming himself from PM and into the leader of the Labour Party. It was a big conference room at Treforest with hundreds in the audience and a noisy atmosphere. We all knew it was the last throw of the dice for both teams of campaigners. He claimed in his speech once again that the final decision was up to them, but that they should not give in to the temptation of leaving him, Tony Blair, with a bloody nose. He also made the repeated assertion that the rules for the unions to cast their votes were exactly the same as when he was elected party leader in 1994 (of course they were, and weapons of mass destruction would be found in Iraq). When the question session started, the formidable Nancy Nicholas from Cardiff West was called. She had positioned herself at the very centre of the hall where the chair could not miss her. We were now definitively moving from *Yes, Prime Minister* to *No, Prime Minister*. Nancy nailed it. 'Why, Prime Minister, do you keep repeating this nonsense about the unions having the same rules now as they did five years ago when you and John Prescott were elected? Surely you recall then that the unions had to have one member one vote ballots? But now they don't.' Once a headteacher, always a headteacher, that was Nancy Nicholas. With people like Nancy in the audience, I could stay quiet. Deference to the Prime Minister simply didn't occur to her, and Blair had to waffle desperately to talk his way out of her question.

With the ballot forms going out early, we now had to scramble desperately to get our telephone canvassing teams ready to operate the rest of that week. When political parties or trade unions organise postal ballots, the tradition is that three-quarters of those who vote do so on the Sunday morning after receipt of their forms. Having been stacked on the mantelpiece for a few days, only very keen participants will fill in their forms during the weekdays or on the Saturday. Come Sunday, there's a bit more time to get organised. So that week was critical. Thanks to Liz Lewis's phone call, we hacked back some of the advantage of surprise that the other side had – it had been a dirty trick to draw the date forward, but I think we got back into our telephone canvassing stride pretty quickly.

My campaign gained a big boost on 2 February, the day of the final Blair visit, which was when the UNISON members ballot result came out and showed me winning by three to one. Peter Hain had to tie himself in knots trying to explain it – he should have said fair dinkum on a good win to Rhodri and his team, and left it at that. But he didn't – he blamed my advantage on the Trotskyite fringe being so influential within that union.

And what was Ron Davies up to in those final weeks? He was trying to make a comeback! He drew a good audience at two public speaking events at the Institute of Welsh Affairs and the Royal Society for the Protection of Birds; he also announced his backing for Alun Michael, which was hardly surprising given that Alun had promised in public that Ron would have a job in Alun's presumed first Cabinet. In his excellent book on the campaign between Alun and me, Paul Flynn, MP for Newport West, refers to Ron's support for Alun as an indication that Ron had calculated the angles on a potential return to his inheritance as leader of the Welsh Assembly as being far better under Alun than me – in other words, Paul has essayed, Ron could work it out that if I became leader, I would be there for a very long time. If Alun became leader, then an accident of politics might befall him – as did indeed happen. Then Ron might have fancied his chances – it is certainly true that Ron has always calculated the angles to the third decimal place, but all on pure speculation. My guess, for what it's worth, is that Ron could see that Alun was far from certain to be elected. If he wasn't elected and the Welsh Executive met up with the Labour Group to elect a leader, then Ron may have thought the mistrust of me among the Welsh Executive arising from the bruising nature of the contest, might lead them to vote for him. Who knows?

The last major piece in the jigsaw was the GMB union block vote. How were they going to cast it? They certainly didn't conduct a ballot. Did they take soundings from the membership? We know two things. The first is that two GMB branch officials representing Cardiff City Council employees in the GMB – Kenny Daniels, leader of the Direct Labour Organisations, and Roy Thomas, who represented the municipal dustmen – organised a petition and had it delivered during their lunch hour to the GMB Regional HQ at Williamson House on Newport Road. The petition demanded that the votes of their members be cast for me. The other account of the run-up to the GMB casting its block vote comes from the then Welsh Office Minister Jon Owen Jones, MP for Cardiff Central, who has always been convinced that there was some kind of skulduggery involving the GMB vote and a connection with the blocking of his attempts to reform the heavily loss-making DLOs (the Direct Labour Organisations carrying out council house repairs), especially the one in the Rhondda Cynon Taf local authority. Jon was keen on reform of the loss-making DLOs, which didn't happen, and it seems Alun and the GMB were involved in some obscure way. Alun then got the GMB vote. All that anyone has been able to find out subsequently about the GMB's modus operandi on decision day is that all the paperwork on how the union cast its block vote was taken out of Williamson House and handed over to Leo Abse and Cohen, the union's solicitors, for safe keeping in a vault somewhere. No prying eyes were ever to be allowed to see it. Once I had blown my chances at the AEEU delegate conference in Swansea, and once the GMB block vote was thrown onto the scales, my path to victory became a calculable impossibility.

There had never been such media interest in a political event in Wales. When Alun and I were taken to a side room on the top floor of St David's Hotel to be told the result by Anita Gale, the party's Welsh Secretary, we were then supposed to make our way down to the ground floor to the waiting hundreds of supporters of both campaigns, along with this vast bank of media folk of every description, and from every country and continent. But there was a problem in that the lifts had decided not to work, so we had to walk down eight floors of fire escape staircase to get to ground level. We made our speeches. I was as upbeat as it is possible to be. I had lost, but I'd won all the OMOV ballots, which gave me a moral victory. Alun had won under the electoral college three-thirds rules, but the victory was to prove pyrrhic when he resigned twelve months later. In all my media stuff that day, I avoided going overboard on the moral victory theme because there was going to be a tough election to fight in early May.

During the May election campaign, Alun did his thing as party leader with Peter Hain pulling all the strings. Peter asked, nay begged me to introduce Alun Michael at a pre-election rally in the Little Theatre in Rhyl. I took the view that I had to do it – I could have refused on the grounds that I'd been stitched up – and though this request from Peter was a bit of a cheek, I got on and did it. We had to try to win that election.

It may have been that my willingness to play a full role in that election rally is what prompted Peter to ring me up three weeks before the election informing me that he wanted to include two or three ideas of mine in Labour's election manifesto. I asked how long I had to send him my shortlist, and he said I had about forty-five minutes – they were going to press that day! I said to Kevin Brennan that we had to get our thinking caps on, and that this offer meant one of two things. Either the flow of ideas in Peter's own well had run dry, or that he meant it as a conciliatory gesture that would bind me into the government that my whole campaign team hoped we would help create after the May elections.

On election day, I swept the board in Cardiff West. The other parties didn't get a look-in. I had achieved such a high profile that I won piles of votes from other parties for my David vs Goliath efforts. There was a huge sympathy vote, and I had no inkling of what was going on elsewhere until, at about three in the morning, a frantic Jane Davidson rang me to say that Wayne David had lost the Rhondda! She had only just managed to avoid a recount in Pontypridd, but with a majority of only five hundred votes. In the meantime, Plaid Cymru was insisting on a recount in Cynon Valley. Labour had lost RCT Council to Plaid, and the whole of RCT was an electoral disaster area.

That was the strangest election ever. We had done sufficiently badly that our newly elected party leader had been able to get in on the regional list for Mid & West Wales, but we'd done so badly in the Rhondda that if Alun Michael did fall, Wayne David wouldn't be there as an alternative to me. So, if Alun fell, it would have to be me.

# six

# Getting the Show on the Road 1999–2000

T HE VERY FIRST AND unquestionably historic elections to the National Assembly for Wales took place on the first Thursday of May 1999. For good or ill, they coincided with the Welsh local government elections. But what did the results show? To say the results were confusing wouldn't cut it at all. It was a curate's egg of a patchwork quilt of a mixed bag, if ever I saw one.

Three things stood out for me. First off, Labour had lost some heartland seats. Take Neil Kinnock's old stamping ground of Islwyn – rock solid Labour from top to toe, gone to Plaid. Same in the Rhondda – rock solid as you could get (although Plaid had done very well there in a by-election in 1967), actually gone to Plaid this time, as had the Council. Llanelli had gone to Plaid too, whereas in the good old days Labour majorities of over 20,000 had been the norm.

What saved things for Labour was the healthy vote in the Labour/Tory marginals strung along the coastal belts along the M4 and the A55. Tony Blair had taken all of them in the New Labour landslide of 1997, and they'd all stayed with us in 1999. The Vale of Glamorgan, Cardiff North, the two Pembrokeshire seats and the Vale of Clwyd and Clwyd West in the north had gone to Labour, but how was it possible to win Cardiff North and lose the Rhondda in the same election? The impossible had happened.

While I was at my count in Cardiff West, at around three in the morning, I had a panic-stricken phone call from Jane Davidson, the Labour candidate in the neighbouring seat of Pontypridd, and who was later my Education Minister. Jane said Plaid was thinking of asking for a recount, as the results in the other two seats in Rhondda Cynon Taf were looking disastrous for Labour. We'd scraped home in Cynon Valley by five hundred votes and we'd lost the Rhondda. Jane's voice was breaking with the emotion of it all.

I knew there were powerful local factors in RCT. It was Wales's second largest local authority, constituting the old coal-mining area north of Cardiff. The Labour Council was unpopular, especially in the Rhondda where the Nant-y-Gwyddon waste disposal site was toxic (certainly politically). Plaid were campaigning on a promise to close it down – there's nothing easier than campaigning on a promise when you never expect to have the power in your hands to redeem it!

Llanelli was the most confusing result of all – Labour fought very hard to win the seat, but the Labour Party establishment needed us to lose it! How so? Well, Alun Michael's late arrival as a Labour candidate, after all the constituency selections had been completed, meant that he could only get a nomination on the regional list. And the only region where Labour could possibly win any regional list seats was Mid & West Wales. Under the system of voting for both the Welsh Assembly and the Scottish Parliament, the closer you got to a clean sweep of the constituency seats in a region, the less chance you had of getting any regional list seats.

In Mid & West Wales, comprising the two mainly rural counties of Dyfed and Powys, Alun as head of the regional list had a fighting chance of getting a seat, but not if Labour won the two Pembrokeshire seats, Carmarthen East & Dinefwr, and Llanelli. If Labour had won those four seats, then Alun, the designated Labour leader and First Secretary, wouldn't have a seat. The Labour hierarchy must have had a Plan B in the event of Alun failing to get into the Assembly – my guess is that the Stop Rhodri candidate to emerge in the way that these things happen would have been Wayne David, the former MEP. The realists might have suggested bygones ought to be bygones, and that Rhodri should be allowed to get on and do the job. The ultra-loyalists would have retorted by questioning whether all their hard work to stop Rhodri had been in vain, if only to capitulate now.

Anyway, Labour candidates Richard Edwards did win Preseli-Pembrokeshire and Christine Gwyther did win Pembroke South–Carmarthen West, but Chris Llewellyn lost Carmarthen East & Dinefwr and Ann Garrard lost Llanelli, and Alun Michael got in to the Assembly. Labour had lost enough constituency seats in the Mid & West Wales region to be entitled to one list seat.

The Tory Party had been wiped out in Wales in the Westminster election of 1997, as it was again in 2001. However, the party was reborn in 1999 via two political institutions they actually disapproved of – the first being devolution, and the second being proportional representation. Only one Tory was elected in a constituency – David T. C. Davies in Monmouth – but the Tories did win eleven list seats. That gave them the right to public funding for their Group office for press and policy work, and it put them back in business. The only thing that kept the party from having to switch off the lights at the UK level was Michael Ashcroft's generosity. PR and devolution gave the Tory Party another kind of Ashcroft blood transfusion – it gave them a springboard, at least in Wales and Scotland, despite the MP cupboard being bare.

Labour was by far the largest party, with 28 seats out of the 60 – 27 of them constituency seats out of 40, and just one out of 20 regional list seats. Labour was therefore destined to be in office, but not in power, and Alun Michael had to go about the job of choosing the Cabinet for his minority government. He invited me to his office, that is the Secretary of State's office on the first floor of Cathays Park.

Built in 1937, the original Cathays Park Welsh Office building is an example of stripped-down classicism. I'd worked in the building back in the mid-1960s, and now I was going to discuss the membership of Alun and Wales's first ever Cabinet. This really was going to see history being made. I sat on the comfy sofa, and Alun with his lists on one of the matching chairs.

The meeting started very oddly – I was up one minute and down the next. Alun told me straight off, 'I want you to do Economic Development and European Affairs.' Yippee! I thought inwardly, just the job I'd always wanted. Then he added, bringing me crashing back down to earth, 'Of course, this is the job I had in mind for Wayne David, but sadly he's not available now. I was going to ask you to be the Deputy Presiding Officer!'

That was the one job I would have absolutely refused under all and any circumstances – a non-ministerial non-job. I didn't tell Alun that, because it was now purely academic. The strange thing was that since it was all now academic, why did Alun feel the need to tell me anyway? I puzzled a lot about that afterwards. It was a gratuitous insult in a way, telling me that I wasn't his first choice for Economic Development.

Was Alun trying to tell me that the Labour hierarchy still didn't want me to be a Minister? There could be two reasons if that were the case. Anyone as utterly loyal to Tony Blair as Alun could argue that, if Tony Blair didn't choose me as a Minister in 1997, then it had to apply in 1999 as well (otherwise, it would have implied criticism of Tony Blair's judgement).

The second, slightly more Machiavellian, explanation could have been that if I had taken on the Deputy Presiding Officer role, I would never have been in a position to take over from Alun should he fall under the proverbial bus. So, in telling me openly that I wasn't supposed to be in his Cabinet at all, Alun might have been hinting that blocking me was still official Labour strategy, but that it wasn't a strategy he supported fully. So, reading between the lines, Alun was now extending some generosity in putting me in the Cabinet, despite the risk that I would be around if anything happened to him.

We had a long discussion about all the other Cabinet jobs. Andrew Davies (Swansea West), as ex-Labour Party staffer, was a natural fit for Chief Whip and

Business Minister. His neighbouring AM Edwina Hart (Gower), having worked in a bank in her early days and ex-chair of the Wales TUC as well as being a redoubtable character, was well suited to the Finance Minister job. Jane Hutt was a shoo-in at Health – Alun knew Jane well from various causes and charities they'd worked on together, such as the Cardiff Broadcasting Company.

The first row Alun and I had was over Ron Davies. I was sufficiently emboldened by this point in the discussion (and after the non-offer of the Deputy Presiding Officer non-job!) to put my foot down. I said that Ron was damaged goods, but Alun's counter-argument was that if Tony Blair had seen fit to appoint Ron to his Cabinet in 1997 and then re-appointed him in his summer reshuffle of mid-1998, then surely, by analogy, Ron must be worth a job in the much smaller pool of talent available for the Welsh Assembly's first Cabinet.

I was adamant that Ron's moment of madness in the bushes on Clapham Common (and all of the other stuff that I had become aware of) had already done so much damage to the whole devolution project in Wales that he had to be kept out. It wasn't about ability – Ron had plenty of that – it was about reputation. We would be a laughing stock (or, if you were cynical or anti-devolution, even more of a laughing stock!).

Alun accepted my view in the end, but insisted that Ron should be given something. The 'something' he got wasn't ideal from my point of view – it was the Chair of the Economic Development Committee, which meant, in effect, that Ron would be scrutinising me, and that might be very tasty. The result was even worse than I had feared, because Ron carried his burning resentment around like a ball and chain that his rightful inheritance to be running Wales under devolution had somehow been taken away from him – or, as I would have put it, had been thrown away by him entirely of his own volition.

This question of Ron's job arose again the following week when Alun and I met up in Cardiff Bay to finalise the list of committee chairs, after much to-ing and fro-ing with the opposition parties on which committees they wanted to chair. This time, it was Alun who stood firm on the issue of what to do about Ron. This meeting was much more hurried. I was standing next to Alun's desk, looking down at his list – luckily, I have a skill that I rarely call upon, which is to read documents upside down. Once I'd deciphered the list, I twigged that Alun was not going to give Sue Essex (Cardiff North) anything, not even the Chair of the Environment and Planning Committee. I exploded. Sue was the best qualified person in Britain, let alone Wales, to do that job. I would have much preferred her to be doing the equivalent job in the Cabinet, but Alun was not even going to give her the committee chair! 'You can't do that!' I shouted, 'You've got to give Sue the Chair of Environment and Planning!' Alun reconsidered, and crossed off Christine Chapman (Cynon Valley) from the list, and put Sue's name in her place. Tough on Christine, but in my view Sue was much better suited.

The key thing about Alun's first and only Cabinet was its geographical spread. Coming from North Wales originally, then being the MP for Cardiff South since 1987, and now having scraped into the Assembly as one of the regional AMs for Mid & West Wales, you could understand Alun's obsession with geographical fairness. Andrew Davies and Edwina Hart represented Swansea constituencies; Tom Middlehurst (Alyn & Deeside in Flintshire in North Wales) was doing post-16 education; Peter Law (Blaenau Gwent) was doing Planning and Environment, and Rosemary Butler (Newport West) was doing Education 3–16 years, the last two both from Gwent; Chris Gwyther representing Pembrokeshire was doing Agriculture; and finally, Jane Hutt and I represented the Vale of Glamorgan and Cardiff respectively. Geographical balance – the Cabinet represented every part of Wales.

I took a different view when choosing the Cabinet fell to me – I chose big hitters and hoped they would turn out to be well distributed across Wales (though they weren't). Alun wanted a well spread-out Cabinet and hoped they would turn out to be big hitters – it's for others to judge how big they did hit.

A religious service was held in Llandaff Cathedral to bless the new Assembly and to wish it well. All the new AMs and many Welsh MPs came along to join in the fun. Paul Flynn MP for Newport West, whose diatribe *Dragons led by Poodles* had taken on Tony Blair's interference in the Labour Welsh leadership race, came out of the cathedral chortling and hooting with laughter. 'That proves it', he said, 'there is a God after all!' What got him so excited was that the reading Alun had been given by the friendly archbishop started with the phrase, 'You did not choose me. I chose you.'

Key to those early Cabinet meetings was the seating plan that emerged – not by design, it just emerged. Alun would sit halfway along the Cabinet table, as happens with the PM in No. 10 Downing Street. I was always sat at the end of the table, the ideal seat, because any time I wanted to come in I could catch Alun's eye very easily. Looking back, I think that bit by bit I became Alun's undeclared deputy, simply by dint of where I sat. Here's an example. Alun was describing a problem with some aspect of Health policy, but he was stuck for the right word to explain why we couldn't be doing everything – 'We can't …', he said, then stopped –'Micro-manage everything?' I said –'That's it, we can't micro-manage everything!' Alun really seemed very grateful.

Actually, micro-management was one of the problems. Alun remained Secretary of State until the end of July, when Paul Murphy was appointed. But even after that, the Secretary of State way of working carried on – all decisions made by Ministers (Assembly Secretaries, to use the title at the time) were not in fact decisions until Alun had seen the outgoing decision letter and approved it. Three weeks' worth of letters would pile up on his desk, despite his brilliant use of all the modern office technology available. The same went for his workaholism

– he would come in at eight in the morning and rarely leave before nine in the evening. On top of that, he would be on the case before coming in to work, and he would work at home into the wee small hours. But if you don't delegate, the backlog still piles up. Possibly in reaction to Alun's micro-management, I may have allowed my Ministers too much latitude.

Sometimes, Alun would delegate a task to me that he might have been better doing himself, and sometimes it went the other way. In June, I deputised for Alun at the Queen's Birthday celebrations in Paris. I spoke French, Alun didn't – it wasn't his kind of thing anyway. The Foreign Office had gone out of their way to give the whole occasion a Welsh theme, and it was a massive opportunity for Welsh food and drink producers to showcase at one of the key social and political occasions in the Paris calendar.

The benefit for me and for Wales was that the Foreign Office was showing off Welsh devolution to the political elite in France – the sub-text was 'catch this, you Frenchies, bet you never thought we Brits could pull off this devolution lark so efficiently!' The FCO was also hinting to me that Wales would always be treated as equals of visiting UK Government Ministers – we need never think that we should have our own little embassies or ambassadors, it's all there for us from the good old FCO!

I tried to picture whether the French could ever have done the same in reverse. Think of Bastille Day and the French Ambassador's Residence in London – might they have a Breton-themed celebration? Would the Ambassador have stood shoulder to shoulder with a visiting Breton Regional Trade and Economy Minister to receive the salute of a French military band? I have to pat the Foreign Office on the back for going for that Welsh-themed garden party in June 1999. Of course, we didn't constitute any kind of threat to the Foreign Office.

That's why the FCO could be so quick off the mark. Of all the Whitehall Departments of State, the Welsh Assembly did not compete with FCO as it might do with a home department. You could argue, if you were of a nationalist stripe or a conspiracy theorist, that we were being captured by the FCO. If we were being treated as a new kind of UK Government ministry, we were buying into a subliminal message that Wales and Scotland were a part of Britain, and that was how it should always stay. On the other hand, the FCO wanted to bang the drum on how smoothly the pan-Celtic devolution exercise had gone – it was a UK success story, the UK had evolved almost overnight from a unitary state to a part-federal one almost without batting an eyelid.

So, we could work well with the Foreign Office because they wanted to show us off as a British success story, and we posed no existential threat to them. At the other extreme was the Department for Communities and Local Government (DeCLoG), the Deputy Prime Minister John Prescott's new super-department. We did for Wales almost everything that they did for England. We were a competitor and a comparator, and therefore a threat. DeCLoG was one of a tiny handful of UK Government departments that were basically an entirely England-only operation. It got nasty occasionally, perhaps especially at official level, where DeCLoG had inherited Henry VIII powers – that is, the power to pass a special type of secondary legislation via the Committee system upstairs in the House of Commons – which had the same effect as primary legislation. It was clear to us that we had inherited the same power as well. DeCLoG said we hadn't, we said we had, and couldn't work out whether it was officials going rogue or whether John Prescott or other Ministers had told his vast army of officials to keep an eye on us and stop us exercising any powers of real significance.

That came to affect me more when I became First Minister. In 1999, it was all about me running the ship and enjoying getting to know my department at the Assembly, including the quangos like the WDA and the Wales Tourist Board. The head of it was Derek Jones, many years later the Permanent Secretary, who had been a senior figure in the DTI in Whitehall. He and I couldn't have hit it off more if we'd tried – not every new Minister got on with the top official they found themselves having to work with, but I did.

From my first tour of the teams in the department at Cathays Park, I knew I'd arrived exactly where I wanted to be. I could have imagined being a civil servant among them, but I had a different job. I had to give them both political and policy leadership.

It wasn't all plain sailing though. What I was most sceptical of was the Baglan Energy Park. On my first day's tour around the project sections, the team responsible told me with confidence that the energy park would produce 6,000 new jobs. I asked them how they could be so sure – it sounded an awfully high figure to me – but they said it was a middle estimate. I could rely on the 6,000 jobs figure.

Actually, it became clear that no jobs would arrive at the Baglan Energy Park, but I eventually found out why the estimate was so unrealistically high. Helen Liddell, by then the UK's High Commissioner in Australia, told me the background story. In 1997, the incoming Blair Government had issued a moratorium on new gas-fired power stations. The American multi-national industrial behemoth GE had wanted to build their first ever H Series combined cycle gas turbine power station at Baglan, on a site vacated by BP. It had been part of BP's exit strategy from South Wales to secure GE's brand new and revolutionary design of power station on the former BP Baglan site. Then along came the moratorium.

US President Bill Clinton received a phone call from 'Neutron' Jack Welch, the legendary boss of GE, asking for his help in getting around the moratorium. Clinton rang his good friend Tony Blair, and asked (or maybe told) the PM to lift the moratorium for GE. That's how things are done in the US, I suppose. I could imagine Clinton smooth-talking Tony Blair over this – 'For God's sake, Tony, lift the moratorium for this power station, I've got Jack Welch on my back!' Anyway,

GE got their permit to build the power station, but the exemption case from the moratorium had to be very special. Electricity from the power station could be supplied over the fence directly, and without paying a grid charge, into energy-intensive industries which could all go on the empty Baglan Bay site (now renamed the Baglan Energy Park). Hence the need for the 6,000 jobs estimate.

Before the power station actually opened, I asked to visit the project site (I was First Minister by this point). I was curious about why the US President had phoned the British PM about it – had to be on a par with a moon shot, didn't it? Bill Cooney, GE's site director, took me around – a lot of guys in overalls with spanners sticking out of every pocket, trying to tweak the turbine blades to get them to run in perfect harmony. With the tour over, I walked back with Cooney to the car park past a row of Portakabins stacked four-high – he said that was where all the design engineers worked. I replied to say that I ought to go in there, as the tour wouldn't really be complete without meeting his engineering team.

Cooney said, 'Very sorry, sir, you can't go in there. You don't have an American passport!' 'Hang on a minute', I riposted, 'we are in Port Talbot, in Wales, and I am the First Minister, I don't need a passport to go anywhere in Wales!' 'I'm afraid you cannot go in there without breaching the US Export Control Act', Cooney replied, 'this is sensitive technology, only US citizens allowed in there.' I wasn't giving up. 'So you're telling me that since those Portakabins were put there, no non-US citizen has been in there?' 'Absolutely right', he said, 'nobody … oh, hang on a minute, nobody except the delivery boys from Domino's Pizza!' Now I knew where the First Minister of Wales stood – somewhere beneath Domino's Pizza delivery boys!

Another area of my responsibilities was overseas trade. The old Welsh Office had for years carried out trade missions to encourage small and medium size enterprises to develop into exports. We left all trade missions in Europe to the Cardiff Chamber of Commerce – they were very good on the trade and export paperwork and in running training courses for exporters. Anywhere beyond Europe was Welsh Office – now Welsh Assembly – domain, and the departmental export team wanted to double the number of trade missions. They thought having a devolved government would help open doors in distant countries where Wales didn't have a high profile.

Kuwait was chosen. Ten to fifteen companies were needed to make a reasonable mission, and two things stuck out when they presented me with the list. It included no companies from North Wales, and there were two companies from England. I objected. 'The *Daily Post* will have my guts for garters if we publish this list – this is the first trade mission since devolution, and we'll have to cancel it if there are no companies from North Wales!' The English companies were easier to explain as simple reciprocity – Welsh companies could go on English trade missions, and vice versa. Anyway, back came my officials a week later with a North Wales company keen to go.

Great, problem solved, except that when I read the publicity bumf from the North Wales company it seemed that its main product was bacon-slicing machinery. 'Hang on', I told them, 'I asked you to get me a North Wales company interested in exporting to a Muslim country like Kuwait, and you come up with a company that makes bacon-slicing machinery! I'd rather have bad headlines in the *Daily Post* than a fatwa in Kuwait!' None of these issues had ever arisen before devolution, there was basically no scrutiny of the detail of how trade missions were organised, it was just the old Welsh Office getting on with its job. Neither the press nor MPs would have dreamt of getting involved in that level of detail, but now we were living in a totally different world of transparency.

Anyway, go to Kuwait we did after the company from North Wales had rewritten its publicity material to emphasise its machines' beef-slicing excellence.

The Kuwaiti knowledge of Wales was pretty sketchy. This wasn't much of a problem to the trade missionaries, but it was a problem for me doing my round of the radio and television studios. The basic problem was that in Kuwait there was no real distinction between the Royal Family (in this case the Emir), the Government and the State – so they thought the Prince of Wales owned and ran Wales, and since we were now running Wales they wanted to know what we'd done with Prince Charles!

They also had a vague idea in Kuwait that Wales had the longest place name in the world. So on English language channels I had to repeat endlessly Llanfairpwllgwyngyllgogerychwyrndrobwll-llantysiliogogogoch! They loved it. They couldn't get enough of it!

Back at home, meanwhile, one of the stranger aspects of my job was being scrutinised by the Economic Development Committee, chaired by Ron Davies, of course. Ron is a very able guy, but what made his scrutineering tricky was the still-smouldering resentment at not being First Minister. Lobbyists used Ron and the Committee to try to get changes made to suit them. No surprise there, except that I found out that Sir David Rowe-Beddoe, the Chairman of the Welsh Development Agency, was among the lobbyists, and Sir David worked for me. Now he was using Ron to try to get the Trade & Export Promotion unit within my department to be transferred to the WDA. For Ron, as the author of the Bonfire of the Quangos policy, to support this was all a bit rich.

It was the disloyalty of the WDA's Chairman that astonished me. Sir David just didn't seem to have grasped the new political realities at all. The WDA had already rather naughtily built up a Global Trade promotion unit, duplicating what the civil servants already did, and I decided we had to sort out that ragged edge and head off any other duplication ideas. I got the WDA to transfer all the staff they had in their unauthorised duplicate unit into the civil service. Then, to prevent any hard feelings at the WDA, I transferred a handful of civil service staff doing technology support into the agency. Most importantly, a clear instruction was given to Sir David *never* to lobby Ron or anyone else on the Committee again. The WDA was working for me now!

Some aspects of the portfolio worked very well in the early months. I had a phone call from an old friend, Glenn Massey, in the summer. Glenn was the top man on inward investment for Price Waterhouse, and had a client who was thinking of building a factory and was inclined towards Wales. The company was Britax Rumbold, who had a factory in Carshalton making high class aircraft seats. The Britax Rumbold site was hemmed in and couldn't be expanded, and even if the site could be expanded it would struggle to get the labour.

When we met in my not terribly swish office in Cathays Park, the Britax Rumbold MD told me he had flown back and forth on BA transatlantic flights and nodded off countless times watching the WDA's catchy little ads on the aircraft cabins' main screens. So what he wanted to know was what kind of grant we could offer Britax Rumbold? It was good to get a reasonably big catch under our belts early on in the life of devolved Wales, and they got a good deal.

That initial Britax Rumbold project was for a factory and design and drawing office, and would employ 350 people. It was that last bit about the drawing office that made it particularly attractive to me. Wales had historically had too many branch factories – pure production units, and the decisions on the future of those factories are always made elsewhere. Branch factories have no control over their destiny, and often close down in a recession.

Anyway, Britax Rumbold got a top grant to build a new factory in Cwmbrân. Some commentators were cynical about inward investment and government grants – the LG project had given inward investment a bad name, but Britax Rumbold gave it a good name. Having started off with 350 jobs, at the last count it was employing over 1,000 and now belongs to French aerospace giant Zodiac.

The long-term problem was that I thought Wales's industrial economic regeneration could be achieved simply by more and more Britax Rumbold-type projects, we just needed to clone that success. The magic combination of the WDA's marketing spend on BA planes and elsewhere, and our grants from within the department under Section 7 of the Regional Selective Assistance, as it was called, plus Glenn Massey's book of contacts, would surely do the trick. But the project for reconstruction proved to be something of a false dawn. I thought, far too optimistically as it turned out, that we could attract a project like that once a month or, at worst, one every quarter.

The strengthening pound didn't help at that point. The market was changing rapidly as 1999 turned into 2000, and labour-intensive industries were already looking not to invest in Wales but in the ex-Warsaw Pact countries, and Poland in particular. Those countries were not in the EU then, and wouldn't become EU Members until 2003, but business leaders simply assumed the latter was just a matter of time.

Indeed, in February 1999, three months before the Assembly had come into existence, Lucas-SEI had covertly shifted its electronic wiring harness operation from Ystradgynlais at the top of the Swansea Valley to Poland, all over the course of a weekend. That was a canary down the mine keeling over if ever I saw one. So not only were the ex-Warsaw Pact countries serious competitors for footloose inward investment projects, they were suitably attractive for already established companies in Wales to shift their machinery and move out. This threat from eastern Europe was before anyone in the West really appreciated how powerful China was going to become in manufacturing. The rise of India as a software developer of choice, in the meantime, and as a location for call centres being offshored was only dimly perceived. How could Regional Selective Assistance in West Wales and the Valleys compete with wage levels in Poland, which were one sixth of those in Wales? Or one tenth of our wage levels when it came to Dewhirst a little later moving their clothes manufacturing plants to Rabat in Morocco.

Still, I was happy as a bunny rabbit as Economic Development Minister. I felt it was what I was born for. I just loved the interplay with my team of civil servants, and even when I was in the kind of political hot water I had with Airbus I still enjoyed going to work every day. The problem I had with the Airbus A380 project was serious. Airbus and its British partner BAe Systems, who made the wings in Wales, wanted to build a super-jumbo to break Boeing's monopoly on big civil passenger planes. They had come up with the A380, much bigger even than the Boeing 747, 500 seats instead of the 747's 400. Breaking the Boeing monopoly in big planes was important to Airbus, because every airline had to have a jumbo jet element in their suite of planes – and every airline had to have Boeing salesmen in through the door because they were the only guys selling jumbos.

Launching the A380 was a colossal undertaking, financially and logistically. I think the total investment was going to be €11 billion. The French Government was as hugely enthusiastic as the German to fund a big chunk through Repayable Launch Aid – that meant the governments would put in the money which would be repaid out of a levy on each aircraft sold. The Spanish Government was also up for the challenge, so that Spain could continue to make the tail section.

BAe Systems had always built Airbus wings at its sprawling complex at Broughton, six miles west of Chester on the English border. BAe was a partner of Airbus, but still a separate company. It had a 20 per cent share in the Airbus consortium. The company had developed a funding model for their piece of the A380 action, involving a Repayable Launch Aid loan from the UK Government totalling hundreds of millions, combined with a £25 million grant from (you've guessed it) the Welsh Assembly, to be paid via Regional Selective Assistance.

All these applications had to go through the Welsh Industrial Development Advisory Board. My officials were certain that the project didn't fit the scheme

– no additionality. WIDAB agreed with them. I didn't have any power to override that decision, and I'm not sure I would have overridden it anyway. 'No additionality' meant that you couldn't show how the grant would make any difference to where the company located the jobs.

It would have been far simpler to ask the UK Government for more Repayable Launch Assistance, but, instead, we in the Assembly (and me in particular) found ourselves the subject of a vitriolic campaign using the North Wales card. The *Daily Post* was at it hammer and tongs. The trade unions at the plant questioned the use of having a Welsh Assembly if it couldn't come up with £25 million towards the cost of the new A380 wing factory in Broughton. And Ron Davies in his capacity as Chair of the Committee came up with the line that I was showing my naivety in not finding a way of overriding the advice of the WIDAB. From his eighteen months' experience as Secretary of State, he claimed there were ways and means to override that advice.

Of course, the fact was that if we could have justified paying out the £25 million, we would have loved to, simply because the Broughton plant was in northeast Wales, culturally the least empathetic part of Wales towards the whole Welsh devolution project, far more oriented towards Liverpool and Manchester than Cardiff. Another reason for not shifting on the no additionality ergo no RSA grant argument was that the army of lawyers employed by Boeing was always on the lookout for further grounds to prove that Airbus was state subsidised. They were only too keen to haul Airbus and European governments before the World Trade Organisation. If we had bent the rules on RSA, the Boeing army of lawyers would have jumped on us.

I have to give full credit to Alun Michael for backing me all the way during this impasse, despite the bad PR it was giving us in North Wales. The same goes for my Cabinet colleague Tom Middlehurst, whose constituency of Alyn & Deeside was dominated by the wing factory. Once I had explained the RSA rules to Alun, he accepted why we couldn't pay a grant.

So Glenn Massey was called in by my officials to broker a solution. First, he was told that we could find some money, but not via RSA, and it shouldn't be £25 million in case it would look like a fiddle. Second, it shouldn't look as though we had caved in to bullying by the company (or the *Daily Post* for that matter), as we couldn't be seen to be doing a climb-down. Glenn came up with a solution that kept everybody happy, and kept Boeing's lawyers off our backs. The company received a £13 million Building Grant via the WDA towards the hundreds of millions the new factory would cost, and £6 million as a training grant. Everybody happy. With time, I gradually became very matey with the senior directors of BAe Systems, including the Executive Chairman Sir Richard Evans, for whom the adjective 'ebullient' could have been invented. Before he retired, he called me into his head office eyrie in Victoria and, among other things, he explained to me that he was the only one of his many siblings from Caerwys in the Flintshire hills who couldn't speak Welsh as a result of having been parked during the war with an auntie in Blackpool. Even more fascinating industrially, he told how the boss of Boeing, Harry Stonecipher, had once told him over dinner that he wished the Broughton plant in Wales could build the wings for Boeing!

I hadn't anticipated spending so much of my time turning down projects. Largesse would make me and the new Assembly popular, but I kept having to say no. The WDA wanted to pay a £10 million grant towards the costs of a property company asking for yet another bash at redeveloping Swansea central shopping centre. The grant was above the WDA's delegated spending limit, and it required departmental approval. Turning the grant down actually proved popular in Swansea, so strong was the local opposition, and there was no anti-Assembly campaign in the *Evening Post*. Mind you, Swansea shopping centre still hasn't been redeveloped two decades on! The other big scheme that I rejected was in Brymbo, just north-west of Wrexham, where the steelworks had closed fifteen years previously. The application argued that there would be coal recovery and, eventually, a housing and playing fields scheme, but the figures were a mess and we said no. The department was being treated as a soft touch – there were no protests and no campaign in the *Daily Post* on that one.

By the time the A350 project came along a decade later, we were far better prepared for any complexities. We loved the company, and I think the company loved us. No argy-bargy. By then, the psychological shift had happened in how the Airbus wing factory and its workforce saw itself – in 1999, the plant was always known as BAe's Chester factory, but by the mid-2000s it was known as the North Wales factory (or the Flintshire factory, or the Broughton factory). Psychologically speaking, it had become Welsh. The English–Welsh border hadn't moved – the factory was always six miles west of the English border, and the proportion of the workforce commuting daily from England hadn't changed (just below 40 per cent) – it was the psychology that had changed. The plant had a Welsh identity that it never had before, despite the row over the earlier grant rejection.

Looking back at those early months of devolution before I became First Minister, I used to ask myself – and, looking back now, I still ask myself – were we, in the eyes of the Welsh public, cutting the mustard? I don't think we were. The Assembly had, after all, had a breech birth with a wafer-thin majority in the referendum of 1997; then Ron's moment of madness on Clapham Common; then the poisonous nature of the contest between Alun Michael and myself for the Labour leadership after Ron's resignation. Even if we had been led by the Archangel Gabriel, our public approval rating would have struggled to get up to scratch. On top of which, Labour was hamstrung by only having 28 seats out of 60 in the Assembly, and minority governments cannot impose themselves. The three opposition parties could lie in the long grass like tigers waiting to pounce – they had the votes if and when they could combine their strength. On top of which, we suffered from the curse of NAAG.

NAAG was the National Assembly Advisory Group. You might think that NAAG stood for something far more prosaic than that – it had been set up to prepare the Standing Orders for the Assembly in the interval between the Government of Wales Act legislation being passed by Parliament and the Assembly elections in May 1999. The new Assembly Members would be able to change those Standing Orders, but only with a two-thirds majority.

When I later asked the now sorely missed Val Feld, who was a member of NAAG and the AM for Swansea East, how the group had come up with the Standing Orders it wrote for us all, she said, 'Well, we looked at how Parliament operated, and our usual guiding principle was to do the exact opposite!'

As one of the seven ex-MPs who were now AMs, I was always nervous about sounding like a dyed-in-the-wool House of Commons soak, but I did think the diffusion of accountability was quite dangerous. It made us seem like a Boy Scout camp in which we all had a bit of a sing-song around the camp-fire, and then a decision would somehow emerge. Very jolly, but not very effective.

With each Minister being a Member of the Committee that scrutinised his or her work, it was hard for the public to see a clear chain of command and responsibility for decisions. That isn't to say it could never work – it was never going to work for me with Ron being the Chair of the Committee – but with Tom Middlehurst as the Minister for post-16 Education and Cynog Dafis (Plaid Cymru, and another ex-MP) as Chair of that Committee, there was good accord. You could agree a policy on merging colleges of further education and school sixth forms. But such ease of scrutiny was a rarity.

Even worse than the diffusion of responsibility was the procedure for mounting votes of censure against individual Ministers. These votes of censure could not get rid of a Minister, but certainly were means for a free hit against a Minister believed to be unpopular, which might destabilise him or her. I can recall nothing in the Standing Orders that set out the legitimate grounds for a vote of censure. To me, common sense implied that the Minister should have done something pretty bad – lying to the Assembly, or a finding of maladministration by an Assembly Committee against the Minister, for example. In the absence of any guidance, opposition parties could simply gang up and, worse still, it would feed a media expectation that votes of censure (and later votes of no confidence) were what the Welsh Assembly was all about.

The first victim of the vote of censure was Chris Gwyther, the Agriculture Minister. Her appointment had been criticised right from the off because she was a vegetarian and Welsh agriculture was overwhelmingly livestock-based. The grounds for the votes of censure against her were spurious, but the three opposition parties had the votes to pass it. The Labour Group was furious, convinced that Chris had been picked on because she was a woman. The move against her was without a doubt destabilising.

The votes of censure also reminded the three opposition parties that they had another, even bigger weapon, namely the vote of no confidence. Now, the vote of no confidence procedure bequeathed to us by NAAG was the opposite of the vote of censure. A vote of censure just slapped the Minister in the face, but the vote of no confidence got rid of the First Secretary – it couldn't precipitate an election as it would do in Westminster, but it simply took out the First Secretary.

So, Reggie Side was the unelected 61st Member of the Assembly! And Reggie was definitely lurking the corridors of the Assembly that autumn – if the three opposition parties could come up with some *casus belli* as a reason for ganging up, they had the votes to get rid of Alun Michael (but not of the Labour administration). The party in government would then have to come up with an alternative nomination for the top job.

There was a steady build-up of tension between the Alun Michael leadership and the other three parties over the issue of Objective One funding. West Wales and the Valleys constituted almost two-thirds of Wales and, from 1 January 2000, it would qualify for an extra £300 million a year of funding from the European Regional Development Fund for the next seven years. That would be of no use in Wales unless there was match-funding in the shape of extra Public Expenditure (PES) cover from the Treasury – that is, a concession that this extra £300 million a year from Europe would be *in addition* to the normal Barnett Formula funding that Wales received anyway. Previous recipients of Objective One funding had not had any extra PES cover from the Treasury. In the 1993–9 round of Objective One funding, Cornwall, the Highlands and Islands of Scotland, South Yorkshire and Merseyside had all received Objective One funding by their sponsor departments in England and Scotland robbing Peter to pay Paul. In Wales's case, with two-thirds of the country being in the Objective One area, you could not possibly switch money around within the Welsh Barnett Formula total – you would have to rip significant sums out of Education and Health budgets to fund it, which was unthinkable in Wales. The previous Objective One areas had constituted less than 10 per cent of the total population of England or Scotland, but for Wales it was almost two-thirds. With no match-funding, Objective One would be a curse rather than a benefit in Wales.

The people of Wales wanted a promise on all this before January 2000, but the Treasury was unbelievably reluctant to do anything in advance of the Public Expenditure Statement due in the summer of 2000. It remains a mystery to this day as to why Tony Blair wasn't able to influence Gordon Brown to release some kind of letter of comfort that would have defused the issue.

In Tony Blair's autobiography, he refers to me as a 'Brownite', which I most certainly am not – but I wonder whether Blair might have entertained the conspiratorial thought that Gordon Brown refused to act early on the Objective One match-funding issue because, secretly, Gordon wanted me and not Alun to be First Minister. If that were conceivably true, it would be the first I've ever heard of it!

So, these were the principal elements in the build-up to the vote of no confidence against Alun Michael, set for 9 February 2000. The overt reason was match-funding for Objective One; the covert reason was the way the other three parties were gradually building up to a joint operation against Labour Ministers, having developed a taste for it with votes of censure and, then encouraged to combine for the big one, the nuclear option, the vote of no confidence.

The established pattern was that the Tories went first, caring less as they did for the question of damaging the institution itself (the Lib Dems and Plaid Cymru did have a care on that issue – the Assembly and its good name meant a lot to them, but politically they couldn't afford to be outflanked by the Tories either). The Tories on their own had tabled the first censure motion against Chris Gwyther for 15 September. The second censure motion on Chris with the backing of all three parties was down for 19 October. Likewise, the first motion of no confidence against Alun Michael as First Secretary was tabled for 2 November, and again that was the Tories acting alone. As night follows day, you could anticipate that the next motion would have all three opposition parties backing it, and that's what happened on 9 February 2000.

While the Labour Group was united in being scandalised by the attempt to bully Chris Gwyther out of office, there wasn't the same sense of pulling the covered wagons into a circle over the no confidence vote. There were tensions within the Labour Group going back to the Labour leadership election. The leadership team was quite lop-sided in a way – if you just looked at the Cabinet, only Peter Law and Tom Middlehurst had been Alun supporters in the Labour leadership contest. The four Junior Whips and the four Special Advisers really acted as Alun's Praetorian Guard.

The four Special Advisers were absolutely ultra-loyal to Alun, having been appointed by him. Their jobs would disappear the day he left, so they were naturally ultra-loyal. They were Gareth Williams (politics) Andrew Bold (policy), Delyth Evans (speech-writing) and Julie Crowley (press, PR and spin-doctor-in-chief). The back-benchers were fairly evenly divided, some anxious to see Alun move on and out, others anxious for him to stay, and some in the middle.

The Cabinet had evolved a strong team spirit. Although I would have counted most as my supporters back in the 1998–9 leadership contests, it didn't affect our team-bonding. We'd had an away weekend at the Abernant Lake Hotel in Llangammarch Wells, in the heart of Wales, to get to know each other. We'd had an away-half-day at the Rhondda Heritage Park Hotel. Both occasions had gone well, without necessarily achieving a great deal. We all got on, that was the main thing, and we didn't want to be destabilised. But there was obviously trouble brewing in the New Year.

The autumn had brought the Rugby World Cup to Wales, with the final between Australia and France taking place at the brand new Millennium Stadium. Wales didn't do particularly well in terms of rugby, but there was a lot of pride that we could host such a big sporting event. The Queen would be coming to Cardiff to present the winners' and losers' medals, coincidentally on the same day as the results of the Australian Republic Referendum. I did the colour piece for the *Today* programme on the morning of the final, and pointed out that the Australian captain John Eales was a prominent supporter of an Australian Republic. Thus, if Australia won the final and the Queen 'won' the referendum in Australia as well, she could say na-na-na-na-na to John Eales as she handed him the World Cup – but if the republic side won, John Eales might be saying ta-ra to her. Anyway, Australia won, but the Queen doesn't do na-na-na-na-na, and John Eales is the perfect gent anyway.

On that *Today* programme interview, I'd also mentioned that two of the other VIP Royal Box guests would be Lionel Jospin and Tony Blair, the prime ministers of France and of Britain. I'd light-heartedly said how important it was not to get their names mixed in case you ended up calling them Tony Jospin and Lionel Blair! Anyway, the strange thing was that the only booing I can remember during the whole occasion came when the television cameras did a shot at half-time of the two PMs chatting away – whether that was French rugby fans booing Jospin, or British fans booing Blair, I will never know.

Someone else must have been listening to *Today* that morning. My job during the match was to get to the Ford of Europe hospitality box at half-time, to meet the boss of Ford Europe, Nick Scheele. That meant clambering over the rows of seats to enter the Ford box. As I passed the Welsh Water box, I was practically dragged in by a squat little man with a very persuasive heavy Australian accent, desperate to know exactly what lay behind my falling out with Tony Blair. I explained that Blair and I used to get on extremely well ten years before, but that Blair had used and abused all the weight of the Labour Party machinery to block me from winning the leadership in Wales.

As the chap kept asking me more and more questions, I was doing my best to answer. And then suddenly it all came to me – 'Wait a minute, I know who you are, you're Pete the Priest, aren't you?' 'That's right', he said. He was Peter Thompson, the Anglican Christian guru who had had such a massive influence on the young Blair at Oxford, when Thompson was a Rhodes Scholar. As a student, Blair was searching for something – half of him wanted to be a rock star, and half of him wanted to be the Archbishop of Canterbury (or, later on, of course, the Archbishop of Westminster!). Pete the Priest used to lead impressionable young students with a bent towards the church on reading parties at various country houses, designed to see if they really had the vocation.

Anyway, once I figured out who he was, I had some questions for him. He had been a kind of substitute father figure for the future Prime Minister when Blair was particularly vulnerable, having lost his mother Hazel in a very untimely way, on top of the huge stroke his father had had earlier. When Hazel died, the Blair family had been living in Radyr, my home village. Indeed, the Blair residence was next-door to where my old piano teacher Helena Evans lived!

I asked Pete the Priest how well the young Blair had coped with his mother's untimely death, and of his father's ferocious courtship of practically every eligible widow and divorcee within five miles of Radyr to replace Hazel. I wondered if the whole episode had nudged the young Blair into this religious vocation phase. Pete did recall Tony saying his old man was acting a bit strangely vis-à-vis the replacement for Hazel issue. We packed a lot into that five-minute chat. I still don't know why he was so determined to grab and pump me for information on my relationship with the PM – I can't imagine he would have gone to that trouble if he thought Blair was dead right to block me from the leadership in Wales.

While the Rugby World Cup was a welcome diversion and a great opportunity to put Wales on the map, the realities of trying to run Wales with a minority government were ever-present.

The massive hurdle we had to cross that autumn and winter was the 2000–1 Budget. The Finance Minister Edwina Hart negotiated intensively with the Plaid Cymru leader Dafydd Wigley, to see what was needed to get Plaid to support the Assembly's very first Budget – or at least to get Plaid's AMs to sit on their hands and let the Budget pass through.

If we failed to pass the Budget, then a budget could be imposed on us by the Secretary of State and that would be a humiliation. In the end, the Budget went through with the promise of a new cottage hospital for the southern edge of Dafydd Wigley's Arfon constituency, the area of the Llŷn Peninsula around Porthmadog. The cottage hospital and the £20 million or so allocated for it stayed in the Budget – the allocation rolled forward from year to year, because no one could identify a suitable site for the hospital! What wasn't in the Budget was any reference to the vexed issue of match-funding for Objective One. That rumbled on right through the Christmas holidays, and you could sense that the three opposition parties were building up to something.

What could Labour do about it? Alun's Praetorian Guard hatched a plan of sorts. If the vote of no confidence was put down, Labour would make it plain that it would not nominate anyone else for First Secretary. The problem with this as a plan was that the Standing Orders of Assembly required the Cabinet, in the event of a successful vote of no confidence against a First Secretary, to go away and meet and come up with a replacement nomination. So, the Praetorian Guard strategy was to defy the Standing Orders.

Of course, the Standing Orders were bonkers, but could Labour simply defy them? You could see how bonkers they were by the simple fact that the three opposition parties could, in theory, vote out the replacement First Secretary just as easily as they might be able to vote out Alun Michael – indeed, they could run through the entire membership of the Labour Group in twenty-eight successive weeks if they wanted to. That would destroy the Assembly as an institution, but the Standing Orders allowed it. If Alun Michael couldn't get the UK Government to come up with the Objective One money, what was the likelihood that any other First Secretary could do better?

One thing the Standing Orders simply didn't provide for was the Cabinet refusing to nominate anyone as replacement if a First Secretary lost a vote of no confidence. Some Labour back-benchers who had picked up on rumours of the plan to refuse to nominate a replacement, and who had never been convinced about Alun's leadership style anyway, were desperate to meet me.

Two of them – my eventual successor Carwyn Jones (Bridgend) and his close friend John Griffiths (Newport East) – wanted a meeting to express their concerns. This was tricky. It had to be discreet, so we chose the Red Lion pub in Bonvilston. Public enough in a way, but nowhere near Cardiff Bay. Unknown to the media and the chattering classes, it was an old coaching inn on the old Roman road across Glamorgan.

I was in a difficult position. I was happy as Larry doing my job in Economic Development. If Alun were deposed by a vote of no confidence, I might hypothetically be interested in taking over, but not if I was only going to last a week before Reggie Side struck me down as well. No thank you.

I told Carwyn and John to hold their horses – there had been no discussion in Cabinet about the plan to refuse to nominate a replacement candidate for First Secretary if Alun fell. That strategy certainly didn't seem workable to me, because the Standing Orders were so clear. The Cabinet would be obliged to come up with another name. I told them to keep their cool, because the issue was bound to come up before the Labour Group, if and when the threatened motion of no confidence was tabled with the support of all three opposition parties. The two of them seemed very het-up coming into the pub, but by the time Carwyn and John left they seemed reassured that there was no Cabinet plan to mount a putsch against the Standing Orders.

Their state of mind showed how difficult it was to manage a divided Labour Group. That unenviable job fell to Andrew Davies, the Business Manager and Chief Whip. The Chief Whip's job involves using every legal trick in the book to get the government's business through, and even more so to keep the government in existence. It also means very occasionally having to tell the boss

– namely, in this instance, Alun – that the party is not willing to march in the direction he wants.

When the motion of no confidence was eventually tabled for debate on Wednesday, 9 February 2000, it did indeed have the signatures of the three opposition parties. So the balloon had gone up. Alun would in all probability be voted out. Although it hadn't been discussed or mooted in Cabinet, the little circle around Alun swung into action. They persuaded Ann Jones (Vale of Clwyd), to issue a press release in her capacity as Labour Group Chair claiming that the Labour Group was totally and unanimously in support of Alun's leadership, and that its support would continue whatever happened in the vote on the following Wednesday.

Those like Carwyn and John were furious that this press release went out in the Labour Group's name, without any discussion having taken place within the Group. The Chief Whip was now in an impossible position – Alun wasn't in a good position either. His senior Special Adviser and strategist Gareth Williams, and his Principal Private Secretary Lawrence Conway, were in Edinburgh. They came back as quickly as possible. Alun discussed with Gareth how to put into action the plan for Labour to hold the line against making any other nomination – they also thought that a final effort should be made to appeal to the Lib Dems, the one opposition party that might be persuaded to haul off the dogs.

Andrew Davies and Edwina Hart asked to meet me covertly on the Sunday, as the Group was in danger of splintering. It was the Red Lion in Bonvilston again. Well, it was a nice pub and it was on their way home to Swansea! They told me that I must keep my head down, which was fine by me – I had no intention of sticking my head above any parapet.

The next day, I was out walking the dog in Michaelston-le-Pit when I bumped into the Assembly's Presiding Officer (equivalent of the Speaker at Westminster), Lord Dafydd Elis-Thomas, who had rented a house in the hamlet two hundred yards from ours. I invited him over to my house that night for some curry leftovers – I wanted to see how the land lay.

Dafydd was delighted to come over – although not so delighted about the curry leftovers, I suspect. He said that the vote of no confidence would have to proceed. It was technically in order, and there were no possible grounds for ruling it out of order. I nudged the discussion around to the hypothetical issue of what he would do if (a) Alun were voted out, (b) I took over, and then (c) a vote of no confidence in me was put down the following week (the latter a very likely possibility, I guessed, as no match-funding would be forthcoming from Westminster).

Dafydd responded that such a second motion would be clearly vexatious and that it would bring the Assembly into disrepute. It would be an abuse of the Standing Orders. He said that his primary concern was to protect the good name of the Assembly, and that he would rule a second motion out of order.

All very statesmanlike and logical and well thought through. Then Dafydd spoilt it all by saying, with a sly wink, 'And you're the one the people of Wales wanted in the first place anyway!' I might have agreed with him on that, but it was not his job to say it! He could think it privately and it was very convenient for me, but he shouldn't say it. At one extreme, you could suggest that the Presiding Officer, himself a Plaid Cymru Assembly Member, was arrogating to himself the right to choose the Labour leader. One motion of no confidence to dispose of Alun Michael is in order, while a hypothetical second motion of no confidence against Rhodri Morgan is vexatious and out of order.

When the Labour Group met on the Tuesday morning, all hell broke loose. The Chief Whip Andrew Davies announced that the press release purporting to show that the Labour Group would die in the last ditch for Alun's leadership to continue, regardless of the vote of no confidence, should never have gone out. All future press releases issued by the Chair of the Group in the Group's name first had to be approved by him. There was a sharp intake of breath around the table. Here was the Chief Whip blowing a hole in the strategy of sticking with Alun come what may. Yes, that was part of his job because it was the only way to stop the Labour Group from splintering, but from that moment on Andrew was considered a traitor to the cause by the Praetorian Guard. The Group never even got to discuss the strategy of refusing to nominate a replacement, if the vote of no confidence in Alun succeeded.

Alun did ask Andrew Davies to approach the Presiding Officer on the Tuesday afternoon to inform him that Labour wasn't going to nominate a replacement. The Presiding Officer, Dafydd Elis-Thomas, was adamant that he could not accept Labour re-nominating Alun if the vote of no confidence passed as that would clearly be contrary to the Standing Orders.

When Andrew got back to Alun's room to report what the Presiding Officer had said, the Special Adviser responsible for PR and press, Julie Crowley, came into the room and started shouting at him – Andrew demanded that Alun get his Special Adviser to stop screaming at him – Andrew was only doing his job – but for the group around Alun, the Chief Whip was now a dead man walking.

Indeed, later that afternoon, ITV Wales's chief political reporter Jo Kiernan (and much later Carwyn Jones's Chief Special Adviser) asked Andrew Davies whether he was about to be sacked. He would more than likely have been, but for an intervention by Cardiff North AM Sue Essex (as an AM, Sue was outside the Cabinet but a figure who commanded huge respect).

By Tuesday teatime, I think Alun and his team of advisers had pretty well given up on the idea of Labour re-nominating Alun if the vote of no confidence were lost. They turned their attention to seeking the help of No. 10.

At Alun's request, Tony Blair invited the leader of the Liberal Democrats Charles Kennedy for a cosy chat in No. 10 on that same evening. According to Charles

Kennedy, he received quite a few of those invitations, usually when the PM needed Lib Dem help. If it wasn't terribly important, then Charles would be firmly told, 'Terribly sorry, Charles, but Cherie absolutely cannot stand the smell of cigarette smoke around No. 10.' If the favour needed was a bit more substantial, Blair would allow Charlie a few discreet fags. If Blair was desperate for Lib Dem help, as he was on this Tuesday, the PM would practically light the cigarette for Charles and hunt down a choice of ashtrays for his approval! Then down to business. Could Charles persuade the six Welsh Lib Dems to abstain on the vote of no confidence against Alun Michael? Charles had to turn him down – ashtray or no ashtray. He explained to the PM that the Lib Dems were an ultra-democratic and fully federal party, that he had no influence and that the six AMs would do whatever they chose to do.

What the Lib Dem Group of Six did do at around seven that evening was hold a meeting at Crickhowell House, the Assembly building, just the six AMs and the Group Secretary Mike Hines. At the same time, Alun Michael invited the Secretary of State Paul Murphy and me to his room on the top floor of Crickhowell House, along with Gareth Williams. It was in one way slightly odd for him to invite me to be at his side on that fateful evening – Mills & Boon potboiler writers love that word 'fateful', but it was certainly apposite on that evening, which might quite possibly be Alun's last as First Secretary.

I'm not sure if he suspected that if I was at home, or roaming free in the political ether, my supporters might be trying to get messages through to the Lib Dem Group to sit tight on the vote of no confidence. Perhaps, as is most likely, he realised that his period as First Secretary was coming to an end, and that I was his probable and natural successor. Hard to say for sure.

The arrangement with the Lib Dems was that Gareth Williams would text Mike Hines every half hour or so to check if there were any developments. After each exchange of texts, Gareth would go to the second floor and Mike Hines would emerge from the Group conclave. The two of them would chat for a couple of minutes, then Mike would go back in and Gareth would return to the fifth floor and report to Alun, Paul and me.

Sometime around eight o'clock, after another two fruitless forays by Gareth down in the lift, Paul Murphy couldn't stand the tension any more and suggested we should all have a drink – 'It will help pass the time, and at this rate we could be here all night!' Alun said he was sure there were a couple of bottles in the First Secretary's drinks cabinet – he produced a bottle of white from the fridge and red from the cabinet, and then revealed that he had no idea where the corkscrew was! Paul and I collapsed laughing, and Paul chipped in, 'Well, I certainly know where the corkscrew is in my office!' Off went Paul to hunt down the corkscrew from beyond the atrium dividing the two wings of the building. He was soon back and we had a couple of glasses of wine while Gareth Williams, duly texted Mike Hines and popped down to see what was happening.

Alun, Paul and I chatted about everything and nothing. The three of us had shared an office at Old Palace Yard when we were first elected as MPs in 1987, and had no problem finding things to natter about. The tense one in our company was Gareth Williams, of course, which was not totally surprising – if Alun was out of office the following day, Gareth would be out of a job too.

Was there ever actually a chance that the Lib Dem Group of Six would throw Alun that precious lifeline? Were all these mini-meetings between Gareth Williams and Mike Hines outside the Lib Dem Group office just a charade? I knew that the personal relationship between the leader of the Lib Dem Group, Mike German, and Alun was pretty dreadful, going back to their time together (though personally very far apart) on Cardiff City Council.

I had never served on Cardiff City Council. I'd hardly ever been in the Members Room, but most ex-and serving Cardiff councillors developed a certain comradeship that overrode party affiliations, a kind of Members Room masonry. But not so with Alun and Mike – there was always a nasty edge to their confrontations across the Assembly Chamber floor. Whether it was actually true (as some alleged) that it was Alun who passed on some gossip to Georgette, Mike's first wife who was also a councillor at the time, which eventually led to their divorce, I have no way of knowing. At around nine o'clock, back came Gareth from yet another quickie meeting with Mike Hines, to tell us the Lib Dem Group had gone out for a curry. So that was that! It was how Alun Michael's period as First Secretary effectively came to an end – the Lib Dems went out for a curry, while Alun, Paul and I went home.

The following day, the motion of no confidence in Alun took precedence over all other business. It was quite unlike the votes of no confidence against the Callaghan Labour Government in 1977 and 1979 – success in those motions precipitated a general election. In the Assembly, it was different. Reggie Side could wield the axe, but the Labour Government would carry on. It was a totally crazy procedure.

The three opposition party leaders launched their attack on Alun for his failure to procure match-funding for Objective One. When it finally came to Alun's turn to respond, he didn't have any rabbit to pull out of his hat – no last-minute letter of comfort had arrived from Gordon Brown promising the millions required – Alun was as angry as I have ever seen him. Strangely, a lot of his anger was directed at the Presiding Officer, presumably for failing to rule the motion of no confidence out of order. Alun did produce half a rabbit out of his hat, though, right at the end, by declaiming that he wasn't going to hang about waiting for the vote – he was resigning.

With that, he bunched up his speech notes and threw them at the Presiding Officer. Fortunately, they fell well short. Dafydd Elis-Thomas, the intended target, then quickly consulted the Chief Clerk, before announcing that, resignation or not, the vote would have to proceed. It duly did, and although Alun had by now left the Chamber, the vote went against him.

Business was then suspended for an hour while the remaining Cabinet Members trooped upstairs to the fifth floor for a well-earned cup of tea, to be followed by a discussion of what to do next. On the way up in the lift, Tom Middlehurst and Peter Law, Alun's two main supporters in the Cabinet, collared the Business Manager Andrew Davies to suggest that he should be interim nominee as First Secretary – effectively, the last roll of the dice by the Stop Rhodri movement. Andrew was very firm with the two of them, however, that the nominee had to be me.

When the Cabinet did reconvene, there wasn't much discussion. Andrew Davies nominated me, and Tom Middlehurst seconded it. That was how he, Andrew Davies as Business Manager, was able to announce to the full Assembly after the hour-long tea break, that I was the Cabinet's unanimous choice to be the new First Secretary. The job sort of fell into my lap.

I think it would have been very different if Wayne David had not been defeated in the Rhondda constituency the previous year. By February 2000, Wayne's defeat seemed an age ago, and it just seemed to be accepted by everyone on the Labour side that I was the natural choice – an assumption that even seemed to include all those who had worked so hard to keep me out of the job in 1998 and 1999. Even the Labour establishment now seemed to want me to take over. If ever proof were needed for the old adage 'Three tries for a Welshman', then here it was!

There was a brief hiatus between being nominated as interim Labour First Secretary and becoming the real thing the following Tuesday. Welsh Labour rules meant that I had to be approved by the Welsh Executive Committee, where most of the machinations of the Stop Rhodri movement had taken place. But not any more. The Stop Rhodri movement had simply evaporated, and I was now welcomed with open arms by those who had gone to inordinate lengths to stop me. Under their emergency procedure, I was approved as the only nomination by the Labour Cabinet and the Labour Group of AMs. There were no whispers from anyone that the three opposition parties might combine their 31 votes to block me when the full and final nomination would be put before the Assembly.

While the Welsh Executive did all the necessary confirmation for my nomination, I took possession of the fifth floor – the First Secretary's room, which was huge because it doubled as the Cabinet Room. During earlier Cabinet meetings, I had noticed there was a water stain on the ceiling – we were on the top floor. There was obviously a roof leak. The building was being rented from Grosvenor Waterside, the property arm of Associated British Ports, and Crickhowell House had been built as a kickstarter for the Cardiff Bay project, developed for a public sector client in the hope that the private sector would follow suit. Crickhowell House is an L-shaped building. The Assembly side was all in the west-facing arm of the L, and the Secretary of State's side was all in the south-facing arm. John Redwood, in his time as Secretary of State for Wales in 1992–4, had grouped together some NHS back-office functions into a quango, and plonked them into the then new building. When the Assembly came along, this quango (with its eight hundred-odd civil servants) was broken up to make way for us. Not a very elevating story, but the least that Grosvenor Waterside could have done was to provide a roof for the fifth floor that didn't leak, where the First Secretary might be expected to entertain potential inward investors.

I knew some of the quango staff, who had warned me that Crickhowell House was a truly bog-standard building. They were right. The owners had made several desultory efforts to fix the water leak, but it kept coming back. I read the Riot Act, exercising my full authority as First Minister for the very first time, over a leaking roof. The faulty roof tile was duly fixed, and the water stain never came back during my ten years there. Nevertheless, it didn't feel right that we were in hock in this way to a private landlord that you had to beg to fix the leaking roof above the Cabinet Room. Governments should never be in such a position.

The jobs of Special Advisers depend entirely on the discretion of the First Secretary. When Alun resigned on the Wednesday, the four Special Advisers had their passes to access fifth floor unceremoniously withdrawn. Of course, I could have chosen to reappoint one or two of them, but most of my Cabinet colleagues thought the four Special Advisers had acted too much as a palace guard around Alun and had thrown their weight around in trying to protect his and their jobs. They came as a package anyway, and it would have been invidious to choose one for re-appointment at the expense of the other.

Alun's resignation affected not only his office as First Secretary, but as Regional AM for Mid & West Wales too. This had the strange effect of catapulting one of the four Special Advisers, Delyth Evans, Alun's speech-writer, into the Assembly as the replacement Regional AM for Mid & West Wales. Under the regional list type of PR we had adopted in Wales, instead of a by-election on the resignation or death of a regional AM, the next name on the party's list at the previous election is automatically promoted. And it was Delyth who had been second on the Labour list in Mid & West Wales.

Alun simply disappeared from view. He was still an MP, as indeed I was, and he returned to the back-benches in the House of Commons. The next time I cast eyes on him was two weeks later at St Woolo's Cathdral in Newport, when Rowan Williams was being inaugurated as the Archbishop of Wales. The process to inaugurate an archbishop for the Church in Wales is different to the Church of England. In England, if a bishop becomes an archbishop, then that bishop moves to York or Canterbury. In Wales, on the other hand, if a bishop becomes an archbishop, he doesn't not have to leave his diocese. Rowan Williams was Bishop of Monmouth, and became Archbishop of Wales without having to leave Monmouth.

Anyway, as I approached St Woolo's after closing my Saturday morning surgery, it was a little embarrassing to find Alun sitting next to the Secretary of State Paul Murphy in the front row. Alun was in my seat, the usher whispered to me, so another seat had to be found for me in the second row. I wouldn't have missed a Rowan Williams sermon for anything, with its usual coruscating warnings to all holders of powerful offices of the perils of power going to your head and so forth. Of course, he was not Archbishop of Wales for long before Tony Blair pulled him across the border to Canterbury – I don't think he was ever happy in that job – temperamentally, Rowan was far more suited to running a disestablished church, as in Wales, than an established one, as in England.

I don't remember feeling any elation at the prospect of becoming First Secretary in the formal and full meeting of the Assembly that came after the long weekend. I had no doubts that I could do the job – I wouldn't have run twice for the vacancy if I didn't think I could do it – but it was simply the minority position that the Labour administration was in. How long would I last?

Despite the earlier vaguely encouraging words from the Presiding Officer that he wouldn't accept vexatious motions of no confidence, I wasn't sure the three opposition parties would be able to hold back now that they had tasted blood. Why should they, given that I could do very little about the Objective One match-funding issue. I rationalised the whole situation by saying that if I lasted a week, I lasted a week; if I lasted a month, I lasted a month; if I got a year in the job, that'd be pretty good. I would be reliant, in effect, on the presumption that Plaid Cymru and the Lib Dems would have sufficient regard for making devolution a success that they would not be over-keen to make common cause with the Tories again.

My message to the Assembly in accepting the full nomination on the Tuesday was not very high-flown with rhetoric about missions and visions. My priority was stabilising the ship and providing good government. Tony Blair rang me that evening to congratulate me – he was so friendly you would think he'd been my greatest backer in the two leadership contests. He said that my opposite number in Scotland, Donald Dewar, rang him every three or four weeks to chew the fat and that he'd be happy to find the time to do the same with me.

Another striking thing about that conversation with Blair was his assumption that we would immediately be moving to a coalition with the Lib Dems (as was the case in Scotland, of course). Where did that come from? Did Blair just assume that the Scottish way of doing things had to be the right way, and that Wales should follow suit? In which case, had he pressed the same idea on Alun Michael to enter into coalition with the Lib Dems back in 1999, after our initial elections? And had Alun offered such a deal to Mike German and been rebuffed? Or could it have been the other way around? It could all have come from Roy Jenkins, of course. The early noughties were the Roy Jenkins years in the Blair premiership

– Blair met regularly with Roy Jenkins back then to discuss electoral reform and the realignment of the left to combine against the right, and so forth.

Then again, it could have been that Blair didn't want any more drama from Wales – enough Welsh *Sturm und Drang* already! Couldn't blame him really, after all, when Alun had resigned the previous Wednesday it had happened at around three in the afternoon, just as PMQs was starting. The Tories had picked it up off their Blackberries, and Blair was totally blind-sided, which was verging on humiliation for him.

Anyway, once we did sign a coalition arrangement with the Lib Dems in October of that year, we had only travelled eight months down the track, but it seemed to be in a different century.

# seven

# Earning Respect
# 2000–2003

SETTLING IN AS FIRST MINISTER involved a lot of almost domestic duties. I quickly got to know my private office, and they got to know my habits – that meant my constant need for coffee to get going, especially in the morning. But more important than the coffee was my computer illiteracy. Everything would have to be in paper form – the office had just got used to Alun Michael being a computer whizz and, though I wasn't exactly a computer Luddite, I was far from mastering the technology.

Les, my driver, a key member of the First Minister's team had driven for Alun, and for Ron Davies before him. For years after giving up being a Cardiff taxi driver, Les had driven for the late Wyn Roberts (MP for Conwy, then Baron Roberts of Conwy), the longest serving Minister in the Thatcher and John Major era. I explained to Les that I worked pretty long hours, but I was not a world-class workaholic like Alun. I wanted to be in the office by nine in the morning, not eight, and I explained that I had no problem doing a big box of letters and reading material, but nobody should expect emails from me at two in the morning!

One thing I did have in common with Alun was that I was a stickler for good flowing grammatical English in the letters going out in my name, with bureaucratic stiffness avoided. Whereas Alun had seen every letter before it went out from any Minister, I told them to discontinue that practice – I was going to trust the Minsters to tweak their own letters. My private office could pass it on to all the other private offices the message about sounding less bureaucratic, but sticking to proper grammar.

The only letters going out from other Ministers that I wanted to see were the ones with wider policy implications, and it was up to my private office to work out the best way of being aware of what was a standard ministerial letter and one that had wider implications. I was definitely not reading all those letters – that was a definite no-no!

Everybody seemed happy with these changes and Les, the driver, did confide that my style of working was going to be good for his health. Not only had he picked my predecessor up at 7:40 am every day, to chauffeur him in from Penarth to the Bay, but Les had then routinely been kept waiting in the drivers' room until nine in the evening. Alun would very often call him mid-evening to ask him to nip over for two of Harry Ramsden's best – one fish and chip portion was for Alun, and one for Les. One of the consequences was that Les thought he'd put on three stone since this habit set in.

I asked if we could freshen up the First Secretary's room – I was going to spend a lot of time in there, and it bore the heavy imprint of Alun's home background. In other words, all the paintings on the walls were by Kyffin Williams. One Kyffin was enough – six was too depressing. I wanted a bit more variety, and I got a selection of portraits and industrial landscapes to offset the one Kyffin.

What officialdom wanted from me, in the meantime, was a public address, a speech to the masses of civil servants whose morale had collapsed and pride of working for the shiny new institution of the Welsh Assembly was at a low ebb. Most of the civil servants wished they were back working at the old Welsh Office. Permanent Secretary Sir Jon Shortridge was very keen that I address a mass meeting of as many of them as could safely be gathered together in the public foyer and stairwell at Cathays Park.

So my address was timed for two o'clock on my first Thursday in office. At about half past one, I developed a splitting headache and I felt totally stressed out – I had never expected anything like this. There were stress hormones coursing around my brain and body. I told Anna and Rose, my two Private Secretaries, that the speech to the assembled thousands of civil servants would have to be called off. 'If looks could kill' – they might have been looking *through* me – and I risked letting everybody down. They told me that civil servants from the out-stations were already on their way to Cathays Park to hear my speech, so it was next to impossible to call the whole thing off. I got the message – splitting headache or no, I had to go through with it.

'Okay', I said, 'can you get me two aspirins and a cup of tea?' They duly supplied them and I gulped down the aspirins with the tea, stole a ten-minute power nap on the office settee, and thank goodness for that settee. I slept like a baby. The headache disappeared. Les drove me up to Cathays Park and it was an amazing sight to see more than fifteen hundred civil servants filling the entire foyer and all around the first floor.

Bull by the horns as ever, I tried to grapple straight away with the low morale issue. I essayed a joke about it. I told them I knew, as things stood, that nobody wanted to boast about working for the Welsh Assembly. If your mother was chatting to her neighbour and she asked her what you, the son or daughter, was doing now, your mother would probably say something like, 'Oh, he's a piano-player in a brothel!'

They all seemed to enjoy or at least understand the joke, and I fell back on the fact that coming from a similar background I was also 'one of them'. Some of the older ones might actually remember me from my time as a civil servant thirty years previously, and I saw a handful of the greyer heads nodding. What I was really trying to get across was that I was going to lead them, I was going to try to establish the authority of the government and make it respected and loved by the people of Wales. Most importantly, I didn't want the gap, the dreaded three-mile-wide gap between us Ministers in the Bay and officials in Cathays Park, to cause problems. We were going to provide scandal-free effective government for Wales, which would transform the way the public thought of devolution. That mass assembling of Assembly civil servants, I'm glad to say, now still continues, at the beginning of each Assembly term – although, mercifully, the piano-player in the brothel joke is now redundant. I don't know if this mass meeting with the civil service has been tried in Edinburgh or in Stormont, but it is now a Welsh fixture.

Becoming First Secretary struck home in many ways in those initial days and weeks. I realised that I wasn't going to have the time to continue jogging three or four times a week. Jogging had been a part of my life for almost half a century, and apart from when Julie and I had three very young children very close together, with all the sleep deprivation that followed, I had always run or jogged. It was part of me. I was sixty when I took up the reins of government, and I was certainly slowing down. My joints were achier than ever before, and I simply didn't think I would have the time to run any more. Looking back, that was probably a big mistake.

If I wasn't going to be jogging any more, I would need to be more disciplined about walking the dog. Well, I took my dog for our first walk along the lanes around Michaelston-le-Pit on the Tuesday night after being voted in as First Secretary. I had lived on the edge of the hamlet for sixteen years. Even by the year 2000, the agricultural character of the village was being watered down and replaced by a more suburban feel – the cowmen and farmhands who had been the backbone of the place for aeons had now retired. There were no young farmhands around.

A curious but very revealing thing happened on that walk, which was the first I had taken as head of the Government of Wales. One of the retired cowmen was also out walking his dog – I'd seen him around the lanes for years, hundreds of times, with and without our dogs, and we'd always exchanged pleasantries. This time he said 'Noswaith dda' to me, which is 'Good evening' in Welsh – and you could have knocked me down with a feather. Clouded by assumptions about the

Anglo-Norman Vale of Glamorgan, I had absolutely no idea he spoke Welsh, but he'd obviously decided that since I was now head honcho in Wales it was time to start speaking to me in Welsh! We got chatting, and it turned out that he was a native of Capel Bangor, a very Welsh-speaking village north of Aberystwyth on the road to Machynlleth. He had been transferred to Michaelston during the war under the Direction of Labour scheme, when Britain was desperate to increase the production of milk. Having always conversed together only in English up until then, we always spoke in Welsh after that until he passed away. Something relating to the Welsh identity issue had clearly clicked in his mind on the day of my election as First Secretary.

The following night, I had a previously agreed booking to speak to the Institute of Welsh Affairs at the prestigious Temple of Peace, right next-door to our Cathays Park main office complex. The Institute is Wales's best-known think tank, where the audience would normally be just a handful of think-tank groupies and lecture tasters. Now the media and others were there in droves to check me out.

I spoke on Welsh devolution pretty fluently and without any notes for about forty-five minutes. I was pleased that the audience was rapt in attention – not so pleased in the reporting of it. That is to say, there wasn't any. No written copy supplied in advance. No spin doctors bigging up the key points. Therefore, no coverage. Too damn difficult to pick out the bones. I just had to accept that there was a huge penalty from my style of public address without notes. I preferred eye contact with the audience to using a written text and advance spinning by a team of press officers. Anyway, my eyesight had deteriorated to the point that I couldn't look at a text in front of me and make eye contact with the audience – I could have tried bifocals, but didn't really want to go down that road. It seemed I would just have to accept that my speeches wouldn't get reported, however good or bad the content.

On top of my stubbornness in not providing written texts of my speeches, there was another issue. Around the year 2000, most journalists stopped going to meetings to actually listen to politicians' speeches – now they just sat in front of computer screens all day long. I was about twenty years too late with my idiosyncratic style of speaking without notes, but I wasn't going to change my modus operandi. Until my Clear Red Water speech at Swansea University in November 2002, I never worked off a written script with odd bits and key phrases supplied in advance to the media by spin doctoring. Even then, I wandered off-script and never reached the much-spun Clear Red Water part of the speech! Still, the intention was there.

By the Thursday of that first week, I was getting pretty knackered. Again, there was a previously agreed booking to address the Pontrhydyfen Welsh Society – Cymdeithas Gymraeg Pontrhydyfen. Les, the driver, was keen to go because he had an old friend living in the village, and I agreed not to pull out. How glad I was that I did stick to the booking – or the 'gig', in popular parlance – they had gone to so much trouble to prepare for my visit.

Pontrhydyfen is eight miles north of Port Talbot, so less than an hour from Cardiff. It's famous worldwide as the home village of Richard Burton – or Richard Jenkins, 'Rich' as he was always known in the village. Actually, Pontrhydyfen is also famous in Wales because it has kept a strong Welsh culture, perhaps stronger than most South Wales industrial villages, and one of the key movers and shakers in Cymdeithas Gymraeg Pontrhydyfen had written an englyn, a four-line poem in strict metre, in my honour.

After the poem had been read out and I'd made my speech, we all sat down for a traditional Welsh supper at a scrubbed long wooden table. I sat among members of Richard Burton's family. On my way home in the car, I mused that when Tony Blair became Prime Minister three years previously, had he ever enjoyed that experience of a poem being written in his honour. As with my conversation with the retired cowman in Michaelston-le-Pit, it was the special Welsh character of Wales that struck home. Maybe there was something called Welsh identity, after all – it hadn't emerged in the referendum on devolution but, beneath the surface, it was there.

While I was still trying to come to terms with the demands of the job, the dreaded New Building Project reared its ugly head. I needed time to think about that little conundrum, but time was in short supply. In that first fortnight of me being First Secretary, my officials wanted my written authority to issue a cheque for one million pounds as a progress payment to the Richard Rogers Partnership.

I have to admit, I was not a big fan of the Richard Rogers Senedd design. It didn't look like the centre of devolved government to me – it looked too much like a Tesco hypermarket. On top of that, it made no allowances for the micro-climate of Cardiff Bay with its occasionally ferocious south-westerlies whipping in from Penarth Head. And, above all, it was three miles – three miles too far for my taste – from Cathays Park, the Welsh Whitehall in the civic centre, which had been practically sitting there for a century waiting for the Welsh Westminster to arrive.

I was reluctant to issue the million pound cheque because, once I did it, even though it was only a progress payment, I would then be committed to the whole Richard Rogers building as well. I didn't know if there was any alternative available, but I just needed to pause and examine the possibilities. The civil servant in charge of the building project nearly had a fit when I told him I wasn't going to authorise issuing the cheque – he just about told me that I couldn't do that, it was too late to go back, and we would be in breach of our contract with our landlords, Associated British Ports (ABP) via their property subsidiary Grosvenor Waterside.

The deal that Ron Davies had agreed in 1998 was that the rent on the interim HQ Crickhowell House would be kept low provided the future Assembly committed to a new HQ building on the adjoining site. ABP would then be able to recover its loss on the low rent through the enhanced capital values of all the land surrounding the new Assembly building. We were the anchor tenant in an urban regeneration scheme, but the whole idea gave me the creeps. *Ychafi!* Completely undignified for a newly-created and elected devolved government to be pawns in a property play – far too banana republic for my way of thinking.

But whatever my moral and practical objections, I was perhaps too late to stop it. The officials in charge of the project insisted that if there was to be a pause, we had to forestall ABP being in a position to sue us for breach of contract. I didn't know the chairman personally, but at least I knew his name, a Swede called Bo Lerenius. The building project team was having kittens about setting up the phone call, but I told them to relax – the Swedes were all good democrats, and they would realise they were dealing with an elected government and not with run-of-the-mill commercial property clients. Bo Lerenius would understand. I couldn't get over the attitude of my civil servants who thought we were in hock to ABP – I told them we were a government and I was the head of it.

In the event, Bo Lerenius was as nice as pie and understood the situation perfectly. If I needed time, I could have it. We chatted about my month-long stay in Sweden in 1955 in the southern province of Skane (recently made famous worldwide by the popular *Wallander* series of books and television programmes).

The biggest question was whether there was any way of reactivating what had been the original Cardiff City Hall option for the Assembly. Being only three hundred yards from Cathays Park where all our officials worked, it was undoubtedly the best location, not too close and not too far. The legislature on one side of the park and the executive branch of government on the other, it was ideal, except that negotiations to buy City Hall from Cardiff City Council had completely broken down in 1998.

Even the threat that the entire Welsh Assembly set-up could go to Swansea instead of Cardiff hadn't moved the regime at City Hall. Ron Davies tried everything, working via the District Valuer to try to set a price for the estate that gave something to the Council and to the incoming Welsh Assembly, but it was almost impossible to put a value on City Hall once the project team had decided that the Council Chamber couldn't be used for the Assembly Chamber.

Ron had tried negotiating with Council Leader Russell Goodway, with his Permanent Secretary Rachel Lomax and the Council's chief executive present – Ron had even tried just him and Goodway in a room together, just two Labour politicians trying to hammer out a deal. I knew that if Ron couldn't do a deal with the Council leadership, it was even less likely that I could. My only hope was that the Council had maybe eighteen months of a cooling-off period, since the breakdown of negotiations, and I'd give them a few more months with the hint that, if there was any movement, then I was open for a deal.

One of the fundamental difficulties was that the Council Chamber was too small and unsuitable without alteration. But it was also incredibly beautiful, and Grade 1 Listed. It was full of history, couldn't be altered, and was therefore discounted for its suitability to be the new Assembly Chamber. The public gallery was far too small for a transparent new democracy; likewise, you couldn't fit new technology into the seating of the Council Chamber. The new Assembly was expecting to go paperless and to be as high-tech and electronic as possible, and therefore the brand new Chamber would have to be dropped in on the north side of the foyer. Then, as soon as you took out the cost of that new chamber, you would have to net the cost off the valuation that you could afford to pay for the City Hall – which left almost nothing for the City Council to build itself alternative accommodation.

On the City Council leadership side, there was very little appetite for devolution at all – a case of this town ain't big enough for both of us. If the Assembly was there in Cardiff, it would mean another bunch of politicians taking away the oxygen of publicity from the Council leaders. So, I was caught between a rock and a hard place. There was no approach from the City Council, and I wasn't going begging. We'd have to go back to trying to think of cheaper ways of building the new Assembly on the ABP site, and the alternative proposals on that site, including building over the car park, were very problematic.

No less problematic, as it turned out, was the Richard Rogers building itself. It didn't function as a magnet for other office blocks to be built next-door, so ultimately I don't think the whole anchor tenant idea worked for ABP. The entire package was eventually sold off to Aviva, the insurance and pension fund giant. I don't think there was any urban regeneration gain in the long run for the public or private sectors, and the whole thing was a shambles, but I'd come into it too late to be able to come up with a cost-effective alternative. I had to recognise the limits of the powers of the First Secretary.

The problem with the new building only emerged when we bought the pause to an end, and told the Richard Rogers Partnership to crack on with it. The tenders for the first work packages came in spot on, as per the quantity surveyors' predicted prices. So, they covered the groundworks. So far, so good.

A few months later, the tenders came in for the first phase of superstructure work packages for the walls, floors and the roof. But, horror of horrors, they were double and treble the quantity surveyors' estimates, which were anyway for much bigger sums than the groundworks.

Edwina Hart and I went through everything with the project team. The explanation for the bids being so high was that the sub-contractors were including a substantial sum for designing the walls and so on, not just in the construction. All these details were meant to have been there in the design specifications supplied to the potential bidders, but evidently the contractors tendering for the work didn't think the detailed design had been done. Should that have been the responsibility of the Richard Rogers Partnership, or of the structural engineers Ove Arup?

I had a mole inside Arup's, a Labour activist who was also a structural engineer of high talent. He wasn't working on the Assembly building himself, but knew everything going on in Arup's Cardiff office.

Ove Arup is one of the most prestigious structural engineering consultancies in the world. When a construction project gets into difficulties on the design work, you normally sack the structural engineers and call in Arup's. But what are you supposed to do when Arup's are already your structural engineers? That's when you could run into really serious problems.

According to my mole, the Arup team had not been able to solve the problem of all the wavy lines in the Richard Rogers design – I was told that they couldn't find a way of fixing the walls to the roof, and the floor plates to the walls. All the sub-contractors wanted the kudos of working on a prestige project like this, but they didn't want to go bankrupt in the process, and that was why they were putting in high bids to include an allowance for finishing the detailed design, as well as for the construction. So, against this backdrop, we felt we had to sack Richard Rogers.

We might comfort ourselves with the thought that, as bad as our new Assembly building project was going, I never felt it ran as completely out of control as the new Scottish Parliament project did (which finished up at a cost of £426 million). I still thought of the problems over our new building as a second-order issue. A bigger problem was how to nurse devolution from being the sickly child that it was into a government commanding authority. We were still too close to being the talking shop that the anti-devolution campaigners had predicted – we were unstable, subject to the threat of motions of censure against Ministers and votes of no confidence against me.

The press and public in Wales had become so used to seeing these kinds of procedural antics as being the highlights of what went on down in the Assembly that expectations had grown that devolution amounted to little more. I wanted us to think more governmental, to sound more governmental, and to act more governmental – I wanted to see to see if I could get more of a divide between the legislature in Cardiff Bay and the actual work of governing Wales. The heart of governing Wales had to be in Cathays Park, with the heart of the scrutiny process taking place in the Bay.

I tried as much as possible to get my Ministers to change their focus and normal place of work from the Bay to the Park. That was impossible when the Assembly was sitting, of course, but the Assembly only sat on Tuesdays and Wednesdays, and then only in the afternoon. Cathays Park was where officials and Ministers could really get to know each other and get things done – it was where they would pick up feedback on what was working well and what wasn't. If Ministers were infrequent visitors to Cathays Park, they would never be seen to be in charge of the departments they ran.

Again, here was another limitation on the First Secretary's powers. Everyone was naturally focused on devolution taking place in the Bay, which was where the Assembly was. I lost count of the number of meetings I arranged with the Wales CBI or the Wales TUC or whoever in my office in Cathays Park and, as the minutes ticked by and the start-time for the meeting slowly expired, still there was no sign of our guests. The explanation was always the same. They'd assumed the meeting was down in the Assembly – it was where everything happened, wasn't it?

It drove me up the wall, but people had got it firmly into their heads that Cathays Park was where you used to go to see the Secretary of State. Now, you went down the Bay to see the First Secretary or any other of the Ministers. I tried to drill it into everyone's head that for Whitehall read Cathays Park, but for Westminster read Cardiff Bay. And if anyone asked where Wales's No. 10 Downing Street was, then the reply should be that Wales was far too small to have one of those!

There had been fairly strong rumours that back in the day, before Clapham Common, Ron Davies had intended to designate the Pierhead building as Wales's Downing Street. The Pierhead building is next to the Assembly building, now named the Senedd, and the Wales Millennium Centre. It's a really beautiful Gothic Revival building – I don't know if it could ever have provided living accommodation as well as a place to work for the head of the government, and anyway, living accommodation would only be required if the First Secretary (or First Minister) didn't already live in the Cardiff area.

The Scottish First Minister, for instance, has always had the use of Bute House, the Edinburgh townhouse of the famous Marquess of Bute, who was at one time the richest man in the world, and who in Wales had developed the coal industry and the docks and half the city of Cardiff. A strange coincidence, that. I had certainly had meetings with Jack McConnell and Alex Salmond at Bute House; Henry McLeish I met at his executive suite in Leith Docks.

The nearest we had in Cardiff to Bute House was the one-bedroom IKEA-furnished flat on the first floor of Cathays Park, next-door to the old Secretary of State's office. Most officials working in Cathays Park, let alone members of the public or press, didn't even know it was there. The flat was carved out of some offices for the use of Nicholas Edwards, Tory Secretary of State between 1979 and 1987. He and his wife, Ankaret, used to find the journey from Westminster to his Pembrokeshire constituency too long and tiring. Edwards's successors, Peter Walker (1987–90) and David Hunt (who did the job twice, 1990–2 and 1994–5) also used it, even arranging for willing civil servants from the private office to baby-sit the kids there! John Redwood must have been spooked by the jazzy

Swedish wallpaper, and insisted on being driven back to his home in Wokingham every night while he did the job between 1992 and 1994.

I never had any use for it, except that the bathroom was very handy for a shave or a quick change of shirt for an evening engagement. For sleeping, I absolutely had to be in Michaelston-le-Pit. By the time I retired in 2009, the flat had been converted back into offices.

I did reflect, though, that if I had lived in Holyhead or Wrexham and couldn't get home in the evenings, we would have had to create that flat in Cathays Park if it hadn't already existed. Then the fuss over the cost of creating it would have made the headlines for months – it would have been described as a luxury pad, the IKEA furnishings would somehow have become designer chic or whatever – it only showed the totally different world we now lived in. There had been no fuss at all when Nicholas Edwards had it converted for his convenience, it just got done. Now we were living in a much more transparent world. The best of transparency meant that if you converted three offices *into* a flat for the head of the government, it was a potential scandal, but if you converted a flat for the head of government *back into* three offices (as happened in 2005), then you shouldn't expect any credit for it. That was the nature of the beast.

I had a lot of help in trying to knock our fledgling government into some kind of shape from Lawrence Conway and Kevin Brennan. Kevin (my eventual successor as MP for Cardiff West) complemented me either consciously or instinctively – if I got a bit headstrong, he would advise caution, and I'm sure that if I'd been ultra-cautious he would have been advising me to go for it! He became my interim Special Adviser. And, like Kevin, Lawrence Conway had the immense advantage of being on my wavelength from the off. Lawrence had been around the block a few times, he was a Welsh Office lifer. He knew all the officials, their strengths and weaknesses, and he had a very tough streak too. I'd come across him once or twice when I was an MP – he'd done the Cardiff Bay Barrage Bill, and he'd done child protection – he had a real interest in lots of policy issues. Lawrence's greatest asset for me was his encyclopaedic knowledge of how the civil service side of our new-fangled set-up worked. He knew which officials were keen on making devolution a success and which were much happier in the old Welsh Office days.

You had to distinguish between the Westminster–Whitehall model, in which the person carrying the title of Cabinet Secretary is in fact the uber-Permanent Secretary. That person is the *primus inter pares* of all the departmental chiefs. With our system, the Permanent Secretary Sir Jon Shortridge was the head of the Civil Service. Indeed, he still attended the weekly prayer meetings of all the permanent secretaries in London, chaired by the (Whitehall) Cabinet Secretary. More recently, Whitehall has shifted over to something much closer to our model, with the head of the Civil Service being effectively separate from the head of Policy Co-ordination. A complication for Sir Jon was that he was also head of those civil servants who had applied for jobs serving the Assembly Members' side of things down in the Bay – the committee clerks, the Members Library, and so on. Parliamentary clerks and librarians are definitely not civil servants in London – working for Parliament is a separate service from working for the Government. Wales was too small for that kind of separation, but it did mean a difficult relationship for Sir Jon with Dafydd Elis-Thomas the Presiding Officer, in which I had to intervene from time to time in order to keep the peace.

Lawrence was ideally suited for the freelance and more Machiavellian side of being Cabinet Secretary – the eyes and ears of the First Secretary. He had the sensitive political antennae and the eyes in the back of his head to know what was going on. He could bridge the gap between the Park and the Bay to perfection, and likewise the gaps between Ministers, their private offices and the departments they were running.

Should Sir Jon as head man of our civil service have continued to attend those weekly prayer meetings with all the other civil service chiefs in Whitehall? Did it tie him in and, by analogy, tie us in far too much to pre-devolution ways of thinking? I think it was right to step away. I don't know whether the Scottish Permanent Secretary went at the same time as Sir Jon; the Northern Ireland Permanent Secretary was not in the home civil service (Northern Ireland started off life in 1922 with an entirely separate civil service).

The real question that lies behind all of this is whether the New Labour Government, having given away power through devolution to the three Celtic nations, was anxious to take it back again by all manner of benign threats, bribes and devices. Again, I don't think so. To begin with, we did have the Joint Ministerial Committee, on which representatives of the three devolved governments would meet with their Westminster counterparts and swap experiences on what was going well and not so well in public service delivery. Tony Blair would chair the meetings himself for the first two or three years, before he got bored. We had one such meeting in Cathays Park in the summer of 2000, on the issue of Health. It was in those early days that the JMC was important, because the Northern Ireland Assembly and Executive was periodically suspended. When it was in motion, it was very important to the Unionist side of the Executive to feel that it was still definitely part of the UK system of government.

Although helping Northern Ireland Unionists to feel that the power-sharing executive wasn't leaving them on the outside of the UK was useful, it had to be balanced by the need to be distinctive in our approach – otherwise, there was no point in having devolution. I had mentioned this in my speech to the Institute of Welsh Affairs, that we in Wales did not automatically think autonomy. The Scottish Office had been around for a century longer than the old Welsh Office, and the Scots' default position was to do something distinctively Scottish. The Welsh Office default position, in the meantime, was to follow Whitehall. That was why Lawrence Conway's intelligence on which of our senior officials were devo-enthusiasts and which were devo-sceptics was so useful – we had to build up a cadre of people who could grow beyond 'follow Whitehall' as the default option in Wales.

Another problem was that the senior civil service was entirely male, pale and a bit stale – I did have several forthright discussions with Sir Jon Shortridge over this, and made a few suggestions about how we might break into this all-male senior management team, including swaps with outside organisations to bring in fresh thinking. Sir Jon was cautious about any of my suggestions to swap one of our mandarins (male) for a prominent professor from Cardiff University (female). No Minister wanted to work with the male mandarin in question, but there were lots of practical problems with the swap idea. Professorial pay had dropped well behind mandarin pay, and no university could possibly afford him unless we made up the pay difference. Furthermore, with the Research Assessment Exercise rearing its ugly head, how could any university afford to take on a pro-vice chancellor or head of department who couldn't possibly be expected to publish any kind of research paper that could earn RAE brownie points?

But the main bone of contention between me and Sir Jon was that he thought we were trying to politicise the civil service. I thought he was being a stick-in-the-mud. There was a strength of feeling inside the Labour Cabinet, which was very gender-balanced, about the male, pale and stale issue – the sense was that the machine we had inherited was not fit for purpose. We had to try to increase the authority of the government at the heart of the Assembly, and to increase the capacity of the Assembly itself to scrutinise its government.

What was totally crazy was that we were pushing the twenty-two local authorities in Wales to move away from the old committee-based model to a Cabinet and Scrutiny model, but at the same time the model we had inherited from the Government of Wales Act and the NAAG Standing Orders was the old-style local government model. We had persuaded twenty-one out of the twenty-two local authorities to go for the Cabinet model, although many back-bench councillors hated it. Powys, the ultra-rural county in the middle of Wales, was the only one not to go for Cabinet and Scrutiny, so deeply entrenched was the committee system there. There were no political party representatives on the Council, and most seats were uncontested at election time.

There was a lot of support from the Tory Group in the Assembly for moving away from the NAAG committee system and for increasing the degree of separation of powers and functions between the executive branch of the Assembly and the legislative branch. This was because they didn't want their voters, still overwhelmingly devo-sceptic at the time, to tar the Tory AMs with the brush of decisions made by us in the Government they fundamentally disagreed with. And quite right too!

Nick Bourne, by then the Conservative leader in the Assembly following the resignation of Rod Richards, wanted a clearer separation, and so did we. That's why we were able to make such good progress on stretching the elastic of the Government of Wales Act and the Standing Orders without actually breaking them. Five years later, we did get to full legal separation of government and legislature, but in 2000 we were seeing how far we could stretch the separation under the 1998 Government of Wales Act.

Devo-sceptics outside the Assembly were furious when we changed the working title of the executive branch to Welsh Assembly Government. They thought we were assuming airs and graces. The letters poured in from the green ink brigade to the local evening newspapers – they had never accepted the referendum result anyway. Ron Davies attacked the name change in a question-time session, claiming that 'Welsh Assembly Government' was the equivalent of the UK Government being called 'British Parliament Government'. Technically correct, I had to concede, but I was surprised that a politician with avowed republican leanings preferred the slightly anachronistic title of Her Majesty's Government.

There was much less of an adverse reaction to the other name change – namely me becoming First Minister instead of First Secretary, and the other members of the Cabinet becoming Ministers instead of Assembly Secretaries. Because what I was doing was nothing more than bringing us into line with Scotland, people seemed to accept it more easily. The public did understand what a minister in a government was, but they didn't necessarily understand what an Assembly Secretary was.

One of the most difficult things we had to administer was the new Objective One programme, bringing an extra £300 million a year for seven years to the part of Wales covering two-thirds of the total in area, and with a population furthest away from the English border and with the lowest GDP per head. The official name for the zone getting the assistance was West Wales & The Valleys – a bit of a misnomer, as a huge chunk of North Wales was included too.

We finally got the match-funding in the shape of extra Public Expenditure Statement cover over and above Barnett Formula, all agreed in the PES in the summer of 2000. This was the problematic area which had forced the resignation of my predecessor. I had kept the Economic Development and Europe brief – no one was exactly begging me to be given the job – and I also took the chair of the Programme Monitoring Group for Objective One. This was one of those strange neither fish nor fowl European-style jobs, quasi-ministerial rather than ministerial. Objective One was meant to run via a partnership between government, the private sector and the voluntary sector. Each area was meant to come up with ideas that would lift the Objective One area by its own bootstraps.

The PMG was not there to administer the funds, but to monitor *how* they were being administered – that was a recipe for confusion, almost as bad as the

Assembly's Standing Orders! The rules of the European Regional Development Fund meant the private sector could get in on the act, but was not able to be the direct recipient of ERDF grants – it was a really cumbersome system of doing economic development, which was a shame because that extra £300 million a year was a useful supplement to the overall budget. There was no extra money available to aid local government in finding some pump-priming money in their area to get the Objective One programme off the ground.

The manufacturing sector was not in a healthy state in that summer of 2000. The newly-introduced euro currency was heading south while the pound sterling was heading north, strengthening all the time because it was a useful hedge against the woes of the euro. The pound being too strong was a problem for the steel industry and for the clothing industry, because both were so labour-intensive. One of Marks & Spencer's main suppliers was a company called Dewhirst, which made sensible slacks for M&S in a complex of factories across West Wales – Cardigan, Fishguard and Lampeter all had Dewhirst factories. But the company announced they were closing all their operations in West Wales, taking out two thousand jobs across eight small towns, and transferring everything to Rabat in Morocco where labour costs were less than a tenth of those in West Wales.

The high pound was not only accelerating that inevitable drift towards lower labour-intensive countries, whether in Eastern Europe or North Africa, but it was making Wales less attractive for inward investment. Everything was set up for West Wales and the Valleys to pick up a large share of any inward investment that was around – if you had Objective One status, it carried with it Tier One status as well. Tier One meant you could offer the maximum level of grants to induce footloose investment to come to West Wales & The Valleys – the equal of the highest grant that could be offered anywhere in the EU. But if the pound was in the wrong place, the companies would be reluctant to come, grants or no grants. The Welsh economic structure, with its high dependence on manufacturing, was vulnerable, especially as the manufacturing wasn't in the high-tech sector. Objective One funding and status wasn't able to counteract much wider factors like the magnetic force of low labour cost countries and the high pound.

While we were making progress on the separation of powers, executive branch from legislature branch, there was no movement at all on the historic realignment of Welsh politics. That was dead. It had always seemed to be pie in the sky to me anyway. It had certainly been part of Ron Davies's dream, which he'd tried to explain as an inevitable consequence of devolution. When he famously said that devolution in Wales was a process not an event, one of the deeper meanings behind that phrase was that political parties would break up and reform in different coalitions. Working in a devolved setting would gradually see the more devo-enthusiastic wing of the Labour Party in Wales merge with the more radical and less farmer-dominated wing of Plaid Cymru, pick up some Lib Dems on the way, and the occasional individual Conservative, to form a Red Dragon/Red Flag phalanx to push Wales's ship of state along.

Ron had enjoyed all the covert meetings he'd had with Dafydd Wigley and Richard Livsey, the Plaid and Lib Dem leaders in the House of Commons, and perhaps been taken in by the positive mood music of cooperation that was generated. The meetings had started before the 1997 general election, then continued in the run-up to the referendum, and during the passage of the Government of Wales Bill in 1998. Ron was operating very much on his own in those meetings – he certainly didn't want me there (maybe he thought I couldn't keep a secret).

You couldn't blame Ron for having realignment on the brain in 1996–9. Tony Blair, in those heady days just before and after the landslide win in May 1997, was into some kind of realignment project too. His idea was to realign the left in British politics, so that the Tories would theoretically find it almost impossible to get back into power. It was the period in which Roy Jenkins and Paddy Ashdown had almost as much influence on Blair as Peter Mandelson, and that's saying something!

Far from any break-up of the traditional party structures, we did in Cardiff finish up with a coalition with the Lib Dems by the autumn, though it wasn't part of any grand plan – it just crept up on us really. It's true that Kevin Brennan and the Cabinet Secretary Lawrence Conway did visit Scotland to meet their opposite numbers in the spring of 2000 – a natural, fraternal thing to do anyway, rather than being part of a deep-laid plot for Wales to copy the Lab–Lib Dem coalition government in Edinburgh.

Lawrence did make a detailed note of how coalition government worked in Scotland. His view was that there was a stark choice for our chances of survival as a minority government for another three years, staggering on from budget to budget in a very wobbly state. By August, one of my newly appointed Special Advisers, Mark Drakeford had started regular Saturday morning coffee meetings with Mike Hines, the Lib Dem Group Secretary. All totally deniable and with no declared approval from me, but no discouragement either. Seeing how the land lay is how I would have described those meetings. They could have ended with nothing more than a one-off deal to pass the 2000–1 Budget, or something more comprehensive.

Mark came in as one of four new Special Advisers, all appointed through an open process after advertising the jobs. That was something totally revolutionary in the British system. Kevin Brennan had had to stand down very shortly after becoming my interim Special Adviser in order to accept his nomination as Labour's prospective candidate to succeed me as MP for Cardiff West – you couldn't be a Special Adviser and a parliamentary candidate at the same time.

I was looking for a team of really bright policy wonks, not spin doctors, which would help pep up the amount of original thinking on policies suited to Wales instead of simply aping Whitehall. That was a much bigger priority for me than spin doctoring to raise our profile. Before anything else, we had to have a clear message to get across.

Mark Drakeford was an old friend and colleague from Cardiff West, and by this time a Professor of Social Policy at Swansea University. He had been a South Glamorgan County Councillor while I was cutting my teeth as a new MP after 1987, and he had also been my parliamentary agent in the 1992 election. I now tasked him to sound out the Lib Dems, which would need to be done so discreetly that, if nothing came of it all, there would be no trail back to me or other Ministers.

So, those informal Labour–Lib Dem chats took place on Saturday mornings through August, and by September Mark was able to supply me with a summary note on where we stood. The terms of a potential agreement were evolving. Labour's programme for government would remain in place in its entirety, to be supplemented by an additional set of priorities that could be agreed by both parties. The content of the policy programme seemed to pose less of a problem than the political arrangements necessary.

The leader of the Lib Dems in the Assembly, Mike German, was apparently adamant that there would need to be another Lib Dem in addition to himself in the Cabinet on the grounds that, without corroboration from one of his party colleagues, the Lib Dem Group and the wider party would not accept his account of what we were up to in the Cabinet! Moreover, he would wish to be both Deputy First Minister and Minister for Economic Development – for a Lib Dem party with just six Assembly Members, those were considerable demands.

Getting those demands through the Labour machinery would expend a lot of my capital. I recognised that much, but by the late summer I thought that I was better established in my leadership of Labour in Wales and my security of tenure as First Minister. Mike German met me face to face for the first time in mid-September, and we closed off the remaining policy differences and agreed the political arrangements. We both agreed that confidentiality should be observed until early October.

The Labour Party Annual Conference took place as usual in Brighton in the final week of September. On the Monday morning, Mark Drakeford travelled down to Brighton with the Health Minister Jane Hutt bringing a near final draft of what became the partnership agreement between Labour and the Lib Dems. More urgently, they brought a pair of proper shoes for me to wear when I made my first big conference speech. I had left for Brighton straight from tidying up the garden, wearing only my mud-caked gardening shoes!

With nice shoes on, suitable for mingling with the Brighton fashionistas, Mark, Jane and I went through the document in a seafront coffee house. I approved it, but then I had to show the relevant bits to each Minister. Rosemary

Butler, then schools Minister, met me in the flat in Brighton Julie and I had rented for the week. Rosemary was happy that there was nothing in the policy document which ran contrary to her intentions; Jane Hutt had already seen and assented to the bits in her portfolio; so with Health and Education out of the way, Mark returned to Wales to get the other Cabinet Ministers who weren't in Brighton to look at the sections relevant to their portfolios.

By the time I returned to Cardiff on the Thursday evening, the policy side was all tied up with the Labour Cabinet Ministers. Now for the tricky bit – the Cabinet reshuffle partially to make room for the presumably two Lib Dems, and to bring in the Labour people I would have chosen in May 1999 had I been First Minister at the time. Because I had kept the Economic Development portfolio, it was not difficult to give it up and make way for Mike German. One other place became available when Tom Middlehurst decided he didn't want to be in a Labour–Lib Dem coalition Cabinet, so it freed up another space but meant I had no one from a North Wales constituency in my Cabinet and that was a major representational issue.

I definitely wanted to keep Tom, an active member of the Cabinet, and though I didn't want to carry on without him I had to. I suspect he wrongly thought he was going to be reshuffled out, and decided to go before he was pushed. Without a Minister from North Wales, I had to designate myself to the role, which logistically meant a lot of journeying up to North Wales on Thursday nights for engagements all day Friday.

The situation with Peter Law, the only other Alun Michael supporter in the Cabinet, was the total opposite to Tom Middlehurst. I wanted Tom to stay, but he wanted out; I wanted Peter Law out, but he would have much preferred to stay. I had to get Peter to step down as Minister for Planning and the Environment regardless of whether we were forming a coalition or not. I had by then read the Local Government Ombudsman report into a planning scandal in Blaenau Gwent Borough Council, involving harsh criticism of Peter speaking on behalf of a planning application about a piece of land in which he had an interest. To compound the matter, Peter hadn't declared that interest.

It made horrifying reading. Even if I could have been persuaded to give Peter another job, he certainly couldn't have continued being responsible for Planning. I did find out subsequently that Alun Michael as my predecessor had been strongly leant on by the Local Government Ombudsman for Wales, Elwyn Moseley, not to appoint Peter to the job back in May 1999. The Ombudsman had taken it upon himself to contact Lawrence Conway, then Alun's Principal Private Secretary, to draw his attention to the strength of the criticism of Peter Law's conduct as a councillor and to try effectively to blackball him from being Planning Minister.

Alun's view at the time was that he had enough on his plate – what with the criticism of his appointment of Chris Gwyther as a vegetarian Agriculture

Minister – and the length of time which had elapsed since the scandal on Blaenau Gwent Borough Council seems to have stayed Alun's hand.

When I read the report in the summer, I wasn't sure if I should get Peter out of the Planning job immediately. I had some discreet enquiries made as to whether there was anything in Peter's conduct that was causing concern to his officials. There wasn't. They were more than happy with him as a Minister. There were some rows over expenses, but not over land and planning. So it wasn't urgent to have him moved, but it would definitely happen in the first reshuffle.

When I called Peter in to tell him the bad news, I should probably have explained to him that I'd done my background reading on the strong criticism of him in the Ombudsman's report. I didn't do that because I should probably have moved Peter out of his ministerial job the day after reading the report, mind you. I chose the alternative course, and told him that we were going to go into coalition with the Lib Dems and I needed the headroom to make it all possible, and we needed the coalition to give us budgetary stability through to 2003. Peter was not happy about going to the back-benches.

It was with a heavy heart that I had to call in Rosemary Butler to tell her I needed to shift her out of the Cabinet to make room in the reshuffle. I explained that I wanted to merge the two Education Minister jobs, split between schools (which she did) and post-16 (which Tom did), into one fully-fledged Education Ministry. I explained that I couldn't envisage her doing that job, but I was confident that she would do a superb job as Deputy Presiding Officer. When she eventually became the actual Presiding Officer a few years later, I think she proved me right.

But in the year 2000, I had reckoned without the wiles of Ron Davies – something I should never have done. The skills he had learned in the Labour Whips Office in the House of Commons during the mid-1980s enabled Ron to outwit me easily. As soon as he heard what was afoot regarding Rosemary and for the Deputy Presiding Officer's job, with the previous holder of that post, Jane Davidson, becoming the Education Minister, Ron called in John Marek, the former Labour MP and by now AM for Wrexham. He told John he had just the job for him – and he was right about that. Marek defeated Rosemary Butler for DPO by a single vote. Rosemary took it very well, but I was furious that I had let down a very good loyal friend. Still, Rosemary went one better a few years later by becoming a very well-liked Presiding Officer.

Not long before all this, John Marek had been to see me on a one-to-one basis to ask why he hadn't been very promptly made a Minister in my Cabinet after I'd taken over from Alun. He thought that since he had the extra kudos of having been an MP and an opposition front-bencher, let alone one of my most prominent backers in the contests against Ron and Alun, he should have had some reward.

John asked if MI5 or MI6 had contacted me to block his path to preferment, explaining that early in his career as the MP for Wrexham he had accepted several invitations to attend receptions at the Czech Embassy. Having a Czech father, he considered it only natural to accept those invitations, without realising that Czech Embassy receptions were used by the KGB as a soft option in the entrapment of inexperienced MPs for the Soviet cause, MPs who would never wilfully attend a Soviet Embassy reception. He'd fallen for the Czech invitations. Nothing untoward had happened, but was sure that he was on some kind of MI5 watchlist.

I had had to explain to John that my reasons for not choosing him as a Minister had nothing to do with any warnings from the intelligence services. He had displayed a snooty attitude to his fellow members of the Labour Group of AMs, implying that because they hadn't previously been MPs they couldn't properly understand how politics worked – he'd even been hissed at in one Labour Group meeting for remarks of that kind. Neither MI5 nor MI6 nor the KGB for that matter, had ever been in touch with me about him.

Even before my reshuffle and the forming of the coalition, we had initiated some moves to make the government closer to the people. Advertising the Special Adviser jobs was just one such move. Taking the Cabinet around Wales was another. After these Cabinet meetings, we would have open mic sessions at which the general public in whatever part of Wales we were meeting had the chance to put questions to all of us Ministers. We started to publish the minutes of our Cabinet meetings after a six-week *cordon sanitaire*, and introduced our own non-statutory version of Freedom of Information, all pretty standard in Sweden, but revolutionary in the UK back then. I also appointed three Deputy Ministers, who weren't able to be paid anything over and above the AM back-bench salary. Now, did any of these moves make the Assembly less unpopular in the eyes of the general public? Perhaps there was a little bit of a drip-drip-drip effect, maybe the us-and-them gap closed half an inch, no more than that.

Just to demonstrate the kind of hostile attitude the Assembly had to negotiate, the *South Wales Echo*, Wales's largest circulating newspaper at the time, used to compile fairly regular telephone polls on people's opinion of the Assembly – practically a free hit for the paper and the public to express dislike of the spending on the new building, or even of the closeness of the referendum result three years previously. The questions all varied on the theme of 'What do you think of the Assembly?' or 'How do you rate the Assembly?' The polls and the coverage of the results were run by Phil Nifield, one of the old-school *Echo* reporters who also doubled as the municipal correspondent covering the City Council beat as well. Phil used to call me for a comment on the terrible phone poll results – wasn't it a disgrace that the Assembly had such appalling approval ratings?

Fair play to Phil, he was a fair-minded guy, and I finally persuaded him to do a poll asking a completely different set of questions. I suggested a three-way question set out as follows: 'Marks out of 10 for (i) Tony Blair and his Government in Westminster, (ii) Rhodri Morgan and his Government in Cardiff Bay, and (iii) Russell Goodway and his administration in City Hall. The results on this were comforting to a modest degree: Tony Blair scored 7/10, I scored 5/10, and Councillor Goodway was right off the scale (at the bottom end, that is).

It proved the point at least that much of our apparent unpopularity was not that the public thought we were doing an awful job, but that they still perceived the Assembly as a new-fangled, costly and unnecessary bunch of politicians whose functions they weren't yet acclimatised to. They knew that Her Majesty's Government in London paid the pensions, ran the economy and so forth; they were familiar with the Council running the schools and emptying the bins; but they weren't too sure what we did.

It was an odd summer and autumn in other respects. One week, I might be attending an incredibly prestigious lunch at Lancaster House, the Foreign Office's conference centre next to Buckingham Palace, and then the following Sunday night I would be enjoying a quiet couple of pints of bitter with my regular drinking companions in the White Hart, a totally unreconstructed (and sadly now closed) Cardiff Dockland boozer. I was determined to maintain as much as I could of my previous and precious way of life – I was pretending that I could be First Minister without it changing who I was.

I remember a glittering pan-European Summit lunch at Lancaster House particularly well, staged to inaugurate and celebrate the start of the United Kingdom taking over the six-month rotating Presidency of the European Council of Ministers. What Tony Blair had done was to invite the whole European Commission to lunch with the entire UK Cabinet, plus the First Ministers of Scotland, Wales and Northern Ireland.

I was at the far end of this monster Lancaster House dining table when, quite suddenly, all eyes were on me. Stavros Dimas, the Greek Member of the Commission, sitting right opposite Tony Blair, had half-jokingly challenged the PM as to why they were being served 'Welsh Feta'. Just imagine how you would feel if you were at a lunch in Athens and were served Greek whisky. I don't think Tony Blair could think of a suitably witty euro-response, so he flung the ball to me – 'How did you manage to get this Welsh Feta on the menu, Rhodri?' Then, to give me breathing space to think up an answer and with a wave of the arm in my direction, he added, 'Rhodri Morgan is First Minister of Wales.' You'd think we were the best of pals and one of the great political double-acts in the business, all past enmities forgotten.

I offered my Euro-joke response – 'Well, we have nine million sheep in Wales and only three million people, and if we don't keep our sheep happy we might face a *coup d'état* from the sheep!' Chucking some French into a joke makes it a Euro-joke, not a British joke, and it halted the protest about us crude Brits despoiling a thousand-year-old Greek tradition by serving Welsh Feta. Three or four people laughed, and Blair looked suitably grateful.

Whereas you could argue that those invitations to attend lunches and dinners at the heart of the political establishment were an attempt to show off how devolution had been handled in the UK, there was an obvious danger that my Celtic opposite numbers and I might become some kind of adjunct Ministers in the UK Government, albeit of a new and exotic kind. That danger of incorporation could ultimately mean London had given away power to Scotland, Wales and Northern Ireland with one hand, and subliminally taken it back with the other. Donald Dewar and his sadly short-lived successors and I might be Labour First Ministers, but we were not government payroll extras, except at our peril!

The UK Government automatically put me and my Scottish and Northern Irish opposite numbers on the invitation list for a meeting of COBRA, the emergency planning and security committee. I recall sitting two seats away from Sir Stewart Menzies, Head of MI5 in the aftermath of 9/11. The meeting was chaired by the Home Secretary David Blunkett. Following Sir Stewart's threat assessment, the Home Secretary turned to where he had been told I was sitting. He asked, rather too pointedly for my taste, 'Rhodri, you've got an awful lot of Iraqis and Libyans studying science at … what's that place called … the University of Glamorgan.' I could only blurt some kind of jokey reply, 'Oh, don't worry, David, we'll only be teaching them the usual rubbish!' – which was a bit unfair on the University of Glamorgan, but I'd been given no prior notice that the question was going to come up. I couldn't think what else to say!

Keeping my feet on the ground was perhaps less of a problem than the dangers of subtle incorporation. I walked into the White Hart one Sunday evening, and before I could get to where my friends were sitting I had to pass through the alcoholic remnants of a Gypsy wedding. A very short, stocky and powerfully built thirty-ish young Gypsy picked me up on recognising me – he had an iron grip around my buttocks, lifted me up as high off the ground as he could, and started whirling me around and around shouting 'Rhodree! Rhodree! King of the Welsh!' There was nothing I could do about it until his exhaustion took over, except to tell myself inwardly, 'Well, I bet this never happened to Tony Blair!' The White Hart was a million miles from Lancaster House.

Apart from the one occasion in the Joint Ministerial Council in Scotland, when the Prime Minister criticised my rumpled linen suit and John Prescott did his big brother in the playground intervention to defend me, there never was another outbreak of old enmities between Blair and me. I mercilessly took the mickey out of him every time I introduced him to the delegates at Welsh Night at Labour Party conferences. He always took it in good part. I remember looking across to Cherie when I was doing my mickey-taking introductions, and her face would be a study in oriental immutability behind which I imagine she was frantically trying to work out what I was going to say next.

At one particular Welsh Night, Cherie was particularly rapt at my account of how things had changed in the fourteen-year interval between me and Tony graduating from St John's College, Oxford (our shared alma mater). 'Take careers advice', I said. When I was about to leave St John's, the careers tutor barked at me, 'Do you want to make a lot of money in the City?' When I told him no, he replied, 'Right, it's school-teaching for you. Next please!' but when Tony was about to graduate, careers advice was all done with the aid of a huge Bletchley Park-style super-computer, which could match any student with any job they wanted. So, when the young Blair said, 'Well, the problem is, half of me wants to be Mick Jagger and the other half wants to be the Archbishop of Canterbury', the careers don responded, 'Righty-ho, young man, let's put that into the computer and see what it comes up with – here we go – job required 50 per cent international rock star and 50 per cent Church of England primate!' After a lot of whirring and chuntering, out of the machine comes a slip of paper with on it the words, 'Only job found answering that description: Leader of the Labour Party'. The relief on Cherie's face that nothing worse had popped out of the computer was a treat to see.

The other priority project I had on at that time was to try to get some positive press coverage, or at least a bit of interest, in our goings-on in the London media. This was the other side of the drift to incorporation risk. The more I was treated as an adjunct Minister of State in Her Majesty's Government, the harder it was to get the press and media to write about something we were doing that was distinct from the New Labour project. It was all very well sitting two seats away from Sir Stewart Menzies at COBRA meetings, but could we get the press to report on what the Welsh Assembly was actually doing? The only coverage Wales and Scotland were getting was about the overspending on the two new building projects. Worse still for the Scots, they did have a huge administrative problem in 2001 with the examination papers and results. It cost the Scottish Education Minister Sam Galbraith his job. Sam was a part of the 1987 intake of MPs like me, a lovely guy and a brilliant brain surgeon to boot. The problem lay within the Scottish Qualifications Authority, but he felt he had to resign, and that certainly drew publicity. God forbid that we in Wales should have any problem of that magnitude.

Anyway, favourable press coverage from the London-based media was far less of a priority for the new Scottish Government than it was for us. Most Scots get their news from Scottish media, while most people in Wales get their news from UK and London media. Could we get the people to take an interest? I think that we had it worse than the Scots – there was a far greater degree of underlying respect in England for the Scottish devolution project than for what was happening in Wales. The respect might be tinged with loathing as well, but at least it was there. Not so for Wales. The put-down was seen as the only appropriate way of covering Wales. In the summer of 2000, I was asked to go on *Newsnight* to be interviewed by Jeremy Vine. No particular agenda items, just that *Newsnight* hadn't done anything on Welsh devolution and they thought it was time they did out of an obscure BBC-ish sense of duty. I was to be the first item on the programme, and was asked to be at the unmanned studio in BBC Llandaff by 10:20 pm. I would be out by 10:40 pm.

I told my Special Adviser Kevin Brennan, 'You come up with me, you can prep me on the way and we'll have time for a swift pint in the Heathcock pub next to BBC Wales HQ after I've finished.' Now, once you're in an unmanned studio, you're a bit like a cosmonaut, all strapped into your seat waiting for take-off, totally powerless. Well, as it urned out, the interview with me wasn't the first item. It wasn't the second either, or the third or the fourth. The promise of a quick pint in the pub post-interview had long disappeared by the time they finally wedged me in, just before 11:15 pm. Last item on the show! What made it far worse was the snooty introduction from the usually harmless Jeremy Vine – 'Now, please don't switch off your sets, we're going to do an item on the Welsh Assembly.' By now I'd been hanging round for so long that I was fit to tie down, and the gratuitously insulting intro was the straw that broke this particular camel's back.

I exploded and gave him the rough side of my tongue, a withering dressing-down for the supercilious tone of his introduction, and I went on and on about the metropolitan elite frequenting their Hampstead dinner parties and knowing absolutely nothing about life beyond the M25 and caring even less. I just about held it together.

The upshot was that I then received a grovelling note of apology from said Jeremy Vine asking if I'd like to come to lunch the next time I was in town. Just my point really – I would have to go to London in order to receive a lunch by way of an apology from *Newsnight*, whom I'd just accused of not really being interested in what went on beyond the M25! I couldn't think of anything worse and I don't think I bothered replying. All I knew about Jeremy Vine was that he was as big a Christian as Tony Blair, and that he chaired the Christian Broadcasting Fellowship. Not the kind of person I could imagine myself going for a pint with in the Heathcock pub in Llandaff next-door to BBC Wales – the same pint that he and his dozy producers had prevented me from having that dreadful night!

The same thing happened when Nick Robinson, now co-anchorman of the *Today* programme, but then a BBC political reporter, interviewed me in that summer of 2000 on the roof of the Millbank studios. An opportunity that turned to dust, because I couldn't imagine how he would interpret one of my replies. I'd explained to him that the Assembly only had secondary legislative powers, and it was therefore particularly difficult for AMs to develop their oratorical skills when all they could speak on was stuff like the Sheep and Goats Identification Wales Order 2000 (Miscellaneous Provisions)! Listening to an hour's debate on that was like watching paint dry or grass grow. When Robinson reported my reply, it was to the effect that my Assembly colleagues couldn't make a decent speech for toffee.

I think the real problem is that the London political press community is still finding it hard to come to terms with a multi-polar Britain. Reporters are in their comfort zone in and around the House of Commons, popping over to No. 10 Downing Street for Prime Ministerial press briefings from your Bernard Inghams or Alistair Campbells, before trooping off to Blackpool or Brighton for the party conference season, and then back to Westminster. The emphasis in 'press pack' is on 'pack'. They might from time to time visit an unknown town for a by-election, but apart from that they can wallow self-referentially in their comfort zone. Westminster and Whitehall is the world they have to mediate to the great unwashed mass of punters.

Then suddenly someone comes along and upsets the system with the news that there is going to be another Parliament in Edinburgh and an Assembly each for Cardiff and Belfast – now cover them as well! How much background knowledge of politics in Scotland, Wales and Northern Ireland are these reporters going to need to cover the new asymmetric UK? As little as they can get away with, basically. Devolution was a blasted nuisance to the Westminster press gallery.

I recall the Irish Taoiseach Bertie Aherne telling me firmly that I should never trust the media, with maybe one or two exceptions, and Neil Kinnock was another who had warned me early on that the British press was utterly untrustworthy. My problem was that I had always thought of myself as a media-friendly politician, both as an MP and as an Assembly Minister, and I'd never considered myself cynical about the press. But I became more cynical by experience.

The best and worst example of this came some years down the line in 2007, after that year's elections had not gone so well for Labour. We were down to 26 seats in the Assembly, still by far the largest party, but well short of a majority. There would be lots of negotiations taking place over the following couple of months. Labour was negotiating with the Lib Dems to begin with, and then with Plaid Cymru. Simultaneously, the Lib Dems, Plaid Cymru and the Conservatives were discussing the formation of an Anybody But Labour (ABL) coalition – it was called the Rainbow coalition, its members popularly known as the Rainbow Warriors, and they only failed to get into office by a whisker.

I was the caretaker First Minister. No one was quite sure which of the two sets of negotiations would reach the finishing line first. I had to attend the Wales TUC Annual Conference in Llandudno, while there was a crucial meeting of the Welsh Lib Dem Executive in Llandrindod Wells to approve and confirm the shape of the Rainbow coalition. Kirsty Williams almost single-handedly managed to scupper it by picking up delegates here and there, with her father in another car picking up some others, to deliver the votes that blocked the deal.

I had received the news that night, in my modest little hotel beneath the Great Orme in Llandudno, that the Lib Dem Executive had voted against the Rainbow Alliance. So, I was surprised to read in *The Times* over my breakfast that the Rainbow Alliance was going ahead after approval from all three non-Labour parties. *The Times* had jumped the gun. Fair enough, in one way. The early edition of *The Times* distributed in North Wales probably went to press at around eight in the evening, so their options were to avoid covering the story, or to try and guess the outcome of the Lib Dem meeting. Nobody could complain about *The Times* getting it wrong, but it was the vitriol directed at me that was a bit of a shock, especially when I saw the by-line. It was Greg Hurst, someone I remember in the Welsh press corps covering parliamentary stuff for the *South Wales Argus*, and I'd always got on well with him. I'd fed him stories. I'd never done him any harm.

You'd assume from Greg's piece outlining my political obituary that I was his lifelong and bitterest enemy. I wasn't just Old Labour – I was antediluvian Labour, he wrote. Of course, by the time I was reading all this I already knew that the Rainbow coalition was not going to proceed, and it was a rather delectable experience to read in *The Times* that I was toast while spreading my marmalade! That marmalade on toast tasted really good!

I know it's not rational, but I couldn't help wondering what I had ever done to Greg Hurst – why was he writing this nasty stuff about me? Nothing, really, except good riddance and goodbye! Perhaps I should always have carried a card to keep on my breakfast table sitting next to the newspapers, bearing the wise words of American sage H. L. Mencken: 'The relationship between the journalist and the politician should be like the one between the dog and the tree!'

Of course, following the defeat of the Rainbow coalition in Llandrindod Wells the previous night and my very enjoyable breakfast in Llandudno, I had to fly back to Cardiff mid-morning from the tiny airstrip at RAF Valley on the tinier plane that did the North Wales–South Wales service. When I reached Valley around ten-thirty, ready for the eleven o'clock flight south to be re-nominated as First Minister in the Assembly that afternoon, things didn't look promising. DELAY read the flight notice board. Anyway, we eventually got on the plane, only for the pilot to climb out of the cockpit and into the passenger cabin with a gloom-laden expression. There were probably about ten passengers in there. He said he was terribly sorry, but they couldn't get the left-hand side battery to function to kick-start the engine on that side. Could we please all get out and push? Not quite. 'Could you please all get out of the plane, and back into the little terminal? None of you have got anything important on down in Cardiff today, I hope?' 'No', I responded, with a world-weary air, 'just forming a government, that's all.' I don't know to this day whether my plea produced an extra-special effort from the mechanic, but about half an hour later the plane was flying and I reached the Assembly in time. That was quite a day!

The bleaker the press coverage the Assembly got, or that my Government got, or that I personally got – or, indeed, the blanket absence of any coverage of us in the UK media – the more I treasured the slightest positive press coverage we did get. Such occasions were rare, but one really notable occasion was when Rory Bremner complimented me on my speech at the official opening of the new Senedd building in 2006. Someone tipped me off that I'd featured on the *Rory Bremner Show* on the Sunday night after the Royal opening of the new building – I was incredulous at first, but it did apparently happen. I didn't even know the Royal opening was covered live on television outside Wales. Anyway, out of the blue, Bremner had said that if anyone wanted to know exactly how to make a speech on a prestigious occasion like that, they should watch a video of my speech – he said it was a minor masterpiece of its kind, or something to that effect.

Then, a year later, I actually bumped into Rory Bremner himself at the Celtic Manor for one of the pre-Ryder Cup Gala Dinner events organised by Sir Terry Matthews. I was walking into the main ballroom-cum-dining room with Sir Terry, when Rory suddenly appeared at our side. He was the evening's master of ceremonies, and I asked if it was true that he had made that reference to my speech on his show. He confirmed that he had, and then turned to Sir Terry and jerked his thumb towards me – 'I don't know why you got me to do this gig for you tonight', he said, 'that's the guy you should be having!'

If I had to think what Bremner considered noteworthy about my speech, it might be that he could appreciate just how difficult a speech like that can be – and for two reasons. The first is that the speech can't over-run its two-minute limit, you can't waste a word. Second, any speech in the presence of Her Majesty, the Duke of Edinburgh and the Prince of Wales can fall hopelessly flat if it's too stiff and sycophantic – on the other hand, if it comes over as flippant, it will be seen as disrespectful and someone will have your guts for garters. You have to pitch it exactly right, or you're dead.

Making the Queen laugh at jokes or even smile with enthusiasm isn't easy, partly because you have to supply the text of your speech to Buckingham Palace forty-eight hours in advance, which means either she or her staff will have already read your speech. Spontaneous laughter is off the agenda. Well, the Queen didn't exactly have a fit of giggles at my speech, but she did join in the ripples of amusement running around the Assembly Chamber once or twice.

I think she most enjoyed my joke at the expense of the Presiding Officer Dafydd Elis-Thomas, who had taken a bit of stick at his choice of the name Senedd for the new building. Some people didn't like the word because it was too Welsh and, indeed, too crypto-nationalist. The word *senedd* itself is the accepted modern Welsh word for parliament. I tried to defuse all that criticism by essaying, 'Some have found fault with the choice of Senedd as the name of the new building. I can assure your Majesty that we will not be following all the practices of the original Senate of Ancient Rome – especially that bit where the head of the government gets stabbed in the back by a bunch of guys wearing sandals!'

Rory Bremner would have understood just how much effort goes into compressing everything into a couple of minutes. No speech-writer can actually help you with a speech like that, it has to be all your own work. I was like a bear with a sore head for a week beforehand, trying to work out what I wanted to say, and getting a clap on the back on the *Rory Bremner Show* made all those writer's block headaches worthwhile.

Getting the *South Wales Echo*, never a fan of the Assembly, to run the headline 'How Rhodri Made the Queen Laugh!' was pretty satisfying as well – I imagined they would probably have much preferred the headline 'Another Ghastly Faux Pas by Gaffe-Prone Rhodri!'

The last piece of uncovenanted positive press coverage came not long before I retired. It was in the summer of 2009. There had been much agonising going on in No. 10 Downing Street as to where Gordon Brown should spend his summer holidays in the UK *en famille*. I don't remember where John Major had spent his summer holidays during his six years as Prime Minister. The years since 1997 had been very different – it used to be, 'Where are Tony and Cherie going this summer?' Now it was, 'Where are Gordon and Sarah going on their summer hols?'

*The Guardian* ran a third leader column telling Brown to stop messing about – why couldn't the Blairs and Browns of this world follow Rhodri Morgan's example? Everyone knew that Morgan and family spent their annual holidays in Rhodri's caravan in Mwnt near Cardigan, and that was that. No fuss. No bother.

Holidaying in Mwnt has been a massive part of my battery-recharging process, without which nobody can do a 24/7 job like First Minister. That's how it was, long before I became First Minister, and it continues to be so long after retirement. Combine the impact of having a caravan you can repair to in the summer (without having to book) with the impact of the get-togethers of my expanding brood of grandchildren that seemed to come along like clockwork in most of the years I was head of the government – one in 2000, one in 2001, one in 2002, two in 2003, one in 2006, and another again after my retirement in 2009 – and it meant I had another life outside politics. I often wonder how I would have kept my bearings if I'd been in a family with no children, like Alex Salmond and then Nicola Sturgeon. It must be much more difficult to get away from it all. I can understand why horse-racing and betting took up such a big part of Alex Salmond's life. That was his relaxation, while caravanning and the ever-expanding hoard of grandchildren was mine.

Down on Mwnt beach, it was brilliant for battery-recharging that people never lobbied me on the beach. I could just swim, read, do the crossword, have a nap (very important in the afternoons), and everyone who knew who I was also seemed to know that I was to be left alone. I needed the down time! On one occasion, a young man with a baby in his arms came over to me. I think I must have started to give my 'I'm off duty' glare, because Julie started to pinch my leg. Anyway, it turned out that all he wanted to say was that his company, Control Techniques in Newtown in mid-Wales, had increased exports by 50 per cent in the past year. Of course, I'd have been pleased with a whole queue of people on the beach if I could have a guarantee that they all wanted to pass on that kind of good news. But I'm undyingly grateful to everyone I shared Mwnt beach with during that decade for leaving me and Julie and the rest of the family to enjoy ourselves unbothered. So the advice of *The Guardian* to No. 10 was spot on. Get a caravan – but maybe not in Mwnt, please!

There is no question in my mind that the turning point in public regard for the Assembly came in the autumn of 2000. The combined effect of my reshuffle with the formation of the Partnership Government with the Lib Dems gave us stability and strength. Getting Sue Essex and Jane Davidson into the Cabinet was essential. My measure of whether to appoint someone to my Cabinet was to ask if this or that person would pass muster as a potential Minister in a UK Cabinet, or at least at the next level down as a Minister of State. Could I imagine them answering questions effectively in the House of Commons? The importance of that test was that my Ministers might very well have to deal with Whitehall Ministers or even at times visit Brussels, especially in Agriculture, where the four UK Agriculture Ministers were treated as practical equals.

Putting the final touches to the coalition meant that we had to have two Lib Dems in the Cabinet. There was one evening at my home in Michaelston-le-Pit that would enormously puzzle those who believe the world of politics consists entirely of greasy pole clamberers. Keeping me company was my team of Special Advisers, plus the Cabinet Secretary Lawrence Conway. I was trying to appoint Deputy Ministers, albeit unpaid, who would be all Labour. A number of telephone calls to the candidates resulted in several refusals. They were unavailable for selection. Mike German was on his way down the A470 from North Wales to join us – he was definitely joining us in the other sense, he was coming into the Cabinet. The A470 is a difficult route for driving, but more notably it is well-nigh impossible to carry on driving and maintain mobile phone reception. Mike had Jenny Randerson in his car, his desired candidate to keep him company in the Cabinet. In his first phone call, Mike said Jenny just wouldn't do it. From time to time, the Lib Dem pair would get on to another stretch with good reception and call back to report that Jenny was still adamant that she wouldn't join the Cabinet. Each time we started discussing alternatives, the line went dead again. Mike and Jenny were practically parked in my driveway in Michaelston-le-Pit when he finally called again and said, 'She'll do it!'

The basis for the coalition was a policy agreement and a rules of engagement paper, setting out how we intended to treat the post of Deputy First Minister, which didn't exist in statute. Whereas the Scottish Deputy First Minister Jim Wallace did occasionally take First Minister's Questions in the Scottish Parliament, my memory is that Mike German never did the same in Wales. It didn't matter how far away I was from Cardiff on a Monday night, or how ropey I might have felt, it was always a maximum priority four-line-whip issue for me to be there and take First Minister's Questions.

The reason for that was that fault-lines had opened up across Wales with the Labour Party, where large sections of the party simply found it difficult to reconcile themselves to the coalition. Their dislike and mistrust of the Lib Dems was such that they would rather we staggered on until 2003 with a minority government losing budgets and having legislation rejected, rather than admit even two Lib Dem Ministers into the inner sanctum of government.

The strongest opposition to the coalition came in those regions where Labour was dominant in local government, but where the Lib Dems and their pavement politics had begun to make inroads. It probably didn't help that one of the canards doing the rounds when the campaign against me becoming the Labour leader in Wales was at its height, especially in the contest against Alun Michael, was that victory for me would mean the death of local government in Wales. Now that I was leading Labour into coalition at the Assembly, it was construed as proof of this lame accusation, and in Scotland Labour had already agreed to switch the voting system in local government elections from first-past-the-post to the single transferable vote (STV).

This came up when I was going around Wales meeting the local membership and explaining why we had gone down the coalition route. I tried to be as clear as possible that I was meeting them to *explain* what we were doing, rather than to ask them to ratify the decision, before it was set in stone. Many of those who came to the meetings nevertheless seemed to think that if they expressed their anger sufficiently strongly it could have the effect of vetoing the whole coalition idea.

Perhaps the best and worst example of this was the meeting for Labour members in south-east Wales held in Newport Civic Centre. Sir Harry Jones, the Leader of Newport County Borough Council, was one of the genuinely big beasts in the world of Welsh local government. He accused me of treachery and described the partnership agreement as a 'betrayal' of the entire Labour movement. He and his councillor colleagues, who had packed out the meeting, rehearsed and repeated the usual arguments about the Lib Dems being totally unreliable partners, that they would seek to grab the credit for anything good that happened and wouldn't be seen for dust if anything bad happened, and the dreaded Trojan Horse of PR voting in local government – they seemed to be utterly unaware that Scotland even existed, let alone that civilisation had not come to an end north of the Scottish border despite eighteen months of Labour–Lib Dem coalition.

None of their arguments held much sway with me. From my knowledge of coalitions, the risks lay heavily with the minority party. Furthermore, I had ruled out changing the voting system in local government – it was going to happen in Scotland, but we had ruled it out in Wales. The Lib Dems had not pushed it once I'd made it clear that it was undeliverable.

I had to be very patient in taking my message around Wales. Opposition soon faded because the wider membership and the public were generally okay with it, but there was a legacy of deep-seated resentment on the assumption that I'd pushed it through, and it rebounded on the head of Mike German a year later.

### The Five Fs: how crisis management changed perceptions

The autumn and winter of 2000–1 saw a series of crises afflict the UK, with Wales right in eye of the storm for most of the time, as though they were sent to try us. Very few were directly to do with our devolved duties – none involved the implementation of Labour manifesto commitments, and what was required was nothing more than simple common-sense good government and crisis management. If we could deliver, then the talking shop accusation of the anti-devolutionists in the 1997 referendum could well go away.

With a lot of barely poetic licence, I invoked the Five Fs. Of course, I only did that in August 2001, by which time even the biggest crisis of them all, foot-and-mouth (which I'll get on to later), was a distant memory.

It all kicked off with the *fuel* tanker drivers' dispute over the price of DERV in September 2000, the first really awkward test for the Blair Government. The tanker drivers were joined in their go-slow protests by the small hauliers, claiming that they were losing business and making huge losses all because the price of DERV in the UK was wildly out of line with its price on mainland Europe.

Nothing could be further away from our devolved responsibilities in Wales than fuel duty. But the new political realities were that the go-slow drivers wanted to start their rolling blockade from outside the Assembly. We were *there* in a way that the Secretary of State for Wales in Cathays Park under the old system had never been. We had visibility and, what's more, we were no distance from the oil tanker depots on Cardiff Docks.

So the lines of trucks and tankers kept on coming, driving up and down at two miles per hour from the Docks to the Assembly and back. They wanted to speak with someone from the Assembly to air their grievances, so Sue Essex agreed to meet them. This was a month before I reshuffled her into my Cabinet. She was the Chair of the Planning and Environment Committee, and had previously run Cardiff City Council. She knew how to run a meeting. She was a good listener and had a natural empathy for anyone engaged in a protest of some kind. She also carried enough natural gravitas to deal with desperate hauliers and stroppy tanker drivers alike.

With Sue in charge, the situation would not disintegrate into a Blair and Brown bashing session. Much better for her to meet them than me or any of my Ministers – I didn't want to split hairs, but I had to stay out of something that I could do nothing about. Still, I didn't expect protesting truckers to make distinctions on devolved and central government issues – all they understood was that there were a whole lot of politicians inside that Assembly building. It would have been inflammatory not to agree to meet them at all. There was a lesson to be learnt for the future. With the Assembly being so new, any social or economic grievance would naturally gravitate towards it, and though we might only be responsible for *half* of the public money spent in Wales, we very well might have to deal with *all* of the grievances!

'Grievance' wasn't always the right word, though. Quite often during that Trials of Job period for the Assembly, in the autumn and winter period 2000–1, we were dealing with natural disasters. The fuel tanker drivers' dispute was followed quite quickly by the huge disruption of the entire UK rail and freight system caused by the Hatfield disaster. While the safety inspectors and Railtrack got on with the painstaking job of working out why the failsafe systems had failed at Hatfield, a maximum speed limit of 30 mph was imposed on all InterCity rail travel. The Cardiff to London train journey took more than four hours instead of two.

Then came the massive rainstorms of October and the flooding that followed. Two county roads were completely washed away in Wales. One was the Horseshoe Pass route, heading north from Llangollen towards Ruthin. The other was the Bwlch Road over the mountain from Maerdy in the Rhondda Fach Valley to Aberdare. The Dee and Alyn rivers in north-east Wales overflowed as well. I had an almost spiritual experience at Bangor-on-Dee (Bangor-is-y-Coed in Welsh, literally Bangor-beneath-the-trees), which is protected from the river by levees, elevated mud banks, as the river passes by the town on its way to Chester and the Dee estuary. I was asked by the community council to see how close the river was getting to the top of the levees. Culturally and geographically, Bangor-on-Dee is very much part of the Cheshire Plain. I'd read somewhere that if the river hadn't changed its course a couple of centuries ago, the whole of the Maelor salient, including Bangor-on-Dee, would be in England. But it was still in Wales in 2000–1, so we gathered in the town square and walked across to the river bank, and up onto the levees. The Dee was in spate alright, racing along towards Chester at one hell of a lick. It was in the evening, and the river's dark brown colour made it look even more menacing. The townspeople and I just stood there watching the river level inch upwards, willing it to stop rising and to recede. And it did, with just two inches to spare! I have no idea what we'd have done if the water had carried on rising. Run for our lives, I suppose!

What also struck me about that quasi-spiritual experience was that the people of Bangor-on-Dee had, in all probability, voted overwhelmingly against devolution. I doubted if any of them had ever been to Cardiff in their lives but, in their hour of need, they wanted the First Minister of Wales with them. The crisis did help them grasp something of what devolution was all about.

Steel was the next crisis to hit Wales, with the announcement from the Anglo-Dutch steel company Corus that they were going to close the heavy end of Llanwern steelworks. Llanwern is not a giant steelworks by the latest world standards (3 million tonnes of liquid steel per year, rather than 7 million or more), but it was very big by UK standards, and thousands of steel jobs were going to be lost. It was shocking just how quickly things could deteriorate. In September 2000, Corus had announced that the £30 million re-line of the big 10,000 tonnes-a-day blast furnace at Llanwern was going ahead. We knew that the Corus strip mill operations based mainly in South Wales were losing money, and that the Dutch end was profitable. It was mostly down to the scissors effect of the high pound and the ailing euro. However, as at September, Corus's senior management had been persuaded that they should ignore these freak currency effects, ride out the storm, and keep both Port Talbot and Llanwern going while the currency fluctuations ironed themselves out.

By January, the head of the Corus strip mills operations John Bryant had suddenly gone, and the blast furnace re-line was cancelled. John Bryant was very loyal to Llanwern, which was his local works in many ways. The bosses of the combine had simply lost patience. They couldn't wait for Britain to make up its mind about joining the euro or whatever, and the axe was swung. Llanwern would lose its actual liquid steel-making side – the rolling mills would stay, with slabs being rail-hauled the forty miles east from Port Talbot to Llanwern to be reheated and then rolled through into coil or strip, or even galvanised.

At Rodney Parade, the historic Newport RFC ground on the banks of the River Usk, I was the guest at a rugby match of the industrialist Tony Brown, who had sunk a lot of money into Newport both industrially (via his Bisley office equipment factories) and into the rugby team. Just below the committee box in the West Stand, where I was sat with Tony Brown and the local AM John Griffiths, one of the punters turned around and looked up at the row of VIPs. He spotted me, and shouted out, 'Save Llanwern, Rhodri!'

It was very touching that a guy on the terraces thought it was in my gift to save Llanwern, though it was well beyond my powers. What would have saved Llanwern was a more competitive level for the pound relative to the euro – maybe a deepwater ore port as well. Llanwern was an amazing works in many ways, but the cost penalty for double-handling all of the raw materials was the reason why neither John Bryant, nor I, nor anyone else could save Llanwern.

They had barely got going in demolishing the blast furnaces, coke ovens and steel-making vessels in November 2001 when the blast furnace explosion happened at Port Talbot. If the decision to close the heavy end at Llanwern had been put off for a year, it would have at least an extra five years' lease of life because of the aftermath of the Port Talbot explosion. What with Allied Steel & Wire in Cardiff, and the old Guest Keen iron and steelworks going into administration, it seemed that steel's massive role in Welsh industrialisation over two centuries was coming to an end. The bad times were concentrated into 2000–2 period, although they came back with a vengeance in 2016.

But things could have been so much worse. The blast furnace explosion killed three, and badly burned fourteen others. When the Health & Safety Executive report into the causes of the explosion was published several years later, it described how but couldn't exactly explain why the blast furnace exploded. The blast furnace weighed about five thousand tons, and lifted about two inches into the air by the force of the blast – it was barely credible good luck for the works and for the town that it came back down again to rest on its foundations without tilting over at all. If it had keeled over, the gas pipes including the carbon monoxide pipe would have fractured. If that had happened, a silent killer cloud of odourless and colourless heavier-than-air gas would have wafted over the tightly packed terraced streets hard up against the boundary fence. I discussed this with the area director of the Health & Safety Executive, Terry Rose, after the report came out. 'Christ, Terry', I said, 'you're telling me that this could have been the Welsh Bhopal?' There was no dissent with my comparison with the Union Carbide disaster in India that had killed thousands.

More by luck than judgement, the major disaster that could have been didn't happen – but it could have. I remember going down to Port Talbot to see Dr Mark Carr, the Corus plant director at the works, the day after the explosion. His face was white as a shroud. He left the steel industry not long afterwards to become Chief Executive of the British Sugar Corporation. After my discussion with Terry Rose about the possible catastrophe if the carbon monoxide pipe had fractured, I could understand why Dr Carr had such a ghostly pallor that dreadful day.

When I had first joined the old Welsh Office as a young regional economist back in 1966, the industry employed 75,000 people. Throughout 2001 and 2002, the agonies of the industry seemed never-ending – the closure of the heavy end at Llanwern, the cold mill in Shotton, the tinplate works in Ebbw Vale, and the outright closure of the Bryngwyn coating plant at Gowerton. The final end of iron and steel-making at Llanwern came on 26 June 2001; the blast furnace explosion at Port Talbot was in November 2001; Allied Steel & Wire went into administration on 10 July 2002.

That this non-stop flow of bad news wasn't exactly the death knell for the steel industry was due in some part to the decision of the Health & Safety Executive, along with the Crown Prosecution Service, who didn't blame company negligence on Corus's part for the explosion. The company's insurance claim was therefore valid, and in a way the company was able to start the revival of the industry by using the insurance payout to build a brand new blast furnace, bigger than the one which had blown up.

Likewise, the assets of Allied Steel & Wire in Cardiff were bought by CELSA, a Barcelona-based family steel company. After a twelve-month period of grace, the Rubiralta family behind CELSA did invest heavily in a new electric arc steel-making plant to produce the billets that could then be re-rolled into bars and reinforcement for concrete and so forth.

The explosion at Port Talbot paradoxically led to a wave of investment in the plant, nothing was going to bring back those who lost their lives or restore to health those who were badly burned, but that was despite the best efforts of the Plastic Surgery and Burns Unit at Morriston Hospital. Again, there came a stroke of luck that may have saved some of the industrial injuries from being totally devastating, when one of the A&E consultants at Morriston happened to be driving along the M4 alongside the works at precisely the moment the explosion happened. That consultant described to me afterwards how, as he heard the bang and saw the clouds of dust and smoke rising, he realised that industrial injuries were a probability. He pulled off the motorway and drove straight into the works to offer to help. He was taken straight into the scene of devastation, and was able to triage everyone hurt or burned at top speed for onward transport to Morriston Hospital as the ambulances and helicopters arrived.

Bizarre accusations were subsequently thrown at me in the Assembly, during the course of urgent questions on the explosion, by two AMs – Tory Alun Cairns (now Secretary of State for Wales), and Plaid Cymru's Janet Davies. They must both have known that responsibility for industrial health and safety was completely undevolved – it came under the H&SE, an arm's length body even from the UK Government. Nevertheless, the two of them implied that I was in some obscure way complicit in the explosion. I was asked to divulge the contents of meetings I had had with Corus – but disclosure was impossible, because no company would ever hold any kind of commercially confidential meeting with me again if the contents of a meeting were divulged subsequently. Because of the political cauldron atmosphere of the Assembly, it was seen as acceptable to accuse me of hiding something relevant to the causes of the explosion – a smear like that was not just below the belt, it was straight out of the political sewer.

When Allied Steel & Wire went into receivership in 2002, I had to take part in one of the most difficult mass meetings I've ever known. The workforce wanted a meeting with the ISTC, the main steel union, to see if there was any way forward.

It was arranged at the Railway Workingmen's Club on Sanquhar Street, Adamsdown, just around the corner from the steelworks. The ISTC leadership asked me to be there with them in anticipation of an angry mood and, my goodness, they certainly got it. It certainly couldn't be otherwise, with a thousand or so men all without jobs and their pensions under threat.

All the chairs had been removed from the hall to make room for everyone, so it was a thousand men with no future, all standing up and wanting explanations. You could cut the atmosphere with a knife. I got there a little late, as agreed in advance, after closing my Saturday morning constituency surgery in Ely, before driving across Cardiff to Adamsdown.

I joined the ISTC leaders up on the stage – we were the ones in the suits, no one on the floor of the hall wore a suit – and we as surrogates for the company's management were the objects of the mass anger against what had happened. They wanted someone to blame.

Despite the tinderbox atmosphere, things didn't get out of hand. It was one of the supreme tests of my political skills to avoid letting that meeting boil over, but allowing steam to be vented for an hour of more by a thousand people. That was tough. The union leadership was incredibly grateful afterwards that I'd come along, because my presence had taken some of the heat off them.

Eventually, a year or so later, many of those at the meeting did get their jobs back, but without any continuity of their accumulated pension entitlement. Older workers were a bit more agitated about the loss of those company pension rights, whereas the younger ones understandably prioritised getting their jobs back.

Because the ASW (now CELSA) steel complex is plainly visible from the Assembly, there is a certain symbolism about the co-location of heavy industry and Wales's new democracy. Although I had been desperate for the Assembly to be in the Civic Centre of Cardiff, I'd lost that battle, and then I felt we had to exploit our co-location with the smokestack world that had powered Wales forward since the Industrial Revolution.

On one occasion, the Saudi Ambassador to the UK was paying an official visit to the Assembly. As normal, after the official part of the meeting was over, I took our VIP guest out to the little balcony outside my office on the fifth floor. I always did this unless it was raining to get some photographs with official visitors, because the views from that balcony were fantastic.

Anyway, as I swung round to show the Ambassador everything from the Somerset coast in the distance to the Norwegian Church where Roald Dahl had been christened, we alighted on the view of the steelworks. 'A steelworks?' asked the Ambassador, 'You should not have a steelworks next to your main seat of government! You should have all your civic buildings around here.' So, I gently chided him – it was vital that we did have a steel plant next-door, because it reminded us at all times how important heavy industry was to Wales now and had been since

1750. I made my point: 'Either driving past the long blue rolling mill building on the way down to the Assembly, or seeing it every time I bring a VIP out to the balcony, is a salutary reminder of who we are governing Wales for.'

Pointing out the Coal Exchange building, amid the jumble of Mount Stuart Square half a mile away, was always a key part of my aerial guided tour from the balcony. There were two reasons for pointing out the Coal Exchange. It was there that the first ever £1 million cheque in UK financial history had been signed, in 1906, when coal exports were at record level and the US Navy had ordered a huge quantity of Welsh dry-steam coal from a consortium of Welsh coal traders in the Exchange. It didn't happen in London, it happened in Cardiff, and that was hard for some to believe.

The second reason was that in 1979, when the first referendum on Welsh devolution had gone down in flames by an adverse 4–1 vote, the Coal Exchange was the building designated at that time to have housed a new Assembly.

I liked the balcony as a safety valve from too many back-to-back meetings in my office. It was like a walk in the fresh air, or at least a walk on deck, as a relief from cabin fever. We didn't have the Downing Street Rose Garden, just that little balcony.

In the aftermath of the Six Nations Grand Slam won by captain Gareth 'Alfie' Thomas and coach Mike Ruddock's Wales XV in 2005 – the first Grand Slam for Wales in twenty-nine years, courtesy of Gavin Henson's wondrous last-minute penalty goal against England and Gethin Jenkins's fantastic length of the field charge-down try against Ireland – I did toy with the idea of an open-top bus tour on the Sunday morning, after which it could have culminated with the team and me appearing together on that balcony with a crowd down in Roald Dahls Plass and in the space between the Assembly and the Wales Millennium Centre. It didn't happen, in part because the balcony was a bit too high from ground level, and too small – far from ideal from a safety point of view.

I floated the idea in the WRU President's Lounge over the tea and biscuits that followed the Irish game, when the Grand Slam was safely in the bag. South Wales Police Chief Constable Barbara Wilding was against it. What about the insurance? Where and how could the supply of enough police officers be organised overnight? Fair point. The then chairman of the WRU, David Pickering, wasn't keen – the players wouldn't be in a fit state to be swaying on an open-top bus the morning after – they'd all be looking for a long lie-in, assuming they'd managed to get to bed at all. Fair point again, so I dropped the idea.

But it is one of my regrets, looking back. The Welsh public would have loved it, I think, because we had waited twenty-nine years for a Grand Slam. People might have a moan at me for not organising the open-top bus on a contingency basis sometime well ahead of the final match that clinched the trophy – but actually, no! The last thing you should to do is organise a victory parade before the victory is sealed. It might have spooked the Grand Slam match. So, if it was ever going to happen, it would have to have been organised at the last minute, on the Saturday evening, and that was next to impossible. But I still regret not pushing harder for it.

I often experience similar regret every time I drive past City Hall – 'That's where the Assembly ought to be', I always think, in a building that exudes national self-confidence. For me, it bespeaks governmental authority and democracy ten times better than the little exercise in exhibition architecture that is the Richard Rogers Assembly building. To my eye, the Senedd building is a bit of candy floss, and the regret that I have is that I didn't have the time to find a way to compulsorily purchase City Hall via a CPO. Then we would have seen how much compensation Cardiff City Council was entitled to and got on with adapting City Hall for the Assembly's use. But I didn't do it.

Other regrets I have when I look back include not pushing harder for the fluoridation of water. I was in favour of doing so, but in the key period when I wanted to push it, the Health Minister Edwina Hart was strongly opposed. Wales's poor record on cavities in children's teeth can only be addressed by fluoridation. And then another regret is the failure to push on and re-open the chain of Skillcentres that had been privatised by Michael Howard in the early 1990s when he was Secretary of State for Employment. I did push for it to be in the first Wales Labour manifesto in 1999, but when I became First Minister in 2000 I was persuaded that the further education colleges would go berserk if we reintroduced the Skillcentre alternative for adults who were way too old to start apprenticeships to acquire craft skills. What the old Skillcentres had provided was a totally different way of becoming a bricklayer or fitter or whatever. In further education colleges, you were taught by lecturers, but in the Skillcentres you were taught by instructors who could give you all the basics in six months. Then you went out into the world with eighteen months of work under supervision on a building site or factory as an improver, before you could call yourself a craftsman (it was almost exclusively 'man' in those days). Anyway, I thought it was one of the worst privatisations of the many that happened under Margaret Thatcher and John Major because Astra Training, the company that bought the chain of Government Skillcentres, closed them all down in an act of wanton destruction. I didn't push that one hard enough either, but you can't win them all.

## The Awkward Squad

Among the things about which I have no regrets is my leadership or management of the Labour Group family from 2000–3, despite the presence of the Awkward Squad, which comprised three individuals and an occasional fourth.

I've already mentioned John Marek, who thought he should have been in my Cabinet from the off and suspected the dark hand of the intelligence services (not true). He won his seat of Wrexham a second time, but this time as an Independent rather than a Labour candidate, in 2003. He defeated his former staffer Lesley Griffiths, who had been selected to replace him, but she beat him when the whole episode was repeated with the same line-up in 2007. John then formed his own party before joining a tiny new party called Forward Wales with a left-wing anti-Blair activist named Marc Jones – so John went from a one-man political party to a two-man party! Then when that also proved short-lived, he seemed to drift out of politics altogether.

One thing I have no regrets about is declining, at Dafydd Elis-Thomas's invitation, to join the drinking circle that he, John Marek and the later disgraced Lib Dem Mick Bates (AM for Montgomery) belonged to. They met up in the Members Tea Room to while away the long evenings, given that Assembly business was usually over by five-thirty, knocking back a good few bottles of plonk, and then the official cars of the Presiding Officer and Deputy Presiding Officer would transport everybody home without any worries over drink-driving and the breathalyser. I am not against politicians enjoying a few drinks after a hard day's work but, to be honest, I couldn't think of anything worse. I politely declined the invitation, despite Dafydd El telling me that it would be healthy for the Assembly if there was less of a gap between the Cabinet and the Presiding Officer.

Dafydd El did spend most Wednesdays in the House of Lords, and John Marek would then take over the Presiding Officer's Chair, but he still didn't have much to do. As a result, John would come up with barmy ideas for which he could be confident that I would get the blame. The barmiest was to buy speculatively the quarter-acre plot south of the Assembly for future expansion. It was only a quarter of an acre, but very valuable, and when the public got wind of the proposition it went down like the proverbial lead balloon. And, of course, it was assumed that I was behind the idea. I must have been, because I was Mr Assembly, wasn't I?

Whereas John thought he should have been selected by me as a member of the Cabinet, Ron Davies thought he should have been running the Cabinet selections himself anyway. He never got over not being the First Minister. The Caerphilly constituency Labour Party did re-select him to stand for the Assembly in 2003, and if the *Sun* newspaper had not nabbed him in a highly embarrassing episode of 'badger-watching' just off the M4, I presume he would have got back into the Assembly for another term.

After the moment of madness episode on the wild side of Clapham Common at the end of 1998, Ron claimed to have undergone a course of psychological treatment to cure him of his compulsion towards risky behaviour. Well, he certainly started the course, but I'm not sure he ever finished it. Anyway, it constituted a useful tool for him in responding to the question every Assembly Labour candidate had to respond to, which was the dreaded questions, 'Have you got any skeletons in the cupboard which, if they emerged into daylight, could embarrass the Labour Party?' Ron did, by hook or by crook, get through the re-selection procedure.

But when the *Sun* found him wandering suspiciously around a lay-by somewhere near Bath, it was all too predictable. The leopard had not changed its spots, and whatever psychological treatment he had undergone, it had not had the desired effect. He couldn't be allowed to stand again, and though there were many in the Labour Party who felt strongly sympathetic towards the badger population, they didn't extend that sympathy to Ron.

There then followed some agonised negotiations with Jessica Morden, then the General Secretary of the Welsh Labour Party and more recently the MP for Newport East, and with Brian Curtis, the Chairman of the Party, to oblige Ron into pulling out of his candidacy. Ron was invited to the Labour Party Wales office in Transport House to meet Jessica and Brian after the badger episode, and Ron explained that he had just bought an expensive house with a big mortgage. Brian Curtis took Ron into the photocopier room to try and sort it out man to man. Whatever was said in there, Ron agreed to resign his candidacy. Brian Curtis, a hard-nosed railwayman's trade union official, could be very persuasive. The key point was that Ron would only stand down if the payment protection insurance policy on his mortgage could be activated. Jessica Morden was unhappy about providing the necessary designer-letter of comfort to Ron's bank that would trigger the mortgage payment protection – Ron needed a letter to say that he had effectively been forced to give up the candidacy, whereas if he just resigned his mortgage payment protection wouldn't be activated. Jessica did what she had to because it was absolutely necessary in the reputational interest of the Labour Party. So I guess Ron Davies is the only person in Wales who was glad to have been sold PPI – he really did need it.

Anyway, as soon as Ron knew the insurance on his mortgage was in the bag, he stood down. The experience was probably quite searing for Jessica, and I don't think she ever felt the same about being General Secretary of the Welsh Labour Party again. When the vacancy for Newport arose with Alan Howarth standing down, Jessica threw her hat in the ring and was selected. I couldn't blame her. When you apply to become the organisational chief of the Labour Party in Wales, there is nothing in the job description indicating that you might have to write a letter on behalf of a badger-loving Assembly Member with an uncured addiction to compulsive risk-seeking behaviour, all in aid of facilitating activation of his PPI policy. That wasn't what Jessica had signed up for.

Ron did make a comeback of sorts in 2006, when the unpopularity of Labour post the Iraq War was at its height, as an Independent councillor for the

Machen Ward on Caerphilly Borough Council. Ron and his colleague unseated the two Labour councillors, and were then able to do a deal with Plaid Cymru. Those two Independents from Machen had the two votes on the Council that Plaid Cymru needed to give them control. In return, Ron earned himself a Cabinet job – not in the Assembly Cabinet, of course, but at least it was a Cabinet job – the Economic Development & Urban Regeneration portfolio on Caerphilly County Borough Council.

In a very small way and only extending to Caerphilly, Ron had achieved the realignment of Welsh politics post-devolution that he had dreamt of.

Peter Law, the third fully paid-up member of the Awkward Squad, was a more interesting case than Ron Davies and John Marek. He was not an MP when the Assembly came into being, although he did become one later on, of course. So I hadn't come across Peter until we had a candidate's get-together in Baverstock's Hotel on the heads of the Valleys Road in March 1999 – a stupid date to arrange a get-together because it clashed with a Wales vs France rugby international in Paris. During the final tea break, we all watched a bit of the second half, some with greater avidity than others. Wales were playing rather well under Graham Henry's wise guidance. I disgraced myself by staying behind in the little lounge – I just had to see out the rest of the game. Alun Michael reconvened us all with fifteen minutes of the match left to go – he just wasn't interested in rugby at all. Anyway, despite several attempts to throw the game to France right at the death, France seemed determined to throw the game back, and Wales won 32–31.

In high spirits, I re-entered the room as the naughty boy creeping in at the back, thinking others would want to know what had happened. Peter Law was in full flow, giving it everything in as good an exhibition of sycophancy as you could ever wish to hear – or rather *not* wish to hear. It was totally over the top, pretty much proposing Alun Michael for sainthood, 'Without Alun's outstanding leadership, none of us would be here today … etc. etc.'

Of course, it was tough for Peter having to adapt to life on the back-benches after the Labour–Lib Dem coalition came into being, but still he spoke frequently and with great fluency in the Assembly Chamber. I would say that he was the best natural orator we had in the Assembly, regardless of party, and he could get up at the briefest notice and speak without hesitation on any subject. But he was very frustrated. I was desperate to find some outlet for his talent, but with so few seats in the Assembly the flexibility wasn't there.

After Labour's 2003 victory and the new Assembly Labour Group of thirty had assembled for a joint session of a fairly celebratory kind with the Welsh Labour Executive, Peter's was the only dissenting voice. While all the other Labour AMs saw it as a victory, Peter saw the prospect of four more boring years with nothing to do on the back-benches. There was animus against me there, that was clear.

When Llewelyn Smith, better known in the Welsh style as Llew Smith, Peter's opposite number as MP for Blaenau Gwent, announced his intention to retire well ahead of the 2005 General Election, Peter wanted to go for it. I had no problem with that – it would solve a problem for me – but a sub-committee of Welsh Labour's executive decided it should be an all-woman shortlist. Peter, I am sure, thought I was behind it – to punish him in some way – but I hadn't even been consulted and, if I had been, I would have advised against an all-woman shortlist in Blaenau Gwent. It was asking for trouble. Labour chose Maggie Jones, a senior Unison union official, originally from Cardiff, and she didn't go down well. She was seen as an imposed candidate, while Peter was considered one of us by the people of the area.

Peter then left the Labour Party to run as an Independent, and won quite easily in the end. There was an almighty twist in the story that happened half-way through the campaign, however, when Peter was found to have a very substantial and malignant brain tumour. He had only months to live. We all assumed that he would abandon the candidacy to concentrate on his health and his family.

Peter's oncologist at Velindre Hospital in Cardiff, Wales's leading cancer hospital, recommended that he should be given access to one of those wonder drugs that can extend the life of cancer patients, but which cost the earth. In England, there would have been access to the Cancer Drugs Fund, but in Wales we had decided not to have an equivalent fund because drugs only form 10 per cent of cancer treatments – surgery and radiotherapy form the other 90 per cent. But this was not seen to be relevant in Peter Law's case – he needed access to this wonder drug, and that was that.

Peter received the drug, and I only found out long after retiring that my office had sorted it all out without telling me – they thought it was better that I didn't know, and it was all done as quickly and discreetly as possible.

I had spoken to Peter at the stage where we had assumed that he would abandon his candidacy, advising him to take it easy and to concentrate on managing the treatment and the inevitable side effects, and to spend as much time with the family as he could. But Peter saw things differently. He knew he would get a huge sympathy vote in Blaenau Gwent for his bravery in ploughing on against the odds, and that he would win the election, perhaps getting in a year's service as an MP while the tumour was in remission. His wife and family would get an excellent pension from the House of Commons. Personally, I wouldn't have gone on with a brain tumour, but Peter knew exactly what he wanted to do.

Should I have made it my business to make sure that Blaenau Gwent was not forced to have an all-woman shortlist? That would have meant Peter could have walked it at the selection conference, and become the MP for Blaenau Gwent with a massive majority, and he would no longer be my problem. When the issue of the brain tumour arose, I would have felt a greater responsibility for finding an appropriate solution to that problem, though I don't know if my office would have felt able to sort out Peter Law's access to the wonder drug. No, I think it was probably for the best that I was kept out of it.

The only other time the Cabinet Secretary decided it was better not to inform me on a matter was when the fake anthrax package was delivered to me. It eventually resulted in a two-and-a-half-year sentence for a sacked Cardiff chemistry teacher, Nicholas Roberts. The actual incident took place at a time of maximum security panic on both sides of the Atlantic, just two months after 9/11, when a package containing suspicious looking white powder was addressed to me, and duly opened by one of our correspondence clerks – she had a screaming fit, and went home. The Cabinet Secretary, Lawrence Conway, thought his correspondence clerks should show some resilience in that kind of situation.

Anyway, I was protected from this information in case I didn't show the necessary resilience, and Lawrence also wanted to keep the whole incident below the political radar. In a relatively small capital city like Cardiff, however, news travels along multiple localised grapevines as much as by official media.

I was in the Cornwall pub in the middle of Grangetown for my usual Sunday night libation, when one of my friends surprised me with his greeting as I sat down. 'Gorgeous Gertie nearly got you then!' What was he talking about? Well, they knew all about the fake anthrax package even though I didn't, and I had to feign total ignorance on security grounds. It turned out that the perpetrator was a well-known local character, given to wearing ladies' frocks and parading up and down the main drag in Grangetown, where the Cornwall pub stood – he spent his days playing the accordion and painting in a studio in nearby Tudor Lane. Everyone knew of him, a wacky former-chemistry teacher who certainly had enough scientific knowledge to be able to put together a fake anthrax package. At his eventual trial he was judged mentally fit to plead, although that came as news to many in Grangetown!

Those three together – Ron Davies, John Marek and Peter Law – made for a lot of instability in the Labour Group during that period of the Labour–Lib Dem Partnership government between October 2000 and May 2003. They didn't consciously act in concert, rather being individual malcontents who all disapproved of my leadership, not really a Gang of Three. That wasn't the issue. I did notice, as did all other members of the Labour Group, the soft shoe shuffle around a quarter past twelve every Tuesday afternoon, when one or two, and now and again all three, would leave the Labour Group meeting fifteen minutes early – they wanted to provide their client friends in the media with some juicy tidbits, anything controversial or vaguely embarrassing, any disagreements that had surfaced during the Group meeting, getting their retaliation in first!

Very occasionally, Tom Middlehurst would join this group of malcontents. Whereas all the others eventually left the Labour Party, I could never imagine Tom doing that, a dyed-in-the-wool Labour man and well-schooled in the code of loyalty instilled in old-school Labour local government groups. The Labour Group in the Assembly was a halfway house between Labour groups in local government and the Parliamentary Labour Party. In councils, Labour groups would usually meet on a Monday night, when business for the week ahead would get an airing and votes would be taken to determine the Labour Whip on each matter. Then, each member of the group would have to abide by the Whip or else, bound by the majority decision even when it went against them, but at least they had their say and vote in the group meeting before the Whip was decided.

There's nothing like that in Westminster. The front-bench determines the Whip. It is explained at a weekly meeting, but only in order to explain rather than to have an open discussion on the matter. The Minister, or Shadow Minister when Labour is in Opposition, never expects to have his or her recommended Whip rejected after a democratic and open discussion – that only happens in local government, not central government

We tried to find a halfway house in the Assembly. Ten out of our twenty-eight AMs on the Labour side had been councillors (that included Alun Michael before he resigned). Although I'd been an officer in local government, I had never been elected as a councillor – perhaps it was a good thing, perhaps not. For some Assembly Members, old council habits die hard.

Tom's fierce loyalty to his local government past surfaced in a way that caused a massive but temporary rift between the two of us over the Wales European Centre, the WEC, a hybrid outfit in Brussels, which acted as the eyes and ears in the EU for us, local authorities and universities, and some business and voluntary organisations in Wales. The WEC was a joint arrangement, involving no separation between the civil servants working for the Assembly with accredited status, and the others sharing an office with them but working for other bodies.

The result of this joint arrangement was that the UK Government's EU Embassy in Brussels, UKREP for short, could brief the Scottish Executive's officials but not ours. What the Scots had was two back-to-back offices, but with passwords to get into the governmental office. That's where I was desperate for change in the Brussels set-up. We had to get a properly accredited office that would have diplomatic cover, so that it could share official government information. But Tom was having none of that, he wanted WEC to stay exactly as it was.

Splitting the WEC office so that the governmental half had governmental authority was an exact parallel to what I was trying to do in the Assembly itself – it was the whole point of the establishment of the working title of Welsh Assembly Government, however cumbersome the title was. It went deeper than a campaign slogan, and I could see afterwards what this was all about. Tom and other local government leaders, the heavies, especially on the Labour side, had either been promised or had assumed a promise that devolution would mean a novel kind of partnership state in Wales, with responsibility shared between the sixty AMs and Labour local government. They would be equal partners. Perhaps it wasn't just a way of getting councillors to vote for Alun Michael rather than me. Indeed, it had also perhaps been a way of getting councillors to campaign for a Yes vote in September 1997 (very few Labour councillors had campaigned for devolution back in 1979).

This equal partnership idea was a constitutional absurdity. The job that the Assembly had to do was to take over the powers of the Secretary of State for Wales and all the quangos that came under him. There was not the slightest suggestion that local government was going to share those responsibilities with the Assembly – conversely, there was no suggestion either that the Assembly was going to take over the functions of local government.

Whatever the arguments about our mandate, the situation we faced was that the heavyweight leaders of local government in Wales thought they were running Wales with an unofficial status of equality with the Assembly – the Leader of the WLGA, Harry Jones (Newport), believed it; Noel Crowley, leader of Neath Port Talbot, believed it; Jeff Jones (Bridgend) believed it; Tom Middlehurst probably believed it too, and was therefore on the lookout for signs that we were downgrading local government from this self-assumed status of equal partners.

That's why the relatively minor issue of splitting the WEC into two halves became such a *casus belli* between Tom and me. There was no going back, however, and no regrets over the issue. I was totally confirmed in my view of the necessity of the split, when the head of UKREP told me at last that he could brief my officials exactly as he already had been briefing their Scottish opposite number.

As a result of the change, Des Clifford became Wales's first ever fully accredited man in Brussels, and could rightly claim that he was Wales's first proper diplomat since Gruffydd Young, the emissary appointed by Owain Glyndŵr to carry the historical Pennal Letter to the King of France in seeking his military assistance to pursue the Welsh rebellion of 1400–10 against English conquest.

Disabusing the corps of Labour councillors of the myth of the equal partnership model was at the heart of the problems I had in selling the coalition with the Lib Dems (coincidentally also referred to as the Partnership Government). They eventually got their revenge with the Mike German Welsh Joint Education Committee expenses row, even though the equal partnership model of how to run Wales was by then in its death throes. This was a year into the coalition government. The row concerned allegations against the Deputy First Minister, Mike German, but related to his time as an employee of the WJEC before 1999.

The WJEC, or 'Welsh Joint', was the original Welsh quango, belonging to the twenty-two Welsh local authorities. Its basic job was to set and mark examination papers for GCSEs and A levels, but unlike its Scottish equivalent, the SQA, the WJEC was not a statutory monopoly. Schools in Wales had every right to choose the English-based examination bodies like the OCR (not-for-profit) or Edexcel (for-profit). Conversely, English schools could opt to sit WJEC examinations if they so chose.

When John Redwood had reorganised Welsh local government into twenty-two all-purpose county borough councils in 1994, the councils had asked if they could convert the WJEC into a statutory monopoly like the SQA. This would remove some of the financial risk from the councils that were about to start their new future, but they were told no because they were in a market place. The WJEC had to go out into the market and generate income from outside Wales as well as from inside.

Mike German's job had been to generate income especially from Europe, which meant he had to go around Europe finding collaborative ventures that the WJEC could participate in and generate some income. By 2001, Mike was Deputy First Minister and Minister of Economic Development & European Affairs. The WJEC, in the meantime, was very much under the control of Labour councillors and some of them hated Mike German's guts – either for personal reasons, or because they hated the idea that the Lib Dems had usurped their dreamt-of function of a partnership in running Wales.

Someone in the WJEC, presumably on the financial side, must have tipped off one of the councillor heavyweights on the committee board that among Mike's many journeys across Europe had been one to Vienna, which happened to coincide with a meeting of the Liberal International in the same city. And it so happened that among the delegates to that Liberal International was Jenny Randerson, Mike German's colleague in our coalition Cabinet. The hound dogs of the investigative journalist community in Wales were given the basic story, and then told to go find!

This resulted in two of the most excruciating meetings in which I had to participate during my decade in power, with no civil servants or even Special Advisers present at either. The first meeting was with two of the real Labour councillor heavies, Jeff Jones and Noel Crowley. Jeff was the one who was a big wheel in the WJEC, and he had a certain degree of resentment against the Assembly because he'd failed to get on the panel of Labour candidates for the first Assembly elections in 1999. That had been a hard blow to Jeff, which was understandable after being named in the press in 1998 as the probable Education Minister in Ron Davies's first Cabinet. To go from being the Education Minister-elect in Wales's first ever Cabinet to not even being a candidate was a massive come-down. It must have been a blow to the solar plexus as well as the ego.

Noel Crowley, who with Newport Council Leader Harry Jones was the most traditional of the Welsh Labour leaders, suggested that we evict the officials from our meeting so that we could sort out this Mike German business once and for all, man to man. It was now going to be the mythic co-determination model of how Wales should be run in spades – but for the very last time!

I was told by Jeff and Noel that I should sack Mike German from my Cabinet, and if that caused the collapse of the Labour–Lib Dem coalition, so be it. Mike was guilty as charged, as far as Jeff and Noel were concerned, of all manner of expenses naughties while working for the WJEC. Jeff claimed to have stone-cold proof from the finance department of the WJEC, and that it was my job to bat them off to give space and time for any investigation required to get to the bottom of the allegations. There were procedures to follow in pursuing any evidence of historic irregularities, and I could then consider any real evidence that emerged from those investigations.

Jeff Jones presumed that he was the only person in the room who knew anything about the workings of the WJEC, and it was at times like this that I was eternally grateful to have WJEC blood coursing in my veins. I told Jeff and Noel that my mother had worked for the WJEC since the 1930s, marking Welsh Language and Literature A level scripts, and I could see their faces fall as I recalled that when my mother started working as an exam marker the body was still called the Central Welsh Board, and A levels were still called Highers. I knew then that I'd won my point, and it took the wind out of their sails. I might be without any officials to help me, but I could call instead on my mother, in spirit if not in body. Jeff and Noel didn't have a monopoly of knowledge of how the Welsh school examination system worked.

The second meeting was even more of a nightmare. I had to call in Mike German and Jenny Randerson, our two Lib Dem Cabinet colleagues, to question them on whether they'd shared a room or if anything untoward of that kind had gone on in Vienna during the Liberal International beano. It was the innuendo swirling around the whole issue – I was sorry, I said, but I did have to ask them if any of it might be true. Was there anything that, if it emerged to the light of day, could cause embarrassment to my administration?

Again, there were no officials present to take notes. I think Mike and Jenny knew that I was not enjoying asking them these questions, any more than they were enjoying answering them. They both assured me that nothing untoward had gone on, and I accepted their word. I had to. The important point was that they had given me their personal assurances that there had been no impropriety.

To this day, I do not know what triggered the involvement of the South Wales Police who added their weight to the investigations carried out by the audit experts of the WJEC. Mike and I had agreed that if and when the police got involved in any investigations, he would have to stand down from the Cabinet *pro tempore*. The police did announce that they were going to investigate, and Mike stood down and hired his own legal team. It cost him many thousands. He had to sell his comfortable semi in Roath in Cardiff, and instead buy a new house twenty miles north of Cardiff in the old mining village of Markham, in the Sirhowy Valley. You got an awful lot more house for your money in Markham than in Cardiff, and it was pretty painful for Mike to move house.

It must have been pretty painful too for Jenny Randerson as the sole remaining Lib Dem in the coalition Cabinet. She hadn't been enthusiastic about joining the Cabinet from the outset, but had gone along with it. And she couldn't pull out now that Mike was suspended from his public duties, because it would look as if she had no confidence that Mike would come through the investigations and return to the Cabinet.

For exactly those reasons, I didn't initially reshuffle the Cabinet. Eventually, the police investigations took so long that I had to fill the Economic Development job rather than continue to do it myself pro tem. I appointed Andrew Davies as Mike German's replacement, so when Mike was eventually cleared of fraudulent expenses claims I couldn't possibly reverse the reshuffle. So, for the final year of the coalition, Mike was Rural Affairs & Agriculture Minister.

My gut feeling all along was that there wasn't much in the allegations of expenses fraud. I had phone calls at home in the evenings from ex-WJEC staff who explained the background to the vendetta against Mike German. His year-long unavailability to the Cabinet cast quite a shadow over the workings of our coalition, but we survived. Jenny Randerson held the relatively light brief of Culture Media & Sport, plus the Welsh Language, for the whole of the two and a half years, from October 2000 until April 2003. Its Westminster equivalent, the DCMS, was sometimes referred to as the 'Ministry of Fun' – I don't think Jenny found it much fun, but she stuck it out. She was probably helped in that one of our Cabinet's weaknesses, namely that we were too Cardiff oriented, actually became a strength. Jenny knew so many of the Labour women in the Cabinet from having served with them on Cardiff City Council or South Glamorgan County Council.

The real driver for the Welsh Lib Dems was that their Scottish opposite numbers were in government in a Labour-led coalition. The Welsh Lib Dems would have felt bereft if they were not in government in the same way – they wanted to be able to look their Scottish counterparts in the eye, and say 'We're in government too!' It was also very much part of the sales patter of Lib Dem leaders in Westminster that the party was already in government in Scotland and Wales, and they were therefore to be to be taken seriously as a party of power rather than a fringe outfit of sandal-wearing vegetarians. By the time of writing, of course, the Lib Dems may have a much more downbeat perspective on the alleged advantages of being in a coalition government, whether in Westminster or in Wales!

## The Foot-and-Mouth outbreak

I've mentioned the search for stability via the formation of the Labour–Lib Dem coalition but the real prize, if only we could earn it, was the respect and affection of the public in Wales as providers of proper competent government. Crisis management is a test of whether you've got what it takes. I've mentioned the Five Fs over the autumn and winter of 2000–1. A bit of a stretch to call them all Fs, maybe – the fuel tanker drivers' dispute, the flooding, the freight trains (which were actually the passenger trains), the ferrous metals – but everyone can guess the final F because it was the big daddy of them all, the foot-and-mouth disease outbreak that dominated everything the Assembly did until August 2001.

It's easy to measure just how big the impact of FMD was when you recall how the General Election called for May 2001 had to be deferred by a month because some farmers would be unable to vote due to livestock movement restrictions. Quite literally, the farmers wouldn't be able to get to the polling stations! That was in Devon, not in Wales, but here in Wales we were certainly seriously affected by the outbreak of the disease. The first cases in Wales came in Anglesey, and they emerged on Day 2 of the UK crisis, and the outbreak highlighted very early on one of the most difficult flashpoints in managing the FMD outbreak – the problem of where to bury the carcasses of the cows and sheep that had to be slaughtered.

From that Day 2 onwards, we were obviously going to be on a crisis management footing, regardless of the fact that animal health was not a devolved issue in 2001 (it is devolved now). That's the difference between *de jure* and *de facto* government. In theory, we could have turned around and said to the farmers whose stock and livelihoods were threatened by FMD, 'Sorry, chaps, nothing to do with us. Animal health responsibility lies with Margaret Beckett at the Ministry of Agriculture in London!' But there was never any question of doing that. The weight of public expectation was that animal health was devolved in Wales just as much as it was in Scotland. There was never any hesitation on our part. We were in, and that was that.

If we had taken the narrow view, we would have quite rightly been accused of a dereliction of duty. We would have been seen as choosing to be a talking shop, or even a student debating society, rather than a seat of government. It wasn't a material consideration back then, but if we could show our capabilities as doers rather than just talkers in combating the crisis as well as it was being responded to in England and Scotland, we would earn the respect of the public in Wales. We did have to divert a substantial number of civil servants in responding to the outbreak, and there was a huge amount of ministerial input, mainly by the Minister of Agriculture Carwyn Jones, and myself.

Apart from the diversion of civil servants, the oddity about FMD was that we did not have to meet the costs. The bills were all paid by Margaret Beckett because in law animal health wasn't a devolved issue. We had all the resources of the state at our disposal to control the disease – not just the state Veterinary Society and the money, but the army as well.

If you had told me when I took over in February 2000 that, just a year later, I would have an army brigadier breezing into my office in Cathays Park and cheerily greeting me with the words, 'Good morning, First Minister! And what can I do for you today?' you could have knocked me down with a feather. But that's what happened. It even became the norm during the spring and summer of 2001, a sign of how far we had come in that short time. Even army brigadiers want politicians to give them marching orders. So, if you're the army brigadier sent down to Wales to help the civil power, you search out the people with the authority to get your instructions on where to deploy the troops. The people with the authority in this instance were Carwyn Jones and me, not the Secretary of State nor the Agriculture Minister back in London.

Margaret Beckett was a very devo-sceptic English Minister (still a very good friend), but she had her hands so full with trying to halt the spread of the disease in England that I'm sure she never spent one second thinking about whether the arrangements for combating FMD in Wales were entirely clear, constitutionally speaking. She just needed as much help as she could get.

Anglesey was the early Welsh hotspot. The Council had to come up with a carcass burial site, but the Council on Anglesey was the most dysfunctional local authority in Wales. Nobody seemed to run the island. Yes, there were other councils with dysfunctional departments, but on Anglesey the *whole* council was dysfunctional. To knock some sense into them, we hired a tiny private plane to take the Secretary of State for Wales Paul Murphy, Carwyn Jones and myself up to meet the Council leaders. They simply had to find somewhere to burn and bury the carcases. The problem was that on Anglesey, there were no real council leaders – they seemed to be fifty councillors and fifty leaders.

Our scheduled meeting was in Llangefni on the Sunday morning with the chief executive and nominal leaders of the Council – unfortunately, all the other councillors, who had absolutely no allegiance to the so-called leadership, were having a sit-in in the Council Chamber demanding that we meet them as well. We would not have got off the island in one piece if we had refused to meet the body of the kirk down in the Council Chamber. If there was going to be a solution for the burial site problem, it couldn't happen on Anglesey without some kind of airing in the Council Chamber.

The three of us agreed to go down and parley, and an hour of bilingual chaos ensued. We just had to ride out the storm. While the local AM and MP Ieuan Wyn Jones and his close friend Bob Parry, Chairman of the Farmers Union of Wales but also a local councillor, sat quietly in the audience, we three Ministers listened patiently to a huge amount of stage-managed indignation, which was itself the consequence of the breakdown of political leadership on the island. Still, I didn't actually dislike that kind of political rough-house, and I was certainly grateful that both Carwyn and I were fluent in Welsh.

The scale and seriousness of the FMD outbreak was really brought home on the flight back to Cardiff. We stopped off in our tiny plane on a minuscule airstrip at Welshpool in Montgomeryshire, in the heart of one of the other two disease hotspots in Wales. The descent to the airfield was like entering a war zone, with palls of smoke rising from funeral pyres dotted across the countryside from the incineration of sheep and cattle carcasses, a truly ghastly sight. We reached the pub in Welshpool for our get-together with farming and community leaders, and the atmosphere could not have been more different from the chaos in Anglesey. In Welshpool, everyone seemed united in doing the job of finding the right sites and, indeed, we'd seen the signs on our descent in the plane that they had already found plenty of those sites. In such a livestock-dominated area, nobody played nimby politics.

Eastern Monmouthshire was the third hotspot. I visited this war zone one-on-one with David T. C. Davies the local Tory AM. We met local farmers in a pub near Grosmont, right in the top north-eastern corner of the county, very close to the Herefordshire border. We'd seen all the funeral pyres up-close this time, not just from the air, and I'm not sure what was more disconcerting – the smoke rising from the pyres, or the guys in the white suits who were carrying out all these incineration ops. Again, it reminded anyone who looked of television series about chemical warfare or post-nuclear Armageddon scenarios.

Although Carwyn Jones was the Minister in charge and was utterly committed to making a success of it, I did occasionally pop into the ops room in Cathays Park. There was even a visit from Tony Blair. If it was so important that the planned General Election was postponed from May to June 2001, it was sufficiently important to make a visit to Wales obligatory for the PM. When he got into the Cathays Park ops room, I introduced Blair to our top team. There was the Minister Carwyn *Jones*; then there was the agriculture department's chief civil servant, Gareth *Jones*; then there was the Chief Vet, Tony *Jones*; then finally the liaison official linking with the police and the army, Neil *Jones*. By the time the PM had reached the fourth Jones in a row, I saw the Blair eyebrow rise a couple of notches, 'Rhodri, have you set up all these Joneses just to take the piss?'

The ops room was pretty impressive. It was the length of a cricket pitch. On the top of the enormous table in the middle was a huge one-inch scale map of Wales with military-style flags marking the location of each affected farm. In each corner of the room were the four different teams – the army, the police, the animal health vets, and the agriculture officials. Only the last team, the agriculture officials, was devolved. But at no time during the Prime Minister's visit did Blair ask either Carwyn or me how we were getting on. Neither did he ask whether we were doing anything different in bio-security measures from MAFF policy. In fact, there were a few differences emerging, but the recommendations to do one or two things differently came from our vets who, in theory, worked for and were paid by MAFF, but had effectively devolved themselves. The key thing that we were doing differently was to allow livestock farmers with two or three separate land holdings to move livestock from one holding to another, provided that they followed very precise extra bio-security measures. Such movement wasn't allowed in England, but farms with upland and lowland pastures not contiguous with each other were far more common in Wales than in England. We didn't discuss this with the PM – we were keener to tell him what we were doing, rather than have him cross-questioning us. All Blair knew was that we'd been given the use of the army to help the civilian teams, and that was job done as far as he was concerned. The visit was symbolic rather than practical. It was to show that he was interested in whether Wales *was* coping, not exactly in *how* we were coping.

What was particularly difficult for us in Wales was not the disease itself, but the impact it had on tourism. The National Parks weren't closed, but they were no-go areas for walking and climbing, and so they might as well have been closed. The countryside was effectively shut for business throughout the spring and summer of 2001. No footpaths and no trails meant no tourists.

Come mid-May, we had a massive decision to make. Would we have to cancel the Hay Literature Festival? Now that's what you call a big decision. Murphy's Law (nothing to do with Paul Murphy) dictates that if you have an outbreak of a major infectious disease, it will always occur in the most inconvenient place at the most inconvenient time, and so it was with Hay in May. A farm in Llanigon had an outbreak of FMD – Llanigon is the little parish south of Hay, on the way up towards the spectacular area of common land known as Hay Bluff. This outbreak occurred about ten days before the festival opened at the end of May bank holiday weekend.

Of course, the literary folk who descend from all over the world on the Wye Valley town for the festival don't themselves carry any bio-security risk. The bio-security risk lay in the transmission of infection with all the travelling back and forth to the hotels and pubs by the guests and the suppliers of food and drinks to the festival.

The risks were huge. If the disease spread up the hill from Llanigon to Hay Bluff, the consequences would be unimaginable. There were no fences up on the Bluff, it was just one enormous common. Half a million sheep grazed it. The rule about slaughter was that if you had an outbreak on a farm, you had to slaughter every animal on that farm. In theory, therefore, although the regulations had not been written with common land in mind, one sheep with FMD on Hay Bluff common meant we would have to slaughter half a million sheep. And, in addition, where on earth would we bury the carcasses? It was off the scale. It was unimaginable!

Our new friends in the army came up with a solution. They reckoned they could get their engineers to run a fence along the lower slopes of Hay Bluff to seal it off from the affected farm in Llanigon. Because Welsh mountain sheep are the world's best at getting under, over, around or through any fence anywhere, the army offered to bring in the Brigade of Gurkhas to patrol the fence, and we gladly accepted the offer. The fence was put up. The Gurkhas patrolled it. FMD never reached Hay Bluff common. The annual trans-migrational trek across the Serengeti Plain from Hampstead to Hay of the wildebeest – in this case the Oscar Wildebeest – could go ahead unhindered.

In July, to try to assess how badly countryside tourism was being affected, Julie and I spent a few days in mid-Wales going from B&B to pub and hotel. They were grateful for any trade at all, the impact of FMD had been horrendous. Visitors could drive around as we were doing, looking at the mountains, but couldn't climb them or walk anywhere in the open countryside. FMD chopped the tourist trade off at the knees.

Just before the outbreak came to an end in August, we had a repeat of the Hay problem with the Brecon Jazz Festival. There was an outbreak just off the main A470, the main road from Cardiff and thence to Brecon over the top of the Brecon Beacons. This was where the outbreak occurred, just off the road on the way down to Brecon after going through the Storey Arms Pass. Could we take the risk? Should we cancel the jazz festival just to be on the safe side? We decided to flood the area with vets and police, and installed those shallow sheep-dip trays full of disinfectant. Every car going along the A470 went through the disinfectant tray and all went okay. It needed to. The Brecon Jazz Festival was much the most precarious of all the major cultural festivals in Wales and it could have ill-afforded a cancellation.

FMD did eventually peter out by the end of August. I think we had earned our spurs. We had made our decisions and had done more than cope. We had had three major hotspot outbreaks, but FMD had never blown out of control in Wales as we were told by our vets it had done in Cumbria. We had operated as a true government and had shown that we were not a talking shop. We could run a country when the chips were really down.

Although the FMD outbreak didn't die out until August, the General Election in June delivered another New Labour landslide. It wasn't totally routine for Tony Blair, though. There was an extraordinary incident in Rhyl during the campaign. The background was that if Labour was re-elected, it was very likely that a Private Members Bill would pass into law banning the use of pack dogs to kill foxes and other wild animals. The Countryside Alliance knew that time was probably up for centuries of countryside tradition, but it was not going to give up its pastime without a fight – and when I say fight, I do mean fight.

We were already only too well aware of how determined the Countryside Alliance was to pursue its campaign of civil disobedience over the prospects of the ban on fox hunting. The previous autumn, Labour Party Wales had held a fundraiser at the Mercure Holland Hotel on Newport Road in Cardiff, and the Countryside Alliance had turned out in big numbers. The police had corralled the protesters on the north side of that very wide road, with the hotel on the other side. But they'd managed to break through the police lines, and had blockaded the front of the hotel. You could only get in through the back entrance – luckily, I knew all the back lanes. So I snaked in and rang up Carwyn Jones, who was still at the Assembly building, wondering if it was safe to approach the hotel. I gave him precise instructions on which back lane to use and he got there okay.

Not so lucky was Secretary of State Paul Murphy, who was one of the keynote speakers at the fundraiser. Because he had not long before been in the Northern Ireland Office as a Minister of State, Paul had very close diplomatic protection at all times. His police detail had been told to park up in a lay-by about five miles east of the hotel, and await further instructions. After hanging about in the car park for half an hour with no sign of the return to good order on the road in front of the hotel, Paul was getting impatient and told the diplomatic protection officer accompanying him, 'I think we ought to make a run for it, I'm sure it will be alright.' 'I have to advise against that, sir!' came the reply. 'The crowd hasn't dispersed yet.' So Paul asked, 'If we get there and one of the protestors approaches the car as I'm getting out, what will happen?' 'I'm afraid I would have to shoot him dead', came the deadpan reply. Paul could just imagine the headlines in the following morning's papers – 'Man Killed Outside Labour Party Fund-Raising Dinner Hotel!' – 'Take me back to Cwmbrân', said Paul, 'I don't think it's worth the risk.'

With that level of ferocity of protest by the Countryside Alliance in the background, there was a pre-election rally in North Wales at the Little Theatre in Rhyl. As the Deputy Prime Minister John Prescott was born and bred in next-door Prestatyn, affectionately known as the thinking man's Rhyl, he was the obvious choice as the star turn, and I was down to introduce him. I ate my pre-rally Italian plateful of comfort food to get me in the mood, and set off on the five-minute walk from the middle of Rhyl to the Little Theatre on the other side of the main London–Holyhead railway line. By the time I reached the Little Theatre, there was pandemonium. If I had been there five minutes earlier, I would have witnessed the Prescott left-jab incident at close quarters. What I saw at first hand was the immediate aftermath. You could cut the atmosphere with a knife – Jessica Morden, the Welsh Labour Party General Secretary, was in tears, head in hands, 'They'll sack me for this, I'll lose my job, I'm finished!'

I still don't know how she thought she could be held to blame for what had happened, but I did understand how she felt. The New Labour dictum was that things must not be allowed to go wrong, no deviations from the script. The egg thrown at the Deputy Prime Minister's head at point-blank range had provoked a fight-or-flight response in John – and if you knew John Prescott at all, you knew that the 'flight' part would be entirely superfluous! The egg had certainly been in flight for a millisecond, and the classic British straight left-jab thrown at the camp follower who threw the egg had now flown around the world from the many satellite trucks parked up at the Little Theatre. One flying egg and one punch wasn't much more than a scuffle really, but a huge story in the middle of an election campaign.

We agreed to postpone the start of the rally for John Prescott to talk it all through with Tony Blair. John was taking it all pretty cool. No one had died. No one had been taken to hospital. What he'd done was an instinctive act of self-defence. I didn't see how he could be blamed. But would Tony Blair see it that way? We certainly knew that the Tory press would have a field day. If there was any blame, it fell at the feet of the Countryside Alliance and the North Wales Police.

When I got to the dressing room, the scruffiest dressing room I'd ever been in, there was the Deputy Prime Minister stripped to the waist having a wash at the Belfast sink in the corner. As he washed and shaved and found his change of shirt, we started to discuss how we should play the issue during the rally, which would include my introduction. We'd not got very far when the Prime Minister's call came through … Oy vey, many oy veys, Blair was not happy!

It's passing strange when you can hear one side of a conversation (in this case, Prescott's replies), but you can't hear the other person speaking (in this case, Blair's interrogation). You have to interpolate. I'm sure that Alistair Campbell was similarly interpolating at the other end of the line in No. 10. For instance, when Prescott came out with his epic line –'Yes, but you're you, Tony, and I'm me!'– you could work out that Blair had put it to his deputy that 'Whatever the provocation, you shouldn't have hit the guy, you're the Deputy Prime Minister, for goodness sake!' On and on it went like that, trying to figure out the best way to play it all down. Prescott was solid as a rock – he had no alternative – 'When someone throws an egg at your head from about two feet away, it bloody hurts, Tony! The public will understand.'

And, by and large, Prescott was right. It was one of those tough against tender issues, where there was no way Tory right-thinking newspapers would be able to cast the punch-throwing Prescott as a metrosexual liberal lefty peace-loving cissie. The incident did cause a lot of amusement, but it didn't harm Labour's prospects of re-election. Most people believed Prescott was perfectly justified in socking the guy who had thrown the egg, and in so doing calling on the skills he'd picked up decades previously on the amateur boxing circuit in North Wales.

**July 2000**, with Prys and Huana Morgan at Swansea Brangwyn Hall, to receive the Swansea University Honorary Fellowship for Huana at the age of 95.

**October 2000,** the Partnership Agreement coalition Cabinet with the Liberal Democrats.

**2001**, with Tony Blair during the General Election campaign.

**March 2002**, Ground Zero, New York.

**2003**, launching the European Year of Disabled People.

**2003**, the Service of Reconciliation at St Augustine's Mission, Rorke's Drift, South Africa.

**2005**, celebrating the first Wales Grand Slam since 1978.

**2007**, with the Prime Minister of New Zealand, Helen Clark.

**2008**, with star pupils at Fitzalan High School.

**Summer in the early 2000s**, *(left)* on Foel y Mwnt.

**June 2009**, *(below)* conquering Snowdon with Lawrence Conway.

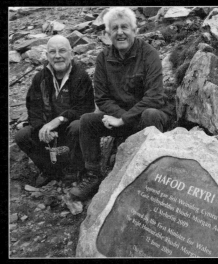

HAFOD ERYRI

**May 2016**, with Julie at her Cardiff North count.

**June 2016**, (*above*) the EU referendum campaign in Pontypridd, with Paul Murphy, Carwyn Jones and Peter Hain.

**June 2016**, (*right*) campaigning during the EU referendum with grandson Jaydon.

We had to get through the rally, although by then it had no more relevance than the play being performed on stage on the night Abe Lincoln was assassinated – 'But apart from that, did you enjoy the play?' Well, it was a bit like that – 'Apart from the egg and punch, did you enjoy the rally?' I made a joke in my introduction that Prescott's home town Prestatyn was about to be renamed Prescottyn in honour of the local boy done good.

The true significance of the incident was that New Labour remained incredibly popular. The Tories still had no MPs in Wales, and the huge army of Labour MPs was redoubled in its determination not to be intimidated by the Countryside Alliance, and to push ahead with the ban on fox hunting to become law in that 2001–5 Parliament – as indeed it did.

Tony Blair has been asked on many occasions what he regrets most about his period as premier. At various times, he's suggested his biggest mistake was blocking me from becoming Welsh Labour leader – he's also referred to the failure to dissuade his vast army of MPs from passing the fox hunting ban – his latest favourite is Freedom of Information, which he describes as a curse – he's yet to get round to the Iraq War!

In 2001, we couldn't get away from animals. Foxes, cattle and sheep – you name it, we had it on the agenda. Forget about FMD and remember the long-running problem of Bovine Spongiform Encephalopathy, BSE, which had been causing a fair amount of panic for everyone involved in the food chain for years. The BSE brain disease could incubate for thirty years after eating dodgy hamburgers, but at least BSE had not jumped species – you could only get it from eating beef or cow offal, or at least that was until a huge panic in the Ministry of Agriculture's Weybridge Animal Health Laboratories in late 2001. What appeared to have happened was that a specimen of sheep brain stored in a lab refrigerator had shown evidence of Transmissible Spongiform Encephalopathy, TSE, the generic name for the family of brain diseases of which BSE was just the one you got from eating infected beef.

Now, if it had been confirmed, it could in theory have meant that all seventy million sheep in Europe would have to be slaughtered. A panic meeting of all four UK administrations was convened in Weybridge to agree on a strategic response. Wales's representative was Dr Mike Simmons, who was a very canny public health medic and official, and Carwyn and I had a lot of faith in his nous. At the meeting, Simmons asked how certain it was that the TSE-infected specimen in the lab fridge was in fact a sheep brain. The others in the room all looked at him with withering incredulity – what on earth was this guy from Wales talking about? Of course it was sheep brain, this was the Weybridge Animal Health Laboratory, not some shed out in the backwoods! 'Well', said Simmons, 'my Minister, Carwyn Jones, is insisting that the brain specimen be re-tested to check that it really is sheep brain.' The incredulity at the stupidity of this request gradually gave way as it became obvious that nobody was going home until the brain specimen was re-tested. The running of British agriculture was now in a multi-polar world, with the four Agriculture & Food Ministers working for different governments.

When the results of the re-test returned, the specimen was found to have been cow brain all along, but with the sheep brain label wrongly attached to it. So, if our man Mike Simmons hadn't been there, the issue remains one of the great what-ifs. What would have happened? It doesn't bear thinking about. That's the subject for another dozen PhDs to work out the potential consequences if Mike Simmons hadn't been so insistent.

I received the phone call from Carwyn to say the specimen was cow brain after all and that slaughtering seventy million sheep in Europe – ten million of them in Wales – was off the agenda. I decided to phone the *Western Mail*. It was about half past eight in the evening, and I was at a function in the Rhondda Valley. A bit late for a front page to be changed, but I decided to tell all. Now, I did feel a bit of sympathy for Margaret Beckett, because it was a source of acute embarrassment for her as the Minister with direct responsibility for the Weybridge Lab, but still it was a unique set of events. Devolution had proved its worth, not just for Wales but for the UK and indeed for rural Europe. That was a definite first. You wouldn't think that a specimen of animal brain in a lab fridge could have constitutional significance, but it undoubtedly did in this case, and the story did need to be in the public domain.

I knew Margaret Beckett would be furious. She was. I couldn't help that. She was always a devo-sceptic, both in opposition and as a Minister. I got on really well with her and with her husband Leo, but that mix-up in the labs and its potential implications dwarfed everything that foot-and-mouth had thrown at us, overriding considerations like affiliations and political embarrassment. It had to be put out there because, in a most unexpected way, devolution had been validated.

### 9/11 and the Inter-Faith Forum

The aftermath of 9/11 in Wales was disturbing. Although the long-term residents of the old coal exporting seaports of Cardiff, Newport and Barry may wear rose-coloured spectacles about how good our race relations were, there was a tangible deterioration after 9/11. Mothers going to collect their kids from primary school wearing traditional garb or any kind of non-Western dress were being shouted at by the brainless, 'Terrorist' being a broadly-flung epithet. Some mosques were daubed with the same underlying message.

Archbishop Rowan Williams, only eighteen months into his role, and Catholic Bishop Peter Smith of Cardiff, were regular attendees from the start at the

Inter-Faith Forum. Although the Muslim faith community has no official hier-archy, there was a Muslim Council for Wales, in which the Sunni–Shi'a divide seemed not to play a part. The only divide that did play a small but disruptive part in the forum for the first few years was the one between Evangelicals and the traditionalist Christians. All the other Assembly party leaders attended the forum as well.

Rowan Williams is not world famous for keeping everything simple, but he did get the most important achievement of the forum spot on. Incredible though it may seem, before the forum existed, he didn't have the telephone numbers of any leader from the other faiths, not even the Christian ones. If we achieved nothing else we did achieve direct lines between them. The significance of that achievement emerged when the Danish-origin depictions of the Prophet Mohammed appeared for the first time in the UK, in an unbelievably obscure publication, *Y Gair – The Word*, a minuscule monthly magazine for vicars and curates of the Church in Wales. The inevitable fuss it provoked was very effec-tively damped down by the telephone tree we had assembled and supplied to all the faith leaders.

But 9/11 inevitably began to have an effect on everything, including the design of the new Assembly building. In July 2001, we had sacked Richard Rog-ers as the architect in charge, and work on the building was suspended until we could get a fixed-price design and build tender for completion of the building. Taylor Woodrow won the tender in July 2003, and took on Richard Rogers as a hired-hand architect, a much diminished status compared to being the architect in charge. On top of that, after 9/11, the security wallahs had advised that the Rogers design had far too many windows and sight lines for snipers perched on nearby rooftops.

Every window space with a line of sight into the Chamber, especially if that line of sight allowed access to a sniper shot at the First Minister's seat, had to be filled in with solid wall. The same applied to the new bullet-proof glass screens separating the public gallery from the AMs in the Chamber below – awful, really, when the public gallery was meant to symbolise the new open transparent democracy for Wales (and the lack of any such symbolism had been one of the main reasons for the rejection of Cardiff City Hall). The overall cost of all the post-9/11 design changes recommended by the security team probably added £10 million to the final cost, which was about 15 per cent of the total!

Anywhere Tony Blair went, he was now surrounded by heavy security pro-tection, and this struck home forcibly in November 2002. The PM's entourage had asked us to host a major Tony Blair speech on Europe, which was itself an intriguing request. It was a major honour for us in Wales to host a major speech on Europe by the Prime Minister, with me to introduce Blair, and what he was going to say on Europe was going to be big – that's all we were told. There would be the usual Labour fundraiser with Tony Blair as the star guest later in the evening. With our election coming up the following year, the funds raised would be most acceptable.

For the major speech itself, we had to procure a selection of sixth-formers, including a fair proportion from ethnic minorities, plus business leaders and councillors. The audience had to look right because the speech was so important, easily the most important the PM had ever done on Europe. It wasn't that difficult in the end to work out that it was going to be the speech in which Blair would announce to the world that Britain was going to join the euro. It couldn't be anything else really.

But it all turned into the ultimate political damp squib, an unbelievable anticlimax. Two things ruined it. The small distraction was that the Fire Brigades Union was on strike. Now, the location we had chosen for this extra-special speech was the Old Library in central Cardiff, a great downtown location, but also a great location for picketing and loud protest. You could definitely hear the noises off from the FBU in the narrow alley alongside the Library building. What killed the occasion absolutely stone dead, however, was that Gordon Brown had vetoed the whole announcement. So it just never happened. Blair was left making the most boring waffle-impregnated speech on Europe he or anyone else had ever made (and that's saying something) and, although I say it myself, my introduction was far more interesting. Poor old Blair had no speech left to give.

The replacement speech must have been concocted at the last minute, because the PM was an hour late starting the show. It could have been last-minute negotiations between Blair and Brown on what, if anything, he could say on the euro. It could have been last-minute scribbling. But the people I really felt sorry for were the sixth-formers who had been hand-picked to look just right on the television cutaway shots on the news that evening. I simply cannot imagine them wanting to attend a political meeting ever again after that.

The post-9/11 world also provided an insight into how the security team around the PM did its work. Around noon on the day of the big speech, Tony Blair and I had met up for the first time to go through timings. This was an hour before the actual big event, and I was accompanied by Professor Mark Drakeford, now a Minister in the Welsh Government, but back then my main speech-writer and Special Adviser. Mark was dressed down in his normal 1960s polytechnic sociology lecturer super-casual gear, tie-less, sloppy sweater, and jeans. Blair was accompanied by a military chappie from central casting, positively bristling with short-back-and-sides briskness and authority.

When I introduced this military man to Mark, it became apparent that he had no idea what 'Special Adviser' meant. It evidently wasn't in the training manual. He simply assumed that Mark was the Wales equivalent of him, and that the dead casual clothes were clearly a master-stroke of disguise intended to throw nefarious enemy agents off the scent. So, when I introduced Mark my Special Adviser, Blair's military man didn't bat an eyelid.'Ah, just the chap', he said,'now where do you want me to position my team of snipers?'This was delivered with a kind of vague glance and a wave of the arm in the direction of nearby rooftops above the shops and offices. Now, Mark Drakeford has some great virtues, but positioning a team of snipers is definitely not one of them. Planting lettuce seedlings on his allotment is more his game.

The fundraiser was no less surreal. Because the FBU was on strike and demonstrating outside the hotel building, the Welsh trade union Executive members, who in normal times would never miss a Labour fundraiser, felt they couldn't attend.

Tony Blair was in a strange, self-absorbed kind of mood. Not surprising, in light of the events earlier. I think I made things worse with my introduction. I still don't know what compelled me, but I re-told the Nativity story as if it had been repackaged by the New Labour press machine, with Mary and Joseph finding no difficulty getting a room in a new hotel funded by the Ministry of Overseas Development, the baby Jesus being born safe and well in a new PFI-financed King Herod Memorial Maternity Hospital, the shepherds celebrating the timely arrival of their CAP Sheep Premium payments from Europe, and the Three Wise Men finding their way to the baby's bedside with ease thanks to the latest sat-nav! The problem, I said, with a Nativity story like that was that it was so boring it would never have made the *Jerusalem Post*, let alone the Bible!

Blair disapproved strongly. Perhaps he suspected I might be implying that he was King Herod, or perhaps the baby Jesus. So his speech, coming straight after mine, started with a stern warning that nobody should make jokes about the Nativity. Okay, it was poor taste to say the least, not my funniest routine ever. I'll give Blair that.

The Assembly Business Minister Andrew Davies thought differently. As we left the dinner, he told me that my new take on the Nativity was the funniest thing he'd heard in years – 'Did you see the look on Blair's face? Priceless!' And that was how the day Britain *didn't* join the euro ended, less between sublime and ridiculous than ludicrous and hilarious, just as it had begun.

Whereas getting Gordon Brown and the Treasury to agree that the time was ripe to join the euro was difficult, I certainly thought the time was ripe to push on with the reshaping of the Assembly. Back in the Labour manifesto of 1997, and in the referendum and 1998 legislation, we had secured a modest devolution settlement, and I had no hesitation about trying to move things on. That was how the Welsh people saw devolution – 'You prove yourselves to us and we'll grant you a bit more rope and a bit more responsibility' – a bit at a time. We'd earned our spurs in 2000–2.

So the debate on the separation of powers took place in 2002 with a lot of cross-party support. The original legislation setting up the Assembly was weak in providing for clear government to be accountable to the Assembly. There was elastic in the wording of the statute, and we used it to make Ministers clearly responsible for decisions and to have to justify them to the legislature.

Was the Assembly a legislature anyway? I remember on several occasions hearing Blair say that the Assembly didn't have legislative powers, being rather an executive model of devolution. Now, although the law was one subject where Blair knew more than I did, it emerged that the secondary legislative powers that we did have could be pretty useable. It wasn't always the Sheep & Goats Identification Wales (Miscellaneous Provisions) Order 2000 – we did the Assembly Learning Grants, for example, via secondary legislative powers, and that was big stuff. When we had a sizeable proposition we wanted to legislate on, the rigmarole was always the same. We'd ask our cleverest lawyers if we could get this done via secondary legislation.

The lawyers would always reply, 'Weeell, we would feel much more comfortable if we could do this via primary legislative powers, then we would be absolutely clear of any legal challenge. But, if you are willing to accept some risk, we could just about do it using the powers we do already have.' And that was almost always good enough for us – 'Go for it', was the call to arms. The alternative of going cap-in-hand to the Secretary of State to get our legislation into the Queen's Speech was very unattractive for two reasons. First, in having to justify before MPs *why* we were doing something different to England, English MPs would be bound to consider whether their constituents would be envious, for example, of Welsh students getting a maintenance grant when English students couldn't. Second, there was always a glut of bills lining up for the annual hopper to get into the Queen's Speech. At the Assembly, we regarded secondary legislative powers as a quarry, and if you looked hard enough you could usually find a way of doing what you wanted to do. We lacked the status of the Scottish Parliament, but we made up for that with invention.

The next step was the Richard Commission, a cross-party and no-party commission set up by the Labour–Lib Dem coalition, but with strong support from Plaid Cymru and a pretty healthy level of support from the Conservatives. Its purpose was to look at the powers and structures of the Assembly – it couldn't rewrite the powers approved so narrowly in the referendum in September 1997, but it could look at whether the Assembly had the powers to do the job.

It nearly wasn't the Richard Commission at all – it might have been the Patchett Commission instead. My first choice was a professor at Cardiff University, Keith Patchett, who was involved in writing constitutions for all sorts of new states. I'd been to visit his house in Cyncoed, in Cardiff, where he'd had an annexe built so that young clerks and lawyers from countries that were emerging into the world could learn the art of constitution-writing. When I visited, a team from the Palestinian Authority was there learning the pros and cons of different types of constitutional arrangements. It was fascinating to watch.

But I was eventually persuaded that a commission produced by and for the Assembly would have to carry clout in Westminster, and if it recommended any changes in the legislative powers of the Assembly then a commission chaired by a technical expert like Keith Patchett wouldn't carry the required weight.

My Special Advisers and the Cabinet Secretary Lawrence Conway insisted – and I accepted – that I should let them draw up a shortlist of political figures, the name of any one of which on the eventual report would make the corridors of Whitehall and Westminster sit up and take notice. That's how I eventually found myself on the phone discussing terms with Ivor Richard, a former Labour leader in the Lords in 1997–8 who had therefore been a fully-fledged member of a Blair Cabinet (albeit for only just over a year). I didn't think his early reshuffling out of the Cabinet was any indication of a big falling out with the Prime Minister, rather it was just one of those things that happens in politics, as I knew only too well myself!

Ivor Richard was also the guy that I had found myself competing with, back in 1985, for the Labour nomination for Cardiff West. I do emphasise competing *with* rather than *against*, because there is always a fraternal sense in seeking nomination for a parliamentary seat, and it could so easily have been Ivor rather than me who was elected in 1987.

The membership of the commission was pretty revolutionary. We asked each political party to nominate one member each, and then we asked the public to self-nominate if they were interested in serving. So, five members came onto the committee via the public appointments procedure, and it gave us a very balanced membership, very committed to the work of the commission.

It was well into the next term of the Assembly before the commission finished its work. All of its recommendations were eventually implemented, with the exception of the increase of numbers of AMs from sixty to eighty. I knew as soon as I read that part of the report's conclusions that implementing the recommendation would screw up any chance of getting the other conclusions on law-making powers through – the people of Wales were simply not ready to accept any argument for *more* AMs, however logical the reasoning over increased work on the legislative front needing more legislators to carry it out. Keeping the public on our side was the only way to make progress.

Another area where I felt we did have the backing of the majority in Wales was for taking the Welsh message overseas. I still treasure the conference pass I was given at the Johannesburg Earth Summit in August–September 2002, which announced me as FIRST MINISTER UNITED KINGDOM – and that was according to the United Nations! The Earth Summit was in the main for fully-fledged members of the United Nations – the ones with their own plastic name tags declaring who they were and their own official glass of water. But there were so many fringe events at the conference that other sub-national states or regions like Wales could attend – we were there with the Basque Country, Western Australia and so forth, plus a number of South African provinces.

What amazed me was how many African delegates knew about the formation of our not-for-profit water and sewerage company, Dŵr Cymru – Welsh Water. They wanted to know how Wales had managed this takeover, but they had sadly got the wrong end of the stick as regards the price of water supply and sewerage treatment – they all thought that water was now free in Wales! Far from it. It still has to be paid for, but at least no one is making a profit out of it. Which is rather different. The African delegates were a bit disappointed. I made some enquiries as to how so many Earth Summit delegates from sub-Saharan Africa had not only heard of Wales but knew that our Welsh Water model was a new not-for-profit structure. Evidently, what had happened was that the International Monetary Fund at that time was pressing a lot of semi-bankrupt African countries to privatise their water supply companies, which would raise funds and commercialise the collection of water charges. I had my fifteen minutes of fame on a variety of African radio stations, explaining how we had taken the water and sewerage industry in Wales out of the conventional private sector and into the not-for-profit sector. But, unfortunately, water was not free in Wales, and the Welsh model was unlikely to be the escape route from the harsh demands of the IMF for more privatisation.

The formation of Welsh Water in July 2001 with its not-for-profit structure was an example of Welsh exceptionalism. When Nigel Annett and Chris Jones had formed the company the previous year, they had no more than a twinkle in their eye about actually succeeding in acquiring the company from Western Power. It was fortunate for the two of them that Western Power didn't want the water and sewerage side of the business they had bought – they only wanted the SWALEC part.

What we then had to do was persuade the regulator, the Chief Executive of OFWAT, that we definitely wanted this new entirely bond-financed model with no shareholders to be given a go in Wales. Initially, OFWAT was reluctant. The regulator told us that he couldn't carry out his job as regulator unless there were enough privatised water companies to compare efficiency – they had to have ten companies to draw up a league table in order to see who was best at what. If Welsh Water was funded with no shareholder dividends being paid out, comparisons would be harder. The regulator also seemed worried about the contagion risk – if it was successful in Wales, might not some of the English regions ask for something similar? Sue Essex, our Environment Minister, told the regulator that devolution had to mean something, and our position was clear – we were very keen on him giving approval to the new model Welsh Water company, still in the private sector but closer to a mutual than a conventional company, with shares floated on the Stock Exchange. The regulator reluctantly agreed.

## Clear Red Water

In the final six months of the Assembly term, thoughts inevitably turned to the issue of disentanglement. We would soon be involved in drawing up a Labour manifesto, the first time the party manifesto would be drawn up by us as a devolved Labour Party. The 1999 manifesto was drawn up by Labour Ministers in the old Welsh Office, and therefore Ministers in a Westminster Labour Government – mostly by Peter Hain, in fact.

Now disentanglement was to prove to have two meanings. The obvious one was how a coalition Government comprising Ministers from two parties starts the process of separation, so that those two parties are free to compete for the affections and trust of the electorate. We wanted to be free, and so did the Lib Dems. Mike German had been back in the Cabinet since July 2002, but in a diminished role as Rural Affairs Minister, and as the smaller party they had an even greater need than we did to distinguish themselves in writing their manifesto.

There were no rules about disentanglement. Coalitions were so rare in Britain that you had to learn on the job, but precedents could certainly be found in Ireland. By a happy coincidence, there was a British–Irish Council being held in Dublin Castle that autumn. There was also a general election pending in Ireland. So we could see at first hand just how the majority party Fianna Fáil, led by Taoiseach Bertie Aherne, could separate from the Progressive Democrats ('Progos' for short) led by the Tánaiste, the Deputy Prime Minister and redoubtable Mary Harney.

Our two-day visit was incredibly instructive. While Bertie and Mary were nice as pie to each other and to us at the British–Irish Council, the newspapers were full of attacks by Mary on Bertie – quite personal ones too.

I'd never met Mary Harney before, but she was as sharp as a tin-tack. I knew Bertie pretty well by now, so it was Mary, the Deputy Prime Minister, that I closely kept track of. She, via the Progos' press machine, was bashing six bells out of Bertie over plans to replace the much-loved Lansdowne Road with a new national stadium for Ireland to cover just rugby and football rather than all of the Gaelic sports. Whereas Lansdowne Road is in the very leafy Dublin Southside suburb of Ballsbridge, the new stadium would be in the heart of working-class Northside. It was to be funded by a huge donation from J. P. Magner, he of the Coolmore stud, one of Ireland's wealthiest men and apparently a friend of Bertie's, but it was all subject to the Government matching the Magner donation. So the Progos had christened the new stadium project the 'Bertie Bowl'. It wasn't actually in Bertie Aherne's constituency, mind you, but next-door in the very ungentrified Northside.

These attacks on Bertie and the 'Bertie Bowl' soubriquet were meant to imply there was a bit of a smell about the project. And yet, however personal and nasty the attacks, they had absolutely no effect on the excellent working relationships between the Prime Minister and his deputy. It was all par for the course in the run-up to an Irish general election.

Back home, I honestly didn't think we would have much of a problem in distinguishing ourselves from our Lib Dem partners in the run-up to May 2003 and the Assembly elections. If anything, we might have a more tricky job disentangling ourselves from some of the policy directions being put forward by the New Labour Government, which was now well into its second term in Westminster.

I was particularly concerned by one line in Tony Blair's speech to Labour's Annual Conference in October 2002, when he predicted with great fanfare the end of the bog-standard local comprehensive – that was the line Alistair Campbell had pushed heavily for the media. You heard it everywhere, but what did it really mean? If you put all the emphasis on 'bog standard', you couldn't disagree – every parent and politician alike would want an urgent turnaround for a failing local school. But if you put the emphasis on the end of the 'local comprehensive', well, we certainly had problems with that. I don't think for a minute that Tony Blair and Alistair Campbell had given any thought to the fact that we in Wales were the ones facing elections the following May – Blair had already won his new mandate in 2001.

The problem with our secondary schools was falling pupil numbers. We had 220 secondaries, but really only needed 200 at the most to avoid wasting resources on empty classrooms. Demand for Welsh-medium secondary education was rocketing, there was a small rise in demand for Church in Wales schooling (though that sector was tiny), but demand for conventional state secondary education and Catholic education was falling fast.

There was very little demand for grant-maintained status. The last thing we needed were new providers coming into the system, when our priority was trying to solve the surplus places issue. There was no demand for academies, city technology colleges, specialist arts or sports or technology schools – what most people actually wanted was a good quality 'local comprehensive'.

At our Inter-Faith Forum earlier that year, we'd had a good discussion about the role of faith schools in Welsh education. The Conservative leader Nick Bourne had quite fairly but slightly mischievously raised the issue of why we in Wales were not pushing the role of faith schools in the provision of secondary education, when our opposite numbers in Westminster were hell-bent on it. Archbishop Rowan said he was keen on an expanded role for the Church in Wales diocesan schools. I explained our policy as best as I could remember it – we were not in the business of closing down faith schools, and if there was proven demand for an additional faith school then it would get funding. But we didn't see faith schools as part of a general policy of rebranding or replacing struggling schools, so we weren't pushing faith schools.

To give an example of the weak demand for faith schools in Wales, we found ourselves approving plans for a new faith secondary school in Wrexham. Neither the Catholic Church nor the Church in Wales had enough pupils on their prospective books to justify a new school but, if they built one faith school for both Catholic and Church in Wales kids, then they had the numbers! No way could you turn down an original idea like that.

Archbishop Rowan had advocated at the Inter-Faith Forum, with utmost courtesy and gentleness, the case for a new Church in Wales secondary school in Aberdare to serve the northern valleys area of Glamorgan. He wasn't advocating a change across to the New Labour policy, which was a London answer to a London problem. This is in no way to underestimate the extent of the success of the London Challenge in turning around educational standards in London – of course, it was helped by the huge gentrification of the East End, the Teach First Initiative, the incredible hunger for success by immigrant families for their children, the brilliant job prospects for school leavers with qualifications, and the vast new private coaching and tutoring industry providing the back-up to what the schools were doing. It's hard to put your finger on the causes of the success, but all credit to Estelle Morris and the various other Education Ministers for the turnaround in London education standards.

The only occasion I can remember discussing with Tony Blair the differences between our approach in Wales and the New Labour approach was in a car ride from the Copthorne Hotel on the western edge of Cardiff up towards the M4. I waved my hand in the general direction of Glanely School, a quarter of a mile away and in my constituency, which had been a failing school for years. It was losing pupils hand over fist, teachers were demoralised and there was high absenteeism (not just among the pupils). It needed a really good turnaround expert headteacher, probably one with the skills of Archangel Gabriel. Parents with any aspirations for their children living on the catchment area of the sprawling Ely council estate would run a mile rather than let their children go there – the school has by now been rebranded, merged and had its fair share of new heads without, so far as I know, being effectively turned around.

To be absolutely fair on Tony Blair, he didn't try to lecture me on how well New Labour's policies were doing in England, and in London particularly. He knew that London was a bit of a one-off because the economy there was expanding so quickly. He knew that Wales was a one-off too, because of the ever-increasing demand for Welsh-medium education. So there was no attempt by Blair to lean on me.

I had still to find a way of getting across to the public that much of the drift of Tony Blair's second term was not for us in Wales. Like Scotland, our culture in public service provision was different. Following Blair's 'end of the bog-standard local comprehensive' line in his party conference speech, the need to differentiate ourselves was urgent.

The alternative was to make a major policy-cum-philosophy statement. We could define our own approach, our own Welsh Labour public services delivery model – neither Old Labour, nor New Labour, but Welsh Labour!

Mike Sullivan, Professor of Social Policy at Swansea University, agreed to host our statement. Mike was a close friend of my senior Special Adviser Mark Drakeford, who drafted the speech to set out our Welsh Labour alternative to the emerging New Labour model. Wales didn't want the user of public services redefined as a consumer exercising choice of where to send children to school, or which hospital to choose for a hip replacement operation.

The Welsh alternative was to move away from the quasi-market and pseudo-choice to a 'we're all in this together' approach. The *citizen* amounted to much more than a *consumer* exercising choice: the citizen was also the taxpayer and voter who had communally created the services in the first place, and was the ultimate owner of the public service facilities. Whereas the consumer in England, especially in southern England, might have the means to choose between the private school and the state school, the same was far less likely in Wales. I think the figures showed that seven per cent of all school provision in England was private, but only one per cent in Wales. And similarly restricted options were evident in health, too. Although private health insurance was quite common in Wales, and private wards in NHS hospitals had proliferated, it was straight NHS provision that the overwhelming majority of people in Wales looked to in the event of any health crisis in the family.

It was very exciting to try to encapsulate our ideas in writing in a coherent manner that could reasonably be described as a political philosophy. As Mark and I bounced the drafts back and forth, that philosophy gradually took shape in the office as my Clear Red Water speech. But I had three problems.

First, there was my off-the-cuff presentational style – I would always go on a stage with nothing more than a few scrappy notes scribbled, often at the last minute, on odd bits of paper, and then I'd wing it. That style, however, wouldn't do this time. I had to have an actual speech prepared, and I had to deliver it. To be fair, my only departures from the winging it style were my conference speeches, where I did use the autocue. Sadly for me, any speech drafted by a former university lecturer is automatically going to last fifty-five minutes, the length of a university lecture. That was a very long time for me – not to mention the audience – to maintain concentration.

The second problem I had was that the speech might upset a lot of Welsh Labour MPs. It was a risk I had to take. BBC Wales had a default position whenever

I said anything remotely controversial, which was to run my remarks past Welsh Labour MPs for comment – the last hangover of the colonial mindset in Wales. Anyway, the consequences of that were that any speech by the First Minister of Wales could only be considered newsworthy for BBC Wales if it was attacked by Welsh Labour MPs as a departure from New Labour orthodoxy. Well, I had no wish to upset Welsh Labour MPs. After all, I'd been one myself! But in no way, though, did they or No. 10 have a veto over my vision for the upcoming Assembly election, nor did they have a right to advance consultation on its content. The 2003 Assembly elections were not being fought by MPs.

(In a parallel universe, Tony Blair and Alistair Campbell would have shown me the text of the PM's 'bog-standard comprehensive' speech to the Labour Party conference in October 2002, to check if its content might complicate things for me in the May 2003 election.)

My speech, then, was actually bigged up by a spin doctor in advance of its delivery – the Clear Red Water speech – and the key passages in it were released to interested journos the night before. That was itself a rarity for us in Wales. A healthy audience turned up for its delivery in the Faraday Lecture Theatre at Swansea University, and I did my best to stick to the script.

The ultimate irony, however, was that I never even uttered the 'Clear Red Water' part of the speech after all the bigging up. This was my third problem – the actual killer phrase didn't occur until very late into the long speech, by which time I was doing my key summing up of all the ideas. I was also starting to feel very hungry. On the way into the lecture theatre, I had noticed the usual Swansea University buffet (nothing too sumptuous, but very filling!) all covered in clingfilm and laid out on tables in the foyer. So when I got to the fiftieth minute of my lecture-length speech and realised that there were still six pages left to go, I skipped to the last page and did a quickie executive summary. I told everyone that it was time at last for us all to traipse out of the theatre and gorge ourselves on all the brainfood waiting for us beneath the clingfilm. And that was that. Then I realised I'd skipped the page with the 'Clear Red Water' bit in it – thank goodness that part had been released to the media the night before, I thought!

The following day, as anticipated, BBC Wales submitted my speech to Welsh Labour MPs for their approval or non-approval. The nearest headline the BBC could manage to 'Rhodri Morgan Sets Out His Stall for Next Year's Assembly Elections' was 'Westminster Labour MPs Attack Rhodri Morgan's Clear Red Water Speech in Swansea'. Right, there was one particularly ludicrous example of this warped way of thinking. In the speech, I had said that that 'the market was amoral', and one of the Welsh Labour MPs seemed to have got very worked up about such an absolutely bog-standard definition of what a market is, as it would be taught to all first-year Economics students. The market works via a hidden hand. But in order to qualify an attack on my speech, 'amoral' had either deliberately or ignorantly casually been replaced by 'immoral', not the same meaning at all – amoral is morally neutral, immoral is nasty and naughty.

Totally pathetic. It didn't matter in the end. And the attacks from my erst-while Westminster colleagues may have helped publicise the speech. It didn't matter either that I never reached the Clear Red Water part of the over-long speech, because we had achieved our differentiation from New Labour. I wasn't knocking New Labour, as it was obvious the Blair strategy was working a treat in southern England, where Labour normally couldn't get a look in. Our key objec-tives in Wales were different. We had to win back parliamentary seats in Rhondda, Islwyn, and Llanelli, while holding on to the gains we had made in 1997 and 1999 in Wales's two coastal belts.

Sometimes, you had the right candidates to win those key marginal seats – sometimes, less so. Sometimes, you might frustratingly hear that candidates you admired and could envisage being promoted to the Cabinet after a year or so had missed out on a nomination by one vote! Curses! But if I had tried to interfere, it would have been flung right back at me – 'You didn't like it when Tony Blair interfered, did you?'

The only time I did interfere, albeit in a very small way, in a selection confer-ence issue was in a parliamentary context rather than an Assembly one. It wasn't even interfering, really, but persuading somebody to throw their hat in the ring. It was in 2002 when the MP for Ogmore Ray Powell had died. As regards the par-liamentary vacancy created, there was no obvious local favourite son or daughter and, indeed, Ray Powell's daughter Janice was already the Assembly Member for the constituency. Neil and Glenys Kinnock pushed the candidacy of Jan Royall, who was Neil's former secretary and would later be Labour leader in the Lords. Janice Powell backed the candidacy of the Leader of Cardiff City Council, Russell Goodway. I was worried, in the meantime, that either of those two as candidates would open the door to a very strong challenge from Plaid Cymru's Bleddyn Hancock, who was the Welsh regional secretary of the colliery overmen's trade union NACODS – he was a ready-made local Valleys Boy candidate.

I rang up Huw Irranca Davies, who had been an impressive candidate for Labour in Brecon and Radnor in the 2001 General Election. He said no first off, adding that he really wanted to serve in the Assembly and that he had a young family. I told him opportunities don't always come along at the most convenient times, they just come along at random, and you have to grab them when they're there. So, eventually, he threw his hat in the ring – I was slightly surprised at my powers of persuasion.

It became widely speculated on the political grapevine in Ogmore that I was backing Huw Irranca Davies's candidacy. Then I got a phone call out of the blue from one of the leading lights in the area, Jeff Jones, previously leader of the local council, which surprised me. It was a call to thank me for persuading Huw Irranca Davies to stand, because if Russell Goodway had become the candidate there would have been a real danger of losing the seat to Plaid Cymru. Jeff explained that the people of these Valleys had an unprintably low opinion of Russell Goodway – it doesn't matter whether what they thought of Goodway was correct or not, it was simply what everybody in the area thought. Likewise in the case of Jan Royall, said Jeff, widely seen as an interloper with no knowledge of the Valleys, looking for a safe seat. Very rarely have I had praise for interference in a selection process. I don't know – perhaps it was a bit easier for me to interfere when it had nothing to do with an Assembly candidate selection.

You had to accept that some outstandingly talented Assembly Members could succumb to illness just as you were thinking very seriously of finding a place for them in the Cabinet. Val Feld was one such. She had been head of Shelter Wales before being selected for Swansea East at the 1999 Assembly election. She had become Chair of the Economic Development Committee to replace Ron Davies after the badger-watching episode had terminated his career.

Val's tragic and ultimately terminal illness deprived us of one of our most talented Members -one who definitely had Cabinet potential, cut down in her political prime. She certainly passed my test of 'Would this person be eligible and credible to be a Minister in a Westminster Government?'

It would have been deeply satisfying if we had managed to reach the end of the Assembly term without a scandal but, sadly, we did not. Of course, diehard opponents of devolution would no doubt quote the overspend on the new Senedd building as a scandal in itself – it was quite a saga, but whether it was also a scandal was debatable. We had deferred the main problem of execution and completion until the second Assembly term, and the eventual cost at just less than £70 million was not small beer but, compared to the £430 million spent on the new Scottish Parliament building in Holyrood, our build out-turn cost didn't look so bad. I realise that your own officials are always going to point to problems elsewhere to deflect blame from themselves. Our project director on the new Senedd building told me, 'The difference between our project and the new Scottish Parliament is that both buildings are well over budget, but the Scots have lost control of theirs and we haven't!' That reminded me of what our chief vet had said about foot-and-mouth in 2001 –'We never lost control of our three hotspots, but in Cumbria it's just blown!' In the advice you get from your own officials, it's always better in Wales!

The genuine scandal we did have at the end of that first term involved the Pop Factory project. It was a £2 million scandal – significant, but not huge. The public money had come from one of our very few new quangos, the skills and training agency ELWa. It went to Avanti Media, a husband-and-wife media company, which wanted to branch out into media training and to do it in the heart of the Rhondda Valleys. The project did have a lot going for it. Because the size of the contract at £4 million exceeded ELWa's delegated spending limit, it had to be countersigned by the Minister of Education, Jane Davidson. There were some mild warning signs when Jane's civil servants described the proposed spend as 'novel', which was a warning to the Minister to think carefully.

I first got wind of the problem from the Economic Development Minister, Andrew Davies, who had in turn picked up a whisper that all was not as it should be. The rumour mill was saying that Emyr Afan and Mair Afan, the aforementioned husband-and-wife team who owned Avanti, were out of their depth.

It all blew up in the first few months of the 2002–3 financial year. Avanti, the company which owned the Pop Factory and had dreamt up the Pop Cafe as a music and multi-media training offshoot, had called a halt and repaid £2 million. The row was over how it had got that far, and it rumbled on for six years. Because there was European Social Fund money concerned, the European Commission and their audit services got involved, and so did the Wales Audit Office. It's still a bit of a puzzle how ELWa had signed such a big contract with such a small company.

Looking back, my theory is that the structure of ELWa was too weak to cope. We had allowed it to be set up with only a virtual head office, with Enid Rowlands appointed to chair, a formidably bright woman. Enid wanted the job, and we were very keen for her to do it. She was also a passionate North Walian, and would never have taken the job if it involved moving from North Wales to South Wales. With that, there would have been disproportionate disruption if we had set up the new ELWa headquarters in North Wales, because most of the staff lived and worked in South Wales. Enid had backed the idea that ELWa could operate with only a virtual head office, but looking back now, I believe there wasn't enough command and control from ELWA's senior management.

The Pop Factory and Pop Cafe together was a great concept in the right area of Wales, and it generated a huge amount of goodwill. But it simply overstretched the management capability of Avanti. Too bad we lost our clean record over the £2 million that couldn't be recovered. Again, if we follow the comparison with Scotland, the Pop Factory scandal was nothing next to the cock-up over the setting of school-leaving examinations perpetrated by the Scottish Qualifications Authority, a far larger scandal that cost my old friend Sam Galbraith his job.

### Run-up to the 2003 Election

Provided we could distinguish our style of government from the new frontiers of New Labour in Westminster, I thought we could reach the first re-elections to the Assembly in reasonable shape.

We'd had our first death of a sitting AM, and the late Val Feld had been replaced by Val Lloyd at the Swansea East by-election. Richard Edwards (Preseli Pembroke), and the first cousin of Huw Edwards, anchorman of the BBC's *Ten O'Clock News*, had become ill with a form of leukaemia shortly after being selected as a candidate for the first elections in 1999. It was always going to be a struggle for survival for Richard to fulfil his undoubted potential – unless a miracle cure could be found, that is. He seemed to have managed to cheat death on innumerable occasions, but chose not to stand again in 2003.

Richard was much more of an ideologue than Val Feld. If Val had survived long enough to hear my Clear Red Water speech, I'm sure she would have approved of it. Richard went much further, however, he was positively exuberant about it despite his debilitating medical problems. He sent a copy of the speech to Roy Hattersley, who then paraphrased it with generous attribution in his article in *The Guardian*.

That in itself was some measure of how far the New Labour project had spread across the political spectrum. Roy Hattersley, along with the late John Smith and George Robertson (later Secretary-General of NATO), had been among the leading lights of the right of centre Solidarity Group within the Parliamentary Labour Party. The Tribune Group, of which Neil Kinnock had always been a member, was the soft left faction. I had joined the Tribune Group when I'd been selected in 1987 – nothing odd in that – but the real curiosity is how and why Tony Blair (from 1983), Peter Mandelson and Alan Milburn (both from 1992) and other New Labour acolytes of theirs had ever joined the Tribune Group. Tony Blair, with Peter Mandelson whispering constantly in his ear, had shifted the whole paradigm to the right, while people like Roy Hattersley and me had stayed roughly where we were before!

When it came down to writing the manifesto for May 2003, Welsh Labour's own policy-making machinery had produced some workmanlike sets of proposals. What they hadn't done was give me anything eye-catching to win back the Labour heartland seats we'd lost in 1999 – Llanelli, Islwyn and Rhondda were etched on my eyeballs exactly as the loss of Calais had been for Mary Tudor. We would need a few more sessions in my home over slices of takeaway pizza to come up with something suitably eye-catching to win back those seats in the Labour heartland.

One suggestion was free prescriptions for all. Although we remained in coalition with the Lib Dems until the end, their back-benchers – Kirsty Williams in particular – were hard at work gearing up for attack Labour mode. Fair play, they were trying to carve out their own distinctive policy territory, just as we were. They were banging on about the free prescriptions issue all the time, and campaigning for an extension of the categories of such illnesses as diabetes that received free prescriptions, to include half a dozen others.

The Lib Dems were certainly right to point out the lack of any medical logic in the free prescriptions list – cancer wasn't on it, for example – but extending the list would be like opening Pandora's box. You couldn't justify the list that we had inherited from the 1960s (diabetes was a later addition to that list), but once you admitted the list was a nonsense and you were going to review it, there was no way you'd ever be able to close it again. The lobbying pressure from chronic conditions not included on the free scripts list would be never-ending. You either kept the list as it was, or you returned to free prescriptions for all. So we went for the complete abolition of charges.

Prescriptions had been free when the NHS started in 1948. Nye Bevan, Harold Wilson and John Freeman had all resigned from the Attlee Government in 1951 when charges were imposed on prescriptions in the emergency Budget of Hugh Gaitskell. Labour had made them free again in the 1960s, then reimposed charges in the 1970s.

This time around, the charges would be abolished only in Wales, although Scotland and Northern Ireland were thereafter soon to follow suit. The Welsh Lib Dems must have been tamping mad when they found out we had trumped their ace, but we didn't simply abolish the charges as a riposte to the Lib Dems. I was in favour of abolishing charges because it would help the low paid. It boosted the Welfare to Work agenda – if you were on welfare and saw a minimum wage job advertised in caring, cleaning or catering, but you suffered a chronic condition like asthma, you'd be far more likely to take the job if you could continue with access to free prescriptions.

Further afield, the invasion of Iraq was upon us pretty much as the election campaign was getting underway. Leaving aside the wider global and ethical issues, the invasion cut both ways for Labour in Wales in terms of electoral advantage or disadvantage. Tony Blair made a very welcome change in the normal parliamentary practice by insisting on having a positive vote to back his invasion plans. He broke the precedent for British Prime Ministers to declare war by using the Crown Prerogative, with no vote in Parliament. He also added an unstated rider to the wish to have an affirmative vote in support of the invasion. It was getting the Labour Whips to let it be known that if a majority of Labour MPs didn't support the vote on invading Iraq, the Prime Minister would have to resign! The Government's argument was that Blair could not be seen to be relying on Conservative MP votes to get the affirmative majority vote.

As the Iraq War invasion only began on 20 March 2003, it was far too early for the latent and later unpopularity of the Iraq War to affect our elections. If anything, by sheer good fortune rather than by design, we actually probably benefitted from support for the war at the start of it by what was known as the Baghdad Bounce!

The controversial nature of the PM's decision to fall in behind George W. Bush's regime change policy didn't harm us electorally, but it did cause internal ructions for the Labour Party with resignations from membership in ever-increasing numbers, especially in the rural and coastal west and north of Wales. We regained Llanelli, Rhondda and Islwyn, and held all the New Labour gains along the M4 and the A55 coastal belts. We lost Wrexham though, where John Marek had responded to being de-selected by running successfully as an Independent. Labour's total number of AMs went up from 28 to 30, which enabled me to take one of the quickest and easiest decisions I ever had to make. I could form a majority Labour Government, with confidence that I could implement our manifesto. We had no need for the Lib Dems or anyone else in coalition – we'd earned a mandate, and we'd give it a go on our own. Of course, having 30 AMs didn't mean we had a majority – it was an exact half – but wild horses wouldn't have stopped Dafydd Elis-Thomas of Plaid Cymru from continuing as Presiding Officer, and that meant that we could rely on our 30 exceeding the 29 total available to the three opposition parties.

I was sixty-three years old and in robust health. The job was a huge strain, but there was no reason why I wouldn't be able to take the people of Wales on the journey to a deeper, higher and wider form of devolution over the four years through to 2007. My idea of devolution hadn't changed, it was the same as I had set out in my speech in the first week of my First Ministership to the Institute of Welsh Affairs. In Wales, unlike Scotland, people were not that ready for devolution because they didn't 'think devolved'. In civic and in civil society, in industry and in the voluntary sector, Wales was a land of branch offices and branch factories. The norm in Wales was to put up draft decisions to a London Head Office for approval. Wales needed a devolved Assembly in order to get used to a devolved way of thinking.

We'd written our own manifesto. No one at Labour Party headquarters had even asked to see it or to approve it – it was the complete opposite of the 1999 manifesto largely written as a pre-pack by Peter Hain as a Welsh Office Government Minister.

Marks out of ten for that first term? I'd set our objectives deliberately low. After the dreadful beginning to the Assembly, with more drama, scandal, farce and tragedy than a fistful of soap operas, my main (but not only) ambition was to get rid of the drama, provide solid administration – scandal-free, if possible. We had to show that the canards put up by the No campaign predicting in the September 1997 referendum that Wales was incapable of governing itself were wrong. Welsh devolution, if I had anything to do with it, would not be characterised by jobs-for-the-boys appointments, sweetheart public sector contracts, by North Wales fighting South Wales, by Welsh speakers unable to agree on anything with monoglot English speakers. Modest objectives, you might say, but we had to get the show on the road before the low self-confidence level of the population of Wales could ever begin gradually to rise. The people of Wales would start believing that they could make decisions just as soundly as people in England or Scotland.

There were problems in Health and Education bubbling beneath the surface. Money was not the problem per se. The arrival of devolution had happily coincided with the opening of the purse strings by Gordon Brown from May 1999, and our budget in cash terms went up by 10 per cent a year, compound over the four years 1999–2003. If you strip out inflation, it still went up by over 7 per cent a year in real terms. We were never to see budget increases like that again.

The problems bubbling away beneath the surface were over how best you remedied Wales's chronic health problems. In England, the decision was made to cut the waiting lists for hips and knees, cataracts and varicose veins, etc. Would the same really make sense in Wales? With a much smaller middle-class component in the population and, conversely, a much higher working-class component and our high retirement Costa Geriatricas in rural Wales, it was the chronic conditions like heart disease and arthritis that were our biggest problem. Whether it was the legacy of mass employment in the mines, or poor lifestyles with excessive smoking and drinking and too much fried food, it was clear what we needed to address in Wales. England could target elective surgery waiting lists – Blair wanted to put the private healthcare outfits under severe market pressure by offering prompt service for your new knee on the NHS – but we needed to do that too while simultaneously changing people's attitudes to the dangers of smoking, obesity, inactivity and poor diet.

Likewise in education – we had far too long a tail of low attainment in our schools, of kids who could only read poorly by the end of primary school, while too much resource was going into the maintenance of empty schools and classrooms. I didn't think we had a mandate to remove the local authorities' control over schools, but how many of the twenty-two councils really knew how to effect a turnaround in a failing school? Not many, I feared. And it was nothing to do with the size of the authority – Cardiff, the biggest authority in school population, was among the poorest performers.

Whereas I think I'd managed to get rid of the awful whiff of salacious scandal and internecine intra-party rivalry, I don't think I'd give myself more than 6½ out of 10 for that first term. Could I do better in 2003–7?

# eight

# The Heyday That Wasn't
# 2003–2007

THE SECOND ASSEMBLY could hardly have started better for Labour. The four heartland seats lost to Plaid Cymru in 1999 – Islwyn, Rhondda, Llanelli, and Conwy in the centre of the North Wales coastal belt – were regained. We'd lost Wrexham to John Marek in the meantime, and we had won Alun Michael's regional seat in Mid & West Wales only because we had lost Llanelli. With Dafydd Elis-Thomas more than happy to keep his place as Presiding Officer, and John Marek likewise as Deputy Presiding Officer, Labour had a majority of one.

So, I got down to the work of putting together an all-Labour Cabinet at my home in Michaelston-le-Pit, with my Cabinet Secretary Lawrence Conway and the four Special Advisers. At the end of a farm lane, just outside our tiny hamlet, we were well away from the prying eyes of the media – the nearest thing to working in total secrecy you can have in Wales. I ordered three pizzas to keep us going through a long evening. When the pizzas arrived half an hour later, the delivery man took one look at the table of advisers at the far end of the kitchen and, as I got my money out, said chummily, 'Picking your Cabinet, are you?'

When we'd finished the pizzas and got our reshaping of the departments and the reshuffling of the individuals all sorted out, we repaired down to the Docks and the White Hart.

By the evening's end, I had a bit of a glow. What a wonderful country Wales is, I thought to myself, where you can pick a Cabinet after winning an election and then go for a drink in a boozer that hasn't been modernised. Is there any country in Europe where you could do that? I don't think the second term of the Assembly that was to unfold proved to be half as rose-tinted as I imagined it might be that night. Nothing disastrous happened, but it was not the great success it should have been.

A very telling statistic about 2003 came to light a year later. Traffic on the M4 around Newport had been rising consistently at three per cent a year – hence the congestion at the dreaded Brynglas Tunnels. In 2003, that growth rate dropped to one per cent. Why was that? Well, it was because of the transfer of manufacturing to the ex-Warsaw Pact countries of Eastern Europe that were now entering the European Union. And the second half of the pincer movement causing a wave of factory closures was the rise of China as a manufacturing super-power. The first arm of the pincer had been anticipated, but the second had not.

The war in Iraq turned from giving us a Baghdad Bounce at the May 2003 elections to a big negative after that. It applied in Britain just as much as in Iraq, as the original warmth of welcome for the British troops by the mainly Shi'a population in southern Iraq around Basra turned sour. The only place where it was almost unalloyed good news was in the northern area populated by the Kurds, who took advantage of the weakness of the central authorities in Baghdad to devolve power to themselves – they weren't given it, they took it, and Kurdistan came into existence.

There were two key tests as to whether the invasion would deliver a positive legacy for the Americans and their allies – and for Bush and Blair especially. The first was whether the de-Ba'athification process was as successful as de-Nazification had been in Germany and Austria after 1945; the second was whether any weapons of mass destruction were found. In my annual end of summer term meeting with the Prime Minister at No. 10 in 2004, the hunt for the WMDs was still in full cry, but nothing had shown up. I didn't like to ask about this acutely painful issue, but Blair raised it with me. 'WMDs will be found there, Rhodri!' he asserted, with that little bit of false emphasis on top, indicating that what he really meant was that he'd be out gong farming if they weren't found! As indeed they weren't. But it was the ghastly failure of the de-Ba'athification process that had the greater long-term adverse consequence for Iraq, making the country pretty well ungovernable. I met a unit of Welsh troops at a reception in Cardiff City Hall after their return from a second tour of duty in Basra, and they told me how dreadful the task of night patrols had now become. They mentioned patrolling the line of the electricity supply, checking on the pylons and transformers, when they found a gang of half a dozen militant Sunni Ba'ath guerrilla fighters trying to saw through the base of the pylon with a hacksaw!

If you rendered completely unemployable in perpetuity anyone who had been a civil servant or electricity worker under Saddam Hussein with obligatory membership of the Ba'ath Party, then you would never get the basic services working in Iraq. How could the Bush administration neo-cons (like Wolfowitz and Cheney and Rumsfeld) not see that? Why didn't we do the same in Iraq as we had done in de-Nazifying Germany? And did Tony Blair have any miti-gating influence over the neo-cons around Bush? I nearly got involved myself. Jack Straw phoned to ask if I would consider going out to the emerging statelet of Kurdistan – they needed advice, he said, on exactly how to manage the rela-tionship between regional and central government. I greeted this as a welcome conversion for the notoriously devo-sceptic Jack Straw, and I told him I would definitely consider it, but I heard no more. To be honest, the Kurds didn't need me or anybody else to advise them, although many of the Kurdish leadership cadres had actually studied in Welsh universities. But I don't think I would have found working on regional-central government relationships with American neo-cons good for my stress levels. In any case, we were going to have plenty of problems on the regional-central government relationship in Wales, let alone Kurdistan, when the Richard Commission reported in 2004. Maybe the Kurds would be able to provide us with a few lessons.

The only direct fall-out on me was actually nothing more than a fiercely hos-tile audience in Aberystwyth on *Question Time* in early 2006, when I was trying to answer the question of whether we the panel thought the exit strategy in Iraq had been properly thought through. Leanne Wood cleverly turned it into an attack on me for not giving a clear statement on whether I supported the war in Iraq or not. Yes, I had been an MP, but I wasn't one in 2003 and so I hadn't had a vote on the issue. But the *Question Time* episode also raised the awkward boundary line that Plaid loved to exploit on me keeping out of Tony Blair's bailiwick and, in return, him keeping out of mine. But Plaid sympathisers in the audience kept on and on, saying I was the leader of Wales and therefore the people of Wales had a right to know whether I was for or against? It was exceedingly uncomfortable. The Iraq War had turned from being a popular war into a very unpopular one, and has remained so ever since. That's one of the reasons why I can't stand to watch or listen to *Any Questions* or *Question Time*, which they are made for over-simplified sloganising. When this particular *Question Time* ordeal was over, David Dimbleby and I walked towards the refreshment room and he asked me, 'Rhodri, what on earth was that all about? I kept wanting to move on to the next question, but the producer was yelling into my earpiece, "Keep it running, keep it running".'

Then we had the Labour Party Conference in Bournemouth, made immensely sad by the death of Gareth Williams, Lord Williams of Mostyn, who had done several years in Tony Blair's Cabinet and was posthumously voted the best life peer of all time. His fellow lordships absolutely loved his steady hand, his sense of humour and his huge respect for others' opinions. Gareth had suddenly passed away at sixty-two and, of all the barrister turned politicians I have come across (including John Smith and Tony Blair), if I ever did have to hire a defending bar-rister then it would be Gareth. Gareth had first come to national attention in the Jeremy Thorpe trial, where he tore the whole of the prosecution case to shreds while defending George Deakins, the Port Talbot one-armed bandit operator. At the committal hearing, Peter Taylor (later Lord Taylor the Lord Chief Justice) had laid out the prosecution case based on an admission of guilt by Jeremy Thorpe in a taped telephone conversation. In it, Thorpe had admitted the need to have Norman Scott bumped off, but also that he, Thorpe, believed he had immunity because he was the only person in Britain who had slept with both Princess Margaret and Antony Armstrong-Jones! Gareth saw his opportunity to insist that the tape be made public in its entirety as it was all relevant to the eventual trial. Once Gareth insisted on publication of the tape, of course, the prosecution couldn't proceed because the tape had to be kept secret to protect the Palace.

Gareth's funeral took place in the middle of the party conference, and the RAF flew the whole of the Cabinet plus me (it was an odd experience for me to be an honorary member of the Blair Cabinet for the afternoon) from Hurn Airport in Bournemouth to Brize Norton in Oxfordshsire in a transport aircraft, which involved being strapped into the walls of the fuselage in troop carrier fashion, and the noise was pretty unbearable. We were then bused across to the parish church in Great Tew, the village where Gareth and Veena lived. Gareth was a huge loss to the Lords and to Welsh and British politics. The man who had the House of Lords eating out of his hand.

I met up again with Robert Carr, the Labour New South Wales premier (not the New Labour South Wales premier) in the course of a trade mission to Australia during the 2003 Rugby World Cup. Carr was a big moderniser, but not a privatiser. He believed that a Labour premier should use all his or her contacts with the trade union and labour movement to get things done, and he explained it to me thus: 'We delivered the Sydney Olympics in 2000 through the trade union movement. I told them that if there was any backsliding towards the old slapdash "She'll be right, mate" Aussie trade union attitude to finishing a job properly, then I'd have to start outsourcing everything to private companies. But if they delivered, we'd hold all the contractors to trade union labour first.' To me, that seemed much more sensible than the messages I was hearing from Westminster. Bob Carr's approach would have been considered impractical in the UK, but I didn't think it was so problematic in Wales. Even before I'd made my Clear Red Water speech in Swansea in 2002, I had heard Bob Carr talking about his approach to deliver the Sydney Olympics via a tough but fair approach to the New South Wales trade unions. I think you could say that his example was one of the inspirations for my 2002 speech!

I then went on to Canberra in 2003, a centre of government not trade, but a huge number of computer service companies had sprung up around the capital (as has happened on a far larger scale around Washington DC). A lot of such companies wanted to go beyond the confines of the Australia–New Zealand market pretty quickly. So, two things every visiting UK Minister has to do in Canberra: the first is to make contact with the federal parliament and government, and the second is to have dinner with the British High Commissioner. I skipped the first because I was a devolved rather than an HMG Minister. My opposite number was the Mayor of the Canberra Municipal Authority, but I didn't really fit there; I certainly didn't meet the Canberra Tourist Authority, which was said to be still seething in the wake of a Max Boyce joke at his Sydney Opera House concert (which seemed pretty innocent to me, 'Tonight, here in Sydney, it's half past nine, while in Canberra it's last Thursday afternoon!').

You could see why it brought the house down in Sydney. There's a sort of static quality to life in Canberra. Take my dinner at the official residence of the British High Commissioner, Sir Alistair Goodlad, who I remembered as Government Chief Whip under John Major. Anyway, we had our dinner at a long table, with Sir Alistair sat at the head at the far end, where I could only just see him. I was seated at the other end, opposite Lady Goodlad. In between the two ends there were journalists and academics and policy wonks. We had not long finished our soup when Lady Goodlad waded in on Michael Howard in what was another of those far more weird than anything I've seen on *Yes Minister* moments. It was only a year since Michael Howard had taken over as Conservative leader in Opposition after the booting out of Iain Duncan Smith.

'He's hopeless!' said Lady Goodlad, in a really plummy Dame Edith Evans voice, 'Absolutely hopeless! He's never going to beat Tony Blair. And do you know why he'll never beat Tony Blair?' I wasn't sure if she expected me to egg her on or not, but there was no stopping her anyway. 'It's the way he speaks. It's that awful accent of his. He's pretending to be pukka but *we* all know he's not, don't we?' This was now turning more Nancy Mitford than Edith Evans. 'There's one word that gives the game away', she went on, 'he can't say the word *people* properly. He says it as *peepul*! And, Mr Morgan, do you know why he always says *peepul* instead of *people*?' I was trying to get the words out, 'Well, he was brought up in Llanelli, wasn't he …' before I burst out laughing, when Lady Goodlad charged on – 'It's because he's Romanian!' I just looked around, gobsmacked, wondering what on earth the crème de la crème of the Canberra intelligentsia made of all this. While Max Boyce had joked in Sydney that it was 'last Thursday afternoon' in Canberra, this was more like *last Thursday afternoon in 1924*. Talk about the Last Night of the Poms! I did half-heartedly put forward the case for the more obvious Llanelli explanation, but Lady Goodlad very firmly claimed that she had a friend who was an expert on the Romanian language and they had both agreed that the exotic Eastern European explanation was the right one. Does it matter what impression the UK political elite makes in countries like Australia? Does our representation at High Commission level appearing half a century out of time create an impression of the UK as a museum piece?

It isn't easy to get across to the rest of the world that Wales is a great place to live, study, play and invest in. Should we emphasise the vision of Wales as a country with the ancient Celtic language, the Eisteddfod, the ancient Red Dragon Flag and the laws of Hywel Dda? Or should we advance Wales as the cosmopolitan modern country proven by the 1841 Census to be the first in history to have more workers employed in industry than in agriculture? Cardiff is where the first ever £1 million cheque was signed in 1906. Not a claim London can ever make. Is it possible to have an image of modernity and antiquity glued together?

What I wanted to do in the whole of that second Assembly was to promote Wales tied to my ideal of it as a modernising country, the ideal location for high-tech industry and research establishments. I had no idea if I was cut out to be that kind of super-salesman, but I had to give it a try. I would never get another chance like this. The Richard Commission Report was also coming out, which was bound to cause some political management problems for me. Ivor Richard had done a brilliant job, with the secretary of the Commission Carys Evans, to turn the other nine Commission members into a unified body. It took seven years to get from the publication of the report in 2004 to the arrival of legislative powers for the Assembly, which was at the time of commencement of the fourth Assembly in May 2011. It was a tortuous process, but get there we did.

What the Commission recommended was a build-up to full legislative powers in the devolved areas; what precisely the mechanism should be, and whether it would require a third devolution referendum, the Richard Commission left to the political process. The Commission was silent on that point. Apart from increasing the numbers of AMs from 60 to 80, one other of the Commission's recommendations has been left in abeyance, namely the switch from one form of PR voting, the Additional Member system, to the Irish single transferable vote system.

Looking back now, the key achievement of the Richard Commission was clear. There was barely any opposition to the legislative powers question when it was put to the Welsh public in the referendum in March 2011. Recalling the strength of opposition in September 1997, not to mention the ferocity of the opposition in 1979, the absence of a No campaign in March 2011 was a remarkable tribute to the degree of unity within the Richard Commission on its main recommendation. There was a window of opportunity in 2011, and the margin and ease of victory in that referendum was remarkable. It could not have happened much before 2011, and that window seemed to have slammed shut with the subsequent rise of UKIP. Still, the key cause of that switch in political opinion came on the side of the Conservative Party.

It was hard to find a Yes-voting Conservative in 1997, but there were plenty in 2011 and some had indeed become fully engaged in running the Yes campaign. I'm not sure if that was down to the influence of the Conservative leader in the Assembly, Nick Bourne, and his nominee on the Commission, Paul Valerio – if there had been any huge opposition to the idea of legislative powers for the Assembly among the Tory grass roots, then both Nick Bourne and Paul Valerio would have been accused of going native. Anyway, that dog didn't bark.

In 2004, the key step for us as a Labour Government in the Assembly was how to get discussions moving towards the British Labour manifesto for the general election expected the following year. Peter Hain and I had many friendly up and downers on this, as we tried to find a compromise that would keep the Welsh Group of the MPs happy (including some notable devo-sceptics such as Paul Murphy and Don Touhig, the MPs for the adjoining Gwent Valleys constituencies). If we could find a way forward which didn't engender opposition in that quarter, we could still hit road blocks among devo-sceptic Ministers like Jack Straw, John Prescott and Margaret Beckett. The Welsh Labour Executive was broadly in favour of moving forward on legislative powers, although it wasn't unanimous. In the end, the Executive agreed a form of words that went through a recall annual conference at the Holland House Hotel in Cardiff. It was written by Peter Hain and me, almost like those parlour games where each individual in a pair writes one word then passes the baton to the other person for the next word. If we didn't write alternate words, we certainly wrote alternate sentences, and the compromise was voted through unanimously. It proved to be the basis for Labour's manifesto in the 2005 General Election. Jack Straw did throw in a block late on, and I had to call Blair to intercede. That phone call overrode the Jack Straw problem, and we got back on track. My impression was that the Prime Minister was convinced of the readiness of the Assembly to take on legislative powers – what helped, ironically, was that the PM wrongly thought that we only had executive powers. I had tried and failed over the years to stop Blair describing the Assembly as a purely executive body – I kept having to remind him that we had done quite a lot with our secondary legislative powers. Luckily, I never succeeded in that particular mission. Blair thought we only had executive powers and that we ought now to get legislative powers – that was the very broad brush grasp that he had. So, the Labour manifesto of 2005 was delightfully flexible, but it did say that a Labour Government would increase the legislative powers of the Assembly. It was vague, though, about how (as well as when and how much). There was no mention of a referendum to validate any new powers.

There was more cooperation with the UK Labour Party over the preparation of the 2005 General Election manifesto on waiting lists for non-urgent treatment. My old friend John Reid, from the 1987 intake of MPs, had become the Health Secretary after Alan Milburn's sudden resignation. In some ways, it was an odd appointment, because John was a Scottish MP and was now Health Secretary for England. His writ didn't run in Scotland. But John loved the job because, as a dyed-in-the-wool Unionist, if he could run the English NHS with shorter waiting lists than Scotland, it would be one in the eye for the devolutionists and especially the crypto-Nat tendency among them. He met me in his room in the Commons, and took me through the process by which he had arrived at the 18-week target for maximum waiting times between GP referral and treatment. There didn't seem to be any medical basis for choosing 18-weeks, it was a matter of eyeballing the management of the NHS in England. 'They told me that 22-weeks was the shortest they could do. I told them we had to do better than that, and they came back and said they could do 20. They were sure I'd agree to 20, nice round figure and all that, but I gave them the cold stare treatment. If you can't get below 20-weeks, I'll have to find some people who can. Then, a week later, they came back with 18, and I did the deal on 18.'

John's other big idea was that competition in delivering faster treatment for hips, knees, cataracts, piles, hernias and varicose veins – the classic non-emergency waiting list conditions – was an essential part of keeping the whip hand over the NHS. John was willing to overlook the first problem that the private sector didn't train surgeons for its own use, let alone for the NHS – it was a one-way ticket for independent (that is, private) treatment centres, which took surgeons from the NHS or imported them from abroad. Doing no training meant that their productivity per hip or hernia was of course going to be higher. The second problem with these treatment centres was that they wouldn't accept the elderly and frail who had multiple-condition problems – their ideal patient was a fit and active forty-year-old who had dislocated a shoulder skiing. The south of England was full of patients like that, but Wales was not.

The 18-week waiting time guarantee was going to cause us a huge perception problem in Wales. Inevitably, it became the Gold Standard (even though there was no medical basis for it), and people in Wales looked with envy across the border at the 18-week waiting time, which actually became accepted as the proper length of time that anyone should have to wait. If Scotland or Wales had come up with 14-weeks, there wouldn't have been the reverse effect – English patients wouldn't look across Offa's Dyke wishing they lived in Wales. For a small country like Wales, it's what happens over the border in England that sets the standard. That's rooted deep in our psychology. By the time of the 2005 election manifesto, we had come up with our 26-week target, but applied it to *all* referrals and not just to GP referrals. The 18-week target in England only applied to GP referrals; consultant-to-consultant referrals and therapists' referrals were excluded in England. It was hard to establish rock-solid figures, but our all-in referral target might have increased the patient numbers in our waiting time targets by some 40 per cent! Not that you'd know it from the press coverage.

This raised one of those difficult interfaces between central and devolved government. I took the view that, in practical political terms, Labour in the Assembly had to come up with a plan to cut waiting times before the 2005 General Election.

We couldn't avoid the issue that NHS waiting times were pretty central to Labour winning a third term. Our 26-week maximum waiting time was very carefully thought through, and my guess that a great deal more thought had gone into it than the eyeball-to-eyeball meetings John Reid had so graphically described to me. But that wouldn't convince the Welsh public, 90 per cent of which believed that 26-weeks rather than 18-weeks was either a decision made to save money or because the NHS in Wales wasn't up to the job and was too disorganised. No independent treatment centres, ITCs, were opened in Wales. We had to import quite a lot of expertise from England to help run the Waiting Time Initiative, and it was funded by a special supplement to the regular Health budget. I would hold monthly meetings with the Health Minister Brian Gibbons and the waiting times team, which included many recruited from the Bristol area, to see where and in which specialties we had continuing problems. Once the long waits and lists had been contracted to a 'new normal' size, the projection was that the special funding would stop and that the Health Department budget would bear the strain from then on.

As far as strain goes, there was a fair amount in relationships over these regular monthly meetings. I had reshuffled my Cabinet in 2005. Jane Hutt had become exhausted after almost six years as Health Minister, the toughest portfolio in the Assembly set-up because the Health budget is enormous compared to any other, 40 per cent of the total with an ever-increasing share. Jane had transferred to Business Minister and Chief Whip and, in her place, I had appointed Dr Brian Gibbons who had most of a career lifetime's experience as a GP in the Valleys, and who was quite happy working with me on the delivery of the 26-week waiting time pledge. The strain only came with the period after the arrival of the Labour–Plaid Cymru coalition Government in July 2007. The new Health Minister in succession to Brian was Edwina Hart, who preferred to be given a job to do and the money to do it, and then to go away and get on with it. I much preferred her modus operandi as well, but this was an exceptional case because of the profile and the financial structure.

The third area where there was an intertwining of the work at our devolved level was over the subsidiarity sections of the Treaty of Lisbon, which came into effect at the end of 2009. Peter Hain was the Foreign Minister representing the UK Government in the treaty negotiations, and Gisela Stuart, latterly a leading light in the campaign to leave the EU, represented the British Parliament in the legislature strand of the talks. The subsidiarity question was of huge political salience in the treaty discussions. It meant that, for the first time, the European Commission could be told to back off if enough national parliaments voted to tell the Commission to drop a proposed EU law on the grounds that the problem was better left with the member states themselves to solve. That's what subsidiarity meant. But the even bigger breakthrough was that the meaning of 'parliament' could also be taken to be a devolved legislature like ours in Wales. Peter Hain told us that the FCO was all brilliant minds when it came to conventional diplomatic questions, but not so well clued up on new domestic arrangements like devolution. Peter borrowed one of our top experts at the Assembly, and got him to write the key part of the Treaty of Lisbon addressing subsidiarity to the regional governments! That was a new experience for our officials and, no doubt, for the FCO – the exact reverse of what had happened half a century earlier, when a senior FCO wallah had been brought in to rewrite *Wales: The Way Ahead* because no one in the infant Welsh Office was up to the mark.

When the Government produced its White Paper on the new European Treaty to ratify and implement Lisbon, we were exercised in ensuring that Wales was definitely in the list of regional parliaments with legislative powers that had the right to be informed in advance of draft EU legislation on areas where the competence had been devolved. The French Government was equally as desperate to keep its regions *out* of this process – that's why the sub-clause 'with legislative powers' had been put in. It all got very heated just to make absolutely certain that Wales was accepted as a region with legislative powers.

The Treasury phoned my Private Secretary on a Saturday afternoon, when she was shopping in Sainsbury's, and agreed to send her a draft copy of the relevant sections. She'd offered to download it at home, print it off, and get it to me that evening – but Julie and I were going to the New Theatre to see *Blood Brothers* starring Linda Nolan, she of the many sisters (Julie had a granny-sitter booked to look after her bed-ridden mother from 7:30 pm until 10:30 pm). Right, so my secretary said she would bring the printed copy to the foyer of the New Theatre at 7:20 pm, and I could then take it home to read after the musical, and let her know if any changes were required. All went well as far as her delivering the document to me – then everything went wrong. The fire sprinkler unaccountably started to drench the safety curtain and the stage – Linda Nolan came on dressed as Mrs Mopp in wellies after ten minutes, to inform the audience that the sprinkler had malfunctioned and they wouldn't be able to carry on until everything had dried out. The performance started about half an hour late, which meant Julie and I would have to go before the final curtain to relieve the granny-sitter. I still don't know how *Blood Brothers* ends! It's a wonderful musical and, if the ending is as good as the rest of the show, we did miss something.

Julie and I got home after sneaking out of the theatre as discreetly as we could. For the very first time, I had worn this new pair of combat pants which had huge zipped pockets that I'd stuffed the document into. Horror of horrors, when I unzipped the big-zipped pocket at home, the top secret document was missing! I realised that what I'd assumed to be a pocket wasn't a pocket at all – it was the zip to remove the lower part of the trouser leg to turn the trousers into shorts. The document had fallen straight down my leg, and onto the floor of the theatre (where it still presumably lay). How would I ever be able to explain that to Prime Minister Gordon Brown? Again, one of those moments that *Yes, Prime Minister* would never have concocted! I had to jump back in the car – I was going to have to look in all the rubbish bins – but what eventually saved me was the late start and the number of curtain calls Linda Nolan and her co-stars had taken. I got into the theatre after the audience had only just left, but before the cleaners had started work, and there was the document still lying untouched on the theatre floor! Saved from humiliation. I didn't dare push my luck and ask for lots of changes to the document, not after that nerve-wracking experience.

I did ride my luck more than once that year, and sometimes your luck runs out. The invitation to attend the sixtieth anniversary commemoration ceremony in Normandy seemed innocent enough at the time. I asked Edwina Hart if she would like to represent the Assembly, because it clashed with the final of the Welsh Open Golf Championship, which I always attended to hand out the prizes with Sir Terry Matthews. Edwina was a war baby like me, but in a totally different sense. I was a war baby in that I was born in September, just after the war had broken out, and I could just about remember D-Day. Edwina was way younger than me, but both of her parents had been in the services during the war. Nobody took the slightest bit of notice of these arrangements until the very end of a press conference taking place in Scotland with my opposite number Jack McConnell. Out of the blue, Jack was asked by a journalist if he was going to attend the sixtieth anniversary of D-Day. He replied to say he wasn't able to go because of a golfing dinner in St Andrews, and then all hell broke loose. Some journalist in Wales chose to ask me exactly the same question, and I gave a remarkably similar answer to the one Jack gave about the golf, and the response too was remarkably similar. All hell broke loose – even Edwina rang me up saying people in her constituency were telling her that she shouldn't go, and that she should tell me to go instead!

The row in the world of the media and politics was never-ending. There was no way out really. If I changed my mind and said I was going at the last minute, it would give the media the impression that they were running Wales – but if I didn't go, I was upsetting a lot of people who thought I was being disrespectful to D-Day veterans and those who had fallen in the land invasion. I decided that the best thing to do was sit tight – I believe Jack McConnell was persuaded to go – but I thought it would set a dangerous precedent to change my mind. So, I attended the Welsh Open final, and handed out the trophy as usual – there was a bit of booing with cries of 'You shouldn't be here, Rhodri!', but that was replaced by applause by the time the prize-giving was in full swing. One golf fan reminded me of what his late father had once said to him: 'Respect the dead, but look after the living.' I don't know where that saying comes from, but I know I found it comforting at the time.

Again, a few weeks later, I seemed to have plenty of time coming into Builth Wells for Her Majesty the Queen's official opening of the Royal Welsh Show. I was only half a mile from the showground when the traffic ground to a complete halt – nothing moved an inch – if I had got out of the car and walked that last half mile, I'd have been at the showground in plenty of time. Terry Grange, then Chief Constable of Dyfed Powys, was good enough to explain to me afterwards what had happened. He had decided to give Her Majesty the full works in terms of police car and motorcycle escorts, which meant that all other traffic in the vicinity of the Royal Welsh came to a complete halt. It actually would have been much faster walking – I wasted half an hour in a stationary car. By the time I got there, the official opening had been and gone. Luckily, Carwyn Jones had been present on my behalf, but the big story of the day became my alleged snubbing of the Queen. I've had the full works myself in terms of motorcycle police escorts in Dublin and New York, but I've never asked for it in Wales because it creates an unnecessary barrier between us and them. But boy! does it make a difference – I've been in the Prime Ministerial Jaguar with reinforced bomb-proof roof in the company of Tony Blair and Gordon Brown, from Cathays Park to the Bay in five minutes through heavy city traffic. A remarkable experience, but I think the people of Wales would rather I was late now and again instead of having police sirens howling through their neighbourhoods just to let them know the First Minister is in town.

In the future, maybe there will one day be a report recommending that the First Minister has an official residence, like the Prime Minister at No. 10 or the Scottish First Minister in Bute House. Even before the emergence of the new-found climate of suspicion of all politicians since 2010 and the expenses scandal, people in Wales have been particularly suspicious of anyone putting on airs and graces. It's the age-old *gwerin* and *crachach* problem, the us-and-them problem writ large. Welsh Ministers do important things, but don't have any defence and security or foreign policy responsibilities, and that's why a whole generation will have to go by before police escorts and official residences will appear on the agenda.

The relationship with the Royal Family does need examination before the Royal Welsh episode. When I first became First Minister, during a Royal visit to Cardiff University to open some new laboratories, time was found to give Her Majesty and me three-quarters of an hour together – it was just an ice-breaker, really, but I had thought that the Palace would press us for some kind of an arrangement for regular briefing, maybe once or twice a year. The PM provides a weekly briefing when Parliament is sitting; neither Her Majesty nor Wales needs anything like that, I suppose. We Ministers in Cardiff were not Ministers of the Crown until 2007, but even after that date the meetings to advise the monarch didn't take place. I had an open mind either way. If the kind of things we do in the Assembly are not considered sufficiently important by the Palace to bother Her Majesty with, then fair enough. She's got plenty on her plate. And she's an avid reader of official papers anyway. Even on the day of my alleged snub to the Queen at the Royal Welsh, she and I spent most of the next four hours together discussing horses. There were never-ending parades of Welsh cobs doing all kinds of prancing and cantering manoeuvres in front of us. The one thing I definitely knew about the Queen was her love of horses, so, if I had given any offence to her by being sort of late, I'd try and get back into her good books by wittering on about horses. I got quite dewy-eyed and romantic about my grandfather growing up on the smallholding above the Swansea Valley, breaking in horses from about the age of seven onwards.

The decision by the Palace authorities against any regular briefing to Her Majesty may have been caused by the vague and unspoken idea that briefings should be with the Prince of Wales instead – and things did kick off that way. Twice a year to begin with, and then once a year, and then tailing off to nothing, I would get an invitation to Highgrove to discuss anything and everything with the Heir to the Throne. He didn't really want briefing from me on what was happening with the Assembly. It was rather an opportunity for him to press me on his favourite topics – like homeopathic medicine, elimination of badgers (Highgrove was in a bovine tuberculosis hotspot), and the need to return to traditional principles in architecture and urban and village design. He quickly realised he was going to get no change out of me on homeopathic remedies – they were not going to be available on the NHS in Wales, and that was that! We weren't going to go in for a badger cull in Wales. But I did have some sympathy with the Prince on the architecture issue, and I accepted his invitation to visit Poundbury in Dorsetshire, a new (albeit twee, it has to be said) attempt at village retro community design. There is no equivalent of Dorsetshire in Wales, but the Prince of Wales Trust did help enormously in establishing what the redevelopment of the BP Llandarcy oil refinery site was going to look like at the new Coed Darcy village (though it was never going to be Poundbury-on-Neath). It had a knock-on effect eventually on the regeneration of the oil tank farm on the Jersey Marine road west of Swansea, where the new £450 million campus of Swansea University has been built.

The only time I thought that the relationship between the monarch and the Welsh First Minister was strained ever so slightly was on one occasion in Haverfordwest, at the Pembrokeshire County Hall. It wasn't at a private meeting – more of a loose scrummage, with maybe half a dozen invitees surrounding Her Majesty and me. Somebody mentioned Pembrokeshire's famous epithet of 'Little England beyond Wales', and I pointed out that it didn't apply to north Pembrokeshire, which was more 'Little Wales beyond Little England beyond Wales'. I said the distinction in language and ethnic origins goes back to the Normans. Her Majesty seemed disconcerted and got quite sharp, asking 'Does all this matter now?' Well, of course, it still does and I was trying to be as helpful as a First Minister could be, but she didn't want my advice. I just had to shrug my shoulders on that one.

I don't know how the relationship has worked out between Her Majesty and the Scottish First Minister. I'm sure it was much easier in Scotland, because the new Scottish Parliament building was built on a site cheek-by-jowl with the Palace of Holyrood. I don't know if there are regular briefing meetings between the Scottish First Minister and the Queen, though Scottish Ministers have been Ministers of the Crown from 1999, not just from 2007 as is the case with us in Wales. As an overall judgement, the relationship in Wales was excellent, especially after the very jolly occasion of the official opening of the new Senedd building in 2006. It's just one of those aspects of devolution that needs ongoing attention.

I was perfectly capable of self-inflicted wounds by not thinking cutely or acutely about an issue. When the term of office of the Assembly's Counsel-General Winston Roddick QC neared its end, he didn't want to renew, and we were not going to fight to retain him either – most of us Ministers thought the job of Counsel-General was a bit overblown in both status and title. Anyway, as was normal, the Permanent Secretary presented me with the four names on the short-list to succeed Winston. I told Sir Jon Shortridge that the only name on the list I had heard of was Gerard Elias QC. Sir Jon had every right to assume that he could proceed to the final stages of the appointment process, safe in the knowledge that if Gerard Elias came through I would be fine with the job being offered. A couple of weeks later, Sir Jon came back to say the job was about to be offered to Elias, but by this time I'd had one of those 'What have I done?' moments. I had heard of Gerard Elias for two reasons – the first was that he had played a leading role in the North Wales Child Abuse Inquiry chaired by Sir Ronald Waterhouse ten years previously; the second, which had bubbled under the surface but without bursting in my conscious brain was that he was a past officer of the Dinas Llandaf Lodge of the Freemasons! As was Winston Roddick, the current holder of the post!

Why I hadn't twigged straight away when his name first came up, I shall never know. Tiredness is the only possible excuse, but no excuse really. It was my own damn fault. I knew all the names of the past officers of that Lodge by heart – they were imprinted inside my eyeballs. The man I'd originally defeated to win Cardiff West as an MP, Stefan Terlezki, was another name on the list. Gwilym Jones, the guy Julie had defeated in 1997 to become the MP for Cardiff North, was another. The full list was like a roll-call of prominent Tory councillors and MPs, or by now ex-MPs, defeated by members of the Morgan family. Now, Winston Roddick was on the list, but he was certainly not a Tory. He had been a Liberal parliamentary candidate. I had no idea of Elias's politics, but I couldn't stomach the idea that this Lodge was so powerful that two successive Counsels-General, the first two in the history of devolution in Wales, were both part of that gang! Sir Jon, in the meantime, was very hurt. My change of mind had offended a principle of appointment within the UK Home Civil Service. Ministers do not choose senior officials – they are, unlike in local government, chosen by the Civil Service Commission. The Minister has the right to object to a proposed candidate on grounds of incompatibility, but may not choose the appointed candidate. This preserves the neutrality of the civil service. It made it politically easier when it emerged that Gerard Elias had been a legal adviser to groups who wanted to preserve fox hunting with packs of dogs, but it made it far more difficult to handle politically when the next best candidate coming forward was Malcolm Bishop, a top QC in London, albeit a North Walian by birth and upbringing, who turned out to be a former Labour parliamentary candidate and came with a reference from the Lord Chancellor Lord Irvine! The excrement wasn't just hitting the fan by now – it was threatening to block the entire ventilator shaft! In the end, the Cabinet decided that we had no need for such a highfalutin position as Counsel-General, and did without. That mini-crisis was all my fault.

Later that year, I had my only experience of a brown envelope incident, but of such indescribably Welsh rural innocence that I have treasured it ever since. I had always wanted to visit the Ifor Williams trailer plant in Cynwyd, outside Corwen, on the A5. It was the classic example of a Welsh family business and a market leader in horse boxes and trailers. No summer drive through Wales is complete without getting stuck behind an Ifor Williams-badged trailer. It was an all-too-rare example of a successful and sizeable Welsh family business, world-beating in product design and engineering. Wales had far too few such firms, and the UK was little better. I went around the factory with Ifor's son John and daughter-in-law. The founder, old man Ifor Williams himself, still designer-in-chief, was waiting for us for the cup of tea and compulsory slice of buttered *bara brith* (traditional Welsh fruit loaf), before we wended our way back to Cardiff. As he was finishing his tea, Ifor passed me a brown envelope. 'Just something for you to enjoy', he said, 'my wife insisted.' I opened it with trepidation, but there was no bung inside. What was inside was a poem written on a sheet of paper. Ifor's wife had won the competition the previous night at the local Welsh poetry circle with a poem on the set subject of 'On the Appointment of Mike Ruddock as the National Coach of the Welsh Rugby Team', and Ifor was now presenting the poem to me. It could only happen in Wales, I thought to myself, mightily relieved. If only we had fifty strong family-owned businesses like Ifor Williams Trailers Ltd exporting all over Europe in the Welsh economy, we'd be alright.

But that wasn't our history. We had plenty of the two extremes – the corner shop family businesses that were never going to go beyond employing members of their own family, and then the giant British Steel and the National Coal Board behemoths – but there weren't enough middle-sized companies in Wales. Ever since the Wall Street Crash of 1929, Wales had been trying to attract employers from outside – the Holy Grail of inward investment had been a branch factory to put into an advance factory unit of 10,000 or 25,000 square feet, but that market was now dying out fast. We had to quickly move up-market. We needed to get the software designers, because the hardware makers were all moving to Eastern Europe or to China. We had a major success with Logica moving to Bridgend, creating 750 software jobs – Logica was regarded as the number one in British software, and its founder Dr Martin Read was on countless government committees addressing the needs of the IT industry. But the company lost its way during the financial crash, and was bought out by CGI, a Canadian IT giant that is still investing in the Bridgend complex. Logica choosing us proved to be a huge win for Wales.

The build-up to the 2005 General Election, Tony Blair's third and last, was poisoned for Labour in Wales by Peter Law standing as an Independent and defeating Maggie Jones, our official party candidate, who had come through an all-woman shortlist. She was Welsh, but didn't sound it – she was not the authentic voice of the Valleys, as I had described Huw Irranca Davies in 2002. Once it became known that Peter was terminally ill with a brain tumour, it made the electors of Blaenau Gwent even more determined to vote him in. It was the same Welsh sympathy for the underdog that had helped me in 1999 and 2000, and this time in spades in Blaenau Gwent. The net result was that Blair was returned with a majority, but Labour in the Assembly actually lost its majority – we went down to 29 AMs after Trish Law, Peter's widow, won the Assembly seat that he had left vacant.

The important consequence of Blair winning again was that we could set to work to implement the 'new improved legislative powers' that Labour had promised in its manifesto. We had to find a way in which there was sufficient parliamentary involvement in the process of creating a new Welsh law that no new referendum for it would be required – but it should not involve Parliament scrutinising the draft law line by line. That had to be a job for the Assembly, not Parliament, and the whole procedure had to be agreed in time for the next Assembly elected in May 2007 to take on the new powers. Since the new procedure we devised only lasted for one term, there is no objective way to measure how effective it turned out to be. The Assembly would have the right to draft a summary of the law it wanted to pass, and then send it to the Secretary of State to process; the Secretary of State would then convert that summary in to a 'long title' describing the purpose of the draft Assembly Measure. It would then be put through Parliament via the Order in Council procedure; Parliament could object to it, but could not amend it or ask for more details. The principle of it could be debated for an hour and a half and, if nobody objected, it would whizz back along the M4 to go through the full legislative processes in the Assembly. That meant the Assembly debated the principle of it and line by line and clause by clause. Of course, it had to be within our devolved areas of competence, such as Health or Education or the Environment.

In 2006, Peter Hain and I gave evidence to the Welsh Affairs Select Committee on the new procedure for Assembly legislation that the UK Government wanted to introduce. Those who were viscerally opposed to devolution, like David Jones (briefly a member of the Assembly, but a cold fish out of water there, and now a Brexit Minister in Theresa May's government), attacked the proposals as far too radical and requiring another referendum. I put the point to him a referendum should only be held to decide *who* governs rather than to decide *how much* you are governed by an institution. It would be over the top to have a referendum every time you wanted to shift something by a few degrees. There were some who thought this Legislative Competence Order procedure was the thin end of the wedge leading to the unrestricted power to legislate that was introduced four years later in 2011 (but that was, in any case, subject to an easily-won referendum). It's pretty difficult to mount a thin end of the wedge argument against constitutional changes proposed in the UK, because the UK constitution is littered with wedges – thin ends, loose ends and anomalies of every shape and size. That's the price of an unwritten constitution. You can indeed change the constitution without even an Act of Parliament. For example, English Votes for English Laws (EVEL) was introduced just by a change to House of Commons procedure, and yet it has huge implications for the balance of the constitution.

Legislative Competence Orders (or LCOs, as they came to be known) came in ready for use by the 2007 Assembly. Until then, we only had the right to pass secondary legislation, or to request Parliament to pass a full and proper law for it on the Assembly's behalf. That is how the Children's Commissioner for Wales Act of Parliament was passed – and also how the Anti-Smoking in Public Places Bill got nowhere, because Parliament didn't agree with that one.

The other big change in how Wales was governed was the implementation of the bonfire of the quangos that Ron Davies had announced back in 1998, and which I had announced on the last day of the summer session in 2004 would actually happen. I had said then that having so many quangos running Wales plus 60 Assembly Members doing the same was clearly unsustainable. In a way, the quangos were on borrowed time for those first six years of the Assembly. In the end, establishing the primacy of the democratically elected body over the appointed boards of the quangos had to be sorted. Most of the quangos were happy to become part of stronger government departments, working to Ministers rather than to appointed boards. But one quango in particular did not. That was the Welsh Development Agency. I would be told that the WDA had built up a brand, and that if I wound up the WDA I would sacrifice that brand value. Then I would talk to top industrial executives who would tell me that *Wales* was the brand, not the WDA – the WDA was rather the message. It was one of the commonest mistakes in marketing, the confusion of brand and message – I remember Sir David Prosser, the long-term and much-admired head of Legal & General telling me that.

The second problem was that the WDA was paying its staff 20 per cent more than the equivalent civil servants. The WDA had doubled its number of staff from around 450 to 900 during the life of the Assembly and that, combined with the 20 per cent pay above equivalent civil servants, was a big cost burden. It couldn't continue. Again, there was an element in the WDA that believed they were a different beast to the humble clock-watching pen-pushers in the civil service. Yet I'd been on dual purpose export trade and inward investment missions overseas to Australia and South Africa, and I'd seen no tangible difference in the commitment of the staff who serviced the trade missions or who put up exhibitions (all of them civil servants) and those who worked on the inward investment side (who were not civil servants – WDA staff being classed as crown servants).

The upshot of the change we intended to unify the economic development function went through. Letters to the newspapers from disgruntled ex-WDA staff still pop up from time to time, but they hark back to a presumed golden age – but in that particular golden age, the WDA would actually have been totally ineffective without the Section 7 Regional Selective Assistance grants, which were administered by civil servants in the Economic Development Department.

When the LG development was signed off in South Korea in 1996, during the William Hague era as Secretary of State for Wales, it was supposedly going to be the largest inward investment in the history of Europe. The delegation that went out from Wales comprised Derek Jones as head of the Economic Development of the Welsh Office (more recently as Sir Derek Jones, Permanent Secretary and Head of the Welsh Government machine) and Barry Hortop, the then Chief Executive of the WDA. Since most of the LG development eventually never happened, what to do with the shell of the huge semi-conductor silicon chip foundry posed a huge inherited problem for the Assembly. There was a brief period in 2005 during which another semi-conductor operation might have taken the foundry for its original chip-manufacturing purpose. It was a joint venture between Intel and Micron to make flash memory chips, officially a fifty-fifty joint venture but, as with all such apparently equal partnerships, one side is slightly more fifty than the other. Unfortunately for us, Micron had the edge in the partnership as they had the technical expertise in flash memory chips. Intel wanted in and Wales, in the sense of Newport and the empty LG building, was in a worldwide final shortlist of two. We were competing against Singapore and no one else. The top secret project had the codename Operation Tulip.

Micron already had five factories producing silicon chips in Singapore. Micron was a very American company, based in Boise, Idaho (which was a quiet little state capital of only 30,000 people back when I had stopped there for a few days in crossing America in 1962). Apparently, Boise had ballooned to 150,000 people by 2005 due in no small part to Micron's incredible rise. Now, Micron's rigid company culture told them to stick with what they knew, which was Singapore. But

Intel was much more cosmopolitan, and favoured Newport. The key advantage for Wales was that the building was already there, and all you had to do was fit it out. If the joint venture consortium needed to get to market quickly, then we were in with a very good shout. On the other hand, if they had the time to build from scratch, then the cluster of five factories that Micron had already built in Singapore was going to become six. I had a lot of involvement with meeting the executive teams. It is hard to describe how one bunch can seem to hit it off so well with you while another can be so hostile. That's how it was with Micron. I met their project manager in the WDA's box at a rugby international, and the one thing we had going for us was that he was called Rod Morgan. But after the initial small talk about our similar names, I could not get through to him – he was going through the motions.

I've never been entirely able to get out of my mind whether there was anything more I could have done to persuade Micron to favour Wales. Maybe I should have gone out to Boise. But I did the next best thing, which was to ask Tony Blair if he would call Rod Appleton, the boss of Micron and a former US Collegiate tennis champion, and use his great powers of persuasion on him. Blair's prestige in America was sky-high at the time, and I reminded him of the high stakes phone call that Jim Callaghan had made in 1976 to Harold Polling, the boss of the Ford Motor Company in Detroit, to persuade him to commit to the new engine plant in Bridgend. 'Could you please work the oracle with Rod Appleton?' I did ask Tony Blair afterwards how the call had gone, and he replied, 'Well, we spoke mostly about tennis!' So, yes, maybe I should have gone out to Boise, but neither the Blair nor Morgan magic worked. The market slowed down a little, and Micron didn't need the plant in any sufficient hurry for Newport to come on the cards. The company took its time and built in Singapore, and the saga of the Newport LG white elephant rolled on for a few more years. I'll admit that William Hague is a very well-respected after-dinner speaker, and he's also very witty, but I doubt if he had figured out a way of coming up with any jokes suitable for an after-dinner speech audience about LG and the taxpayer-funded white elephant he left behind for us to try to sort out.

The highlight of that year for me was almost accidentally getting into *Dr Who*. One of the many achievements of Menna Richards as Controller of BBC Wales was to get BBC network to accept pitches from BBC Wales to make series for network. It's cause for regret, perhaps, that most of these series made in Wales could theoretically have been made anywhere. They were not set in Wales – they were shot in Wales. When a series was very dependent on special effects, as *Dr Who* was and is, BBC Wales accepted that for the initial phase they would need to bring outside experts from London. One evening I arrived at the BBC Wales television centre in Llandaff for an interview on the late night news. I was met at the door by a new and very young meeter and greeter who seemed to know who

I was – she told me she'd take me straight to makeup. I followed her to this huge makeup studio I'd never seen before, and she left me there. Soon afterwards, a young man came in and introduced himself. He said he'd start straight away, and it would probably take no more than two and a half hours! 'No, surely, it can't possibly take more than a few minutes? In any case, I'm due on in five!' 'I'm a pretty fast worker', said the guy, 'but to make you look like a tree, it really is going to take over two hours.' Me? A tree? Suddenly the penny dropped, *Dr Who*! The makeup artist was a blow-in from the Big Smoke, that's why he didn't recognise me! Having the first ever male makeup artist I'd ever met at BBC Wales was not part of some new policy of getting away from gender stereotypes in employment practice. It was the *Dr Who* effect. I asked for directions to the bog-standard makeup room, no bigger than a barber's shop normally, and all was resolved. Within a year or two, all of the special effects people working on *Dr Who*, *Merlin*, *Sherlock* and *Casualty* were locally trained, but not back then just as the production boom in Welsh-produced network series was kicking off.

The low point of that year, or indeed any other year, came in an unseemly row over the Remembrance Day annual service and parade, normally held at the Welsh National War Memorial in Cathays Park at the heart of Cardiff's formal civic centre. The ownership and upkeep responsibility for the War Memorial is anomalous in a way – it is a Welsh National War Memorial, but it's owned and looked after by Cardiff City Council. When the annual Service of Remembrance takes place every November, the occasion is always organised by the City Council, and the service doubles up as a Cardiff municipal Service of Remembrance in addition to being a national all-Wales service – but it is run by the City Council. There had never been any problems in adapting this dual function ceremony to the realities of devolution. All the party leaders were invited every year to lay wreaths. The Presiding Officer and the First Minister had a special standing alongside the Lord Mayor of Cardiff, in a rough approximation of the service held at the Cenotaph in London. But this time, we received no invitations. I was mystified. I rang Bernard Schwarz, President of the Welsh Branch of the British Legion, and asked if they'd received their invitations. He said they hadn't, and that the invitations were indeed very late, 'I'm not sure what that man is playing at! I'd better get on to the Council.' I assumed 'that man' referred to the Council leader, Councillor Goodway. Anyway, the following week I received a request for an urgent meeting at my office from two of Councillor Goodway's chief lieutenants, councillors Gordon Houlston and Lynda Thorne. I don't know if it was at their request that no one else was present, or if there just happened to be nobody else around – neither special advisers nor regular civil servants from my private office, which happened occasionally – so I was on my own.

I asked them why none of the party leaders in Wales or anyone from the British Legion had received their usual invitations to the Service of Remembrance, and Gordon Houlston said, 'Rhodri, there's got to be something for the Council in this as well!"What are you talking about?'I protested, and Gordon replied to say that the Council was looking for support for their application to the Privy Council for the functions of Lord Mayor and Council Leader to be merged. 'Gordon', I said, 'we're talking about the Remembrance Day service!' And the meeting came to a close without any handshakes. So, we had to organise a last-minute Service of Remembrance at Llandaff Cathedral instead. It wasn't great to be absent from the usual Service of Remembrance followed by the parade in front of City Hall – we couldn't do a compulsory purchase on the Welsh National War Memorial, obviously, and we were almost back to the position Ron Davies had been in in 1998, trying to secure Cardiff City Hall for a reasonable price from Councillor Goodway.

The following year everything returned to normal. Nothing more was heard of the application to the Privy Council to merge the functions of Lord Mayor and Council Leader in Cardiff.

The Government of Wales Act did get onto the Statute Book in 2006. Part 3 of the Act implemented the halfway house idea for the Assembly to issue a summary of a piece of law that it would like to pass to the Secretary of State for Wales; if not objected to in Parliament, it returns to the Assembly. That took effect in May 2007. Part 4 of the Act contained the full monty ability to legislate within all of the devolved fields without the need to seek consent from the Secretary of State and Parliament, but it could only come in after a referendum (and no date was put on the implementation of a commitment to call that referendum). To my mind, the best way to think of Part 3 is as transforming of the Assembly into a legislative body, but with L plates fixed clearly on its back bumper. To remove the L plates and get a full licence would require a majority in a referendum. Future historians will argue over whether the removal of those L plates between 2007 and 2011 was caused simply by Labour having to enter into coalition with Plaid Cymru in July 2007, or by the conversion of large swathes of the Conservatives in Wales to supporting more powers for the Assembly. A third possibility is that it was MPs in Westminster, including those who in 2005 and 2006 wanted to keep the parliamentary apron strings tightly tied around the Assembly, eventually got bored and said, 'To hell with this – let them get on with it down in Cardiff!'

Historians of the constitution may also query why the original Government of Wales Act 1998 was such a half-baked Act of Parliament that it required a rewrite just eight years later, and then another rewrite ten years after the second one. That is a lot of time for the UK Parliament to spend on Welsh devolution, trying to make sure it's a process when it should have been an event. But divining exactly what the Welsh public really wants from its own Assembly, Senedd or Parliament, is not easy for mere mortals. It even baffles opinion pollsters and focus group experts.

Now and again, you get a reminder from the people of Wales that they don't do deference to the First Minister – not even when they may be working for you! I was being driven up to Llandudno to meet the head honchos of the Wales TUC, the Welsh secretaries of the four big unions, in the bar of the main conference hotel for a drink at nine-thirty. I needed to check on how our partnership model with Wales's trade unions was working (this was my attempt to replicate what Bob Carr had done in New South Wales to deliver the Sydney Olympics in 2000, on time and within budget, in cooperation with the trade union movement).

About eight o'clock in the evening, the journey north was going well, when suddenly traffic on the A470 just north of Machynlleth ground to a dead halt. We didn't move for ten minutes. As usual, some kind of herd instinct takes over, and everyone starts to get out of their cars. Part of that response is the need to stretch the legs; part of it is the fear of missing out if those who get out of their cars might discover some piece of valuable information that gives them the edge. There is no mobile phone coverage in the valley heading north from Machynlleth to Dolgellau, so you're only going to get information by wandering round. Eventually, a green-uniformed official-looking person with a clipboard came into view, talking to drivers in little knots as he walked down the static queue of cars. I know I should have stayed out of this – I was onto a loser here, because it was a trunk road for which the Welsh Government bore responsibility, but I still couldn't help going over to join the knot of frustrated drivers.

'What's going on?' I asked – highly original.
'We've got to stop all the traffic because we're doing a bat survey', came the reply.
'Why d'you have to do a bat survey now, in the evening? Can't you do it in the middle of the night when there's no traffic around?'
'No, you can't', came the firm response, 'you can only do a bat survey in the twilight, that's when the bats all come out.'
I wasn't letting go. 'Yes, but why do you have to do a bat survey right here?'
'It's because you can't do the road improvement to straighten out these bends until we've done a bat survey.'
'Well, whose idea is this road improvement work?'

'Yours', came the deadpan reply. Not 'Yours, sir', but quite correctly 'Yours!' Plain and simple, and that was that really. I climbed back into my car with my tail between my legs. I never did manage a pint in Llandudno with the top guys of the Wales TUC. Never pretend to be a big shot in Wales. It doesn't pay.

There is no effective road between North and South Wales. The mountain ranges make it well-nigh impossible. If devolution had occurred in 1979 via the first referendum, and not 1999 after the second one, I can easily imagine that blasting a route through the mountains to knock ninety minutes off the journey time from Cardiff or Newport or Swansea up to Llandudno or Wrexham or Bangor would have happened back in the day. The 1980s was the golden age of big road-building projects, and the need to unify Wales in the era before the internet might have prompted a new devolved Wales in 1979 to give top priority to a fast north–south road.

By the time devolution did happen in 1999, however, the age of heroic road-building projects of national significance was over, so improvements to the A470 were really quite modest – more a matter of removing pinch-points than anything else. The M4 got a lot more attention because it carried far more lorry traffic. The M4 bore a massive commercial load, as did the A55 across the North Wales coast. East–west is where the great weight of commercial traffic needs to go in Wales, not north–south.

The question of how to relieve the strain on the dreaded Brynglas Tunnels in Newport and provide a resilient future-proofed M4 across South Wales prompted the Economic Development and Transport Minister, Andrew Davies, and the head of the Highways Division, Robin Shaw, to prepare a presentation for me on the right solution. The new road involved a high-level crossing of the River Usk passing over Newport Docks. The key feature was that it was not intended to be built using taxpayers' money. It was going to be paid for by road pricing. The UK Department of Transport was at that time going gung-ho for road pricing as the way of the future. The funding of the new road would be done Singapore-style, via electronic tags deducting a toll fee from your bank account every time you used the road. But, more than ten years later, road pricing still hasn't happened. In the meantime, a slow-down took place that wasn't appreciated at the time of the presentation of the case for a new M4 around Newport. The previously inexorable three per cent annual traffic growth on the M4 went into a stagnation decade, which lasted from 2003 to 2013. It was also not appreciated that fears at the time over the resilience of the concrete pillars carrying the M4 over the River Usk immediately east of the Brynglas Tunnels were misplaced – further engineering studies made it apparent that they were not about to fall down. But now that traffic has resumed its previous annual growth, something certainly needs to be done to provide more resilient capacity around Newport.

Not all of the key spending decisions in which I was involved were in the mega-millions bracket like the M4. There might have been a couple of million here and there, but they would involve a new budget line. Why would I get into budget decisions involving a few million when I disliked any hint of micro-management? It was usually the result of lobbying. Scientific researchers had pointed out for me the anomaly that in Wales, though not in Scotland or England, a scientific or medical research team that won a contract from the Wellcome Trust and the other medical charities had no way of covering the overhead recovery charged by their university. In Scotland, if you won the contract, the Scottish Government would pay the overheads. In Wales, a really successful researcher might be told not to bid for any more contracts because the university was unwilling to continue to cover the overheads (which could amount to 40 per cent on top of the grant). Scottish universities were already far more successful than Welsh universities at winning contracts from medical charities, and we in Wales weren't exactly helping our researchers catch up. The Finance Minister Sue Essex and I discussed this problem, and designated £3 million into a new budget line in order to stop disadvantaging our universities in this way.

Another example was the £2 million a year for the fissure sealant programme, which I managed to get doubled to £4 million. The fissure sealant treatment protected the teeth of children with heavily cavity-damaged teeth against future damage. Now, deprived communities have high levels of cavities in children's teeth, and Wales performs badly in this respect, so perhaps I should have pushed the fissure sealant programme a bit further (especially if we were not going to go in for fluoridation).

The £2 million that Sue and I designated to clear the accumulated shortfall in the Aberfan Memorial Fund was a huge decision, although the sum might seem relatively modest within the overall £15 billion annual Assembly budget. Micro-management can sometimes work, so long as you don't make a habit of it.

I appointed myself Science Minister, given that simply putting £3 million annually into the budget to cover the overheads of parent universities was never going to be enough to get science in Wales fully up and running. What it meant in practical terms was that three times a year I would chair a meeting of all the vice-chancellors of those universities with a significant science research record. I wanted to get them to give me some idea of where the star researchers or research teams of the future might be emerging, and in which subject areas Wales was strong and might reach international quality given a bit of backing. These meetings were not a great success, partly because Cardiff University's vice-chancellor never attended; Swansea University's vice-chancellor always attended, but Cardiff University was by far the biggest player, and not attending signalled some lack of respect either towards me and the office of First Minister, or towards the other universities in Wales. It vitiated the whole exercise.

Research Council money is not devolved. Scottish universities are not the only ones who outperform – the Golden Triangle of Oxford, Cambridge and London do the same. Likewise, it isn't only Wales that has under-performed – the Midlands and North of England, and Northern Ireland, do the same. Getting Welsh universities' science into the critical mass so that grants would start flowing was a long-term job, but at least we did make a stuttering start. That effort was stepped up by the appointment of Professor John Harries and, more recently in my successor's time, by Professor Julie Williams in the role of Scientific Adviser to the First Minister; and then by the Sêr Cymru appointments of star professors, both from overseas and from within the Golden Triangle. The picture is now looking healthier in Wales than it has done for a long time. In 2007, the global perception of science in Wales received a massive boost when Sir Martin Evans won the Nobel Prize for Medicine for his work on stem cells. Sir Martin became President and subsequently Chancellor of Cardiff University, although the Nobel Prize was awarded for work he had done some decades earlier at Cambridge. But very few people drill that far down into the detail, and what most people saw was that a Welsh scientist had won the Nobel Prize!

My reason for moving into the promotion of science in Wales and of Welsh science outside Wales was because we couldn't rely on our traditional industries to provide employment. When I had started out as a young civil servant in the old (but at that time actually infant) Welsh Office in 1966, Wales had a labour force of 100,000 coalminers and 75,000 steelworkers. Within twenty years of the ending of the coalminers' strike in 1984–5, there were very few mines left open and the labour force of the steel industry had fallen under 10,000 (steel was probably not making money either, so worse was likely to come). I had always been a doubter of the merger of British Steel and Royal Dutch to form Corus in 1999 – many of my friends in the industry had described it as a marriage made in heaven, but I couldn't see it. The pound being far too strong relative to the euro didn't help, and that in particular was a huge problem for the strip mill side of the business, where the operations in South Wales and Shotton in north-east Wales were in direct competition for orders with the better-placed Royal Dutch strip mill and tinplate complex in Ijmuiden in Holland. This internal competition within Corus wasn't a problem for the Scunthorpe and Yorkshire-based long products division, because the Dutch end of Corus didn't produce long products.

I was relieved in a way when, in October 2006, Corus agreed to be taken over by Tata of India. The Dutch end of the operation had always seemed to me to be looking down on the South Wales UK strip mill operations – if you keep banging on about being more like Ijmuiden, all you end up doing is to depress morale rather than improve performance. The Tata people never had that kind of approach. The Indian steel culture seemed to be more encouraging. When the overall boss of Tata Steel, Mr B. Muthuraman, came over to visit the Welsh operations for the first time, I was invited to meet him for an hour at a conference room at Cardiff Wales Airport, before he flew back to India in Tata's corporate jet. We did a *tour d'horizon* together of Tata's newly acquired works in Wales, and I told him what my impressions were of their strengths and weaknesses. The very Dutch boss of Corus's strip mill operations, Rauke Henstra, who had set up the meeting was there as well.

During the visit, I mentioned the existence of the long-held dream of exploiting the coking coal reserves at Margam, which could be mined in such a way as to bring the coking coal directly up into the works stockyards. The coal at Margam was known to be perfect for making coke for the steel industry. 'Nobody told me about this!' said Mr Muthuraman, looking angrily around the room. Rauke Henstra didn't know where to look – the mainly Dutch bosses of Corus didn't want to know anything about the coking coal on the doorstep of the Port Talbot works. It didn't fit into their picture of how a strip mill operation should work. The Indian view, on the other hand, was to develop steelworks on top of either an iron ore reserve or a coking coal mine, and import everything else to the site.

All of this was before the financial crash of 2008, which left some industries totally unaffected. The defence industries were one such, but we had few of those in Wales. General Dynamics was such a rare bird, and had located its R&D and manufacturing centre on top of an old coal mine at Oakdale in the Gwent Valleys, to carry out the re-tendered Bowman contract to provide modern secure radio communications for the British Army. The best thing that the Labour Defence Secretary Geoff Hoon did was to have the courage to remove the contract from GEC-Marconi in Chelmsford, who were making no progress with it. It was re-tendered and won by a little known Canadian subsidiary of General Dynamics. The Canadian bosses came to have a look at the Oakdale site and loved it – it looked just like Calgary, they thought. They were cautioned that attracting top-notch designers and software clever-clogs to the Welsh Valleys wasn't easy and, fortunately, they advisedly chose to ignore the point. They delivered Bowman on time, and didn't experience any recruitment problems, which led to a rather pleasant and unexpected pat on the back for me as Taff One representing the whole of Wales from Sir Peter (now Lord) Levene, the MoD's Head of Military Procurement.

It was brilliantly choreographed by Sir Peter at Kensington Palace, after a service in St Paul's Cathedral to celebrate the one-hundredth birthday of HRH the Queen Mother. All the invitees had been ferried back from St Paul's to Kensington Palace in a fleet of posh works buses. Then, when everyone was poised with a cucumber sandwich and a cup of tea in hand, out came Sir Peter with it, very deliberately, loud and clear. With half of the entire British establishment in the room, he said his piece so that they could all hear him. 'Congratulations to you, Mr Morgan. We all owe Wales a debt of gratitude. The people of Wales working for General Dynamics have done a magnificent job for Britain on the Bowman contract!' There was an exclamation mark after every word. Blimey! I hadn't expected that! What was interesting to me was that the Head of Procurement for all the Armed Forces should see me as a national surrogate for the thousand-odd staff working at the Oakdale site. I don't think he would have viewed the Secretary of State for Wales in quite the same light.

Early in 2007, the Ministry of Defence gave Wales another boost almost out of the blue, when it announced that the Metrix Consortium had won preferred bidder status in the race to win the 25-year contract to provide the technical training for all three armed services. In the end, it proved to be another LG, a will-o'-the-wisp, rather than another Bowman. It never happened. Preferred bidder status meant that it was Metrix's to lose and, in a way, they never did lose it. It was simply a casualty of the financial crash. Banks and property companies drew in their horns. As a result, it just became a PFI too far – as another Labour Secretary of State for Defence, Des Browne, explained it to me, 'We were desperate to do something to repair the damage done by taking those 3,500 skilled jobs out of St Athan when we shut down the Defence Aviation Repair Agency.' Losing DARA had indeed been a huge blow, and the manufacturers all hated St Athan. Anyway, the great plan for the Defence Training College for all three services never got off the ground – it became clear that it never would after the 2010 General Election and the George Osborne cost-cutting emergency Budget.

As our own elections of May 2007 approached, I had to make my intentions plain. How was I to avoid the Tony Blair trap in the run-up to the 2005 General Election? Blair was, in turn, trying to avoid the Thatcher trap of going on and on. Blair had baffled everyone by saying in 2005 that it was his last election, and that he wouldn't be seeking a fourth term in office – but he also said that he would be serving for the full term if elected for a third time. That was a nonsense, and everyone knew it. He would have to finish sometime *before* the election to allow his successor the opportunity to be chosen by the Labour Party, and for that successor to bed in. I was always of the ten-years-maximum school of thought, and I definitely didn't want to hang on beyond my sell-by date only to be pushed out by impatient younger colleagues. So I went for the public announcement that this May 2007 election would be my last. If I were to remain First Minister after the election, I would hope to finish roughly two-thirds of the way through that term of office, and give a successor plenty of time to settle in, and to stamp his or her authority on the administration plans for the period after 2011. Privately, I didn't believe the lame duck theory propounded by experts who have never been there, but it was a risk I was willing to take.

The four years from 2003–7 should have been the high point of my time in office, but I don't really think they were. I really did have some potential capital after our 2003 election strategy, though I'm far from sure that I made the most effective use of that capital. I loved the job alright, but it may be that running a Welsh Government in a coalition set-up actually put me on my mettle and kept me on my toes far more than the phantom idea of running Wales on a bare majority ever did.

# nine

# Working with Plaid 2007–2009

I T WAS NEVER GOING TO BE an easy election for Labour in 2007. Party morale wasn't high – we had lost a lot of members over the Iraq War, and it seemed to have debilitated the party especially in the western half of Wales, west of the River Llwchwr in South Wales, and west of the Clwydian range in North Wales. In these areas, our core active membership was mostly retired and far more likely to be *Guardian* than *Mirror* readers!

The Labour strategy as far as possible was to retain what we held. We were always going to struggle to keep the 30 seats Labour had won in 2003, which had in any case gone down to 29 with the mid-term defection of the late Peter Law in Blaenau Gwent. The only way that I could see of minimising our losses was to try to emphasise that the only alternative to a Labour Government was a ramshackle coalition of Conservatives, Plaid Cymru and Lib Dems. I was accused of irresponsible scaremongering by flagging the dangers of an unsustainable Anybody But Labour (ABL) coalition, but I thought I had irrefutable logic on my side.

If the people of Wales wanted to vote for an ABL coalition, that was their indisputable democratic right. My warnings were simply to the effect that voters needed to understand that they were choosing not just a local AM and a regional AM, but that they were indirectly also choosing a party and a First Minister to head up a government for Wales. If they wanted a coalition, nobody was going to stop them, but if they didn't actually want a coalition they should vote accordingly for me and for Labour – not a great and inspiring message to get across, I have to admit.

That was perhaps why the people of Wales didn't overly heed my so-called irresponsible scaremongering. By the Friday after election day, on 3 May, clearly with no majority party, we had a right mess to sort out over who was going to run Wales. We hadn't done well, but we had done a hell of a lot better than in Scotland, where Labour had finished up with one less seat than the SNP, though the nationalists were miles off having a majority. In Wales, Labour had 26 AMs elected out of 60, 24 in the 40 constituency seats and 2 in the list seats.

Now, when you've been the party in power with 30 seats (falling in 2005 to 29) and then you drop to 26, the commentariat is bound to say that you've lost the election. For the purposes of the negotiations that now had to take place to try to form a government, it was important to make sure that the more optimistic view also got an airing. Labour had manned the barricades and come out with a respectable result. In terms of a Westminster election and the first-past-the-post system, we had cruised home, winning 24 out of 40 seats. All other parties had mustered only 16 between them. We all knew it wasn't like that really, but we had to whistle to keep our spirits high. If we accepted for one second the sales patter that we had lost (as was the case in Scotland), it would compromise Labour's strength as a negotiating partner – we were by far the largest party, but well short of a majority.

Alex Salmond in Scotland, in a numerically far weaker position than me, was able to move into minority government because the SNP was accepted as having *won* the election. But if 47 MSPs out of 129 was a *win* for the SNP, then I had won a landslide with 26 out of 60! It just wasn't seen like that, of course, simply because Labour in Wales was coming down from a position of power and the SNP in Scotland was in the ascendant. The SNP becoming the largest party was seen as granting the party moral authority to form a minority administration. No way was I going to be able to do that, whatever the comparison with Scotland told you mathematically.

So, Wales was in a mess. How could we get out of it? How long would it take? I didn't know in early May that it would take two months of three-dimensional chess to sort out, and that it would cost me my health. I had made it clear that I wouldn't be standing at another election – 2007 was my last, I was sixty-seven at the time of the election and couldn't countenance standing again at seventy-one. I was one of those dead lucky politicians who had never known election defeat – I had won Cardiff West three times in a Westminster election, and three times in Welsh Assembly elections. I had faced huge struggles in all sorts of other ways in my late-starting political career, but at least I scored six out of six in elections.

I had also made it clear that if I did get the backing to carry on as First Minister, I would not be serving a full term because I would certainly not carry on beyond the ten-year mark in February 2010. Tony Blair had caused all sorts of problems by fudging this issue in 2005 when he'd won his third term – I'm sure that Blair's advisers had told him that, if he set out some kind of future timetable for stepping down, he would become a lame duck.

That was very poor advice in my eyes, and I did the exact opposite. I don't think I was ever conscious of a lame or even a one-legged duck problem – in other words, of my instructions not being followed because colleagues in the Cabinet and civil service were looking ahead to the day when I'd be gone.

There is a genuine problem here in how to draw a career in political leadership to a close. It usually happens when you lose an election – you've been defeated, and you resign. You could, of course, draw the curtains and die in office. Or yet again, your own colleagues might decide you've been around too long, and they defenestrate you (I'd seen it happen to Margaret Thatcher in 1990). None of these three alternatives – defeat, death or defenestration – held any attractions for me. If I could figure out a way of doing it, I wanted to leave office on my own terms. I wanted to disprove Enoch Powell's dreaded dictum that all political careers ultimately end in failure!

It wasn't just that issue driving me, though. The other reason for being so firm on this point of not standing again for election after 2007 was to do with my father's health problems thirty years earlier. Although he'd had a very serious heart attack when he was fifty (I was seventeen and lived through every minute of it), my father had made a very good recovery, eventually to finish up as Deputy Principal at the university in Swansea. He would have retired at sixty-seven if he hadn't been leant on to stay on for another year. He'd agreed to that, and I always thought it was a year too long. In the end, he never enjoyed the retirement that he should have had.

I don't know if it's a common thing for sons to compare actuarial longevity with their fathers, but I certainly did. I was now sixty-seven, my father's age when he'd been persuaded to work on for another year. I was confident that I was fitter at my age than my father had been because I'd never smoked. But, on the other hand, I thought I shouldn't push it too hard so that I could hopefully enjoy a reasonable retirement. With so many grandchildren, I was determined to have a retirement, preferably lasting years rather than months. Indeed, one of my children had reminded me very pointedly about what I had told her about my father damaging his health by working that one extra year! Sometimes, you have to take heed of what your children tell you.

Sorting out the mess left by the inconclusive election result took two months, but it actually felt like six with all the twists and turns. As Labour was still by far the largest party in the Assembly, we had to take a lead, but that was against every indication that the other three parties were going to have a jolly good try to form an ABL coalition (just as I had warned during the election campaign). One of my jobs as caretaker First Minister was to open up the services of our civil servants to help the grouping of the other three parties, in order to cost their proposals to see if a coherent whole could be made of it. I didn't have a problem with that. It was a long-standing tradition, although more usually done before the election.

I continued as caretaker First Minister in line with rule changes to the Government of Wales Act 2006. In the 1998 legislation, which governed the first two Assemblies, the First Minister and the Cabinet were not Ministers of the Crown (as Westminster and Scottish Ministers were); by 2007, we were. The practical effect was that we all remained in office as caretaker Ministers until we could form a government, or until we were evicted by someone else who could. Of course, as caretakers we couldn't take any political initiatives, but we could provide a little bit of guidance to officials and we could have responded to civil emergencies if there had been any. That's all. But possession in politics may not be nine-tenths of the law, but it is perhaps seven-tenths!

The other three party leaders would come into the Cathays Park headquarters of Welsh Government for meetings arranged with the teams of officials assigned to them, and then go down to the Bay or to their party offices, or indeed home, to work up their proposals to another decimal place. Labour Ministers left over from the 2003–7 Assembly were in their normal ministerial offices with their normal private office support, and transported by ministerial cars to ferry them home. There were still letters to be checked and signed. It was the phoney war period during which you could have scripted a BBC series called *Yes Minister, But For How Long?*

We politicians from all four parties thought we had twenty-eight days to form a government, as set out in the Wales Act; if nobody could form a government by 31 May, there would have to be fresh elections, and the very thought elicited groans all round. Fresh elections would have dealt a huge blow to Welsh self-respect and to the already fragile esteem in which the Welsh political class was held, let alone to devolution itself. Nobody had any money left to fight another election either, so it wasn't so much 'perish the thought' as 'keep that thought at the front of your mind'!

It actually took sixty-odd days to sort out the stalemate – well over twice the twenty-eight day maximum allowed by law. And I threw in a heart attack at the end to spice things up, just when it looked as though the drama was gently abating to an orderly conclusion.

As Labour was the largest party, we engaged in the search for potential coalition partners, the Lib Dems being the most marriageable. In Scotland, Alex Salmond could move ahead with his very minority government simply because there was no other alternative way forward. The Scottish Lib Dems had boxed themselves in during the election campaign with an undertaking that they would feel obliged to negotiate after the election only with the largest party, which turned out to be the SNP (with one more MSP than Labour). But even without that rash promise, a new Labour–Lib Dem coalition might have found it hard going, because they only had 62 MSPs between the two parties (46 Labour and 16 Lib Dems), well short of the 65 required for a majority. Looking ahead to what happened in 2011 when the SNP did win a majority, the rash 'largest party only' campaign promise by the Scottish Lib Dems still looks like an episode of chaos theory – a tiny thing at one moment in time, which turns out to have huge unforeseeable political consequences down the line.

The Welsh Lib Dems had made no such rash promises to box themselves in. They were happy to negotiate potential coalition deals with Labour as the largest party, while simultaneously working to stitch together a three-party deal with the Tories and Plaid Cymru. In that set-up, Plaid Cymru leader Ieuan Wyn Jones would have been the First Minister, and the Conservative leader Nick Bourne would have held the purse strings as Finance Minister. The attraction for the Lib Dem leader Mike German was that he would be the only one with previous ministerial experience (having been Deputy First Minister for two and a half years under the Labour–Lib Dem coalition during the first Assembly term) and so he would perhaps expect to be deferred to on the grounds of ministerial experience. That would compensate for the lack of clout arising from only having 6 AMs in his Lib Dem Group, out of the total of 33 belonging to the three parties trying to knock together this Rainbow Alliance.

Being the only one with that special top-dog status of experience in government from this potential three-party coalition may have made the non-Labour tie-up preferable to Mike German. He might have seen it as offering more job satisfaction than would returning to a Labour–Lib Dem coalition. The Lib–Lab alliance in Westminster from 1977–9 was widely remembered as not having benefitted the Liberal Party.

All of that perhaps explains why our negotiations with the Lib Dems lacked something. It never felt as though we were going to reach a successful conclusion. Mike German was putting more effort into other negotiations in another room in the same building, and I really don't think we on the Labour side made a better bid to bring the Welsh Lib Dems into coalition with us. It was the other avenue into government that offered something a bit special to Mike German.

His problem was the rest of the Lib Dems in Wales. They didn't universally share his enthusiasm – the Rainbow Alliance with Plaid Cymru and the Tories might suit him personally, but the Lib Dems were an ultra-democratic party and he couldn't just sign on the dotted line off his own bat. He would have to get the approval of a special body, comprising the 6 Assembly Members and the Welsh Lib Dem Executive, each member of which had one vote.

Things reached tipping point on the night of Wednesday, 23 May. Still eight days to go before the drop-dead date of 31 May, when new Assembly elections would have to be called. The Lib Dem Group and Executive met in Llandrindod Wells, right in the heart of Wales and not an easy place to get to – equal pain shared by all from South Wales and North Wales. My political career hung by thread that night, and so did Mike German's incredible plan.

Putting to one side for a moment the suspicions among rural Welsh Lib Dems on the party's Executive about Mike German, he didn't actually have the full support of his Assembly Group of 6. Two of them – namely Peter Black (a regional list AM from Swansea) and Kirsty Williams (AM for Brecon & Radnor) – didn't seem to be backing the Rainbow Alliance proposal.

In the end, Labour's survival as the lead party in government and my survival too depended on whether Kirsty Williams or Mike German could muster the most warm bodies to attend the Lib Dem Executive meeting. Not everyone in a position of king-making power is young, fit, active and in full possession of a driving licence. Lifts have to be offered, zig-zag routes negotiated to collect sometimes quite elderly Executive members from different parts of Wales, and you can't be late for the meeting with your cargo of Executive members wedged into the back seat of your car, otherwise the vote will already have taken place. Kirsty Williams did a hell of a good job.

Kirsty was determined to block the Rainbow Alliance deal. Why was that? Well, Brecon & Radnor is seventy-eight miles from top to bottom, a classic and very rural sheep-farming Lib Dem/Tory marginal, fringing old coal-mining rock-solid Labour territory at its southern edge where it borders the Swansea Valley. Now, if those voters in Labour territory switch tactically to vote Lib Dem in order to stop the Tories getting in, then Kirsty wins. But if they suspect the Lib Dems are somehow in with the Tories in a Rainbow Alliance, then they'll stick to voting Labour and Kirsty loses the seat.

In the middle of May, the Welsh think tank, the Institute of Welsh Affairs, had conducted a seminar in the Assembly building on how to break the deadlock created by inconclusive election results. I decided to attend myself, Kirsty Williams represented the Lib Dems, and Adam Price MP was present for Plaid Cymru. It was a bit risky for me as caretaker First Minister, because it was a bit of a free-for-all with Q&As from the press, and every kind of political nerd, geek and camp follower in attendance. But I saw no reason to hide away and, as it turned out, it was one of the best decisions I made in those very tense two months.

I said nice things about the Lib Dems and how it was only natural that we should try to work with them. Adam Price jumped on me straight away, and accused me of 'showing a bit of ankle' to Kirsty Williams – I snapped back to chide him for using dreadfully inappropriate language like that (which was no better than the equally inappropriate, ill-advised and demeaning 'cheap date' jibe made by Public Services Minister Leighton Andrews in the Assembly in 2016). Adam Price could see the threat to the Rainbow Alliance plan, which was not going to go through without the Lib Dems united behind it. If anti-Rainbow Alliance Lib Dems like Kirsty were quite clear in their own minds that Labour wanted a coalition arrangement with them, it would strengthen their resolve to block the Rainbow Alliance.

And that was what happened on the fateful night of 23 May. It was the numbers of bums on seats in the back of Kirsty Williams's car and, I believe, her father's car that scuppered the Rainbow Alliance which had by now been renamed the All Wales Accord. From my narrow point of view, to survive as First Minister it wasn't necessary to have signed a coalition deal with anyone by 31 May, but I did have to prevent an anti-Labour alliance from gaining traction. To be fair to Adam Price, MP at the time and AM now, an undoubtedly very gifted politician in so many ways, he had spotted the one big flaw in the Rainbow Alliance, which was that the Lib Dems weren't united on it. Adam couldn't do anything about that, but he knew it was an ultimately fatal flaw. Still, to paraphrase the Duke of Wellington after the Battle of Waterloo, it was a damn close-run thing!

I heard the news that the Welsh Lib Dem Executive had failed to approve the Rainbow Alliance while having a quiet late-evening pint in the bar with my Cabinet Secretary in Llandudno – I think we had an extra pint at the bar on the back of it. My time as First Minister was not over and done with, and here was a chance to let the brain free-wheel on how next to proceed. After all, we were no more than halfway towards the formation of a stable government. The reason for being 180 miles north of Cardiff in Llandudno at a time of acute political drama was that I had been addressing the Wales TUC Annual Conference – whether I was only an interim and totally powerless First Minister or not, I had to address the Wales TUC Annual Conference, it was an absolute must. It could very easily have been my last official duty, but there was never any option about being in Llandudno for conference.

I've described elsewhere how much I enjoyed my hotel bacon and egg breakfast early the following morning, especially reading the premature piece in *The Times* by Greg Hurst, describing my political demise as being thoroughly deserved because I was not just Old Labour but antediluvian Labour. *The Times* had decided it knew how the Lib Dem vote would go, and didn't actually wait for the result! My toast and honey did taste particularly good that morning.

I talked over the options with the Business Minister ('Leader of the House', in Westminster parlance) Jane Hutt. She and I agreed that we needed to strike and at a moment of maximum weakness in the Rainbow Alliance and with only a few days to spare before the witching hour of 31 May. Jane could put my name down for First Minister the following day. All I had to do was get back to Cardiff as soon as possible – I was booked on the morning flight from Valley airstrip on Anglesey to Cardiff Airport and, although it was quite a long run across Caernarfonshire and Anglesey to reach Valley, we made it in good time. It was a twenty-seater 'bush' aircraft, and on I got to buckle in for the next closely-averted mini-disaster (I won't repeat that episode), and we were able to set off. Never was I so grateful that there are people like that aeroplane mechanic who saved the day about the place in Wales, people with the skills that I never had, people who could get a recalcitrant aeroplane engine firing up and whirring away.

So I made it to Cardiff in time to be re-nominated as First Minister, with no other nominations. That didn't mean the stalemate was over, of course. All it did was avoid new elections. In addition, it gave me a little more psychological advantage of possession in nine-tenths of the law. And meanwhile, there was pandemonium among the Welsh Lib Dems. The anti-Labour faction in the Welsh Lib Dems had secured enough signatures to call a special conference to reverse the Executive's decision, with the vote due to take place on the Saturday night. The Young Turk element among the Lib Dems was all very anti-Labour, grouped around the party's new-found strength in local government following notable election victories in 2004 (when they wrested control of Cardiff, Swansea, Newport and Wrexham from Labour). Having taken control of Wales's big cities and towns from Labour, it was a natural follow-on ambition for them to want to wrest control of the Assembly as well.

I invited the press round to my house in Michaelston-le-Pit for a barbecue that day. If this weekend was the end, well, I wanted to go down out in the open and not skulking around in hiding. One of the big advantages of bringing everyone to Michaelston-le-Pit was that there was virtually no mobile phone reception in my house or in the garden, which made for a relaxed kind of evening. I was quite fatalistic about the whole thing. If the vote went for the Rainbow Alliance, and therefore against my survival, well, I'd had seven and a half years as First Minister. There was no point in being greedy or regretful.

Nick Speed of ITV Wales was the only one among the press gang who broke ranks and climbed up on to the five-barred gate that opened out into the field, just so he could get mobile reception. So it was he who broke the news that the conference in Llandrindod Wells had supported the Rainbow Alliance and that, therefore, I was effectively out of office. The other journalists thought this poor form – to accept my hospitality in the first place, and then to do an 'I can exclusively tell you that Rhodri Morgan's career as First Minister is over' report!

So how did I survive? Two things clinched it really. First of all, the recall party conference of the Welsh Lib Dems in Llandrindod Wells did indeed back the ABL alliance, but it didn't destroy the perception that the Welsh Lib Dems were sorely divided over it. Plaid Cymru wasn't unanimous either. The same factors were at play. Just as Kirsty Williams needed Labour tactical votes to keep her Brecon & Radnor seat, so the Plaid Cymru AM for Llanelli, Helen Mary Jones, couldn't win that seat back from Labour if there was any suggestion of colluding with the Tories. The Plaid Cymru leadership wanted reliable partners – the Welsh Lib Dems were too divided to be reliable – and then you had the drum-beat of dissent from those who wanted Plaid to position itself to the left of Labour.

And then you get one of those purely accidental moments to top everything off. The Cabinet Secretary Lawrence Conway was cycling down to the Bay from Cathays Park, through St John's Square in the city centre. Coming in the opposite direction, also on his bike, was the Plaid Cymru Chief Executive, Dafydd Trystan. They both dismounted and stopped for a chat. Dafydd wanted to check whether our position indicating that Labour wouldn't rule out working with Plaid Cymru was really genuine. Lawrence was suitably cautious as a civil servant, but he said that if Plaid was at all interested it should probe and pursue things a bit further. What came next all stemmed from there really.

When Lawrence arrived at the end of his journey at the Assembly building in the Bay, he was in quite an excited state. Had he perhaps gone too far for a civil servant, even one in a highly political job like Cabinet Secretary? Or had he actually managed to plant a seed that could provide a way out of the stalemate? He spoke to Mark Drakeford, and they both came into my office. This was urgent business. Lawrence certainly didn't get any kind of reprimand from me for exceeding his remit – it was, after all, very much the job of the Cabinet Secretary to seek solutions to the stalemate.

Lawrence then went from the First Minister's Office on the fifth floor (the top floor of Crickhowell House) down two floors to the Plaid Cymru quarters, to see their leader Ieuan Wyn Jones. That happened with my approval. Mark Drakeford and I both agreed that the problem for Plaid was they thought Labour in Cardiff Bay couldn't possibly do a coalition deal with them unless we had permission from Tony Blair – they had little grasp of how devolved we were.

Lawrence explained to Ieuan that if Plaid was interested in a coalition, then so was Labour – and coalition would mean entering government, not a Lib–Lab pact as happened in Westminster in 1977–9, or a confidence-and-supply arrangement as Labour in New Zealand had negotiated with other parties when in a similar minority government position – it was absolutely necessary to be clear on that.

There was a little bit of history to the New Zealand issue going back to the beginning of May. On the Friday, the day after the election, I'd had a long chat on the phone with the Rt Hon. Jonathan Hunt, the New Zealand High Commissioner. We'd struck up a friendship during one of his visits to Cardiff to watch Wales vs New Zealand All Blacks. I knew he was close to the Prime Minister Helen Clark. He had given me some flavour of how she had struck the various bargains with the various minority parties to construct a workable government, while being well short of a majority in the New Zealand Parliament. Jonathan asked me if it wouldn't be better for me to speak to her directly. He said it wasn't that difficult to overcome the huge time zone differential, and that I should ring her that evening at nine, when it would be nine in the morning in New Zealand. He gave me the PM's number, and said he'd give her notice of what the call would be about.

Clark's main message was that minority government wasn't such a big problem – you just had to work hard at all the details. Psychologically, it was a huge boost for me to hear her being so positive about constructing alliances that could bring sustainability in government. What she said about Plaid Cymru's position was highly relevant – 'If I was Plaid Cymru, I wouldn't enter a coalition with Labour. All the recent history is that voters punish junior parties in a coalition, so they will do badly in the next election! They'd be better off with a confidence-and-supply arrangement. Offer them that!'

The advantages to both sides in a confidence-and-supply arrangement is that the junior party agrees to support the major party in any vote of no confidence and over the Budget, and does so in return for consultation and negotiation rights over the Budget and legislative programme. So, we decided to sound out Plaid Cymru. Mark Drakeford, although my senior Special Adviser, had retained his Chair in Social Policy and, more importantly, his own office in Cardiff University. Mark invited Adam Price, Plaid Cymru MP and policy and strategy guru, to his professorial lair – the perfect setting for some totally unattributable, wholly deniable, poker-playing. But the meeting didn't go well. Confidence-and-supply held no interest for Plaid Cymru. In Adam's view, Labour was not being serious and needed to appreciate how weak its position was – far too weak to monopolise all the ministerial positions. Plaid felt Labour was fobbing them off, with a mess of pottage, although actually we thought we were protecting their long-term electoral interests.

Of course, the driver was the comparison with Scotland. Alex Salmond was going to be First Minister. He was forming an SNP Government! That was an historic achievement. Plaid had clearly not achieved anything like that massive electoral breakthrough, but they did not want to be seen to be lagging too far behind the SNP. That was why the Rainbow coalition, with a Plaid Cymru First Minister lining up alongside Alex Salmond in photo shoots, had such a hold on them. They were willing to pay the price of coalition with the Tories because they were desperately keen to see that headline: 'Nationalist First Ministers in Scotland and Wales!'

So, back to the happy chance meeting of cyclists in St John's Square at the end of May. By now, I had been re-nominated without a challenge as First Minister on 25 May. I had taken advantage of the situation to appoint proper (rather than caretaker) Ministers. I only appointed five, so that it was clear to any observer in another party (Plaid Cymru or Lib Dem) that I had left room for them to join in. The 'come hither' sign had been hoisted. But having a Labour Cabinet in place relieved the time pressure. We had a real government in place, not a caretaker one, and negotiations could take as little or as long as was needed. But possession was by now well above nine-tenths of the law – the Rainbow Alliance had been knocked on the head.

It meant for me that I was going to go on – not on and on, however, as Margaret Thatcher had fatally promised the nation in 1990, prompting the grey suits to encircle with unsheathed daggers. I was never going to stand for office again, but I now had a fair chance of being able to retire at a time of my own choosing, if Labour and Plaid Cymru played their cards right. That was the big prize for me. The disputes breaking out around No. 10 and No. 11 Downing Street that summer only reinforced my view that all the precedents of staying for too long in office had led to disaster.

But my first priority for June was how to get the Labour Party to back the idea, in broad principle first, and then in detail. I was sure that there would have to be a recall party conference – we hadn't done that when the coalition with the Lib Dems had been signed in October 2000, and there was still resentment over it. What we were now proposing was going to cover a full Assembly term of four years, not just two and a half.

I made another phone call to Helen Clark on the other side of the world – I gave her a progress report, and asked if she had any Cabinet Ministers about to visit the mother country who wouldn't mind coming down to Cardiff to explain every in and out – and do and don't – of coalition government to the Welsh Labour Executive. 'Rhodri', she boomed in that wonderful contralto voice of hers, 'I've always got one or two of my Cabinet Ministers visiting the mother country!' We settled on her Health Minister, Pete Hodgson.

Negotiating teams were set up with Plaid Cymru. The key thing was that I didn't attempt to do the negotiating with the Plaid leader Ieuan Wyn Jones. I left the hard yards to Jane Hutt, with Jocelyn Davies in the opposite role for Plaid. They both liked each other and there was a bond of trust, and obviously no macho posturing. I couldn't have guaranteed no macho posturing if it had been me and Ieuan. Mark Drakeford and Simon Thomas did the more detailed stuff and all the writing up – Simon was an ex-MP, who was by then Plaid's policy chief. The idea was that with the time pressure off, we could really assemble a fully-fledged programme for government. On our side, we didn't want anything taken out of our manifesto. We could add things from Plaid's manifesto, but not *instead of* what we had in ours. Still, we did want this bible of the inter-party agreement to cover all four years of the 2007–11 Assembly term.

As I wasn't doing any of the negotiating, my job was to sell the principle of the deal with Plaid to the Welsh Labour Party in the weeks ahead of the recall party conference, at which time we could seek approval for the finalised document.

So, to get the Welsh Executive of the Labour Party on board. As early as 12 May, we had secured a broad approval from the Welsh Executive that we should try to stay in power by coalition or some other New Zealand-type arrangement. Pete Hodgson then came to Cardiff for a Q&A with the Executive – it was a bit of a whirlwind visit to Wales for him, catching the 17:15 pm from Paddington, and

I met him at Cardiff Central to take him to watch Cardiff Blues vs Leinster at the Arms Park (we missed the first ten minutes). Luckily, the Blues, with Nicky Robinson very much to the fore, did the business 26–11. We met a freshly-showered Xavier Rush, the former-All Black who captained the Cardiff Blues team, straight after the match. Then it was off to Barry and Jane Hutt's re-election victory party, and home to mine by midnight. After breakfast, we took a walk around Michaelston-le-Pit for an hour or so. Pete was a vet, and wanted to learn as much as he could about the local farms, local cattle and sheep, and their various ailments. Then finally, mid-morning, off for the eleven o'clock meeting of the Welsh Executive in Transport House. He caught the train back to London at around one.

What his visit did was to reinforce the opinion that the party with the most MPs or AMs has to take the lead in forming a government, and that there's more than one way to skin a cat. Of course, there were die-hards and purists around in the Labour Group at the Assembly, and among the grass-roots membership, who felt Labour should go into opposition. They thought that if we couldn't rule on our own, then we should ask the opposition parties to see if they could run Wales – and when the latter enterprise would fail, everything would collapse and fall back into our lap. Nobody on the Welsh Executive seemed to follow that school of thought, though. I don't know how they would have reacted if we had said on 12 May that we were seeking a coalition with Plaid Cymru, but they knew we had tried to renegotiate a coalition with the Lib Dems first and that those talks had failed. What gave the Welsh Executive its special flavour was that there was a high percentage of trade union officials on it, and the overwhelming view of trade union leaders in Wales was that we should find a way of staying in power. The Pete Hodgson Q&A reinforced that view –'Share some power if you have to, but stay in power!'

I kept repeating that to all the hustings meetings arranged for me round Wales in June, as we inched closer and closer to a coalition agreement with Plaid Cymru. The kinds of questions thrown at me in these sessions didn't really relate to the content of the likely agreements on policy programmes. It was more a question of the visceral dislike and distrust almost amounting to loathing towards Plaid Cymru and its members –'You don't know what they're like when they're in charge', I was told in north-west Wales.

I was trying to reassure the membership that having Plaid Cymru as junior partners in government didn't mean that the Government of Wales was then effectively a nationalist government. Did the association with Plaid Cymru in a coalition make us, the Welsh Labour Party, a crypto-Nat party? 'Crypto-Nat' was just about the worst insult your internal enemies inside Labour could throw at you – Peter Hain, in managing the campaign for Alun Michael for the Welsh Labour leadership back in early 1999, had made sure that this particular epithet was lobbed at me. Now, eight years later, could I persuade those members who might have suspected it that I wasn't a crypto-Nat now and that I never would be? The reality was that we were simply unwilling to go into opposition if there was any viable alternative.

They were tough meetings. The roughest meeting of all was with the Welsh Group of Labour MPs, followed by an even rougher set-piece with Neil Kinnock. Just one-to-one. Neil and I had been good friends for forty-four years, but as far as I was concerned he'd always had a blind spot on devolution. For his part, I'm sure he thought I was a crypto-Nat or somesuch.

We reached the stage by the end of the month where we could put the completed document, the 43-page *One Wales* bible, to the Labour Group in the Assembly for approval on 27 June. The Plaid Group did the same. Now, we could make preparations for two recall party conferences.

That recall conference date was set for a Friday night, 6 July, choreographed with Plaid Cymru's recall conference taking place on the Saturday morning. If it had been the other way around, then some wavering Labour members might swing against the whole deal if they saw enthusiastic Plaid members jumping for joy on television screens at the prospect of their party getting into government.

Come the Friday night, about four hundred delegates present in the wonderfully conspiratorially-named CIA (the Cardiff International Arena) – now the more humdrum Motorpoint Arena (Motorpoint did pay money to buy the naming rights – don't think the CIA ever did). The atmosphere was pretty good-natured. Pat Brunker, a salt of the earth activist from the Rhondda, was Labour's Chair that year. A no-nonsense and very Valleys kind of person. I sat next to her. With odd whispers here and there, we both agreed that the last impression we wanted to give was that anyone wanting to speak would be denied the opportunity; and, again, provided they didn't really do a five-act play, they shouldn't be cut short either.

The consequence was that six delegates from the Islwyn constituency in the Gwent Valleys raised their hands to speak, and every one of them made their speeches. Islwyn was Neil Kinnock's old seat. Neil himself, by now of course Lord Kinnock, wanted to speak and, though you could have argued that he wasn't a delegate, much better to let him do as much damage as he could, and he certainly barn-stormed. I think he went over the top, but that's how passionately he felt. Maybe some of the barn-storming was because he knew the power had slipped away from him, and there wasn't much he could do now about the new direction of politics in a Labour devolved Wales. Anyway, counting Neil, there were seven speakers from that one constituency of Islwyn – I'm not sure if anyone who wasn't from Islwyn actually spoke *against* the proposed coalition deal with Plaid Cymru.

At the special conference, I spoke last and I did try and pick up and answer the points the doubters and naysayers had made. It was all the thin end of the wedge and Trojan Horse stuff that I had to contend with, nationalists as junior partners in government today equals Welsh independence in twenty years' time, something like that. I didn't need to make a barn-stormer of a speech, and I didn't try. I just had to reinforce the conference's trust in me. Whatever the headlines in the media in Wales about historic breakthroughs for Plaid etc., it would be me and Labour in charge.

As happens in these kinds of conferences, most of the delegates had already made their decision on how they were going to vote, so my speech probably didn't make that much difference. The coalition deal went through by well over three-quarters of the votes, but with the added bonus that it wasn't the trade union votes overriding the constituency votes – over 60 per cent of the constituency vote was in favour too. The final count had 78.4 per cent of the total votes being cast in favour, which was beyond my wildest dreams.

After the overwhelming victory, I wanted to go out to talk to the press, and all the delegates wanted to go home or sample the beverages available in the innumerable fleshpots and hostelries clustered all around the CIA. But there was a rather curious tailpiece which we had to sit through first, a wind-up speech by the Secretary of State Peter Hain, which had been added to the schedule.

I must admit that I wasn't paying full attention to its tenor. All I had running through my head was *78.4 per cent! 78.4 per cent! 78.4 per cent!* Beyond my wildest dreams, it was all I was able to concentrate on, until I heard Pat Brunker hissing in my ear, 'What the hell does he think he's doing?' Peter was delivering the most downbeat speech you could ever imagine, making it clear that the Westminster end of the Labour Party would be watching in case it all went pear-shaped and that, if it did go pear-shaped, no one should say we hadn't been warned.

I told Pat to relax and let it go. It wasn't going to change the result one bit. It just took a tiny little bit of the flavour off everything. Looking at it from Peter's point of view, he was also thinking *78.4 per cent! 78.4 per cent! 78.4 per cent!* but coming to an opposite conclusion to me. He was thinking, 'The Welsh Labour MPs strongly opposed to the deal have been smashed, and I must lift their spirits somehow.' Otherwise, the Welsh Labour MPs might feel humiliated that nobody had listened to their advice. After all, they were the ones Peter would bump into in the corridors of the House of Commons and in the Welsh Group of the PLP every day of the week. I think Peter had even been suspected himself of being a crypto-Nat once or twice, so he had to prove to the Welsh Labour MPs that he was on their side.

The Saturday came and went, with Plaid meeting in Pontrhydfendigaid in the rural depths of Ceredigion, halfway between Aberystwyth and Devil's Bridge – about as different a place from Cardiff as you could find.

So, I could relax at last knowing that all I had to do was concentrate on media appearances, the choice of Cabinet Ministers, and ponder what Plaid might be looking for.

Yes, I needed a nice relaxing weekend. Julie was leaving me at home to recharge my batteries. She was meeting her cousin, who worked at the Roman Museum in Caerleon, with the children and grandchildren so that I could sit down and do nothing or jot names down on paper opposite Cabinet jobs. I made myself a cold salad lunch with some delicacies – chili peppers stuffed with feta cheese – and sat slumped in front of the television. I had a nap. Then, at about three-ish, I decided to take the dog for a walk.

I had only just crossed the stile into the field, no more than two hundred yards from the house, when I felt a pain in my chest. And this was when my brain divided itself into two halves – the optimistic half said, 'It's those chili peppers, you've got indigestion, you've always been a bit allergic to chillies.' The pessimistic half of my brain said the precise opposite, 'This pain is different from any pain you've felt before, it's not indigestion, you're having a heart attack.' Precisely the same scenario I had gone through half a century before with my father, in October 1957. Heart attack was the correct diagnosis back then as it was now. What made me plough on, walking away from the house and away from access to a phone, I will never know. I rationalised it all by telling myself I'd walk on a bit and see if the pain might ease – it surely couldn't be a heart attack. The pain did ease off a bit and I carried on walking. The dog was enjoying himself. It was a lovely day. I didn't want to spoil the dog's fun, after all.

I had been walking about half a mile when I came to a little hill. As I climbed, the pain came back, but this time much stronger than before. Now I had no doubt, it was a heart attack. I had no mobile phone, and there was no mobile reception in the area anyway. There were quite a few families around with their kids and other dogs splashing around in the brook, but there was no point dragging them into my bother and asking for help. Somehow, I had to get back to the house and dial 999, so down the hill and to the footbridge over the Cadoxton brook I crept, walking very slowly, thinking about how stupid I'd been. 'Talk about the crucifixion coming three days after the resurrection!' All my own fault this time, and nothing to do with Tony Blair.

Putting one foot cautiously in front of the other, I started on the journey back. I became desperately tired. I really wanted to just lie down in the grass and go to sleep, but I knew I couldn't do that – I would probably never wake up. I had to keep going. It must have been half past four when I climbed over the five-bar gate in front of the house, unlocked the door sat in front of the television again, and dialled 999.

Even then, the huge effort of concentration I had mustered to get back to the house must have taken half my brain away. When I spoke to the telephone operator, she asked, 'Are you having any difficulty breathing? Are you short of breath?' I was panting like mad, but still managed to answer, 'No, I'm breathing okay.' Fair play to her, she said, 'Well, you sound pretty short of breath to me!' 'Yes, I am', I said. 'Right, I've marked it urgent, we'll get the ambulance round there straight away', she replied. I gave her the rather complicated instructions to get to our house, and sat back to wait.

I had totally forgotten that I had a family. I didn't ring Julie or the children – I'd forgotten they existed. It was just me, the heart attack and the ambulance – my entire world. It was October 1957 again, just waiting for the ambulance. A tiny bit of me still entertained hope that there was a faint chance it would prove to be indigestion after all.

The rapid response vehicle arrived in about five minutes. Its crew administered the GTN spray under my tongue, and I felt better immediately. They did an ECG – no sign of any heart problem. The indigestion hope sprung eternally again. They did an ultrasound – no sign of a heart attack. Still, they were convinced that it was probably a heart attack, so they called for the full-sized ambulance complete with wheelchair to take me to Llandough Hospital (which I could just about see from our house).

The proper ambulance arrived at about five o'clock, and the four paramedics ran more tests and decided I needed to be taken in to hospital, by which time the family members were beginning to arrive home for tea. When she saw the two ambulances in the drive, my daughter was convinced that they'd gone to the wrong house, and she started to redirect them to where they really ought to be. She practically had a fit when they told her it was me they'd come for. And then my son-in-law Bas told me I mustn't conk out, because I'm the only grandfather the kids have! His own father had died many years before.

Then Julie arrived. I still find it hard to explain why I hadn't rung her. All I remember is the effort of concentrating on staying totally relaxed and focused on not doing anything that might cause further damage to my heart – more, that is, than my own stupidity had already caused.

So, by the time they were ready to wheel me out to the ambulance, I was surrounded by an army of my children and grandchildren and four paramedics. Julie came with me in the ambulance, and before six o'clock I was in the Medical Assessment Unit at Llandough. The MAU is a very busy place, even on a Sunday evening, and I was feeling pretty chipper by now. The GTN spray is so effective at opening up your arteries that you almost feel a sense of euphoria – the pain and panic of an hour before seemed long gone.

I should have been in Lawrence Conway's house that evening to seal the deal with Plaid. I was going to meet, in order, my Special Adviser, then the Permanent Secretary Jon Shortridge, and then finally Plaid's leader Ieuan Wyn Jones. When I didn't show up, Lawrence rang my home number, and Bas told him, 'We think he's had a heart attack!'

Again, an ECG showed nothing, and neither did the ultrasound, and the cardiologist Dr Khan explained he was pretty sure I'd had a cardiac episode – but the only proof would be the presence of a certain protein in the blood stream, and they couldn't do the blood test until the next morning because the haematology labs were closed on Sundays. 'I only live five minutes away', I pleaded, 'why can't I go home now, sleep in my own bed, and come back in for the blood test first thing in the morning?'

Dr Khan was very insistent. If it was a cardiac event, heart attack or whatever, there was a possibility of another one. That would be very bad news, especially if I wasn't in a hospital bed with emergency staff on duty to deal with a repeat episode. Having been allocated a bed in the MAU ward, which was a Nightingale-style ward with twenty beds, I then went into the visitors' room to watch television. I felt great. Once again, I asked them, surely I'd be better off sleeping in my own bed – they were getting so fed up by now with my constant requests to go home, that they called a junior doctor, a very determined young woman from Llanelli, to tell me in Welsh exactly why it would be the height of idiocy to spend the night at home, however well I felt and however close to the hospital I lived. It was the combination of her giving me a talking to in Welsh, and her strong and formidable personality, which convinced me that I was indeed staying the night.

About half past eleven, I decided to that it was bed-time. I walked down the MAU ward to the bed allocated to me. There was a computer on my bed with a policeman tapping away on it, as he sat on the visitors' chair. When I told him I wanted to go to sleep, he joked, 'Oh, you're not taking away my desk, are you?' 'Afraid so', I said, 'doctor's orders, beauty sleep, all that stuff.'

The policeman wasn't there to guard the First Minister – he was there to guard a 'person of interest' in the bed opposite mine, a young man lying fully-clothed on his stomach, completely sparked out. He was going to take a long time to wake up but, when he did, that policeman's job was to make sure he answered some questions and didn't do a runner.

I hadn't slept in a dormitory since my days youth hostelling – if you're not used to it, it's not easy to sleep with twenty others in the same room. I did manage to fall asleep by one o'clock, but was awake again at half past – the young man opposite had now woken up, and his solicitor and family were around the bed arguing loudly over his rights with the policeman. My rights to a decent kip didn't come into it, nor the rights of the other eighteen patients on the ward. I tried to shut out what they were arguing about – once you start following legal arguments, you'll never be able to return to the land of nod. After half an hour of that, quiet broke out again until about six o'clock.

Then, at six, the elderly lady in the bed next to me started wailing for both God and Jesus to come and save her – she was very confused – and that set off one or two other ultra-confused old ladies who didn't know where they were. It was morning in the MAU. The young man in the bed opposite had disappeared.

I had my blood test at eight, and the results came back within the hour confirming the cardiac event. The marker protein was there. Dr Khan returned, not totally displeased that his very educated guess had turned out correct, and I asked him again why nothing kept showing up on the ECG and ultrasound. All he could tell me was that hearts come in all shapes and sizes, and so do heart attacks and suchlike. He wanted more tests on ever-more powerful ECG and ultrasound, before making a final decision on treatment.

By mid-morning, I was moved out of MAU to a quiet medical ward. More tests showed nothing, but the protein was there. I'd had some kind of heart attack, but what exactly was it? Dr Khan was very reassuring –'We don't have the capacity to do angiograms or angioplasty here, so we're going to move you to the Heath' – which was short for the even bigger University Hospital of Wales. 'I'm recommending that they do an angioplasty', he said, 'that's when they insert a wire into a vein in your wrist, and send a little camera device up into the arteries around your heart. That way, any blockages can be located and dealt with, it's a very safe procedure.'

Then followed the only point at which I think I had preferential treatment (of sorts). Instead of bringing the ambulance back to the main MAU entrance, where there was a stack of media, they wheeled me round the hospital to the tradesmen's entrance on the north side, and that's how they got me out of Llandough without photographers scrambling to get a shot of the infirm First Minister.

At the Coronary Care Unit, my cardiologist Dr Nick Ossei-Gerning went through all the details of angioplasty, saying, 'As there is no information on your heart coming through from the ECG and the ultrasound, we don't know what we are going to find when we get the camera in there. We think we will find a blockage or two, and then we can insert two or three stents. They are spring-loaded little devices – they'll hold the blocked arteries open, and strengthen the walls of your arteries where there's a weakness.'

While I was having more tests done, Dr Nick took Julie to his consulting room to talk her through the risks, but told her not to worry about a thing. He was a very positive kind of guy – 'It's not open-heart surgery', he told her, 'it's a procedure, we don't need to cut him open, it'll only take forty minutes or so.' Julie couldn't help being reassured – compared with what she'd seen of full monty open-heart surgery up-close when she had been allowed to observe Mr Magdi Yacoub operating at Harefield Hospital, what I had to go through did not indeed sound that risky.

I went to theatre for the angioplasty at four in the afternoon. I was fully conscious. There was no pain, just discomfort of the heartburn type as the wire was pushed along the vein to reach my heart, shoving away the blockage, and putting in stents. I was given a choice of music – Beethoven or the Treorchy Male Choir. I went for Beethoven. Dr Nick kept telling me to follow the whole thing on the television screen – but I was too thick to follow – and to stop me panicking, I was given a kind of substitute wife to hold my hand and say nice things while it was all going on.

Everything went smoothly in one sense, but it took a lot longer than forty minutes. Despite the best efforts of my substitute wife, I did lose my nerve and broke down in tears, sobbing 'Can I have Julie in here?' I wasn't brave. What it was like for Julie in the relatives' waiting room when it went past the hour, I do not know. Dr Nick explained the extra time was taken up trying to wedge the stent into one of the blockages, because it had occurred right on a fork in the artery. Y-shaped stents are trickier to fit.

But the sense of new wellbeing after they wheeled me back to the ward was phenomenal – they tested my lung function, blowing into a tube, and it was back to normal.

After Julie had gone home, I had a dozen or more rubber suction electrodes fitted to every part of my torso and legs. I tried to sleep. It shouldn't have been that difficult compared with the MAU over in the other hospital – my bed was curtained off from the main Coronary Care Ward outside, not that quiet, but privacy wasn't a problem. What made sleeping difficult was all the electrodes. I was, in effect, trussed up like a Christmas turkey. I like sleeping on my side, but that was impossible with the rubber suction discs all over me. I like turning a lot in my sleep, but that was impossible too. I reckon I eventually got to sleep around five in the morning.

Before six o'clock, there was a huge security alert just outside my curtains. A man had gone berserk. 'Put that glass down', I could hear the night nurse saying to this guy on the rampage, who was high on drugs. 'I saw what you did, you bitch!' the crazed man was shouting. 'Now, please put that glass down …' the nurse kept pleading. I thought he had picked up a tumbler, but no such luck – what he had in his hand was a shard of glass he'd smashed out of the porthole in the locked end-door of the ward. The stand-off continued for a good half-hour, until finally security arrived. I will never again hear a bad word said about the nurses at Heath Hospital.

When all had calmed down, the staff came in to tell me about it. The three intensive care units at the Heath are all next-door to each other – the Paediatric Intensive Care Unit, the Adult Intensive Care Unit, and the Coronary Care Unit. I was in Coronary Care. At night, the same team of nurses does the observations on all three sets of patients, after which the end-doors for that floor can be locked. But the patient who had gone berserk was either a junkie or had reacted horrendously to some cocktail of drugs, and had become paranoid and delusional.

He had tried to escape from the floor, but had found the door locked so he smashed the porthole window. Then he pulled out a shard of glass from the broken window, and went on the rampage just outside the curtained-off area inside which I was trussed up like a turkey. What might have happened if an already delusional berserk patient had pulled away the curtain and found the First Minister of Wales lying there, I cannot imagine. All that had been going through my head was, 'Please, do your best, nurse – don't let him fall through the curtains, I'm trussed up, I can't fight back, and I can't escape!'

Once all that excitement was over, Tuesday was actually a wonderful textbook recovery day. Lots of visits from the family, including grandchildren, and my brother coming up from Swansea. Lawrence Conway and Mark Drakeford came to see me, and we discussed a little Cabinet business – not much, just keeping me in touch – and I caught up on lost sleep.

I slept like a baby through Tuesday night, and there were no disturbances. The next day, I went down to the maternity ward to look in on one of my Special Advisers, Jane Runeckles, who had just given birth to her first-born son overnight. The medics discharged me on Wednesday afternoon and told me, 'Three weeks complete rest!' But they knew what was coming next – 'I've got to form a government first, then I can have my three weeks rest!''Okay, okay', they replied, 'but can you find a stress-free way of forming a government?'

I think it was difficult for any of my appointees to the Cabinet to argue with my job offers. No one wanted to be responsible for my relapse – I think they had been given pretty strict instructions by my private office that they were going to be in the Cabinet and should be satisfied with whatever I offered, whether they wanted it or not. They were told that I would be resting for three weeks – they could get on with their portfolios, but 'whatever you do, don't upset the First Minister!' Everyone was in and out in five minutes, and even those inclined to argue for a bigger portfolio or a more impressive-sounding title (and, let's face it, some politicians are like that) were very well behaved.

Appointing the Plaid Cymru leader Ieuan Wyn Jones as Deputy First Minister and Minister for Economic Development & Transport was not going to produce an argument, because Lawrence Conway had already discussed it with him. Ieuan wanted a big portfolio as part of the coalition agreement – but what was a big portfolio? Ieuan wanted Finance, but he was dissuaded. Of course, we didn't know in July of 2007 what horrors were around the corner when the banking system went pear-shaped and Lehman Brothers collapsed in 2008. Finance would have been very bad news for Plaid to have as a portfolio when that happened. Economic Development was bad enough with closures and job losses all around, but Finance would have been far more difficult.

The tricky thing about coalitions is that a First Minister has to ask incoming Ministers from another party whether they have any skeletons in the cupboard, which, if leaked to the local media, could cause embarrassment to the Government. Plaid's Elin Jones wasn't a problem, well respected and elected as the Assembly's Presiding Officer in 2016. But, in contrast, there were rumours to the effect that the other Plaid Cabinet Minister, Rhodri Glyn Thomas, had some specially-fitted IKEA cupboards in his office that were *packed* with skeletons – but we skirted around this issue with rapidity, and a wink and a smile on both sides, with my excuse being my need for complete rest, doctor's orders!

So, we now had a Cabinet. We had a Government and the summer recess would soon be upon us, which was when I would be able to reach the period of rest and recuperation that the doctors wanted. I shared with them the wish that their handiwork of inserting stents into my coronary artery would not be ruined by any foolishness – if I could have gone straight down to the caravan in Mwnt, then I would have done so, but that wasn't possible, I just had to get a bit of First Ministering done first.

What the doctors emphasised was diet, exercise, and de-stressing my life. The first two I could get away with straight away. I had been given the British Heart Foundation diet sheet. Julie and I followed it religiously for about two years and, fair play, my waistline did shrink a lot. No curries, no Chinese takeaways, no pizza, no gravy on cooked dinner – that was all common sense.

Exercise wasn't a problem either. Walk a hundred yards on day one; double it to two hundred yards the next day, four hundred yards the next, and so on. Of course, there had to come a point at which I stopped this doubling up, otherwise I'd be walking Land's End to John o' Groats before the month was out! It settled down at around five miles a day, including three or more steep hills, steep enough to produce at least one bead of sweat on my forehead. My dog, William Tell, thought it was Christmas every day! The hills around my home village could have been designed to provide heart rehab walks – some lasting an hour, others an hour and a half exactly.

I could fit in this rehab with finishing off all the work of getting the coalition government up and running. I tried to do it in a non-stressful way. Appointing junior Ministers was not a problem, but it was a different story when it came to Special Advisers. Ieuan, my new Deputy First Minister, came to see me with a problem. He wanted to appoint his spin doctor without telling me who it was, but I told him that was impossible because the appointment had to be made by me – otherwise the Special Adviser wouldn't get paid at the end of each month. The rules hadn't been written with coalitions in mind. In fact, they weren't written with devolution in mind. Actually, in strictly legal terms, Tony Blair was still responsible for appointing all our Special Advisers! De facto, he had delegated that to me.

Now Ieuan was telling me that I had to accept a *fait accompli.* He couldn't tell me the name of his chosen Special Adviser because the person concerned was in a sensitive position – couldn't resign until certain that the job was there for the taking, and wouldn't be able to *un*resign, as it were, if I was to bilk at the name. Well, I pride myself on being able to figure out what cards are in the other person's hand when it comes to anything going on in Wales, but my pseudo-encyclopaedic knowledge of all matters Welsh let me down on this occasion. I blame the heart attack! Still, I should have worked it out – BBC Cymru Wales! Where else was there a politically-neutral body with a lot of Plaid sympathisers? Anyway, after a lot of umming and ahing, I accepted Plaid's *fait accompli* and the person concerned turned out to be Rhuanedd Richards, previously the face of *Newyddion*, the news service provided by BBC Cymru Wales for S4C – by 2007, she was more like the news editor of *Newyddion*. Rhuanedd was the daughter of Phil Richards, a barrister and almost perpetual Plaid Cymru parliamentary candidate in the Cynon Valley. And, as it happens, her mother's caravan was only about ten pitches along from ours in Mwnt. The Welsh connections again!

What I did learn from that particular episode was that Ieuan might think the best way to deal with me in coalition was to present me with a *fait accompli* and test my nerve every time. So, I made up my mind to be prepared for that tactic, and to squash it next time around, if indeed there was a next time.

I made it to the summer break in one piece. More exercise and more rest and relaxation and healthy food, and I was confident now that I would be able to be in tip-top nick by the time the summer recess was over. There was, however, a problem. My GP asked where I was going on holiday, and I said I was so much looking forward to walking and swimming in the sea at Mwnt, preferably with dolphins. 'Oh, no, I don't think so – the cold water could give you another heart attack, I couldn't be responsible for that', she said, 'why don't you try the Med? The water's much warmer there, ideal for someone in your condition.' 'No', I insisted, 'I've always gone swimming in Mwnt!' She must have seen the tragedy queen look on my face. 'How about wearing a wetsuit?' she asked. 'Wetsuits are for cissies', I insisted, 'my grandchildren wear them, but I'm from the pre-wetsuit generation! It would take me so long to get into a wetsuit that I'd have no time left to get in the sea!'

Anyway, we went round and round the houses over the Med vs Mwnt issue, and in the end we compromised on me wearing a T-shirt as a kind of poor man's wetsuit, and swimming not in Mwnt but in Aberporth, the beach next-door to Mwnt, where the water is half a degree warmer.

And that's what we did that summer. The first time I went in, Julie and I were very nervous. I walked into the water with baggy T-shirt over my bathing trunks, I just inched into the water bit by bit, got used to the temperature, avoiding any kids that might look like they fancied splashing me, and got under just for a few minutes. The following day, a little bit less nervous – it was just like walking one hundred yards to start with, then doubling up to two hundred yards, and so on.

It wasn't such a smooth progression on the walking and hiking side. One day, I got totally tricked by the Ceredigion coastal footpath, now proudly part of the Wales Coast Path. In the summer of 2007, the all-Wales coastal footpath was still a work in progress. I always tried to find circular routes, so I walked two miles west of the caravan, and then down to the edge of the cliff. Then, I confidently turned back to the footpath only to find that it petered out after the first hundred yards. I pushed on through the brush and gorse bushes. Luckily, I was wearing jeans – or maybe unluckily. If I'd had shorts on, I would have had to turn back long before I got totally stuck. I kept thinking the famous coastal footpath had to be there somewhere. 'It must be just over there, no, over there …' Well, it just wasn't anywhere! After ten minutes of pretending to be Indiana Jones with a bus pass, I had to admit to myself that I was stuck. I couldn't move. I couldn't move forwards, sideways or backwards. I was on an impassable stretch of hillside, covered with an untamed jungle of gorse and blackthorn bushes woven tightly together with rampant brambles.

I had passed the point of no return – I just had to get to the top of the hill – I stopped worrying about my cardiologist's handiwork – I was beyond panic – I went into a kind of catatonic state! I was going to get up to the top of the hill, however long it took me to push my way through the undergrowth, forcing one leg forwards a few inches, then the other. It was the longest fifty yards I've ever walked, more like swimming against a strong current, and I was light-headed with relief when I finally found the path.

The stents were undamaged and so was I. In July and August 2007 I was definitely the cat with nine lives.

Getting back to work in the middle of August meant getting stuck into the best way of delivering the One Wales agreement with Plaid Cymru. Personally, I always had a mental block about calling it the 'One Wales agreement'. When I was told that this was the name the Labour negotiating team of Jane Hutt and Mark Drakeford had agreed with Plaid, I told them to come up with something better. 'One Wales' had something of a *yuk* and *ychafi* factor for me – as a war baby, it was redolent of the Nazi 'Ein Volk, ein Reich, ein Führer' slogan. But I allowed myself to be overridden. I was told Plaid was very keen on 'One Wales' – not exactly a dealbreaker if I vetoed it, but more trouble than it was worth to go back to Plaid and try to find something catchier and less numinous (at least as I saw it). Looking back now, I think Mark Drakeford was right to persuade me, and I was right to give way on this, but even now I still can't see the 'One Wales' strapline without cringing.

Now, what about the content of the One Wales agreement? Was it difficult for Labour to swallow the Plaid Cymru elements that were in there? There was stuff in there about improving the rail services between North Wales and South Wales – not that difficult to do, with specific subsidies to Arriva Trains Wales, tied to increasing the number of stops, number of trains per day, timetables and so on. These were common-sense service improvements, but you had read that common-sense commitment to improving rail services in the context of Plaid's view of Welsh geography. North to South good – East to West bad. That sums it up really. On the Labour side of the coalition, we occasionally joked about a Plaid adviser coming up with a scheme to widen Offa's Dyke to fifty miles in order to provide Wales with the east coast it so sadly lacked. We cracked these kinds of jokes only when there were no Plaid negotiators present, of course, it just relieved the tension. I'm sure it happens in every coalition.

Hospital reorganisation in Wales had been the hardest part of the coalition agreement to negotiate. It had been electoral poison for Labour candidates in May's election, and there was much resentment among Labour candidates who had lost their seats where Plaid candidates had described themselves on the actual ballot paper as 'Plaid Cymru Save Withybush Hospital'. It was a tactic Plaid had copied from the SNP, who put 'SNP Save Kirkintilloch Hospital' on ballot papers, which might have been dirty politics, but it was legal and remarkably effective. Plaid didn't win seats on the back of it as the SNP had done, but the tactic certainly cost Labour some seats.

We had to get a form of words into the agreement which didn't imply that there would be no change in the disposition of hospital services across Wales from 2007–11. That would make no sense. So what the agreement stated was that no changes would be made unless and until alternative community hospital provision was in place. Changes in hospital provision is still immensely difficult.

The pressure to get on with reorganisation of hospital services was made worse by the European Court of Justice decision to count on-call time as working time under the Working Time Directive. In our district general hospitals with only four hundred or fewer beds (of which we had half a dozen in Wales), it became very difficult to recruit junior doctors. If their on-call time was counted as working time, they wouldn't get enough experience of any specialist work in a six-month or twelve-month house officer post (F1s and F2s as they are now called). That would in turn endanger Royal Colleges accreditation from those hospitals as suitable places for training. The Working Time Directive was intended for truck drivers, not junior doctors in training. Anyway, Plaid didn't want to put forward their ideas for reconfiguration of hospital services, and they blocked all of our proposals. On affordable housing, another big feature of the coalition agreement, we did make more progress, but it was painfully slow.

The big prize for Plaid Cymru in signing the deal with us was to implement the recommendation of the Richard Commission to give the Assembly full legislative powers in devolved areas. Labour had put the promise of law-making powers for the Assembly, restricted only by which fields were devolved to the Assembly, into its 2005 manifesto. So it was going to happen, but putting it centre stage in the coalition agreement made it safer that it wouldn't be forgotten. We had done Part 3, involving Legislative Competence Orders, but the issue was when to implement Part 4 and when to trigger the referendum that would enable the next step to be taken.

The Plaid Cymru segment of the coalition made a very big deal of having secured a guarantee via the One Wales agreement that Labour would not only support a motion to implement the law-making powers part of the Richard Commission recommendations, but would also campaign with enthusiasm to get a win in the referendum.

With the Conservative Party in Wales also supporting law-making powers, it turned out to be the easiest referendum to win in my entire political career. In a way, the problem was that there was hardly any opposition at all. I had retired as First Minister by the time of the referendum in February 2011, but I was still heavily involved in chairing the Yes campaign steering committee.

It was psychologically important to Plaid Cymru that securing this commitment to full law-making powers via the referendum route provided them with the justification for pulling out of the so-called Rainbow Alliance with the Tories and Lib Dems. The combined strength of all three of those parties didn't match up to two-thirds of the Assembly. To implement the law-making powers section of the Government of Wales Act 2006, you had to have a motion that required the support of two-thirds of the Assembly, and then a referendum.

What Plaid Cymru gave up in abandoning the Rainbow Alliance and coming in with Labour was the chance for Ieuan Wyn Jones to be First Minister. As First Minister, Ieuan would have been able to have lots of photo shoots with Alex Salmond, the new First Minister of Scotland, together the two History Boys.

But around the Members Tea Room and the canteen, where journalists gossiped with party staff and dirt was dished, a very different story also emerged. Alex Salmond and Ieuan Wyn Jones were both cut from very different tartan. Self-doubt never afflicted Alex Salmond – 'ebullient' didn't adequately describe his personality, he never had a nano-second's hesitation in grabbing the reins of government in Scotland despite being miles short of a working majority. No problem! In fact, Alex probably thought he could run Scotland, the European Union and the United Nations all at the same time, while still finding the time to place shrewd bets on the winner of the three-thirty race at Lingfield Park! That was Alex. The contrast with Ieuan Wyn Jones could not have been more marked. Did Ieuan really think he was ready to be First Minister? Did his colleagues at the top of Plaid Cymru think he was ready? The feedback we were hearing was that it might be better for him to start off as Deputy First Minister, learn the ropes, grow into the role, with some even saying he could learn a bit off me – at least learn what not to do! Anyway, the upshot was that Ieuan would be more comfortable as Deputy and, if Plaid was seen to deliver really well through its Ministers, the next step in the rise of the party would be something more like the SNP at the 2011 election. With plenty of experience of government, Plaid might hope to become the largest party in the Assembly.

Immediately after the forming of that Government, with me laid-up at home for the first week, Ieuan had been sworn in as Deputy First Minister. It was a week before I was fit enough to come into the office to form the joint Cabinet. Being sworn in as Ministers was a new experience for us all. In the first two Assemblies, Welsh Ministers were not Ministers of the Crown. But, under the new legislation creating a Welsh Assembly with go-faster stripes from 2007 onwards, all Welsh Ministers had to be sworn in as well. I imagine that Her Majesty does the swearing in for Westminster Ministers, but we were sworn in by a judge on her behalf.

It was providential for me, then, that Ieuan could be sworn in as Deputy First Minister on 10 July, although still without a Cabinet job, and he could represent Wales on 11 July at the ninetieth anniversary of the Third Battle of Ypres in 1917. Ieuan was there with all the dignitaries at the Menin Gate. For anyone from Welsh-speaking north-west Wales, the Third Battle of Ypres had added poignancy because of the death of the poet Hedd Wyn, the Bard of the Black Chair at the National Eisteddfod held that year in Birkenhead, by which time he had been killed in battle. Ever since then, the 1917 festival is known in posterity as the Eisteddfod of the Black Chair.

The following day, Ieuan was able to deputise for me and represent Wales at the British–Irish Council in Stormont, the home of the most problematic of the three devolved bodies in the UK. With that meeting being in Stormont, it also had extra significance because the Northern Ireland Assembly had been through another suspension and return to direct rule, but it was now back in business.

So Ieuan, as Leader of Plaid Cymru, had a flying start to the role of Deputy First Minister as a result of my illness. The following week on 19 July he received his portfolio as Minister for Economic Development & Transport, which was the heavyweight portfolio he wanted. One of two other Plaid Cymru Cabinet Members, Rhodri Glyn Thomas, took the prize for Plaid Cymru of Culture, Sport & the Welsh Language, the equivalent of Westminster's 'Ministry of Fun'. If Ieuan had a heavyweight portfolio, then his colleague had a lightweight one, but it carried huge cultural significance for Plaid Cymru. Everybody happy, for now anyway. Elin Jones was the third Plaid Cabinet Member, and she became Minister for Agriculture & Rural Affairs (and Labour had to accept that this meant a change in policy on badger culling).

Little did we know, of course, that the worst recesssion since the Hungry Thirties was just around the corner, and that came to dominate everything. The early months were, with the advantages of hindsight, something of a fool's paradise. Coalitions are like marriages, you are bound to have rows in among the good times, and I remember having a fleeting thought during one meeting with Ieuan and his Special Adviser Simon Thomas (former-MP for Ceredigion), and Simon's Labour 'oppo' Mark Drakeford. The meeting was conducted entirely in Welsh, and the fleeting thought was very untypical of me – roughly to the effect that Owain Glyndŵr must have dreamt six hundred years previously that, one day, this was how Wales would be governed.

I don't think we had a big row in the marriage until October. As Minister for Economic Development, Ieuan was going to lead a trade mission to India. Fine. No problem. Then I found out he was taking his wife Eirian with him. I said no. The message was relayed very firmly that in the eight years of the Assembly's existence, no Minister had ever taken their spouse with them on official business – no one had thought to ask, in fact – so that was that, Eirian couldn't go.

The message was then relayed back to me that it was too late – Ieuan had told his wife that she was coming. 'Here we go again', I thought to myself, 'it's the *fait accompli* technique!' I had been waiting for it. So another message, even clearer than the last one, spouses going on ministerial visits isn't going to happen, and that's that – Ieuan will have to tell his wife. Eventually, we compromised, with Ieuan taking his wife but paying for her airfare and any expenses – you always compromise in coalitions and marriages if you're going to make them work.

While we were getting our coalition government bedded down in Wales, things were not exactly quiescent up in the Big Smoke. In the summer of 2007, Tony Blair's hands and fingers had finally been prised away from the levers of power in No. 10 by Gordon Brown. Blair had done just a shade over ten years – he would probably have liked to do another year to break Margaret Thatcher's record, but that was not to be.

Blair had sacked a lot of Labour Ministers at Cabinet and junior level during that decade, and passed over quite a few others, including me of course. It all mounted the pressure on him eventually to go. The ex-Ministers he had reshuffled out and the non-Ministers he had never chosen were all cheering. But should I have been one of the cheer-leaders? In his autobiography, *A Journey*, as I've previously said, he described me as a Brownite. I don't know where he got that from – I can only guess Blair was getting me mixed up with Kevin Brennan, my successor as MP for Cardiff West, who certainly was a Brownite and one of those active in giving the PM the hurry-up sign in 2007.

I couldn't really fault Blair's conduct in helping make devolution work during the years when I was First Minister and he was Prime Minister. He was never a convinced supporter of devolution in Wales, nor in Scotland as far as I could tell. The bit of devolution that he threw himself into with all his energy and phenomenal stamina was Northern Ireland – the Good Friday Peace Agreement cemented his international reputation at the very start of his premiership. Although the Northern Ireland Assembly had a very on-and-off existence in its early years, it got there in the end and it was set up a year ahead of either the Scots getting their Parliament or Wales its Assembly.

Looking back over Blair's decade in power, he remains an enigma. How did anyone elected as an MP on the 1983 Labour election manifesto move so much to the right during the next twenty-odd years? Yes, he was a chameleon, but also a barrister trained on the taxi-rank principle that you can make a brilliant speech to the jury regardless of your private views on the defendant. It's an occupational hazard for barrister-politicians. But I never felt the same kind of hazard with John Smith or Gareth Williams, for example, who were both barrister-politicians too – Gareth especially, coming so late in his career to politics. John and Gareth both seemed rock-solid in their beliefs. Blair never did.

Maybe 'chameleon' is the wrong word. Most great barristers need a really good instructing solicitor to detail them on the case, and then they go off and turn whatever sow's ear it happens to be into a silk purse. Blair's instructing solicitor for most of his time in No. 10 was Peter Mandelson – that's how the New Labour project was dreamt up. In 2003, Blair's instructing solicitor was, maybe, George W. Bush – a personality trait, I can only assume, is the reason why Blair didn't take a more independent line with Bush when he called from Air Force One after 9/11 and made his plea, 'Yo, Blair, World War III has just started! Are you with us or against us?'

Blair should have fended off just as Harold Wilson had done with President Johnson over the Vietnam War. Why couldn't Blair have done the same with Dubya throughout that disastrous period from 9/11 and leading up to the invasion of Iraq? It baffles me to this day.

I enjoyed a very good relationship with Tony when he was starting out in the Shadow Cabinet in November 1988, when Neil Kinnock gave him the Energy brief, shadowing the newly rehabilitated Cecil Parkinson and the Bill to privatise the electricity industry. I was one of Tony's shadow junior Ministers, and we lived in each other's pockets during that twelve-month period. Later on, we had the big falling out over why he never wanted me in his Government in 1997, and then the attempts to block me becoming First Minister. But then, once I was actually in the job, the old friendship resumed. I'll always feel in his debt, because he did deliver on Labour's commitment on devolution, despite his efforts to block me.

If Tony Blair was a reluctant devolutionist led into it via the glory of bringing peace to Northern Ireland, Gordon Brown was the exact opposite. Gordon was an utterly convinced devolutionist from way back, and an avid follower of the John Smith theory of the settled will of the Scottish people. Yet, when Alex Salmond won his right to form a minority SNP Government in May 2007, Gordon went right off the whole thing – his beloved Scotland was now in the wrong hands.

The problem for us in Wales was that the much tighter attitude from London towards Scotland actually hurt Wales and my Labour-led Government far more than it hurt Scotland. Scotland had a cushion of generous funding far greater than ours, and an economy and social structure that was far easier to pay for. Elderly people retired *away* from Scotland, but they retired *to* Wales; the Scottish birth-rate was well below ours in Wales, so fewer children to educate; the proportion of the workforce in white-collar employment was identical to England's, while it was very blue-collar in Wales.

So when the new Prime Minister and his new Chancellor of the Exchequer, Alistair Darling, agreed to meet me, Alex Salmond, and Peter Robinson and the late Martin McGuinness, the two First Ministers from Northern Ireland, to discuss why the Olympic Games was being exempted from the normal workings of the Barnett Formula and some other funding issues, I led on the Olympics. I could see why you could at least make a case for exempting the sports facilities – such as the athletics stadium, the velodrome and the aquatic centre – but it was plainly absurd that the transport and urban regeneration spending across east London should be exempt. Gordon was seething. Alex Salmond was enjoying himself far too much, seeing a Labour politician like me laying into two Scottish Labour head honchos like Gordon and Alistair, and allowing Alex the luxury of an occasional smirk or two.

But no joy whatsoever.

Gordon just could not overcome his loathing of Alex Salmond – some of it loathing for Alex personally, some of it for the SNP, and maybe that bit of the loathing was spiced by the accursed SNP getting into minority government by that one single seat in the Scottish Parliament.

So, Wales got it in the neck as collateral damage from Gordon's desperate desire to scotch the Scottish nationalists. In that meeting of the three devolved administrations to protest about the exemption of all expenditure on the Olympics from the Barnett Formula, Alex Salmond had raised the issue of borrowing powers for Scotland. The Treasury line was that all the borrowing would have to come out of the block grant. I said, rather foolishly looking back, that in Wales we were already borrowing small amounts to support economic development via Finance Wales, our in-house quasi-bank investment subsidiary. Then, within about a month, the Treasury had closed the loophole, and all of Finance Wales's borrowings were deducted from our block grant! I should have kept my mouth shut. We all thought we had the Treasury's agreement to disregard Finance Wales's borrowings from our block grant – they had certainly agreed this verbally, and I was assured there was no problem because we had it written down on paper as well. But horror of horrors, no one could find the piece of paper on which the Treasury had agreed to disregard the borrowings, and we were stuffed.

You could see what had happened. After the meeting with the Prime Minister and the Chancellor, Alex Salmond must have set his officials to task on how to achieve parity of treatment for Scotland compared to Wales. He wanted borrowing powers for Scotland as well, with the same disregard, when the block grant was calculated. The Treasury had then refused, and was no longer going to disregard Finance Wales's borrowings – Wales had been penalised, while the intention all along was to stop the SNP getting away with something. And it didn't help matters after the fruitless search for the elusive written agreement with the Treasury that our own civil servants said Finance Wales's borrowings should have been deducted from the Welsh block grant in the first place.

When I heard that last little contribution, it was one of those I-nearly-fell-off-my-chair moments. How could any civil servant in the Welsh Government want to 'give' £200 million back to the Treasury? Rules! That's what drives some civil servants. Anyway, setting up Finance Wales was one of the most creative things we had done during my decade in power, but we had kept it below the radar and allowed it to grow organically, building up its lending expertise. Its growth path would have been better and smoother if I'd kept my mouth shut at that meeting, or if we'd found that bit of paper with the Treasury's agreement on it. There have been lots of attempts to build up something similar on both sides of the right–left divide at a UK level – everyone wants a British Investment Bank. Launching the concept is quite easy, but building one up to be a serious player with the right skill-sets is much harder.

I couldn't get through to Gordon Brown on policy issues. I could travel in a car with him and get on great – I remember one such journey from Newport through the Torfaen constituency, then Islwyn and then on to Cardiff North. It was the May 2007 elections, so Gordon was still Chancellor at the time. He was like a sponge as I told him about the key points in the industrial history of this and that valley. He loved my story about Andrew Carnegie coming to Blaenavon with a cheque for £250,000 to buy the worldwide rights for the Gilchrist–Thomas process for smelting high phosphorus iron ore for use in bulk steel-making. Carnegie is supposed to have said that when the history books would come to be written, what the two cousins Percy Carlyle Gilchrist and Sidney Gilchrist Thomas had achieved in Blaenavon would be accounted as far more important than all the doings of all the Kings and Queens of England! 'Ah …' said Gordon, 'you've got to remember that Andrew Carnegie was a very committed republican!' The other highlight was me telling Gordon that the school visit we were doing in Cardiff North was at Heol Llanishen Fach, the birthplace of Oliver Cromwell's grandfather, Morgan Williams. 'So', he laughed, 'this is the birthplace of the Revolution!' We decided not to use that line with the assembled press.

That, in many ways, summed up the personality differences between Gordon Brown and Tony Blair. Gordon's idea of a perfect holiday was three weeks buried in the archives of the Widener Library at Harvard University, studying the history of a mega-industrialist like Carnegie; whereas Tony's ideal holiday was three weeks in a borrowed palazzo belonging to a modern-day plutocrat like Silvio Berlusconi. Gordon was Protestant ethic personified – that wasn't how Tony saw the world or his place in it.

I certainly found it quite difficult to get close to Gordon. Everyone complained about it when he was Chancellor of the Exchequer. He had his coterie, his

Praetorian Guard, of Ed Balls, Charlie Whelan, Ed Miliband and Geoffrey Robinson. And although the Praetorian Guard had broken up by the time he got to No. 10 in the summer of 2007, he was still difficult to get close to.

In late 2007, I remember a half-finished conversation when Gordon started to tell me how the coming year was going to be pretty horrendous – then he suddenly stopped talking when he remembered I wasn't part of the Government, let alone his inner circle. He hadn't exactly let the cat out of the bag – maybe just let the cat's head out of the bag and then tried to stuff it back in there. It was halfway between the collapse of Northern Rock and the fall of Lehman Brothers – the wholesale money markets had effectively closed, and all the horrors of the sub-prime mortgages and the grossly overvalued CDOs (the collateralised debt instruments stuffed with sub-prime) were starting to come to light. I found myself in Gordon's inner circle for a split second, and then I was back out of it again.

It reminded me of a similar experience with Tony Blair a few years before, when he started to tell me all about a serious back problem he was being treated for. Then he looked at me more closely, realised who I was – in other words, neither a member of the UK Government, nor a member of his inner circle – and stopped mid-sentence. Both were odd experiences, reminding me of the unusual position I occupied, simultaneously inside and out.

It certainly drove me and my staff nuts that the Labour leader in Scotland, Wendy Alexander, albeit the Leader of the Opposition in the Scottish Parliament, had such good access to Gordon Brown when he was PM. Wendy was definitely part of Gordon's inner circle, though she wasn't running the country – Alex Salmond was, and I had to have a working relationship with Alex. He didn't come to Cardiff, but I certainly went to Edinburgh early on in his First Ministership to try to enlist his support for reforming the Barnett Formula. I knew there was very little chance of it, but I had to try. Alex's blunt reply was that he would only consider joining in the call if he was given access to a chunk of the North Sea oil and gas reserves and revenues.

Gordon tried to enlist my support for getting the Scottish Department of Agriculture & Fisheries to be given the lead role in looking after Ag. & Fish. for the whole of the UK. This was because MAFF, the Ministry in London, was universally recognised as the pits of Whitehall. Alex and I were both ex-civil servants, so I understood the problem, but I also understood it would never happen. I also thought it was such a bizarre thing for Alex to aim for as a nationalist, because it would tie Scotland's government far more closely into the governance of the UK. I told him I thought he should go for just the 'fish' part of Ag. & Fish., and Wales could then bid for steel rather than the whole of Trade & Industry. Anyway, nothing came of it, though I still puzzle about the logic of it for an SNP First Minister.

Whatever the possible merits of the Scottish Government and Welsh Government taking over any part of UK civil service administration on fish, steel or anything else, everything got buried under the tsunami caused by the collapse of the banking system in 2007–9. It was a hellish time for Gordon Brown to be taking over as Prime Minister – likewise for Obama in the USA and, in our small way, the Labour–Plaid coalition.

For the first year, it wasn't absolutely clear whether the political system could contain the runs on the banks like Northern Rock and the Bradford & Bingley, and the threatened complete drain of money from RBS NatWest (which in 2007 was ranked as the largest bank in the world).

The only person who got it right in 2007, and made his views and fears crystal-clear to me, was Peter Griffiths, Chief Executive of the Principality Building Society. He said he was frightened, and when I asked what he meant, he replied, 'House prices are so way out of line with wages, there's going to have to be a huge downward correction in house prices, a crash', he warned, 'and I don't know what the fall-out is going to be.'

Unlike Scotland, Wales did not have the headquarters of two major banks like RBS NatWest and HBOS; unlike Newcastle, Bradford or Halifax, no city in Wales had a major de-mutualised building society that had turned itself into an aggressive mortgage lender. The Principality had never gone in for privatisation – it had expanded but at nowhere near the breakneck speed of Northern Rock, which had created thousands of jobs in mortgage administration in Newcastle and Sunderland. As a result, Wales did miss out on thousands of those financial services jobs, but thank goodness we did. There was no Welsh contribution to the crash of the banking system! Our hands were clean, for whatever good that did us, when the storm hit.

Others had a very different and far more sanguine view of impending doom. At one early meeting of the Joint Ministerial Committee, the get-together of the First Ministers with the Prime Minister, Alex Salmond complained bitterly about how little Lloyd's Bank had paid for HBOS (when HBOS was on the verge of going down) – 'It's an absolute steal, Rhodri!' was his verdict. I said that I didn't think there was anyone around who would have paid a penny more for it, and he replied, 'No, maybe not, but on a five-year view they've got it very cheap!' That was just a classic example of tartan-tinted spectacles. You can't take a five-year view when you're about to run out of money. Perhaps if Wales had had two massive bank HQs, I might also have let myself be tempted into wearing dragon-tinted specs. Anyway, the consensus now is that Lloyd's Bank nearly went down itself because of taking over HBOS at far too *high* a price.

Late in 2007, I primed our Permanent Secretary Sir Jon Shortridge to ask a few pertinent questions at the weekly 'prayer meetings' he attended with all the UK heads of department. 'Why are the public finances not in surplus?' I told him to ask.'Surely, after a long period of sustained economic growth since 1997, house price growth, and share price buoyancy, when if not now would there ever be more tax receipts than expenditure?' Sir Jon did raise it with his Treasury opposite number Sir Nick MacPherson, who told him that the expected surplus had never arrived due to the unexpected fall in tax receipts from North Sea oil and gas.

So, there was this perfect storm brewing, and the UK wasn't in great shape to withstand it. The ex-building societies up north had all gone mad on their mortgage lending practices – 125 per cent mortgages, for heaven's sake! North Sea tax receipts, which had bailed us out since 1979, were now in serious decline. Then the US Government decided not to bail out the busted Lehman Brothers, because it didn't fall into the too big to fail but too stupid to succeed category. Leman Brothers could be allowed to go down – it was the cost of judgement that shattered the epoch, and the whole house of credit cards collapsed.

Then why was Wales affected so much? Wales didn't get any bail-out money because there were no banks in Wales to bail out. What Wales did get was the extraordinary fall-out from the failing banks on hire purchase, therefore on the purchase of cars, and therefore on the purchase of steel. More jobs in Wales were lost in manufacturing than in financial services as a result of the collapse in the banking system. Manufacturing remains below where it was in 2008, whereas financial services are way above pre-crash levels. There's no logic to it, but it's historical fact.

When the recession hit its full stride after the Lehman Brothers collapse, in Wales we had to adopt an all-hands-on-deck approach. Eventually, it was going to mean less money for public services after years of expanding budgets. In the short term, there was no attempt to cut back on public expenditure – if the state had tried to cut back just as the private citizen and the private sector of business was cutting back, it would have been disastrous. The UK followed a Keynesian approach of keeping money pumping into the economy to try to stabilise the ship. There would be a reckoning, but it would not be in 2008–9.

We had an Economic Council for Wales, which paralleled the Economic Council for the UK that Gordon Brown chaired. Paul Murphy as Secretary of State for Wales was the link between the two bodies. Construction, especially house-building, was completely up the spout, and retail wasn't much better. The next-door building to the Assembly happens to be HQ for the British and Irish end of Atradius, one of Europe's leading credit insurance companies. It had originally arrived in Cardiff thirty years previously, as the short-term credit arm of the Export Credit Guarantees Department (ECGD). Half an hour talking to the boss at Atradius brought home to me the level of the carnage on the high street and the building sites.

The same applied to a conversation I overheard in a little timber yard in Splott, which I patronised whenever I needed a small carpentry job doing in the house. A plasterer was being served ahead of me. 'I've never known anything like it. I've been in the building trade all my life. One minute I'm working for Bovis in Ferry Road on a big housing scheme, and then the job gets stopped, just like that, and everyone I've rung says there's nothing doing anywhere. Not even in London. Nothing. It'll be years before we get back to normal. I don't know what I'm going to do, apart from doing up my house!'

For me personally, I was glad in one sense that I had not retired just before the recession hit. It would have been like running to the hills just as things were getting rough. I think the all-hands-on-deck approach did lift morale in the business sector and more widely in society – we were going to get through it somehow. Being a 1939 war baby, I had no direct experience of the Hungry Thirties, but boy! I'd had it drummed into me by my mother and father about just what an appalling time in Welsh history the Hungry Thirties had been. It was the last full-blown recession caused by a banking collapse, and all I could think to myself throughout that crisis in 2008–9 was that there would be no return to the Hungry Thirties in Wales. Maybe I set the bar far too low in that sense, but at least I think we passed that particular test.

Of course, Gordon Brown may have been too complacent about the build-up of a house price bubble, but he was the right man for the job of ensuring no collapse of the world trading system. He made this awful *faux pas* in Parliament of announcing that we had 'saved the world' when he clearly meant to say we'd 'saved the world's banking system'. I'm not sure how well Gordon got on with President Obama, the presidential handover from Bush to Obama having taken place in January 2009, in the eye of the storm with General Motors on the verge of going under!

Gordon had the right experience, even though he couldn't run an office for toffee – his office was completely dysfunctional. I once spoke about this problem with Sarah Brown's business partner, Julia Hobsbawm, when Julie and I met her at the Hay Literature Festival. Julia told us that the Brown team wanted her to join his office to help get it organised, but in the end she decided against because even the Archangel Gabriel wouldn't have been able to sort out Gordon's office!

I had always held annual meetings with Tony Blair just before the summer recesses. There were never any problems. I'm not saying we solved any of the world's top priority issues, but the meetings did at least take place. The channel of communication between PM and FM was always there and always respected. When Gordon arrived, we could never agree a date for an annual meeting, and then we could never agree a time, or if we did agree a date and a time then Gordon would never stick to it. I was left sitting in an ante-room next to the executive office, meant to be organised like Mayor Bloomberg's bullpen hive of cubicles in New York.

Sue Nye, Gordon's brilliant assistant and an old friend, brought me several cups of tea. She even took me into the office to show me the banks of 24/7 News Channel television screens high up on the walls, and loads of clerks and secretaries busy at work. No actual Gordon, though. Another time, I was asked to wait for him in the Downing Street Library. It was a dreadful room. Very chilling. After half an hour of no show (which felt like an hour and a half), I decided to leave. As I was walking down the stairs, Gordon came bounding up and greeted me like a long-lost brother in arms. There must have been some kind of closed circuit that alerted everybody that I was leaving, and Sue must have hurried him, 'Gordon, quick, up those stairs, Rhodri's leaving!' There was no excuse for it, really.

I think we made a fair fist of it retaining as many jobs in Wales as we could under appalling circumstances. What we did differently from England, Scotland and Northern Ireland was to introduce a short-time working subsidy scheme called ProAct. We had first introduced what we called our *ReAct* scheme in October 2008, designed to help individuals who had been made redundant to be retrained; what *ProAct* did, starting two months later, was to help companies who only had enough work for half a week or three days to retain the workforce while waiting for the upturn. ProAct subsidised workforce training, on the job or off-site, for the remaining two days in each week.

Our officials worked their socks off to come up with a scheme that would pass muster with the European Social Fund. It wasn't original. It was a rip-off of something the German and Dutch governments had introduced. It was widely admired, and why it wasn't introduced across the rest of the UK, I will never know. I once asked Peter Mandelson why the Department for Business hadn't introduced it, and he mumbled something about Wales having the advantage of European money. I still think the real reason was that we had better officials who were not easily daunted by being given a very short timescale to create something workable.

They were the ex-ELWa officials who had become civil servants two years previously following our 'bonfire of the quangos'. They did fantastic work, which didn't just save thousands of jobs – it meant also that the companies were more competitive when the eventual upturn came. It often struck me that, because of the importance of manufacturing in Wales, we had to run the country as though it were a part of Germany. I think that's why the scheme wasn't introduced in England, because it was particularly suited to manufacturing. Unfortunately, making things was seen as old hat in London.

Those final two and a half years of being the First Minister weren't all *Recession Recession Recession*. There were occasional flare-ups of coalition management. In the summer of 2008, for instance, we had to manage the Plaid Cymru Cabinet member Rhodri Glyn Thomas out of the Government. He was a minister of religion, but anything but the stereotype of a Welsh Nonconformist minister.

Rhodri Glyn Thomas was a fully paid-up member of the unholier-than-thou ten-dency – he had expended one life earlier in the summer by reading out the wrong name in announcing the winner of the Welsh Book of the Year (I didn't mind if he wanted to become a bit of a laughing stock, but not in my Government please!), and then he went one better with a saunter into a pub next to the Assembly with a lit cigar despite the smoking ban in public places! He resigned with good grace.

After a series of rows with the Deputy First Minister Ieuan Wyn Jones about the sharp behaviour of his more than feisty spin doctor, Rhuanedd Richards, Ieuan asked, 'Do you want me to sack her?' 'No', I said, 'I just want you to instruct her what she's supposed to do.' I did get the impression that it was the other way round at times though!

The central cause of strife was that Rhuanedd had sneaked out a press release claiming for Plaid Cymru all the credit for the Jeremie Fund (a European initiative for funding small and medium-sized enterprises), where Wales was piloting the scheme for the whole of the EU.

Then we had an utterly unbelievable episode in Llangollen, which the local AM Karen Sinclair, recovering at home from leukaemia, brought to my attention. I could barely believe it at first, and indeed it would have been thrown out as far too fanciful by any self-respecting Welsh television company pitching for a drama commission. It involved a Chinese martial arts instructor called Pol Wong, who had instructed a few dozen local Bruce Lee wannabes in Kung Fu. Then he went on to tell his pupils that their Welsh heritage was under threat from too much local house-building intended to be marketed to buyers from across the border, and organised them in marches through the town togged out in martial arts gear – all of which would just be an expression of free speech, except that one of our officials was involved in trying to use public funds to refurbish a redundant local hotel as the training centre for the Welsh heritage-defending Kung Fu club. With the official in question being in Economic Development, it meant that it was the job of Ieuan as Deputy First Minister to sort it out.

I think my last contretemps with Ieuan came over the Kemble passing loop on the Great Western main line between Paddington and South Wales. Now, you'd be correct to point out that Kemble is in Wiltshire. Anyway, by the time I became involved, Ieuan had already paid part of the cost of the feasibility study into this extra passing loop, to improve service resilience during engineering works. When the Department for Transport came back to us to fund a share of the actual building of the loop, I knew absolutely nothing about the sub we had sent to the DfT for the feasibility study, but I was furious when I found out about the proposal to give the DfT money towards the cost of the actual works. 'No, Ieuan', I insisted, 'Look, the DfT is trying to rewrite the terms of the devolution settlement. The main line isn't devolved. If it had been devolved, we would have given the funding from the start to cover the costs.' By 2009, all the UK home departments were starting to feel the squeeze. If they could get us to chip in for part of their budgets, their cuts wouldn't be as severe. But we were feeling the same squeeze and we knew there was much worse to come. So it had to be a definite no!

I think 2009 was the crossover year, when all governments, central and devolved, were starting to realise what was to come. The Keynesian reaction to the collapse of the banks to try to make credit available again, and to foster trade and keep unemployment from going through the roof, was coming towards the end. The payback period of getting a handle on government borrowing was soon going to start.

That was why the reaction to the H1N1 Mexican swine flu outbreak was such a good case in point. Money – £1.2 billion of it – was thrown at the problem as if there were no tomorrow. According to the Dame Deirdre Hine evaluation report, it was all textbook response. There was, said the report's author, unanimity among politicians that the UK must acquire huge stocks of Tamiflu to alleviate the symptoms. Preparedness was the key to it. Now, no politician would dare risk losing credit with the great British public by having bought too large a stock of anti-virals – but God forbid that you should be last in the queue at the drug company's sales office when you wanted to get your order in, if and when the pandemic exploded.

This unanimity didn't include me. I only participated in one teleconference with the UK, Scottish and Northern Ireland Health Ministers. This was when the Assembly's Health Minister was ill and, possibly because I was soon to leave office, I had become a non-person. When Dame Deirdre came to interview me personally during the compiling of her report, I explained how baffled I was that there was no reference in the minutes of the teleconference to my disagreement on the Tamiflu policy.

Wales was in an anomalous position to begin with. Whereas Scotland and Northern Ireland had a devolved responsibility and a budget for emergency planning, Wales did not. Indeed, it still doesn't. So, the UK Government was responsible for emergency planning for England and Wales – this was why Wales had never been given a budget for emergency planning. But Health was our most important responsibility. Theoretically, if the UK Government wanted to buy in huge stocks of Tamiflu just in case the pandemic balloon went up, those stocks would have to cover England and Wales. Then, if they were really needed, the Welsh Government would buy its requirement from the UK Government to treat those who were ill.

Anyway, what had struck me during the teleconference as I listened to Nicola Sturgeon as Scottish Health Minister, along with her opposite numbers, was that money was not an issue and that we *had* to get the Tamiflu. My concerns were dismissed and not minuted, and my subsequent concerns passed on in person to Dame Deirdre were not included in her report. I had become a non-person, I didn't exist.'All politicians' were agreed that the UK must get all the Tamiflu stocks it could – but I wasn't.

It turned out to be a complete waste of £1.2 billion which the UK plainly didn't have. It was spent in order to reassure the public that all the UK authorities working together had a master-plan, and that we in the UK would be alright if the pandemic hit.

My scepticism about the UK Government machine's response to the threat of flu pandemics had been fuelled a few years previously when the threat reared that H5N1 avian influenza might bring down civilisation as we knew it. I attended the COBRA meeting chaired by the Home Secretary Charles Clarke, and the good thing about the meeting was that officials were all mixed up with us politicians around the table. I found myself next to Sir David King, the Government Chief Scientific Adviser – the two officials we politicians most wanted to hear from were the specialists, Sir David himself and Sir Liam Donaldson, the Chief Medical Officer. Unfortunately, they were in complete disagreement over their advice. As Sir Liam spoke on the medical priorities, Sir David was muttering away to me that Sir Liam plainly didn't understand the science or the mathematics. The mathematics was in modelling how the avian influenza would spread, and that determined whether wise action for the reduction of its impact was to get prophylactic doses of the Tamiflu to all health workers, key public service workers, school teachers and so on. The same number of people would contract the bird flu in the end, but it was just that it would take longer to pass through the population. There was at least a case for arguing that it should be allowed to run, that it was all very mild. Professional disagreement seemed by now to be extending to personal dislike.

My final year or so in office had a very stable Cabinet. If Rhodri Glyn Thomas was Plaid Cymru's Boris Johnson, his replacement Alun Ffred Jones was more in the Theresa May serious person mould. Not that Alun Ffred was humourless, but he was a really safe pair of hands. As we'd settle into our chairs for Cabinet meetings, grabbing our tea and fruit slices or biscuits, I would usually try to make the Plaid colleagues feel as welcome as possible with a few jokes in Welsh (the majority of the Cabinet didn't speak Welsh). I might even give them useful tip-offs (such as when the wine section at ASDA was running a half-price promotion offer on Patagonia Malbec).

I hadn't really decided exactly when I was going to step down. Mentally, I had made a note that my notional decade would be up in February 2010, and that would allow fourteen months for my successor to bed in. I thought fourteen months was feasible for whoever it was to choose his or her own Cabinet and put their own stamp on things. Somebody in BBC Wales had the allegedly bright idea of following me round for my final twelve months in power with a fly-on-the-wall camera. I had no objection to the idea but, as soon as we talked about it in a bit more detail I realised that my idea of my last twelve months and the BBC Wales team's idea were a million miles apart. They seemed to think that my last year would have a kind of ceremonial character – their vision was that my private office would draw up a list of my favourite legacy projects, like the Wales for Africa programme, and I would then visit one of these every fortnight and say goodbye and presumably receive gratitude from the citizenry involved in whatever scheme it was. But I wasn't intending anything like that. I would just carry on without any thought of retiring until my last day in office. That would be it really. BBC Wales did do their fly-on-the-wall, but I think it fell pretty flat.

A much simpler retrospective made by ITV Wales was broadcast on S4C, and it involved less fuss but came over as a much punchier programme – at least it did to me. It didn't obsess over legacy, that was the key difference. Far fewer people saw that one on S4C because it was all in Welsh, but that's part of the glory of being a bilingual nation.

If I had had in mind any kind of schedule of legacy marker visits in that last year, to put my stamp on any list of top ten achievements, then Wales for Africa would have featured highly. But that simply wasn't how I intended to spend my final year as First Minister. Wales for Africa had kicked off in 2006, but really got going late in 2007 when we launched the Gold Star project. It was a community-based programme, aimed at stimulating Welsh communities with a link to sub-Saharan Africa to meet certain quality standards in how they contributed to meeting the Millennium Development Goals.

Well after my retirement, I bumped into Paul Boateng, originally a colleague of mine from the 1987 intake of Labour MPs. By 2012, he had retired from the lower house of Parliament, and had then been British High Commissioner to the Republic of South Africa. By now, he was in the *other* house of Parliament, the upper house. In our conversation, the subject of the Wales for Africa programme came up and, much to my astonishment, Paul said that everyone in the field in sub-Saharan Africa knew that the Wales for Africa programme was far superior to anything done by the Department for International Development – a bit of a shock to me, albeit a very pleasant one.

Wales was still going through the mincing machine of the recession. The world trade system and the world's banking and credit system were very sickly children throughout 2009. We also had some practical personnel problems to manage – if we hadn't managed them pro-actively, we could have finished up with Sir Jon Shortridge, Lawrence Conway and me all retiring at the same time.

Sir Jon could be spiky in his defence of neutrality of the civil service against all political threats, real and imaginary. He feared possible politicisation attempted during the difficult transition phase to devolved assemblies and parliaments in 1998–9. He especially treasured his weekly attendance at the get-together of all the permanent secretaries in Whitehall, a reminder to everyone that the Welsh and Scottish civil service was still part of the UK Home civil service. Anyway, Sir Jon retired first in April 2008, and he was replaced by Dame Gillian Morgan, previously Head of the NHS Confederation. There were not that many *wo*mandarins in the history of the UK civil service, and certainly none in Wales. Where Sir Jon was not so hot was on avoiding the male, pale and stale character of the senior civil service in Wales. He had got very upset with me over the Gerard Elias issue, which I've already described, but overall we got on well. We did share a similar background, having both been planning officers on the staff of the Department of the Environment – me in the 1960s and he in the 1970s.

When the Cabinet Minister for Industry and Universities and Science (DIUS) John Denham rang me six months after Sir Jon retired to ask if Jon was an okay person, I said yes without hesitation. John Denham described his problem to me and said, 'Rhodri, I've had to be my own Permanent Secretary for a month now, bloody nightmare! I urgently need a short-term fix. We're thinking of asking Sir Jon to come out of retirement for a few months. Any thoughts?' I gave John a little list of Jon's strengths and weaknesses, and then he got the job pro tem.

It's an odd relationship between Ministers and civil servants, because Ministers have no responsibility for staff matters. Sir Jon was our Head of Service in Wales. But in the public's eye the First Minister was responsible for everything. If anything went wrong, even in staff management, it was still seen as the First Minister's responsibility.

That personal responsibility extended to architecture and IT projects. On the new Senedd building, we had sacked Sir Richard Rogers because the tender prices for the superstructure packages were coming in two or three times higher than the estimates. It was down to Edwina Hart, and we had to find a way out – were we right to hire Taylor Woodrow who would in turn bring back Sir Richard by the tradesmen's entrance as a hired-hand architect? The alternative was to accept a really interesting bid from a Welsh firm of architects – Stride, Treglown and Davies – fine if all went well, but if it had all gone wrong the entire architectural establishment in London would have turned on Wales. They would have reminded everyone that back in John Redwood's day, twenty years earlier, Wales had collectively rejected the late Zaha Hadid's design for the new Opera House. We would never have heard the last of it, and that's why I decided to play safe.

Likewise, when the Merlin IT contract came up, the cheapest bid by a long way came from the Siemens-led contract. They had held the contract before, again going back to the old Welsh Office days, when it was called the OSIRIS contract. We all agreed that the IBM-led contract was far more imaginative, and my gut feeling was to go with IBM, but it wasn't the lowest bid. If we had accepted the IBM bid, I would have had to write an explanatory letter to the Chairman of the Public Accounts Committee explaining why I hadn't gone with the cheapest tender.

I still think my gut instinct was right, but I agreed to go with the Siemens consortium. It turned out to be nothing but trouble. Siemens had clearly bid too low in a desperate attempt to retain the Welsh Assembly business, and the only way they could make any money was by under-resourcing it. Our officials would complain that systems weren't working properly, and Siemens would agree to lay on more senior staff for trouble-shooting. All would go well for a while until, a few months later, the senior trouble-shooters would be replaced with more junior staff, and then Assembly staff complaints would start all over again. It was like a roundabout with not much magic to go with it. I knew that I should have been brave and gone with the IBM bid, but it would have been against official advice and I didn't quite have the bottle to do it.

Dame Gillian Morgan had never been a civil servant, but she knew the corridors of Whitehall inside out. She had very firm views on health matters, but was willing to listen and learn about most other issues. I got on well with her, as is nearly always the case with individuals you appoint in the first place!

An unusual request for a favour arrived at my office from the deposed Prime Minister of New Zealand, my good friend Helen Clark, whose advice I had found such a boon in May 2007. Now she was out of a job after three terms of office, and not expecting ever to run again for office in New Zealand. Did I have any influence with Gordon Brown? She would want his support in applying to work with the United Nations or any other international body lacking a chief executive, and she was obviously leaving no stone unturned by ringing me up! 'I've proved that I can run things, Rhodri', she said, and that was true. And I did speak to Gordon on her behalf. Eventually, she did get her wish – she became head of the UN Development Programme, though I doubt my chat with Gordon had much to do with it (I'd be absolutely thrilled if it did, mind you, I owed Helen a favour).

The highlight from the fun point of view during that last year was climbing to the summit of Snowdon to open the new summit café, Hafod Eryri, in June 2009. It was a wonderful way to test how complete the recovery was after my heart problem. I had been completely discharged by my cardiologist, Dr Ossei-Gerning, who had shown me the video images of my heart muscle. He said admiringly – of his own handiwork as much as of my heart – 'That's a good squeeze!' He never needed to see me again. That really was fantastic news for me.

Walking up Snowdon following the knife-edge of the Crib Goch trail wasn't that easy, but I was fit enough from all the walking I had done around Michaelston and Mwnt to make it to the summit with no trouble. It was a great day out with members of the Ramblers Association keeping us company. Mountaineering fanatic and former Cabinet member Alun Pugh (Alun had lost his seat in 2007) and my Environment Minister Jane Davidson were there as well. Doing an interview at the summit for Radio 5 live on their morning programme was the icing on the cake. If you've never had heart problems, it might be difficult to understand exactly how euphoric my feeling of full recovery was.

Soon after that, I had my long-awaited meeting with the Labour General Secretary in Wales Chris Roberts to discuss my retirement. I wanted to do the ten years, but if we had an internal election it would take up energy and money resource that really ought to be channelled into the next general election, which was due in May 2010 at the latest. My tenth anniversary on 9 February 2010 was uncomfortably close to May 2010, so in the end we settled for 9 December 2009 as a far more practical retirement date.

I said I wasn't going to endorse anyone. Whoever wanted to stand should go for it, and there would be no attempted anointment and no interference from me. Actually going and handing over the seals of office was far less difficult than others seem to surmise. It was what I had always planned, to go before I was pushed! I invited many of the journalists who had followed me around during much of that decade over to the house for a barbecue in the garden and coffee indoors. One BBC Wales blogger later commented that it was hard to believe I was really going to give up power voluntarily until that evening, when I was spotted drinking my coffee from a large mug bearing the legend, 'I'd rather be in the shed'. I think one of the grandchildren had bought it for me. It was a real grand-dad's birthday present – it even had a slot to park your dunking biscuit in! That last was most definitely not me, but 'I'd rather be in the shed' was me to a tee. Not golf. Not bowls. But the shed. And maybe with the piano stool.

After the announcement on 9 December 2009 in the Wales Millennium Centre that Carwyn Jones had been elected as my successor, I was free. I was the Assembly Member for Cardiff West, but it was Carwyn's turn now to bear that 24/7 weight on his shoulders. I know it sounds a bit fanciful, but I did finally feel my shoulders lifting up about two inches. The worry beads that had coursed around my veins for ten years weren't there anymore. I definitely felt free as a bird for the first time in almost ten years. High office – who needs it?

# ten

# No Back-Seat Driving
## 2010–2017

I WAS SEVENTY WHEN I GAVE UP the burdens of high office. I still had sixteen months to go before the third Assembly term came to an end early in 2011. My heart was giving me no problems, and I was keeping pretty strictly to my British Heart Foundation diet. I'd had the warning in 2007, and I didn't want to throw away my chances of a happy retirement by going on for too long. Happy the man for whom the bell tinkles before it tolls.

I didn't have much in the way of other health problems to spoil things, although my hearing was no longer a hundred per cent. I had been struggling to hear women's voices, particularly in the Assembly Chamber – when your hearing starts to deteriorate, it's the high-pitched sounds and the letter s that tend to go first. Sometimes, I'd have to make an educated guess at what a woman AM had asked during my weekly question session at Tuesday lunchtime. If I could see their faces, I could lip-read, which was a huge help – but if they were looking down at a piece of paper, I couldn't lip-read and just had to guess. I found it an irritation, but I don't know if anyone else noticed.

My plan was to step down from the pressures of a flat-out full-time job gradually. I had heard too many stories – of men especially – going from working all the hours God sends to doing nothing in their retirement all in one go, supposedly to enjoy their pension. But then they didn't last six months because the change in lifestyle was just too drastic. My plan was to step down from the front-bench and move to the back-benches, and then to see what other opportunities arose while taking it easy. Time for a coffee and a browse through the papers in the morning, and no rushing off to work. Every day like a Sunday morning. What could be nicer?

Although we'd struggled in the 2007 election, the Labour–Plaid Cymru coalition which had emerged from it was a reasonably stable organism. I hadn't backed either my successor Carwyn Jones or one or other of his two rivals, Edwina Hart and Huw Lewis, for the party leadership in Wales. I thought it was healthy that Labour members had a wide choice and had made up their own minds to elect Carwyn, rather than me trying to anoint a leader who would supposedly stick to my agenda and protect my legacy. Carwyn was roughly the same age as my children, so Labour had jumped a full generation in making its choice. As far as I could judge Carwyn's innermost thoughts, I guessed he would be more than happy to soldier on with the Plaid coalition, and the same would have been true if Edwina Hart had won. Huw Lewis might not have seen it in quite the same way. Huw had done me a few good turns back in the days of the two leadership contests, sometimes nipping up the two flights of stairs in the lunch hour from Labour Party Wales HQ, where he worked as an organiser on the second floor of Transport House, to my lair on the fourth floor to update me on the latest bit of skullduggery planned by the party hierarchy to spoke my wheels – but Huw had also been the only AM in the Labour Group to vote against the Plaid coalition.

I went on two back-bench committees. The one I chaired was the European and External Affairs Committee, and one I sat among the ranks was the Legislation Committee. Although I was determined not to be a back-seat driver, calling Carwyn every whipstitch, I did make a slight exception over the Children's Rights Measure, which was halfway through its legislative stages, when I finished my First Ministerial stint. The purpose behind the Measure was to incorporate the United Nations Convention on the Rights of the Child into all our laws and actions as a government. The officials had never liked it, because they feared that we would be making a rod for our own backs with queues of lawyers claiming that every move we made was in breach of the UN Convention. I had heard on the grapevine that as soon as I was out of the door, those same officials had come back and had another go at watering down the draft to restrict its application.

That watered-down version of the Children's Rights Measure then came down to the Legislation Committee for our scrutiny. The voluntary sector with a special interest in children's rights was scandalised by the weakening of the scope of the law. The committee, with me taking a strong role in pushing for reinstatement of the original phrasing, changed the wording back to what it had been when I was still First Minister, and this time around there was no further attempt was made to dilute it. Not really an example of back-seat driving, more a retired First Minister rising zombie-like from beyond the grave to restore legal wording! It was sheer chance that I was put on that committee. Nobody volunteers to be on the Legislation Committee – it's considered to be a fairly low form of Assembly pond-life. I could have stood on my dignity and told the Labour Whip that

I wasn't willing to serve, but thank goodness I duly did what I was told, and the committee did make a difference.

The top priority in those early months after I had stepped down was Julie's campaign to keep her Westminster seat in Cardiff North at the May 2010 General Election. Julie was a very popular Labour MP in a highly marginal seat, but Gordon Brown was not a popular Prime Minister. The personal dislike of him kept coming up on the doorstep, even more so after the incident in Rochdale when the microphone was accidentally left on in his car as he referred to a pensioner who had given him a difficult time as a, hysterical bigot.

Right at the end of March, on the last day of the Parliament, Julie managed to get her Private Members Bill on the Regulation of Sunbeds voted into law by a very narrow squeak. It's a very rare honour to get a Private Members Bill voted through onto the Statute Book – you have to have a fair degree of backing from the government, and you have to navigate your way past the opposition of the small handful of Tory back-benchers whose hatred of all law and regulation is such that they make it their business to block everything they can. On the very last day of the session, the two houses of Parliament and the Government have what they call the 'wash-up' session. Some draft laws fall at that stage, but Julie's Sunbeds Bill became law pending the signature of Her Majesty the Queen.

What put the top on the teapot was that Julie and I had been invited to spend that evening as guests of Her Majesty and the Duke of Edinburgh at Windsor Castle. So, as we enjoyed our pre-dinner drinks with the Royal couple and the other invitees, Julie was able to thank Her Majesty for signing her bill into law. Julie asked when exactly the document to sign had been presented before the Queen, and how many of these last-minute laws did she have to process. The Queen told us that she had pre-signed them all the previous day, and then her flunkeys and parliamentary clerks discarded the ones that didn't survive the wash-up, even though they bore the Queen's signature. She seemed to indicate approval of the sunbeds regulation law, while the Duke of Edinburgh was very much himself. He harrumphed, 'What a load of rubbish! People ought to have more sense than to fry themselves in those sunbed machines!' I was comfortable in my skin as the spouse of an MP. Being the ex-First Minister didn't really count at Windsor Castle.

Sadly, that was Julie's last day in Parliament, because she lost at the general election by 192 votes, beaten by the Conservative Jonathan Evans, a Trade Minister under John Major and an ex-Leader of the Conservative Group in the European Parliament. He told me at a social occasion six months later that the Tories had put a huge effort into winning the seat because they wanted to destroy 'Brand Rhodri Morgan'. This was all news to me – I didn't realise I had a brand – but Julie restored the status quo the following year by winning the same seat back quite easily as an Assembly Member at the 2011 elections, and then doubled her majority in the 2016 elections. If there is a Brand Rhodri Morgan, the flag is still flying thanks to Julie's campaigning skills.

But what is that brand? We should put aside all that stuff about Old Labour, New Labour, Antediluvian Labour or, as I prefer to call it, Classic Labour. With the advantage of hindsight, the Morgan brand is best summarised as Default Option Labour. In Scotland, until recent years, the default option was to vote Labour; now it's SNP. In Wales, despite the Brexit vote shock, the default option could still be to vote Labour. I hope I contributed something to the retention of that Labour loyalty by staying as close as possible to the people. As the fall-out from the Great Depression still continues, and the earnings of blue-collar workers in manufacturing and construction lags below 2007 levels, that relationship with Labour has been under huge strain – the Trump phenomenon has capitalised on disillusioned blue-collar voters in the American mid-western rust belt, while the strain in support for social democratic parties and values has hit Europe, and this is all part of the fall-out from the 2008 economic downturn. It's a struggle to retain the trust of blue-collar workers when the economic recovery hasn't reached them.

A few years ago, I had a discussion with then Labour Shadow Cabinet Minister for Welsh Affairs Owen Smith about why Labour in Wales hadn't had the catastrophic drop in support as it experienced in Scotland. He said it was because I had kept Plaid Cymru at bay – I had 'stood in Plaid's shoes', he said. He didn't mean it as a compliment, mind you. I'm an instinctive devolutionist. And that doesn't make me a crypto-Nat. There has to be a middle-ground filled by devolution, halfway between unionism and nationalism. There's nothing to apologise for in trying to define that middle-ground with enthusiasm, and I don't see why it should be treated with suspicion, especially when the example of the collapse of Scottish Labour is there to hand.

It's the other side of the coin of the mythology that I am in some way a lost sheep from the Plaid Cymru fold. Just after being elected in 1987, I was interviewed jointly with Ieuan Wyn Jones, who would be my Deputy First Minister in the Labour–Plaid Cymru coalition twenty years later. The two of us were new boys, and Gwilym Owen of BBC Radio Cymru was doing the interview from Bangor. Gwilym was an old-school interviewer, unusual in Bangor for not being an instinctive nationalist and, since he didn't know me at all, his first question completely threw me. 'Why are you Labour?' he asked, bold as brass, 'I'd have thought with your background you'd be one of those Plaid Cymru yuppies!' My reply was that my father was the son of a collier and the brother of a collier, and I could only presume that any assumption about me in various crypto-Nat forms was because my father wasn't a collier but a professor of Welsh!

Julie comes into this as well. I bumped into a Plaid Cymru councillor on the street in Dinas Powys many years ago, who was out leafleting with a party colleague new to the village. He introduced me to the new activist and said that, of course, I would have been one of them had I not been tempted away by this beautiful local girl who was strongly Labour. Well, yes, I was tempted by Julie, but I was never tempted by Plaid Cymru. Not a lost sheep at all! It's all in the perception. For some Welsh Labour MPs, there was this sense of a loss of control over Labour in the Assembly, which had emerged in the run-up to the recall conference in July 2007. Not only was there a fear of contamination by working with Plaid in the coalition government, but also of the long-term implications of the referendum to de-restrict the Assembly's power to pass laws in all the fields devolved to it.

That referendum, the third in the history of Welsh devolution was scheduled for early March 2011, two months before the Assembly elections. I was asked to chair the Yes campaign. Daran Hill was the secretary. It wasn't exactly a doddle, but compared with the nightmare of campaigning in 1979 and the struggles of the close shave of 1997, it was remarkably easy. The key was that it was supported by 95 per cent of the Welsh Conservative Party. David T. C. Davies, the former AM, now MP for Monmouth, and Chair of the Welsh Affairs Select Committee in the Commons, maintained his visceral opposition to devolution and therefore to any expansion of devolution. But really, most Conservative activists followed the pro-devolution stance of Nick Bourne, the party's leader in the Assembly. I had enjoyed the pleasure of working with Plaid and Lib Dem activists in 1997, but working with enthusiastic Tory activists in getting leaflets out was wonderfully mind-boggling.

The official No campaign to enable the BBC to maintain its general policy of a balanced presentation in a referendum campaign was taken up by Rachel Banner from, yet again, the Islwyn constituency and her 'True Wales' campaign organisation. She didn't have the authenticity and appeal that the two Rhondda housewives and leaders of the Rhondda Valley section of the No campaign, Betty Bowen and Carys Pugh, had had back in 1997. They were both very hard to counter, and were actually fifteen years ahead of their time (in purveying an anti-politics, anti-chattering classes 'we are the little people' message, they pre-empted the Brexit vote and the rise of UKIP). Rachel Banner was more highly qualified, but Betty and Carys could put themselves over as true representatives of the people, attacking the chattering classes in leafier parts of Cardiff.

We should not have been quite as surprised that the Welsh Conservatives were so active on the Yes side. They owed so much to the Assembly for revitalising the party. The Welsh Conservatives had not supported the use of a proportional representation system of voting, and had opposed the Assembly itself, but it was the Assembly that put them back in business (as it much later seemed to put UKIP *in* business). For most of the Assembly's existence, the Welsh Conservatives have only won a small handful of directly elected AMs, but that has been hugely supplemented by regional AMs, which in turn gives the party Group status in the

Assembly to employ researchers and press officers. Suddenly, the Tory party in Wales was in business. Whether that sense of owing something to the existence of the Assembly was the key for Tory support on the Yes side in the 2011 Assembly, I don't know, but it just made our task in winning the vote remarkably easy. There was a window in March 2011, and the Yes campaign was able to climb through it.

With the referendum out of the way, I could retire. I didn't have a moment's regret that I wasn't there to take advantage of the new law-making powers – nice though it might have been to be present and witness the Organ Transplant Presumed Consent going onto the Statute Book. When I haven't been writing a newspaper column and this book, off and on for the past five years, how do I spend my time? Well, aside from cutting the grass, a lunchtime sandwich and preparing an evening meal for Julie for when she returns exhausted from her self-inflicted madcap hectic schedule at the Assembly and in Cardiff North, I look after my chickens. Sunday morning soft-boiled eggs from our very own hens with toast in bed are a weekly treat.

And aside from these domestic duties, I've been Chancellor of Swansea University for five years. I can't claim the credit for the idea, but I've had a bird's-eye view of the new £450 million Bay campus taking shape on the Jersey Marine road, on the site of the old BP oil tank farm. There is a huge amount of building still going on, but several thousand students in Engineering and Business Studies are already on-site, soon to be joined by those studying Mathematics, Computer Science and Law. Actually, I can take a tiny bit of the credit. When I was in my final sixteenth months in the Assembly, the European Investment Bank (EIB) wrote to me in my position as Chair of the European & External Affairs back-bench committee, to ask if I could write to public bodies in Wales explaining that the EIB had millions of pounds available to lend for good quality low-risk infrastructure projects that would benefit Wales, its economy and society. I duly did as requested. The only body that I know to have responded was Swansea University, who ended up borrowing £120 million from the EIB at very low interest rates in two tranches. What Swansea University's top management told me was that it wasn't so much the two slugs of £60 million and the low interest rates that made the difference, but it was the way borrowing money from the EIB had opened the doors to other lenders. They all wanted to lend money coming in behind the prestige of the EIB as an institution.

There was only one dodgy moment in developing the new campus. That was when a very senior civil servant from the Assembly advised the university against developing the second campus on the grounds that it was 'too big for Wales'. Now, I've had the immense pleasure of seeing a project deemed in some circles as 'too big for Wales' come to life – on time and on budget! But it's an instructive commentary on the age-old question of whether we in Wales incline towards a self-deprecating cult of mediocrity with a fear of aiming high. A lack of real self-belief afflicts us, possibly, when it comes to doing something world-class – quite the opposite of Scotland. A retired medical professor recently raised the question with me. In the bad old days, she and I recalled the appalling treatment of Joe Jacobs in the late 1960s, who was turned down for the Chair of Paediatrics in the School of Medicine at Cardiff. He emigrated to Canada in 1969 to continue his world-class career in Toronto. As a world-class paediatrician, he was considered just too good for Wales, despite being a local boy done good. Now, that would never have happened in Scotland.

The only regret I have about not being appointed a junior Minister in the Welsh Office in 1997 is that I wasn't there to prevent the departure back to Italy of Francesco Musumeci, a truly world-class paediatric cardiac surgeon. He and the cardiologist Graham Stuart were providing a world-class service for hole-in-the-heart babies for Wales's tertiary paediatric cardiology service, just at the time when the nearest alternative service at the Bristol Royal Infirmary was collapsing because of high death rates in one of the worst scandals in the history of the NHS. Musumeci was one of my constituents, and came to my surgery to explain how he was blocked at every turn from developing the service. He wanted to do heart transplants for adults, but the medical establishment told him, 'No, we're not doing complicated stuff like heart transplants, this is Wales remember!' Musumeci was appealing for my help, but there was nothing I could do. He went back to Italy, and Graham Stuart went over the bridge to help rebuild the service in Bristol after the disaster. Paediatric heart surgery was closed down in Cardiff, never to return. I don't honestly think that whole shabby episode would have happened if the Assembly had been in existence, because of the greater level of transparency – but the Assembly was still two years away. Unlike the US Cavalry riding over the hill, we got there just too late.

I do believe we have seen an emerging change in our national self-confidence over the past couple of decades. I saw it fairly early on in the Tsunami Concert in the Millennium Stadium in 2004. We in the Assembly Government had only helped the project in a very small way, and it was really all down to the drive of the stadium manager Paul Sergeant and the musicians who took part. Twenty-one acts appeared on stage, seven of them from Wales, an even bigger musical jamboree than the one to celebrate the arrival of the Assembly in May 1997. What really brought home its significance for me was an article written by a journalist from *The Scotsman* newspaper who had come down to cover the event in 2005. His basic line was how on earth had the Welsh managed to organise something really tremendous like this when Scotland had just been frittering around on the edges. The purpose of the concert was to raise money for the tsunami victims, not to make the Scots envious, but it was a fascinating in-depth commentary on two national psychologies, one that was used to self-confidence, and another smaller nation with a deep-seated lack of it.

The Scots must have been even more envious during Euro 2016, of course, but the behaviour and national pride of the huge army of Welsh fans in Bordeaux, Toulouse, Lyon and Lens was a marvellous indicator of how far we've come. The fans all enjoyed themselves hugely, but they behaved as if they belonged on the European stage. The behaviour of Wales football fans on overseas visits was previously on a par with England fans – binge-drink and then smash the place up and fight the locals. In 2016, the Welsh fans had matched the Irish as the most popular to have in the tournament's city centres.

What then to make of the Yes to Brexit vote in the referendum? Was that a primal scream from the council estates and the former mining valleys, the have-nots in Welsh society? Or the lack of an effective media in Wales to channel a distinct debate different to England's? On the surface, the vote in Wales looked awfully similar to the vote in England. Maybe, if you dig a bit deeper, it wasn't quite so similar, what with the demographics in Wales signalling so many indicators for a high Brexit vote, including many retirement areas along the Welsh coast and many industrial areas where the normal balance between the middle-class and the working-class is just not present.

The danger for Wales post-Brexit is that the vote has released a Little Englander nationalism across Offa's Dyke which is not about wanting a return to the nation state – the nation state is the UK. It's much more about the rise of Little Englander, it's about England and not the UK, or at best England plus those pesky Celts on the fringes. More usually, it's England and sod the Scots, forget the Welsh and ignore Northern Ireland – and that isn't much of an alternative to the European Union for Wales. Actually, we may be making too much of the pro-Brexit vote in Wales. It may be no more than an expression of frustration that, eight years after the banking crisis of 2008 kicked off the depression, wages in manufacturing and construction still haven't returned to 2007 levels. But we are living in far more uncertain times than ever before, with more of a threat to the heart of devolution that Wales can find its own identity as a nation in a family of nations that make up the United Kingdom.

I've always been enthusiastic about devolution. People are normally passionate about nationalism or unionism, but a bit subdued about expressing a strength of feeling about Welsh devolution. That's because it's a middle way, and that's why it has suited me so well. I am an enthusiastic gradualist. I didn't offer charismatic leadership to Wales, but I always wanted to be sure that Wales was ready to travel in the same direction as me. I didn't want to march towards the summit of a distant mountain peak, only to look behind me to find that Wales had not followed. That was not my style.

What I hope I did do was to lead the transition from the appointed state to the elected state. Here's an illustrative story that explains what I mean. In 2003, I visited Velindre, the cancer hospital where my grandmother had been one of the very early patients. I was the First Minister so, naturally, I travelled in the official Volvo car. I entered the main reception area and the chairman of the Velindre Hospital Trust and all the Trust board members were there to meet me, the 'line-up' as they call it, for the handshake and the official photographs for the local paper, before the chairman of the board showed me around his hospital. Such moments always depressed me – they made me feel like a cross between a minor Royal and a performing monkey – definitely not like the head of a government accountable to the people of Wales. Fortunately on that day, the situation was saved by a guy in a wheelchair waiting for me at the end of the very first corridor. It was Dave Campbell, dying of cancer maybe, but with a rasping voice that I could hear loud and clear. 'Come on down, Rhodri, I'm going to show you around. I know all the patients and all the staff!' I knew Dave from when he had been a Labour councillor and a steel erector before the cancer got hold of him. We left the chairman of the board to his own devices, while Dave gave me the people's tour of the hospital. And that moment summed up for me the transition from a Wales of quangos to a Wales of direct accountability to the people.

The Wales we had before 1999 was run by people appointed on quangos. This carried with it all the overtones of acceptance of a colonial psychology. It implied that we weren't clever enough or responsible enough to run our own affairs. Of course, if we do run our own affairs we will make mistakes and learn from them – but at least they are *our* mistakes. We have taken responsibility for them. Yes, it's much easier to let England or London or their appointees in Wales make the decisions, and then we can blame them for anything that goes wrong. That's colonial psychology. But I do believe we've grown out of that now that we're well into the second decade of devolution, by gradually easing Wales forward three or four steps from the moderate amount of devolution we started with to where we are now. Others may disagree, but I hope I was the right man in the right place at the right time. Getting away from the cult of mediocrity was a key element in putting the colonial psychology behind us.

The former Health Minister Brian Gibbons is the son of the late Hugh Gibbons, who was a Fianna Fáil TD in the Irish Parliament. When Brian came with me to a British–Irish Council meeting in Dublin, the Irish contingent made a big fuss of him, having all known his father. He told them that I was the 'Welsh de Valera' – from my father's experiences during his one-year stay in Dublin in 1927–8, early in the life of the Irish Free State, he would not have considered the 'Welsh de Valera' epithet to be a compliment. But Brian certainly meant it that way. 'You know', he said, 'the Father of the Nation and all that.' Well, I never made the journey from revolutionary gun-runner to Prime Minister to President, thank goodness, so I think I'll let the de Valera issue lie.

I don't underestimate how important the crisis management period was back in 2000–1, especially foot-and-mouth, to persuade the people of Wales to take us seriously as a government rather than a talking shop. We redeemed promises made by previous governments of both colours, totally unfunded promises – I'm thinking of the Mid-Valleys Hospital in Ystrad Mynach, the Swansea Medical School, the Wales Millennium Centre, the Hafod Eryri café on Snowdon, and the Children's Hospital for Wales. We cast our net far wider than before in copying good ideas that worked. Previously, it had been England that we copied. Now, we stole the 5p plastic bag charge from Ireland, the Learn Through Play nursery curriculum from Finland, the Children's Commissioner concept from Sweden, the short-time working subsidy scheme ProAct from Germany and, after my time, the organ donor law from Belgium and Spain. On the reduction of hospital waiting times and lists, we unashamedly did continue to borrow from England. I can't think of a single Welsh innovation that was truly original, but what was important was that they were mostly innovations within the United Kingdom. That's what Wales never did before devolution, to break with colonial-style thinking.

There have been plenty of disappointments along the way, of course. The PISA results are a particularly acute form across Wales of a wider UK phenomenon of falling behind South-East Asia where, in the tiger economy countries, tiger mothers push their tiger children to achieve tigerish results. Canada has shown that Western countries can do it too. And then there was the collapse of the Defence Training College project at St Athan after the Metrix Consortium had won the preferred bidder stage, which was another huge blow. I also still wonder if I should have pushed harder for fluoridation of water.

So, when I'm not writing, I try to learn to play the piano after a break of sixty years. I'm not on the public-speaking circuit at astronomical fee levels, as some of the retired fraternity are. There's no call for speeches from ex-First Ministers of Wales. In a small way, I am in the private sector. I always wanted to have a job in the private sector, but somehow the opportunity never arose until after I retired, so I do now have a non-executive directorship in a stem cell-based biotech company, which I find very exciting because it's so different. I keep half a dozen chickens at home, three of which were hatched and looked after from birth by me. There's absolutely nothing wrong with retirement. I'm doing alright.

# Index

A55 157, 257, 281
Abbott, Diane 112
Aberaeron 117
Aberfan Memorial Fund 282
Abernant Lake Hotel 172
Abertillery 67
Aberystwyth 8, 9, 45, 62, 104, 188, 261, 300
Abraham, John 75
Abse, Leo 42
abseiling 91
Adams, Colin 76
Advisory Council for Wales 51
AEEU 147–9, 154
Afan, Emyr and Mair *see* Avanti Media scandal
Agricultural Halls 102–3
Aherne, Bertie 208, 247, 248
Airbus 167; A350 169; A380 project 167, 168
Ainger, Nick 106
Aldermaston marches 49
Alexander, Wendy 317
Allan, Tim 109, 112
Allied Steel & Wire (ASW) 217, 218, 219
Alyn & Deeside 161, 168
Amalgamated Society of Woodworkers 73
American Embassy 49

Andrews, Leighton 292
anti-apartheid movement in Cardiff 45, 49, 110
Archbishop of Wales 181
Arfon 174
Armstrong-Jones, Antony, 1st Earl of Snowdon 262
Arthur Andersen 74, 110
ASTMS 75
Ashcroft, Lord Michael 159
Ashdown, Paddy 199
Assembly *see* National Assembly for Wales/Welsh Assembly
Assembly elections *see* Welsh Assembly elections
Assisted Areas 55, 57
Associated British Ports (ABP) 180, 190, 191
Association of University Teachers (AUT) 33, 71, 72
Attlee, Clement 20, 27, 83, 256
Australia 106, 163, 170, 173, 246, 262, 263, 276
Australian Republic Referendum 173
Avanti Media scandal 253–4
Aviva 191

BAe Systems 167–8 169
Baglan Energy Park 163–4

Baker, Kenneth 95
Baker, Stanley 76
Balls, Ed 317
Bangor-on-Dee 215, 216
Banks, Tony 84
Bannister, Roger 58
Barber, Tony 72
Barnett Formula 171, 197, 315, 317
Barrett, Lorraine 141, 142
Barron, Kevin 88
Barry 26, 27, 44, 54, 64, 65, 80, 92, 95, 240, 298; Community Hospital 111
Basildon 95, 96
Bastogne (Battle of the Bulge) 138
Bates, Mick 222
BBC 1, 9, 26, 70, 102, 126, 290, 333; *Ten O'Clock News* 255; BBC Radio Cymru 332; BBC Wales 7, 46, 72, 207, 250, 251, 277, 278, 308, 324, 325, 328; Board of Governors 107; Director-General 97; Gallery/ *Newsnight* 47, 135, 207; *Question Time* 261; *Dr Who* 277: *see also Today* programme
Beckett, Margaret 115, 132, 232–3, 240, 265
Beer, Professor Sam 39, 50
Belfast 208, 238
Benn, Tony 147
Berkeley, California 40
Bevan, Aneurin (Nye) 4, 20, 81, 256; 'Nye for Prye' 49, 55
Bevan, Bill 71, 72
Bevins, Anthony 82
BHP 70
Birt, John 97
Bishop of Monmouth 181: *see also* Williams, Rowan
Bishop, Malcolm 273
Black, Peter 292
Blackhurst, Chris 112
Blaenau Gwent 143, 148, 161, 225, 274, 287; constituency Labour Party 143; council 59, 201, 202
Blair, Cherie 88, 94, 116, 178, 205, 206, 211

Blair, Hazel and Leo 101, 102, 174
Blair, Tony 18, 30, 37, 42, 60, 61, 81, 83, 85, 96, 97, 102, 104, 106–13, 115, 116, 118, 119, 120, 134, 138, 139, 159, 160, 161, 163, 171, 173, 182, 189, 195, 199, 204, 205, 206, 207; Alun Michael leadership 131–6, 144–6, 148, 149, 151–3; Alun Michael resignation 177–8; Blair's babes 113; impact on the Assembly elections 157; Iraq 48, 100, 152, 256, 260; John Smith, death of 101–3; NHS, attitude towards 258; Pete the Priest 173–4; Rhodri's appointment as First Secretary 182, 183; Ron Davies leadership 123–9; Rhodri's snub 113–14; Rhodri's reflections 313–14; working for Blair 86–8, 93–4
Blunkett, David 205
Boateng, Paul 81, 325
Boeing 167–9
Bold, Andrew 172
Booth, Cherie *see* Blair, Cherie
Bourne, Nick 197, 248, 265, 291, 333
Bournemouth (Labour Party Conference) 68, 86, 97, 262, 263
BP 81, 163, 271, 334
Braggins, John 139
Braithwaite, Sir Roderick 99
Brandon, Jim 104
Brecon Jazz Festival 236
Brecon & Radnor Constituency Labour Party 104, 252
Bremner, Rory 210, 211
Brennan, Kevin 101, 121, 124, 128, 131, 135, 137–40, 149, 151, 154, 194, 199, 207, 313
Bridgend 23, 34, 73, 86, 148, 175, 228, 274, 277
Brighton (Labour Party Conference) 54, 103, 118, 120, 133, 147, 200, 201, 208
Bristol 53, 65, 96, 141, 267, 335
Britax Rumbold 166

British Legion 22, 90, 278
British Rail 49, 57
British Steel Corporation 58
Brooks, Jack (Lord Brooks of Tremorfa) 42, 45, 67, 89
Broughton 167–8, 169
Brown, Craig 84
Brown, Gordon 42, 86, 96, 101, 102, 111, 112, 114, 127, 132, 171–2, 179, 211, 242, 243, 258, 269, 270, 313, 314, 315, 316–18, 319, 320, 321, 327, 331
Brown, Nick 114
Brown, Tony 216
Brunker, Pat 299–300
Brussels 20, 58, 61, 62, 63, 65, 68, 70, 71, 212, 227, 228
Bryant, John 216, 217
Brymbo 169
Budget 256, 285 (National Assembly for Wales) 171, 174, 198, 199, 202, 213, 258, 267, 282, 296, 319
Burgham, John 118
Burns, Dave 84
Burton, Richard 189
Bush, George W. 48, 100, 257, 314
Butler, Rosemary 161, 200–2

Cabinet: Lib Dem coalition 200–2, 212, 231; Plaid coalition 300–1, 306, 307, 312, 321, 324; Shadow Cabinet 86, 87, 88, 93, 94, 101, 112, 113, 122, 127, 314; UK 20, 22, 48, 51, 87, 104, 107, 114, 120, 121, 125, 127, 204, 245, 253, 261–2, 313; Welsh Assembly 126, 143, 149, 153, 159, 160, 161, 172, 174, 175, 180, 196, 200–1, 203, 213, 214, 247, 259, 267, 273, 290, 296
Cabinet Secretary 194–5, 199, 212, 213, 226, 245, 259, 293, 295
Caernarfon 40, 104, 293
Caerphilly 55, 122, 123, 129, 222, 224
Cairns, Alun 218
Callaghan, Jim 42, 44, 45, 46, 47, 49, 50, 66, 69, 72, 81, 91, 179, 277;

Chancellor 48, 54; stepping down as MP 67
Callaghan, Michael 47
Campaign for Nuclear Disarmament (CND) 49
Campbell, Alistair 116, 129, 145–6, 208, 238, 248, 251
Canterbury 182
Canton 56, 68, 74
Cardiff 1, 50, 92, 104, 108, 161, 193, 199, 201, 208; 36 Churchill Way 42; Charles Street 42; Alexandra Hotel 43, 45; Angel Hotel 75; Beti Rhys's bookshop, Castle Arcade 34, 137; as capital city 55; Canton Police Station 56; Cardiff Docks 6, 7, 204; Cardiff East MP (1945) 20; Cardiff Fraud Squad 50; Castle Arcade 137, 140, 144; Castle Gate 122; Churchill's Hotel 101; City Hall 59, 108, 190, 191; Coal Exchange 220; Conway Road 69, 70; Cornwall pub 226; Cowbridge Road 57, 73, 74; Cyncoed Road 43; East Moor steelworks 58, 59, 61, 63; economic history of 55; ethnic diversity of 55, 56; European assistance 55, 64; European Commission Office, Cathedral Road 61, 62, 63, 65, 70; European Summit (1998) St David's Hotel 107, 150, 154; GMB Regional HQ Newport Road 153; Gordon Road, Lord Mayor's official residence 21, 22; Marcello's pizza 137, 144; Market 24; Glamorgan cricket ground 25; Marriot Hotel 91; Ninian Park 76; Ocean Club, Tremorfa 43; Old Arcade pub, Church Street 14; Plasnewydd Ward 56; Railway Workingmen's Club 219; Rhiwbina 93; Roath 56; Royal Infirmary 29; Royal Mint, Llantrisant 51; Rugby World Cup 173; Sophia Gardens 45, 46; Splott 46, 49; Temple of Peace 188; Tiger Bay 46; Transport

House, Cathedral Road 75, 99, 122, 134, 135, 140, 223, 298, 330; twinned with Stuttgart 90: *see also* Canton; Cardiff Bay; Cardiff City Hall; Cardiff University; Cathays Park; Chapter Arts Centre; Ely; Fairwater; Grangetown; Llandaff; Morganstown; Radyr; Riverside; Roath

Cardiff Bay 107, 160, 175, 180, 189, 192, 193, 195, 204, 295

Cardiff Bay Barrage 79, 84, 86, 89, 194

Cardiff Bay Development Corporation 89, 107

Cardiff Central 72, 86, 93, 122, 125, 141, 153

Cardiff Chamber of Commerce 164

Cardiff City Council 50, 59, 99, 133, 141, 149, 153, 179, 190, 191, 203–4, 215, 221, 231, 252, 278; City Planning Department 50, 53

Cardiff City Hall 59, 75, 108, 109, 190, 191, 204, 221, 241, 260, 279

Cardiff North 41, 42, 44, 54, 72, 89, 93, 113, 116, 125, 141, 157, 160, 177, 272, 316, 331, 334

Cardiff RFC 25

Cardiff South & Penarth 42, 43, 44, 46, 54, 67, 72, 125, 133, 141, 142, 161

Cardiff Technical College 72

Cardiff West 27, 57, 67, 72, 73, 74, 75, 76, 95, 96, 101, 122, 125, 133, 141, 152, 155, 157, 194, 199, 200, 245, 272, 288, 313, 328

Cardiff University 43, 149, 196, 244, 270, 282, 283, 296; Student's Union 43

Cardigan 198

Carmarthenshire Adult Education Residential Centre, Ferryside 74

Carmarthen by-election (1966) 15

Carmarthen East and Dinefwr 145, 158

Carr, Robert 262

Cathays Park 72, 104, 128, 159, 163, 166, 186, 188, 189, 192, 193, 195

Cathcart, Earl 60, 78

Central Electricity Generating Board 87

Chapman, Christine 160

Chapman, Sydney 77

Chapter Arts Centre 56

Charles, Prince of Wales 165, 210, 271

Chataway, Chris 55, 58

Chernobyl 71

Chief Whip: Alistair Goodlad 263; Andrew Davies 159–60, 175–7; Jane Hutt 267; Nick Brown 114

Chilcott Inquiry 100

Child Support & Disability Living Allowance 99

Chris John Estate Agents 43

Christian Broadcasting Fellowship 207

Church of England 181 206

Church in Wales 16, 181, 241, 248, 249

Churchill, Winston 20, 23, 83, 101, 138

city regions (Severnside/Humberside/Tayside) 53

Civil Service/servants 14, 50, 51, 54, 55, 56, 58, 62, 87, 89, 99, 104, 105, 106, 108, 126, 128, 144, 151, 163, 165, 167, 181, 186, 187, 189, 190, 193, 194, 195, 196, 227, 229, 232, 233, 234, 254, 257, 260, 273, 276, 278, 283, 289, 295, 316, 317, 318, 321, 325, 326, 327, 334

Clapham Common 119, 123, 125–7, 133, 144, 160, 169, 193, 222

Clark, Bill 47

Clark, Helen 295, 297, 327

Clause Four 103–4, 112

Clement, John 51

Clinton, Bill 163

Clwyd, Ann 62, 97

Clwyd South 73, 74

Clwyd West 98, 150, 157

Cobbett, William 96

Cobert, Carol 69

COBRA 205, 206, 324

Common Market 63

Connolly, Brian 61

Conservative Party, The *see* individual politician references

contraceptive pill 53
Conway, Lawrence 176, 194, 195, 196,
    199, 201, 212, 226, 245, 259, 295,
    302, 306, 325
Conwy 185
Cornwall 171
Cook, Robin 65, 79, 101, 106, 108, 112,
    132
Cooney, Bill 164
Cooper, Graham 39, 40
Cooper, Jilly 140
Countryside Alliance 326–9
Corbyn, Jeremy 112, 114
Cornford, John 110
Costin, Dr W. C. 36
Cox, Jo 100
Crickhowell House 178, 181, 189
Cromer, Lord 48
Crowley, Julie 172, 177
Crowley, Noel 228–30
Cuban Missile Crisis 38, 39
Cunningham, Jack 95
Curtis, Brian 223
Cwmbrân 118, 166, 237
Cymdeithas Gymraeg Pontrhydyfen
    188–9
Cynon Valley 155, 158, 160, 308

d'Albuquerque, Professor 15
Dafis, Cynog 170
Dafydd ap Gwilym 15, 33
Dahl, Roald 7, 219, 220
Daily Express 80, 95
Daily Mail, The 80, 95, 102
Daily Post 164, 165, 168, 169
Daily Telegraph, The 80
Damazer, Mark 116
Daniels, Kenny 153
Darling, Alistair 77, 103, 315
Dartford-Thurrock Crossing Bill 77, 79
David, Wayne 41, 121, 127, 139, 155,
    158, 159, 180
Davidson, Jane 90, 143, 155, 157, 202,
    212, 254, 327
Davies, Andrew 159, 161, 175, 176, 177,
    180, 231, 243, 254, 281

Davies, Angharad 128
Davies, D. T. M. 51, 52, 55
Davies, David T. C. 158, 234, 333
Davies, Huw Irranca 252–3, 274
Davies, Janet 218
Davies, Jocelyn 297
Davies, Ron 41, 96, 101, 104, 105,
    106, 112, 118, 119, 120, 132, 138,
    140, 143, 144, 145, 149, 153, 169,
    185, 189, 190, 193, 197, 198, 199,
    202, 222–3, 224, 226, 229, 275, 279;
    Chair of Economic Development
    Committee 160, 165, 168, 170, 253;
    leadership contest 119–33
Davies, Teifion 118
Davignon Plan for the steel industry 63
Department for Communities and
    Local Government (DeCLoG)
    162–3
Department for Trade and Industry
    (DTI) 55, 56, 58, 163
Department of Energy 87, 88
Deputy First Minister: Mike German
    200, 213, 228, 229, 291; Ieuan Wyn
    Jones 306, 307, 311, 312, 322
Deputy Ministers 203, 212
Deputy Presiding Officer 159, 160, 202,
    222, 259
Devolution: development of LP
    position for Wales 1990s 104–5;
    differing views across Wales
    168; diverging LP policies 109;
    foundation stone 50; maturing
    257–8, 264; opposition support for
    182; reaction of UK Government
    departments 162; settling down
    187, 192, 198, 203; UK media
    coverage of 206–8, 210; views
    within the Welsh Government
    civil service 194, 195, 196
Devonald, Bryn 73
Dewar, Donald 81, 82, 101, 106, 118,
    120, 121, 127, 182, 205
Dewhirst 198
Dexter, Ted 46, 47, 48
Dimas, Stavros 204

Direct Labour Organisations 153, 154
Dixon, Don 98
Dinas Powys 53, 54, 56, 64, 65, 79, 80,
    99–100, 332; Millbrook Road 61;
    Youth Club 90
Dobson, Frank 88
Dodd, Ken 96
Downing Street 115, 126, 131, 135, 148,
    161, 163, 177–8, 193, 208, 211, 212,
    220, 238, 251, 260, 270, 297, 313,
    314, 317, 321; switchboard 115, 134,
    135; reception 148
Drakeford, Mark 141, 142, 199, 200,
    201, 242, 243, 250, 295, 296, 297,
    306, 309, 312
Driver and Vehicle Licensing Agency
    (DVLA) 51
Duncan, Smith, Iain 263
Dŵr Cymru 246
Dylan Thomas Centre, Swansea 5

Eales, John 173
Ebbw Vale: constituency 4; steelworks
    58, 63
Ecclestone, Bernie 114–15
Economic Development and European
    Affairs (Assembly Secretary for)
    159, 167, 175, 197
Economic Development Committee
    160, 165, 168, 170, 253
Edinburgh 6, 55, 66, 101, 176, 187, 193,
    199, 208, 317
Eisteddfod, Inter-College 3
Eisteddfod, National 13, 264, 312
Edwards, Gareth 25
Edwards, Richard 158, 255
Edwards, Huw (Labour candidate) 95
Edwards, Huw (television presenter)
    255
Electoral Commission 47
Electoral reform 183
Electricity, privatisation of supply 85,
    87, 89, 99
Elias, Gerard 272–3, 326
Elis-Thomas, Lord Dafydd 176, 177,
    179, 195, 210, 222, 257, 259

Elizabeth, The Queen Mother 23, 284
Elizabeth II, Queen of Great Britain
    and Northern Ireland 23, 86, 162,
    173, 210, 211, 270–2, 312, 331
Ely 21, 57, 73, 75, 76, 91, 92, 95, 96, 219;
    'Ely Bread Riots' 91, 96; branch LP
    68; council estate 57 69, 249; link
    road 64; Pethybridge Road Youth
    Centre 91; Youth Club 90
Emlyn-Jones, Alun 27, 44
Energlyn, Lord 60
Energy Select Committee 85
England, Joe 65
englyn 189
Essex County Council 78
Essex, Sue 141, 160, 177, 212, 214, 246,
    282
Ethelred the Unready 111
Euro currency 98, 109, 198, 216, 242,
    243, 283
European Commission 20, 59, 61, 62,
    63, 65, 66, 68, 70, 71, 147, 204, 254,
    267; Wales receptions 64, 65, 66
European Council of Ministers 204
European Economic Community
    (EEC) 64
European Parliament elections 63
European referendum: (1975) 20, 63;
    (2016) 336
European Regional Development
    Fund 64, 171, 198
European Social Fund 68, 254, 321
European Summit 107–8, 204
Eurosceptics 98, 104, 111
Evans, Carys 264
Evans, Delyth 102, 150, 172, 181
Evans, Gwynfor (Carmarthen by-
    election 1966) 15
Evans, Helena 174
Evans, Jonathan 331
Evans, Sir Richard 168–9
Evans, Roger 95
Evans, Roger Warren 143

Fabian Society 50
Fairwater 69

Falconer, Dr Alan 34, 35, 39
Fawkes, Guy 49, 79, 113
Federal Reserve 48
Feld, Val 122, 170, 253, 255
Fellowes, Danny 151
ffitch, Sir Rodney 80
Finance Bill (1987–8) 82
Finance Minister 160, 174, 282, 291
Fire Brigades Union (FBU) 147, 242, 243
First Minister of Scotland 82, 118, 121, 193, 204, 311, 315, 317, 318
First Minister of Wales 10, 15, 18, 32, 37, 45, 82, 123, 164, 165, 169, 172, 181, 185, 193, 197, 200, 201, 204, 205, 208, 209, 211, 216, 221, 222, 233, 241, 245, 251, 257, 270–2, 280, 282, 283, 285, 287–94, 296, 303, 304, 306, 311, 313, 315, 318, 321, 325, 326, 330, 331, 337
First Secretary 120, 124, 125, 127, 131, 151, 158, 171, 172, 174, 175, 178, 179, 180, 181, 182, 186, 187, 188, 189, 191, 193, 195, 197
Fish, Michael 81
Fishguard 13, 198
Flynn, Paul 78, 143, 153, 161
Follett, Barbara 79
Follett, Ken 79
Follick, Frank 40
Foot, Michael 64
Ford Motor Company 173, 277
Ford, Anna 97
Ford, Phil 136
Foreign and Commonwealth Office (FCO) 40, 52, 53, 100, 107, 108, 162, 204, 268
Formula 1 motor racing 102, 114, 115
Forster Education Act (1870) 18
Forte, Rocco 107
France 10, 70, 162, 173, 224, 228
Freedom of Information 203, 239
Freemasons 272
French Government 167, 268
Frost, David 97

Galbraith, Sam 206, 254
Gale, Anita 154
Galloway, George 77
Garrard, Ann 145, 158
GE 163–4
General Elections: (1945) 14, 23, 27; (1951) 20, 26, 46, 47; (1955) 28; (1959) 42; (1964) 46; (1966) 41–2, 52, 54, 64; (1970) 42, 54; (1974) 50; (1979) 64, 179; (1983) 64, 73; (1987) 74; (1992) 88, 94, 95; (1997) 74 108, 112, 113, 199; (2001) 232, 234, 236, 252; (2005) 225, 265, 266, 274, 285; (2010) 89, 285, 328, 331
General Management Committee (GMC): Cardiff South & Penarth 44, 48; Vale of Glamorgan 54
George, Lloyd 16, 27, 44
Germany 6, 34, 70, 100, 115, 167, 260–1, 321, 338
German, Mike 179, 182, 200–1, 212–14, 228–31, 247, 291, 292, 321
Gething, Vaughan 150
Gibbons, Brian 267, 337
Gibbons, Hugh 337
Glais, Swansea valley (father's family) 1, 5, 16, 24, 145
Glamorgan cricket ground 25
Glan-y-Môr Secondary School, Swansea 5
Glasgow University 82
GMB 69, 142, 147, 153–4
Goodway, Russell 115, 190, 204, 252, 253
Goodwin, Dick 38
Gorbachev 100
Gould, Philip 117
Government of Wales Act: (1998) 170, 196, 197, 199, 279; (2006) 275, 279, 290, 298, 311
Gow, Ian 100
Gower 41, 160
Gower, Sir Raymond 27, 28, 44, 54, 64
Grangetown 67, 226; *Grangetown Gondolier* 84; link road 64
Greenham Common 49

Gregory, Janice (née Powell) 78, 252
Gren 107
Grocott, Bruce 126
Grosvenor Waterside 180–1, 189
Griffiths, Ceri 62
Griffiths, Gareth 34
Griffiths, Jim 51, 52, 128
Griffiths, John 175, 176, 216
Griffiths, Lesley 122, 222
Griffiths, Peter 318
Griffiths, Win 62, 101, 112
Grist, Ian 86
Gruffydd, Professor W. J. 14
*Guardian, The* 93, 119, 144, 211, 212, 255
Gullam, Malcolm 123
Gwaelod-y-Garth: Welsh
     Congregationalist Chapel 12; *The*
     *Englishman who went up a Hill but*
     *came down a Mountain* 22
Gwynne Jones, Alun (Lord Chalfont) 38
Gwyther, Christine 158, 161, 170, 172,
     201

Hague, William 107, 108, 115, 276, 277
Hamilton, Neil 66
Hain, Peter 95, 119, 125, 129, 149, 150,
     153, 154, 247, 257, 265, 268, 275,
     298, 300
Hancock, Bleddyn 252
Hancock, Jim 118, 133
Harry Ramsden's fish and chips 186
Harle, Annabelle 148
Harlech beach 60
Hart, Edwina 160, 161, 174, 176, 191,
     221, 267, 269, 326, 330
Hart, Julian Tudor 79
Harvard 18, 35, 37–9, 50, 66, 146, 316
Hattersley, Roy 85, 89, 112, 255
Haverfordwest 104
Hay Literature Festival 235, 320
Hayes Tabernacle, Cardiff (Baptist
     Sunday School) 12, 22
Haynes, Frank 88
Hayward, Byron 143
Healey, Denis 147
Heathcock pub 207

Heath, Ted 57, 59, 63
Hemingway, Ernest 30
Henderson, Doug 110
Hengoed 62
Hennessey, Frank 84
Henry VIII powers 163
Heseltine, Michael 83
Hicks, Robert 84
Hiles, Herbert 15
Hill, Daran 333
Hill, David 85
Hines, Mike 178–9, 199
Hodgson, Pete 297–8
Hoey, Brian 70
Holmes, Ann 80
Honeyball, Mary 69
Hoon, Geoff 284
Hopkins, Ken 104–5, 108
Hopkins, Tony 53
Houlston, Gordon 278–9
House of Commons 1, 19, 42, 45, 58,
     73, 80, 81, 82, 84, 87, 90, 102–3,
     113, 119, 126, 146, 149, 163, 170,
     181, 202, 208, 212, 225, 275, 300;
     Cloisters 78
House of Lords, views on non-elected
     chamber 60
House of Lords Scrutiny Committee,
     evidence to 59
House of Lords 116, 147, 222, 262; 1
     Old Palace Yard 78–9, 113
Housing Bill 82, 84
Horton, Nick 129
Howard, Michael 221, 263
Howarth, Alan 83, 223
Howells, Kim 95, 97, 103
*HTV* 125 (*Wales This Week*) 106–7
Hughes, Aneurin Rhys 62
Hughes, Cledwyn 52
Humphrys, John 49, 146
Hunt, David 89, 193
Hunter, Anji 94, 101, 108–9, 131
Hurst, Greg 209, 293
Hurst, Michael 35
Hutt, Jane 160, 161, 200, 201, 267, 293,
     298, 309

Hybrid Bill: Cardiff Bay Barrage 84, 85, 89; Thurrock-Dartford 77, 79

Illsley, Eric 78, 113
IMF 48, 77, 79, 246
*Independent, The* 72, 82, 112
Industrial Development Advisory Boards 57, 58, 167
Ingham, Sir Bernard 116, 208
Ingram, Adam 81
Institute of Welsh Affairs 153, 188, 195, 257, 292
IRA 3, 57
Irvine, Lord 116, 273
Islwyn 133, 157, 252, 255, 257, 259, 299, 316, 333
ISTC 147, 218–19
ITV 125 (Wales) 177, 294, 325

James, Stan 66
Jenkins, Arthur 20
Jenkins, Clive 75
Jenkins, Roy 20, 62, 66, 182–3, 199
Jewish ex-Servicemen's League 90
James, C. L. R. 42
Joint Ministerial Committee (JMC) 146, 195, 205, 318
Jones, Ann 176
Jones, Carwyn 175, 176, 177, 232, 233, 234, 237, 239, 270, 328, 330
Jones, Dan 28
Jones, Sir Derek 163, 276
Jones, Elin 306, 312
Jones, Gareth 234
Jones, Gwilym 93, 272
Jones, Dr Gwyn 106–7
Jones, Sir Harry 213, 228, 230
Jones, Ieuan Wyn 291, 302, 308, 311, 313, 332; coalition talks 295–7; Deputy First Minister 307, 312, 322
Jones, Ivor (Mr and Mrs) 43
Jones, Jeff 228–30, 252
Jones, Jon Owen 72, 93, 153–4
Jones, Maggie 225, 274
Jones, Neil 234

Jones, Tom (Deputy Cabinet Secretary) 4
Jones, Tony 234
Jones, Wyndham 22
Johnson, President Lyndon Baines 48
Jospin, Lionel 173

Karlin, Miriam 75
Keays, Sara 87
Kennedy, Bruce 106–7
Kennedy, Charles 177–8
Kensington by-election 80
Kent County Council 78
Kiernan, Jo 177
Kinsale Hall Hotel, Flintshire 111
Kinnock, Glenys 45, 65, 75, 76, 86, 96, 140, 252
Kinnock, Neil 41, 42, 43, 44, 45, 46, 58, 64, 67, 74, 75, 79, 80, 81, 85–8, 96, 101–3, 112, 150, 157, 208, 252, 255, 314; 1987 Cardiff election rally 75, 76; 1992 General Election 95; becomes leader 6; 1985 Bournemouth speech 86; flat with Rhodri 27; Plaid coalition 299; resignation 97
Kinnock, Rachel 75
Kinnock, Stephen 75
Kitson, Paddy 42, 43, 44, 49, 140
Kuwait 164–5

Labour Group 151, 153, 170, 172, 175–7, 180, 203, 221, 224, 226, 227, 298, 299, 330
Labour Party 39, 44, 45, 50, 51, 54, 65, 71, 72, 82, 87, 101, 115, 127, 139, 164, 223, 227, 257, 285; Annual Conference 54, 55, 56, 65, 68, 82, 86, 97, 103, 111, 112, 118, 120, 133, 147, 200, 201, 205–6, 208, 251, 260, 262, 263; Blair-Prescott ticket 138–9; Campaign Group 112; Clause Four 103–4, 112; devolution 97, 104–5, 110–11; General Secretary 124; how to get on 42; machine 135, 173; National Executive Committee

101, 133, 134; newly-formed 7;
Solidarity Group 112, 255; Tribune
Group 112, 255
Labour Party Wales *see* Welsh Labour
Lake District 96
Lampeter 198
Lancaster House 204, 205
Latsis, John 111
Lavernock Point 54
Law, Peter 161, 172, 180, 201, 202, 224,
225, 226, 274, 287
Law, Trish 274
Lawson, Nigel 72, 81, 85
Legislative Competence Order (LCO)
275: *see also* Government of Wales
Act 2006
Leo Abse & Cohen 42, 154
Lerenius, Bo 190
Levene, Lord Peter 284
Lewis, Inspector 92
Lewis, Liz 151, 153
Lewis, Saunders 13, 14, 15
LG investment 107, 166, 276, 277, 285
Lib Dems *see* Liberal Democrats
Liberal Democrats 93, 104, 105, 172,
177, 200, 208, 257, 287; coalition
199–201, 212–14, 228–30, 247,
255–6, 297; National Assembly Lib
Dems 176, 177–9, 182, 183, 198, 199;
Rainbow Alliance 290–4, 298, 311
Liberal Party 16, 18, 27, 44, 62, 64, 65,
66, 83, 146, 272, 291; University of
Wales MP (1943) 13, 14; Annual
Conference Llandudno (1982) 64
Liddell, Helen 163
Littlewoods (Cardiff) 45, 55, 56
Livingstone, Ken 78, 112
Livsey, Richard 105, 199
Llandaff Cathedral 161, 279
Llandaff Cathedral School, Cardiff 7
Llandough Hospital 111, 302, 304
Llandrindod Wells 208, 209, 291, 293
Llandudno 64, 65, 208, 209, 280, 281,
293
Llanelli 51, 143, 145, 157, 158, 252, 255,
257, 259, 263, 294, 303

Llanfairpwllgwyngyllgogerychwyrn-
drobwll-llantysiliogogogoch 165
Llangefni 233
Llangollen 215, 322
Llanigon 235–6
Llanstephan Castle 74
Llantrisant 51, 55, 58
Llewellyn, Chris 145, 158
Lloyd, Peter 107
Lloyd, Val 255
Llŷn Peninsula 13, 174
Local Government Ombudsman 201,
202
Local Government Reform Bill (Wales)
104
Lomax, Rachel 106, 144, 190
London Marathon 90
Lords and Commons Tennis Club 83
Lucas-SEI 167

M4 65, 73, 93, 94, 126, 157, 218, 222,
249, 257, 260, 274, 281; Kinnock car
crash 65
Maastricht Treaty 98
Mabbutt, Dr 35
MacDonald, Lord of Gwaun Ysgor 27
Mackay, Andrew 81
Maesteg 117
Major, John 86, 98, 101, 102, 104, 108,
111, 115, 144, 185, 211, 221, 263, 331
*Mail on Sunday, The* 70
Mandelson, Peter 95–6, 97, 102–3, 109,
112, 199, 255, 314, 321
Mann, Tom (leader of 1889 London
Dock Strike) 12
Manning, David 99, 100
Marek, John 140, 202–3, 222, 224, 226,
257, 259
Margaret, Princess, Countess of
Snowdon 262
Marks and Spencer 198
Marquand, Hilary 20
Marquand, David 20
Massey, Glenn 166, 168
Maxton, John 88
Mates, Michael 83

Matthews, Jack 25
Matthews, Sir Terry 210, 269
Maudling, Reggie 46, 72
Mawhinney, Brian 121
May, Theresa 60, 275, 324
McAlpine 111
McAuliffe, General Anthony 138
McCarthy, Mike 140
McConnell, Jack 193, 269
McDonagh, Margaret 124, 138
McFadden, Pat 135
McFall, John 78, 113
McGuinness, Martin 315
McLeish, Henry 193
Melbourne Olympics (1956) 58
Menzies, Sir Stewart 205, 206
Merseyside 89, 152, 171
Mid & West Wales Regional List 144,
    150, 155, 158, 161, 181, 259
Michael, Alun 18, 72, 78, 79, 119, 126,
    132, 133, 168, 169, 171, 181–3,
    185, 186, 201, 202, 213, 224, 227,
    228, 259, 298; leadership contest
    138–51, 153–5; Assembly elections
    158, 159; the first Cabinet 159–62;
    resignation 172–80
Michaelston-le-Pit 79, 94, 129, 130, 133,
    176, 187, 188, 189, 194, 212, 259,
    294, 298, 327
Middlehurst, Tom 161, 168, 170, 172,
    180, 201, 227, 228
Miliband, David 109, 112
Miliband, Ed 124, 317
Millbank 101, 126, 139, 145, 207
Migration Watch 53
Militant 68, 74
*Mirror, The* 97, 110–11, 151–2
Mitchell, Andrew 85
Mitchell, Austin 85
Monmouth 181; by-election 94, 95;
    constituency 158, 333
Monmouthshire 4, 51, 234
Moore, Will 32, 33, 34, 36, 43
Moores, Peter 56
Moreia Chapel, Ynystawe 3, 5, 19
Moseley, Elwyn 201

Morden, Jessica 223, 237
Morgan (family name) 9
Morgan, Reverend Bob 92
Morgan, Esther (great-great-great-
    grandmother) 18
Morgan, Dame Gillian 326–7
Morgan, Gwyn 61–3
Morgan (née Rees), Huana (mother)
    1–11, 16, 21, 23, 24, 27, 29, 30,
    31, 40, 41, 44, 71, 77, 86, 230 320;
    Saunders Lewis 13; Welsh poetry
    and politics 15
Morgan, Hubert 68
Morgan, Hywel **Rhodri**
    1992 GE defeat 95–6
    1997 referendum campaign 116–17:
        *see also* referendum
    1999 Assembly election results 157–9
    2005 Labour Party manifesto,
        waiting list targets 265–7
    2011 referendum 264: *see also*
        referendum
    abseiling 91
    Alun Michael's first Cabinet
        159–62, 172
    Alun Michael's resignation 172,
        176, 179, 180
    announcement of retirement 285,
        288–9
    Awkward Squad/gang of three
        221–7
    becoming a PPS 85
    becoming an MP 74–6
    becoming First Secretary 180–3
    being 'Labour' 332
    birth 6
    Blair hustings in Cardiff 101–2
    Blair snub 113–14
    Blair relationship 205, 243, 313–14
    Blairite / Brownite 102–3, 171–2
    Britishness 25
    build up to Alun Michael
        resignation 171–2
    Cardiff Bay Barrage 79, 84, 86, 89,
        194
    Cathays Park *see* Cathays Park

civil service 51, 58, 194–6, 326:
see also civil service
Classic Labour 332
Clear Red Water 188, 247–52
coalition with the Lib Dems
200–31, 247
coalition with Plaid Cymru 30,
295–300, 306–13, 322, 330
cousin Nia 141
cousin-in-law Ray 145
crypto-nat 298, 332
D-Day commemorations 269–70
deference deficiency 74
early experiences of political
figures 20, 21
early ill-health 9, 10
early political influences 15, 16,
26, 27
early political life 42
economic and political view of
Cardiff in 1970s 55, 59
eleven-plus 22
Elizabeth II, Queen of Great Britain
and Northern Ireland 270
entering frontline politics 66, 67
evidence to House of Lords
Scrutiny Committee 59
finding his feet as an MP 77–89
first experiences of LP in Cardiff
43, 44, 45, 46, 47
first job, WEA 41
first leadership contest 119–25
First Minister 32, 37
first and last months as First
Minister 185–8, 204, 328
first political meeting 27, 28
first Shadow team job for Blair 87–8
fishing for salmon 60
Five Fs 214–18
foot-and-mouth crisis (FMD) 214,
232–6
getting to grips with being an
Assembly Secretary 163–9
Goon Show, The 26
Gordon Brown, reflections on his
premiership 313–21

Harvard 37, 38, 39
heart trouble 301–8
holidays see Mwnt
House of Commons maiden
speech 19
House of Lords, views on
un-elected chamber 60
how to write a speech 210
influence of Julie on his career 56,
66
Inter-Faith Forum 240
joined the Labour Party 42, 44,
140
Julie see Morgan, Julie
Labour leadership contest 330
Maastricht vote 98
manifesto (2005) 265–7
marriage, children and move to
Dinas Powys 53, 54, 56, 61, 68
media coverage 70–1, 72, 84, 106–7,
108, 110, 112, 115, 134, 188, 204,
206–8, 211, 269, 325
meeting Blair about leadership
126–7, 131
meeting Julie 43
move to the DTI 56
moving to Cardiff 43, 59
naming of 8
National Labour Party Conference
54, 65, 68, 112, 120, 147, 205,
206: see also Labour Party
Annual Conference
National Service 35, 36
new Assembly building 189–92:
see also Senedd
NHS 10, 26
not going to Winchester College
29, 30
not in the ministerial team 109,
112, 113
Objective One funding see
Objective One
Oxford University 32–7
Public Administration Select
Committee 114, 116
quangos see quangos

Rainbow/Anybody but Labour
  (ABL) coalition 208, 209, 287,
  290–4
reflections on relationship with
  Blair 173–4, 313–14
religion 12, 22
rugby *see* rugby
run up to second leadership
  contest 133–6
running 57, 75, 90, 110, 187
schooling 22, 23
second leadership contest 137–55
selection in Cardiff West 67–70
son-in-law 302
stepping down 324
Suez crisis 26
town planning 50, 59
travelling after Harvard 40
trip to Moscow 99–100
views on devolution 58, 97, 104–5,
  188, 192, 198, 203, 212, 215, 240,
  243, 249, 257–8, 279, 336, 337
Wales for Africa 325
Welsh Assembly Government
  name change 197
Welsh identity 60, 108, 326
working in the Welsh Office 50–4
Morgan (née Edwards), Julie 47 49, 92,
  95, 96, 112, 116–17, 122, 125, 126,
  128, 130, 134, 144, 152, 201, 212,
  236, 268, 272, 301, 302, 304, 305,
  307, 308, 320, 334; first meeting
  43; Julie's career 56 66, 89, 93, 113,
  331–3; Julie's mother, Grace 50,
  54; Grace on Blair 94; marriage,
  children and family life 5, 53, 54,
  46, 61, 129, 187
Morgan, Ken 45
Morgan, Morgan (great-great-
  grandfather) 17
Morgan, Piers 151
Morgan, Prys (brother) 6, 7, 9, 10, 11,
  21, 22, 24, 25, 27, 30, 32, 35, 36, 41,
  66, 71, 77, 86, 111, 140, 306
Morgan, Sally 131–2
Morgan, Thomas John (father) 1–8,
  11, 12, 14, 16, 18, 20, 21, 27, 29,
  37, 40, 61, 71, 86, 145, 320, 332,
  337; heart attack 30, 31, 32, 40,
  289, 301; Professor of Welsh 41;
  Registrar of the University of
  Wales 15; rugby 2, 3, 6, 24, 25, 26,
  32; Saunders Lewis 13–14; Tribunal
  of Conscientious Objectors and
  Reserved Occupations 14
Morgan, William (paternal
  grandfather) 2, 9, 16
Morganstown, Cardiff 7
Morley, Elliot 78
Morris, Jenny 47
Morriston Hospital, Swansea 10, 17,
  218
Moscow 99, 100
Mowlam, Mo 86
Mrs Gill's Nursing Home, Connaught
  Road, Roath, Cardiff 7, 8
Mrs Stanford's Academy, Radyr,
  Cardiff 7, 28
Mungham, Geoff 149–50
Murphy, Gerald 50
Murphy, Paul 78, 97, 161, 178, 182, 233,
  235, 237, 265, 319
Mwnt 116, 211–12, 307–8, 327
Myerson, Aubrey 59

NALGO 42
Nant-y-Gwyddon waste disposal site
  158
National Assembly Advisory Group
  (NAAG) 170, 171, 196, 197
National Assembly for Wales 107, 119,
  167, 169, 182, 214, 218, 219, 227,
  232, 271, 297; building capacity
  for 50, 264–5; building capacity of
  192–3, 196; credibility of 203, 206,
  207; first elections to 157, 158; new
  powers after GOWA (2006) 274–5,
  279, 310, 333; public view of 204,
  212; separation of powers 195–8,
  243–4; Standing Orders 170, 174,
  176, 177, 197–8; votes of censure/
  no confidence 170–2, 175–80, 182,

192: *see also* Welsh Assembly;
Senedd
National Assembly Labour Party
*see* Labour Group
National Audit Office 106
National Coal Board (NCB) 51, 66,
273
Neath 145, 271 (by-election) 93, 94, 95
Neath Port Talbot 228
Neill, Lord 115
new Assembly building *see* Senedd
New Labour 103, 106, 112, 115, 116,
125, 134, 146, 157, 195, 206, 236,
238, 239, 243, 248, 249, 250, 251,
252, 254, 255, 257, 314, 332
New Orleans 39–40
Newcastle 91, 110, 318 (City Council)
50
Newport East 83, 175, 223
Newport Leisure Centre 125
Newport West 73, 143, 153, 161
NHS 73, 79, 80, 86, 109, 110, 181, 250,
258, 271, 335; 2005 manifesto 266–7;
free prescriptions 256; Rhodri's
first recollections of 10, 26, 32;
Welsh Labour manifestos 109
Nicholas, Nancy 152
No. 10 *see* Downing Street
Nolan, Lord 115
North Sea (oil and gas) 85, 317, 319
North Wales 14, 28, 44, 60, 73, 74, 140,
150, 151, 161, 164, 165, 168, 169,
199, 201, 209, 211, 238, 239, 254,
257, 260, 272, 281, 287, 291, 311
Northern Ireland Assembly 82, 120,
195, 204, 205, 208, 237, 256, 282,
312, 313, 314, 315, 321, 323, 336
Norwich North 69
NUM 71 142, 147
Nye, Sue 321

O'Sullivan, Tyrone 142
Objective One funding 171, 172, 174,
175, 179, 182, 197, 198
*Observer, The* 12
Okey, Robin 49

OMOV (One Member One Vote) 124,
138–9, 143, 147, 152, 154
Open University 72
Ove Arup 192
Owen, Dickie 16
Oxfam 79
Oxford 91
Oxford University 15, 18, 30, 38, 39,
41, 43, 60, 72, 115, 116, 174, 206,
282; Labour Club 44; Templeton
College 74, 110: *see also* Morgan,
Hywel **Rhodri**, Oxford University

Paddington 55, 57, 86, 148, 297, 322
Palace guard *see* Praetorian Guard
Paris 162, 224
Parkinson, Cecil 87, 314
Parry, Bob 233
Patchett, Keith 244–5
Patnick, Irvine 98
Paxman, Jeremy 47, 135–6, 146
Peabody Coal Company 70
Pearce, Edward 96
Pembrokeshire 123, 147, 157, 158, 161,
193, 271
Penarth 186, 189
pension increase 50
Permanent Secretary 106, 144, 163,
186, 190, 194, 195, 272, 276, 302,
318, 326: *see also* Jones, Sir Derek;
Lomax, Rachel; Morgan, Dame
Gillian; Shortridge, Sir Jon
PFI 77, 106, 243, 285
PES *see* Public Expenditure System
Philip, Duke of Edinburgh 86, 210,
331
Pierhead building 193
Plaid *see* Plaid Cymru
Plaid Cymru 13, 14, 15, 30, 105, 144,
145, 155, 157, 158, 170, 172, 174,
177, 182, 198, 199, 208, 218, 224,
244, 252–3, 260, 261, 287, 291, 292,
294, 321, 322, 324; Carmarthen
by-election 15; Coalition 267, 279,
295–300, 306–13; University of
Wales MP (1943) 13, 14

Pithouse, Andy 57
Plain English Society 146
Plank, John 38
Poland 8, 9, 99, 166–7
Poll Tax 83
Pontardawe County School 2
Pontllanfraith 97
Pontrhydyfen 188–9
Pontypridd 42, 143, 155, 157; address
    in Graigwen 43; by-elections 27, 95
Port Talbot 1, 2, 19, 75, 123, 164, 189,
    228, 262; steelworks 58, 63, 216,
    217, 218, 284
Poulson, J. G. 50
pound, the (sterling) 166, 198, 216, 283;
    devaluation of 48
Post Office 52
Porthmadog 174
Powell, Jonathan 109, 110, 115
Powell, Ray 78, 252
Powell Davies, Mervyn 33, 34
Powell, Janice see Gregory, Janice
Powys 158, 196
Praetorian Guard 109, 172, 174, 175,
    177, 181, 317
Presiding Officer 176, 177, 179, 182,
    195, 202, 210, 222, 257, 259, 278, 306
Prescott, John 102, 118, 132, 146, 152,
    162, 163, 205, 265; the punch 237–8
Price, Adam 292, 293, 296
Price, Tom (headmaster at Rhymney
    County School) 4, 5
Price Waterhouse 166
Prime Minister's Questions 81, 85, 86,
    111, 115, 183
Prince Charles see Charles, Prince of
    Wales
Principal Private Secretary 176, 201
Private Finance Initiative see PFI
ProAct 321, 338
proportional representation 213, 264;
    Tories lease of life 158–9, 333–4;
    National Assembly system 181
Prosser, Sir David 275
Public Administration Select
    Committee 114, 116

Public Expenditure System (PES) 171,
    197
Pugh, Alun 150, 327

quangos 107, 111, 163, 165, 181, 228,
    229, 253, 275, 321, 337
Queen see Elizabeth II
Queen Mother see Elizabeth, The
    Queen Mother

RAF Valley 209
Radford, Brian 121
Radyr 1, 6, 7, 10, 20, 37, 67, 68, 101,
    102, 137, 138, 141, 174; church
    rooms 27, 28, 38, 46; Heol Isaf 6, 11,
    20; school 21, 22, 23, 27; Women's
    Institute 30
Rainbow coalition see Morgan, Hywel
    **Rhodri**
Randerson, Jenny 212, 229, 230, 231
Rapport, Cecil 90
RCN 152
Rebecca Riots 17
Red Lion pub, Bonvilston 175, 176
Redwood, John 104, 118, 181, 193, 229,
    326
Rees, Dorothy 27, 28, 38, 44, 46
Rees, Idwal 6
Rees, Jane (maternal grandmother)
    10, 11, 12, 16, 18, 19, 22, 24, 28, 29,
    336
Rees, John (maternal grandfather) 11,
    16, 18, 19, 28, 29, 30, 271
Rees, Thomas (maternal great-
    grandfather) 17
Rees-Mogg, William 18
Rees-Mogg, Jacob 18
Reid, John 77, 81, 265–7
Referendum on Welsh devolution
    274–5; (1979) 32, 97, 104–5, 220,
    281; (1997) 32, 109, 116, 117, 118,
    120, 148, 169, 189, 197, 199, 203,
    214, 243, 244, 257, 281; (2011) 264,
    265, 279, 310, 311, 333, 334
Regional Development Grants 51
regional policy 55, 57

Regional Selective Assistance 166–8, 276
Repayable Launch Aid 167–8
Research Assessment Exercise 196
Rhondda Cynon Taf (RCT) 154, 155, 157–8
Rhondda 6, 34, 127, 150, 154, 155, 157, 180, 215, 240, 252, 254, 255, 257, 259, 299, 333; Heritage Park 172; Labour Party 104, 113
Rhydlafar 10, 86
Rhyl 154, 236, 237
Rhymney 4, 5, 15, 62
Rhymney Coal & Iron Company 4
Rhymney County School 4
Richard Commission 244–5, 261, 264, 310, 311
Richard Rogers Partnership 189, 191, 192, 221, 241, 326
Richard, Arthur 22, 66
Richard, Ivor (Lord) 22, 66, 68, 69, 70, 78, 245, 264
Richards, Ceri 20
Richards, Menna 277
Richards, Rod 28, 98, 103, 107, 197
Richards, Rhuanedd 308, 322
Richards, Sioned Mair 150
Ridley, Nicholas 58, 83, 84
Riverside 67, 68, 69, 73
Roath Furnishing Company, Cardiff 4
Roath Ward Labour Party 44
Roberts, Huw and Julia (neighbours in Michaelston-le-Pit) 128–30
Roberts, Michael 42, 46
Roberts, Nicholas 226
Roberts, Wil 44
Roberts, Wyn (Baron Roberts of Conwy) 185
Robertson, George 112, 255
Robinson, Geoffrey 317
Robinson, Nick 207–8
Roddick, Winston 272
Rodgers, Bill 50
Rodney Parade 216
Rogers, Allan 41, 62, 63, 113
Rogers, Richard see Richard Rogers Partnership

Rolls Royce 57
Rommel, Manfred 90
Rooker, Jeff 96
Rose, John 90
Rose, Terry 217
Rowe-Beddoe, Sir David 165
Rowlands, Ted 42, 54, 104
Royal Mint 51
Royall, Jan 252–3
Rugby 9, 12, 16, 25, 28, 32, 46, 81, 89, 136, 173, 174, 216, 220, 224, 247, 273, 277, 295, 298; Byron Hayward 143; father playing 2, 3, 6; Gareth Jenkins 220; Gavin Henson 217; Graham Henry 224; grandfather 16; Mike Ruddock 220, 273; Oxford 33; playing with his father 24; rugby player or a politician 32; World Cup 173, 174
Rumbold, Sir Anthony 52, 53
Runeckles, Jane 306
Ryder Cup 210

S4C 103, 308, 325
Sackville, Tom 90
Salmond, Alex 82, 84, 85, 193, 211, 288, 291, 296, 297, 311, 314, 315, 317, 318
Scheele, Nick 173
Scholar, Sir Michael 37
Schroeder, Chancellor Gerhard 131, 133
Scotland 51, 58, 82, 88, 106, 107, 109, 114, 120, 121, 127, 146, 159, 162, 182, 197, 199, 205, 213, 214, 232, 250, 254, 256–8, 265, 266, 267, 269, 272, 281, 282, 288, 290, 296, 311, 313, 314, 315, 317, 321, 324, 332, 335, 336; devolution to 97, 104–5; Highlands and Islands 171; media coverage of 206, 208
Scott, George 62
Scottish Convention on devolution 104
Scottish National Party see SNP
Scottish Office 51, 53, 105, 195
Scottish Parliament 120, 158, 192, 213, 244, 250, 270, 315, 317

Scottish Qualifications Authority 206, 229, 254
SDP 20, 50, 67
Seaview Labour Club 65
Second World War 1–10, 13, 20, 21, 22, 24, 28, 35, 36
Secretary of State for Wales 105, 124–5, 151, 174, 193, 214, 274, 279; Jim Griffiths 51, 128; Cledwyn Hughes 52; Nicholas Edwards 193; Peter Walker 58, 193; David Hunt 89, 193; John Redwood 104, 118, 181, 193, 229, 326; William Hague 107, 276; Ron Davies 105, 119, 122, 127, 129, 144, 168; Alun Michael 132, 151, 161; Paul Murphy 161, 178, 182, 233, 320; Peter Hain 300; Alun Cairns 218
Seligman, David 67, 140
Senedd 189–92, 193, 206, 210, 220, 221, 241, 253, 272, 279, 326
Severnside Physical Planning Unit 53
Sharp, Ruth 44
Sharpe Pritchard, parliamentary agents 59, 60
Shawcross, Sir Hartley 83
Sheehan, Chris 140
Sheeran, Ed 141
Sheep and Goats Identification Wales Order 2000 (Miscellaneous Provisions) 207, 244
Sheepmeat Regime 63
Sheffield Rally 95
Short, Clare 106, 112
Shortridge, Sir Jon 186, 194, 195, 196, 272, 302, 318, 325
Simmons, Dr Mike 239–40
Sinclair, Karen 322
Skinner, Dennis 77
Smith, Chris 101
Smith, John (friend and Vale of Glamorgan MP) 28, 64, 79, 95, 111
Smith, John (leader of the Labour Party) 81, 82, 86, 97, 98, 100–3, 104, 112, 124, 147, 255, 261, 314
Smith, Llew 41, 225

Smith, Neil 107
Smith, Owen 332
Smith, T. Dan 50
Snowdonia 71
SNP 104–5, 288, 290–1, 296, 310, 311, 314, 315, 317, 332
Social Chapter 98
Socialist Health Association 109
Sofia, Bulgaria 100
South Glamorgan County Council 45, 59, 200, 231; Parliamentary Bill 59
South Wales Echo 22, 47, 91, 92, 107, 144, 152, 203, 211
South Wales Electricity Board 99
South Yorkshire 171
Spanish Civil War: early memories of his father 12; Saunders Lewis 13, 14; neighbours' experience 21
Spanish Government 167
Special Advisers 172, 181, 194, 199, 212, 225, 229, 245, 259, 278, 306, 307
Spectator Parliamentarian of the Year 116
Speed, Nick 294
Sporle, Sydney 50
St John's College, Oxford University 32, 34, 35, 37, 40, 206
St Woolo's Cathedral 181–2
Standing Orders see National Assembly for Wales
Strangers Bar 58, 82
Starkie, Dr Enid 34
Starovoitova, Galina 100
Stead, Peter 47, 64
Steel, David 64
Steel 216; Brymbo 169; CELSA 218; Corus 216; Davignon Plan 63; East Moors 55, 58, 59, 61, 63; Guest Keen 59, 217; industry state-ownership 58; proposed programme of closures (1970s) 58, 59; Shotton 58, 63, 217, 283; steelworkers in Cardiff 55; steelworkers union 61; Tata 283: see also Allied Steel & Wire; Ebbw Vale; Llanwern; Port Talbot

Steel Privatisation Bill 82
Steele, Chris 100
Steinbeck, John 30
Straw, Jack 96, 110, 132, 261, 265
Sturgeon, Nicola 211, 323
Stuttgart 90
Sully Hospital 56
*Sun, The* 80, 93, 95, 102, 152; Ron
    Davies 222–3
*Sunday Times, The* 12
Sussemilch family 1, 21
Swansea: AEEU delegates meeting
    148, 154; Bishopston 41–2, 79, 122,
    123, 124, 154, 161, 169, 176, 190;
    Peter Black 292; Cabinet geographic
    balance 161; civil servants 51;
    family connection 1, 2, 3, 5, 6; Val
    Feld 122; Guildhall 149; leadership
    nominations 123–4; location for the
    National Assembly 190; Tom Mann
    open-air meeting 12; mother's
    house 86; Second World War
    military hospital 10; John Smith
    79; Swansea Docks 19; Swansea
    Medical School 338; WDA city-
    centre development proposal 169
Swansea City Council 5 (Liberal
    Democrat control) 294
Swansea East 122, 145, 170, 253, 255
Swansea University 6, 41; Saunders
    Lewis, Chair in Welsh 30; Peter
    Stead, Professor of Cultural
    History 13, 15, 47, 64; Clear Red
    Water speech 188, 251, 262; Mark
    Drakeford 200; Mike Sullivan 250;
    Science Research 282; father's
    position as Deputy Principal 289;
    Chancellor 334
Swansea West 77, 159
Swansea Valley: family origins 1, 2, 3,
    16, 145, 271; Lucas-SEI 167; border
    with Brecon & Radnorshire 292
Sweeney, Walter 98, 111
swimming in the sea: Lavernock Point
    54; Prys 9; Mwnt and Aberporth 308
Swinnerton-Dyer, Sir Peter 71

Taff Vale Railway Company, Cardiff 7
Tahiti 107
Tanner, Haydn 25
Taoiseach 208, 247
Tarbet, Steve 72
Taylor, Dari (MP) 28
Taylor, Nev 118
Terlezki, Stefan (MP) 67, 73, 272
Thatcher, Denis 70
Thatcher, Margaret 19, 57, 72, 79, 81,
    83, 84, 85, 88, 94, 104, 106, 118, 185,
    221, 285, 289, 297, 313
*Thick of It, The* 98
Thomas, Jeffrey 67
Thomas, Gareth 150
Thomas, George 67, 73, 113
Thomas, Rhodri Glyn 307, 312, 321,
    322, 324
Thomas, Roy 153
Thomas, R. S. 25
Thomas, Simon 297, 312
Thomas, Terry 105, 142
Thomas, Watcyn 6
Thompson, Peter 173–4
Thorne, Lynda 278
Thorpe, Jeremy (trial) 261–2
*Times, The* 18, 38, 77, 84, 86, 209, 293
Tobacco advertising 115
*Today* programme 49, 114, 115, 116, 138,
    146, 173, 207
Tonyrefail 28
Tories *see* individual politician
    references
Touhig, Don 133, 265
town planning 42, 50, 59
trade unions 7, 65, 104, 138, 152, 168,
    262, 280: *see also* individual trade
    union references
Transport & General Workers Union
    (T&GWU/TGWU/T&G) 68, 75,
    118, 120, 123, 124, 133, 140, 147,
    148, 151
Transport House 75, 99, 122, 134, 135,
    140, 223, 298, 330
Treasury 40, 58, 97, 171, 243, 268,
    315–16, 319

Treaty of Lisbon 267–8
Tredegar 4 (Town Band) 81
Trethowan, Ian 47
Tribunal of Conscientious Objectors
    and Reserved Occupations 14, 15
Tribune Group 112
Trotman, Dickinson, Sir Aubrey 72
Trump, Donald 100
Trystan, Dafydd 295
Tugendhat, Christopher 66
Turner, Muriel 75
Tylerstown Leisure Centre 113
Tŷ Mynydd, Cardiff (home of Roald
    Dahl) 7
Tŷ'r Cymry Welsh-medium school 21

UKIP 53, 66, 264, 333
Ungoed-Thomas, Lynn (MP) 27
United Nations Convention on
    the Rights of the Child (UN
    Convention) 330
UNISON 147, 153, 225
University College Cardiff 71, 72
University College of South Wales and
    Monmouthshire, Cardiff 4
University Grants Committee 71
University of Glamorgan 134, 152,
    205
University of Wales 13, 14, 15, 30, 45
University of Wales Institute of
    Science and Technology 72
University of Warwick 49, 71
Upper Clyde shipbuilders sit-in 57
Utah Mining Company 70

Vale of Clwyd 157, 176
Vale of Glamorgan 27, 64, 65, 98, 111,
    144, 157, 161, 188; by-election 28,
    79, 95; moving to 54
Valentine, Reverend Lewis 13
Velindre Hospital 10, 24, 225, 337
Vietnam War 48, 49, 314
Vine, Jeremy 207

Wadge, Amy 141
Wakeham, John 87, 88

*Wales: The Way Ahead*, economic plan
    for Wales 51, 52
Wales CBI 193
Wales European Centre (WEC) 227–8
Wales Joint Education Committee
    (WJEC) 29, 228–31
Wales Millennium Centre 193, 220,
    328, 338
*Wales on Sunday* 136, 152
Wales Tourist Board 163
Wales TUC 160, 193, 208, 280, 293
Walker, Peter 58–9, 106, 193
Wallace, Jim 213
Walters, Professor Alan 85
Walters, Donald 111
Wandsworth Council 50
Ward, David 102–3
Welch, Jack 163
Welsh Assembly 18, 104–5, 117, 118,
    120, 121, 127, 128, 135, 144, 153,
    158, 160, 162, 167, 168, 170, 187,
    190, 206, 207, 227, 312, 327, 330:
    *see also* National Assembly for
    Wales; Senedd
Welsh Assembly elections (2003) 251,
    259
Welsh Development Agency (WDA)
    106–7, 163, 165–6, 168, 169, 275–7
Welsh Government 53, 187, 280, 285,
    290, 316, 318, 323; development of
    identity 194–5, 227; name change
    197, 227
Welsh identity 117, 169, 188, 189, 264,
    280, 336
Welsh Industrial Development
    Advisory Board (WIDAB) 167–8
Welsh Labour 133, 222, 237; 1999
    Assembly results 157–9, 169;
    fundraising dinners 18, 237, 243;
    HQ 133, 135, 140, 223, 330; leader
    119, 120, 124, 127, 129, 133, 135,
    177, 206, 330; Lib Dem coalition
    213; manifesto 109, 116, 154, 221,
    247, 257, 265; officials 142; on
    devolution 104–5, 112, 198; Plaid
    coalition agreement 30, 298–300;

recall Conference (2007) 299–300;
rules 139, 180; twinning 125, 142;
Welsh Labour Conference 30;
Welsh Labour Executive, WEC 134,
138, 150–1, 180, 265, 297–8
Welsh language 8, 14, 16, 17, 21, 30,
49, 75, 187, 188, 189, 231, 312; Tŷ'r
Cymry 21
Welsh National War Memorial 90
Welsh Office 50, 51, 52, 53, 54, 104, 105,
106, 107, 113, 120, 164, 165, 186,
194, 195, 283, 326, 335
Welsh Parliamentary Labour Party
139, 250, 251, 265
Welsh Society (Dafydd ap Gwilym),
University of Oxford 15
Wentloog Industrial Park 59
West Wales and the Valleys 167, 171,
197, 198
*Western Mail* 8, 9, 28, 129, 152, 240
Westminster School 83
Whips 77–9, 93, 98, 172, 202, 256
Whitchurch Grammar School, Cardiff
1, 11, 22, 33, 66
Whitchurch bypass 34
White Hart pub 204, 205, 259
White, Michael 119–20
Whitehall 51, 52, 53, 57, 131, 144, 162,
163, 189, 193, 194, 195, 196, 200,
208, 212, 245, 317, 325, 327
Wigley, Dafydd 105, 174, 199
Wilding, Barbara 220
Williams, Alan 77
Williams, Bleddyn 25
Williams, Brandon Rhys (Lord of
Miskin Manor) 80
Williams, David (*The Rebecca Riots*,
1955) 17
Williams, D. J. 13
Williams, Gareth (Cardiff West CLP
Chair) 68, 69, 75

Williams, Gareth (Lord Williams of
Mostyn) 261–2, 314
Williams, Gareth (Special Adviser to
Alun Michael) 172, 176, 178–9
Williams, Ifor (Ifor Williams trailers)
273
Williams, Kathy 40
Williams, Meurig 41
Williams, Rowan 181, 182, 240–1
Williams, Shirley 50
Williams, Kyffin 186
Wilson, Harold 20, 38, 42, 46, 48, 50,
76, 81, 256, 314
Wilson, Joe 140
Wooding, Neil 121–2
Woodward, Shaun 83
Woodward, Will 144
Worker's Educational Association
(WEA) 41, 50, 65, 139
*World at One* 150
*World in Action* 97
World Trade Organisation 168
Wrexham 117, 118, 122, 140, 169, 194,
202, 203, 222, 249, 257, 259, 281,
294
Wright, George 123, 124, 133, 147, 151
Wynne, R. O. F. 13
Wynne-Jones, G. V. 46, 47

*ychafi* 49, 151, 190, 309
Yeltsin, Boris 99
*Yes Minister* 98, 263, 290
*Yes, Prime Minister* 98, 150, 152, 269
Ynystawe, Swansea Valley (grand-
parents' house) 1, 2, 3, 5, 9, 10, 19
Ysbyty Gwynedd 86
Ystradgynlais 167
Ynysybwl 100

Zodiac 166